Jean Lefebvre de Cheverus painted by Vicomte Greys,
preserved in Saint-Seurin Basilica, Bordeaux.

Jean Lefebvre de Cheverus

1768-1836

Annabelle M. Melville

THE BRUCE PUBLISHING COMPANY
MILWAUKEE

NIHIL OBSTAT:

    Very Rev. Msgr. Francis J. Lally,
    Censor deputatus

IMPRIMATUR:

    ✠ Richard J. Cushing, D.D., LL.D.,
    Archbishop of Boston
    August 6, 1958

Jean Lefebvre de Cheverus

For the successors of Cheverus in the
United States, England, and France

FOREWORD

WHILE one hundred and fifty years is a small measure of time in the life of the Church universal, it is nonetheless one which in a local context can be seen as a matter of real significance. In 1808, when the Diocese of Boston was established, the American Republic was scarcely two decades old and so we have been able to observe the Church and the nation expanding side by side under the blessings of a benign Providence.

Who could have foreseen that in a century and a half the twelve hundred Catholics in Massachusetts, of which Father Matignon spoke to Bishop Carroll, would have grown to number in excess of two million? The story of the growth of the Church in New England is a glorious one and it is certainly appropriate that for its full understanding we study it in its beginnings. The early years of the diocese were those in which Bishop Cheverus ruled as spiritual shepherd and it would be difficult to imagine one better suited for the task. An *émigré* from France, driven out by the excesses of the Revolution in that country, he brought the full influence of his own native culture and immense personal charm to the service of the faith here.

In the light of later and less happy developments it is good to be able to recall the cordiality with which he was received in these parts by the older settlers. The Catholic Church in Puritan Massachusetts, where Congregationalism was still the religion of the establishment, must have seemed to them a strange sect of which they had heard only the most direful reports. Into this climate came a young French priest of aristocratic background and good education to minister to the small number of Catholics in the area, a group largely made up of Indians in the settlements of Maine, who had been converted somewhat earlier by the French. It is a credit to the leaders of the community at that time, and no small tribute to the Bishop himself, that his friendly ways and his dedicated piety soon won the admiration of all and promptly set at rest among informed people the sad tales of "Romanism" which had circulated for generations.

vii

The story of Bishop Cheverus in Boston is only a small part of the total story of his life for he returned to his native land and served the Church there in various capacities until finally he was named Cardinal Archbishop of Bordeaux and indeed a Peer of France. The pages that follow will describe the details of this great and fruitful life and I would not wish to intrude upon them or the distinguished scholarship of Dr. Melville which is there represented.

I do feel, however, that there is a very important contemporary relevance for this biography of the first Bishop of Boston. Published in this sesquicentennial year it brings to mind a personality who in the space of a very few years accomplished great things for the Church in America. There is a lesson in the fact that love of neighbor, rooted in the love of God, clearly worked wonders in transforming human dispositions even in an unpromising climate. Bishop Cheverus taught us once again that the truly Christlike character is the best witness to the Faith and he demonstrated how that love, which we traditionally call charity, conquers all things.

I am happy to be able to contribute a few words of Foreword to this important and impressive biography which I have encouraged Dr. Melville to write for this anniversary year. Those who are familiar with her other biographies — those of Bishop Carroll and Mother Seton — will not need to be reminded of her competence as an historian and her skill as a writer.

For my part I am pleased that both author and publisher were able to add this significant item to our jubilee celebration. Many readers will, I am confident, draw from these pages new inspiration for the apostolate of our times and they will recall, too, how Providence does not fail to call from the bosom of the Church great and good men who answer in labor and grace the necessities of every age.

✠ Richard J. Cushing
Archbishop of Boston

PREFACE

IF, LIKE wars, biographies may be thought of as emanating from causes both immediate and remote, a new life of Jean Lefebvre de Cheverus may join the category of other debates over inevitability. The present writer has been intrigued with him since he first crossed the pages of a biographical study of his American contemporary, *Elizabeth Bayley Seton*, and Cheverus continued to hold his charm through the researches connected with his superior, *John Carroll of Baltimore*. In simple justice, to say nothing of fond affection, sooner or later Jean Lefebvre de Cheverus was sure to be given the center of the stage.

A new biography of Cheverus was also certain to be written for more extensive reasons. Since the year after his death in 1836 not a single new study has appeared of the man who was not only the most eminent of the suffragan bishops of Archbishop Carroll, but who was as well, after his return to France in 1823, unique among prelates in his relation with three successive kings of France. The influence of Cheverus may still be felt in every one of the New England states where he was the founder of the first Catholic churches beyond Boston. The mark of Cheverus remains in England where he founded at Tottenham the first Catholic chapel since the Reformation. In France, the elevation of Cheverus to the Roman College of Cardinals marked changes in Franco-Roman relations, in Church-State relations within the nation, and even in the ceremonies attending the conferring of a cardinal's hat. When, moreover, to his significance for national histories is added his personal example of remarkable virtues it becomes apparent that the life of Cheverus merits reassessment for reasons transcending geography and time.

André-Jean Marie Hamon, S.S., in 1837 published his first edition of the *Vie du Cardinal de Cheverus* under the pseudonym of "J. Huen-Dubourg." In its third edition, 1842, this work was judged so worthy by nineteenth-century French standards that it was crowned by the Académie Française with a prize of 2000 francs. In 1839 Robert M. Walsh published in Philadelphia a translation with appended American documents, and in the same year in Boston E. Stewart also published a translation with minor corrections of American details. Taking note of the American corrections, Hamon himself revised the *Vie* and it went through seven French editions altogether by 1883. Briefer biographical sketches of Cheverus, either French or American, are all based largely on this one study.

Although the Hamon *Vie* remains a remarkable work in its veracity, the pious effusiveness of style common to his century may detract from the modern reader's interest and enjoyment. A second drawback lies in its scanty treatment of the Boston era of the career of Cheverus. Three fifths of the public years of his life were spent in the United States, and a balanced study should strive for some such proportion. Since the scholarly *History of the Archdiocese of Boston* appeared in 1944 there is no difficulty in supplementing Hamon's work in this respect. Another substantial contribution to Cheverus lore made since Hamon's last edition went to press was the publication from 1903–1907, in the *Records* of the American Catholic Society of Philadelphia, of over one hundred letters of Cheverus which throw new light on his personality and character. With the recent contributions of French scholarship to a better understanding of the Restoration Era, of the history of the Church in France; with excellent new biographies of religious and lay contemporaries of Cheverus, it is possible to present more vividly the background from which the man cannot be totally separated.

In spite of these incentives to an enlarged study of Cheverus, his twentieth-century biographer faces a serious handicap which was not present in Hamon's day. The result of the Separation of Church and State in France in 1905, as far as ecclesiastical archives were concerned, was to greatly decimate the available documentary evidence. In Montauban the episcopal archives retain no Cheverus materials, while the archives of Tarn-et-Garonne possess less than a dozen documents. The episcopal decrees are still extant at Nègrepelisse but if it were not for Camille Daux' *Histoire de l'église de Montauban* which was admirably documented prior to 1886 it would scarcely be possible to re-create the years Cheverus spent in that diocese. The situation in Bordeaux is slightly better since the episcopal and municipal archives each have a few documents and the departmental archives preserve a fairly large collection.

In addition to the loss of documents owing to changes in Church-State relationships, the Cheverus materials suffer from the fact that the American materials are barren in regard to scores of letters addressed to Cheverus. It is possible much of this material was lost in the shipwreck of 1823, when Cheverus was returning to France; but, whatever the cause, many letters which would have clarified his relations with important friends are no longer extant. The biographer must laboriously fill in the details of a picture only half-sketched by existing documents. When all the hazards are admitted there still remains an ample testimony that Jean Lefebvre de Cheverus lived a varied and fascinating life, in a manner still full of meaning for a later century.

The writer is immeasurably indebted to the Most Rev. Richard J. Cushing, Archbishop of Boston, for his interest and generosity which not only prompted this undertaking but opened doors both in Boston and in France. To the Very Rev. Francis J. Lally and Rev. John Grant of the Boston *Pilot* this work owes its particular impulse at this time.

In the critical development of the manuscript special credit must go to the Right Rev. John Tracy Ellis of the Catholic University of America, for his incomparable advice touching all phases of the work; to Rev. Guillaume de Bertier de Sauvigny of the Institute Catholique de Paris for his expert opinion and suggestions relating to the French phases; to the Right Rev. Philip Hughes of the University of Notre Dame and Rev. John Rudd of Flint, North Wales, for their contributions to the English chapter; and to Dr. Clement C. Maxwell of the Bridgewater Teachers College for his critical reading of the whole.

The work of research for the American materials was made possible by the co-operation and limitless courtesy of the Right Rev. Robert J. Sennott, Chancellor of the Archdiocese of Boston; Rev. John Broderick of the Creagh Research Library, St. John's Seminary, Brighton; Rev. Thomas T. McAvoy, C.S.C., of the University of Notre Dame; Rev. Salvatore M. Burgio, C.M., of the Mother Seton Guild, Emmitsburg, Maryland; Sister-Archivist of the Saint Joseph Central House, Emmitsburg, Maryland; Sister Archivist of Mount Saint Vincent on the Hudson; and all archivists who in the past assisted in the use of materials deposited in the Department of Archives and Manuscripts of the Catholic University of America, St. Mary's Seminary of Roland Park, Maryland, Mount St. Mary's Seminary, Emmitsburg, and the Archives of the Archdiocese of Baltimore.

In France research was greatly facilitated by M. le chanoine E. Moura, Archiviste de l'évêché de Bordeaux, without whose unlimited kindness the writer could never have accomplished so much in so short a time; in Bordeaux fine assistance was also given by MM. Martin Descot and Alain d'Anglade of the Archives Départementales, and MM. Xavier Védère and Claude de Rocher of the Archives de la ville de Bordeaux, and M. l'abbé Pierre Brun, then at the Cathedral of Saint-André, and M. Raoul Cousté, Archiviste en chef, Journal *Sud-Ouest*.

In Montauban search was assisted by M. le chanoine Gayne, Archiviste de l'évêché; M. le chanoine Prunet, Curé de Saint-Orens; M. René Toujas and Mme Jeanne Naurouse of the Archives de Tarn-et-Garonne; M. Dufor of Maison Dufor-Quercy; and the personnel of the Bibliothèque Municipale.

In Paris M. l'abbé Chalumeau, C.M., gave access to books at the community house of the Prêtres de la Mission, 95 Rue de Sèvres. Work at the Archives Nationales was simplified by the kindness of M. Bernard Mahieu, Archiviste, and his able staff. M. Roger de la Massonnais, a descendant of the Cheverus family, offered invaluable aid in tracing genealogy and family portraits. The staff of the Bibliothèque Nationale offered services too numerous to list.

For individual kindnesses in translating, lending books, running down odd identifications, and services of that nature the writer is grateful to Rev. Charles J. Metzger, S.J., of West Baden College; Rev. Francis S. Shea of St. Ann's, West Bridgewater; Dr. Jordan Fiore of Bridgewater Teachers College; Miss M. A. Rea of Islington, Massachusetts; the late Mrs. John J. Ryan of Haverhill, Massachusetts; and the students of history classes of Bridgewater Teachers College.

ANNABELLE M. MELVILLE

Bridgewater Teachers College
Bridgewater, Massachusetts
1958

CONTENTS

JEAN LEFEBVRE DE CHEVERUS

CHAPTER I

A YOUTHFUL PRIOR

ON THE very last day of December, 1779, in the fifth year of the reign of Louis XVI of France, *Monsieur,* Louis-Stanislaus-Xavier, brother of the King, Duke of Anjou, Count of Maine, and the bearer of other noble titles, conferred a benefice on a young native of the ancient Province of Maine, a boy not quite twelve years old and so small in size he scarcely passed for ten. There was really nothing unusual about it except, perhaps, for the size of the new prior. And the men of the Lefebvre de Cheverus family were short, as every one in the town of Mayenne could testify.[1] Jean Lefebvre de Cheverus had recently been tonsured in the seminary chapel of Le Mans by Bishop François-Gaspard de Jouffroy de Gonssans on September 19, and now that he was in minor orders he was eligible to see to it that two weekly Masses were offered in the Chapel of Our Lady of Pity at Torbéchet.[2] The benefice had already been held for thirty years by another Lefebvre de Cheverus, his great-uncle, Vincent-Gilbert.[3] The modest income of 710 *livres* would enable young Jean to continue his ecclesiastical studies with less sacrifice on the part of his family.

Simple benefices such as the one conferred by *Monsieur* were common enough. France in 1779 was still a decade away from the Revolution that was to bring profound changes to the French Church. The old methods of supporting the clergy were still more feudal than modern. One needs a vivid imagination today to understand what degree of union of Church and State existed under the Bourbon monarchs of the Old Regime. Yet, in a special sense, the clergy were no expense to the State. Their properties in France were estimated at three billion *livres;* they collected taxes as well, in the form of the tithe.[4] Indeed,

1

the credit of the Church in France was said to surpass that of His Most Christian Majesty's government.[5] And it was not to be wondered at, when one considered that the Church was exempt from the onerous direct taxes: the *taille,* the *capitation,* and the *vingtième.* The princes of the Church lived in a style second only to that of their King. Their palaces in cities like Montauban and Bordeaux were the grandest in the city.[6]

It must be recalled, of course, that the Church in the eighteenth century rendered two major services that are today performed by the State. Public aid in the form of hospitals and bureaus of charity, and education were the province of religion. It must be remembered, too, that the lower clergy who formed the majority were country priests and lived simply if not in actual poverty. If the French bishops enjoyed great influence because of their noble birth, their wealth, and the nature of their functions, the lower clergy enjoyed prestige by reason of their morality and intellectual superiority to their parishioners.[7] And not a few of the latter held simple benefices which guaranteed a fixed income to the titulary while requiring no care of souls beyond some required good work or prayers for the dead which the original founder of the benefice had meant to perpetuate.

The naming of candidates to benefices was a right usually reserved to the heirs of the founder. The presentation of a candidate to the chapel of the castle at Torbéchet had belonged to the Seigneur of Torbéchet. When René-Pierre Deschamps, the successor of Cheverus' great-uncle, died in 1779 the Duchess of Beauvilliers named a candidate, Antoine-Jean de Clinchamps.[8] But she had forgotten that she no longer possessed this right. At the time she became Dame du Sonnois et de Peray on August 9, 1763, she had relinquished to Louis XV some of her seigneuries, Torbéchet among them. The right to present candidates had since passed to the Count of Maine.[9] The brother of the king thus, on the recommendation of one of his council members, Pierre Gerbier, presented the name of young Cheverus who took possession of the benefice on April 29, 1780.[10] Cheverus continued to enjoy the small benefits of Torbéchet until 1792.[11]

The new prior of Torbéchet was Jean-Louis-Anne-Madeleine Lefebvre de Cheverus, the eldest son of Jean-Vincent-Marie Lefebvre de Cheverus and Anne-Charlotte Lemarchand de Noyers. He was born on January 28, 1768, in the parish of Notre Dame de Mayenne, of a family distinguished in public service.[12] The Lefebvre family seems to have been originally from Saint-Hilaire-des-Landes but had settled in

Mayenne at an early date. The elder branches took their names from the land of Cheverus, of Champorin, and La Provotière. Jean's grandfather, Jean-Louis Lefebvre de Cheverus, had been a judge's *conseiller-assesseur* at the ducal bar of Mayenne. His uncle, Julien-Jean Lefebvre de Champorin, was first a lawyer and then a lieutenant-general at the same bar. In 1778 he became mayor of the city. Jean's father in his turn would serve as civil judge in Mayenne and as a lieutenant of police. Another uncle, Louis-René Lefebvre de Cheverus, was pastor of Notre Dame de Mayenne.[13]

Young Jean de Cheverus had two brothers: Julien-Madeleine and Louis-Anne, and three sisters: Anne-Renée-Hélène, Michelle-Françoise, and Marie-Clotilde.[14] The six children enjoyed a happy home in pre-Revolutionary Mayenne and developed affections which neither time nor distance would ever threaten. While she lived, Anne Lemarchand de Cheverus gave her sons and daughters by example and precept a fine Christian training. Gentle by nature herself, she could never use severity with her children. Yet she had that rare understanding in dealing with them which produced both obedience and love. It was a very real punishment in the Cheverus home to be excluded from the family evening prayers. Jean grew up a gentle and very loving lad, and he bore these two marks, gentleness and loving kindness, to his grave. Although his mother died when he was only sixteen, Jean de Cheverus never forgot her, and even in his old age, whenever he spoke of the duties of parents to their children, he always cited her example.[15]

Young Jean's earliest formal education was gained at the local *collège* in Mayenne where he led his classmates in both study and play. The school which had been founded in 1560 by Geneviève Tronchay had taken the title of *collège* thirty years later; under Jacques Gouttard, the principal during the years Cheverus attended, it was admirably suited to the preliminary education of a French boy destined for the Church. Jean's success in his studies brought him two rewards which made it possible to continue his further study in Paris. The noted lawyer, Pierre Gerbier, was impressed by the young Cheverus of Mayenne and, as we have seen, was instrumental in securing the benefice of Torbéchet for Jean in 1779. That same year, on November 11, Bishop Gonssans of Le Mans awarded him one of the scholarships of the diocese for the College of Louis-le-Grand in Paris.[16] By the time Cheverus had finished his schooling at Mayenne in August, 1781, coming home with several coveted prizes, his mother was quite reconciled to the thought of separation from her eldest son.[17]

The doors of Louis-le-Grand in 1781 were not open to everyone. To be admitted was an honor; to stay there several years lent an air of privilege. To enter as a *boursier* or scholarship student meant meeting the severest requirements set by four examiners and Principal Denis Berardier.[18] The year Jean de Cheverus entered the college there were 526 scholarship men, most of whom owed their appointments to merit rather than to mere accident of birth. Although the college of Louis-le-Grand came to be called the "Seminary of the Revolution" because it numbered among its students in the decade from 1775–1785 Robespierre, Camille Desmoulins, Saint-Just, Pilot, and du Tertre, it was also the cradle of notable careers in charity and religion, including as it did such men as Legris-Duval, Cheverus, and a future Bishop of New York, John Dubois.[19] The college furnished the principals of the most renowned colleges of the realm: Douay, Cambrai, Beauvais, Saintes-Puy, and Châlons-sur-Marne. Prelates chose their vicars-general from its graduates; and Louis-le-Grand furnished the most astute lawyers to the courts of Paris and the provinces, as well as doctors to the faculties of medicine.

The college had a venerable career behind it and had weathered many a storm since its institution in 1560. Known as Clermont until 1682, after its founder Guillaume du Prat, the Bishop of Clermont, it was renamed after Louis XIV in the year of its second foundation. The Jesuit system based on the *Ratio studiorum* published in 1599 suffered very little change until 1762. In that year a court order of August 6 expelled the Jesuits from France and Louis-le-Grand, like St. Omer in Flanders, lost its Jesuit teachers.[20] The enemies of the Society of Jesus installed themselves joyously in the Parisian college and many changes naturally ensued. In the library Pascal and Voltaire were placed beside the Jesuit fathers Rapin and Geoffrey; Corneille rubbed covers with Bossuet and Fénelon. Both profane and religious authors were now studied in three languages, and Latin gave way to French as the language of the students.

For all the changes, Louis-le-Grand was still without equal for philosophy, theology, and law. In the 1780's the theologians were more than one fifth of the college and the methods of teaching were still those of Jesuit days. Each week the students of theology appeared before the superiors of their house to give their sermons. The chief change lay in the fact that they could no longer complete their studies at Louis-le-Grand, as in the old days, but must go on to a major seminary. The *boursiers* in theology, however, could with the consent of their superiors continue to receive their scholarships for three years after they passed on from Louis-le-Grand.[21]

The school year began in October and ended in August but vacations varied from forty to sixty days, depending on the age of the students. Apparently those whose intellectual efforts were more strenuous were believed deserving of longer holidays. Each week had two days of rest. Sunday, of course, was one of these, but the other could be any day of the week. Students rose at 5:30 and retired at 9:00. Classes lasted for two and a quarter hours, morning and afternoon, with a conference hour from 6:15 to 7:15 each evening. In size the classes ran about thirty students, and the new freedom which prevailed in the post-Jesuit era allowed for a while greater noise and disorder than formerly.[22] But by the time Cheverus entered, the directors had already begun to return to a policy of firmness. All recreation was carefully supervised, and when a class went for a walk they took a clearly defined route and proceeded at a pace neither too fast nor too slow. There were youthful misdemeanors, naturally. Upperclassmen sneaked out over the roofs at night; forbidden books were smuggled in under greatcoats. But when contrasted with the years after 1789 the quarter-century before was an exemplary era. Indeed, when contrasted with the large and turbulent student bodies of our own century, the sober young men in their wigs, which were worn from the time of Louis XIV until the Revolution dethroned even petty tyranny, presented a picture more suggestive of youthful judges preoccupied with affairs of state.

From the point of view of physical comfort the young collegians were certainly not indulged in riotous living. The furniture of their small dark rooms was simplicity itself, functionally insuring that the chamber should be used for sleeping and nothing else. The dual problem of heat and light was never solved. Candles were kept under lock and key; and a chimney that heated without belching clouds of smoke, or a window that closed with exactitude, was a rarity. Chimney fires all too often required that Cheverus become as skillful in fire fighting as in theology.

Although there were four meals a day, the food was meager and monotonous. Dessert was all too often apples, even though twice a week prunes were expected to work their good effects. Lentils and string beans were daily honored, and there were eggs, eggs, eggs. "One did not attempt to exhaust the one hundred and ten ways of accommodating eggs," was wry humor at Louis-le-Grand. Yet the health of the students was, in general, excellent. Illnesses were light and on an average only one boy died in any school year. These nourishing if dreary meals were taken in large refectories near the kitchen at heavy tables lined with massive benches. A note of elegance was preserved in the rows of gleaming silverware and cups engraved with the names of the colleges which had been combined to form Louis-le-Grand: Arras, Autun, Beauvais, Lisieux, and the rest. It was never quite the same after the Revolution replaced the costlier metal with pewter and tin.

The whole system at Louis-le-Grand was centered around three ideals which left their lasting imprint on Jean de Cheverus; religion, devotion to monarchy, and discipline. Even a cursory glance at the college life of the 1780's makes it much easier to understand Cheverus in later life. Certainly, in no man did the ideals of the Old Regime institution come to more perfect fruition after that regime had passed away. Although the Jesuits left Louis-le-Grand, religion did not. Only the Roman Catholic religion prevailed. Masters, pupils, and servants, all had to profess it, and anyone outside the faith was outside the college.[23] Baptism was not enough. Daily practice was rigorously required. Confessions were made at least once a month, and more than half the student body went more often. First Communions were attended by particular solemnity and were preceded by a half-week of retreat. Boys were grounded in the precept that true charity was a reflection of God's tenderness for man. "True courtesy does not consist in vain formulae of compliments or in exterior demonstrations alone, but takes its root in charity which ought to unite us all, one with another." Politeness belonged to all, servants and strangers, as well as to relatives and friends. Gentlemen avoided sarcasm, disdain, hauteur, and raillery at all costs. Religion demanded it.

After religion came patriotism, and in Cheverus' time king and country were synonymous. National meant royal, and to love France meant to revere her monarch. The college seal quite naturally bore the king's arms. All that concerned the royal family deeply interested the young men at Louis-le-Grand. President Rolland d'Erceville could say truly on the occasion when the king's portrait was given to the college, "This portrait is engraved in all hearts here in ineffaceable characters." Occasions honoring the monarch were graced with speeches in Latin and Greek delivered by youthful orators who imbibed love for monarchy at the same springs which quenched their spiritual thirst. The young *boursier* from Mayenne found it as easy to love his king as to love his God. The altar and the throne were objects of his devotion to the day he died.

The third ingredient of education was discipline. The voice of the bell was the signal for every common action. No one left the study room without permission, and his absence was timed. Exclusion from a class was the gravest matter. Parents were informed and the student had only fifteen days to make his peace. A scholarship could be canceled; and if the student were not a boarder he could be expelled. Although talking was allowed under the new administration, meals were still eaten in silence with reading the rule. Each had his place and kept it all year long. Together with an emphasis on emulation this discipline brought results.

Emulation was fostered by rewards, chief of which were the "Charlemagne," the annual prizes, nominations to the university, university grades, and qualification for other schools. The annual prizes were books engraved with the arms of the house and were distributed amid impressive musical and artistic accompaniments. The "Charlemagne" was the most coveted reward. It was a legacy from the old University of Paris which came to Louis-le-Grand after 1763. A student who remained at the head of his class from the opening of school in October was invited to a banquet given on January 29 in honor of the old emperor, to whom legend attributed the founding of the University of Paris. For the duration of the evening each student summoned to the feast was an emperor himself. It was the high occasion of the year and turkeys suffered noticeably in consequence.

The first autumn that young Cheverus went up to Paris he was accompanied by his father. It was a trifle out of their way, but they stopped at Le Mans to call on Bishop Gonssans who was responsible for the scholarship that the young student was to enjoy. Once arrived in Paris they called upon Gerbier in Rue des Théatins. The celebrated lawyer was no longer on *Monsieur's* council, but now served the university council. His greatest years of glory were behind him. The brilliant oratory and charming facility which had made him outstanding both in the Parlement of Paris and before the commission of the interregnum between parlements was fading into increasingly frequent displays of ill-humor. His last years before his death in 1788 were rather sad ones.[24] But courtesy and gratitude compelled the Cheverus men to call upon him and Gerbier was delighted to see the younger man whose talents had attracted him previously. He insisted on presenting him to his royal patron, the brother of the king. The impressionable Cheverus was filled with awe at seeing a Bourbon at such close range. *Monsieur*, who was twenty-six at the time, was enormously diverted at Gerbier's suggestion that this small chap be named his Chaplain Extraordinary, a title that went with the Priory of Torbéchet. He displayed an unusual gentleness toward Cheverus, whose candor and good manners he found quite charming.[25] Jean left with something close to hero-worship flooding his young heart. The inculcation at Louis-le-Grand of devotion to the royal family found a very ready subject in one *boursier* matriculating in 1781.

Once established in his quarters in Rue St. Jacques, Cheverus quickly became popular with his classmates and teachers. There seems never to have been a time when he was not a lovable person. It is not surprising that his preceptors liked him, for he was a serious student from the very beginning. He went to Communion every eight days, and attended all the religious exercises with happy regularity. No roof-top escapades found him involved. When Bishop Gonssans visited the college to find out how his protégé was getting along the reports were unanimously enthusiastic, and he returned to Le Mans convinced that, "My little Abbé de Cheverus will one day be the outstanding subject in my diocese."[26]

Yet he had, with all his deep piety, a personality that other less serious students found irresistible. For so small a lad he had a fearless self-possession and manliness. In spite of his achievements he was so modest the lesser lights minded not at all. His infectious humor and evenness of disposition naturally drew others around him. Already, in those adolescent years which in some bring "growing pains," Cheverus was that steady, glowing spirit that cast an effulgence on all who moved within his range. If this seems strong language, it is simply because the whole record of his life demands it. No one who knew him at Louis-le-Grand ever forgot him.

For his own part, Cheverus found two particular friends while he attended Louis-le-Grand. One was his classmate, René-Michel Legris-Duval, a *boursier* like Cheverus but a few years older and almost a veteran at the school, having entered while he was only eleven. His brief career was to be inextricably woven into the history of French charitable foundations. When Cheverus went on to the seminary of the Oratorians, Legris-Duval went to the seminary of Saint-Sulpice. Both friends were ordained the same year; both were devoted to the Bourbons and refused to collaborate with the Revolutionary upheaval.

When Louis XVI was arrested Legris-Duval courageously left his place of retirement in Versailles and went boldly to Paris. "I am a priest," he declared. "I have learned that the king is condemned to death. I come to offer him the services of my ministry." Louis already had a confessor, as it turned out, and Legris-Duval was to no avail publicly known to be in Paris without proper papers. But old loyalties of Louis-le-Grand days served him in good stead. Some of his former classmates, now connected with the Republican regime, arranged his return to Versailles.[27]

Like Cheverus, Legris-Duval rejoiced at the restoration of the Bourbons after the fall of Napoleon, and shortly after the entrance of Louis XVIII Legris-Duval was the preacher at a funeral service held at Notre Dame de Paris in memory of the former monarch. He promoted the work of the Savoyards, encouraged a society for visiting the sick in hospitals, and began the work of reclaiming young prisoners. His greatest zeal was for the French missions, both foreign and at home. Refusing all honors, he died on January 18, 1819, after exhausting his meager store of health. When five years later Cheverus, by then Bishop of Montauban, had occasion to preach himself in the interest of the missions he recalled the past briefly for his audience. Speaking of his beloved schoolmate he said, "He honored me with his friendship; and in his youth, condescended to associate me with his works of piety and zeal. Blessed friend, if I could be your echo at this time, all hearts should be moved, and your work perpetuated!"[28]

A second friend of those years was the Abbé Antoine-Jean-Baptiste Augé, a more advanced theologian who was only one step removed from his doctorate. There was an odd custom in practice then, that candidates for the doctor's degree must present a young man to uphold publicly the candidate's thesis. Although by the 1780's it was a notorious fact that the candidates deserved no credit for their proxy's performance, the custom held. Augé needed only this public defense of his thesis to complete his requirements. His choice fell upon the reluctant Cheverus. Because Augé had been so kind to the younger student, accepting his confidences, advising him on spiritual problems, guiding his first months at college, Cheverus could not refuse. So in March, 1786, he appeared in public to uphold his friend's thesis with such facility of reasoning and elegance of language that both Augé and Cheverus were singularly distinguished.[29] Augé became a doctor at the Sorbonne, and in later years was well known in Paris. With the Archbishop of Paris, Hyacinthe de Quelen, he served on the commission named in 1825 to lay plans for a central house of higher ecclesiastical studies, was made archdeacon of Notre Dame, and became vicar-general to Quelen at the height of that prelate's career.[30]

Cheverus had no difficulty in securing admission to a major seminary. Although Jean-André Emery, the superior of Saint-Sulpice, offered him a free place in the seminary selected by Legris-Duval, Cheverus preferred to take the entrance examination for the seminary conducted by the Fathers of the Oratory, Saint-Magloire. Saint-Magloire dated back to the reign of Louis XIII, having been founded in 1618, and many a bishop of the Old Regime had been educated there.

It was at Saint-Magloire that the scholarly side of Jean de Cheverus found its early fulfillment. Here the sacred Scriptures were read and re-read, sometimes with joy that dissolved in tears. He learned Hebrew so that he might study the Bible at its fountainhead. His Greek was kept in practice by his study of the Church Fathers who had used that classical mode of expression. His Latin brought him in contact with the queen of studies, theology. The *De locis theologicis* of Melchior Canus became his favorite model and he grew so fascinated by its niceties of style that he rejected a classmate's suggestion that he might also learn English.

Nicolas de Mac-Carthy, who was a close friend at Saint-Magloire, told Cheverus he ought to learn English, and offered to teach him Mac-Carthy's mother tongue. Mac-Carthy had been born in Dublin on May 17, 1769, the son of an Irish nobleman who later took refuge in Toulouse for religious reasons. When their seminary days were over, Mac-Carthy became a Jesuit and a brilliant orator who was to preach in Bordeaux while his seminary friend Cheverus was archbishop of that city; but all of that was in the future.[31] In the 1780's Cheverus could not foresee that one day he would come to speak English with greater ease than French, and he refused his friend's offer in order to pursue those studies which he believed most immediately useful to a priest destined, as he hoped, to minister in the Diocese of Le Mans.

The days at Saint-Magloire sped swiftly by. In 1789 he was a subdeacon and acting as a master of conferences at his old college, Louis-le-Grand. On October 7, 1790, he was made deacon. In after years Cheverus recalled that happy time as "blessed years . . . the fairest of my life. Happy days when my duties were so easy, my days so serene, my soul so tranquil. . . ."[32] Yet he was a deacon scarcely more than two months when he was ordained to the priesthood in the last public ceremonies of that nature to take place in Revolutionary Paris. Bishop

Gonssans with prophetic insight was beginning to fear that the ferment of reform permeating the National Assembly of France might make ordinations difficult, if not impossible, in the very near future; and he procured from Rome a dispensation allowing Cheverus, who was not yet twenty-three, to receive holy orders in December. And so it happened that on December 13, the deacon of only a few weeks wrote, "I am on retreat at Saint-Magloire Seminary until Saturday night, and I shall probably leave Sunday for Mayenne."[33]

On December 18, 1790, Jean Lefebvre de Cheverus was ordained to the priesthood and left Paris for his boyhood home. He celebrated his first Mass on Christmas, at the midnight service at Notre Dame de Mayenne.[34] In the ordinary course of events it should have been the beginning of a permanent and peaceful ministry in the city of his birth, among the friends and the relatives who had awaited his return with such affectionate anticipation. Instead, on the very next day the government in Paris decreed that all priests must take an oath to uphold the Civil Constitution of the Clergy. The decision now faced by the earnest new priest could alter the course of his life.

CHAPTER II

NON-JURING PASTOR

THAT first Mass on Christmas Eve was the happiest occasion that the Abbé de Cheverus would know in many years. It was not only that a first Mass is a wonderful and holy thing for any new priest, offered among the people he has known from infancy, the fulfillment of a host of dreams cherished through long years. But this Mass was offered by a priest who had not yet made the harsh decision which put himself beyond the pale of the constitutional demands of his government. After February 12, 1791, he would belong to the large throng who refused to take the oath in support of the Civil Constitution of the Clergy, and in Mayenne he would be thenceforth a marked man.

There is no way of knowing now what Cheverus thought of the political rush of events that marked his last years at Saint-Magloire. Surely, being in Paris, the very heart of the Revolutionary impulse, seminarians must have been aware that the world they had known in youth was undergoing radical changes. The year that Jean de Cheverus returned to Saint-Magloire as a subdeacon had witnessed the opening moves that impulse inspired. As early as January 24, 1789, parish assemblies in Mayenne had been convoked in preparation for the meeting of the Estates General that year.[1] The royal decree summoning these assemblies broke the precedent of a century, and the session which opened in Le Mans, the episcopal city, on March 16 was marked by solemnity and prayer. In the abbey church of La Couture the *Veni Creator* was sung and Bishop Jouffroy de Gonssans offered a Mass of the Holy Ghost. Following the reading of the king's letter the three estates went to their separate chambers and continued to deliberate twice a day for two weeks thereafter. The clergy with 942 voters met at the Jacobins; the nobles with 458 sat in the

Oratory; the 354 members of the Third Estate remained at La Couture. In the parish meetings in Mayenne, Cheverus' own city, representatives worked busily from March 1 to March 8 preparing their *cahiers* of grievances. Respect for Louis XVI was generally present, but the winter just ending had been exceptionally hard on the underprivileged classes and suggestions for reform were radical.[2]

The clergy of the Province of Maine agreed that the good of the nation might now require same sacrifices. But this modest view was unacceptable to many of the electors at Le Mans. In all three assemblies there was great tumult. The clergy themselves very nearly failed to elect their own bishop a delegate, and the closing sessions on March 30 gave ominous warning of the future religion would face in the Diocese of Le Mans. Bishop Gonssans was more than usually earnest in his pastoral of April 18, urging prayers for the general meeting scheduled for May 5, 1789.

The news of the fall of the Bastille in Paris on July 14 reached Mayenne four days later. There was very little surprise in the city, and much less dissatisfaction. The mayor, Cheverus' Uncle Julien, gave a speech, and the citizens formed a civilian militia to keep order. Over in Le Mans the bishop prescribed a Forty Hours' devotion for the state of the nation to begin on September 20. But the clergy were scarcely more disturbed by the event than the average man. When the National Assembly abolished clerical privileges in August bishops rivaled each other in generous acquiescence, and the Archbishop of Paris proposed a *Te Deum*. As late as September 28 the clergy were still consenting freely to the surrender to the treasury of all ornaments of precious metals not essential to the sacred rites of the Church.[3]

But by the time of the October opening of classes at Saint-Magloire an indefinable change was coming over the nation. Anticlerical passions were beginning to awaken, and ecclesiastical deputies to the Assembly began to receive insults. And the subdeacon from Mayenne, hurrying on his way from Porte St. Jacques where Saint-Magloire was located to Louis-le-Grand to act as master of conferences, heard the word *calotin* sneeringly hurled after men in clerical garb. By November 2 the National Assembly had a substantial majority in support of a measure to place Church properties at the disposition of the nation. As Count Mirabeau put it, priests were now public officials. The first sale of ecclesiastical property was decreed on December 19, and this latest "reform" was under way. The clergy still did not raise strong objections. In the Diocese of Le Mans both the bishop and the pastors

asserted that this deprivation would be accepted without a murmur.[4]
For Jean de Cheverus the chief change for the moment seemed simply
that his revenues from Torbéchet would now be paid by the treasurer
of the District of Mayenne.[5]

It is a matter of history that the French clergy of the Old Regime
deserved criticism in many areas. The Diocese of Le Mans in 1789
had an excellent bishop in Jouffroy de Gonssans. But the memory
of his predecessor could not be erased. Louis de Grimaldi had offered
a notorious contrast. Not only was it rumored that ladies of pleasure
had been received at the episcopal palace, but people still lived who
recalled his passion for hunting in red coat and white stockings and
the day when, meeting a procession chanting the Litany of the Blessed
Virgin, he had spurred his horse and driven through the devout
crowd.[6] The deplorable episcopate of Grimaldi had nearly ruined
clerical discipline, and the heroic efforts of Gonssans did not have the
success they deserved. Although most of the clergy of the province
were from profoundly Christian families, followed serious studies, and
performed a laborious ministry, the quiet virtues of the many had
far less effect on heated imaginations than the memory of former evils
and the scandal brought by the few.[7]

The regular clergy, too, those living in seclusion by hallowed rules,
came in for their share of hatred. Although they constituted scarcely
one tenth of the total, the Diocese of Le Mans included abbeys of
Benedictines, Augustinians, Chartreux, Dominicans, Cordeliers, Recol-
lets, Capucines, and Minims.[8] To these were added the secular congregations: the Lazarists of the Seminary of Coëffert, the Oratorians
of the Collège du Mans, and the Eudists of the seminary-college of
Domfront-en-Passais.[9] There were many religious women in the diocese
as well. On February 13, 1790, the French Assembly abolished religious
orders; it was this law of secularization which finally brought a definite
schism between the clergy and the government. The prelates of France
could no longer acquiesce. From their point of view the civil authority
was now infringing on the rights of the Church. When the Declaration
of the Rights of Man introduced beyond any shadow of a doubt the
principle of indifferentism to religion, the schism was permanent. As
one French historian has expressed it, "On the ruins of the Gallican
Church, and in opposition to it, the Assembly was to organize another,
the Constitutional Church. Thus was to be consummated, after temporary union, the divorce . . . between Catholicism and the Revolution."[10] It needed only the decree of July 12, 1790, establishing the

Civil Constitution of the Clergy, to complete a national church independent of both king and pope.[11]

The abolition of the former provinces of France and the creation of eighty-three *départements,* taken together with the Civil Constitution of the Clergy, brought immediate changes to France. The decree of the Assembly that there should be as many dioceses as *départements* meant that fifty-two episcopal sees were now abolished; of the eighty-three left a grouping was to be made under ten metropolitan sees.[12] Of 160 bishops of the Old Regime only seven supported the Civil Constitution of the Clergy, and of these seven only four actually governed dioceses. Of the latter, Talleyrand of Autun resigned his see and thus eighty new constitutional prelates were to be elected.[13] With few exceptions the non-juring hierarchy quietly left the field to their elected successors. "The Gallican Church had now been decapitated as well as cut off from Rome and the king's protection."[14]

The Province of Maine in which Mayenne was located now became part of two new *départements,* Sarthe with its capital at Le Mans, and Mayenne with its capital at Laval. The city of Mayenne had hoped to become capital of the latter and Uncle Julien had been one of the unsuccessful agitators toward that end. When the directory of the Département de Mayenne was organized on July 7, 1790, Lefebvre de Champorin was chosen one of the members; two years later he had risen to vice-president of the directory.[15] It was natural that Uncle Julien should settle in Laval, the new capital.

Since the episcopal sees now coincided with the capitals of the new political divisions, the city of Mayenne belonged to the Diocese of Laval rather than to Le Mans. Cheverus' new diocese had the questionable distinction of being one of the first to have an elected bishop. The faithful were in an excruciating quandary those first months after the creation of the constitutional church. Although the king had signed the Civil Constitution on August 24, 1790, it was eight months before Pius VI made clear the Roman attitude toward the new state of affairs in the French Church. In the interim the new directors of the Département de Mayenne were primarily anxious to prevent disorders. Finally, on November 16 the procurer-general distributed circulars announcing that an election would take place on Sunday, December 12. This was the precise situation at the time that Deacon Cheverus began his retreat at Saint-Magloire prior to his ordination.

On the day appointed for the election only 295 of the 425 electors met in Trinity Church. A high Mass was celebrated, and then the clergy withdrew. Pierre Sourdelle de la Valette, the presiding officer, opened with a speech lauding the work of the National Assembly of Paris, and the Civil Constitution of the Clergy in particular. France, he shouted, was now returned to the methods of the primitive Church; scandal at last was at an end. He then called for nominations.

Three names were popular but a third ballot finally elected Michel Thoumin des Vauxponts.[16] Vauxponts was a vicar-general of the Bishop of Dol, Urbain-René de Hercé, and a friend of Uncle Julien's. Both Vauxponts and Hercé were natives of the city of Mayenne and the former, in spite of considerable personal fortune, lived very simply in Cheverus' native city. Lefebvre de Champorin who had helped elect his friend was delegated to go and escort him to Laval. But Uncle Julien returned from Mayenne alone with the news that the bishop-elect refused to serve. Yet scarcely had this news been made public when word reached Laval that Bishop Hercé had prevailed upon his vicar-general to accept.[17] In the end, this news, too, was refuted. Vauxponts consulted Rome and when Pius VI forbade him to accept he obeyed. And this was the situation when the newly ordained Cheverus began his sacerdotal career.

It is difficult to conceive a situation more perplexing to a man of Cheverus' age, temperament, and vocation. Under ordinary circumstances he could have entered the active period of his ministry with little confusion. As a priest he was prepared to obey his ecclesiastical superiors; as a Frenchman he was prepared to give devoted service to his king. By nature, Jean de Cheverus was endowed with an almost eager veneration for discipline and authority. At the same time, his youth and recent ordination filled him with impatient zeal to begin his service to Church, monarch, and fellow man. A half-century earlier it would have been possible to serve all three consistently with the same ministry. But now confusion reigned. It was not certain that Louis XVI, in spite of his signature, required his priests to accept the new order in ecclesiastical affairs. Until March 10, 1791, Cheverus could not know, either, whether Rome would approve. More immediately, there was the question of his own superior; did he still take orders from Jouffroy de Gonssans, or was he supposed to wait until a new constitutional Bishop of Laval accepted his election? French priests ordained in 1790 began their careers under most unenviable auspices; within two brief years, for most of them, life within France itself was not even possible.

The city in which Cheverus hoped to begin his work comprised two

parishes in 1791: Saint-Martin and Notre Dame. The pastor of the
latter was his uncle and baptismal sponsor, Louis-René de Cheverus,
who had been at Notre Dame since the year Jean was born. The
older Cheverus was in extremely poor health, and his nephew was
welcomed as a sorely needed assistant.[18] Neither of the relatives, however, was destined for service at Notre Dame very much longer. His
uncle had from the first consistently refused to adhere to the new
constitutional regime, and on February 12, without waiting for the
official attitude of Rome to be announced, young Jean also refused to
take the oath prescribed by the law of December 26, 1790. Five days
later an election in Sarthe named Jacques-Guillaume Prudhomme de
la Boussinière des Vallées bishop to replace Jouffroy de Gonssans; on
March 20, Gabriel-Noël Villars was elected Bishop of Laval in the
face of Vauxponts' refusal.

Gonssans on March 28 pronounced both of the elected prelates
schismatics, but his clergy did not agree in accepting this judgment.
Many remained loyal to their former superior; others awaited the
installation of the constitutional bishops. The radicals among the laity
ignored Gonssans completely. On April 16 in Cheverus' own city a
Jacobin Club was inaugurated in the Church of the Capucines with a
Mass celebrated by a constitutional priest. Jacques-François Bissy, a
lawyer who later led the Terror in the city, pronounced a terrible diatribe
against the Cheverus priests and the other non-jurors of Mayenne.
Schism was now an open fact. The installation of Villars at Laval
on May 31 was the signal for the beginning of disorders and violence.[19]

The first faint rumble of disaster began in Laval on that occasion. The
city ordered a general illumination in honor of the bishop's installation. When several houses refused to comply, stones, clubs, and sabers
were used against the recalcitrants, and when the divisions of the
National Guard from Mayenne who had gone up to Laval for the
ceremonies returned they were in a nasty mood. They demanded that
a general illumination be decreed in Mayenne, and the mayor reluctantly
complied. At eleven that night a crowd of young people began roaming
the streets singing, "Ça ira, ça ira!" Small children and the riffraff
of the town followed in their wake, breaking windows, and beating at
doors of the houses not lighted to their taste. The rioting went on
until two in the morning.[20]

If the townspeople seemed to be forming in hostile ranks, so did
the clergy. Saint-Martin's parish and Notre Dame were separated
by the river which flowed through Mayenne. A single bridge in the

center of town connected them. But the bridge now ceased to be symbolic of communication, for the priests of Saint-Martin took the oath and accepted Bishop Villars. At Notre Dame only one inactive priest took the oath, but both the pastor and his assistants continued to regard Jouffroy de Gonssans as their superior. On Ascension Day many of the parishioners of Saint-Martin, convinced that attending a Mass at Notre Dame would be no sin and not so certain about one at their parish church, tried to cross the bridge. The National Guard and the former rioters met on the bridge at nine o'clock that morning and forcibly prevented the would-be worshipers from reaching the church where Cheverus was offering Mass. From that day on any citizen suspected of sympathizing with the Cheverus priests was insulted and threatened.[21]

By the middle of June the radicals of Mayenne were even violating the sanctity of funerals in their fervor for constitutional priests. A certain Mme Sougé-Lusseau, who was distantly related to the Cheverus family, had expressed the wish before she died that she be buried by a non-juring priest. Her body was taken to and fro, from the cemetery and back, three times by crowds screaming, "Ça ira!" and in the tumult the coffin burst open. Even the constitutional priests were ashamed of their adherents and asked the city magistrates to intervene. The officials replied by banning all religious ceremonies entirely. When the news of the king's flight to Varennes on June 20 reached Mayenne the Terror really began in that city.[22]

Through the first days of confusion and violence Jean de Cheverus conducted himself with courage and equanimity. Although his uncle was now so incapacitated that all decisions had to be made by the nephew, Cheverus staunchly kept at his post. Gonssans sent down from Paris in June a pastoral authorizing his clergy to exercise their functions if need be in private homes instead of the churches.[23] But until well through July the non-jurors at Notre Dame continued services in the church. The two salaried assistants, Cheverus and François-René Esnault, were given the moral support of two volunteers, but when Cheverus and Esnault refused to read the pastoral letter of Bishop Villars of Laval, putting their refusal in writing on July 17, the authorities of the *département* were compelled to act.[24]

It was an embarrassing situation. Julien, the young assistant's uncle of the Champorin branch of the family, was one of those authorities. Further, the actual condition of Louis de Cheverus' health, together with his virtuous conduct over the years, demanded some consideration.

In spite of the animus of the mob, the men serving the nation were still gentlemen and alive to feelings of respect and pity. A suggestion was made that since doctors could testify to the elder Cheverus' condition, and, it was hinted, might show that if he had full control of his reason he might have taken the oath, could he not at least retain the title of pastor that he had borne so long with honor? After all, the conduct of rash assistants did not bind the pastor.[25] The electors were soon to meet to select a constitutional pastor for Notre Dame. A decision from the directors at Laval might keep the position for the sick man while he lived out his few remaining days.

The meeting of the electors took place on August 1 amid incredible confusion. The choir of Notre Dame was filled with "an immense crowd of citizens, women, and inhabitants who were pell-mell with the electors, preventing all possibility of work." The meeting had to be adjourned until three that afternoon. The city officials again asked the *département* to revise the provisional decree regarding the vacancy. People still questioned the legality of the vacancy's existence.[26] Louis de Cheverus was still pastor as the year came to its hectic close.

Then, just three days before his death on January 24, 1792, the elder Cheverus was replaced by Jean-François Hubert Dauvernay, a juring priest who had been chaplain at the Madeleine. Gonssans, on the death of Louis, named Jean de Cheverus pastor of Notre Dame, but the young non-juror was never allowed to take possession of his parish. The jubilant radicals installed Dauvernay, forcing Cheverus to fulfill his functions in private chapels or homes.[27] It was a grim way in which to begin the second year of his priesthood. But the end would be even worse. Within two months he was hounded out of his native city; by autumn he was driven out of France. Yet under the gentle, docile exterior of the small twenty-four year old man there was a streak of steel. Once the decision was made on that February day in 1791, he never faltered. Indeed, if it had not been for his concern for his family he might have remained in Mayenne a hunted priest or a martyr.

A decree of the National Assembly on May 6, 1791, had promised a quasi-liberty to non-juring priests, a liberality for which Talleyrand, the former Bishop of Autun, and Abbé Sièyes, the former vicar-general of Chartres, were largely responsible. Priests who refused to take the oath were still to be allowed to say Mass in the constitutional churches or places furnished by the faithful, but they could administer none of the sacraments nor could they preach sermons.[28] Yet opposition to even this degree of moderation developed in the *départements* almost immediately. In Aisne priests were ordered to leave their houses within twenty-four hours; in Reims they were refused the use of linen, candles, bread and wine. By March 23, 1792, Mayenne went even further and ordered all non-juring clergy to register in Laval and to remain within distance to answer a daily roll call. When Urbain Hercé first heard this news at his brother's chateau his family tried to persuade him to resist, but the Bishop of Dol retorted, "Heaven prevent me from losing such an occasion to confess the name of Jesus Christ."[29] Hundreds of priests left their shelters and families to follow Hercé's example.

Jean de Cheverus did not immediately obey. His concern for the faithful of Mayenne and the responsibility he felt toward his rightful bishop, who had made him pastor of Notre Dame, compelled him to stay even though he had to minister in secret. The scandalous conduct of some of the constitutional priests caused the virtuous Catholics to flock to Cheverus. Over in Saint-Martin's one priest went about the city accompanied by soldiers gathering up children of the aristocrats and baptizing them with such names as "Liberty," "Equality," or "Carmagnole" while a local prostitute stood godmother. The godfather on these occasions was a cleric appointed by the constitutional bishop, Villars, himself.[30] Cheverus could not abandon his fellow Catholics to the tender offices of such scoundrels.

The longer he stayed in Mayenne, however, the more infuriated the radicals became. First they tried to seize him while he was offering Mass, but the faithful crowded around their little shepherd and prevented it. Then, a few days later, rumor said that the authorities would secretly carry him off while he was alone. A crowd of loyal friends gathered around his place of refuge and again foiled the attempt.[31] Finally Cheverus received a letter telling him that if he did not leave Mayenne at once his father's house would be burned to the ground. At last he was moved. Physical threats to his own person were one thing; but his widowed father, and his brothers and sisters, must not be innocent victims however willing. Together with his friend and relative, Jean-Ambroise Sougé, Cheverus fled. The two priests remained overnight in a country house three quarters of a league away, and then on the next day went to Laval.[32]

For more than two months Cheverus lived with his Uncle Julien in Laval, going each day for the roll call of priests at the collegiate chapel along with Bishop Hercé and the 600 or more priests. The calm dignity of Hercé infuriated the Jacobins and apostate clergy of the city and one day they tried to snatch his pectoral cross, but the other priests, Cheverus among them, intervened. Vauxponts, Hercé's vicar-general, answered the daily roll, too. This man, who had only lately been asked to be their bishop, was now accused along with the others of carrying concealed weapons under his cassock. But the non-juring clergy of Mayenne could not be provoked. "They know not what pleasure they give us by enhancing our confessions of Faith," they replied to sympathetic citizens who would have defended them. Cheverus felt it an honor to bear the taunts and gibes of the Jacobins.

But soon the rancor of the Jacobins could not be satisfied by the mere daily roll call. On June 20 when the priests gathered for the daily proof that they had not fled back to their posts of duty the drums beat, a proclamation was read, and without further warning the clergy were herded into the former convents of the Carmelites and Capucines which had recently been denuded with the approbation of Bishop Villars. Not a stick of furniture was left, but the indignant Catholics of Laval rose to the occasion; by nightfall beds, at least, were provided. A few chairs and tables soon appeared, as well. Jean de Cheverus found himself confined in the same cell with Hercé and Vauxponts.[33]

The days that followed were nightmarish. The civilian officials made no provision for feeding the priests crowded into the small cells and corridors, and even the chapels of the convent prisons. The kind-hearted citizens of Laval again came to the rescue with food, but they could do nothing against the horror of the nights. Guards strolled rudely past the reclining bodies of the clergy, ladies of pleasure on their arms, prodding the priests with bayonets, singing obscene songs, or snarling, "You are not fat enough to kill yet," or "Your head will look better under the guillotine!" Often after the worst nights the guards refused to let provisions enter the prisons. There began to circulate rumors that a massacre of the entire group was on foot. It was a known fact that the Jacobins had already demanded the expulsion of priests from France.[34]

Julien Lefebvre de Champorin, now vice-president of the directory at Laval, feared for the life of his nephew and persuaded him to plead his illness to the guards. He himself assured the authorities that his nephew would be under surveillance in his uncle's house. Apparently Uncle Julien was influential enough to merit this favor. In any case, Jean was allowed to go to his relative's home. Julien succeeded in getting a passport for a merchant and the last week in June the small priest, now disguised as a layman, fled to Paris.[35]

His brother Louis was studying law at Louis-le-Grand, but Jean was too well known as a priest in that area of Paris to seek Louis out openly. He went into hiding at an obscure lodging near Saint-Eustache where he spent two miserable months of furtive existence. It was here that he learned that the wish of the Jacobins in May was now law binding all non-juring priests. On August 26 the Paris government decreed that they had eight days to get out of their *départements* and fifteen to get out of France. On May 26, of course, it had already been stipulated that any dissident suspected of favoring invasion of France by foreign powers and denounced by twenty citizens should be expelled. But now the decree fell on all. Any priest who remained in the country after the issuance of his passport was to be condemned to ten years in prison.

After the harrowing weeks of concealment the news was almost a relief. Clerical garb was now forbidden to all except the constitutional priests assigned to parishes. Cheverus' landlord, he knew, was suspicious of the small young man who prayed so earnestly in his room. Cheverus was tired of hiding his breviary every time he heard a step slowing down outside his door. If he could only secure a passport he would gladly go anywhere to be allowed to follow his vocation in peace. He knew that if his uncle or brother could manage it a passport would soon be his.

On Sunday, September 2, he felt a yearning to go over on the Left Bank where the streets and churches were so familiar since his college days, and where Louis might be able to give him some news. It was dangerous, he knew. The Seminary of Saint-Sulpice had been forced to give one of its largest rooms for committee meetings of the Revolutionary authorities. The chapel of the Blessed Sacrament of the splendid Church of Saint-Sulpice, one of the newest in Paris, was now converted into a bureau of enrollments. But every street in the city was dangerous after August 26, and Cheverus was irresistibly drawn to the quarter where so many of his priestly colleagues were held prisoner in the Carmes, and in the abbey at Saint-Germain-des-Prés. His old mentor, Principal Berardier of Louis-le-Grand, was one of the men detained in that area. Jean-Marie Dulau, the Archbishop of Arles, and the Rochefoucauld-Bayers of Beauvais and Saintes were known to be in the convent of the Carmes. The king's confessor was there, too, along with many professors from the university and the superior of the Benedictines.[36]

Suddenly from the direction of Saint-Sulpice a maddened crowd rushed up the Rues Vaugirard and Cassette, pushed into the Carmes, and a horrible sound rent the Sunday afternoon air. Inside the garden courtyard, where the clergy had been sent at two o'clock by the head of the Revolutionary committee of the section, the helpless priests were first harassed by sanguinary shouts of the mob from the cloister windows. But almost immediately seven or eight young men armed with pistols and brandishing sabers entered the garden itself crying, "Where is the Archbishop of Arles?" Jean-Marie Dulau was struck down without having a chance to move from his place of meditation.

Some of the priests fled to the chapel altar and were killed at prayer; some climbed trees or scrambled over the garden walls into the Rue Cassette, but most of them were forced back into the church from which they were taken by twos, asked if they had taken the oath, and upon their negative answers, were assassinated. Of the 160 confined in the Carmes 116 perished in that awful afternoon.[37]

Jean de Cheverus could only guess what frightful martyrdoms were occurring. In frantic haste he darted off in the direction of the Sorbonne and finally reached Rue St. Jacques and his brother's room where Louis insisted that he remain in hiding.[38] No priest was safe on the streets of the Left Bank that terrible day of massacre. All too soon the brothers learned that the events at the Carmes had been only one of many massacres. The abbey at Saint-Germain-des-Prés had over 300 martyrs; the Concièrgerie had 100; Châtelet, La Force, Bicêtre, La Salpetrière, Tour Saint-Bernard, and the Seminary of Saint-Firmin all suffered terrible slaughter. Over 1000 souls had been dispatched in one day. Although the executions fell upon nobles, former officials, malefactors under the common law, and women of the streets, the clergy furnished the greatest number of victims. One question alone was asked. "Have you taken the oath?" The answer "No" meant instant death.[39] There was now no question of delay. Cheverus must, if he could, leave France at once.

Back in Mayenne friends and families had been trying desperately to aid priests out of the country ever since the August decree. After September 5, when the news of the Paris massacres reached the city, anxiety had increased. On September 7 Julien Lefebvre de Champorin presented the directory of the Département de Mayenne an urgent request for a passport for his nephew. "If he had stayed in his region he would have obtained the permission he solicits," he argued. All Jean asked was a passport to go from Calais to England.[40] Up in Paris Louis, too, was feverishly trying to solve his brother's problem. First he got a visa for the merchant's passport Cheverus had used in his flight from Laval. But then he decided that a passport for a man going to England would be safer, and, posing as his brother, obtained it. On September 11 Jean de Cheverus arrived at Calais.[41]

It was the last his family heard of him for many a day. Back in Laval on September 23 the directory received a petition demanding the deportation of a list of priests of Mayenne. The petition was signed by 100 citizens who cited the law of August 26. Jean Lefebvre de Cheverus was fifty-fourth on the list and inconsistently titled *Curé de Mayenne*.[42] But the young pastor whose rights had never been recognized by the petitioners, and whose parish had never really been his, was gone. Three decades would pass before he would see his native city again. Uncle Julien in Laval who had tried to help him would himself suffer arrest as the Terror progressed.[43] The ancient and honorable family of Lefebvre had fallen upon evil days.

CHAPTER III

ÉMIGRÉ IN ENGLAND

THE physical distance which Cheverus traversed from Calais to Dover was the shortest expanse of water separating the shores of his homeland and his first land of exile, and yet in the year 1792 the two countries were never farther removed in those human matters which ultimately shape men's lives. To the French radicalism that effected the September Massacres England presented a conservatism that found Whigs going to the support of William Pitt and the Tories. At the very moment that France, a traditionally Catholic nation, seemed determined to destroy the power of that form of Christianity, England, which had been Protestant since the sixteenth century, now offered Catholics a degree of toleration. Economically, the predominant agrarianism of the French scene was matched by a rising industrialism across the Channel. And a few months after Cheverus' arrival the two nations were in fact at odds; for France declared war on England on February 1, 1793. Never had so few miles of water signified a greater gulf between two ways of life.

Yet, oddly enough, only a few years before Cheverus embarked at Calais these disparities had not been so evident. The earliest phases of the French Revolution had been loudly acclaimed in England. Charles James Fox had exclaimed at the fall of the Bastille in 1789, "How much the greatest event it is in the history of the world and how much the best!" The romantic poetry of William Wordsworth would ecstatically recall, "Bliss was it then in that dawn to be alive; but to be young was very heaven." Dr. Richard Price's sermon which subsequently elicited Burke's *Reflections on the French Revolution* first fell on approving ears as he ventured to see in the French events a con-

25

structive imitation of the glorious English Revolution of 1688. But the jubilation had quickly vanished. As stability and rank were swept away before the French doctrine of equality Burke raised a portentous voice denouncing "the wild attempt to methodize anarchy" and the Revolution became to English eyes a foul, impious, and monstrous thing. Fear of French agents led to such excitement that the British cabinet, without the actual pretext of insurrection, did not hesitate to issue a proclamation against seditious notions in 1792. Two years later Parliament was even willing to suspend that centuries-old principle of *habeas corpus*. Political reform which had briefly raised its head in the first decade following the loss of the American colonies was doomed to languish for the rest of the half-century after the Treaty of Paris of 1783.

The changed attitude toward Catholics, too, was a very recent thing. Prior to the Relief Act of 1791 Catholic life in England had been characterized by poverty, paucity of numbers, secrecy in practice, sporadic persecution, and, in respect to the clergy at least, a lamentable level of culture. During the years that Jean de Cheverus was a student in Paris there were scarcely 56,000 Catholics out of six million people living in all of England and Wales. Joseph Berington sadly admitted, "The truth is, within the past century we have most rapidly decreased," and John Henry Newman later described the Catholics of that period as "not a sect, not even an interest . . . but a mere handful of individuals, who might be counted like the pebbles and detritus of the great deluge." Until the arrival of the French *émigrés* there were no public chapels except in the foreign embassies; private ones, like St. Mary's at Lulworth Castle, were disguised to resemble a mausoleum or some other inconspicuous and innocuous appendage.[1]

The clergy concealed their true character by dressing as laymen and their letters disguised references to their superiors with contrived aliases. The vicars-apostolic were hidden in names like "Cousin Bona" or "Tarleton"; the Pope might appear as "Mr. Abraham" or "The Old Gentleman." The Irish and English Catholics Cheverus came to know had vivid recollections of the Gordon Riots of a dozen years past when embassy chapels were ransacked and the houses of Parliament were visited by rioters protesting the Relief Act of 1778. Only the courageous intervention of the king had ended the plundering and destruction.[2] It was small wonder that the scattered homes of the landed Catholic gentry remained the Catholic centers of England and that the faithful were compelled to depend upon the daring of some large house which risked harboring a priest. The Faith had almost died out in the towns.[3]

By fateful coincidence Cheverus reached England at the very time in history that some amelioration in the condition of the Roman Catholics was legally guaranteed. As a matter of fact, the very month that the first fleeing French bishop reached English shores, Sir John Mitford rose in the House of Commons to introduce an acceptable bill for Catholic Relief. Not that the old laws of persecution were to be repealed; but Catholics were at least to be freed in private life from the old penalties, and religious exercises could be held in public places. The old prohibition against the Mass was removed. "It was for the Catholics the law's permission to exist."[4] Just as English Catholicism had reached its nadir the Relief Act of 1791 and the first trickle of French priests combined to predict the dawning of a new day. By the time Cheverus arrived the sun was above the horizon.

If Jean de Cheverus had been deported with the other clergy imprisoned at Laval, he would have left France from Granville and arrived first on the Island of Jersey with Bishop Hercé and the others he knew from Mayenne.[5] Instead, because he had fled from Calais, he went directly to England without the consolation of friendly companions, and with only 300 francs in his possession. Although there were already a few *émigrés* in England, Cheverus was part of one of the three great waves of clerical emigrants to reach those shores during the course of the upheavals in France. Their precursor had been Jean-François de la Marche, Bishop of St. Pol de Léon, who had arrived on a storm-battered little smuggling vessel at Mount Bay on the Cornwall coast on February 28, 1791.[6] François A. Matignon, who was destined to become Cheverus' dearest friend, had also arrived in London that spring of 1791.[7] Matignon whom Cheverus had known as a professor in Paris was gone from England by September, but Bishop de la Marche who had found refuge at Wardour Castle hurried to London when he learned of the deportation decree of the French Assembly. The three great tides of *émigrés,* those of 1792, 1794–1795, and 1797, found this indefatigable prelate waiting to welcome them and offer his assistance in finding them places of refuge.[8] Cheverus, who was only one of many thousands who descended upon the Protestant nation in the autumn of 1792, was quickly placed near a prominent Catholic family in Oxfordshire.

The story of one small exile nearly disappears in that larger saga of displaced persons. Of the first great exodus following the September

Massacres some 2000 took refuge on the Channel Isles while another 3000 landed at various ports of England. Wearing fantastic disguises and still dazed from the horrors they had seen, they could not help but touch the hearts of the English who received them. One aged bishop was reduced to ill-fitting trousers and a straw hat; a vicar-general arrived in a carter's smock; a simple priest's blood-stained cassock was silent witness to the murderous bayonet thrusts that had slashed him.[9] Many were old; all were bereft. The flower of the clergy of the country from which they had so painfully escaped, they were in English eyes pitiful victims of inhuman persecution. Considerations of religion, nationality, or class, vanished in the undiscriminating gaze of humanitarianism and charity.

The little *émigré* who had arrived from Calais in merchant's guise would suffer cruelly from the natural pangs of violent uprooting. Being French he could not help but suffer. "The language, the amenity of relations, the sociability, the vivacity of race, all that constitutes the temperament of a people . . . climate, soil, even the undulations of the countryside, the inexplicable atmosphere — physical, intellectual, moral — in a word, France," all this was missing.[10] Because of his own nature the ex-pastor of Notre Dame de Mayenne would experience sheer desolation. To a man whose family ties had been so dear the mere separation from his father, from his brothers and sisters, was a wound from which he never recovered. Long years afterward a friend recorded, "He never spoke of his sufferings, during his last two years in France, or his difficulties and privations in England, without being so much affected as to distress his friends."[11] His was a heart from which love flowed naturally and limitlessly. Love had found its former objects in family, king, and fatherland. Now that king was dead, that family torn from him by this harsh exile decreed by the country that had been part of his very being. As young as he was, it is still surprising that the impact of this triple deprivation did not leave upon his sensitive nature a deeper scar than it did.

The great and first love of his heart was always his God and that Will which decreed what man cannot evaluate. From his earliest youth Cheverus had learned to say the *Pater noster* and now, when it required a docility beyond the most exaggerated imaginings of his adolescence, he would and did repeat those words, "Thy will be done." He sought with humility and found with fortitude the consolations that this new, alien world had to offer.

One of these consolations was the magnanimity of his hosts. An

English priest wrote to America that autumn that London was bursting with French *émigrés*. "It is a pleasing thing," he added, "to see Englishmen of all religious persuasions trying to exceed each other in generosity and charity to relieve their distress. If we do not excel in religion, we are at least not lost to feelings of humanity."[12] If an English Catholic saw some novelty in Protestant generosity toward a religion generally detested when practiced by their own countrymen, Frenchmen like Jean de Cheverus were simply grateful. After the indescribable scenes that had passed before their horrified eyes, after the months of harrowing flights from place to place, the serenity of the English countryside and cities, where no bayonets were raised against them, where officers of the peace went unarmed, and where ordinary citizens went quietly about their affairs obedient to law, was like waking from a nightmare. The mere silence was a blessing to ears that had been pierced by the cannibal cries of "Ça ira," the incessant beating of drums, the agonizing moans of the dying. How sweet was the sympathy in English eyes which seemed to say, "You have suffered much. Come, stay. You have nothing now to fear."[13]

Although Cheverus has left no record of his arrival in England, it is not hard to imagine how it must have seemed. Another refugee, the Abbé Barruel, later recorded their impressions.

> Every vessel that arrived with a cargo of these exiles seemed to have been foreseen by the English through an instinct of benevolence. They flocked to the landing places to offer us a lodging or refreshments. Fifty, a hundred of us, arrived at a time. They seemed more concerned for us than we were for ourselves. Where lodgings could not be had, a spacious room was prepared. . . . There they were nourished, visited, and questioned about their needs. Carriages were hired for them, and frequently on the road a gentleman, a lady, or a tradesman paid their expenses at the inn, and sometimes defrayed the whole journey to London.[14]

From king to lowliest subject the nation seemed bent upon outdoing its nobler impulses. George III asked the bishops of the Church of England to start a fund for the French exiles,[15] and Pius VI expressed his gratitude in a letter to Bishop de la Marche saying, "We have thought it fitting to write to you that you may assure the members of the committee of our lively gratitude towards the king and the nation, who in this respect have added new lustre to the Crown and the honour of their country."[16] The clergy of the Church of England responded magnificently to the appeal of the king and their own hearts. When the floods of immigrants threatened to exhaust the first relief funds subscribed Samuel Horsley, who was Bishop of St. David's and one of the most distinguished scholars of the day, rose in the House of Lords to urge:

> None at this season are more entitled to our offices of love than those with whom the difference is wide in doctrine, discipline and external rites; these venerable exiles, the prelates and clergy of the fallen Church of France, endeared to us by the edifying example they exhibit of patient suffering for conscience's sake.[17]

His appeal brought a house to house collection which resulted in the raising of £41,000. Horsley himself had already done yeoman service for the English Catholics in his parliamentary address at the time the Relief Bill was under discussion. His amendment to the bill was believed by many to have saved orthodoxy for Catholics of England.[18]

Horsley was only one, however, of many Anglicans who gave the weight of their office and good will to the *émigré* cause. Dr. John Sturges, chancellor of the Diocese of Winchester where so many priests were sheltered in the King's House until 1796, defended the French from charges of proselytism. "It is natural and commendable for us to be vigilantly on our guard," he publicly announced. "But while we are thus on guard it is but justice to these unfortunate men, not to give admission to complaints against them without proper information or proof." He pointed out that their conduct in general was exemplary in the highest degree and begged his coreligionists to cast no shadow on the "brightest instance of national benevolence" they had recently displayed.[19] Other ministers like Dr. George Gregory, the energetic member of the Royal Humane Society, and Thomas Scott, the noted biblical commentator and chaplain at Lock Hospital in London, were assiduous in working for this most interesting of humanitarian ends.

Catholic prelates were equally zealous, it goes without saying. John Douglass, the Vicar-Apostolic of the London District, was one to whom Cheverus was particularly grateful. After he was gone from England Cheverus told Douglass, "Nothing shall ever blot out from my heart the grateful remembrance of your condescending and amiable friendship."[20] Douglass was revered by the exiles as the bishop who "received them with bounty, directed them by advice, as he edified them by his virtues."[21] He rallied the Catholic laity in a pastoral letter which urged, "Persevere in the work of mercy, and let your abundance supply their want; considering the example they hold out to us, for they have not hesitated to forego every advantage of a worldly nature to preserve their consciences unstained. . . ."[22] He immediately granted faculties to five French archbishops, twenty-seven bishops, and thirteen former vicars-general whom he exuberantly noted in his diary as "the bishops and vicars-general employed by me." It was John Douglass who soon was to dedicate the permanent chapel founded by Jean de Cheverus in Tottenham.[23]

Cheverus had reason to remember Bishop Thomas Talbot, too. Although he was in the jurisdiction of the Vicar-Apostolic of the Midland District only briefly the young French exile could scarcely forget the man who welcomed so many priests from Mayenne, Sougé and Vauxponts among them. By report Cheverus learned, too, that Bishop Charles Walmesley, O.S.B., of the Western District was a devoted friend to the *émigrés*. Walmesley kept in close touch with Thomas Weld who started a Trappist community on his ancestral estate. Thomas Weld already had the honor of having built the first Catholic chapel in England since the Reformation.[24] The advent of the French found him happily giving six monks of La Trappe enough land to maintain themselves. By 1794 he was confiding in Walmesley his intention of building them their own house and proper chapel. "It gives me great pleasure," he wrote, "to find my charity to these good monks of La Trappe coincides with your ideas. They are without exception the living saints of the Church of God upon earth."[25] Although it is unlikely that Cheverus ever met either Bishop Walmesley or Thomas Weld, the three men came to have one bond in common in the person of John Carroll of Baltimore. It was Walmesley who had consecrated Carroll in 1790; it was Weld who furnished Lulworth Chapel for the occasion; and it was Cheverus who became after 1796 the devoted friend of Carroll's episcopal years.

Another priest who worked valiantly for the rehabilitation of the French was John Milner who was destined to become Bishop of Castabala and Vicar-Apostolic of the Midland District. He had come to London in 1791 as a parliamentary agent from Winchester during the debates over the Catholic Relief Bill, but he had enough zeal to defend Catholics both French and English.[26] Not content with establishing a chapel for the 1000 *émigrés* at Winchester, Milner translated and had printed the *Letter of Right Rev. John Francis de la Marche, Bishop of Leon, addressed to the French Clergymen Refugees in England.* At a service in St. Peter's Chapel at Winchester Milner preached a stirring eulogy of Louis XVI on April 12, 1793. A year later he was busy establishing Benedictine nuns at Winchester, after their flight from Brussels on June 22, 1794.[27]

The princes of the churches were not to be outdone by the nobility. Henry, the seventh Baron Arundell, who had first sheltered Bishop de la Marche continued to take refugees into his home. Father Philip Wyndham, his chaplain, commented on the arrival of eighteen priests at Wardour Castle, "I was greatly edified at their behaviour, having come ten miles afoot, and being Ember Day, though they had been three days at sea in great danger of perishing, they could not be prevailed upon to take anything else but a little cabbage, turnips, and such kind of food."[28] Wardour was accustomed to edifying refugees, having accommodated John Carroll two decades earlier when he fled from Bruges in October, 1773.[29] Lady Christine Arundell had the habit of hospitality.

George Nugent-Temple-Granvill, the Marquis of Buckingham, whose residence in Ireland as Lord Lieutenant had overcome his prejudices against Catholics, likewise took up the cause of the newcomers. After Oxford University published a Vulgate edition of the Bible expressly for the French clergy, Buckingham himself subsidized a second printing. His wife, who was a Catholic, started a tapestry factory near Winchester to help the impoverished priests augment their incomes. The names of the marquis and his lady were later carved in marble to express the gratitude of the 700 clergy who enjoyed residence in the Winchester area. Before his own departure for Ireland in 1795 Thomas Wentworth, too, Earl Fitzwilliam, added his support to the *émigré* cause.[30]

As Bishop de la Marche so gratefully pointed out, "These attentions, this liberality, were not confined to any particular descriptions of men, but common to the whole nation . . . to the palaces of the rich and the humble cottages of the poor."[31] Even the children gave their mites. And Charles Burney commented to Fanny d'Arblay that the lists of females interested in this most fashionable of charities were "very illustrious and honorable." He appended enough names, certainly, to prove his point: Lady Charlotte Greville, Lady Ann Dashwood, Lady C. Douglas, and the rest.[32] But more than any other one person the fugitive clergy all revered Mrs. Dorothea Silburn, the widow whose devotion to their needs won for her the name, "Mother of the priests of France." She dedicated her time, her energies, and her fortune to the task of organizing *émigré* aid from the very start. Her house in

Queen Street lovingly nicknamed "La Providence" became the central bureau where Bishop de la Marche and Mrs. Silburn registered an unending stream of unfortunates. Here records were kept of the financial needs of each immigrant, here priests were directed to what were for many of them their final destinations, here was the clearinghouse for the precious news smuggled back and forth across the Channel by families so cruelly sundered.[33] Even after Cheverus had left England for the United States he still made use of her services "to write a line to my family and assure them of my good health."[34] The house on Queen Street became the inevitable channel through which English aid flowed.

The monetary aid was phenomenal. Edmund Burke voiced one of the first appeals saying:

> It is confidently hoped that a difference in religious persuasion will not shut the hearts of the English public against their suffering brethren, the Christians of France; but that all true sons of the Church of England, all true subjects of our Saviour Jesus Christ . . . all persons attached to the cause of religious and civil liberty . . . all these will be gratified in having an opportunity of contributing to the support of these worthy sufferers in the cause of Honour, Virtue, Loyalty and Religion.[35]

Within a few weeks this appeal had produced £33,775. Burke himself with Pitt, William Wilberforce, and other notables attended the meeting summoned by John E. Wilmot in the Freemasons' Hall where the first committee for relief was organized. Wilmot was an unusually silent member of Parliament as a rule; but in the interests of the French he emerged from his author's retreat to organize English charitable impulses. From his home in Bruce Castle, Tottenham, he was to see at close range one result of his efforts; for it was at Tottenham that Cheverus raised the first Catholic missionary altar of that area.[36]

A continuous stream from private sources augmented the public subscriptions. Catholics made a separate collection of their own; so did the women of England. On one occasion the House of Commons replied to Prime Minister Pitt's plea by granting funds without a single dissenting vote. It is estimated that during the years of the crisis Parliament voted about £200,000 a year. When it is recalled that the nation was at war during these years, and against France herself, the heroic charity of the nation looms even larger.[37]

Jean de Cheverus did not rely upon this charity in a direct way. "The little I have," he explained, thinking of his 300 francs, "will suffice until I know the language a little. Once I have learned it, I will earn my own living, even if I must work by my hands."[38] How he wished that he had taken advantage of Nicolas Mac-Carthy's offer to teach him English when they were at Saint-Magloire! He must now learn the language as quickly as possible to prevent his becoming a needless burden on the people whose kindness was daily taxed by arrivals less fortunate than he.

The occupations which the French migrants entered were varied. Some became preceptors of academies, some filled posts as clerks in houses of business. Others resorted to manual labor, working as tailors, clock repairmen, or planting and harvesting in the English fields. But the large majority became teachers and tutors of mathematics, music, Latin, and French; it was in this category that the young priest from Mayenne found his first employment.[39] He settled in Wallingford in Berkshire not long after his arrival in England, and here after January, 1793, he gave lessons in French and mathematics in a boarding school conducted by a Protestant minister.[40] The details of this period of his life are so scanty that it is difficult to reconstruct with much certainty the early months of Cheverus in England. The minister who employed him seems to have been imbued with some of the prejudices that Sturges deplored. He supervised the work of the newcomer assiduously until he assured himself that Cheverus was not guilty of proselytism. But his fears were quickly dissipated. Cheverus was eager only to earn his living. He was an excellent teacher and his quiet virtue was an example the headmaster could only applaud. With candor the latter confessed his first doubts to Cheverus and the relationship was thenceforth a very real pleasure to both men. The students enjoyed helping the little stranger who laughed with such good grace at his own mistakes in his eagerness to master the English language. But he was blessed with a marvelous facility in language, and before the year was out Cheverus not only spoke correctly, but wrote with grace and charm.[41]

His Sundays were spent at Overy, "the place beyond the water" as it was called, not far from Wallingford and just across the Thames from the little village of Dorchester in Oxfordshire. The little settlement which later was included in the Parish of Dorchester was in those days scarcely more than a mill, a substantial farm, and a row of cottages. But the people were Catholics and Masses had been offered there several times a year ever since the days of Henry VIII. A Mr. Davey, who was the courageous chief citizen who had preserved the Faith in most recent years, was more than happy to welcome French *émigrés*. The last regular visiting priest had given up his ministry in 1788 for reasons of health, and Cheverus was an asset to a house in which "all the necessary altar furniture" was lovingly preserved.[42] And thus it happened that the teacher of a Protestant school in Wallingford went on Sundays, "to a place two and a half miles away to celebrate Mass and sing Vespers."[43]

By the end of 1793 Cheverus felt that his English was sound enough to undertake real pastoral duties in his foster fatherland and he approached Bishop Douglass with a plea that he be given an assignment wherever he could be most useful. He boyishly submitted some compositions he had written to prove his competency. But his conversation was enough to convince Douglass that Cheverus was quite capable of fulfilling the functions of his vocation.[44] Overy would not be deserted, for Jean-Ambroise Sougé who had fled to Laval with Cheverus in 1792 was recently arrived from the Isle of Jersey, and not caring to remain at Winchester where he first was sheltered, could take over in the place of his friend and relative. Sougé, in turn, persuaded their compatriot and fellow prisoner of Laval, Michel Thoumin des Vauxponts, to settle in Overy.[45] Vauxponts' name is the only one of the Mayenne priests befriended at Overy to remain on record there, no doubt because he was the only one of the three to remain there until his death. Both Cheverus and Sougé went from England to the United States, and eventually returned to France. Vauxponts, who was older, died in England on March 2, 1798, and through the kindness of his Anglican friend, the warden of New College, Oxford, was buried in the superb pre-Reformation abbey church at Dorchester.[46]

Overy would be well served by the self-effacing Sougé and the scholarly old man who might have been Bishop of Laval if he had chosen. Cheverus was more eager to do the bidding of Douglass than to remain with his friends from home. As dear as memories of Mayenne might be, a place nearer London was waiting where he could at last be a true shepherd of a flock. He had been ordained nearly three years and had scarcely begun to serve in the full sense of his vocation. Bidding an affectionate farewell to his patron at the boarding school, his companion in flight, and his English Catholic friends in Oxfordshire, Jean de Cheverus set out for Tottenham.[47]

An English writer has said of the French migrations:

We cannot but admire and bless the mysterious dispensation of divine Providence in our favour. For just at that critical time when our seminaries had failed . . . a large number of those French priests, who had been driven as exiles upon our shores, remained in England and preferred to labour as best they could in our poor missions. . . . Gladly did our bishops welcome these worthy men and employ them in the work of the holy ministry. . . . Many a congregation now large and respectable, owes its beginning to the humble but persevering labours of some poor French priest generously giving his time, his toil, and his hard earned savings to the great work of salvation of souls in a strange land.[48]

He might very well have had Jean de Cheverus in mind. For the chapel at Tottenham was one of the permanent establishments of that era.[49]

Of the eight chapels established in London alone the most enduring was the one at Portman Square, in Little Saint George Street, dedicated to the Blessed Virgin under the title of the Assumption.[50] Of the chapels established in the outlying districts of the city three at least had permanence. In Hampstead the Abbé Maurel built a chapel which is still in use. At Chelsea another mission was founded by the Abbé Voyaux de Franous and was destined to endure. The third which can be traced down to the present time was the mission in Tottenham some six miles away from London. The brass plate at St. Francis de Sales Church in Tottenham carries this inscription:

> To the pious memory of the most eminent and reverend Jean Lefebvre de Cheverus, first Bishop of Boston in America, and afterwards Cardinal Archbishop of Bordeaux, who, an exile from his native land, here in Tottenham raised the first altar after the suppression of the Catholic religion, A.D. 1794.[51]

When Cheverus arrived in Tottenham in Middlesex he found a pleasant village of between two and three thousand inhabitants.[52] The Domesday Book compiled in the reign of William the Conqueror referred to the hamlet as "Toteham, the land of Countess Judith," but speculation gives an even greater antiquity to the area, claiming a Roman settlement there.[53] By the closing decade of the eighteenth century the healthful and charming settlement had attracted many prosperous Quakers as well as other city merchants. Indeed, Tottenham was reckoned to be one of the largest Quaker populations in the London area and they maintained two private schools and took a very active part in local affairs.[54] Just prior to Cheverus' arrival many poverty-stricken Irish had come to Tottenham, lured by the prosperity of the region. They found work in the market gardens and fields nearby, and lived in modest lodging houses. Together with the increasing number of French exiles they formed a Roman Catholic nucleus which Cheverus was now at hand to serve.[55]

Cheverus began by getting work as a tutor in a Protestant English family living in Tottenham Terrace, White Hart Lane. Until he could get enough money to buy property for a chapel he offered Mass for the Catholics in the back parlor of the Three Compasses Inn in Queen Street.[56] But early in 1794 he was able to buy three cottages at the end of Queen Street, and there Tottenham Chapel was founded. One cottage was used for divine services, one served as a residence for the clergy, and the last was used for a school. Bishop Douglass came from London to dedicate the chapel and on March 19, 1794, Cheverus recorded his first baptism in the Tottenham register.[57]

The cottage rectory soon came to house other French priests. It was the beginning of the hospitality that was to be so characteristic of Cheverus wherever he went. No matter how small his house, how meager his larder, Cheverus was happiest when he could share it with others. One by one other priests from Mayenne came to Tottenham and stayed on to succeed Cheverus in the seven years following his departure. Renatus Salmon, who had been an assistant at Notre Dame de la Couture in Le Mans, Pierre le Tellier, who had assisted at Montenay in Ernée, and Joseph Fillatrais, who first succeeded Cheverus at Tottenham, all followed their fellow prisoner of Laval.[58] It was to them Cheverus left everything but his clothes and a single cassock when he departed after two and a half years among his French and Irish flock.[59]

For a fleeting moment in his second year at Tottenham the young exile dreamed of seeing his homeland and family once more. The prelate with whom he had been confined in the Cordeliers in 1792 was going to try to rejoin his flock. Urbain Hercé, Bishop of Dol, was filled with high hopes that year, for the Reign of Terror seemed to have come to an end. Hercé had been made chief chaplain of the Catholic royalist army which was planning an invasion of Brittany, and at the age of sixty-nine he joined the gallant expedition destined for Quiberon midway between Brest and Nantes. He had already on January 1, 1795, sent a pastoral letter congratulating the non-juring clergy in that area.[60] As spring turned into summer the loyal old shepherd had only the desire, as he said, of "reuniting with the flock divine Providence confided in me." The distance from Quiberon to Dol was scarcely shorter than that from the small peninsula to Laval. Cheverus was filled with a terrible longing to return. Hercé had great admiration for his small friend. He named him one of his vicars-general; if the expedition should succeed, Cheverus would make an energetic assistant to the old bishop. But when Cheverus begged to accompany the expedition Hercé refused.

"No," he said. "I am old, and may risk the few days that still remain for me to spend on earth. But you are young; I could only consider myself culpable to the Church if I exposed it to the loss of the long and useful services you may render it."

"But you are as a father to me," Cheverus protested. "It is the son's duty to attend his father in times of peril. I ought and I will go with you."

But Hercé remained adamant.

"If you follow me," he warned, "you will cease to be my vicar by that very act. Stay here. It is my wish. If the enterprise should succeed, I will send for you immediately."[61]

So Cheverus stayed behind. For his family's sake, whether he realized it or not, it was a fortunate decision. Jean-Vincent de Cheverus had been placed on the list of suspects of the Département de Mayenne not long after his son fled. He left the city of Mayenne with the children who were still living at home, and took up his residence in Saint-Denis-de-Gatines in the district of Ernée farther west. It was not until August 17, 1794, that he was finally removed from the list of those whose loyalty was questioned.[62] Louis de Cheverus was now a soldier in the Battallion de la Montayene, having entered military service from Paris the year after aiding his brother's escape. Julien had since enlisted from Saint-Denis and was training on the *Caton*, lying at anchor in the port of Brest.[63] It could only have been embarrassing politically to the Cheverus men to have it known that their non-juring relative was back in France with the royalist forces in the summer of 1795. True, Robespierre's head had fallen beneath the guillotine. But the Convention in Paris was still wrestling with the task of writing a new constitution for the republic. Napoleon's "whiff of grapeshot" soon demonstrated what kind of welcome any threat of intervention with its work would receive.[64]

For Cheverus' own sake it was fortunate that he resigned himself to Hercé's ultimatum. The expedition which set sail from Portsmouth on June 10, 1795, was doomed. After defeating the French fleet on June 22 the invading royalists approached the barren little promontory and by June 27 some three and a half thousand *émigrés* disembarked near Quiberon. But they wasted precious time trying to occupy the useless peninsula, and by July 19 they were hopelessly cut off from the interior. The English fleet helped nearly 2000 escape; but the rest were taken inland to Auray where they were held briefly. Bishop Hercé and his brother who was his vicar-general, together with a dozen other priests, were confined to the city prison. Then they were moved to Vannes where on July 28 the executions began. Within two days the massacre was complete.[65]

And so the last forlorn hope of re-establishing the See of Dol perished. Its bishop lay dead at the hands of the firing squad of Vannes, his brother by his side. Michel des Vauxponts would live out his few remaining years at Overy, in friendly intercourse with Dr. Samuel Gauntlett, the head of New College, Oxford.[66] The ephemeral claims of the third vicar-general, Jean de Cheverus, were quickly forgotten in the events of the months immediately following the arrival of the tragic news from Quiberon.

The failure of the royalist expedition dispelled any hopes that a brighter day would dawn for *émigrés* in France in the near future. Cheverus was growing restive in Tottenham. There were hundreds of priests flooding the London area after the second great wave set in motion in 1794–1795. Surely there must be some place where his ministry could be put to better use. He voiced his misgivings to Bishop Douglass, but Douglass was loathe to lose the ardent young missioner of Tottenham Chapel.

"Yes," he agreed. "There is a superabundance of priests. But a scarcity of ones like you. I need you. Stay with me."[67]

So Cheverus stayed on in England for another year.[68]

But in the end the Vicar Apostolic of London lost Cheverus. In 1796 an invitation reached Tottenham which seemed to offer genuine enticements. Father François Matignon, the professor Cheverus had known in Paris, wrote from the United States urging his young friend to join him there. Matignon had been corresponding with Cheverus for some months, describing the American field of endeavor. His jurisdiction extended hundreds of miles; he was not only trying to minister to Catholics in the midst of militant Protestantism, but was responsible for tribes of Indians who were pleading for a priest. Matignon's assistant had been working in the southern part of his jurisdiction, but the Indians to the north were in dire need of a missionary. Cheverus was enormously attracted by the picture sketched by Matignon's pen.

At last here was an invitation which predicted an opportunity really challenging to a priest who longed to serve his God where service was truly needed.

Mrs. Silburn and Bishop de la Marche at their headquarters for migrant priests had from the beginning considered the United States as a possible refuge for the French clergy. The Bishop of St. Pol de Léon had written to Bishop John Carroll of Baltimore soon after the first influx caused by the September Massacres. On December 12, 1792, he told Carroll:

> Some priests have a desire to go to New England and to labour under your jurisdiction. The knowledge that I have acquired of that country shows that there are resources for but very few, perhaps twenty priests; also that to be of use they should know English well enough to hear confessions and give instructions in that language. I know that you have some French sections but not many. . . . Still if I have been misinformed, and if that portion of the country offers a wider and better field than I think, I shall be greatly obliged to you if you let me know.[69]

Bishop Carroll replied at once that he could use only four priests at the moment, and that for a while Canada would seem to be a better prospect for the French *émigrés*. "How I wish that it were possible to offer them an asylum here and to employ for the needs of my diocese a like number of your worthy and estimable priests; but . . . you are well acquainted both with my limited means, and with the absolute necessity of some knowledge of the English language for a priest, that he may be any use in the performance of ministerial functions here."[70] Carroll had already authorized the former procurator of the English Jesuits, Thomas Talbot, to make whatever arrangements were necessary for the few priests he could absorb into his diocese. François A. Matignon had been one of those whom Talbot sent.[71]

By 1796, however, Jean de Cheverus was more than competent in the English language, Carroll's chief prerequisite, and Thomas Talbot was quite willing to recommend him to the Diocese of Baltimore. This time the protests of John Douglass fell upon deaf ears. Douglass knew how to acquiesce gracefully. He wrote a glowing letter of introduction to Carroll in Cheverus' behalf.[72]

Cheverus also had a testimonial from the late martyr of Vannes, but he wanted one other. He was still in theory a subject, he believed, of Jouffroy de Gonssans, Bishop of Le Mans. Gonssans was in exile on the continent, and Cheverus wrote to him. As eager as he was to join Matignon it was not his nature to take any step without advice and authorization from all those to whom he owed either courtesy or obedience. The letter he received in reply removed his last hesitation. Although the Bishop of Le Mans feared that the American undertaking might deprive France of an invaluable priest, should the old days and jurisdictions ever be restored, Gonssans could not but admire Cheverus' zeal. Like Douglass', his letter was full of praise:

> We attest that he has conducted himself with zeal and piety as a worthy and commendable minister of God . . . imbued with sound doctrine, praiseworthy for his knowledge and Religion, most attached and devoted to the kingdom and King of France and, because of his zeal for the Catholic faith, undeviating in his love for the Holy Apostolic See as well as in his constant preaching of the divine word and his resistance to the assaults of the impious when violently torn from his parish.[73]

The Latin phrases of the original seem at first glance to carry an ordinary letter of recommendation for any one of hundreds of exiles from France. Yet the longer the life of Cheverus is studied the more these phrases come to describe precisely what he was. His first bishop knew him well in these early painful years of Cheverus' priestly career. Gonssans' testimonial described, however, not only what Cheverus had been but what he would ever be. Many European priests came to the United States in the early years of the Republic, and most came bearing glowing letters of introduction. A considerable number, unhappily, failed to live up to the high promise with which they entered John Carroll's jurisdiction. But Jean Lefebvre de Cheverus, who was soon to be known simply as John Cheverus, never deviated by word or deed from the character given him in 1796.

Love for France was engraved in his heart, as was devotion to her former dynasty. Learning and sound doctrine graced his every phrase. Attacks by unbelievers and the necessity of leaving on more than one occasion flocks he dearly loved found him always gentle, ever submissive. Even on those occasions when he found himself in the minority of his colleagues his devotion to the pronouncements of the Holy See remained undeviating. And always, as assistant, pastor, bishop, archbishop, or cardinal, he remained the young priest Gonssans had described, the pious, zealous, worthy minister of God.

Cheverus had already made a will leaving everything he had painstakingly gathered together for the little chapel in Queen Street "to the priests who live in the house by the chapel and who serve it." The modest little document dated July 17, 1796, tells its own story. He left to the Catholic chapel of Tottenham, "which the Lord had given him the grace to establish," two chasubles, stoles, maniples, and albs, an altar cloth, candlesticks, flower vases, missal, ritual, "in general all that is at this moment in the said chapel for the use of divine service." The pitifully scanty furnishings of his cottage rectory he left to his house-mates from Mayenne. As an afterthought he added, "In case the chapel should be suppressed (which I hope will never happen) I leave every-thing pertaining to the chapel to the Bishop Vicar Apostolic of London. . . . I recommend myself to the charitable priests and the faithful of Tottenham Chapel." The will was signed simply, "Lefebvre de Cheverus, priest."[74]

Like the original apostles, devoid of worldly goods but rich in zeal, he boarded the *Galen* as summer waned and set sail for Boston. As the English shores faded from sight, and the unknown seas surged before the wooden vessel's prow, his mood was melancholy and the tears that welled so easily obscured his view. He had only been in England four years, and he was leaving of his own volition. But for the second time his susceptible heart was wrung by the pain of depar-ture. He had come to respect British institutions, to admire British intellect, wealth, and power. But above all he would never forget the warmth of English hearts. "May Almighty God bless and preserve from all dangers," he prayed, "the magnanimous nation who has received and fostered in her bosom with such kindness all the unfortunate exiles, and myself in the number."[75]

CHAPTER IV

MISSIONARY TO MAINE

On October 3, 1796, the *Galen* put into Boston and the twenty-eight-year-old voyager from London got his first glimpse of the city which was to be his home for the next twenty-seven years. To the many French migrants who passed through New England's most thriving port in the 1790's, Boston still retained "every appearance of an English colony."[1] Their general impression was one of neatness without luxury, but to simplicity of customs Bostonians united "that French politeness and delicacy of manners which render virtue more amiable."[2] John Cheverus quickly came to love this city which combined some of the best features of the two lands already endeared to him. But upon his arrival his chief feeling was one of eager curiosity.

The city seemed overrun with hackney coaches, reputed to be the best in the nation. They clattered over the narrow, crooked streets which were paved from side to side with great round stones. Carts, wagons, and wheelbarrows obstructed passage everywhere. Hucksters of phenomenal hardihood set up their wares in the streets while porters pushed their small handcarts at the risk of being crushed by the carriages recklessly thundering past. Business houses crowded against each other and their signs proclaimed that glass, wool-cards, fishing hooks, and sail-duck were particularly Boston's own. The sail-duck factory alone employed 360 people and kept twenty-seven looms whirring.[3] The noise and confusion were indescribable, but after the long ocean voyage it was enormously exciting to land in the middle of so much life and activity. Cheverus went up past the grain market, a *cul de sac* called Corn Court which reminded him of Impasse Ferou in Paris, where his cousins lived. Corn Court had originally been "a wheelbarrow way of full five feet" but now it was graced by the Hancock Tavern where Cheverus sought lodging.[4]

The next day he eagerly went to meet Father Matignon who was living in Mrs. Lobb's house in Leverett's or Quaker Lane. The talk flew thick and fast; they embraced, they laughed, they wept. How good the old French phrases seemed, the shared recollection of Paris, the Left Bank, the dear names of mutual friends, familiar streets, and former joys. There was a difference of over fourteen years in the ages of the two exiles now reunited in this bustling city of the New World; but they were bound by every tie that joins men when nationality, religion, and intellectual convictions are identical. Although Cheverus had been only a student while Matignon was a professor in the days when they shared the academic world whose center was the Sorbonne, Cheverus had been acquainted with Matignon ever since he "went first to confession to him in his 13th year."[5] Matignon had fled from France a year earlier than the younger man, and had arrived in Boston before Cheverus even reached Wallingford. Only letters had continued their acquaintance begun in Paris. But now in the autumn of 1796 this meeting in the small room in Quaker Lane began an abiding friendship between them; from that day forward Matignon was for Cheverus, "My brother, and my tenderest friend."

The pastor of the Boston Catholics who welcomed Cheverus that day was a remarkable man. While Cheverus was completing his preparatory studies at Louis-le-Grand, Francis Matignon had received his doctorate in theology. In 1787 the older man had been appointed professor at the College of Navarre.[6] Refusing to take the oath to support the Civil Constitution of the Clergy, Matignon had gone to England in the spring of 1791 but had looked almost immediately across the Atlantic Ocean. Thomas Talbot, the former procurator of the English Jesuits, told Bishop Carroll on June 6, 1791, "He wishes much to put himself under your care to be employed by you in your vineyard as you shall judge best. . . . I love him and esteem him." Matignon already knew enough English to be useful in the United States. Talbot, who knew something of Carroll's jurisdiction from the correspondence that the two ex-Jesuits maintained, ventured to suggest that Matignon might do well in Boston since he already knew and respected Father John Thayer, a convert-priest in that area. William Strickland, another English priest who corresponded with Carroll, commented, "Mr. Matignon, whom I am told you have accepted, will be a great addition to your Mission."[7]

In the autumn of 1791 Matignon had returned to Paris to settle his affairs there prior to departing for the Diocese of Baltimore.[8]

He had some difficulty getting passage from France to the United States that winter and it was only by April of 1792 that he finally sailed from Le Havre.[9] His traveling companions were François Ciquart, Gabriel Richard, and Ambroise Maréchal, all Sulpicians, and all destined like Matignon for splended service to the Church in the United States. Their arrival in Baltimore on June 24, 1792, was a day of deep significance for areas as widely separated as Maryland, Maine, Massachusetts, and Michigan. Maréchal was to become the third Archbishop of Baltimore; Richard went to Michigan where he founded the first Catholic schools; Ciquart served the Indians in Maine; and Matignon was to become the founder of the first Church of the Holy Cross in Boston.

Four years after his own arrival in Boston Father Matignon had no dearer wish than to keep his young friend Cheverus with him. The newcomer must, of course, put himself at once under the authority of Bishop Carroll in Baltimore and await his commands. Cheverus did this by letter, forwarding the testimonials he had brought with him from England.[10] Some of these were lost on the way, but Carroll soon learned of Cheverus' arrival and almost immediately decided to send this latest *émigré* to the Detroit territory. Matignon was disconsolate.

John Carroll had very sound reasons for his first decision. The year before Cheverus arrived the Jay Treaty concluded between the United States and England had extended the jurisdiction of the Bishop of Baltimore in the Northwest Territory. The Bishop of Quebec had notified Carroll on January 14, 1796, that the Detroit region was now Baltimore's *frichette* and that the American bishop would have to send the tillers of the soil to that fallow land. Accordingly on March 30, Carroll had appointed Michel Levadoux his vicar-general in the region and had asked Father Levadoux to make a tour of inspection and report to Baltimore on the needs of the territory.[11] Before Levadoux could make his report Carroll received a direct plea from the Catholics of Rivière au Raisin, begging for a priest. The Bishop of Baltimore replied on October 19 that he deeply appreciated their situation, but that he had been waiting for his vicar-general's report before acting. Now he had real hope that a good priest would soon be theirs. If he could not send one from the Illinois area he would try to find one he could spare in the east.[12] The arrival of John Cheverus just at that time seemed providential and it is not surprising that the bishop thought immediately of Rivière au Raisin when he received the news from Boston.

Cheverus learned of Carroll's intention on January 19, 1797, when he received a letter from Baltimore apologizing for sending him to a place "so far advanced into the country that he would only rarely and with difficulty get news from the numerous friends in Europe to whom he was so fondly devoted." It was not truly an American mission; Cheverus would have to wear the cassock habitually because the inhabitants were used to seeing their clergy in a long gown. Carroll hoped Cheverus would be able to reconcile the people, so recently removed from the political jurisdiction of the British king and the spiritual direction of the Bishop of Quebec, to the United States and its laws.[13] Carroll perceived that the formalities of transfer symbolized by the substitution of the Stars and Stripes for the British flag on July 11, 1796, would be succeeded by many complexities. It was a transfer involving old and ingrained loyalties. The people had not only exchanged a French cultural dominance for an American way of life; they had shifted as well from the status of British subjects to citizenship in experimental democracy. The new freedom must not become a pretext for living without the restraints of religion or of civil authority.[14] Cheverus appeared to be admirably suited to a ministry requiring both spiritual service and guidance in cultural readjustment. Carroll's only concern was for the material support of Cheverus on the mission and the immediate costs of a journey westward.

Although Cheverus was unaware of the enormity of the problems facing the Bishop of Baltimore in his lands "beyond the mountains," he replied immediately that he would set off as soon as he received Carroll's order to do so. "Send me where you think I am most wanted," he wrote cheerfully on January 26, "without making yourself anxious about the means of supporting me. I am willing to work with my hands, if need should be; and I believe I have strength enough to do it. I am in good health and not yet thirty years of age." It would be a bit hard to wear a cassock all the time because he was "worth but one," all his other clothing being that usually worn by English missionaries. And then he voiced sentiments which could only endear him to John Carroll:

> I shall carefully treasure up in my mind the advices contained in your letter. I shall use my best endeavours to reconcile the people entrusted to my care, to all the measures of the humane and liberal government they live under. I shall on all occasions shew myself a hearty friend to the interest of the United States and to the Federal government. Everywhere I shall seek the peace of the Country which the Lord will have me dwell in.[15]

Francis Matignon found it much less easy to accept the bishop's plan for Cheverus. The needs of his own region which had prompted his letters of invitation to the missionary of Tottenham had not altered. Quite apart from the selfish delight he had in the companionship of his gay young compatriot, in the four brief months that Cheverus had been in Boston Matignon had seen how sorely his ministry had been needed, what marvelous good Cheverus worked in this Protestant stronghold. On the heels of Cheverus' ready submission another letter from Boston reached Baltimore. Matignon wrote urgently, "I beg you to leave him here at least till autumn unless it is absolutely incompatible with the greatest good of the Mission."[16] It seemed a pity to send him to a French mission when he preached so well in English. "I have noticed several times that a half hour of preparation is enough for him to give an excellent instruction in that language," Matignon explained. "In some ways it has become more familiar to him than his own."

In the weeks that followed Matignon's pleas increased, and Carroll was compelled to reconsider. His respect for the Boston pastor was unqualified and he knew Matignon was no man to urge his own whims. If Cheverus were that badly needed in Boston, this fact must influence an ultimate decision. Carroll was only too familiar with the difficulties that had plagued Boston prior to Matignon's own arrival; he was more than grateful for the work being accomplished there. In the end the Bishop of Baltimore wrote to Levadoux in Detroit, "Mr. Cheverus, whom I had destined for the Rivière au Raisin, meets so much opposition on the part of Mr. Matignon of Boston, and the latter demands conserving him for the country where he is with such strong entreaties, it has been impossible for me to move him."[17] Before another month elapsed John Cheverus was on his way, instead, to the Indians of Maine carrying with him a letter from Matignon which read, "My brothers, the bearer of this letter is a missionary not only approved but singularly esteemed by Monseigneur our Bishop."[18]

Six years after Cheverus died in his native France a citizen of New Hampshire commented in a lecture delivered in Portsmouth:

Among the Indian subjects of his spiritual guardianship, he acquired a most powerful influence. He went down to them in all their degradation, that he might lift them up to light and life. If their extreme debasement defeated his best hopes, he seems to have elicited, even from the squalid remnants of the eastern tribes, some scintillations of their native brightness.[19]

His first biographer, writing only a year after his death, commented, on the other hand:

> Thanks to religion, which inspires and preserves whatever is honorable and delicate, M. Cheverus found, even among these savages, elevated sentiments that might put the most civilized people to blush. He met there grateful hearts which gave him numerous proofs of affection, which he loved to relate, mothers tender and affectionate, children who carried their filial piety even to heroism, great and generous souls that had the most exalted ideas of honor and duty.[20]

Both of these reflections given in retrospect, one by an American, the other by a French contemporary of Cheverus, are doubtless justifiable judgments of an exotic situation involving the sharp contrast of a small, highly cultivated European of one race working among the vigorous, less than civilized people of another in the midst of an almost primeval forest. Yet the faint tinge of racial superiority of the one and the "noble savage" romanticism of the other may obscure the actual truth of the missionary work of John Cheverus in Maine. A clearer view is gained from reading his own letters written from the mission field itself, letters completely devoid of race consciousness or fanciful sentimentality. The Indians of Maine were to Cheverus brothers, men needing God and his ministers, a people living in poverty and speaking a different language, it is true, but always his flock, his friends. Of all the Cheverus letters still extant none is more joyous nor more delightfully infectious in its humor than those he wrote from Maine. They carry neither the theories of the sociologist nor the poetic ecstasies of the tourist in the wilderness. They are the racing, breathless reports of a priest who was incredibly happy to have found at last his own special, limitless field in which to plant, to cultivate, and harvest, and from which to bring his heavy sacks to the granary of his Lord. Every man has a yearning to be needed but none more than the man with the priestly vocation. For the first time since his ordination in 1790 Cheverus had the exquisite joy of knowing that he could carry the sacraments to a people who without his ministry would be bereft. His cup was full to running over.

However pressing the needs of the Detroit territory the New England area needed just such a man as Cheverus proved to be; John Carroll had no reason to regret his final decision. The very year Carroll had been made the first Catholic bishop in the United States the Indians of Maine had been concerned over the need for a priest. The Penobscots on July 19, 1790, told Bishop Jean Hubert of Quebec, "Our heart is sad. Is it not a reason for grief to see men . . . who have not yet received their first Communion? All our young folk have been baptized only by our own hands; as for our dead, we dig their graves and bury them ourselves."[21] That fall they appealed to the "Fathers of the Church in New England" asking that a priest at least visit their tribe. Father Louis Rousselet, who was then one of the priests in Boston, made a trip to the Penobscots in October and had "the consolation of 102 Communions, 65 baptisms, and 12 marriages," according to his report to Bishop Carroll on January 15, 1791.

At the same time that Rousselet was writing this news to Baltimore the Passamaquoddy Indians of Maine were begging Colonel John Allan to help them secure the services of a priest, too. Allan was a man who had been interested in the Indians of Maine ever since the time of the American Revolution. A Scotsman who had settled in Nova Scotia, he had been appointed by the Continental Congress to act as Indian agent in the east, and as a result of his intermediary activities both in Congress and the Council of Massachusetts a priest had been sent to the Maine Indians in 1779. Since the treaty of 1783 concluding the war for independence the Passamaquoddies who lived on the border of British Canada had been neglected, and in their distress had made repeated requests to their old friend to get them a priest. In 1791 Allan helped them frame an appeal to Bishop Carroll which the St. John and Micmac Indians also signed. "It looks as if we were shut out from all the blessings and benefits of our Religion," they wrote. "We pray you, Father of the church in this land, to think of us and send one suitable for our purpose." Carroll assured them on September 6 that he would try to send two priests as soon as possible. "This should have been done much sooner, if I had been informed of your situation," he apologized. "You may depend upon it that you shall always be in my heart and mind." When François Ciquart, who had once been a missionary to some Canadian Indians, arrived in Baltimore with Matignon in June the following year Bishop Carroll had sent him to Maine.[22]

Carroll did keep the Indians in his "heart and mind." He asked President George Washington for federal aid for missionaries to the Indians. In 1792 Washington feared the time was not ripe for missionaries to the western Indians because in that area they were still in revolt and needless martyrdoms might be provoked.[23] In regard to Maine, however, he suggested:

According to the best information I can obtain they are so situated as to be rather considered a part of the inhabitants of the State of Massachusetts. . . . Any application, therefore, relative to these Indians, for the purpose mentioned would seem most proper to be made to the government of Massachusetts.[24]

While Carroll waited for the federal and state legislatures to act the Society of St. Sulpice came to his rescue and offered support to the priests who were sent to the Wabash and Illinois Rivers or to Maine.[25]

For two years Ciquart worked fervently among his Indians. Together with Colonel Allan he succeeded in persuading the General Court of Massachusetts to grant them a permanent home on Atterell's Island. When this turned out to be within British territory ten acres of land at Pleasant Point were substituted. But Governor-General Guy Carleton of Canada eventually coaxed Ciquart back to his domain, to work among the Indians of the St. John River region, and in August, 1794, the Maine Indians were once more without a priest.[26] Although Father Matignon had urged Ciquart to come across the border at least during the Easter season, the need for a regular missionary to Maine was critical by the summer of 1797. Chiefs of the tribes came to Boston in June to plead with both Matignon and the civil government for a priest. And so it was that John Cheverus set out that July on his first journey as an Indian missionary. Even though this first trip was to be a brief one hopes flourished in both Baltimore and Boston. As Matignon told the Indians, "While he is among you, we will be united in prayers that God will bless his ministry . . . and fill you with all kinds of grace, both spiritual and temporal."[27]

Cheverus had not anticipated when he landed in Boston after his passage from England that he was to become such a sailor. The trips were genuine voyages since the Indian settlements lay midway between the Maine towns of Belfast and Portland. Coastwise sailing in midsummer was much pleasanter, however, than a trans-Atlantic passage in the fall. Although the ship was on the high seas part of the time the hours when they skirted the Maine shores gave him an opportunity to glimpse something of its wild beauty and vastness. When he reminded himself that all of this sprawling land was a province belonging to only one state in the federal union he felt again the enormous difference between his new homeland and the tidy, compact nations he had left behind.

Cheverus arrived at Pleasant Point at one o'clock on July 30, 1797, and as soon as he put his foot on the ground the Indians fired their guns in "hearty and moving welcome." Eagerly crowding around the

long-desired missionary they escorted him to the "church" where
Cheverus gave thanks to God for his safe voyage and begged His
blessing on this mission. Then the Indians proudly showed him his
"parsonage house" which they had hastily erected upon receipt of
Father Matignon's letter announcing the prospective arrival of a priest.
Both chapel and rectory were brand new, and stood up on the hill
above the Indian wigwams. The house was ten feet square and eight
feet high; the chapel was as large again. But both rude buildings were
without windows, and possessed one door. It was so dark in the chapel
that Cheverus could scarcely read the missal. The church had nothing
but "a few logs and sticks set crossways to support the bark" on which
the sacred vessels rested; the house had only a table made of rough
boards. In their excited joy over the coming of their missionary the
Indians had completely forgotten that he must eat, and Cheverus was
lucky to have brought with him the barrels of biscuits Matignon had
recommended.

The simple pleasure in their expectant faces Cheverus found irresistible. His was a nature that required affection, and here in this crude
settlement were evidences of a welcome beyond anything he could wish.
To Father Matignon he wrote happily of his dwelling, "*My* house
(and with pride I say it, for it is a long time since I was in a house of
my own), *my* house." He was deeply moved by the little purse of seven
dollars the old men of the tribe brought to him that night. He put his
mattress on the rough table and went to sleep in deep contentment.

The morning brought its joys, too. He was amazed and delighted
to discover in singing the Mass for the dead that the Indians sang
"exactly upon the same tune as we do." The *Kyrie* preserved the Greek
words and they answered the Preface of the Mass in Latin. "What
courage and patience in the first missionaries!" he thought. He had read
some of Father Ciquart's letters on the Maine Indians and found them
very helpful. He spoke gently but firmly on the matter of drinking.
They could not receive Communion "except they had not got drunk
since a very considerable time, about a year." It would probably mean
very few communicants that summer, but he could not expose the
sacraments to profanation. Already the plan he and Matignon had conceived of combining a visit to the Passamaquoddies and to Damariscotta
across Muscongus Bay on this first missionary trip had to be altered.
He would need his three weeks here at Pleasant Point.[28]

To another man the days which followed could have been unbearable.
The weather was frightful. Aside from a few Irish in the surrounding

countryside, and the Allan and Morin families, Cheverus had no one but his Indians. One night Colonel Allan came over and stayed with him, occupying the table "bed" while Cheverus slept on the floor. But the priest slept as comfortably as on a feather bed, he wrote Matignon.

> What others would call hardships are for me luxuries of life and agree extremely well with me. The other night I awoke and found myself nearly swimming in my bed. The violence of the storm had made a hole in the bark at the top of my wigwam. Well, that cold bath braced me, and far from catching cold, I felt stronger and more lively![29]

Matignon had no intention that his little confrere should stay permanently among the Indians. That summer visit in 1797 was meant only as temporary relief for a neglected people. In fact, Matignon would have gone himself if his health had allowed it. The only reason Cheverus could be spared from Boston just then was because Father John Thayer, a former Boston priest, had returned for a time while he awaited his next assignment by Bishop Carroll. Yet Cheverus, after only a few weeks at Pleasant Point, was already hoping this temporary mission could become a permanent charge. He confided in Matignon, "Should the bishop think it proper, I would be happy myself to be appointed to this mission." In the short time he had been here he had baptized fourteen children, more than he had numbered in the six previous years of his priesthood. He had officiated at the first wedding of his sacerdotal career. On the feast of the Assumption there would be a solemn procession in this wilderness. His heart pulsed with love for his flock, so like children in many ways, yet so dutiful "since I have been their Father." He had grown attached to them so quickly that, knowing his own easy tears, he knew he could not leave them without genuine grief. It was a reluctant little man who boarded the ship sailing for Boston on August 20.

The next spring Cheverus determined to start earlier for Maine. His first experience with Indian confessions had convinced him that although they generally remained good Christians during the months right after having been to confession, the absence of a shepherd allowed corruption to creep in. He was anxious to get back to the Passamaquoddies; and this summer he must visit the Penobscots, too, and try to reach Damariscotta. Early in May he left Boston for his second journey to Maine.

Cheverus stayed at Pleasant Point until the end of May, and his return among the Passamaquoddies filled him with mingled emotions. This time he had four baptisms, two marriages, and thirty Communions. This was the "bright side of the medal," finding as on Carmel "plants which do glory to the garden of the Spouse." But there was the reverse side. By now he knew each of his Indian people by name and as individuals. In a long letter back to Boston, written in French because of his excited impatience to describe them all to Matignon, Cheverus characterized each one in vivid little pen portraits which showed the problems a missioner must face. It seems incredible that he could have learned to know each one in so short a time. But the crammed pages of neat French show how anxious Cheverus was over these isolated Christians, how his gentle heart yearned for some amelioration of their situation.[30] He was later a bit ashamed of his garrulous ramblings and told his Boston colleague the next time he wrote, "As I suppose you have had by this time plenty of my nonsense in French, I shall now for variety's sake give you some of it in English!" But his nonsense, as he called it, gives clear proof of the place each one of his flock held in his concern.

He left Pleasant Point for the Penobscots farther north on the Friday morning after unburdening himself in that lengthy May letter. The trip was made by canoe in weather so bad the Indians persuaded him to stop for the night only ten miles from their starting point. There were five canoes in what Cheverus jokingly called "our Squadron." Two were from Passamaquoddy and three from Penobscot. Eight men, three women, and three children accompanied the missionary, camping in the dripping forests the three nights of the journey. Cheverus himself spent one night under cover with a storekeeper who was also the most northern postmaster in the United States. But the other two nights he lay under a canoe on the rain-soaked forest floor, a victim of gnats and flies like the others. He cheerfully denied any inconvenience and assured Matignon, "The last two nights I slept without interruption from the moment I laid down till the dawning of the day." There was no time to build wigwams, of course; and there was not a single log cabin in sight during the whole trip. Nothing but woods and water.[31]

Cheverus may have been drenched as to clothes but his spirits remained undampened. To him the wilderness was not a gloomy sight; the land was almost everywhere covered with fine hardwood trees which in May were beautifully green. There were the occasional grassy glades, as fine as any he had ever seen. He liked to imagine how the country would be some day when it would be settled, indulging "the pleasing idea it might one day become the asylum of the piety and innocence now persecuted almost everywhere." With that hope in mind, and as if to consecrate the new era beforehand, he celebrated high Mass and Vespers with his Indians on Trinity Sunday.

It requires a stolid nature not to feel a keen emotion at the thought of this delicate little "black robe" surrounded by his few Indian traveling companions pausing in the somber woods on a Sunday in June to sing the lovely phrases praising God in His three persons for a land that might ever be a refuge for the oppressed of the Old World and asking His blessing on the unfortunates of the New. To the untutored Indians who sang the responses probably the Mass meant simply that they had a shepherd who was asking for spiritual and material blessings for themselves; but the expansive intentions of the celebrant included the whole world.

With a spirit like John Cheverus' nothing physical could be a hardship. He had only laughter for the rigors of the four-mile portage from the lake to the Penobscot River. Tumbling and falling along the path visible only to the keen eyes of his companions, he commented comically, "I believe I can crawl nearly as well as a snail."[32] When he gave Matignon his lighthearted account of the hazardous journey he concluded, "I am without any *exaggeration* very well in my health. So, my dear Sir, were it even as important to preserve it, as your tender friendship persuades you, be not anxious on that point," and signed himself, "Yours from my heart, J. Cheverus."

The Penobscot village to which Cheverus was going was on an island in the river known as Old Town. In the summer of the year Cheverus arrived in the United States, the government of Massachusetts had made a land settlement with these Indians which left them with Old Town and the islands in the river thirty miles above it. It had been a very shrewd bargain on the part of the state: in exchange for woolens, corn, salt, shot, and rum they had acquired some 189,426 acres which could be carved into nine townships for white settlers. It scarcely required generosity to promise the Indians that they would try to provide the tribe with "a minister of their own religion settled among them."[33] But in the summer of 1798 this promise still remained to be kept.

Cheverus stayed through June at Old Town, hearing confessions six hours a day for a fortnight. It was slow, painstaking work since he still needed an interpreter much of the time. He was just beginning to understand the Indian language, and had much better success with the children. He worked laboriously over a six-page catechism for the ones who were preparing for their first Communion. He hoped to have eight prepared by the feast of Saints Peter and Paul. Here at Old Town, as in Pleasant Point, he was saddened by the corruption the long periods of neglect had caused. He told Father Matignon in a moment of anguish, "Unless a priest is established here, or at least visits here often, all is lost."

But again, as among the Passamaquoddies, he preserved his equanimity and sense of humor. He wrote:

> The wood nymphs have just lighted in my cabin a fire of cedar wood which gives off a truly agreeable odor but whose smoke blinds and suffocates me in the most delicious way in the world. . . . Don't be uneasy, for on coming out of my cabin I will recover sight and respiration.[34]

It sometimes required an effort to write in this vein. Cheverus was still the eager intellect he had been at Louis-le-Grand; he was still the fastidious Frenchman who craved the companionship of his own kind and suffered the separation from his family and native city. Contact with Boston depended on the occasional ships which visited the Maine coast and he was often without Matignon's fraternal messages for weeks on end. When late in June he got a letter enclosing a sermon of Father Thayer's he read avidly and with deep pleasure. Thayer had preached in Boston on May 9, 1798, on the day of fasting proclaimed by President John Adams. His references to the Pope, the persecutions of the Catholics, and unfortunate France brought tears to the lonely missionary's eyes. He was depressed by the reminder that his own family might not even know he was alive and well. He asked Matignon in his next letter to write to Mrs. Silburn in the hope that her contact with former priests from Mayenne might provide a way to get some message through.[35]

But he quickly put his nostalgia aside and began a lengthy history of the mission among the Penobscots. Then he rose resolutely and went about his plans for the *Feu de Saint-Jean* for the next day. June 23, the eve of St. John the Baptist, should have its bonfire, wilderness or not. His French heart demanded this symbol of welcome to the summer season and he later reported proudly that in addition to the leaping flames they had "a complete discharge of artillery, and the hymns of the festival sung while the fire was burning." The Indians loved shooting their guns and the shot furnished by the Massachusetts commissioners enabled them to demonstrate their fervor; the forests rang on all religious festivals. Cheverus wryly recorded, "We walked in procession with great pomp and solemnity on Corpus Christi day and the Octave. Guns were our substitute for Censers and gave in noise to our ears what our noses would have received in sweet perfume."[36]

He was as happy among the Penobscots as he had been at Pleasant Point. If money was even scarcer game was more plentiful. He assured Matignon:

> Plenty of fresh salmon, 2 partridges, 4 pigeons & three turtles have supplied my table with abundance. You see I have no great merit in having sent you a tongue of moose, the less so because I ate a fresh one at Quaddy. . . . I really grow fat. However, if yourself and some other good souls will have it that I lead here a very hard and mortified life, you are welcome to indulge the pious thought.

The puffs of suffocating smoke which nearly drove him from his shelter were still counted blessings in disguise. Did they not drive away the thousands of flying insects feasting upon his face? He philosophized merrily:

> Smoke, which makes everything dry and lean, preserves here my *enbonpoint*. Were it not for its kind assistances I would be by this time nothing but skin and bones. The only thing I am afraid of is that my fine complexion will be spoiled, and that you must own will be a great pity.[37]

He was not destined to become, however, a permanent resident among these questionable benefits. The urgings of Father Matignon, Colonel Allan, and Cheverus himself the year before bore fruit. An Indian delegation which reached Boston in 1798, with Matignon as their spokesman, petitioned the General Court for a regular missionary. Massachusetts now consented to pay $200 a year for a teacher of "good moral and political character" to reside among them.[38] But John Cheverus was not to be that teacher. Neither Bishop Carroll nor Father Matignon could imagine allowing the exceptional talents of the young priest to be monopolized by that isolated and scattered flock. When Cheverus wrote to John Douglass in London that August he said:

> Within these four months past I have visited 2 tribes of Indians at Penobscot & Passamaquady in the District of Maine. Taking the two tribes together there are about 300 individuals men, women & children, all among them above 7 years have come to Confession. 30 men & 89 women have received the blessed sacrament, among

whom 18 for the first time. . . . I offered the Bishop to go & settle among the Indians, but he thinks I am more useful here. I doubt it very much, but I ought not to be judge in my own cause.[39]

He honestly tried to banish any preference from his own mind. A priest went where his bishop sent him; and as the winter progressed it began to appear that the Bishop of Baltimore meant to send him to Philadelphia. But he was anxious that the beginnings he had attempted should not be lost. On February 17, 1799, he gathered together the letters he had written to Matignon from Pleasant Point and Old Town and sent them to Baltimore. He said apologetically that Carroll must skip the trifling and unnecessary passages, but, he wrote urgently:

I have . . . the name of every one amongst them and notes of their good and bad qualities so far as I knew them by their exterior conduct. These notes I will give to the Priest who will go amongst them. I shall even, if he wishes it, accompany him and remain with him for a short time. Should no priest come, I shall visit them again this year if you approve of it.

As for his own future, Cheverus said honestly that he knew Matignon would be grieved should they be separated. "However if you think I shall be useful either in Philadelphia or anywhere else more than in Boston, I shall always be ready and willing to go wherever you please."[40]

Matters very quickly resolved themselves in a way that Cheverus approved and Matignon applauded. Not only was Cheverus allowed to continue in Boston as his friend's assistant, but his "dear savages" received as their permanent priest a man Cheverus had known from his boyhood. In July, 1799, Cheverus accompanied Jacques-René Romagné on the ship leaving for Pleasant Point. Father Romagné was from Mayenne, had been imprisoned at Laval with Cheverus, and had later been an *émigré*, like Cheverus, in England. He was destined to spend nineteen fruitful years among the Passamaquoddy and Penobscot Indians, and by the time Cheverus was back in Boston in September Romagné was already busy with plans for a real church in the wilderness.[41]

Cheverus himself would return many times to Maine, and eventually as a bishop, to the delight of his *chers sauvages*. Colonel Allan had said of these Indians:

They are a very moral people among themselves . . . and admire it in strangers. . . . They soon know a priest, a priest's character.

... When a person is exemplary for his life & conversation — strictly attentive to the duty of his calling — open, affable, free & generous (within the bounds of that distinction to be always observed by spiritual teachers) they will sacrifice all for him, nothing they can do will be too good.[42]

And so Cheverus had found them. The brief years of his dream of living among them were over; but if letters are any indication of a man's heart, they were among the happiest years of his life.

CHAPTER V

A LITTLE MATTER OF LAW

ALTHOUGH the Indian mission held first place in his heart, Father Cheverus never actually spent more than a few months of any one year in Maine. The greater proportion of his time was devoted to his ministry in Boston and among the nascent Catholic congregations within Matignon's jurisdiction. It was a ministry of contrasts, certainly, ranging as it did from the northern wilderness to Boston, the most cosmopolitan city of New England. Massachusetts was not growing so rapidly as the other parts of the Republic in the later years of the eighteenth century; yet, in the decade of Cheverus' arrival its population, excluding the province of Maine, rose from 378,000 to 423,000. Boston itself was a fourth again as large as it had been at the close of the American Revolution, and was fast approaching a metropolis of 25,000. In addition to the immigrants who came to stay, many a French exile passed through its maze of streets including, tradition has it, a future king of France.[1]

Yet, in many respects, the city still resembled an old-fashioned English market town. The sidewalks, where they existed at all, were paved with round cobblestones. Streets went almost unlighted at night, and police scarcely were known. In spite of incessant industry, Yankee ingenuity, and phenomenal thrift the city, like the whole New England area, was relatively poor. The entire banking capital of Boston did not exceed $2,500,000. True, the merchant class enjoyed a prosperity which the French wars did much to augment; but the clergy and other professional men recognized as leaders of the community were eminent for penury as well as piety. Father Matignon's Christmas collection the year of Cheverus' arrival was a mere $32; and the pastors of Protestant churches rivaled his poverty. The Reverend Abijah Weld of Attleborough raised his family of eleven children and was charitable to the poor on an annual salary of $220.[2] Cheverus was never to cherish any illusions of material prosperity in his new post. When he and Father Matignon sponsored a concert on St. Cecelia's Day the first autumn he spent in Boston, they found, on counting the returns, that their efforts had achieved the princely sum of $14.92. If Matignon had not paid for their house taken on School Street out of his own personal money, they might not have had a roof over their heads.[3]

The Catholic congregation of Boston was naturally very small and equally poor. The pastor described it as "almost wholly restricted to the class which our Divine Saviour would have particularly loved to instruct."[4] As a formal religious group the Boston church was only eight years old when John Cheverus arrived, and it was still something of a novelty in the Protestant community. Prior to the American Revolution the New England area, and Massachusetts in particular, had a perduring antagonism toward the Catholic Church, its doctrines, its ceremonies, and its clergy.[5] This was not strange since Massachusetts had been founded by colonists whose Puritan origins in England were markedly hostile to all things Papist. In their new home they had faced on their northern borders a French Catholic power whose threats to their security added political motives to religious reasons for fearing and detesting Catholicism. The course of the Stuart kings in England, too, roused recurring fears that "Popery was craftily to be introduced" against their wishes. The Glorious Revolution in 1688 which had driven Catholic James II from his throne had been followed by enormous relief in Massachusetts, especially since the new colonial charter of 1691 expressly denied Roman Catholics liberty of conscience. The next century found Massachusetts applying English penal legislation to prevent Catholics from exercising any political functions.

The American Revolution had compelled some modifications of this attitude owing to the patriot desire for assistance from French Canada, the northern Indians who were Catholics, and from France herself. General George Washington had at the outset issued his now-famous order against the anti-Catholic celebrations on Guy Fawkes Day or "Pope's Day," lest possible allies be offered an insult "so monstrous as not to be suffered or excused."[6] Massachusetts civilians had not been noticeably swayed by this military decree and it took Governor John Hancock's added exhortations in 1780 to suppress the annual rioting on November 5.

The course of the war, however, brought Massachusetts eventually to a constitutional acknowledgment of the Catholic's right to religious freedom; and the new constitution of 1780 made this legal, at least as far as public worship was concerned. The war, too, brought many Catholics into New England in the persons of the French armed forces and their chaplains. The history of Catholicism in New England from 1780 to 1788 was, indeed, almost exclusively French.[7] Although the French forces left America at the close of the war, a sizable number of French Catholics continued to live in the New England area. French consulates and their staffs, former soldiers and chaplains, and ambitious business entrepreneurs formed a nucleus for future Catholic congregations in the commercial cities.

In Boston the French were for some time too sparse to constitute a congregation and St. Jean de Crèvecoeur reported to his government on September 22, 1785, "I dare say that the French who live in Boston will not think of building a church for several years, as they are the only Catholics in the city."[8] It was, nevertheless, a former French naval chaplain who three years later offered the first public Mass in Boston. Claude Florent Bouchard, who added to his name the title "de la Poterie," on November 2, 1788, celebrated Mass in a dilapidated building at 18 School Street, a building that had once belonged to French Huguenots and then to a group of Congregationalists. Not long afterward a congregation was formally organized and the Catholic Church in Boston had its permanent beginning.[9]

Although there was some good will and much more curiosity among the Protestants who tolerated this departure from the old days of proscription, the next four years of Catholic history in Boston did much to revive the dislike for Catholics and particularly for their priests. Unhappily the Abbé Bouchard de la Poterie and the priests who came after him treated the city to scenes far from edifying. Before the new congregation was two years old it was in public schism led by the priests themselves. The story is too complex and unsavory to repeat here; but the arrival of Father Matignon in Boston on August 20, 1792, was a relief not only to the Catholics of Boston and to Bishop Carroll but to the Protestant majority who might for the first time see an exemplary priest's ministry in their midst. "Tactful healer of schism, gentle remover of prejudice, zealous pastor of souls, prudent administrator of a pitifully meagre church revenue," Francis Matignon in the four years prior to Cheverus' arrival had gone unobtrusively about his work of conciliation.[10]

The congregation remained poor and small. By 1796 it was no

longer predominantly French, however. Crèvecoeur's remark in 1785, as a matter of fact, had been only an opinion. The French were not the only Catholics in Boston during the critical period following the Revolution. The Boston marriage records during those years show many Irish names, and although some were probably those of immigrants from northern Ireland, it is a fact that among the congregation organized by Bouchard de la Poterie there were numerous Irish Catholics. Mrs. Mary Lobb, at whose boarding house Father Matignon was living until Cheverus joined him, was only one of these.[11] By 1796 the French who had been dominant in earlier days had moved on to other places. The records of Cheverus' first years in Boston show a dwindling of French baptisms from one fifth to one tenth of the total.[12] The Irish who replaced them in the congregation of the church on School Street had not yet found it easy to rise very far in the economic world. It is not surprising that they could contribute but meager support to their clergy. None of this mattered to Cheverus. He told Bishop Douglass:

> I live happy with my worthy and amiable confrere, Mr. Matignon. . . . Our temporalities are rather scanty, but still we do not want for what is really necessary, having food and raiment, therewith we ought to be, and we are in fact, perfectly content.

With the books and chalices Douglass sent him from England he felt rich indeed.[13]

The secret of his deep content lay in the felicity he enjoyed in Father Matignon's friendship. Never were two men closer in heart and mind. To see them together immediately suggested the closest bonds that might unite men. A Protestant editor who knew them commented, "Their tastes, their pursuits, their dispositions, were kindred, and they became inseparable. Those who witnessed the manner in which they lived together, will never forget the refinement and elevation of their friendship; it surpassed those attachments which delight us in classical story, and equalled the lovely union of Saul and the minstrel of Israel."[14] Priests who shared their hospitality found them living together like "Apostles and Gentlemen,"[15] and Bishop Carroll saw them as father and son.[16] Matignon, perhaps, described it most perfectly when he said theirs was a friendship "which unites us as one person."[17]

It was natural enough that these two should have been congenial. Both were French, both were possessed of excellent minds trained by the best continental European systems. Both had experienced hazards in their forced departures from homeland and family; both felt an unbounded fervor for ministering in the midst of an alien, and largely Protestant, environment. It was natural enough, too, that each should enjoy the other's complementary personality. Matignon was older, more experienced in the field, and by nature more serious. How could he have resisted the youthful enthusiasm and merry humor of his new assistant who plunged into whatever task Matignon suggested without a moment's demurral? Matignon's fears for the health of his little curate were laughingly rebuked. If the superior fretted about the music for high Mass, the energetic assistant joined the choir and incited the amateur performers to more polished renditions. When the older man worried over the suitability of their living quarters Cheverus reassured him saying, "As far as our lodging goes, do what you can. All I can say to you . . . is that I find everything you do well done. A small hole without a chimney would suffice me."[18] Matignon responded to the irresistible high spirits of his companion and teased Cheverus in his turn, accusing him of being a Jansenist because of his three years under the Oratorians of Saint-Magloire. But it was all in fun. As he told their bishop, "His sentiments, when he is serious, are exactly the same as mine."[19]

But their devotion had deeper roots than the happy coincidences of nationality and culture or the provocative contrasts of age and disposition. The deepest love is rooted in gratitude, the matchless gratitude of the soul, intent upon the pursuit of perfection, finding a fellow whose conduct is an unfailing reassurance of the perfectibility of human nature. "Human nature miraculously restored," the missal promised. These two saw in each other the living, daily testimony. Matignon was endowed with signal virtues: well-tried character, eminent learning, diligence, administrative skill, conspicuous prudence in moderating men's various natural propensities. Cheverus was blessed with indefatigable zeal, an incredible facility and success in preaching, and a personality which marvelously attracted all ranks of people.[20] But over and beyond these marks of eminence, both were graced with remarkable humility. The only rivalry that ever existed between them was that of attributing to the other all the credit for whatever good came of their mutual ministry. Matignon insisted that "the good that has been done here is nearly the exclusive work of Mr. Cheverus"; while Cheverus was so self-effacing that people often confused the two men, and paid Matignon compliments which in all justice were due to his assistant.[21]

With such rapport the sharing of work was easy. In early January of their first winter together Matignon left his assistant in charge of Boston and went to Wrentham to begin mission work south of the city. When he returned he sent Cheverus north to Newburyport where a colony of French refugees had been without a priest's visit for more than three years. Cheverus visited as well some French Catholics in Portsmouth, New Hampshire, and on his return trip stopped in Salem where he baptized the children of an Irish family. After a brief respite in Boston he traveled south to Plymouth in early June, again baptizing an Irish boy, a Michael Fitzgerald. It had been Matignon's intention to go himself to Maine on Cheverus' return, but he was not well and the curate went in his stead.[22]

In addition to his work among the Indians already described Cheverus tried that first summer to reach the other Catholics around Pleasant Point and southward, even hoping to carry the faith to non-Catholics as well. He found some Irish families near the Passamaquoddy settlement and some Protestants who took little pleasure from the only ministers available to them, the so-called New Lights. Cheverus wrote optimistically to Matignon, "I have some hopes of being able to throw some seeds in this wild soil," but it was not much of a beginning.[23] On his way home he visited some Irish families at Bedford, New Hampshire, where he did sow seed which produced fruit, for Theodore Goffe who gave him lodging later became a Catholic. Then a few months of autumn weather later he was reunited with Matignon once more.

And so their time was spent, taking turns at the church in School Street, making their respective mission journeys to the north and south, enjoying the brief reunions in Boston when experiences could be shared and zeal renewed in the sharing. Each fed the other's flame. When Father Matignon made his report to Bishop Carroll on May 1, 1798, he was encouraged. There had been almost 250 Easter Communions, over 100 baptisms, and seventeen marriages.[24] It was no miraculous increase over the previous year but the list of places now being periodically visited was growing: Newburyport and Salem to the north; Wrentham, Carver, Plymouth, and Scituate to the south; Bedford and Portsmouth in New Hampshire; and the Indians in Maine. In the year since Carroll had agreed to leave Cheverus in New England Matignon had felt his spirits soar on wings of renewed hopes for the future of the Church in that area.

It had been a pleasant year in other respects, too. They had enjoyed visits both protracted and prolonged of other priests. Father John

Thayer, Matignon's predecessor in Boston, had joined them for a year in between his labors for the church of Albany, New York, and his departure for the Kentucky frontier.[25] His preaching had been of great assistance when either Cheverus or Matignon was alone in Boston. Father Jean S. Tisserant, an *émigré* from the Diocese of Bourges, came up occasionally from Wethersfield, Connecticut, to share anecdotes or obtain furnishings for his altar.[26] Edmund Burke, who was later to become the first Bishop of Halifax, was such an ingratiating visitor that Cheverus jokingly complained from his Maine mission, "I am . . . glad that you have such good company, although that may occasion some comparisons not wholly advantageous to me !"[27]

The man Cheverus was personally most pleased to welcome to New England was Jean Sougé. Not long after Cheverus left Tottenham Father Sougé decided to follow his childhood friend to the United States. Bishop Douglass wrote to Bishop Carroll, "He is a gentleman strongly recommended to me for his learning, piety, and zeal, and he is intimately connected with Monsieur Cheverus whom I recommended to your Lordship last Autumn."[28] Matignon doubted the Boston church's need for three resident priests in 1797, and Father Sougé in addition did not yet feel competent enough in English to enter the active mission immediately. After his arrival in New York he wrote to Bishop Carroll that he had entered his diocese, and then went to Connecticut to serve as private chaplain to the family of Vicomte de Sibert Cornillon in the Hartford area. After a year both Cheverus and Matignon believed that Father Sougé knew enough English to be used actively in the field, and the Boston superior wrote to Carroll:

> Mr. Sougé . . . has presumably written you these last days to offer his services in the mission. . . . I do not know how much English he knows, but he has enough to have given instruction, when he was in England, to a little congregation to which the Bishop of the Middle District assigned him. An excessively modest disposition has rendered him perhaps somewhat lacking in self-confidence.[29]

If Cheverus hoped his relative and friend would become a permanent addition to the New England clergy he was disappointed. Sougé did enter the active ministry, but not near Boston. Carroll eventually used him in Newtown, Maryland, one of the oldest centers of Catholicism in the United States, where diffidence would present no handicap.[30]

Actually Boston could not have supported another priest at that time, even if the Catholic population warranted two assistants. If Father

Romagné had not been subsidized by the government, even his mission
in Maine would have been virtually impossible. Boston was unattractive
on other scores; the climate was always rigorous for men accustomed
to the more gentle variations in France. In addition, like the other major
ports of the Atlantic seaboard, Boston was periodically visited by the
ravages of yellow fever, the most dreaded plague of the time. Since
the Revolution it had appeared in virulent form in 1791, 1793, 1795,
and now in 1798 Cheverus got his first experience with the panic it
produced.

Very little was known, from a medical point of view, about the causes
of the fever. The most widely accepted view in New York was that
of Dr. Richard Bayley, whose "Report on the Subject of Yellow Fever"
prepared for Governor John Jay in 1796 argued that the unwholesome
condition of ships and docks was largely responsible.[31] Bishop Carroll
in Maryland was convinced that it was brought in from the West
Indies and he said in 1795, "Our merchants are too greedy of gain not
to keep up a continued intercourse with those Islands; and our Maryland legislature, through unpardonable inattention, or some worse
motive, has made no sufficient provision for the preservation of health."[32]
The only remedy commonly practiced was flight from cities where the
fever struck.

When Cheverus returned from his second visit to the Indians he
found Boston in a state verging on hysteria. One third of the people
had already fled, business was at a standstill, and those unfortunates
who had no place to go were beside themselves with fear. The selectmen
had tried to minimize the situation by reporting on August 4 that their
consultation with the physicians of the city showed "but sixteen persons
have died with that disease and but ten persons are now sick."[33] This
attempt at reassurance had small effect since the numbers were every
day increasing. By October more than a hundred had died, and the
little Catholic congregation accounted for nearly a fourth of that number.
It required all the efforts of the clergy of the city to console the sick,
fortify the dying, and bury the dead. With few exceptions, these men
of God, Catholic and Protestant alike, worked with superhuman energy
to bring peace of mind to the terrified Bostonians. Cheverus and
Matignon were "always seen at the post of danger" and their conduct
that fall left a mark which time did not erase.[34] Differences of religion
diminished in the common crisis; but the mutual respect engendered
while the crisis lasted endured. The *Columbian Centinel* reported in

relief on October 20, "Health has again returned to bless our town. And the citizens with their families have very generally appeared, to enliven our late gloomy abodes." In some of those homes the love for two French priests and their unstinting valor was permanently enshrined. In the city generally, there could never again be quite the same virulence of animosity toward the priests who lived in School Street.

Yet animosity did exist in some quarters, and within two years it would enmesh John Cheverus in a legal matter from which, Matignon stoutly maintained, only Providence extricated him. It all came about as a result of his ministry in the Newcastle-Damariscotta region of Maine. Cheverus had first visited there in June, 1798, finding four Irish families sorely in need of a priest. These families were interrelated by both marriage and business, and seemed to offer an excellent nucleus for building up a Catholic congregation. When Cheverus returned from Maine that August he had told Bishop Douglass, "I have visited several Catholic families scattered on the sea coast from New Brunswick to Boston. I have given Communion to 33 individuals of either sex. Wherever I have preached I have had a great many Protestant hearers, but only 4 or 5 conversions."[35] There is no way of knowing how much of this progress was made at Newcastle and Damariscotta in 1798, but a few years later Cheverus wrote from Newcastle to a friend in Mayenne, "I have had the good fortune to found here a little parish. The majority of my lambs are new converts, a great number baptized by my own hands."[36] There is no question, however, that the Kavanaghs, the Cottrills, the Jacksons, and the Hanleys, whom he met on his first visit, furnished the beginnings of what became one of his outstanding missions. James Kavanagh and Matthew Cottrill were business partners in shipbuilding and bridge construction on the Damariscotta River. It was in Cottrill's house that Cheverus offered Mass on his first visit, and in Cottrill's barn that he preached to both Catholics and Protestants.[37] The Hanley brothers, Patrick and Roger, lived farther down toward Pemaquid at Bristol, but the Jacksons had come to Newcastle since their daughter Sarah was James Kavanagh's wife. After Cheverus accompanied Father Romagné to the Indian mission in 1799 he visited Newcastle for the second time and made his home with the Kavanaghs. For five Sundays he offered Mass for the people living around the Damariscotta River, and during the week he visited nearly a dozen other families before returning to Boston in September.

It was this second trip which indirectly involved Cheverus and his pastor in court proceedings, to the surprise and chagrin of both priests. No two men were ever less contentious or inclined to litigation. While the younger man was more amused than angry, his older friend could not lightly disregard the humiliations Cheverus was tendered, although he bore with more equanimity the suit in which he himself was involved. The first suit, which was originally tried before the Court of Common Pleas of Boston on January 7, 1800, revolved about the injustice of double taxation suffered by the Catholics of Maine. According to law the residents of Newcastle were required to pay a tax to support ministers in the town. Until Cheverus arrived on his first visit there had been little reason to protest. Not only were the Catholics unprovided with a priest, but the Protestants themselves had no permanent minister before 1797. The Kavanaghs and Cottrills are even said to have attended occasional Protestant services in the years during which their annual Easter trips to Boston constituted their only contact with ministers of their own faith. But in 1797 the situation changed; Newcastle got a resident minister and the Catholics learned that Father Matignon meant to send his assistant to visit them. Cheverus certainly had hoped to visit Damariscotta before he discovered how much time he needed among the Passamaquoddy Indians. When the ministerial tax next came due James Kavanagh paid it, but he stipulated that it should go to Father Matignon as their proper minister charged with sending them a priest. Matignon never received Kavanagh's $16.02. By the time of Cheverus' second stay in the Newcastle-Damariscotta area, and his five consecutive weeks among the Catholics there, both Kavanagh and Cottrill were more than ever incensed at being taxed to support a minister when their own missionary was obviously in such need and came to them at such personal sacrifice. When they paid the tax in October they told Benjamin Lincoln, the collector, that they would sue to recover the money if it did not go to their own minister. "If we can't get clear as Roman Catholics, then we will turn Baptists," they said angrily. "Then we will certainly get clear!"[38]

Much against his will Francis Matignon became the plaintiff in the resulting suit. Attorney-General James Sullivan was certain the Catholics had a chance for "almost infallible success," and a writ was issued on November 1 against the Town of Newcastle in the name of the Boston pastor. When the trial came up the following January the court decided against the Catholics and charged Father Matignon with costs. Again in spite of private preference, Matignon allowed Sullivan to appeal the case. Again the verdict went against the Catholics and on March 5, 1801, Matignon was assessed the costs of $49.25. Cheverus ironically told Bishop Carroll:

> The Judges of the Supreme Court now sitting in Boston declared unanimously that [they] must pay for the support of said Minister. . . . The Constitution, said they, obliges every one to contribute to the support of Protestant ministers and them alone. Papists are only tolerated, and as long as their Ministers behave well, we shall not disturb them. We were present, Dr. Matignon and myself, and, as you may suppose, listening with raptures to the above and equally flattering speeches.[39]

Matignon could not allow himself the pleasure of sardonic humor when reporting the affair to Carroll. He was much too concerned over the implications of the decision. If the courts were to continue to read into the law the word "Protestant" before every mention of publicly supported teachers or ministers, then religious liberality "so vaunted at the present time," not to say justice, did not exist. "Not only individuals but even an entire Catholic community," he said, "could thereby be forced by law to provide itself with a Protestant minister, which is absurd and an injury to liberty of conscience." He blamed Attorney-General Sullivan for mishandling the case, for arguing it "exactly as I would have desired him to do, if I were the adverse party."

> We believed that the only question would be whether Kavanagh living some two hundred miles from here, could still be regarded as a member of our Church, and on this point we would have been victorious. They made it a general question of law, on which Mr. Sullivan was evidently but little prepared. Thus we are forever deprived of a right, which in a number of places, no one even thought of denying us.[40]

Matignon was more legally correct than the judges who so unanimously pronounced against him. The state constitution specifically prohibited subordinating one sect to another. It further stipulated that money paid to the support of public worship and public teachers should be uniformly applied according to each man's "own religious sect or denomination." By reading the word "Protestant" into the law the gentlemen of the bench had put prejudice before jurisprudence. Nevertheless, this colored reading would prevail for some time to come. In his heart Matignon found it difficult to think charitably of James Sullivan who had handled the case so badly.

Perhaps in this respect the loyal pastor was himself a trifle biased. The truth was, Sullivan was already out of favor in School Street that year, for reasons related to another legal matter involving Matignon's beloved confrere. This second bit of litigation resulted from what had seemed at the time a gala occasion. The second year of his mission work at Newcastle, Cheverus was invited back soon after Christmas. The Kavanaghs desired him to preside over the marriage of Mrs. Kavanagh's sister to James Smithwick on New Year's Day. To his amazement, when Cheverus returned to the Damariscotta region that summer, he was arrested on charges both civil and criminal for having performed a marriage in Lincoln County with "no lawful authority." He discovered that Attorney-General Sullivan had instigated the proceedings before a grand jury at Wiscasset which had returned a bill of indictment. There is little reason to believe that Sullivan acted except in his capacity as the people's prosecutor in the matter, but Matignon told Carroll bitterly, "We have Attorney-General Sullivan to thank for this humiliating and costly prosecution."[41] Matthew Cottrill indignantly furnished the bail of $200 and Justice of the Peace Shearjashub Bourne released Cheverus for trial in October.

Cheverus was not disturbed. If he understood the law he was guilty of no offense. Legal marriages within the Massachusetts jurisdiction required either the offices of an authorized minister or of a justice of the peace residing in the county; if no minister of the happy couple's persuasion could be found in their own county, the law allowed one from the next to act. Cheverus knew he was an authorized priest residing in the nearest county in which one could be found. Furthermore, following the Catholic practice he had seen in England, Cheverus had insisted that the Smithwicks go on January 2 before a justice of the peace to have the marriage civilly ratified. Elizabeth Jackson and her husband were validly and legally married, beyond any doubt in his mind. He went about his mission duties, serenely offering Mass in "a small neat Chapel" Kavanagh had fitted up at his own expense in Newcastle, conferring the sacraments in the outlying settlements, and preaching wherever he found any people ready to listen.

In October at Wiscasset Cheverus found himself "at the same bar with thieves, men guilty of forgery, etc." waiting judgment at the hands of Judges Theophilus Bradbury, Simeon Strong, and Samuel Sewall. Bradbury and Sewall were two of the judges who some months later decided against Matignon in the ministerial tax case; Strong was the brother of the governor whom Matignon described as "rather small

and without ability." Sewall was the only one of the three not openly
hostile to Cheverus. Of the two actions begun against Cheverus in July
only the criminal question was at issues in October. If Cheverus could
be proved not a "settled minister of Boston" he would be subject to
both fine and the pillory. Cheverus was defended by Silas Lee, a member
of the Congress of the United States, and by a member of the Massachusetts legislature who proved that Cheverus was, in fact, a settled minister
of the Catholic Church in Boston. Bradbury who was presiding could
not prevent his spleen from showing, however; in announcing the dismissal of the criminal action he said in open court that if it had been
proved otherwise he would gladly have sentenced Cheverus to an hour
in the pillory and a fine of £80. As it was, Cheverus told his bishop
in summarizing the first trial, "There is still a civil (or rather very
uncivil) prosecution carried on against me for the recovery of a fine
of £50 . . . and this I am afraid I shall have to pay."[42] He was beginning
to perceive that the mere letter of the law was only part of these cases.
When Matignon gave Carroll his account of the affair he added, "Mr.
Cheverus for his part . . . told me 'I was never in better spirits.' I
hope God will recompense him for these little humiliations and more
and more bless his labours."[43]

In the interim between the first and second actions against the assistant both priests prepared as best they could for the civil suit.
Cheverus made a written agreement with the Catholics living in Newcastle by which they recognized him as their pastor and he pledged
himself to fulfill those functions in their regard. The approbation of
Bishop Carroll was obtained for this contract. It could have no retro-
active effect, he knew; but it might at least prevent future litigation.
Until the civil suit came to trial he followed Matignon's advice and
neither married nor baptized publicly in Lincoln County.

Matignon meanwhile asked Carroll to send them a "sealed certificate"
attesting Cheverus' authority to act as Catholic minister in that area
and requested a copy of Carroll's pastoral letter on marriage. Cheverus
had seen an extract from it left by Father Thayer and believed it
might be useful in arguing his case. The bishop dispatched the sections of the decrees of the diocesan synod of 1791 relating to matrimony,
but when Cheverus thanked him for them he commented wryly that
he feared the Latin would be "quite out of the way of most of our
lawyers here, and judges too."[44] Matignon explained to Carroll that
what Cheverus had really wanted was the pastoral of November 10,
1791, regarding marriages before other than lawful Catholic pastors,[45]

As the time for the second trial approached both men were pessimistic. After the negative decision in Matignon's own case in Boston on March 5, 1801, they had even less cause to be sanguine. Cheverus said, "The judges gave us here a little specimen of their good will toward the Catholic Religion and its ministers. . . . I really believe should my former trial come on again these gentlemen would not be ashamed to set me on the pillory."[46] Matignon told Carroll gloomily, "There is every appearance from reports that we will be condemned in the civil action of £50 damages and payment of costs."[47]

But they were both wrong. On July 3, 1801, Matignon wrote gleefully to Baltimore:

> I have the satisfaction of informing you that the civil action against Mr. Cheverus . . . has just ended in his favor. Providence served us in a very particular manner in this matter. Judge Bradbury who was to preside as the oldest, and who had positively declared last year in open court that Mr. Cheverus ought to be condemned . . . could not be present at the court because of a fall from his horse which nearly cost him his life. Attorney-general Sullivan could not be there either and his substitute was found to be the very one who would plead for us. . . . It is regarded as finished.[48]

In late summer Cheverus returned to Newcastle for a prolonged period of active, joyful ministry. Matignon reported proudly to their bishop:

> The progress is most rapid and consoling in the little mission of the East, where Mr. Cheverus has been nearly 5 months. 50 and some communed, there were 30 baptisms in the current year, 5 adults, and far from the corruption of our cities and the infection of Jacobinism almost all there are if not exemplary at least regular and sincere.[49]

Even if the eyes of justice did not always smile with the same steady approval on the Catholics of New England, they were still in the hands of God. As for their shepherds, the little matter of law each had witnessed in his turn only served to strengthen the bonds of affection for each other and for their flocks.

CHAPTER VI

TO GO OR STAY?

EARLY in February of the year that Father Cheverus was exonerated by the court in his New World location he received a letter which recalled him to former loyalties in the Old World, and ushered in a period of nerve-racking indecision. Because of his nature his times of most acute trial were those during which he did not clearly perceive the will of God for him in the particular exercise of his ministry. It was ironic that just as Matignon believed Providence had intervened to keep Cheverus in New England Cheverus himself was presented with the suggestion that it was his duty to depart.

Susceptible as he was to the urgings of family affections and to friendship's demands, devoted as he was to his native land and its former dynasty, docile as he meant to be to ecclesiastical authority, zealous as he remained for the good of souls, he was destined to suffer repeatedly during his life a refined torment peculiar to himself. In 1792 he had experienced just such an anguish in trying to reach a decision in regard to his pastoral obligations at Notre Dame de Mayenne. His flight to England had been made with his mind in turmoil. It had been less harrowing to leave Tottenham, because England had so many priests at the time and the United States so few; that move had been chiefly an exchange of one exile for another, and his first years in New England had offered so many opportunities for fervent endeavor he had been more than content. Rather, as we have seen, he had been as joyful as a missionary could be.

But now, in his fifth year as Matignon's assistant, he faced a dilemma that brought gravest misgivings to himself, months of intense anxiety to his confrere and the faithful, and real concern to his bishop in Baltimore. The crisis was precipitated by his father who was once more back

73

in the city of Mayenne. Jean-Vincent de Cheverus in his letter which reached Boston in February, 1801, enclosed another from the former parishioners of Father Cheverus at Notre Dame begging him to return. Only one of his former assistants, François-René Esnault, had survived the exile of the 1790's and returned to Mayenne where, with a half-dozen aged priests, he represented a mere remnant of the former clergy of the city.[1] Cheverus had promised the Bishop of Le Mans on leaving England that he would return to France "whenever it could be done." Was this the time when his pledge to Jouffroy de Gonssans should be fulfilled?

Conditions in France had changed since the grim days of the September Massacres. Not long after Cheverus had returned from establishing Father Romagné among the Indians in 1799, Napoleon Bonaparte's coup d'état had overthrown the Directory and organized the Consulate. Almost immediately hopes had revived in France that the Church would now see better days. Decrees of December 28, 1799, not only annulled the regulations which kept churches closed except on every tenth day, but also abolished former oaths which had prevented all but constitutional priests from exercising their functions. Now, in order to be an active priest, a simple oath of fidelity to the new constitution was exacted. A decree two days later granted to the mortal remains of Pius VI, the Pope who had died on August 29 at Valence, "marks of consideration for a man who occupied one of the highest ranks on earth." During its return to Rome the body of the late pontiff received all the homage it deserved.[2] By the time Cheverus received his father's letter the new Pope, Pius VII, and the new chief of the French nation, First Consul Bonaparte, were considering a concordat. Napoleon was alleged to have told the clergy of Milan on June 5, 1800, that he hoped to have the good fortune of "removing all the obstacles which could still bar a complete reconciliation of the Church and the French nation."[3]

The situation in Mayenne naturally seemed much brighter. After Bishop de Gonssans finally fled from France in 1794 he had sought refuge first in Holland, then in Münster, and finally in Paderborn. From this last refuge he had sent Charles-François Duperrier-Dumourier back to France to administer his diocese. Duperrier-Dumourier entered his homeland secretly in 1797 and when news reached Le Mans on April 30, 1799, that Gonssans had died at Paderborn the preceding January, five former canons of the cathedral chapter unanimously elected Duperrier-Dumourier vicar-capitulary to administer the diocese during the vacancy of the see.[4] When Cheverus first notified Bishop Carroll of the letter from his former parishioners he told him that Rome had confirmed Duperrier-Dumourier as administrator of the diocese and that it appeared likely he would succeed to the bishopric. "I know him," he added, "and believe he will send me orders to return."[5]

In March, 1801, Cheverus was thus in a quandary. He did not want to break the ties which bound him to the Church of Boston, or to his scattered congregations elsewhere. If he must leave this country it would be with sincere regret. On the other hand, he felt bound by his promise to return to France; yet he could certainly take no step without consulting his superior in the United States. Finally, knowing the many changes France had undergone since 1789, changing from absolute monarchy to limited monarchy, from all forms of monarchy to a republic, first under the Convention, then the Directory, and now a Consulate, how could he be sure that the new regime would prove permanent? As he told Carroll, "We live in times where less than one year is enough to overthrow not only individual projects, but even Empires and Nations. Therefore I look, as yet, on my return as very uncertain. My only wish is to obey the voice of Providence and to go wherever it calls." In replying to Mayenne he explained that he could not leave Boston suddenly but in case nothing should prevent it, he expected he might be able to go "after Easter next year."[6]

Francis Matignon was utterly aghast at the possibility of losing his friend. He told Carroll in a hasty note on March 16 that he could not just then go into details "on the dolorous loss which threatens me in the person of Mr. Cheverus," but three days later he explained his anxiety more fully:

> The loss of Mr. Cheverus, if it takes place, as there is every appearance of, and should I survive it, will be irreparable for me. I have so little talent and strength I don't know how I shall be able to suffice here, especially now that our people have become accustomed to frequent instructions, etc. And in the view of the meagerness of our resources, it will be impossible to think of replacing him. Your paternal goodness and Divine Providence will doubtless dictate what is to be done.[7]

Quite apart from the personal loss he dreaded, Matignon was not at all sure that the present situation in France was one to invite the return of the *émigré* clergy. Like Cheverus, he was still loyal to monarchical principles and in the last year of the Directory had told Bishop

Joseph Plessis of Quebec, "I hope to live to see the monstrous atheistical government of France destroyed, to give place to the restoration of Religion and monarchy."[8] Louis XVIII, the legitimate heir to the abolished French throne, was alive in England, and news from that quarter indicated that he was categorically opposed to the oath of fidelity required to the new French constitution. Through Cardinal Maury he urged the new Pope to condemn the formula and to pronounce in his own favor. The old bishops, too, were not in agreement as to the propriety of the clergy's taking an oath to support Napoleon's government. Episcopal instructions were contradictory. The opposition of the would-be king and Maury, whom he named "Protector of the Churches of France," to the new regime naturally raised doubts in Matignon's mind as to the wisdom of Cheverus' return in 1801. He told Carroll on July 3:

> The silence from England on Cardinal Maury's reply, which I have however read in the *Mireure britannique-francais* makes me doubt its authenticity. My confrere, although resolved not to make the promise, seems nevertheless to be going to return to France. But I believe Mr. Romagné will stay with us.[9]

As he had anticipated, John Cheverus did hear from Duperrier-Dumourier, but there was no clear-cut command to return immediately. It appeared that as yet priests in Mayenne were not being compelled to take the oath of fidelity, and that the administrator of the diocese wished Cheverus' return. But aside from predictions that great changes were soon to take place in the Church in France, Cheverus learned little more than his father's letter had already told him. When Matignon wrote to Baltimore in September he said, "Mr. Cheverus, who left some weeks ago for his mission of the East, is still of the same disposition and waits impatiently for *ulterior* news of France. He is resolved at present not to make the promise of fidelity."[10] When Cheverus replied to Dumourier he assured him of his interest in the parishioners of Notre Dame de Mayenne and of his willingness to return; but he then described the situation Matignon faced in New England and said that advice from "theologians of the first merit" prevented his leaving until a replacement could be found. It would be the following spring, probably, before he could set sail for France.[11]

As the cold, gray days of New England winter arrived in Maine, Cheverus continued his work in Newcastle. No further clarification of the French situation reached him before the new year, not even a word from his father. When he thought of leaving at all he found that he was thinking in terms of another postponement; it would be at least the fall of 1802 before his return to France. When he wrote to Esnault from Newcastle in January he spoke of his obligations in Maine, his duty of preaching during the Lenten services in Boston, the scarcity of priests, and the poverty of the American mission. "Can I leave a number of Catholics here exposed to dying without the sacraments, to losing their faith, abandon a worthy confrere in health so feeble who, if I leave, would have no priest nearer than a hundred leagues?" Without any further knowledge of the new arrangements being made in France as a result of Napoleon's negotiations with Rome, Cheverus did not see how he could leave Matignon for months to come.[12]

As a matter of fact, a great deal had happened in France even if Boston was slow in getting the details. The Concordat of 1801 had been signed by the negotiating diplomats in Paris the day after the national celebration of the Fourteenth of July. Although its provisions have been subject to various interpretations, depending on the individual point of view, certain general facts may be accepted. The negotiations had been understood to represent the proposals of the First Consul and the Roman Pontiff, each possessed of a plenitude of sovereignty. The first article of the concordat asserted two fundamental principles; freedom of religion and the right to public worship. Then followed provisions governing the divisions of dioceses and the nomination of bishops. The spiritual authority was recognized as possessing the exclusive right to delimit the dioceses; in regard to episcopal nominations the former principle of 1516 was accepted. According to this, the kings of France had exercised the right to present candidates who were then invested with spiritual authority by the Church. Now, the First Consul would name the person and Pius VII would give the canonical institution. Nothing was said, however, of what would happen if governmental candidates proved unacceptable to Rome. All the clergy were now to take an oath to obey the government, whereas formerly only bishops had been required to do so. The French government would enjoy all the rights and prerogatives of former regimes as long as the Catholic religion was professed. The state would pay the clergy a "suitable salary."[13]

At first glance the convention marked a triumph for Napoleon. But the Church could find some cause for rejoicing. While the republic recognized the Roman Catholic and apostolic religion as only that of a majority of its citizens, it was more than a statement of fact. "Roman" was used in the full sense of the word, denoting a recognition of papal primacy; further, it connoted that the Revolution had not succeeded in destroying Catholicism or in setting up a national religion. The accord signified the recovery of security after a decade of persecution. This "triumph without precedent of pontifical jurisdiction" predicted the return to a rapport between the French government and the papacy which could heal the wounds inflicted by the Revolution. On Rome's part the ratification was exceptionally rapid. On August 15 the encyclical *Ecclesia Christi* announced the concordat to the Catholic world; and two briefs: *Tam multa* and *Pastoralis sollicitudo,* urged the constitutional bishops and the prelates of the Old Regime to resign from their sees so that the new order could be effected. Nine days later Pius VII named Cardinal Caprara his legate *a latere* to France.[14]

Yet the speed of Roman ratification belied the complexities of the situation. "In reality, each article of the convention contained as many equivocations, calculated or unintentional, as the difficulties resolved." The debate in the general congregation of August 11 in Rome indicated the division of opinion among the cardinals. There was strong feeling that Pius VII had sacrificed too much to the secular power and to the Revolution.[15] In France, on the other hand, although Napoleon ratified on September 8 he delayed for seven months before submitting the articles to the deliberative assemblies. It was not until April 8, 1802, that Paris finally passed a specific law regulating religion in the nation and on April 18 officially proclaimed the concordat at Notre Dame with a *Te Deum.*[16]

The most delicate problem immediately posed by the concordat was that of establishing a new hierarchy. Bishop Carroll in Baltimore got a clue to the troubles in store when he read Father William Strickland's letter from London written the September that Cheverus had gone to Newcastle. The English priest, commenting on the reception of the papal brief *Pastoralis sollicitudo,* wrote on September 29, 1801:

> We have seventeen French bishops in London who last week had four or five meetings to deliberate on their answers. Four only have agreed to resign their sees. . . . The conduct of the majority of the bishops has given no edification either to the English or French.[17]

Louis XVIII urged the *émigré* prelates, "The king relies on the firmness of the majority of the bishops of his realm not to submit to the laws which the Pope, much less the illegitimate government, had no right to impose on them." The eventual tally of Old Regime bishops found thirty-eight refusing to resign while fifty-five agreed. Threats of schism appeared before the concordat was even promulgated in Paris. On December 23, 1801, the *Mémoire des évêques français résidant à Londres* appeared, and the bishops who refused to resign protested even more forcibly in April, 1803, in their *Réclamations canoniques* addressed to Pius VII. The *Petite Église,* as it was called, continued to present its schism until the fall of Napoleon and the *émigrés* finally submitted to Pius VII in 1815. Numerically the opposition was small enough, and isolated. But the French government was pitiless toward any priest rash enough even to correspond with his former religious chief. The constitutional bishops, in sharp contrast, resigned as a body, not so much out of obedience to the Pope as out of complete submission to the secular authority.[18]

The new division of dioceses in France created sixty episcopal sees grouped under ten metropolitans. By the end of April, 1802, the new hierarchy was constituted. Sixteen were former bishops of the Old Regime; twelve were constitutional prelates who had submitted to the Holy See on April 15; and thirty-two were raised from the ranks of the lower clergy, former vicars-general or cathedral canons for the most part, only one of whom was a former juror or *assermenté;* only two of the former constitutional bishops were assigned to sees of major importance. For the most part, although the new hierarchy was less aristocratic, the nominations of the First Consul were excellent. "More scrupulous than the Most Christian King, he admitted not one prelate without faith or morals." He chose men who would be both competent and conciliatory.[19]

The new bishops were consecrated on May 3, 1803, by the papal legate and were then received by Napoleon. Acting with speed and accord they succeeded in establishing themselves without notable opposition by the end of the following eighteen months. But the organization within the dioceses was not equally rapid. The right of defining parish lines and of naming pastors was left to the bishops; but the total number of parishes fixed by law was woefully inadequate. The budget seemed more important than spiritual welfare in Paris, and the new hierarchy found the 3000 or so parishes of France quite insufficient. The need for priests, too, presented an acute problem. Since 1789 there had been few ordinations, and the persecutions, deportations, and voluntary exile had decimated the ranks of those already ordained. The body of the French clergy in 1801 was largely composed of men who were old and worn out by overwork. It would be a slow and arduous task to revitalize both the ranks and the discipline. Almost everywhere material conditions were frightful. Ruined churches, razed steeples, roofs gaping to the rain and snow, rectories alienated or occupied by anticlericals, presented a discouraging picture.

Conditions were probably nowhere more critical than in the diocese from which Cheverus had fled a decade earlier. For ten years it had been divided into two separate dioceses corresponding to the *départements* of Sarthe and Mayenne, with see cities at both Laval and Le Mans. Now, under the new concordat, they were reunited again under one bishop in a jurisdiction that time would prove entirely too large for one prelate to administer. Contrary to Cheverus' expectation, Duperrier-Dumourier was not made bishop. He wrote to Cheverus on June 10, 1802, "We have a very good Bishop, Mgr. Pidoll, suffragan of Trèves. He is going to take possession at any moment. He will be busy fixing the limits of his parishes, and as soon after this work as possible he will name the pastors."[20]

Michel-Joseph de Pidoll von Quintenbach was born at Trèves, November 16, 1734. In 1794 he had been made an auxiliary bishop to Clement-Wenceslas of Saxe, the Archbishop of Trèves. When the French invaded Trèves during the Revolutionary wars Pidoll had fled across the Rhine and had thereafter exercised his ministry at Frankfort, Mainz, and Ehrenbreitstein. On April 9, 1802, he was named Bishop of Le Mans and arrived there on July 7, taking possession of his cathedral four days later.[21] He was installed on Sunday, July 22, at Le Mans, and a month later entered Laval formally to take over the administration of Mayenne. From the very beginning Duperrier-Dumourier was kept on as his vicar-general in that part of his diocese, and it was in this capacity that he urged Cheverus in the summer of 1802, "I summon you in consequence of your pledge, and beg you to leave at once on receipt of this to come and unite yourself to us. It is a question of re-establishing religion in our country and you are needed. Do not hesitate, therefore, I beg of you."[22]

What Dumourier did not say, but what accounts for some of the urgency of his summons, was that the Diocese of Le Mans was rife with factions competing for the pastoral appointments. Long before the concordat was officially in force parishioners were using all the influence at hand to insure the nomination of priests of their own preference. "Never were rivers so hard to cross, never was intemperateness so violent, never was there greater uneasiness among the faithful."[23] Al-

Gilbert Stuart portrait of Cheverus made in 1823, now in the Boston Museum of Fine Arts.

Boston in Cheverus' time.

Cathedral of the Holy Cross, Franklin St., Boston.

St. Patrick's Church, Damariscotta, Maine.

though Cheverus did not receive this letter from the vicar-general of Le Mans until almost nine months later, he may have suspected something of the sort from the impatient letters he received from his relatives, his former parishioners, and Father Esnault. Matignon, with whom Cheverus discussed every aspect of his dilemma, had told Bishop Carroll on January 23, 1802, that both the Catholics and non-Catholics of Mayenne had signed a letter begging Cheverus to return. He relayed Esnault's theories that after all former clergy had resigned their parishes, and the number of parishes had been fixed, the former pastors might be rehabilitated if there were not "too strong opposition on the part of their parishioners."[24]

Cheverus himself said, when writing to Esnault from Newcastle that same month, that he would have no hesitation about returning if pastors re-entered their former parishes by right. But, he went on:

> Since it is necessary to resign (and I give my resignation very willingly for the peace of the Church and authorize you to give it in my name), since it is necessary to await a new nomination, and it is uncertain whether it will fall upon me, ought I not to await the result here, where my presence is actually necessary: Won't the new bishop of Laval desire to put another in a place so important, especially in the case of the reunion of parishes? He will easily find among my confreres some one more worthy of his confidence than I am.[25]

When Dumourier's letter of June, 1802, finally did reach Boston, Matignon was still convinced that there was no assurance that Cheverus would actually return as pastor of Notre Dame. He explained to Bishop Carroll that the summons, "written as it is on the same sheet as his father's, and with no express mention of the new bishop's orders, nor of his parish . . . clearly expresses the *desires of his family* rather than the *real orders* of an *ecclesiastical superior*."[26]

Altogether Cheverus well might have been confused. Added to his unwillingness to take the new oath, his genuine reluctance to abandon Matignon and his people, his uncertainty as to his true superior, there was this other question of the genuine need of his old parish of Notre Dame. He obviously could not be sure of the precise position he would hold if he did return to France. This alone would not have deterred him, however. As he said to Esnault:

> If the good Lord permits it, I want to finish my days in your midst. But I speak in the sincerity of my heart when I assure you that I

would prefer a place as assistant, or any other, to an elevated position. If they name a pastor to Mayenne, I will go with joy to work under him as soon as I can find a nurse to whom I could entrust my children in America. . . . The will of my superiors will always be the rule of my conduct . . . but, today, I do not even know whom my ecclesiastical superiors will be.[27]

His was a most unenviable predicament. To his French exhorters he answered, "My heart calls me to you, but the voice of duty and love for religion seem to require a longer delay than I imagined." It was the nearest he could come to a solution just then. Return to France he would, but not until there was someone to take his place in Boston and some clearer sign of Providence's intentions in his regard.

Father Matignon knew what his assistant was suffering. They were too close for it to have been otherwise. When Cheverus returned from Newcastle after Candlemas in 1802 Matignon promised not to mention the subject again. But in his heart he dreaded fresh importunings from Mayenne which might alter his confrere's resolve to stay in Boston until fall. He tried meanwhile to imagine what Boston would do without Cheverus and proposed to Bishop Carroll two possibilities that had come to mind. The first was the suggestion that Father John Thayer be brought back from Kentucky. Matignon humbly offered to step down and let Thayer assume the pastoral role. Thayer had been in Boston first, he argued, and was his "elder in the Mission." Besides, Thayer had means and the plans for a new church and rectory might progress more rapidly.[28]

If Thayer's return were not feasible, perhaps the New England mission might be placed under the direction of a quasi-Jesuit society which had recently been organized in Europe. Matignon knew that several attempts had been made to revive the Jesuits since their expulsion from France in 1762, particularly since the Revolution. Father Pierre de la Clorivière had secretly founded the Society of the Heart of Jesus; two former Sulpicians in 1794 had founded at Louvain the Society of the Priests of the Sacred Heart; and at Spoleto three years later Nicolas Paccanari had established the Fathers of the Faith of Jesus. These last two had united in 1799 under the name "Fathers of the Faith" under the sign of St. Ignatius. At the time Matignon was searching for a solution some of these "Paccanarists" were in England and he had been in correspondence with Charles de Broglie, one of the founders of the Louvain branch who was now in Kensington. Father de Broglie had gone to England to recruit members for the quasi-Jesuit society in 1800 and it was from him that the Boston pastor got the idea of affiliating with the group.[29]

Neither of Matignon's suggestions received any encouragement from Baltimore. John Carroll had private reasons for hoping Thayer would never return to Boston. Reports from his vicar-general, Stephen T. Badin, in 1801 had led first to Thayer's suspension and then to his being ordered to leave. Although Thayer did not actually leave Kentucky until 1803, Carroll gave not the slightest consideration in the previous year to the suggestion that he be sent back to Boston, much less as Francis Matignon's superior.[30] The notion of affiliating the Boston mission to a quasi-Jesuit organization was equally objectionable. Although Carroll loved the Jesuits as only a man can who has once chosen the Ignatian rule for his vocation, and had suffered personal grief at the suppression of his beloved society in 1773, as Bishop of Baltimore he had consistently opposed any mutilated or modified form of the order in the United States. Only two years prior to Matignon's suggestion he had risked the sharp disapproval of the American ex-Jesuits by opposing their affiliation with this very group.[31] There would have to be a better solution to Boston's needs than either of Matignon's present proposals if Carroll were to agree.

And so the second year of Cheverus' indecision stretched out. In France the concordat was executed, the new bishops consecrated, and the reorganization of the Diocese of Le Mans begun. Cheverus held himself in readiness to leave whenever he received a letter that clearly prohibited further delay. "The first vessel will carry me to you," he assured his former assistant Esnault. But Lent had begun with Cheverus preaching the weekly sermons of the season and he had seen the first date he had fixed for his departure pass. Summer, too, went by without any summons. Again autumn's brilliant foliage gave way to the leafless, snow-covered trees of winter. Only his family continued to plead for his return. As the second season fixed for his return to France passed he became almost tranquil. He promised his father that, perhaps, by next May he would come to Mayenne, if only for a visit. But his thoughts were preoccupied with the new church they were trying to complete in Boston.

Then, late in March of 1803, Cheverus received the note from Duperrier-Dumourier which the vicar-general of Le Mans had written so many months before. It was appended to one from his father, and all the old doubts and anxieties were reawakened. If he did not mean to renounce his fatherland and his native diocese, he read, there was no longer time to weigh matters. Vincent de Cheverus wrote pleadingly, "If a father can believe he still has any authority over a dear son, this would be the occasion to use it and summon him to leave at once to join his family . . . and a father to whom it would add ten more years of life."[32]

Discussing it with Matignon only added to his uncertainty. His friend refused to advise him. His heart was too interested, he said. But Cheverus knew his old colleague was praying for only one intention, that Cheverus remain. After a week of agonizing indecision he took the only step left; he would leave the decision to John Carroll in Baltimore. "My mind is perplexed with doubts, my heart full of trouble and anxieties," he wrote. "Duty, respect, and confidence bid me apply to you for advice and comfort." Then he outlined his dilemma, quoting Dumourier's note in full, and repeating his father's plea. He told the bishop of his own idea of going to Mayenne in May for a visit, but he added:

> The whole congregation here have shown such grief & have so strongly represented the case to me I have promised, if you think I can do it conscientiously, to stay at least till next autumn. Even, if in your opinion, the good of Religion requires my presence here I am very willing to remain in this mission. . . . I must observe that it is uncertain whether I am reappointed to my former station, & under the present circumstance I do not wish it, have even some objections to the oath, though after the decision of the Holy See, I think I would if necessary get over that difficulty.[33]

The truth was he did not know where his duty lay. His father and other relatives seemed to feel that Dumourier's words carried a positive order from his ecclesiastical superior. For his part, Cheverus confessed, he did not see any such order but merely a strong invitation. If Bishop Carroll could only send him a speedy reply he would know what to tell them in Mayenne.

The Bishop of Baltimore was soon in a position to see all sides of the Boston question, for close on the heels of Cheverus' worried request for advice came letters from both the congregation and its pastor. If Father Matignon had hesistated to influence his assistant's decision he had no such compunction where his bishop was concerned. He knew Cheverus would accept Carroll's advice as the voice of Heaven, that the bishop's words would calm his fears. Matignon did not hesitate to to set forth his own convictions:

The more I think about it, the more I am convinced that God evidently destines him for this mission. The strong inclination which he feels to consecrate himself to it, despite the multitude of human motives which . . . call him back to France; his perfect knowledge of the language; talents peculiarly adapted to the mission in this country; his perfect disinterestedness; the tender friendship which unites us as one person and is so useful for doing good together; an infant mission in the East which promises much but will almost infallibly perish unless he continues to cultivate it for many years to come; finally, a series of incidents which since he landed in America, seems to have been arranged by Providence to keep him here . . . all this convinces me that this is his vocation.[34]

But only Bishop Carroll could convince Cheverus that his vocation lay in Boston, Matignon repeated. If the bishop would speak he would "answer the desire of all our Catholics here, many of whom actually wept at the very rumor of his leaving." For the pastor himself it meant granting a new lease on life as well as doing infinite good to this part of the Diocese of Baltimore. It was the strongest letter Carroll had ever read from his loyal subordinate.

Without yet having met Cheverus in person the wise old prelate in Baltimore seems to have known exactly what line of reasoning would best dispel the doubts of the harassed young French *émigré*. Or, perhaps, it was simply his customary facility in dealing with canon law and his habit of impartial judgment. In any case, immediately after receiving the mail from Boston the bishop sat down and analyzed the situation both clearly and forcibly.

He discussed first the question of obligation to the Diocese of Le Mans. A priest was, of course, bound not to abandon his diocese or to enter any other except as prescribed by canon law. "But if events take place, even much less violent than those produced by the late revolution, so that a clergyman cannot hope for support, protection or safety; if his bishop can no longer employ him . . . it appears clear to me that he is no longer bound *in justice* to the service of his former diocese." Carroll did not need to point out that Jouffroy de Gonssans, Cheverus' former bishop, was dead. It was beside the point. The law of preservation entitled *émigrés* to seek elsewhere the protection they could not find in France during the Revolutionary era.

But what of the present situation under the concordat? "The Pope, in his bull for the concordat expressly suppresses and totally extinguishes all the pre-existing Dioceses of France," Carroll pointed out.

This extinction necessarily was accompanied by an extinction of all claims based on their existence. Consequently, both the new Diocese of Le Mans and the parish of Notre Dame de Mayenne were foreign to Cheverus, and he was without any rights extending to his person or services. Then Carroll continued:

> To make an examination of this matter as satisfactory to you as possible, I divested myself, as much as I could, of every personal consideration, and endeavored to view it solely in itself. The result of my reflections has been more satisfactory to my mind, than when I first began them. I am fully persuaded that you are not obliged, by your previous engagements to, or connexions with, your former Diocese or parish, to return to them.

With justice thus disposed of, Carroll turned next to the claims of charity. Did these compel Cheverus to resume the spiritual care of his former parishioners who were so attached to him and needed so much his zealous and charitable ministry? Here Carroll saw even less difficulty. Considering the number of excellent clergymen in France, the many seminaries, the resources of the country, there was little danger of the faithful being destitute of the sacraments. "But what resources will remain for those whom you have begun to train here . . . if you quit your present station? None at all." The claims of charity were clearly stronger in New England. As for the urgings of family, Carroll would give no advice except to say that he had every reason to hope "that the service of God, the extension of the kingdom of Jesus Christ, the salvation of souls purchased by his death, will speak more forcibly than the voice of flesh and blood."[35]

This reply was received by Cheverus on April 20, 1803, and on Easter Sunday he told the congregation in the School Street church that he would stay. To the bishop himself he wrote fervently, "To your clear and forcible arguments I should have nothing to oppose, were I so inclined; but in your decision I see the decision of divine Providence in regard to me and I humbly submit. Methinks it is Jesus Christ Himself who has spoken by the mouth of His venerable Apostle."[36] In Boston he would stay.

As Carroll had predicted, Mayenne did not remain destitute. That very year Augustin-Charles de Paule Gournay became pastor of Notre Dame de Mayenne. Three years later Jean-Ambroise Sougé, who had since returned to France, was named to that post and Cheverus wrote happily to his sister-in-law, Sougette de Cheverus, "I congratulate you on the nomination of your dear and worthy cousin to the parish of Mayenne and I congratulate the whole city on its pastor."[37] With the accession of his friend of so many years on January 29, 1808, Cheverus had no slightest pretext for uneasiness about his former French parish.[38]

The Bishop of Baltimore's judgment seemed vindicated on other scores. The news he got from France in the months that followed convinced Carroll that Cheverus would have found conditions there scarcely better than those which had forced his exile in the first place. He commented to the Bishop of Quebec on July 26, 1806:

> Very late accounts from France speak uniformly of the deplorable state of servility in which the ministers of the Sanctuary are held, notwithstanding the eminent zeal and piety of some of the Bishops and lower clergy. It is grievously suspected, on a close view of the proceedings of the French government, that the plan for the utter extinction of religion is renewed, not with fire and sword, as in the worst times of the late revolution, but by vilifying and degrading it to a slavish obsequiousness to the civil power.[39]

Napoleon made himself Emperor of France the year after Cheverus reached his decision to remain in Boston, and thereafter, the French government embarked upon policies which not only belied the spirit of the Concordat of 1801 but which, by 1809, resulted in the arrest of Pius VII and his captivity for the remainder of Napoleon's meteoric career.[40]

The ultimate justification of Carroll's advice and Cheverus' submission to it came, of course, from the benefits the Church in the United States enjoyed as a result of Cheverus' remarkable labors during the next two decades. Matignon had argued, "God evidently destines him for this mission" and that Cheverus would work "infinite good" for New England. From a human view of things, no prophecy was ever more precisely fulfilled.

CHAPTER VII

A NEW CHURCH OF THE HOLY CROSS

WHEN Father Cheverus thanked Bishop Carroll for his sound advice in the spring of 1803 he added, "We all rejoice here in the expectation of your visit next August."[1] He was referring, as the bishop knew, to the rapidly crystallizing plans for the dedication of a new church for the Boston Catholics. Carroll had already remarked in February in a letter to England:

> Besides other Catholic churches built in certain parts of the United States, where our religion was unknown a few years ago, except from the occasional pulpit invectives against, and misrepresentations of it, a very handsome and large one is nearly finished in Boston, formerly the hotbed of the most rancorous Calvinism. I expect to go thither during the summer, with God's permission, to consecrate it; and would presume to sollicit some donations toward it from the excellent Mr. Weld, if it were not an abuse of his munificent charity to add this to the demands incessantly made upon it.[2]

There was good reason for this happy anticipation in Boston and Baltimore, for, in spite of the humiliations at the hands of the law and the distress caused by Cheverus' bout with conscience over his former parish in Mayenne, Matignon and Cheverus had gone steadily ahead with their project of building a new church for their growing congregation. Neither public opposition nor private unhappiness ever deterred these two from their unremitting efforts to advance the cause of religion and the Church.

There was no denying the need for a larger place of worship. Matignon had done the best he could with the old one. The summer before Cheverus arrived he had spent more than $100 on repairs, mending the pulpit, patching the window frames and pews, and whitewashing

88

the walls.[3] But repairs did nothing to improve the size and Matignon knew they could not stay permanently in the former Huguenot chapel in School Street. "We have been refused permission to buy the little chapel which we occupy," he told his bishop, "and are thus prevented from working toward its enlargement." In 1796 lack of money made the alternative of buying or building a new one out of the question.[4] The second year that Cheverus was with him, encouraged by the optimism and zest of his new assistant, Matignon decided to make a beginning and he opened a subscription for the purchase of a site. But 1798 had proved a bad year for fund raising. The advent of yellow fever so early in the summer, together with the decline of shipping activity during the undeclared naval war with France, had ruined business in the New England port, and all the contributions had totaled a scanty $90, ten of which had been given by a merchant friend of the bishop's in Baltimore.[5]

The first tangible beginning was made in 1799. On the Sunday after Easter the "Reverend Pastors" held a meeting of the entire congregation to consider ways and means for replacing the chapel whose lease was soon to expire. The committee then appointed included the Spanish consul at Boston, Don Juan Stoughton, the three wardens of the church, and three other men of the parish. Cheverus and Matignon were to act as joint treasurers.[6] A second meeting held on April 7 produced pledges exceeding $2,000 with $788 paid in immediately. The largest amount was pledged by Cheverus' good friends at Newcastle, Kavanagh and Cottrill, who gave $500 for land and another $500 toward a building. Warden John Magner came next with over $300, followed by the Spanish consul with $200. The latter expressed the hope that he might later be able to obtain $1,000 from the King of Spain. Three widows pledged $100 each; four little altar boys pooled their resources and gave $1.50. From New Brunswick Father Ciquart, who had once been a missionary to the Indians of Maine, sent down $73. By May the subscription had leaped to $3,202.24. A site, at least, could be bought if one could be found.[7]

Just how they would manage to finance the actual construction of a building Matignon could not predict, but he told Bishop Carroll, "While we have Mr. Cheverus with us, there is room for hope that God will bless his indefatigable labors by conversions more numerous and more important than the few which have been made hitherto." It was foolish to expect any substantial aid from non-Catholics since "We have no one remarkable for his generosity for us, and this aid will hardly amount to much." Meanwhile he and Cheverus had written to both Havana and Martinique, the only places outside the United States where they could hope for anything.[8]

Father Louis William Dubourg to whom Matignon wrote in Havana was too busy on his own account to reply. This French Sulpician who had been in the United States since 1794 had gone to Havana on January 22, 1799, with the notion of establishing a seminary in Cuba. When the Bishop of Havana failed to encourage him Dubourg turned his hopes toward Santiago at the other end of the island, but, here again he met with failure. The spirit in Cuba just then was anti-French and not very conducive to supporting a project of a French *émigré* on the island, to say nothing of donating money to an unknown congregation in New England headed by two other French priests, even if Dubourg had made the suggestion.[9] The plea to Martinique was more effective; eventually $331.14 arrived as a gift from that French island. But little by little the pledges made by the self-sacrificing Catholics of Boston were fulfilled, and on October 28, the congregation were given the happy news that there was a site for sale which they could afford.

The lot which measured seventy by one hundred feet lay at the end of Franklin Square and "appeared to unite cleanliness, decent neighborhood, together with a central and airy situation remote from noise, especially on Sundays." The owners, the proprietors of the Boston Theater, could have sold the lot at a higher price to a tavern or other public house, but they offered it to Matignon for only $2,500.[10] The people quickly approved the purchase of this lot and the transaction was completed in time for the pastor to add his announcement to the other "glad tidings" of Christmas Day, 1799. It was in the happy mood this purchase inspired that the unsuspecting assistant had set out for Maine to perform the marriage of the Smithwicks, and that his confrere had written to Baltimore, "We anticipate with joy the time which will be convenient for you, if you will, to honor us with a visit." They had only $600 toward the building itself but, "counting on divine Providence for the means to continue," they were determined to begin.[11]

And begin they did. On St. Patrick's Day, 1800, unable to contain their national ardor, the Irish began to dig the frozen ground in preparation for the foundations. By April 21 the excavation had progressed far enough to start laying the foundations and Cheverus informed Carroll they awaited his reply to the invitation to lay the foundation stone. But the Bishop of Baltimore had more pressing episcopal duties which took priority. Not only were the troubles in Philadelphia (which he had briefly hoped Cheverus might solve) continuing; but a veritable swarm of hornets buzzed about his head in the form of reports of recalcitrant priests in Maryland, Virginia, Pennsylvania, and Kentucky. He could not allow himself the satisfaction of visiting Boston that spring.[12] The cornerstone had to be laid without him.

During the summer the foundation progressed three feet above the water level, but there the work stopped for a while for lack of money.[13] A new subscription was started on August 28 but President John Adams' handsome contribution of $100 and Haskett Derby's gift of a bell were the only encouragements. "Our Catholics are almost exhausted," Matignon told Carroll. More money must be had if they were to be ready to raise the walls and roof the following summer. "There is no indication that that will take place," he said truthfully.[14] It was not pessimism, only simple realism, to assess the material resources of his flock in this fashion. When he wrote to Baltimore in December after commenting, "Our church remains at the foundations, which we have had difficulty paying for," he spoke of other matters.[15]

The year during which the church building was at a standstill furnished enough to occupy the minds of the two priests, as we have seen. Matignon lost both his suits to recover Kavanagh's ministerial tax, and Cheverus barely escaped fine and court costs in his two trials. Both men were intensely interested in developments in France and were worried by what these events signified for Cheverus. In Boston they were conscious, too, of a bitterness in some quarters directed against their efforts to build a larger church. People who were pleased enough to observe the good influence Cheverus and Matignon exerted over the Irish workers of the city, since it served their private interests to have an orderly, peaceable supply of cheap labor, now found the gaping cellar on Franklin Square a horrid reminder that the ranks of the Papists were swelling. The one bright spot that year was the decision of the General Court to grant Father Romagné in Maine a farm with house, barn, and forty acres of cleared land contiguous to the Indian village or camp.[16] A new attempt to raise funds for the church in Boston, by means of a monthly collection, was painfully slow in gaining momentum.

Nevertheless, the new year began with fresh resolves on the part of Cheverus and Matignon. The latter staunchly asserted that when spring came the walls of the church would begin, even though he had only $5,000 on hand and that twice that much was indispensable for the work, probably three times that amount before they were really through.[17] With his bishop's permission he meant to make a "begging trip" throughout the eastern part of the Diocese of Baltimore. This journey which began on April 23 was a happy thought. Although the other Catholic congregations were engrossed in supplying their own needs, Matignon returned with over $1,000 which he had collected in New York, Philadelphia, Baltimore, Washington, Conewago, and other places.[18] It was less than he had hoped for, but every dollar helped. Matignon exuberantly decided to match the collection with $1,000 of his own personal money furnished by his relatives in France.

Then, in 1802, the example of former President Adams bore fruit. Money began to come in from other non-Catholics, not only in Boston but in Salem as well. The total contributions of the non-Catholics eventually reached $3,454, and even more appreciated by the priests was the friendliness those gifts connoted. The fine co-operation of the Reverend William Bentley of Salem was antidote enough for the earlier harsh strictures of Justice Bradbury in court. But more than all the other sources of funds the ledger remains a remarkable proof of the self-sacrifice of the Irish people of Boston. Of the $16,098 raised for the church before its dedication $10,741 was eked out of the meager earnings of the working people or given by the more prosperous minority. The new church was to be greatly venerated with good reason. It was built with love.

The new Church of the Holy Cross was beautiful in other respects. Its design came from the drafting board of Boston's most illustrious architect, Charles Bulfinch, and showed the influence of his European sojourn and the enthusiasm for Renaissance style which he brought home. The Boston priests had told their bishop on March 9, 1800, "We accept a plan proposed by the most celebrated architect of the city, Mr. Bulfinch, who has visited Italy, to whom this city owes its State House and all the elegant buildings we have." Although the church on Franklin Square has long since surrendered to the onrush of commercial exigencies, a twentieth-century student of architecture can imagine something of its elegance by visiting St. Stephen's Church in Boston which was built at the same time, by the same craftsmen, and from a very similar design. Flemish bond brick, noble entablatures, architraves, lovely façades, and graceful cupolas, all exemplify the Old World grace that marked both churches which Bulfinch designed as the nineteenth century began. St. Stephen's, which was originally the new North Church erected in 1804 for a Protestant congregation at the corner of Clark and Hanover Streets, and Holy Cross on Franklin

Square were architectural sisters, if they were not identical twins.[19] The Boston Museum of Fine Arts still preserves a fine silver urn designed by Mathieu de Machy in Paris in 1789 which bears the inscription: "Presented to Charles Bulfinch, Esqr. Presented by the Catholics of Boston Jany 1, 1806." It was one way of showing appreciation for the kind offices of a great man and his design for a beautiful church.

When it was finished Holy Cross was "very handsome and spacious, and well finished" with a sanctuary both elegantly and richly accoutered.[20] Atop the tower with its jalousied arches was a gleaming guilded cross. Inside, a gallery circled the vestibule anticipating vocal performers at the high Masses. Above the altar a large painting of the Crucifixion by Lawrence Sargent noticeably impressed the non-Catholics who came to inspect what their generosity had helped to achieve. If more refined tastes like those of Jean S. Tisserant found it possessing "many defects," it had the merit in most eyes of being one of the largest canvases painted in Boston. Bulfinch, too, had thought in terms of size. The new building, which was fifty-eight feet wide and eighty-one feet long, was four times as large as the old chapel; and his designs were drawn with the provision for an additional thirty-three feet of length when the need should arise. Everyone agreed that Holy Cross was, "if not the largest, undoubtedly the loveliest church in Boston."[21]

Down in Baltimore John Carroll had followed the reports of the progress in construction with particular interest. Ever since Matignon's visit in the spring of 1802 he had determined that nothing would prevent his going north for the dedication ceremonies. He liked Matignon's way of phrasing the invitation, "If you can visit us in the autumn you will unite the consecration of the spiritual temples by confirmation to the consecration of the material temple." The church was not ready, of course, in the fall of 1802; but already in February of 1803 Carroll was speaking of his forthcoming trip to Boston that summer. Matignon wanted the dedication on August 15, the feast of the Assumption, a day deeply significant in the bishop's life as the anniversary of his consecration. In June, however, a letter from Boston deferred the ceremonies until September 8. The bishop was just as well pleased. By August his friends the Barrys might be in Newport and he could visit them en route. As it turned out, the dedication was postponed once more, and Carroll notified James Barry on August 25, "Dr. Matignon has concluded finally to fix the ceremony on the 29th of September, Michaelmas day." Carroll planned to leave Baltimore at the beginning of September in order "to be at Boston some days previous to the opening of the Church; as it is necessary and perhaps advisable for me to be." He was taking all the *pontificalia* necessary for the occasion and was filled with innumerable anxieties over the best route to follow so that his baggage would not suffer.[22]

In accordance with his plan, the bishop left Baltimore the first week in September; but in Philadelphia he began to suspect that the Devil, who is "always busy to raise obstacles," might be at work. A disturbance in Trenton delayed him in New Jersey where he had not anticipated stopping. News from New York made him change his plans for that city; the quarantine for yellow fever could tie him up indefinitely if he did not find a way to evade it. It was all very perplexing, since by this time the Barrys were in New York and talking of accompanying the bishop to Boston, to witness the dedication, and renew old ties with friends there. In spite of the hurried rearrangements which the fever necessitated, and the Barrys' decision not to go to Boston after all, the bishop arrived at his destination in ample time to perfect the arrangements for the formal ceremonies. Even his precious trunk arrived safely, although it did take Abraham Strong a whole night of wrestling to get it off the ship.

The dedication was quite a sight for Protestant Boston: a bishop in full regalia, four priests in cassocks and surplices, and a line of altar boys marching from Don Juan Stoughton's house to the new church so close by in Franklin Square. But there was more than idle curiosity in the eyes of the on-lookers; there was, for at least three men who walked in solemn procession to the new Church of the Holy Cross, respect and veneration. John Carroll of Baltimore had been in Boston before and had already earned the admiration of the city's leaders. The press had commented on that other occasion, "Boston would congratulate the hour of this Gentleman's return, and will remember with gratitude and pleasure his visit to this State."[24] His frame may have grown thinner during the intervening decade, but the Catholic prelate's reputation had become immeasurably more substantial; and the sight of him now, in miter and brilliant robes, his episcopal staff in his hand, did nothing to diminish the earlier opinion that "under his auspices even the prejudiced view with more favorable eyes a religion he so truly adorned."

For Francis A. Matignon, too, there were powerful reasons for respect. Catholics and non-Catholics alike knew the church about to be dedicated was the product of his ceaseless efforts. Never since his arrival some ten years before had the city seen any of those disturbances among the Catholics that had scandalized Boston previously. His humility, his extraordinary courtesy, his simplicity were bywords. Many of the non-Catholics there that morning had made their contributions chiefly out of respect for the man himself.

Behind the dignified prelate, and abreast of the worthy pastor, came the slight figure of John Cheverus, the assistant who was to preach the sermon on this occasion. The Boston Catholics who had wept at the prospect of losing him, his friends from Newcastle, Newburyport, Salem, and the southern missions, whose children he had baptized, whose stumbling confessions he had heard, whose beloved dead he had buried, all these had only pride and gratitude in their faces as their indomitable shepherd went by ahead of Father Tisserant from Connecticut and the Indian missionary, Romagné from Maine.

John Cheverus was destined to participate in much grander ceremonies, and to speak in far more enduring cathedrals than this church whose paint was scarcely dry. He was to wear robes more elegant and costly than those of the bishop whose garments now were the cynosure of all eyes. But he would never be more beloved, nor more truly happy, than he was in Boston this day in late September. No pontifical high Mass would surpass this *Missa Regia* sung for the first time in Boston on the feast of St. Michael the Archangel; no *Te Deum* ever sounded more heartfelt praise than this one thanking God for the fulfillment of Matignon's dream. The marvelous light of the thousand lamps which illuminated the front of the church later that evening could not rival the glow in one small man's heart for the goodness of his God.

When Cheverus entered the pulpit on September 29, 1803, he was beginning a career as a preacher that has never been excelled in the Diocese of Boston. Tisserant, who heard him that morning, commented later:

> He is generally regarded as the best preacher in Boston, and by many as the best they have heard in America. I, myself, confess that I never heard anyone who made a better impression on me. His eloquence is brilliant, agreeable, full of unction, and captivating. Many who came to hear him out of curiosity were so touched they have become converted.[25]

Matignon wrote to England in 1805:

> God continues to crown with his blessings the labors of my excellent Colleague. Strangers often crowd our church in order to

hear him, and gradually learn to lay aside their prejudices against us. The Church visibly increases.[26]

A wealthy and cultivated merchant visiting Boston from Leghorn wrote to New York in 1804, "Every Sunday our church is crowded by Protestants to hear the sermons of our learned and eloquent Cheverus; and some conversions take place without any murmuring at all."[27]

These Catholics were not exaggerating. Dr. Stephen Blyth of Salem, who was one of these converts, confessed that he found Cheverus "a man of uncommon zeal and uncommon talents. He possessed the language of the country in perfection and thundered it from the pulpit with the eloquence of a Paul."[28] President John Quincy Adams, who was able to resist the theological argument of Cheverus, was sufficiently impressed by his eloquence to record in his diary his recollection of having heard Cheverus "before he was even bishop." Cheverus had been speaking of the heathen who was so astonished at the charity of Christians that he cried out, "Behold, how they love one another!" Cheverus had then remarked that if the same heathen visited Boston in these days he might be tempted to exclaim, "Behold, how these Christians *hate* one another!" At the end of his notation Adams added succinctly, "Cheverus himself is an exception."[29] Josiah Quincy, too, another who could remain impervious to the doctrine but not the delivery of Cheverus, recorded his memories of the little preacher of Franklin Street.[30] Samuel Knapp, the lawyer and editor, said in all sincerity, "The seraphim seemed to have touched his lips with a coal from the altar of the Most High."[31]

Unlike the most successful preachers of his day, Cheverus did not give readings of carefully prepared allocutions. The thoughts he voiced were seemingly extemporaneous, effortless, and welled from a heart full of sympathy for mankind. He was endowed with a clear, melodious voice; he had acquired a splendid knowledge of history and controversial theology, he could draw allusions from literature ranging from the Scriptures to modern French and English authors. His wit was never failing. At the same time his sensibility, his tenderness of heart, could invade his sentences and communicate his own rush of emotion immediately to his listeners. Blyth admired the "thundering" of sound doctrine. Quincy was delighted with the directness of a speaker who would open a sermon with the words, "I am now addressing a congregation that has more thieves in it than any other assembled in this town." Knapp thought Cheverus' best sermon was the one delivered on the release of Pius VII from captivity, a sermon in which the orator "indulged his feelings to the full tide of his delight." But all who heard him found one common pleasure: the sense of being in communication with a mind devoid of intellectual cowardice and a heart filled with a uniform charity toward all. "Within his heart he had room enough for all the sects, all opinions, all parties; it never occurred to him that love could be measured by degrees dependent upon character, rank or opinion. Men, as they were, never ceased to be his brothers in Christ."[32] Words emanating from such a heart were bound to be heard.

Unfortunately for history, aside from recollections of occasional phrases, or newspaper reports of one or two sermons, the sermons of Cheverus are lost. The church on Franklin Street is gone, the pulpit vanished; the ringing voice has been silenced by the tomb. Yet it may be more than a pretty conceit to suggest that in a larger sense the message of the little preacher who graced the brand-new *chaire* of Holy Cross so long ago is still working its effect in the Boston of today.

If the dedication ceremonies were the culmination of Matignon's dream of a larger church and the inauguration of a phenomenal career of predication for Cheverus, they were also the occasion for the commencement of a lively friendship between John Cheverus and his bishop. Cheverus had been eagerly waiting for this encounter, and he had frequently expressed his desire to meet Carroll. "I can hardly express how ardently I wish for a personal acquaintance with you," he had written in April, 1800. "Had my pecuniary faculties allowed it, I would not have remained here three years without going to ask your blessing."[33] In 1803 when he was so confused over his obligations on both sides of the Atlantic he told the bishop, "The hope of seeing you . . . would be a sufficient motive to put off my going to France. . . . You have the goodness to express the wish to be personally acquainted with me, and I assure you that I shall think it a happy day when I shall have the opportunity to pay you my respects."[34] That happy day had now arrived.

It was quite easy for Carroll to comprehend, now, why Matignon had been so anxious to retain his assistant in the United States. It had not been mere French hyperbole to speak of his departure as an irreparable loss. And Carroll was no man to be carried away by one good sermon. In the month which followed he had ample opportunity to see for himself what the addition of Cheverus had meant to his diocese. Together with Father Romagné and Cheverus the bishop went into Maine to visit the Catholic congregations there. At Newcastle it was quite obvious that a solid foundation was already laid. The affection and mutual respect existing between that congregation and the priest with whom they had signed the contract between his two court appearances were unmistakable. Cheverus was radiant watching confirmation being administered to his flock by their "beloved and venerable prelate."

On the way back to Boston the three men had visited Newburyport and shared a memorable pudding there. They stopped in Salem, including in their visits a call on the Reverend Mr. Bentley who had proved so generous to the Boston church fund. Here Cheverus modestly left the floor to Carroll, Romagné, and their host; and the minister in reporting the occasion to his diary devoted his daily jottings to Carroll, whom he had found a "fine man at 68 years of age" able to converse on all subjects as a man of letters, and Romagné, who had expatiated so interestingly on the relative difficulties of Christianizing the Passamaquoddies and the Penobscots.[35]

Carroll noted all these things, the radiant fervor in the presence of the sacraments, the gusto with which the rare good pudding was greeted, the becoming diffidence in social gatherings, and the limitless affection his companion bestowed on all they met. But he was even more intrigued by the underlying, irrepressible humor that made the whole strenuous journey seem like a schoolboy lark. The distances were long, the waters rough, the terrain hazardous much of the way. Yet Cheverus ignored the discomforts of the trip as if they did not exist. It was small wonder the bishop was in good spirits as they started the last leg of their journey from Salem to Boston on October 22. After his return to Baltimore he told James Barry what he had missed by not going to Boston that fall. "You were deprived," he said in contented retrospect, "of much comfort in beholding the progress of religion in that town. There were very particular reasons for me to wish you had come on."[36]

As for Cheverus, he had found his bishop everything he had imagined. His correspondence to Baltimore took on a new tone of warmth and filial devotion. He told Carroll happily, "All, without exception, remember you with grateful affection and gratitude."[37] In the years that followed no birthday greeting was more fervent than the one he sent to his *beau ideal* of what a bishop ought to be, and when the day came for Cheverus to don episcopal robes himself he had only one desire. To the companion of that journey he wrote, "Pray that God may give me the grace to walk *so as I may have your pattern*."[38]

CHAPTER VIII

A CONVERT BY CORRESPONDENCE

THE first winter in the new church found Father Cheverus in a new home as well. While he was away with the bishop on the visitation north of Boston, Matignon had moved their scanty belongings from School Street, and the picture of Louis XVI that Cheverus so cherished now hung on the wall of the house adjoining the church property. Here in the "Franklin Street Convent," as the rectory soon came to be called, Cheverus busied himself with a new printing of the *Roman Catholic Manual* while his pastor reorganized the Confraternity of the Blessed Sacrament.[1] When the church committee met in the new year the recurring hopes for a parish school were discussed. The dedication of the new church had fired them both with new zeal, and by the time Cheverus left in June for his Newcastle mission the older priest was already talking of having an organ especially constructed for Holy Cross.[2]

The Newcastle-Damariscotta congregation that summer was more than 200, most of whom were converts "from among all sects, even the Quakers who are the most difficult to bring over."[3] Cheverus had grieved in his first years in Maine that he had no conversions, telling Matignon disconsolately in 1798, "I am afraid I am nothing but a sounding brass and a resounding cymbal."[4] But Bishop Carroll had seen the way Cheverus drew people, "Catholics and non-Catholics, to himself and, at the same time, to the practice of piety and the setting aside of prejudice against the Church."[5] Now, in 1804, in spite of distances ranging from four to twenty miles, these fervent worshipers swarmed to the little chapel in a barn to offer Mass with their "adored Missionary" on Sunday.[6] In the intervening days Cheverus traveled constantly to reach them in turn.

When he got back in late September he was brown, thin, and worn-looking. Father Tisserant, who was in Boston when Cheverus arrived from Damariscotta with Matthew Cottrill, thought his little compatriot was working too hard and feared he would soon succumb to exhaustion. Privately Tisserant thought, "Unfortunately, he can not restrain himself; the idea of the good he can do prevents him listening to daily remonstrances."[7] If Cheverus himself was conscious of fatigue, it quickly vanished in the interest aroused by a new acquaintance that the three French priests made in Boston that fall.

A month before Cheverus returned, an Italian gentleman, Antonio Filicchi, had arrived from New York to attend to some business of the family firm and to visit his connections by marriage. He was the younger brother of Filippo Filicchi of Leghorn who had married Mary Cowper of Boston a decade and a half earlier.[8] Filippo had spent some time in the United States in the 1780's and had remained a staunch friend of Bishop Carroll's ever since.[9] Now Antonio was in the country, visiting Baltimore, New York, Boston, and Canada. The story he had to tell the men in the "Franklin Street Convent" was a fascinating one; it was a story that all three priests would soon have a part in shaping.

It seemed that the year before, in November of 1803, a William Seton, whose family in New York had mercantile connections with the Filicchi firm, had arrived in Leghorn with his wife and one of their five children. Seton was ill and the voyage, a last desperate attempt to arrest his malady, had proved fatal. Two days after Christmas he had died and on January 21 was interred in the British burial ground at Leghorn. The Filicchis had naturally befriended the young widow and her daughter while they awaited passage back to New York.[10]

Then the story grew more interesting. While Elizabeth Bayley Seton remained among the Filicchis in Italy she had become interested in Catholicism. She herself was a devout Episcopalian and had a good foundation for the doctrinal discussions that followed, and Filippo was almost certain that she had been ready to enter the Church as the hour of her departure from Italy drew near. Antonio decided to go with her to New York, partly to transact business for the firm, but partly to encourage Mrs. Seton in the pursuit of her investigation. They had arrived in New York on June 4, 1804, and Filicchi had remained there until August, keeping in touch with her as often as business concerns allowed.

To his chagrin and deep disappointment, the widow moved further away from her Italian views and closer to the doctrines now more vigorously presented by her own pastor, the Reverend John Henry

Hobart. Filicchi enlisted the aid of Father Matthew O'Brien, an assistant at St. Peter's Church, but Hobart continued to gain ground. As his time in New York grew short Antonio decided to appeal to Bishop Carroll, to whom he had a letter of introduction from his brother. He was unalterably persuaded that Elizabeth Seton must not be lost to the Church and he closed his letter with the words, "I must beg you with all my soul to hasten to come to my relief." When the bishop complied, Filicchi left New York, confident that Carroll's advice would turn the scales. Now those hopes were dashed. The letters arriving from New York showed that Mrs. Seton was more confused than ever.

The longer Filicchi stayed in Boston the more he wished that Cheverus and Matignon could be prevailed upon to influence her. If Mrs. Seton were in Boston she could see for herself what the Church meant in an American community. He wrote to her, "Oh, my good friend, with what worthy clergymen are Catholics here blessed! Their countenance, their conduct, their doctrine are acknowledged almost with enthusiasm by most Protestants themselves."[11] As time went by he became more and more convinced that Cheverus in particular could persuade Mrs. Seton, if anyone could. But Cheverus apparently believed that his bishop's argument could not be improved upon; in any case, he went back up to Newcastle after Christmas without intervening.

It was a terrible winter. Up in Maine the snow was so deep that Cheverus was unable to unite more than four families, the roads being quite impassable. Down in Boston Matignon was conducting the services of the jubilee and worrying in between times about Cheverus. He wrote anxiously to Carroll that he hoped that somehow the bishop had found a way of extending the plenary indulgence of the jubilee to his snowbound friend.[12] The jubilee was already a year late in the United States, Pius VII having proclaimed it for 1804 as a symbol of rejoicing for the peace rendered the Church by the Concordat of 1801. Many of the churches in France had celebrated it in March of that year.

In New York, too, the snows had been excessive and Mrs. Seton had been snowbound herself with her five fatherless children before Christmas. When the jubilee services began in St. Peter's of Barclay Street she was still battling weather as well as spiritual uncertainty. Matthew O'Brien reported to Bishop Carroll:

Mrs. Morris has become a Catholic without any further solicitation and is performing the Stations of the Jubilee with astonishing edification. There are two more ladies converted. Mrs. Seton is yet in the scale. Mr. Filicchi is here and has good hopes. . . .[13]

Filicchi's good hopes were soon to be realized. Mrs. Seton herself finally said to him, "You speak so highly of the Catholic priests in Boston, perhaps it would be best you should give a short history of your dear Sister to the one you esteem most, as I may one day find the benefit of your doing so." Cheverus, of course, already had a short history of Filicchi's friend; but he now received a letter meant to overcome any lingering reluctance to intervene. Filicchi wrote:

> Mrs. Seton, I am in full hopes, will be finally a good Rom. Catholick with her five children. Considering Bishop Carroll too much occupied I have suggested her to have recourse to you in her scruples and anxieties, for instruction, comfort, advice, and she is actually writing to you. You will have, it becomes you, the merit of determining and perfecting the work.[14]

There is no way of knowing what Elizabeth Seton herself wrote to John Cheverus that February, but together with Antonio Filicchi's her letter drew from Cheverus the words which ended all further indecision.[15] He told her firmly that she had debated long enough, had heard enough argument on both sides. She was never for a moment a strong Protestant; she was often, as she herself admitted, a good Catholic.

> I believe you are always a good Catholic. The doubts which arise in your mind do not destroy your faith, they only disturb your mind. Who in this life, my dear Madame, is perfectly free from such troubles? "We see as through a glass in an obscure manner," we stand like Israelites at the foot of the holy mountain, but in spite of dark clouds and the noise of thunder, we perceive some rays of the glory of the Lord and we hear his divine voice. I would therefore advise your joining the Catholic Church as soon as possible, and when doubts arise, say only: I believe, O Lord, help Thou my unbelief.[16]

Like Carroll two years before, without ever having met his correspondent, Cheverus hit upon the precise analysis required to resolve another's uncertainty. The letter which he sent in care of Filicchi was taken immediately to Mrs. Seton. "She accepted it as of a distinguished blessing from God; she prayed, she meditated on it," and therewith came peace of soul. Cheverus had, indeed, the merit of perfecting the work the Filicchis, Father O'Brien, and Bishop Carroll had begun. In later years Elizabeth Seton wrote on the back of the treasured letter,

"Bishop Cheverus' first answer to an earnest entreaty for his advice. Entered the church immediately afterward — March 14th."[17] Of that joyful occasion Antonio Filicchi wrote to Boston that his friend had gone "to our Church, where she had previously been several days at Mass and . . . formally abjured in my presence her past errors, and made the requisite profession of faith of the Roman Catholick Church."[18] Elizabeth Seton told Cheverus:

> My joyful heart offers you the tribute of its lively gratitude for your kind and charitable interest in its sorrows when it was oppressed with doubts and fears, and it hastens now after the completion of its happiness to inform you that through the boundless mercy of God, and aided by your satisfactory counsel, my soul offered all its hesitations and reluctances a sacrifice with the Blessed Sacrifice of the Altar. . . .
>
> You, dear sir, could never experience, but may picture to yourself, a poor burdened creature, weighed down with sins and sorrows, receiving an immediate transition to life, liberty and rest. Oh pray for me, that I may be faithful and persevere to the end! And I would beg of you advice and counsel how to preserve my inestimable blessings . . . directions addressed from a revered source must forcibly impress.[19]

She was already reading constantly the books he had recommended: the Gospel of St. John, the *Following of Christ,* the life of St. Francis de Sales, and the sermons of Bourdaloue.

And so it was that the career of Mother Seton, the founder of the Sisters of Charity in the United States, came to be a part of Boston's history from the moment of her conversion. Antonio Filicchi joyfully warned Cheverus on March 16:

> Taught by me to put the proper value on your advice and spiritual direction, and sensible of your goodness from the manner in which you have been pleased to answer her first application, she will occasionally avail herself of the permission you grant her of addressing you; and to God, I know, you will look for reward of your trouble.[20]

In another year Filicchi would be gone from the United States never to return, but the convert whom he had confided to Cheverus' care continued to follow his advice. From the spring of 1805 until the day she died Elizabeth Seton's friendship with John Cheverus was one most highly valued by them both.

In a worldly or sentimental view of human relations it may seem straining a bit to speak of "friendship" between the New York widow and the Boston priest. Materially, they had nothing to offer each other. Cheverus was powerless to relieve the harsh economic plight of a young widow with five children whose father had left nothing for their support; Mrs. Seton was never at any time able to make generous contributions to the penurious missioner in New England. Sentimentally considered, they had few of those ties which speed friendships on their way. The French *émigré* knew nothing of the New York mercantile environment in which his new friend had spent her life; she in turn, aside from a fluency in his native language, was ignorant of the milieu from which he had come. They had no friends in common at the start other than an Italian businessman who was only temporarily in the country. They had small prospect of even meeting, much less of developing a pastor-parishioner bond.

Yet, among the many warm and enduring friendships that Cheverus enjoyed during his life this was to become one of the most cherished, because there were in fact many reasons for its flourishing. Each had passed through enough sorrow and hardship by then to be able to distinguish between the ephemeral and the more enduring values in earthly relations. Each was in reality an exile from past and beloved connections: Cheverus a physical exile, the convert a spiritual one. Neither ever tried or even wished to close the door on those whom blood and time had united to themselves in former days; both possessed an acute sensibility which enhanced their nostalgia.

They were alike in other ways. In a day when communication by letter was a formal commonplace, both Elizabeth Seton and John Cheverus were gifted with an uncommon facility for expressing their individuality on paper. Although the priest was naturally more restrained than she could ever be, Elizabeth Seton was the person, after Francis Matignon, to whom he confided his personal sorrows with least repression. But the greatest bond, and one which grew stronger with the years, was their zeal for the good of the Church. The delicate woman destined to spend the rest of her life in the isolation of the Maryland frontier, and the little man who, even as bishop, never gave up his exhausting journeys to the isolated settlements of Maine, shared an ardor for souls that revolutionized their respective regions and united their glowing hearts beyond the bounds of space and time.

Cheverus took Antonio Filicchi's admonition in regard to spiritual direction seriously from the start. In her first days within the Church in New York, days in which Mrs. Seton found herself mingling with people quite alien to her former social and economic associates, she had to elevate her mind above its surroundings and she told Filicchi, "Involuntarily my thoughts revert to all you have described Mr. Cheverus to be, and the interest he infuses into his instructions."[21] But Cheverus soon had an opportunity to offer her more than written counsel. In May when Jean Tisserant was in Boston with the news that he was contemplating a trip to Elizabethtown, New Jersey, Cheverus seized the occasion to send Mrs. Seton proof of his interest. Tisserant carried to New York a copy of the new *Manual* whose prayers might help her, and a letter introducing Father Tisserant as both pious and learned, and blessed with pleasing conversation as well. As for himself, Cheverus wrote:

> I hope you continue to enjoy that happy peace which surpasseth understanding. Should it, however, be disturbed by doubts, anxieties, etc., do not get discouraged. In the midst of the storm, and when Jesus seems to be asleep, call upon him with earnestness. He will arise and everything will be calm within you.

He told her not to hesitate to call upon him, through the mistaken fear of writing too often. "I shall always," he promised, "answer your esteemed letters with punctuality."[22]

Cheverus' happy inspiration in regard to Father Tisserant was a very real consolation to Mrs. Seton during her first and most trying year as a Catholic.[23] Through his visits and his letters she learned more of the work of Matignon and Cheverus in Boston, reading with interest his enthusiastic report of the 500 Communions at Easter and the six converts who were baptized on Holy Thursday.[24] Through Tisserant the Boston priests learned more of Mrs. Seton and her "chers darlings" as he called the children. It was plain to Matignon and Cheverus that their compatriot found this remarkable widow as charming as the Italian merchant had described her.

Cheverus was, of course, not concerned with personal charm (whether momentarily obscuring or permanently enhancing) where deepest virtue was concerned. As spiritual adviser to many converts already he was aware of the precise pitfalls Mrs. Seton might encounter, and his letters were directed to that end. When he learned from her that well-meaning Protestant friends were trying to win her back by poking fun at her faith, he advised her to meet attacks on her religion with brief, clear answers; but, in the event the discussions grew heated, she must remain silent since "silence is the best answer to scoffers."[25]

She was enormously impressed by the mental picture she had of Cheverus, created by the enthusiasm of Filicchi and the sincere praise of Tisserant, and nourished by the prescient letters of her director himself. When Cheverus read the unrepressed exclamations of gratitude and praise which flowed from her impetuous pen he grew uneasy, and wrote forcefully, "I must ask as a favor that you will never again write to me anything that has been said in my praise, but pray for me that I may be always sincerely humble."[26] His letter was read in New York with some chagrin. Had she offended him? She wrote the best apology she could, and confided in Father Tisserant that she was afraid she had made Father Cheverus angry. Then it was Cheverus' turn to feel abashed. He hastily told Tisserant:

> She owes me no excuse, but unfortunately, knowing very well that vanity is not dead in me, I begged her not to repeat to me praises made by those I love and respect. It is a temptation too delicate and to which I do not wish to be exposed. Thank you for having told her that I have no anger against her. If some words of mine made her believe it, I beg her pardon.[27]

To Mrs. Seton he explained penitently:

> I am sorry if my letter made you suppose for a minute that I was angry with you. Never have I had any other sentiments toward you but those of most sincere respect and friendship and with those I do and shall always remain.[28]

To prove it, he sent her five volumes of Jean-Baptiste Massillon's sermons on Advent and Lent. It brought to a happy conclusion the only misunderstanding they ever had.

While the convert was getting to know something of the bedrock humility of her Boston friend, he in turn was rapidly learning the details of her own life in New York. When her sister-in-law, Cecelia Seton, remained briefly on the borderline between Protestantism and Catholicism after Elizabeth's own conversion, Mrs. Seton wrote fearfully to Cheverus of the consequences to Cecelia's soul. He reassured her with the Church's doctrine:

> Your beloved sister has been made by baptism a member of the Church. Willful error, I have reason to think, has never separated her from that sacred body. Her singular innocence of mind and ardent piety have also, very likely, preserved her from offending God in any grievous manner, and I hope that in consequence even if she

cannot receive the Sacraments she will be a member of the triumphant Church in heaven.[29]

Father Matignon naturally knew as much of the new convert's affairs as Cheverus and Tisserant. Cheverus through affection — and what his pastor deprecated as a ridiculous respect for Matignon's degree in theology — inevitably referred Mrs. Seton's problems to his colleague. When Cheverus was away on his annual missions the older man filled his role of adviser-by-mail. During the summer of 1806, when the conversion of Cecelia Seton aroused a storm of protest within her family, it was Matignon who consoled Mrs. Seton.[30] Although he wrote fewer letters he assured her, "In spite of my silence I take a very lively interest in all which concerns you; I wish every day at Mass the action of God's grace in all your concerns and a continuation of his favors."[31] It is not surprising that in the major crises in her life Elizabeth Seton consulted both Boston priests with equal confidence, spoke of them usually in one breath, and cited their advice as conclusive justification for her actions. Had not Filicchi told her both in person and by letter, "Dr. Matignon and Mr. Cheverus will always be ready to assist and comfort you with their advice."[32]

It was this advice, of the two men who were as one person, which was largely instrumental in preserving her work for the United States rather than for Canada, where she was first inclined to go after her conversion. Her Canadian idea originated in the beginning because of her desire to have her sons placed in a Catholic school. While Filicchi was in Canada during the summer of 1805 he had been favorably impressed by the college and seminary of Montreal, and on his return he told the Boston priests of the advantages he saw there for the Seton boys. Matignon was already aware of the school's possibilities, having written to England earlier that year:

> The College in Montreal which was unhappily destroyed by fire is now rebuilding upon a larger and nobler plan, and will be fit for the reception of boarders next winter. On account of the wholesomeness of the climate and the moderate terms for board and education, it is expected that many of our Protestant families will place their children there.[33]

As a matter of fact, Matignon a year later was responsible for the Kavanaghs and Cottrills' sending their sons to Montreal. But in 1805 the college was rebuilding more slowly than either Filicchi or his Boston friends anticipated, and Cheverus told Mrs. Seton, "Unhappily they give no hope of the immediate admission of your dear children. Mr. F. will try in Baltimore or in Georgetown and I think he will succeed. His recommendations alone will have great weight."[34] When the boys were eventually placed in Georgetown neither Filicchi nor their mother gave up the Montreal notion, and Mrs. Seton told Matignon that she was now wondering if, when the boys transferred to Montreal, she might find a place in a nearby convent. She asked the Boston priest to get her some information about convent rules there, if he could.

This second aspect of her Canadian plans found no enthusiasm whatever in Boston. Cheverus replied:

> Dr. Matignon sends his respects and desires me to tell you he does not know how to procure the Rules of the Nunneries in Canada. Dr. Dubourg was to converse with you about another project which I should prefer, hoping it would be better for your family and being sure it would be very conducive to the progress of religion in this country.[35]

The other project he referred to was one that he and Matignon had both favored ever since its first mention by William Valentine Dubourg. Dubourg in the days before and after their abortive appeals to him in Havana had been active in the field of education in Washington and Baltimore.[36] Since his return from Cuba he had founded a college in Baltimore as a complement to the Sulpician seminary there, and in November, 1806, he was in Boston energetically trying to raise money by means of a lottery.[37] On his way through New York Dubourg had met Mrs. Seton, who confided in him her dream of entering a Canadian convent or teaching order; Dubourg's ebullient optimism had immediately conceived an alternative. By the time he reached Boston Dubourg had his plan firmly fixed in his mind. Instead of Montreal, Baltimore should be her destination. Her sons could attend St. Mary's College; she could start a school for girls. It was not only possible, but could be accomplished without difficulty.

His enthusiasm was contagious. Both Cheverus and Matignon believed that the New York convert was destined to take a great place in the United States, where it was infinitely preferable that she remain. Matignon wrote to her on November 29, "We are entirely agreed on what Mr. Dubourg has proposed to you." But the Boston pastor was more cautious than the Baltimore college president. There was no urgency. "God has his moments which we need not anticipate," he reminded her. "Prudent slowness only ripens and brings to fruition the good desires which Grace inspires within us."[38]

Mrs. Seton was reluctant to abandon the Canadian dream, however, and tried to enlist Bishop Carroll's support for the prospect her Boston friends discouraged. But Carroll refused her any encouragement. Instead, when told of the Baltimore alternative he said categorically, "Tho I am entirely ignorant of all particulars . . . it is enough for me to know that it has the concurrence of Dr. Matignon and Mr. Cheverus."[39] The approbation of Boston was equally important to Dubourg. As his plans began to materialize he kept Matignon and Cheverus informed, and by the spring of 1808 he told Mrs. Seton:

> I have this moment written at large to our worthy Bostonian friends to submit to their consideration the scheme which now engrosses all my thoughts. Should they approve of it I would be for coming in two or three weeks. . . .[40]

When Cheverus read Dubourg's detailed description of the latest developments he wrote at once to Mrs. Seton that he and Matignon agreed with Dubourg on all points. "We infinitely prefer it to your project of retreat in Montreal," he reiterated.

> Remember that Mr. F. has authorized you to draw from his correspondent in New York any sum necessary to begin a useful establishment, and this same esteemed friend has written to me that money shall not be wanting. You know the sincerity of his offer and you can without doubt avail yourself of it within the limits dictated by prudence, but not with an excessive delicacy or timidity.[41]

The Canadian dream was over. When Mrs. Seton read this letter dated May 12, 1808, she knew she would go to Baltimore. She had meant it when a year earlier she had told Antonio Filicchi, "As you have left me so much in the charge of our Bostonian friends, I will do nothing without their full consent."[42] Canada had never had their full consent; now, it appeared, Baltimore did. On June 8, much less than a month after receiving Cheverus' clear recommendation, she sailed for the Maryland city.

Their exchanges by mail would take longer in the future; they were physically farther apart. But in the realm where their friendship flourished Cheverus and the former New Yorker were close indeed. After the departure of Jean Tisserant and Antonio Filicchi for Europe in 1806, Mrs. Seton had come to rely on those letters from Boston "written in their consolatory and heavenly style with the same patience and charity" she had first found in Tisserant.[43] Matignon and Cheverus had become for her "those persons whose will is my law."[44] From

Cheverus she had learned the meaning of true humility, patience, and confidence in God. She had repaid him by becoming the spiritual sister who substituted for the physical ones from whom he was separated by the wide Atlantic. It was to Elizabeth Seton that he wrote in 1807, on learning of the death of his brother Julien:

> I grieve for him & still more for my aged father who writes to me that I also am almost to him as if I were dead. . . . I have one brother left and three sisters, all married & having families except a sister 21 years of age. I have now hardly any hopes of seeing them in this world. . . . These details your goodness will excuse. I know I am writing to a feeling & friendly heart.[45]

In New York or in Baltimore, her heart would not change. For Cheverus she would always remain "My beloved and venerable sister." The years would prove the wisdom of the advice he gave her in 1808 to keep her for the country that was hers by birth and his by adoption.

CHAPTER IX

RELUCTANT BISHOP

By the time Elizabeth Seton was settled in her new home in Baltimore Cheverus was once again getting ready to go to Newcastle. This year he was more than ever eager to go to Maine, for he was traveling as Matignon's vicar-general with express authorization to dedicate a new church. Through the efforts of the Kavanaghs, Cottrills, and the enthusiastic converts a very neat and elegant little chapel had been built of brick for about $3,000 at Damariscotta Mills. The bell which was to summon the faithful to divine services was the work of Boston's Paul Revere but the benches inside the church were rough hewn from the trees of nearby forests. On July 17, 1808, this labor of love was dedicated to St. Patrick, and Cheverus explained to Bishop Carroll, "The name seemed to gratify our friends here. I liked it myself because it proclaims our Church here is the work of Irish piety."[1] There was a cemetery, too, adjoining the chapel grounds which he blessed the same day. He continued in his letter to Baltimore:

> How happy we should all have felt had we been blessed with your presence. *Oh, that our good and venerable Bishop was here:* was the prayer of every heart and repeated by every tongue. The whole assembly (and it was a numerous and respectable one) were hospitably entertained at Mr. Kavanagh's house and feasted upon their *excellent* mutton.

Only one thing was lacking, a resident pastor. True, Father Romagné spent about six weeks there before Christmas and usually a few more days during Lent. But he was permanently attached to Passamaquoddy where his house, farm, and income from the state kept his first obligation to the Indians of Maine. Seven months a year the Catholics of the

111

Damariscotta region were without a priest and some necessarily died without the sacraments. In addition, recently this area was being "over run with Methodists, Baptists, etc." Cheverus wrote to Baltimore, hoping to get one of the six new priests he had heard were ordained on the last ember week Saturday. A priest could live with the Kavanaghs, he assured Carroll. Only two requirements were really necessary; facility in English and a rugged constitution. Cheverus himself found no inconvenience from the climate, since only the winters were hard; but Father Romagné, who was of a delicate constitution, was often confined to his room.[2]

His plea went unfulfilled. The new priests were too badly needed elsewhere; in 1808 the Newcastle congregation had to content itself with a new church, a new cemetery, and a few months of regularity while Cheverus or Romagné was in their midst.[3] The news Cheverus got from Baltimore when he returned to Boston that fall was of an entirely different nature. Instead of a promise of assistance, Carroll informed him that he had been named first Bishop of Boston!

There is no way of knowing how Cheverus reacted to this news coming at the conclusion of his strenuous trip south from Maine, his stops at Bristol, Hope, Warren, Jefferson, Pinhook, Edgecomb, and Ballestown. Yet it could scarcely have come as a complete surprise. The subject of a division of the Diocese of Baltimore was almost as old as the diocese itself. The first year of his episcopacy Carroll had meant to suggest it to Rome. Although the Holy See had for the time preferred the appointment of a coadjutor bishop with the right of succession Carroll had been told, "Should the Catholic religion . . . spread further . . . it may be necessary for the Apostolic See to appoint more laborers . . . with episcopal jurisdictions." With the accession of Pius VII the subject had been reopened and in 1802 Rome had suggested that four or five new dioceses would lessen Carroll's burdens.[4]

From the time of Carroll's visit to Boston to dedicate the Church of the Holy Cross in 1803 a division of the diocese was a common topic of conversation among the clergy. Carroll evidently talked to Cheverus and Matignon about the best way of fixing the new diocesan boundaries, for Cheverus in later years recalled that the first plan his bishop had mentioned to him was for three dioceses; Baltimore, Bardstown, and New York, with Boston subject to a vicar-general from the Diocese of New York.[5] Carroll certainly corresponded with Matignon on the subject after his departure. Matignon on November 12, 1804, strongly urged subordinating the New England area to New York:

Portrait of Cardinal Cheverus at Tottenham.

The Cheverus plaque in the Church of St. Francis de Sales, Tottenham, England.

Piæ Memoriæ Eminentissimi et Reverendissimi
Joannis Lefebure de Cheverus Primi Episcopi
Bostoniensis in America et postea Cardinalis
Archiepiscopi Burdigalensis qui exul a patria hic
in Tottenham primum altare post eversam Religionem
Catholicam erexit Anno Domini MDCCXCIV
In pace Christi requievit die XIX Mensis Julii
Anno Domini MDCCCXXXVI

R. I. P.

Cathedral of Montauban as it is today.

Cathedral of Montauban in the time of Cheverus.

The Port du Pont at Montauban.

A Bishop presupposes a clergy, a sufficient number of parishes to supervise, ordinations to perform, some provisions for episcopal expenses, etc. The clergy of Massachusetts is reduced to three priests. . . . All the Catholics together amount to 1200 souls; there is no permanent fund either probable or possible.[6]

Carroll must have taken Matignon's views seriously for his next letter to England smacked strongly of the Boston pastor's own words. Writing to Charles Plowden on December 7 he found Rome's preference for four or five dioceses "rather premature, considering the number of clergymen, and the means of support for the different bishops."[7]

Matignon continued to doubt the feasibility of making Boston an episcopal see. When he wrote to England the next spring, mentioning the contemplated creation of an archbishopric with suffragan sees in the chief towns of the union, he commented, "The Bishop is reported to have received from Rome faculties necessary for this object; which, however, it will (I think) be very difficult to carry into execution."[8] Bishop Carroll, however, was more prone to follow Roman leadership on the subject, and when he received a request that summer for concrete recommendations for the erection of new dioceses, he found himself thinking in terms of four in addition to Baltimore. By November 23, 1806, he had completed his detailed memorandum. Boston was first on his list, with jurisdiction over five states: Massachusetts, New Hampshire, Rhode Island, Connecticut, and Vermont. Francis A. Matignon should be bishop.[9]

When rumors of the bishop's recommendations reached Matignon's ears he was aghast. Everyone knew how he felt on this score. Tisserant in 1804 had remarked:

I know that Father Matignon is designated for one of the new Bishops; but I doubt that they can get him to accept it, for, together with other qualities of apostolic men, he has besides the same fear they had of the burden of the episcopate.[10]

Carroll certainly should have known his abhorrence for such an office because the modest pastor, when decrying the creation of new bishops in 1804, had said plainly:

Father Cheverus, I feel sure, would not accept it in the present circumstances. As for myself, the proposition if serious would make me flee to the other end of the world.

I even dare to conjure you, if only for the honor of the episcopal dignity, to put a peremptory end to some rumors which have been spread on the subject. When I compare them with what I am, they humiliate and mortify me more than I can tell you.[11]

He hastened now, on April 6, 1807, to make clear his position. He assured Carroll that he was writing "without any affectation of humility, but with the same impartiality as I would speak to you about another." He spoke frankly of his own handicaps, his miserable memory, the growing weakness of his eyesight, his difficulty in writing in English, his halting sentences from the pulpit. "Finally, I am at present almost incapable of undergoing fatigue, even of a short journey," he pointed out. His incapacity and absolute unfitness for the rigors of episcopal life could easily be attested by anyone in Boston. He then went on to say that Cheverus was all the things he was not. "If he knew that I am telling you this he would not thank me, for he is far from having any ambition for the place," he admitted. Actually Matignon was far from wishing the dignity to fall on his colleague for selfish reasons, he went on; if Cheverus were absent more frequently it would only add to Matignon's burdens, especially in regard to preaching. Nevertheless, he believed Cheverus could be persuaded to accept if the motive of conscientiousness were stressed.[12] It was such a sincere, forthright presentation of Matignon's convictions that Carroll knew the Boston pastor meant what he said.

There was no question in the bishop's mind that if Matignon categorically refused to accept the nomination Cheverus would make a worthy substitute. On June 17, 1807, when he recommended Cheverus to Rome he also suggested that he be temporarily made administrator of the Diocese of New York. If the Holy Father and the Sacred Congregation saw fit to accept the objections of Matignon "who for no reason of self-indulgence but out of a conviction of bodily infirmity refuses to take the burden," then there was no one else to think of than Cheverus who was not only in the flower of age and health but enjoyed as well the highest esteem among all people.[13]

On April 8, 1808, Pius VII by two briefs created Baltimore a metropolitan see and named the four suffragans: John Cheverus for Boston, Richard Luke Concanen, O.P., for New York, Michael Egan, O.F.M., for Philadelphia, and Benedict Flaget, S.S., for Bardstown.[14] These two briefs and a letter to Carroll dated May 25, 1808, were entrusted to the new Bishop of New York who had been consecrated in Rome a month earlier. Then followed months of waiting.

If anything was needed to remind the clergy of the United States that the Napoleonic wars were fatal to free commerce and communication, the two years which elapsed between the creation of the dioceses and the consecration of the new bishops furnished that reminder. From Maine to Maryland the futile attempts of Bishop Concanen to elude these restrictions were a subject of sustained speculation, and news of his whereabouts arrived through varied and amazing channels. Luke Concanen hoped, naturally, to find an American ship leaving Italy for his new destination but as summer came on he was still in Europe. In July he succeeded in getting news through to Dublin that the new dioceses had been officially created and this reached Carroll on September 25, 1808.[15] But in November Antonio Filicchi wrote from Leghorn that Concanen, thwarted in his attempt to leave from Palermo in Sicily, was waiting for an occasion from the more northern port. Filicchi told Mother Seton, "He will bring along with him the requisite Bulls for the consecration of our Cheverus as Bishop of Boston." But this letter did not reach Emmitsburg until a year later.[16] As 1808 ended Carroll had to content himself with letters from Concanen dated July 23 and 26; the Roman documents remained in Italy. Carroll considered Cheverus' appointment settled, nevertheless, and informed English friends that since Matignon refused absolutely to be appointed, the first Bishop of Boston was John Cheverus, "a French priest of great eminence and exceedingly beloved."[17]

Although there remains no record of his reaction to the first news of his appointment, there is no doubt that as winter passed and Concanen remained in Leghorn with only feeble hopes of reaching the United States before spring, Cheverus cherished hopes of escaping the dreaded office. He told Elizabeth Seton on April 13, 1809:

> When or whether I shall go to Baltimore is quite uncertain. Should ever Bishop Concanen arrive, I hope I shall be permitted to remain as I am, and that we shall be placed here under the jurisdiction of the Bishop of New York. This appears to me the best plan for the present, and for many years to come, and if there must be a Bishop of Boston, I ought not to be the man. This affair has given me more anxiety & grief than I can tell. I will say no more about it. I will not dampen your heavenly joys by my gloomy reflections.[18]

He much preferred to contemplate her own good news.

Although Matignon and Cheverus knew Mrs. Seton would have admirable spiritual direction once she settled near the Sulpician priests in Baltimore they both had continued to take an interest in all that concerned her. They had learned with pleasure and very little surprise soon after her arrival in Paca Street that she was thinking of becoming a religious.[19] They had both given hearty approval to a step which "would serve the interests of our precious faith and glorify God in a special manner."[20] As her plans for establishing a community of women to educate Catholic girls and aid the poor took shape they learned that she was yearning to have Father Tisserant return from Europe as their director. When her letter of March 12, 1809, arrived with the news that she would take modified vows on the twenty-fifth, Cheverus had wished intensely that he might be there for the ceremony. Duty, of course, and the solemnities of the Lenten season required his presence in Boston. "But though in Boston," he assured her, "I was with you, and so was Dr. Matignon." He prophesied a great future for her and her "choirs of virgins." He knew Antonio Filicchi and Father Tisserant would rejoice over her profession. "I have no doubt, my beloved and venerable Sister, that He who has begun this good work will bring it to perfection."[21]

Down in Maryland Elizabeth Seton, of course, still regarded the approval of Boston as a recommendation for her actions. In the hope of securing financial aid she wrote repeatedly to the Filicchis that her new project was "greatly approved by . . . dear Mr. Cheverus and Mr. Matignon."[22] But the closed ports of Europe were as unkind to private pleas as to official documents, and in her impatience she asked Cheverus if he could not act in Antonio's name to get money for the infant community. But this Cheverus declined to do. He had no doubt that the Italian would lend a hand to her "holy and useful establishment," he told her, but explained, "I am not authorized to do anything of the kind. I do not even know the name of Mr. Filicchi's correspondent in this country."[23] He would write to Leghorn, however, at the first opportunity. He was quite right in thinking Filicchi would come to her aid. Before the year was out, Mother Seton who was now settled in the hills of northern Maryland received a year-old letter from Leghorn commanding her, "To promote the establishment you intimate so much approved of by Mr. Cheverus and Mr. Matignon you will please draw on our friends, J. Murry & Sons of New York, one thousand dollars."[24] The names of the Boston priests were still sufficient guarantee.

The year which ended on a note of optimism for his convert friend left Cheverus, however, still only a bishop-elect. Carroll wrote to England in June,

We have heard nothing from Dr. Concanen. The rigorous embargo on American vessels at Leghorn & other ports of Italy prevent his coming, & deprive him of the means of correspondence; tho it seems to me that the last difficulty . . . might be easily overcome. Letters to me from Italy to the care of the American minister, or American merchants at Paris, would find their way. Mr. Concanen himself would perhaps be able to obtain a passage from France . . . if the circumstance of being born a British subject did not render the experiment of travelling thro' France rather dangerous.[25]

In September Carroll further commented that roundabout news indicated that Concanen had left Leghorn to return to Rome, and he continued:

Since that, about the last of June or July, my friends in Paris have obtained thro the interest of Cardinal Fesch, & forwarded to him a passport to travel thro France and embark there on board of the first public American vessel with dispatches from any of their ports. The Rev. Mr. Flaget, . . . now the Bishop elect of Kentucky, has gone within the last fortnight to France . . .: perhaps he & Dr. Concanen may come in the same vessel.[26]

Concanen had indeed left Leghorn, but not before he had made copies of the briefs and bulls which he left "sealed up in separate bundles in the care of the Messers Filicchi with directions to forward them immediately, if ever safe occasion offered."[27] Whatever may have been Benedict Flaget's personal motives for going to France that September, his return nine months later with these "authenticated copies" seemed most providential.[28] At least the archbishop-in-waiting at Baltimore thought so. Up in Boston something slightly different had been anticipated, for Flaget had written Cheverus from Paris on March 29, 1810:

Doctor Concanon [sic] has finally informed us that he is en route to Paris since the 26 of this month. He hopes to be with me by the middle of April. No one accompanies him. He congratulates himself that I am still in France to be able to travel with me. It is possible we may take the same vessel, by which I came, to return. That would be then in May this year that we set sail for America. *Fiat, fiat*, for I am very bored in France.[29]

The unfortunate first Bishop of New York never reached Paris, as it turned out. Instead:

Fortified by a passport, he went from Rome to Naples, intending to embark on board an American vessel, which was allowed to bring home the unfortunate American seamen, whose vessels had been so treacherously confiscated in Naples. But Mr. Concanen, on his arrival at that city, was instantly put under arrest & prohibited from going out; which disappointment made such an impression on him that he fell ill, & died in a few days, June 19.[30]

Fortunately for the Church in the land he never reached, he did send to Paris authenticated copies of the important documents, and Flaget carried these duplicates with him when he embarked from Bordeaux.[31] Benedict Flaget sailed from France on June 10, 1810, on the *George Dyer* and arrived in Baltimore on August 10, just two months later.[32] When it was learned that Bishop Concanen was dead and that the originals could not arrive by that channel Carroll decided to accept Flaget's copies of the documents as authority to proceed. At long last the plans for the three consecrations in Baltimore were set in motion.[33]

Father Matignon, anticipating that some definite news would arrive in 1810, went to Newcastle in Cheverus' place in May; but not before he had refurbished the sanctuary of Holy Cross and added a new pulpit and bishop's seat for his reluctant colleague.[34] In Boston Cheverus worked on the second volume of the *New Testament* that he and Matignon were publishing from the French version of Sacy. They had already gotten out the first volume containing the Acts and the Gospels.[35] Flaget's letter did little to console him and he wrote to Bishop Plessis in June, "I recommend myself to your prayers, since I must submit to bear the burden of the episcopacy."[36] By the end of September he knew his consecration was to take place on All Saints' Day, and he wrote to Dubourg in Baltimore that he expected to arrive by October 23 in time to make a week's retreat before *la Toussaint*. "Pray for me," he pleaded, "and beg your holy colleagues to pray for me. In any other circumstances it would be a veritable holiday for me to spend some time among you, but the reason for which I am now going gives me more uneasiness than I can tell."[37] It was some comfort to know Father Romagné would stay with Matignon while he was away, but the purse of $500 which his old friend presented toward his outfit and traveling expenses made him feel excessively embarrassed. How he wished he could exchange places with Romagné and stay in Boston! It was a painful parting.

The three bishops-elect made their retreat at St. Mary's Seminary in Baltimore. Michael Egan, the Franciscan, was already there when

Cheverus arrived on October 23; Benedict Flaget, the Sulpician, came the day after. Egan was consecrated first on October 28, and then it was Cheverus' turn. In the twenty years since John Carroll had first entered Baltimore as bishop there was still no proper cathedral, and the ceremony took place in the small, brick pro-cathedral, St. Peter's of Saratoga Street. Even with the additions that had been made since the first building in 1770 it was not very spacious. But for the small French priest from Boston, who was fast approaching his forty-third birthday, nothing was spared in solemnity of ceremony. Of the three candidates consecrated that year, none was closer to the consecrating prelate's heart. And no one listened more appreciatively to Father William Harold's sermon that Thursday, holding up Carroll as a model of episcopal virtues, than the earnest new Bishop of Boston who had come to revere Carroll as they shared the joys and tribulations of their journey into Maine seven years before. Cheverus agreed with all his heart as the Dominican preacher eloquently exhorted:

> You have not to resort to antiquity for an example of Episcopal virtue. That bounteous God, whose manifold blessings overspread this land, whose boundless mercies claim our warmest gratitude, still preserves for your advantage, a living encouragement to such virtue and a fair model for your imitation. You will seek both in your venerable and most reverend Prelate — you will find both in the Father of the American Church, and under God the author of its prosperity. In him you will find that meekness which is the best fruit of the Holy Ghost, that humility which for Christ's sake makes him the servant of all, that richly polished character which none but great minds can receive, which nothing but virtue can impart.[38]

Three days later Cheverus himself was the preacher at Flaget's consecration in St. Patrick's Church at Fell's Point. He praised the Society of St. Sulpice to which Bishop Flaget belonged, quoting the words of Fénelon on his deathbed, "At a time such as this, when no one is given to flattery, I know of nothing more venerable and nothing more apostolic than St. Sulpice." His fervor brought tears to the eyes of the Bishop of Bardstown and approval to the archbishop whom Cheverus had greeted in his opening as "The Elias of the New Law, the father of the clergy, and the conductor of Israel's chariot in the New World." Father Jean Moranvillé, the pastor of St. Patrick's, was so delighted with the whole discourse he insisted that Cheverus must return to Fell's Point the following Sunday.[39]

Archbishop Carroll scheduled a meeting of the new hierarchy for the middle of November and the interim was a busy time for Cheverus. Carroll insisted that he must meet his relatives and friends around Baltimore. Charles Carroll and his son-in-law, Robert Goodloe Harper, the McHenrys, Bernabeus, and Keatings were only a few of the Marylanders who were charmed with the New England bishop's conversation and personality. There was interesting conversation at the Sulpician house, too. William Dubourg was planning another trip in the interests of the college, this time to Martinique, and he meant to confide his first Communion and confirmation classes to a French newcomer from Rennes. It was Cheverus' first meeting with Simon Gabriel Bruté, one of the travelers who arrived with Flaget in August. Father Bruté was teaching philosophy at the college and trying to learn English at the same time. Cheverus was greatly attracted to the former medical student who had been ordained only two years before. He warmly encouraged Bruté to write to him whenever he could. Then on November 8, at the Sulpician college, all the bishops attended a great banquet in their honor and at which homage was paid to Charles Francis Nagot, the retiring superior of St. Sulpice, and his successor Jean Marie Tessier.[40] On this occasion it was Carroll who lauded the Society, and Cheverus who listened with approval.

Then the more serious work of consultation began. The first and most distressing subject discussed was the captivity of Pope Pius VII. Carroll presented a letter from the prelates of Ireland which the Archbishop of Dublin had addressed to the new American hierarchy the preceding February 17, and they set to work drafting not only a reply to the Irish protest but a joint pastoral for their own flocks. The former was primarily concerned with the defense of Church unity and the authority of the Holy See during the dangerous period of the pope's captivity; the latter solemnly protested that captivity and decreed that on every Sunday and feast day the 120th Psalm and special prayers for the pontiff should be read, and that at daily Masses the prayer for the pope should be added at the collects.[41] They meant, of course, to make public their joint pastoral to the American faithful; as events proved, their letter to Ireland was also printed both in Ireland and in England.[42]

They turned next to those matters which need not wait for the visitation of their dioceses or other extended surveys. They agreed to recommend to the Holy See consideration for their situation which rendered difficult the holding of diocesan synods and making annual visits to their entire dioceses. Further, they recommended to the pope that nominations for vacant sees ought to come "solely from the Archbishop and Bishops of this ecclesiastical province."

By November 19 they had come to formal agreement on all the questions that they could discuss at such a first meeting. It is interesting to find that among such usual topics as provincial councils, diocesan synods, episcopal visits, secular and regular clergy, and the sacraments, the first suffragans also went on record regarding secret societies like the Free Masons, and the use of the vernacular in the Mass and administration of the sacraments. Their agreement, together with the earlier ones of the clergy who formed the synod of 1791, formed the earliest code of canon law in the American Church.[43] After taking a resolve to reconvene in two years the new prelates adjourned their five days' meeting.

After making a hasty trip to Georgetown to see how the Kavanagh and Cottrill boys were getting along in the college where they were now studying, and calling on the archbishop's sister in Washington, Cheverus started off on a journey he had been anticipating for many months.[44] Together with Bishop Egan he was going to visit the Sisters of Charity of St. Joseph in Emmitsburg, Maryland. Egan had several reasons for going, having a niece in the girls' school there and an interest in three Philadelphia women who had joined the sisterhood.[45] But the Bishop of Boston had one primary motive in going; he meant to see for the first time the woman he called "Sister" but who was now Mother Seton.

Elizabeth Seton had been anticipating this visit even longer. Almost as soon as she had learned of his nomination by Carroll she had started expecting him. She wrote excitedly to Filicchi from Baltimore on January 16, 1809, "Mr. Cheverus will be here in a short time. Oh, how happy I will be to see him, dear Antonio! What pleasure we will have in speaking of you."[46] Cheverus had not been so confident when he told her in April that same year, "When or whether I shall go to Baltimore is quite uncertain"; but she had continued to count on seeing him. Her letter to Leghorn in May, 1810, repeated a rumor that Flaget had already arrived from France and continued, "If so, the consecration will bring Mr. Cheverus to Baltimore and of course he will visit the Sisters of Charity. Oh, how happy, happy, I shall be! Maybe he will call me to Boston to settle a branch of us there. To be sure, fine hopes in the brains of your poor sister."[47] By then she had been gone from Baltimore ten months, but she still nourished the notion that the consecration would be followed by his visit.

There is a tradition that when Elizabeth Seton hurried into the room where an unknown and travel-worn small man waited to see her she had no idea who he was, and when in reply to her query he said only, "Mr. Cheverus," she fell speechless to her knees, only able to kiss his episcopal ring in silence. There is ample evidence that she was overjoyed, and that she regained her speech soon after. The night after his arrival she wrote a letter which she intended him to carry to New York; and when it was delivered Eliza Sadler read:

> It will please you to see our blessed Cheverus because he carried your friend and the darlings in his very heart, and we love him with a sentiment not easily described. . . . Look at his purple ring and reflect how often we kissed it, and if you have the happiness to hear him preach you will participate in the consolation I have greatly wished you to enjoy.[48]

After he was gone she commented more temperately to Archbishop Carroll, "I need not tell you our consolation on receiving the blessed Bishops, nor how many benedictions they poured upon us. We have been very sensible of the special favor."[49] To Antonio Filicchi she wrote, "The blessed Bishop Cheverus has indeed been all the way to our mountains to say 'I bless you.' He was like a father to us."[50]

They had a thousand things to say. Cheverus could see how concerned she was about her children's welfare, and was glad Carroll had persuaded her to modify her vows so that she could continue to handle their affairs. He reassured her that he had high hopes for them and "would do all he could for their protection."[51] He learned, too, of her ardent desire to see Mrs. Sadler in New York become a Catholic. But particularly he found that Mother Seton herself was very disturbed about the confusion within her community over the new rules Flaget had brought from France. Her problems were more numerous and complex than in the early days when he had been her chief adviser.

He and Bishop Egan stayed two more days, making their home with Father John Dubois on Mount Saint Mary, where the Baltimore Sulpicians had recently begun a school for boys. Here the talk was just as furious. Although Dubois was four years older than Cheverus, he had gone to Louis-le-Grand and Saint-Magloire in the same decade; they had innumerable memories to recall. Dubois was able to tell Cheverus a great deal about the Sisters of Charity, whose staunch support he tried to be. He wished Cheverus would stay on for a while, even if Egan could not, knowing what it would mean to Mother Seton.

On Friday he sent over a note to St. Joseph's suggesting that she use her influence to get Cheverus to stay at least through Sunday. If Bishop Egan consented to go on alone, Cheverus would remain. "Exert all your insinuating eloquence on the old Bishop," Dubois hinted.[52]

But Cheverus went with Egan on Saturday morning, leaving a little note for Mother Seton. "The Bishop of Boston sends his thanks and respects," he wrote, thinking of her inordinate awe at his episcopal dignity and his sapphire ring. "Never will he forget and begs not to be forgotten in the prayers of his dear Sister." From Conewago where he and Egan next stopped he wrote to Carroll, "We have visited the holy mountain and have been very much edified."[53] When he thought of the two infant establishments, the Sulpicians on the hillside and the Sisters of Charity in the valley, it seemed that the mountain was very holy indeed. How admirable was divine Providence. More than ever, now that he had seen her, he could re-echo his words of April 13, 1809, "I see your holy order diffusing itself in the different parts of the U. S., spreading everywhere the good odour of Jesus Christ, and teaching by their evangelical lives, and pious instructions how to serve God in purity and holiness."[54]

After Cheverus parted from Bishop Egan in Philadelphia he went on to New York, where he delivered Mother Seton's letter to Eliza Sadler and did his best to carry out her wishes that he influence Mrs. Sadler's religious views. He reported to Emmitsburg, "I saw Mrs. Sadler once, delivered your letter, had some serious conversation with her, but saw no prospect of doing anything."[55] Eliza Sadler sent a longer description of his visit, when she wrote to Mother Seton, saying that she had been upstairs when he called but that "the ring excited something of the sensation you wished." She had found in Cheverus all that ease and simplicity she so much admired in so dignified a character. His visit was very short, but as a result of it she went Sunday morning at eight o'clock to St. Peter's in Barclay Street to watch him give confirmation and address the congregation afterward in both French and English.[56]

Although the New York woman and the Bishop of Boston met so briefly they found they had a mutual connection in New York City. Mrs. Sadler went to St. Peter's that Sunday with Mme de Neuville, the wife of Jean-Guillaume, Baron Hyde de Neuville. Mme de Neuville was a very devout Catholic who had been a great benefactress of the Sisters of Charity in France.[57] She had come to New York in the summer of 1807 with her husband, whose Bourbon loyalties had forced him into exile from France that year. After traveling for a time through the western part of the state, and going south to visit friends like the Dupont de Nemours, the Neuvilles had settled in New York City where in 1810 the baron had been influential in founding *l'École Économique* for refugee Dominican Catholic children.[58]

Cheverus was naturally better acquainted with the Boston branch of the family. The wife of Don Juan Stoughton had been a Neuville by a former marriage, and her daughter, Anne Cécile de Neuville, was one of Cheverus' own converts. He had baptized her at the age of seventeen on June 6, 1802, and seven years later presided at her marriage. He confessed to Carroll, "She was to me the dearest of all my spiritual children."[59] In New York, however, Cheverus was very interested in the baron's project which already cared for some 200 and received grants from the New York State Legislature.[60] Whatever the future of Mrs. Sadler's religious convictions, she could not have formed an acquaintance with better people. None of them could foresee, of course, in 1810 that when the Neuvilles returned to France a second time in 1819 Eliza Sadler would be their traveling companion; much less could they have predicted that when the Neuvilles returned for the third and last time in 1822 the baron's negotiations would deprive Boston of its first bishop.[61]

During the week Cheverus spent in New York he had an opportunity to become acquainted, too, with the fine work being done by the Jesuits there. He talked with Father Anthony Kohlmann, the acting vicar-general during the vacancy of the see, and with Benedict Fenwick. The Literary Institute which they conducted appeared to be very flourishing and Cheverus gave them a pressing invitation to open a school in Boston as soon as their numbers and his own resources warranted it.[62] And then he began the last part of his journey home.

The Boston *Gazette* on December 20, 1810, reported that Bishop Cheverus had returned to their midst. On December 22 he formally entered his cathedral and was installed. At least that is how an official description of such an event should read: "The bishop was escorted to the door by all his clergy and given the keys by Vicar General ———, who harangued him in appropriate phrases. . . ." In reality it was a very different event from the grandeur such words conjure up. "The clergy" consisted of James Romagné with whom Cheverus had shared many a hardship in Maine; "the vicar-general" was ailing Francis Matignon, whose valorous endeavors had built the modest church on Franklin Street and whose self-effacement had made his former curate this new bishop. One can only imagine the surge of emotions taking possession of the susceptible heart of John Cheverus as he looked at his old friend that December morning as they entered the Church of the Holy Cross. There was no need to take a resolve that nothing would change between them. Each knew the other beyond all resolutions. The next years together would be simply a continuation of their first fourteen, as confreres, as brothers, and tenderest friends. It was characteristic of Cheverus that when writing to Bishop Plessis after his return to Boston he said of Romagné and Matignon, "I have two co-workers at this moment." Plessis saw for himself when he came to Boston five years later how "Monseigneur Cheverus (after he became Bishop) changed nothing in his manner of life and continued to perform, as formerly, all the duties of priest and missionary, always in perfect harmony with Dr. Matignon."[63] The bishop's miter and crosier had altered nothing in his heart.

In July Cheverus went again to Maine as usual. He spent two months in Newcastle-Damariscotta as he had done for the last dozen years. Then on September 8, 1811, he had the supreme pleasure of confirming 122 of his *chers sauvages,* the Indians of Old Town. Romagné told Carroll afterward of the Indians' delight at this visit from their bishop, "the first perhaps that ever set foot on their island."[64] Cheverus had confirmed more than 400 in New York, and 178 in Boston on the feast of Pentecost, and would confirm thirty-seven more in Newcastle a week later. But for the first time he savored to the full the rewards of episcopacy. Here on this isolated island, among the flock he had once pleaded to be given as his permanent charge, John, Bishop of Boston, was privileged to confer that inestimable sacrament which finishes and perfects the work that baptism has begun. As he made the sign of the cross on each dark-skinned forehead, his thin right hand resting upon the coarse black hair of these men whose names he well remembered, his soul was at peace. Undeserving and unfit as he was, with the help of divine Providence he was bringing to this wilderness the visible sign of grace which makes men witnesses for Christ, "until He comes again in the glory of his Father with the holy angels." Next year he would go to his equally dear Passamaquoddies. Father Romagné was their pastor, it was true. But he, John Cheverus, was their bishop. And a reluctant one no more.

CHAPTER X

THE ALIEN CORN

To SPEAK of the bishop or archbishop of a principal city of the United States in the twentieth century conjures up a vast administrative network which, as one prelate of Boston has commented, perforce arranges that a preponderance of time be devoted to the conservation of the many institutions already established and the creation of new ones to meet the needs of a rapidly expanding population.[1] The many institutions — schools, hospitals, convents, orphanages, and churches — require of the prelate the capacities of an astute executive in corporate enterprise. These enormous and pressing needs have found in this century great and good men to assume the burdens of modern episcopacy. But the experience which the twentieth century man has with the Church and the hierarchy in his own time makes it difficult to conceive what the office "Bishop of Boston" signified in the time of John Cheverus.

His consecration brought no legacy of seminaries, convents, hospitals, and schools. Whatever he might leave to his successor must be created and firmly established during Cheverus' administration. John Carroll twenty years earlier, on entering his own episcopacy, had spoken of the necessity of raising everything "as it were, from its foundations." In the first two decades of his reign he had made notable progress. Saint Mary's Seminary, three academies or colleges for men, a school for girls; Ursulines, Visitandines, Sisters of Charity attracting religious women; Augustinians, Dominicans, Jesuits enlisting men; all these had beginnings by the time the pallium was conferred on the Archbishop of Baltimore. But none of these institutions lay within the jurisdiction assigned to the new Bishop of Boston. Cheverus had not even been able to secure one additional priest for Maine, as we have seen.

From a human view, of the five jurisdictions existing in 1810 Boston was surely the least likely to succeed. Neither of the other new bishops nor Administrator Anthony Kohlmann of New York faced such a paucity of human resources, either in clergy or in laity. Six years after his consecration on that All Saints' Day in Baltimore Cheverus reported to Rome:

> Beside the Bishop, there is only one priest (in the city). . . . The offerings of the faithful and the small payments made for the pews in the Church hardly suffice for food and clothing to this body of clergy.[2]

When Ambrose Maréchal wrote to Rome in 1817 he commented:

> Mr. Cheverus is a light actually hidden under a bushel. Every one here grieves to see this excellent prelate at the head of a tiny parish. Your Eminence may judge by the report sent to him some months ago. He will see by it that there are not more that 1500 Catholics in the entire extent of his Diocese. A vicar-general, for years to come, would suffice abundantly for the care of so small a flock.[3]

After Cheverus returned to France in 1823 one of his episcopal colleagues wrote to Rome, "None of us, indeed, has the least doubt that the smallness of the Diocese of Boston was the chief cause why the Right Rev. Cheverus lent a most willing hand to his transfer from there."[4] However Bishop Dubourg may have erred in imputing motives, and he was prone to err even when the motives were his own, he was right in his implication that all the bishops recognized that the Diocese of Boston was the least of the American sees.

The report of Bishop Cheverus to Rome on February 7, 1817, contained, however, a most significant conclusion:

> I am overcome with shame at the little accomplished hitherto, but there is now hope of much fruit. In this city and other places where a few years ago, the name Catholic Church was, so to speak, infamous, and that of Priest abhorred, we are now looked on with veneration and friendship, kindly regarded and kindly treated.[5]

If Cheverus had little material progress to report, his account contained the clue to one of his greatest contributions to the Church.

Van Wyck Brooks has commented of this period in New England's development, "While there was in the region still a measure of intellectual life, the prevailing tone of mind was conservative and sterile."[6]

Another writer has said when speaking of the same era, "New England was still commonly ranked with the South as the part of the United States where it would be most difficult for Catholicism ever to take deep root; and as even worse than the South, in as much as ignorance of, prejudice against, and hostility towards, the Church were greatest here."[7] Of all the monuments to John Cheverus existing today — the statue in the square of Mayenne, the elegant marble tomb in Saint-André Cathedral in Bordeaux, the portraits in oil in Tottenham, Boston, Montauban, Bordeaux, and Versailles, the stained glass windows, the institutions dedicated to his name — the simple bronze plaque placed by the Protestants of Boston in Franklin Street is probably the most symbolic. During the twenty-seven years of his stay, his person made his name among Catholics and non-Catholics alike a "name never uttered but when hallowed with benedictions";[8] his labors loosened that harsh New England soil from which such abundant harvests would one day spring. The longer the environment of his American years is studied, the more unique his contribution appears.

Cheverus had arrived in the United States at precisely that moment when American feeling in regard to all things French was becoming a political as well as a cultural matter. The presidential election in November, 1796, had given victory to New England's John Adams over an opponent who was branded as a French tool, a French Deist, and a friend of anarchy. The bitterness of the contest was suggested by the small electoral disadvantage Thomas Jefferson had suffered. During the early years of his missionary trips to Maine Cheverus had seen hostility to his nationality growing by leaps and bounds. In 1797 President Adams had been hard pressed to keep the Republic out of war with France. The seizures of hundreds of American vessels by the French Directory's decrees, the infamous X. Y. Z. Affair, and other irritations had led to the abrogation of the treaties of 1778 with France, to the passage of the Alien and Sedition Acts, and ultimately to the undeclared naval war. In Baltimore, in 1798, John Carroll saw anti-French prejudices threatening the very life of the infant seminary in Paca Street.[9] The Fast Day proclaimed by President Adams for May 9, that year, elicited resounding oratory from the Boston pulpits, and Father John Thayer's sermon which Cheverus had read with such interest in the Maine forests was one of the few that had anything good to say of France. After his Phi Beta Kappa sermon in 1798 denouncing French infidelity Dr. John Thornton Kirkland's reputation was assured. From Boston that same summer Cheverus wrote to England, "The

public opinion has undergone of late in this country a very remarkable
. . . alteration. French principles and their abettors are now generally
despised and abhorred."[10] Five months later Father Matignon commented to a friend in Nova Scotia:

> France has irretrievably lost her influence in this country, in spite
> of the Jacobin faction, which daily loses ground; and whatever may
> be the fate of Europe, this country is resolved to maintain her inde-
> pendence against every foreign power, and should war be the conse-
> quence, they are not afraid of it, especially having England for ally.[11]

Although in the simplicity of reasoning which fear produces, many
identified France with what Hamilton called "the disgusting spectacle
of the French Revolution" — that conspiracy against government, religion, and morality — and nodded their heads in agreement with
President Timothy Dwight of Yale when on July 4, 1798, he predicted
as much from Jeffersonian Republicanism; others went farther afield
in their Francophobia and ultimately arrived at vituperative anti-Ca-
tholicism. In Boston, for example, the *Constitutional Telegraph* on May
17, 1800 launched a biting attack on Popery.

> Amidst the many harangues from pulpit and bar against the infi-
> delity and the villany of the French nation, it has been the subject
> of surprise to many serious people that nothing has been said by
> our clergy against the papistical, jesuitical doctrines of the cidevant
> priests of France, and their strenuous efforts to disseminate their
> baleful sentiments.

The author, who signed himself "Layman," went on to show how
England had been repaid for her generosity to French *émigrés* — by an
increase in detestable Popery. In a second article three days later
"Layman" revived all the favorite New England misconceptions of
Catholicism: Pope-worship, saint-worship, the sale of licenses to commit
sin, and the rest, using these as a springboard for a more direct attack
on the spread of Catholicism in Boston.[12] Cheverus was inclined to
refute the "Layman" and wrote a lengthy reply which began:

> A flat denial would be a sufficient answer; the more so, as all
> those calumnies are now-a-days known to be such by every un-
> prejudiced Protestant. For fear, however, that a simple, or prejudiced
> people should construe silence into acquiescence under the heavy
> charges brought against us, I shall address these few words to those
> who have read the Layman's reflections inserted in the Telegraph.

He went on to explain the Catholic's precise relation to the pope, distinguishing between temporal and spiritual power. He replied to the charge of "vicious and impious lives of the Popes" saying:

> We thank God, however, that in this corrupted age, and as it were, to "silence the ignorance of foolish men," such illustrious and unblemished characters have for a long time past filled St. Peter's chair, that people of all Religions have paid an unfeigned homage to their wisdom and virtues. Pius the 6th, in particular, commanded the respect and admiration of his very persecutors. A new Pope has been elected in spite of the predictions of the Layman, and many other Prophets inspired by the same spirit; and we hope that as his election has disappointed those "who had seen vain visions," so his irreproachable conduct will silence the enemies of the Catholic Church.

As for the ludicrous accusation of selling licenses to commit sin, he retorted comically:

> It has been remarked in this very town that, since a place of public worship has been opened for the Catholics, and a Priest has resided here, the people of that communion have, in general, led a more exemplary life than they did before. Strange indeed that, when they had nobody to give them leave to commit sin, they often took it themselves, and since they have a Priest, who encourages and grants them licenses to commit all kinds of crimes, they are perverse and obstinate enough to refrain from vice and immorality![13]

In clarity and wit Cheverus' retort rivaled the best public correspondence of Bishop Carroll himself.[14] But for reasons not evident Cheverus did not send it to the *Constitutional Telegraph;* it first saw public print seven years after he was gone from Boston and reigning as Archbishop of Bordeaux.[15] It may be that Father Matignon feared rousing further antagonism at a time when their new church in Boston was scarcely begun and when both priests were involved in legal difficulties. "Layman" went unanswered in 1800, and those who read him with approbation were very quickly to have fuel to keep their prejudices aflame. That same year an American edition was printed of Thomas Mathias' *The Pursuits of Literature,* which had first appeared in London during the first wave of French migration.[16] This work deprecated the revival of Romish superstition in England, with the attendant "cruelty, tyranny, the impiety" of the Church of Rome. It was all very well, Mathias asserted, to pity and succor the *émigré* priest; but woe to his principles! Matignon told Bishop Carroll on October 14:

The virulence of the author of *The Pursuits of Literature,* which has just appeared here, has helped the secret jealousy of some ministers who use it to persuade many people who have until now treated me with friendship that it was a great deal to tolerate us.[17]

At the same time that their own French origins inevitably caused Cheverus and Matignon to be viewed through the bifocal lens of politics and nationalism, the origins of their parishioners further complicated their position in the New England community. The Irish, like the French, presented a minority which had implications for both party politics and religious animosity. By the time Cheverus was preaching the eloquent sermons from the Franklin Street pulpit his listeners were for the most part anti-British and pro-Jeffersonian Democratic-Republicans. Their deep-seated animosity toward Britain had recently been aggravated by news from Ireland of the "Terrible '98"; the Irish in Boston had heard from the "Old Country" how, after the organized rebellion of 1798 had ceased, the butchery had gone on; that almost every Roman Catholic chapel from Bray to Wexford had been laid in ashes. They knew, too, that Prime Minister Pitt had not succeeded in securing complementary legislation to relieve Irish Catholics at the time of the Union of 1800.[18]

In Boston the anti-Federalists naturally played upon Irish sensibilities, and the politicians lured many an Irish Catholic into the party whose principles were labeled Jacobin, French, and even atheistical. After Jefferson's re-election in 1804, the two rival parties through their respective journalistic channels revived the politico-religious bickering which the subject of French *émigrés* had aggravated a little earlier.[19] Although neither Cheverus nor Matignon became directly embroiled in these more political verbal battles, the dissensions thus provoked did not ameliorate their situation. And to add to their uneasiness while being publicly contemned on the threefold charge of being Catholic, being French, and being pastors to Irish ruffians, both Francis Matignon and John Cheverus were, by training, breeding, and experience, naturally drawn to the Federalist society of the city.

Happily for the first Bishop of Boston, he had no political desires or designs. When he first actually appeared in print, the year before being named bishop, his position was solely that of a defender of the Church. On November 16, 1804, a Bostonian traveling in Europe had written home from Rome his reactions to Catholicism. After his return, John Lowell gave his letter to the *Monthly Anthology and Boston*

Review for publication in February, 1807, but signed it simply, "An American Traveler." Claiming to be charitable in his motives and quite free from prejudice in his heart, he accused the Church of contempt for other Christians, of bigoted intolerance and persecution, of gross idolatry, and, of course, the old charge repeated that indulgences were permissions to commit sins.[20]

On April 7 Cheverus wrote a reply which he signed "A Roman Catholic" and did send to the magazine where it appeared in the April issue. He explained:

I am a Roman Catholick, and in points of doctrine perfectly agree with my brethren in Italy and elsewhere; but neither they nor I hold such a doctrine concerning indulgences and persecution, as you attribute to us in your letter.

Where did you read, sir, from whom did you ever hear, that indulgences are permissions to commit offences? Not, I am sure in any catholick writer, not from any member of our church. Had you asked even the ignorant beggars you met with at Loretto and in other places, whether indulgences authorized them to get drunk, steal, &tc, &tc, they would have looked at you with astonishment, and perhaps mistaken a *christian* for an infidel.

We ourselves publish indulgences in our church in Boston; and if indulgences are permissions to commit offences, let our church be pulled down, and every Roman catholick be banished from this hospitable land. But, I dare say, sir, you do us the justice to believe, that instead of encouraging crimes, we do our best to prevent them, and with the blessing of God, not unsuccessfully. If I am not misinformed, the American Traveler's respectable name is inscribed among the benefactors of our church in this town; I acknowledge it with pleasure and gratitude, and feel happy in assuring you that you have not contributed to the establishment of a school of corruption and idolatry.

Your venerable forefathers fled not from a *popish,* but from a *protestant* persecution. They landed here, and were at full liberty to show what was the spirit of their sect. Was it toleration? Many other virtues they possessed, no doubt; but to this they were utter strangers.

Lord Baltimore, himself a Roman catholick, as well as his companions, fled from the same persecution. See them establishing themselves in Maryland; they will no doubt give strong specimens of popish bigotry and persecution. They opened an asylum, afforded protection, and granted the same civil privileges to christians of every denomination.

Here are my evidences. Judge of them yourself, sir, and give your decision. I am willing to abide by it.

I know, sir, that the children here have not inherited the persecuting spirit of their fathers. Our church in this town is a standing monument of their liberal and friendly dispositions; and the one who addresses you is proud of the friendship, and grateful for the polite attentions of several of them.

We Roman Catholicks cherish a sincere affection for this country and its inhabitants; we abhor the idea of being licensed to commit crimes; and instead of hating our brethren on account of their religious opinion, we wish only to be able to do them every service in our power.[21]

A biographer of John Lowell claims that Lowell "had so much respect for his opponent and for the good work he was doing among his people here, that he would not run the risk of diminishing his influence in the slightest degree, though he thought that his article could be very easily answered."[22] Although the "American Traveler" abandoned the field to "A Roman Catholick" the editor of the *Anthology* attempted to rally the offense by appending his own comments to Cheverus' letter, quoting at length from the *Encyclopedia Britannica* on the subject of indulgences! Dr. John Kirkland added magnanimously that Lowell had the highest respect for both Cheverus and Matignon "whom he wishes to believe incapable of countenancing all the errors and absurdities, which have crept into the practice of the Catholicks in some countries."[23]

To editor Kirkland's comment Cheverus replied gracefully, addressing himself to the Anthology Club, whose organ the *Anthology* was:

Sir:

No man is more averse to controversy than I am myself & I would really be sorry to find in your monthly publication nothing but a bunch of controversial thorns & nettles, instead of a fragrant nosegay of literary flowers which the title promises & the contents generally afford. I think however I must say a few words about your note, but I do not request you should publish them. They are only addressed to you & to the American Traveler at whose request you published the reflections contained in your note.

To know the doctrine of our Church, the books which she approves must be quoted. I know that the British encyclopedia & many other works pass condemnation against us. But I appeal from their judgment to your own candour, if you will but examine my witnesses.

Two of them I take the liberty to send. Examine & cross-examine them, if you have the leisure and patience. . . .

I beg of you, Sir, & of the American Traveler to receive my thanks for the very polite, though in regard to myself very undeserved, manner in which you speak of my venerable colleague & myself. Wishing that every controversy may be carried on & terminate in as friendly a manner as ours

I remain Sir. . . .[24]

The letter was read in the club's meeting on May 21, 1807, and the public aspect of the controversy was over.

The private and personal repercussions of the little exchange, however, were only beginning. From 1807 until the day he died John Cheverus was to experience increasing friendship, in numbers and degree, with the Anthology Club whose rooms were not far from his rectory. The two books which Cheverus sent over in 1807 were followed by many subsequent gifts to the Athenaeum Library founded that year by the Anthology Club. Indeed, the *Columbian Centinel* of January 5, 1820, referred to Cheverus, along with the two Adamses and Governor Dewitt Clinton of New York, as one of the most munificent donors to the library during the first years of its existence.[25] The gentlemen of the club whose membership included such names as Harrison Gray Otis, Josiah Quincy, Theodore Lyman, as well as the Lowells and Kirkland, found they had much in common with the little priest of gentle birth, refined tastes, and extensive learning. Even if they could not concede him victory in religious polemics, they found they could not withhold their respect — a respect which soon became genuine affection. Their sentiments permeated their family circles and were reflected in the demeanor of wives and children, so that one contemporary noted:

Bishop Cheverus numbered among his most intimate friends, a large circle of intellectual females of the Protestant faith, and many of them moving in the higher walks of life. In his judgment and friendship, they reposed implicit confidence; and not only consulted him themselves, but taught their children, that in every painful or delicate exigency of their lives, to call on him for counsel and direction.[26]

There was an irresistible appeal in the stories that circulated about the gentle yet dauntless "Dear little Bishop." People who went by stage-coach to Salem in bad weather found him "always the same kind, affable companion . . . ; his presence and pleasant manner of conversation opened their eyes to the lovable and beautiful character hidden beneath the form and garments of the Catholic priest." On good days he could be seen descending from the ferry and trudging to Salem on foot, in order to give the stagecoach fare thus saved to some deserving poor person.[27] It is not difficult to understand how the Protestant Reverend Mr. William Bentley, D.D., of Salem could record in his diary after the first episcopal visit of Cheverus:

> On Tuesday last, Bishop Cheverus for the first time since his Consecration & for the first time that a Catholic Bishop read mass, confirmed, baptised & performed other duties of the high Office of a Bishop. . . . On Tuesday, I heard his address & it was happy. It was not upon their arguments they were to vindicate the ceremonies or doctrines & to oppose prejudices & jealousies of their rivals, but by their character to destroy all fear.[28]

The word "bishop" was easier to use when it applied to Cheverus whose own character assuredly destroyed all fear.

Josiah Quincy was not likely to forget his first meeting with Cheverus. The Federalist leader of Boston who was destined to become mayor of the city and then president of Harvard was driving one day from Quincy to Boston when he overtook a forlorn foot passenger, drenched and bedraggled, plodding the miry road to town. When Quincy offered the sorry figure a ride he was refused with the remarkable words, "That would be scarcely fair. My clothes are soaked with water and would spoil the cushions of your chaise, to say nothing of the wetting I could not avoid giving you." Quincy insisted, however, and on the ride into Boston learned that his companion was Cheverus, who had been walking back from Hingham where he had gone to perform a priestly office.[29] It marked the beginning of a friendship which Quincy always recalled as "very dear and precious," and which Cheverus deemed a "treasure."[30]

People who lived on Water Street might have been chagrined at another tale Bostonians loved to repeat. Cheverus, it seems, had sent a sick woman a load of firewood, but for days it lay outside her cottage in Water Street, no neighbor volunteering to cut it up and carry it in. Then, one morning before daylight, aroused by a noise in the street, they discovered the Bishop of Boston energetically sawing up the wood and carrying it in. He said to the gaping group that he was there in the dark to conceal the necessity for a bishop's having to do what charitable neighbors ought to have done.[31] It was a reproof not likely to be forgotten.

Children adored him. "His very look was a benediction, the mere glance of his eye was a *Sursum Corda*. That calm, wise, benignant face always had a smile for the little ones . . . and the pockets of that benevolent prelate never knew a dearth of sugar-plums." The children who romped in the alleys off Franklin Street knew two dignitaries — the Spanish Consul, Don Juan Stoughton, and the French Bishop, John Cheverus. Don Juan they respected; Bishop Cheverus they loved.[32] The Stoughton children had reason to be familiar with Cheverus, of course. Their houses were so near, their interests even nearer. Cheverus was often a guest, and through the Stoughtons he made friends with other Bostonians who were not of his flock. Among these was the richest man in town, Gardiner Greene. Greene came to the bishop's assistance on more than one occasion and Cheverus told him, "Aware of your friendship for me & of your sound sense & prudence I could not apply for advice to anybody sooner than to you."[33]

As a man, there was every reason why Cheverus should have been loved. Bishop Carroll had immediately perceived during their first weeks together that personality which "marvelously" drew people to the French priest. His modesty, his simplicity, his complete lack of personal ambition, his integrity, his self-abnegating generosity, all clothed in delightful humor made him a man destined to be revered. But it was as a priest and prelate that he was beloved, as well; for the man and the office were inseparable.

> It was as a moral personality that Cheverus rose to grandeur. A deep, solid, and ardent piety was the core of his character and the mainspring of all his actions. It was a piety of a specifically French flavor, the joyous, smiling piety of a Fénelon, a St. Francis de Sales, a St. Vincent de Paul. Its geniality sprang, of course, from no mere cheerful acceptance of this world as relatively good and no mere natural satisfaction with the pleasant things of life. It was rather the joyousness that comes after a long and harrowing process of self-conquest, self-immolation, when one has surrendered oneself completely into the hands of God.[34]

Wherever his reputation spread, it was always as a priest and bishop that he was known.

It is not surprising that when two men condemned to death in distant Northampton heard their sentence they wrote to Cheverus, "Come to our assistance." The men were James Halligan and Dominic Daley, the year 1806. A Marcus Lyon of Woodstock had been murdered on November 9, 1805, and his body thrown into the Chicopee River. The coroner's inquest accused two unknown transients in sailor's clothes who were on their way from Springfield to Connecticut. Three days later at Rye, Daley and Halligan had been picked up and, although protesting their innocence, had been held for trial before the Supreme Court at Northampton on April 22, 1806.

The whole atmosphere surrounding the trial was one of deep hostility. The fact that the accused men were Irish and Catholics was enough to make them feared and despised in the western Massachusetts town. The newspapers described the men as obstinate and hardened criminals and they were condemned on circumstantial evidence on April 25. Daley's mother in Boston petitioned the governor for a pardon, but no pardon was granted. Cheverus went to Northampton to be with the condemned men during their last days. Although he was not Irish, he was a "Papist" and Pomeroy's Tavern refused him lodging. The wife of the proprietor said fearfully that she "would not have been able to sleep a wink under the same roof with a Catholic Priest." When Joseph Clark, a more courageous Protestant, dared to shelter Cheverus the villagers saw the hand of Providence in the ill-fortune which later befell poor Clark. The death of his wife and the loss of his house by lightning bolt were clear proof that Heaven was "chastizing him for his heresy!"[35]

Cheverus went his daily way to the jail to give Communion to the men and help them prepare for the awful day of execution. With his aid, they prepared a final statement protesting their innocence once more. On the day of the execution Cheverus preached to the largest audience he had yet seen. About 15,000 people, one of his listeners later estimated, crowded inside the Protestant meeting house, or stood outside the open windows to hear what the Papist priest would say on such an occasion. The ministers of the town made a last minute attempt to prevent Cheverus from speaking, but he protested forcefully, "The wish of the dying men is sacred. They asked for me alone; I alone will speak to them!"

He took his text from 1 John 3:15, "Whosoever hateth his brother is a murderer." Then, giving vent to the sorrow and repugnance with which their hatred for the two men had filled him, Cheverus spoke in unmistakable reproof. Ordinarily, he said severely, an orator would be flattered to have so large an audience. "But I am ashamed," he said in tones of righteous wrath. Had death become an amusing spectacle, an object of curiosity? Especially was it disgraceful to see so many women there, avid and eager. "Your eyes," he accused them, "are full of murder. You have forgotten your sex; you have dishonored it and brought it opprobrium." The women, at least, had the grace to leave the scene of the execution after his denunciation.[36] The *Hampshire Federalist* on June 10 described the sermon as "an appropriate and eloquent discourse." It had struck home.

The tranquil resignation of the prisoners also made a deep impression on the non-Catholics who were there that day. Were the men innocent after all? They asked Cheverus, since he had heard their honest confessions, if there had been a mistake. Cheverus seized the question as an excellent opportunity to develop the teaching of the Church in regard to the sacrament of penance and the inviolability of the confessional.[37] Some of his listeners asked him to stay longer, but he was already overdue back east; Newcastle was waiting for its summer missioner as usual. As the little priest made his way home to Boston there were some in western Massachusetts who were reconsidering their first notions of Catholic priests and their doctrines.

In reassessing the impact of Cheverus on the Protestant environment of New England, the matter of conversions naturally raises a query. Did converts in sizable numbers enter the Church? The answer is not easy to come upon. Baptismal records are of little assistance since they do not tell which converts were due to Matignon, to Cheverus, or to mixed marriages. Sometimes whole families became converts after such a marriage. Again, the records give no clue to the number of converts whose non-Catholic baptism was believed valid. It is generally accepted that Cheverus brought many into the Church, and in some cases the converts themselves verify his influence. For example, Dr. Stephen Cleveland Blyth of Salem went directly to Cheverus when his investigation of various religions — in Europe and in the West Indies — roused his interest in Catholicism. When Blyth published an account of his conversation afterward, the dedication of his work read:

> To the Right Reverend John Cheverus, Bishop of Boston
> My dear Lord and Friend,
>   I take the liberty to inscribe my pamphlet to your Lordship. To you it owes its existence; for you (under God) I owe my conversion.[38]

Thomas Walley, Jr., another convert of note, gave credit to both Cheverus and Matignon. Walley had known the vicissitudes of the

Catholic Church in Boston ever since its foundation and after his conversion he said:

> In its beginnings I saw nothing but what confirmed all my early prejudices against the Catholic Church; but I desire to be thankful for the mercy and grace of God, and also for the arrival in our country of those two most excellent men, Dr. Matignon and Mr. Cheverus, who soon gave a different color to all things.[39]

Bishop Cheverus himself, in reporting Walley's conversion to Archbishop Carroll, called the merchant a precious acquisition to the Church. "We have valued him as a friend for years previous to his becoming one of the household of the faith."[40]

Sometimes even ministers were swayed; a Protestant Episcopal minister of Derby, Connecticut, owed his final conversion to correspondence and direct conversation with Cheverus. John Henry Hobart, who by 1819 was Bishop of the Episcopal Church of New York, must have felt some chagrin upon hearing that the man who had once helped entice Elizabeth Seton from his flock was now instrumental in the loss of Reverend Calvin White.[41] Hobart already had reason to regret not replying to questions raised by another minister who had come under Cheverus' influence. Back in 1810, after meeting Cheverus in Boston, Reverend Daniel Barber of Vermont had raised the question of the validity of Anglican orders. Now both Barber and his minister son were Catholics. Although Bishop Hobart could blame the Jesuits of New York for Virgil Barber's defection, the truth was that books Cheverus had placed in the father's hands had been the start of it all. Three ministers gone over to Rome within three years may have had a sobering effect on Hobart.[42]

Conversions, in the end, prove very little. The numbers during the years of Cheverus' ministry seem small by present-day standards;[43] and, quite apart from statistics, conversions are due to the gift of faith which God confers through instruments of His own choosing. The efficacy of the little bishop's labors need not stand nor fall on this test. The ultimate witness to his unique contribution lies in the altered position Catholicism enjoyed as a result of his reign. When Bishop Pierre Denaut of Quebec visited Boston less than seven years after Cheverus' arrival he was showered with kindness and courtesies by the most distinguished persons of the city. "What a difference from the past!" he exclaimed. "Twenty years ago they would have hanged me without even the form of a trial."[44] When his successor, Joseph Plessis, visited

Boston five years after Cheverus was consecrated bishop, the Canadian prelate commented in similar amazement:

> Who would have said, thirty years ago, that the true faith would be known and respected in Boston, the city of all English America the most opposed to Catholicism, the city where, every November, they thought it an act of religion to burn the pope in effigy, and where even the children, imitating what they saw their elders do so lavishly, had their own little popes which they also threw into the fire. . . .[45]

Boston was now a city whose welcome to the President of the United States naturally included the Catholic bishop among the dignitaries attending the chief executive of the nation.[46]

As his episcopacy continued, relations between Catholics and the Protestant majority continued to improve. The Catholic clergy were on the best of terms with the best of people. Lawyers like William Tudor and Samuel Knapp put their sentiments in print. Tudor wrote in his *Letters on the Eastern States,* referring to Matignon and Cheverus:

> They have fulfilled the numerous parochial duties required by the Catholic religion, with apostolical simplicity and evangelical zeal, neither attempting to make proselytes nor to excite controversy; and I presume it cannot be disputed, and I hope it will not be considered invidious to say (circumstances of their congregations being taken into view) that their ministry is by far the most arduous and useful in the town.[47]

Knapp came to feel himself the constant advocate of the Catholic cause with such devotion that Bishop Cheverus came to rely on the lawyer's defense whenever that cause was at issue. Before Knapp founded his own organ, the *Boston Monthly Magazine,* his sympathetic support appeared in the pages of the *Gazette,* the *Palladium,* the *Centinel,* and the *New England Galaxy.*

The physicians of Boston proved as friendly as the gentlemen of the legal profession. Dr. John Warren and Dr. George Parkman performed many a charitable service for the bishop's flock and counted themselves lucky when Cheverus could be prevailed upon to join them socially. A letter from the bishop to Dr. Parkman dated June 27, 1816, is typical of their relationship:

Dear Sir:

Your goodness encourages me to send to you two worthy but poor women living in Charlestown, who have Children to be inoculated. Your charity to them will be the more acceptable, as they are not entitled to the privilege of the inhabitants of Boston.

I would be very happy to join your party tomorrow, but I am under sailing orders, and cannot dispose of a moment.

> Your grateful & respectful Servt.
> John Cheverus[48]

Dr. Warren, who was Dean of the Harvard Medical School from 1816 to 1819, was much more convenient to the bishop after 1815 when the school moved from Cambridge to Boston. Cheverus thought there was no one like Warren for ailments of the eyes, and he quoted Warren as an oracle on other matters as well.[49]

The most numerous friendships were those formed with the clergy of the other churches. Some of these began, naturally enough, as a result of Bishop Cheverus' collaboration with the Seamen's Aid Society which was founded in 1812 by the notable pioneer in social work, the Reverend Joseph Tuckerman of Chelsea, and many prominent Boston laymen and clergy. One of the laymen who attended the meetings of the society recorded later that the Catholic bishop's slight form and humble yet dignified countenance was a powerful influence "in breaking down the prejudices of the sturdy descendants of the Puritans against the Popish name."[50] Working on the projects of the Seamen's Aid Society brought Cheverus in direct contact with ministers like Tuckerman, Charles Lowell, William Ellery Channing, Horace Holley, and Joseph S. Buckminster, not to mention Cheverus' former epistolary controversialist, John Thornton Kirkland, now president of Harvard.

Charles Lowell remained devoted to Cheverus and long after the first Bishop of Boston had returned to France the Unitarian minister informed the editors of the *Christian Register:*

> I knew him well and had frequent and affectionate communication with him. . . . When I was in Rome, I had, as is usual, a formal introduction to the pope. I have often thought how little of formality there would have been if Cheverus had worn the tiara. I have no doubt, from my knowledge of his simplicity and kindness of heart that he would have put his arms around my neck and embraced me, as he did when we parted in Boston. . . .[51]

William Ellery Channing became so fond of Cheverus that when he was called upon to review a new life of Fénelon in 1829 his article became a paeon of praise for Cheverus:

To come down to our times, has not the metropolis of New England witnessed a sublime example of Christian virtue in a Catholic Bishop? Who, among our religious teachers, would solicit a comparison between himself and the devoted Cheverus? This good man . . . lived in the midst of us, devoting his days and nights, and his whole heart, to the service of a poor and uneducated congregation. We saw him declining a great degree, the society of the cultivated and refined, that he might be the friend of the ignorant and friendless . . . bearing with a father's sympathy, the burdens and sorrows of his large spiritual family; charging himself alike with their temporal and spiritual concerns; and never discovering, by the faintest indication that he felt his fine mind degraded by his seemingly humble office. This good man, bent on his errands of mercy, was seen in our streets under the most burning sun of summer, and the fiercest storms of winter, as if armed against the elements by the power of charity. . . . How can we shut our hearts against this proof of the power of the Catholic religion to form good and great men?[52]

Although a firsthand record of Joseph Tuckerman's sentiments toward the bishop are lacking, after Tuckerman became Minister-at-large for the American Unitarian Association and devoted himself to working as a city missionary to the poor of Boston, one of Tuckerman's own disciples, William Ware, commented of Cheverus:

It was a common remark that he did more for the peace and order of the city, through the moral means which he employed, than was effected by all the various machinery of the law. The remark . . . was founded in truth, and it shows the estimation in which the public held his services. He was, in fact, a minister-at-large in the truest acceptation of the term. He lived almost among the poor. . . . His memory, where he lived and labored, will never die. The name of Cheverus will never be forgotten by the poor of Boston.[53]

The Reverend John Pierce of Brookline, who might have been forgiven some resentment over the conversion of Thomas Walley, said of Matignon and Cheverus, "They have both given the most incontrovertible evidence of sincerity in their religious belief. . . . Nor have they manifested great solicitude to gain proselytes from the protestants. . . . In obtaining, as they did, a male member of my Church, I had no evidence of any disingenuous efforts on their part."[54] Others like Thomas Gray of the First Church of Jamaica Plain, Thaddeus M. Harris of the First Church of Dorchester, James Freeman of King's Chapel, shared with the Catholic bishop an affectionate relationship.

One of the last services Cheverus ever performed for a Bostonian was for Harris, to whom he wrote in the month before his death, "Remember me kindly and affectionately to your family; to the Rev. Doctors Pierce and Gray. . . ."[55]

It goes without saying that Cheverus remained unalterably opposed to the doctrines of his non-Catholic friends; no one ever suspected his gentle friendliness of symbolizing a lack of firm conviction. A Protestant might write ruefully, "We had the pleasure of his acquaintance for several years, and always regretted that a man of his capacity, knowledge, liberality and independence, should not have been numbered with the Protestant church."[56] But everyone knew the bishop's tolerance was for men, not for deviations in doctrine. His orthodoxy must have been scandalized at some of the dissensions among his non-Catholic friends, many of whom were involved in the Unitarian controversy which came to a crisis during Cheverus' episcopacy.

In 1815 the *Panoplist* reprinted an English pamphlet on the history of American Unitarianism. It was believed that the information and documents for the pamphlet had been furnished by Dr. James Freeman; and rumor attributed the American reprint to Dr. Jedidiah Morse's instigation. The minister of the First Congregational Church of Charlestown viewed with alarm the similarity he found in English and American Socinianism or Unitarianism. William Ellery Channing of the Federal Street Church denied the similarity, defending the Unitarians against the charges of materialism and humanitarianism. The battle was on! Pulpit oratory became impassioned and the magazines printed lively vindications under a variety of pen names. Cheverus wrote to Father Bruté:

> One of our Congregationalist ministers, speaking from the pulpit last Sunday, declared that the doctrine of the Trinity would soon be as completely rejected as is that of the Salem witchcraft. He was Mr. Horace Holley: and at least spoke his mind clearly. He is a talented and amiable man. But what is religion coming to, when such blasphemies are boldly preached and quietly received by a large congregation! You will note that The Layman is also quite unrestrained. He is a lawyer, Mr. John Lowell, brother of a minister, a member of one of our first families and of the Corporation of the University of Cambridge.[57]

When the bishop made his report to Rome in February, 1817, he concluded sorrowfully, "The Socinian heresy has many followers here, under the name of Unitarians, among the Protestant ministers, in the

University of Cambridge, etc. A large number of the inhabitants both live and alas, die also, without baptism."[58] Especially in the Advent season the bishop grieved for his Unitarian friends. To be deprived of the profound joy of the season was something he could not bear to contemplate. As he wrote to Bruté, "In spite of the Socinians, *Verbum habitavit in nobis. Credimus charitati quam habet Deus in nobis.*"[59] What a blessing was this faith which still believed that God in His love for men had sent the Word to dwell among them.

The Unitarian question had its by-product in a brief renewal of anti-Catholic sentiments among the Evangelical Protestants and the Trinitarian Congregationalists. The *Panoplist* and the *Christian Register* led the attack in 1819; but that stout defender of the Boston Catholics, Samuel Knapp, took to the pages of the *Gazette* and routed the forces of bigotry.[60] His spirited article included, to no one's surprise, a special encomium of Bishop Cheverus. The touchstone of Catholicism in Boston in those years was the little prelate of Franklin Street. Once his name was brought into the arena of polemics the heat of the argument submitted to the warmth of his person.

The readers of this generation who approach the Cheverus era through the corridors of a century and a half of history know quite well that the first Bishop of Boston did not banish religious intolerance from New England forever. He was still alive in France when an Ursuline convent was burned within the Diocese of Boston. After his death Massachusetts would be visited with the virulence of the Nativist or Know-Nothing hatreds in mid-century and the repercussions of the American Protective Association in the 1890's. Not even the enlightenment of the twentieth century has been entirely free from sporadic revivals of prejudice.

The lesson of Cheverus is not so much that he changed the history which came after him, but rather that for the twenty-seven years he dwelt among the alien corn, Boston was the better for his sojourn. In an age when the value of the single life may be lost among the files and statistics of the fetishly venerated group, class, or trend, it is salutary to reconsider the true relation of man to mankind. The generation whose usage bans "heart and soul" as a cliché, and for whom the phrase "person-to-person" suggests only a popular entertainment, may profit from the example of Cheverus. The power of one man in his own time should not be underestimated. And if the influence he exerts is direct enough, flowing unimpeded from a pure heart and a zealous soul, he does, in the end, change history.

In the year of the bimillenary celebration of the foundation of Paris, the Boston Athenaeum chose to mark the event with a display honoring Jean Lefebvre de Cheverus. "It is appropriate," the *Memorial* of 1951 remarked, "that the Athenaeum should commemorate France's greatest gift to the spiritual life of Boston." The display, of course, was arranged in collaboration with men of several faiths; and the *Memorial to Bishop Cheverus* concluded, "This is as it should be, for if any single principle for the guidance of the future were to be derived from the twenty-seven years of Cheverus' ministry in Boston it would certainly reduce itself to the four words — let brotherly love continue."[61]

CHAPTER XI

THE WAR YEARS

THE active episcopate of John Cheverus at Boston extended over a period of thirteen years and falls into three rather distinct phases: the years of painful beginnings largely conditioned by the events which led to the War of 1812 and by the war itself; the years of change which coincided with the wave of nationalism following the war; and, finally, the years of consolidation. Chronologically considered, these three periods came to a close in the fall of the years 1815, 1819, and 1823. The first was particularly influenced by economic factors over which Cheverus had no control, and by the rupture of communications with the Holy See. The second period was marked by the changing relations of the American hierarchy, both in relation to each other and to the Holy See, following the death of Archbishop Carroll. The last years were clearly the "Cheverus era" in that Francis A. Matignon was no longer alive to support and complement the bishop's efforts, and therefore whatever of merit accrues to those years was unmistakably due to the work of Cheverus. Two *leitmotifs* run through the entire episcopacy of Cheverus, however: the unchanging humility of the man who wore the robes of bishop, and the growing conviction everywhere that John Cheverus was "certainly the first bishop of the United States" among the suffragans.[1]

Cheverus began his reign amid economic distress which, though visited upon the whole nation, fell with heaviest weight upon New England. The struggle for economic survival waged by Britain during the decade after the coronation of Napoleon in 1804 perforce involved American commerce. The Berlin and Milan Decrees on the French side, the retaliatory British Orders in Council on the other, provoked the Congress of the United States into measures which proved equally

146

destructive of the shipping interests of the Atlantic ports. We have already seen the disruption of intercourse during the months that Cheverus waited for the arrival of the papal bulls and briefs necessary to his consecration. The same July in which Bishop Concanen died in Naples saw Napoleon ordering the seizure of American merchantmen in that city and the sale of all sequestrated ships and cargoes. Although John Quincy Adams warned President Madison that it was "a trap to catch us into a war with England," the French promise to revoke the Berlin and Milan Decrees led the President to prohibit, for the third time in four years, all commerce between England and the United States.

This action was taken on February 11, 1811, at the very beginning of Cheverus' reign. To be sure, the commercial strictures led to a salutary diversification of industry in New England, and before the war was over John Lowell's brother would have established the first complete factory in Waltham; but the prosperity spawned by infant textile industries was not immediately felt. The only things perceived by the Bishop of Boston and his flock during the first years after his return from the Baltimore consecration ceremonies were poverty and depression. The declaration of war on England resolved by Congress on June 18, 1812, only confirmed the prospect of want, and Cheverus did not try to conceal it. He told Archbishop Carroll:

Many of our poor people have no employment, and all feel the distress of the times, without excepting my good friends, Messrs. Kavanagh and Cottrill, who have met with heavy and repeated losses. I really do not know at present one of my diocesans, to whom I could apply with good grace even for ten dollars. The dear Dr. Matignon and myself have but one purse, but it is now an empty one. However, we live from day to day, and a kind providence supplies our daily wants.[2]

His cheerful humor, as of old, eased many a scanty meal. To Father Matthew O'Brien, who had chosen that year to come and live with him, Cheverus drolly asserted that what they had they would all share, and "when all the bread and meat was exhausted he would take his Crozier and walk with Dr. Matignon in procession to the Almshouse."[3] O'Brien was welcome, if only because he had admitted Elizabeth Seton into the Church while he was at St. Peter's in New York; but he felt some compunction about eating Cheverus out of house and home. "They are abundantly generous and never complain of wanting," he told Carroll in some wonderment. "The more indeed

I consider their circumstances, the greater is my astonishment; like Anthony and Paul, they had one loaf already, but another half has been added in favour of me. I know not whence it comes." And with it all the two French confreres endlessly kept spreading happiness about them. They even took into the small house young Edward Kavanagh and his brother during the winter of 1813–1814 when the financial losses of their father made it impossible for the young men to continue their respective studies in Baltimore and Emmitsburg.[4] Cheverus may have thought it "bread upon the waters," for Edward, at least, appeared to have a vocation. But it took more than an extra half-loaf to feed those hearty appetites.

As the war continued things did not improve. In its second year Cheverus wrote to Baltimore, "The hardness of the times has obliged many of our people to go elsewhere in search of a living, and their absence is but scantily supplied by some few poor people who are now and then added to our Church." Boston was very gloomy that year and Cheverus found his only remedy was to "forget home and look abroad."[5] To Mother Seton he let some of his discouragement show and wrote sadly, "I have not even been able to establish a school for our children."[6] Before peace finally came he told his brother Louis, "The unfortunate war in which we are plunged has changed our flourishing cities into asylums for the poor. If God does not give us peace, commerce by which we solely exist is ruined."[7] Even after the news of the Treaty of Ghent finally reached Boston, the city could not hope for any speedy improvement. "We are breathing since the peace," he admitted, "but we can scarcely hope to see again our former prosperity."[8] It is apparent that the first five years of his episcopacy saw little respite from direst poverty.

These years were critical in other respects. It was all very well to joke about marching to the poorhouse in full regalia, or more seriously to reassure Louis, "Although I am poor . . . I am not in debt, and I am satisfied"; he could not shrug off the signs he saw of more careless virtue which the days of crisis and tension inevitably encouraged. He loved poverty for himself; but when it led in others to evil and wrongdoing his heart was pierced. As bishop he felt an awful responsibility and he wrote in anguish of spirit to the Sulpicians in Baltimore:

> I wish I had consoling news to give you of my diocese, but to
> my shame, I have none. No conversions for a little while, and in-
> stead of a growth of piety, scandals. . . . I have every cause to fear

that my episcopacy is a great misfortune for myself and for this diocese. Have pity on me, my dear Sirs, and pray for me. I have more need of it than you can imagine.[9]

Archbishop Carroll was aware of his friend's suffering over the decline in morality and felt no surprise when he read Cheverus' first reaction to the news of the pope's release from captivity in 1814: "What a pity that amidst so many causes of joy, admiration, and gratitude we must drop a tear of sorrow over this degraded country! I try to hope that miracles of mercy will be wrought also in our favour." From another man the reference to tears of sorrow might have been a figure of speech; from John Cheverus they were a simple admission of literal fact. Mother Seton, too, knew the utter sincerity of his plea to her on January 20, 1815, "Dear & good Sister, pray for the poor Bishop of Boston who can do nothing towards promoting religion & piety in his Diocese."[10]

Added to his worry over the pitiful plight of his parishioners and his sorrow over his own inability to be a worthy bishop Cheverus was constantly, during those first years, intensely concerned over the situation of the papacy. French troops had invaded Rome in February, 1808, and the bull for Cheverus' appointment had been issued after the Swiss Guard was disarmed.[11] Pius VII, a prisoner of the French, had first been taken to Grenoble, then to Savona; by the end of the next year Dubourg was circulating news he had received that the pope had died as a martyr to his confinement on the Island of St. Margaretta near the coast of Provence. His last words, according to Dubourg, were, "Pray and fear not."[12]

The pope was not dead; but when the bishops were consecrated in Baltimore in 1810 Carroll could tell them very little else. An English friend had written only:

Of his Holiness Pope Pius the 7th we know nothing certain. Many contradictory reports are spread concerning him, fabricated by his enemies on purpose to conceal the truth. . . . There is however one report which seems to be grounded on better motives & which I hope will prove true. It is said that the Pope foreseeing the disasters & difficulties to which the Church would be exposed, especially with respect to the choice of a Successor in case of his death, had whilst still at liberty called a consistory of cardinals & with their unanimous concert had nominated the Bishop of Palermo for his successor. If this report be true it will prevent many difficulties and doubts.[13]

Other than this Carroll knew only that the prisoner was still at

Savona, "where he was lodged in a good house with liberty to see anyone who desired it, but always in the presence of French and German officers."[14] Although the new bishops had been more reserved than the Irish prelates in their statement on the pontiff's captivity — "on account of the infancy of our hierarchy we felt a diffidence," as Carroll put it — they had shared equally the anxiety of the whole Church over the future of Pius VII and the throne of St. Peter. It was disheartening to learn from Archbishop Carroll after they left Baltimore, "A letter of October 1, which I received from Rome itself, describes great desolation in that city."[15]

It was natural that Pius VII should become a subject of deepest veneration throughout the Archdiocese of Baltimore. Pictures of him were in great demand and when Cheverus received one from Mother Seton he acknowledged it saying:

> Although we had received some of the pictures of the Holy Father, the one sent by you was not the less welcome. I keep it as my own and look on the writing at the back of it as a valuable addition. Receive my sincere thanks for this new mark of your affectionate kindness.

It was really impossible to have enough of them and the next month the Bishop of Boston had to request ten dozen more from Baltimore.[16] But no number of pictures could substitute for some direct channel of intercourse with the Holy See. The new bishops had no directives from their spiritual head to guide them: they had no certainty that their reports or recommendations would ever reach him. The last tangible proof of the Holy See's concern for the American hierarchy was the pallium for Archbishop Carroll, brought by John Augustus Foster in 1811, and Cheverus found it "not a little remarkable that the British minister should have been the bearer of it."[17] What a topsy-turvy world, when Catholic France held a pope captive and the diplomats of Protestant England became papal emissaries!

The American declaration of war on England in 1812 might have been expected to improve relations with France but it had no appreciable effect on the recourse of the American bishops. Carroll told Plessis in March, 1814:

> It would be gratifying to me, if it were in my power to give comfortable information . . . of the state of the Church, and of our Holy Father. But if any alteration has ensued in the personal treatment of the latter, it is yet unknown to us. When our last advices

left Europe, no mention was made of his delivery from captivity.
. . . In August, my most confidential friend in France wrote to a
third person here for my information . . . that a memorial in my
name and that of my Right Revd. Brethren in the United States
. . . had been with much industry conveyed to & placed in the Pope's
hands . . . but the same friend added, that it was vain to expect
any answer.[18]

Late that month the glad news finally reached the United States
that the allies had entered Paris and that Pius VII was released from
Fontainebleau where he had latterly been held. Archbishop Carroll
told Mother Seton on March 29 of "the intelligence received here
yesterday of the delivery of our Holy Father . . . and departure for
Rome. If this should be confirmed," he added, "our prayers for our
captive Pontiff will be exchanged for a *Te Deum*."[19] On June 3
Cheverus in Boston got the official confirmation and two days later
in the Cathedral of the Holy Cross his *Te Deum* was sung "for the
deliverance of His Holiness and the miraculous and happy events
which have led to it and to the peace in Europe."[20]

Amid all the general rejoicing none was more heartfelt than that
of the Bishop of Boston, who preached his finest sermon that day.
The non-Catholics in his audience, many of them members of the
legislature, were given a glimpse of the place the papacy had in
Catholic hearts. Protestant Samuel Knapp never forgot the occasion
and a decade later still carried a vivid recollection of the bishop's remarks. "Whoever heard him, will never forget his address to his flock
on the news of the Sovereign Pontiff's release. . . . Other joys at the
same moment crowded upon his mind, and he indulged his feelings
to the full tide of his delight."[21]

After suspending the prayers *pro papa* in the Mass Archbishop
Carroll began writing his pastoral letter on the subject of the papacy,
hoping that before it was completed "we may perhaps hear of His
Holiness being restored and received at Rome; perhaps, too, of some
beams of peace shining on us."[22] When Cheverus received his copy
on July 13 he told his metropolitan, "I intend reading it from the
Pulpit next Sunday. Never will my people be more delighted or
edified than in hearing me as your *Echo*."[23] His vibrant voice seemed
indeed to issue from lips touched by a burning coal as he read to
his flock:

My beloved brethren: We have passed days and years of painful
anxiety; for though we did not lose sight of Him, who after declaring

that His Church was built on a rock, and that the gates of Hell should not prevail against it, yet we knew not the term allotted for our chastisement, nor for the return of mercy. That term is now come, and we are bound by duty and sentiment to hail it with accents of thanksgiving and praise. You are convoked together today for the performance of this duty. O my brethren, let it make a lasting impression on you; let the occasion as well as the celebration be deeply engraven on your memory. This is the day which the Lord has made; let us exult exceedingly and rejoice therein.[24]

Yet the day of rejoicing was succeeded by months more of waiting for further news. In October Bruté passed on the news he got from Duc de Rohan-Chabot:

who having been formerly one of the Chamberlains of Bonaparte contrived means to see sometimes at Fontainebleau, and gain his confidence, the Pope; and since had some commission to Italy, which gave him an opportunity of beholding his Holiness' solemn entrance into Rome, of which his letter . . . gives a most splendid and edifying description. . . .[25]

The bishops of the United States meanwhile continued for another eight months without any other satisfaction than the knowledge that their recommendations of 1810 had been received before the pope's liberation.

It is impossible to estimate the degree of detriment this set of circumstances had for the Diocese of Boston. But in two respects the correspondence between Boston and Baltimore during those five years shows how close Cheverus and Carroll were in their thinking on matters affecting the American hierarchy. The first was the matter of the council which had been scheduled to take place in 1812; the second was the problem of the vacant sees in the United States, particularly that of Philadelphia. Both matters were interrelated and both were adversely affected by the rupture of communication with the Holy See.

On August 25, 1812, Carroll wrote to his suffragans reminding them of their resolve to meet in council that November. Immediately upon receipt of this letter Cheverus sent his reasons for opposing such a meeting that year. In the first place, he argued, no news had yet been received from Pius VII, a situation which no one had foreseen at the time the council was planned. In 1812 both New York and New Orleans were vacant sees and could not send bishops. For himself, November was one of the worst seasons for travel and "an objection almost insuperable is expense." He had just returned from two and a half months in Maine and could not in justice leave Matignon again so soon with his colleague so frail in health. "I am more a parish priest than a Bishop," he said quite truthfully.

He was not opposed to the council, only his own attendance, and even that not categorically. Carroll may have mentioned the violent rioting which Baltimore witnessed in July after the declaration of war or perhaps Cheverus had glimpsed a copy of the Baltimore *American* of August 15, 1812, in which Archbishop Carroll had publicly reproved a Protestant sermon with the irate query:

Who would have expected that a minister of the Gospel, instead of endeavoring to calm the violence of passion excited by political contention in this city, would at this time attempt to increase animosity by super-adding the bitterness of Religious invective to the rage of civil disputation?

In any case, Cheverus remarked, "The present distracted state of this country, the shocking scenes . . . induce Dr. Matignon and myself to doubt the propriety of holding our assembly just at this time, and particularly of holding it in your city."[26] But if the council must be held Cheverus suggested that he be represented by an *ad hoc* vicar-general, preferably his "learned, pious, and venerable friend, Dr. Dubourg." He concluded in characteristic candor that he had not forgotten his consecration oath: *Vocatus ad synodum ibo.* "If you order me to come, I must and will obey, but if the above reasons appear to you sufficient to justify dispensing with my attendance, I most humbly and earnestly beg that you will grant me such dispensations."[27]

Carroll, who knew his northern suffragan, found his reasons as sound as Cheverus himself. Baltimore had only to give the word and Boston would come, of that he was certain. It was out of the question to have William Dubourg sit in for Cheverus, since Dubourg was already on his way to Louisiana. Carroll replied at once that no council would be held that November.

Unfortunately, Benedict Flaget was already traveling toward Baltimore before the news of the postponement reached him and Cheverus was most distressed to hear through Flaget's traveling companion, Stephen T. Badin, that the Bishop of Bardstown was somewhat irked at this wild goose chase. Badin hinted, too, that Bishop Egan of Philadelphia favored a meeting, feeling that there were "important matters to be settled." When Cheverus sent his New Year's greetings to Carroll and the *ad multos annos* for his friend's forthcoming birthday that January he explained uncomfortably, "I merely exposed to you my reasons. . . . Had you judged them of no weight, I was ready to go." But he was still of the same opinion, that nothing just then made a council "either necessary or particularly useful." If they were having trouble with the sacrament of matrimony in Kentucky, as Badin suggested, surely the theologians at St. Mary's Seminary could examine the cases and then submit them to the archbishop. "Your decision would become our rule in our respective dioceses," he said. But if Carroll wanted him, Cheverus would come without delay.[28]

He needed no defense as far as Carroll was concerned. Their letters must have crossed, for on December 31 the old prelate had composed a long, chatty letter to his sensible little suffragan, confiding in him some of the problems a metropolitan faced in those trying days. He had been plagued from both sides, by the bishops of Ireland and the vicars apostolic of England, in their current dissensions; each side desiring the approbation of the American hierarchy. While Flaget was in Baltimore Carroll had been treated to all the unpleasant details of that bishop's differences with Badin; Cheverus need not worry that it was merely for the council Flaget had come. As the old year closed the Archbishop of Baltimore was plainly disgruntled and after reading the letter, Cheverus replied at once, offering what sympathetic advice he could respectfully submit:

> I believe with you, that were we even to assemble, we could not with propriety deliver an opinion concerning the unhappy differences between the I.B. and the A.V. All that we can do at such a distance, and with our necessarily imperfect information concerning them, is earnestly to pray G. in his mercy to his Church to bring them to a speedy end.

He went on to say how sorry he was that Badin was at variance with his worthy and amiable bishop. Actually, he was sure, Badin's excited complaints, if they were like the ones he had written to Boston, were only an excess of zeal. The harshness of some of Badin's expressions quite disappeared "in passing through the mild organ of my venerable friend." It was his way of saying that charitable hearts like Matignon's and Carroll's need not remain downcast over Badin's peculiar fervor. As for Flaget and the council, Cheverus wrote:

> I am glad however to find that it was not altogether on account of the Council that the R. R. Bp. of K. came to Baltimore. To go

there myself will certainly be accompanied with real inconvenience, but I beg this consideration have no weight, when you will decide upon this matter . . . my most earnest wish is to shew myself very willing to yield to the opinions & wishes of my R. R. Brethren & above all to yours, Most R. Father. Let me then beg that you will vote & decide for me, send your decision & with heart & soul I shall answer: Amen[29]

Apparently Carroll liked part of the letter from Boston, for when he next wrote to the vicars apostolic of England he told them that the American bishops "did not deem themselves sufficiently informed on the subject . . . to interpose their judgments; which was, I think, wise . . . considering how recent is their standing as prelates of the Church."[30] Flaget's relations with Badin involved more than charity and their dissensions did not end with Flaget's visit to Baltimore. But even though Flaget stayed on there for five months more no council of bishops was convened either that spring or during the rest of the war years.[31] The reluctance of the Bishop of Boston took precedence over any possible advantages the other prelates may have seen in such a meeting.

The matter of the vacant sees was of much greater concern to them all. Carroll said in 1812, "Unless means be found to obtain for ourselves and everywhere else some authority from the Holy Father to fill vacant Sees, and his confinement remain as rigorous as it now is, disorders of great magnitude are to be apprehended."[32] Three years later he was even more worried, telling his friend Plowden, "The See of New York has long been vacant; that of Philadelphia for nine months . . . and N. Orleans stands much in need of one."[33] Cheverus was in Newcastle when he got word that Bishop Egan had died on July 22, 1814. Carroll wrote that "the conditions and distractions of the Church at Philadelphia require immediate attention."[34] Of the three vacancies, that at Philadelphia presented the greatest need for concerted opinion; by 1814 the hierarchy had less reason to fear for New York or New Orleans, since the future of those two dioceses seemed assured.

In 1810 when the last directives from the pope had arrived with Benedict Flaget, Louisiana was given an administrator. Although Charles Nerinckx, whom Rome had named, refused to take the post, Carroll had in 1812 finally persuaded William Dubourg to accept, saying, "In this situation of his Holiness, the difficulties of our communications with him and the necessities of the Church in particular,

I could scarcely take your exceptions into consideration."[35] Dubourg
set out from Baltimore in mid-October "to be Administrator of the
Diocese of Louisiana with all episcopal powers which do not require
episcopal ordination."[36]

New York, too, had a capable administrator in the person of
Anthony Kohlmann, S.J. Furthermore, it was generally anticipated
that as soon as relations with the Holy See were resumed New York
would be given the Sulpician, Ambrose Maréchal, as its second bishop.
It was known in the United States that Concanen had asked Pius VII
to make Maréchal his coadjutor and that the pope "intended to assign
him." Maréchal returned to the United States in 1812 and was generally
considered "worthy of any promotion in the Church." Believing this
measure would be effected, the American bishops were not uneasy
about New York. As for New Orleans, everyone expected that whenever a bishop should prove necessary Dubourg would be named.[37]
But the vacancy created by Michael Egan's death was another matter.

When Carroll notified Cheverus of the Philadelphia vacancy on
August 23, 1814, he said he believed he ought first to consult the
most discreet and experienced priests of that diocese before anything
else was done; yet he wanted Boston's advice. Cheverus agreed
heartily, but, he pointed out that Carroll doubtless recalled that at
the time New York was at issue in 1810 they had all agreed that
Carroll *alone* should make the recommendation for candidates. Cheverus
would like to see the same thing done for Philadelphia, explaining:

> For my part, I am not competent to give my opinion. I am very
> little acquainted with the clergy of Pennsylvania, and I have never
> known exactly what were the difficulties at St. Mary's. . . . What-
> ever we do must be done by letter. The distance and the times do
> not allow of any other mode. But the best mode would be that the
> Venerable Father of the American Church should alone recommend
> whomever in his wisdom he will think most likely to restore peace
> to the distracted church of Philadelphia.[38]

In September of 1814 no one would quarrel with Cheverus' opinion
that the times allowed no other mode than an exchange of letters.
The day after Carroll wrote his letter the British had reached Bladens-
burg in the outskirts of the federal capital. The President had fled
to the woods, leaving his dinner uneaten on the White House table.
On September 12 the British under General Robert Ross were headed
for Baltimore and for a week the metropolitan see city heroically defended itself in "an awful spectacle to behold." The archbishop who was

nearly eighty exclaimed, "Heaven preserve us from another such visitation."[39]

In Cheverus' domain things were scarcely better. Cape Cod was ravaged at Falmouth, Wareham, and Orleans. One Sunday at Salem William Bentley's sermon was interrupted by shouts of, "The British fleet is chasing the *Constitution* into Marblehead!" and the minister had dashed from his church with the others to tug the cannon into position to defend the town.[40] Up in Maine Father Romagné was right in the midst of the British among his Penobscot Indians, and the Passamaquoddies. The British were only on the eastern side of the Penobscot River in which the island of Old Town lay and they were as polite to the Catholic priest there as were the officers and commander at Passamaquoddy. "Neither he nor his Indians have been disturbed," Cheverus told Carroll gratefully.[41]

Cheverus himself kept to his schedule of visits that fall, determined not to leave the Damariscotta mission until September 18. "Otherwise," he argued, "it would be said here, not in jest, but in earnest, that fear caused me to leave earlier; for the people really believe themselves very exposed to the enemy."[42] But when Romagné arrived in Newcastle the bishop persuaded him to come to Boston for a while. The two came by land this time, because Cheverus still meant to stop at Portland and Portsmouth on the way. The rueful bishop wondered at his own precautions for his confrere, once they got home.

Boston that September was beside itself with rage and fear. The rage was for the Federal Government which had taken all the soldiers from her fortifications, leaving the town to defend herself as best she could; the fear was for the attack from the British which was momentarily expected. Paul Revere, a patriot from an earlier defense against the same enemy, was as determined at seventy-nine as he ever was four decades ago that Boston should resist and his name headed the list of Mechanics of the Town of Boston who were now helping "by manual labor in measures for the Defence of the Town and Naval Arsenal."[43] The Bishop of Boston had not the same motives for resisting the British, but he loved Boston as much as any man. Although so lately returned he rounded up 250 of his congregation and side by side with his flock he spent September 27 shoveling and carrying sods in a wheel barrow on Dorchester Heights, while across the way he could see Dr. John Lothrop with his deacons and elders engaged in the same strenuous and frantic work of fortification.[44] There was no larger group at work that day than the men from Holy Cross Parish. Later Charles Bulfinch, speaking for the Selectmen of Boston, thanked them for their voluntary aid for the defense of the town and harbor.[45] But the bishop was even more prompt with his own gratitude and wrote on September 28 to Paul Revere and Son,

> Bishop Cheverus presents his compliments to Messers P. Revere & Son and thanks them for having permitted the men in their employ to work yesterday with him at the fortifications, and for generally allowing them their usual wages as if they had been working for him.[46]

It was not until the panic had subsided and Father Romagné had returned to Maine to spend the winter with the Kavanaghs in New-castle that the Bishop of Boston could reply to the letter written in Baltimore the day he was occupied on Dorchester Heights.

The difficulties Cheverus mentioned in his first letter on the sub-ject of Philadelphia were so confusing it was small wonder that he did not understand them. They dated back to the very accession of Bishop Egan and centered around William Vincent Harold, the Dominican who preached so effectively at Cheverus' consecration. It is not necessary to go into the details of the schism which ensued, but many people believed that Egan's death had been hastened by the troubles in St. Mary's Parish. Leonard Neale, Carroll's coadjutor, re-plied to Carroll's first inquiry in August as speedily as Cheverus, convinced that the disturbed state of the Church in Philadelphia re-quired "an immediate despatch in the business as may possibly be." Like Cheverus, he refrained from making any suggestions as to actual candidates for the see.[47]

Without waiting for a reply from Flaget in Bardstown, Carroll then forwarded to the bishops the recommendations of the clergy he had consulted by September 27. Two names seemed to have the prefer-ence: John Baptist David of Kentucky and William Valentine Dubourg of Louisiana. The only obstacle Carroll saw to these two was, in David's case "the difficulty of removing him from the good Bishop of Bardstown," and in Dubourg's the doubtful propriety of selecting a man who had been acting as an administrator of a diocese immediately dependent upon the pope. Of the two, Dubourg would probably be more willing to accept Philadelphia since he was not happy in Louisiana. Carroll himself then added two other possibilities to the list: Demetrius Gallitzin and Michael Hurley, but the archbishop admitted the former had the handicap of a great load of debts and the latter that of youth.[48]

When Cheverus replied to these suggestions he said at the outset that he recommended whatever two candidates Carroll most approved. "I think myself secure and right in following your Grace," he re-iterated. But he knew the archbishop wanted his reactions and so he gave them. If David's removal were to cause harm to Kentucky, then he thought it "hardly right to benefit Philadelphia at the expense of another Diocese." Dubourg, on the other hand, faced many obstacles where he was and it would not surprise Cheverus if Louisiana were again given back to Spain, who had once administered it. It was very doubtful if Dubourg would be made a bishop where he was right away. As for Gallitzin, the fact that he was heavily in debt ruled him out as far as the thrifty Bishop of Boston was concerned; Hurley, he knew, was "obnoxious" to many of the Philadelphia Catho-lics and it was to be feared that his appointment would not "produce the desired union." Therefore, Cheverus concluded, Dubourg and David in that order should be proposed to His Holiness.[49]

Flaget was even more prompt in replying. His letter of October 10 protested bitterly against the nomination of his chief support in Kentucky. "To make a man a bishop," he said, thinking of himself, "with no priests is a kind of cruelty."[50] As a matter of fact, Flaget asserted, until the United States had more priests no more bishops were needed. Carroll relayed his views to Bishops Neale and Cheverus and to the administrators of New York and Philadelphia. Anthony Kohlmann and Louis DeBarth, "who thought differently." Carroll then sent to Rome triplicate letters in November naming Dubourg and David as candidates for Philadelphia.[51]

Flaget was furious and continued to voice his opposition. In a letter of July 21, 1815, he accused the archbishop of not consulting him. Carroll had only a few more months to live but he retorted in his usually vigorous, yet considered fashion. "Have you then forgot," he inquired pointedly, "both my letter to you on the subject and your answer?" Flaget *had* been consulted and had declined to nominate any one. Carroll continued:

> If I can find Dr. Cheverus' letter, which is preserved, before this goes to the post-office, you shall receive an extract of his remarks on your opinion. Besides the general necessity of preserving the succession of episcopacy in the vacant See, he was influenced by

a view of the unfortunate divisions subsisting in the Church of
Philadelphia, which manifested themselves before good Bishop Egan's
death. The same motives acted on others, who were to concur in
the nomination. . . . Was it to be supposed, after your first answer
. . . that I could wait to refer back to you the discussion with you
. . . and thus protract a decision of any measure towards settling the
Diocese of Pennsylvania?[52]

Although the Cheverus letter referred to was lost to both the archbishop and subsequent historians, Carroll appears to have found it
convincing enough at the time he read it. Once again it was the
Bishop of Boston's judgment which was closest to the thinking of
the Archbishop of Baltimore.

Meanwhile the war with England had come to an end; perhaps
the worst days were past. In February the nation learned the news
of the signing of the Treaty of Ghent, and everywhere there were
fireworks and illuminations. In Boston the bells began to ring right
after breakfast on February 13 and soon the whole town was in an
uproar. Almost every house had a flag out and people set out in
sleighs or on foot to roam the snowy streets shouting happily, "Peace,
peace, peace!" Sleds full of sailors were greeted with deafening hurrahs;
the Navy had won the war. "Ladies were running about the streets
as if they did not know what they were doing, the gentlemen shaking
hands and wishing each other joy. All this time bells were ringing,
canon firing, and drums beating."[53] Over in Franklin Street the little
bishop was as elated as the rest. "It is certainly a happy event," he
said, "and ought to inspire the inhabitants of this country with lively
gratitude to God who grants this great favor as by a miracle."[54] At
Holy Cross they had a way of showing their gratitude for favors; the
Bishop of Boston and his flock would sing one more *Te Deum*
together.

CHAPTER XII

LOSSES AND GAINS

WHILE concerns outside his diocese were strengthening the bonds between the Bishop of Boston and his metropolitan, and while common deprivation and danger drew him closer to his fellow Bostonians, Cheverus plodded the same paths so well worn before the mantle of the episcopacy was laid upon his shoulders. His modest two-story "episcopal palace" was sometimes more crowded than formerly, and the one room that served as his bedroom, reception room, and study drew affectionate complaints from the visitors who were compelled to sit on the bed in lieu of chairs. But as at Tottenham, his house always had room for one more.

Holy Cross did not change either. Briefly, on his return from the Penobscot Indians in 1811, Cheverus enjoyed finding in the sanctuary four Spanish Capuchin friars who had been banished from South America by the revolutionary Miranda, and a Trappist, Father Eugene, all in their religious habits. At the same time Father Michael Hurley from Philadelphia was there and preached a sermon very much admired.[1] For a fleeting moment the small church took on the atmosphere of a cathedral.

These were only passing guests, of course. But in May the next year, as Cheverus was preparing to go to Maine, the Reverend Dr. Matthew O'Brien arrived, "disposed to spend the summer" in Boston. Cheverus wrote happily to Carroll:

> It will be a great relief to my mind that my dear and venerable friend Dr. Matignon has with him an amiable companion and zealous cooperator. In our conversation in Baltimore and in a letter since you seemed to expect Dr. O'Brien would come to us, therefore I doubt not that his being here meets with your full approval.[2]

O'Brien stayed much longer than a summer, as it turned out. Aside from a few months in New York at the end of that year, and again in the spring of 1814, he lingered in the Diocese of Boston until the war was over.

At first O'Brien worked in Boston where he busied himself "making out Sermons en Regle in order to do these folks as much good as possible."[3] Father Matignon still deplored his own preaching and was delighted to have a substitute while the bishop was away on his visitations. When Cheverus was in residence O'Brien cheerfully went to Salem to a congregation so poor he had to pay his own stage fare most of the time.[4] For Salem Catholics it was the start of a new era. Cheverus had been able to stop only occasionally on his journeys back from Maine. He had gone there, naturally, his first year as bishop to confer Confirmation and William Bentley, who watched these Catholic developments with a kindly eye, noted in his diary on April 30, 1811, that it was the first time a Catholic bishop had ever pontificated in his town. Any preaching Cheverus did in Salem in the old days was done in houses like Campbell's in Daniels Street, or Kenelly's in Herbert Street.[5]

After O'Brien had been with them a year in Franklin Street Cheverus decided to make him a resident pastor at Salem, where on special feast days the size of the congregation now led the Catholics to worship in the court house.[6] It soon began to appear that they might even have a church of their own. Father O'Brien told Archbishop Carroll on May 15, 1814:

> A lot of ground is already bought at Salem, and the slender congregation of that place . . . will thrive and become expanded. The confused situation of a chamber (for church services) shocks the prejudice of many, and many declare that had we a public church, they would purchase pews and become incorporated with us.[7]

He was using his trip to New York, on which Cheverus had sent him for the purpose of bringing holy oils to the vacant see, for an opportunity to collect money for a church building.[8]

While Cheverus was in the northern mission that summer O'Brien stayed with Matignon in Boston, all hopes of going to Baltimore on a collection tour blasted by the developments of the war. But after Christmas was past Father O'Brien began to revive his plans for a southern journey.[9] He never returned to Salem, for death called the priest who had received Mother Seton into the Church, and Matthew O'Brien died in Baltimore on October 20, 1815.[10]

O'Brien was not the only clerical newcomer during the war years. In the fall of 1812 Father Francis Xavier Brosius left his school at Mount Airy near Philadelphia to come to Boston. Although Brosius was "no help in the ministry," as Cheverus put it, it was pleasant to have another priest in the area, especially one of such cultivated talents. The Alsatian priest, who had come to the United States with Demetrius Gallitzin, in the same year that Francis Matignon had arrived, was a natural scientist and mathematician. While he stayed in Boston he not only taught mathematics but also edited and published Cavallo's *Elements of Natural and Experimental Philosophy* and *A new and concise method of finding the latitude by double altitudes of the Sun.*[11]

Father Brosius did not live at the Franklin Street residence since several members of his family were with him in Boston. Cheverus did the best he could to get pupils for the ailing priest and told Carroll in December, 1812, "The good & amiable Mr. Brosius has got a few young men whom he gives lessons of Mathematicks. I begin to hope he may be enabled to remain with us. What a pity his health is so precarious."[12] It was not much more than a year later that Cheverus announced, "Mr. Brosius has been approved by the University of Cambridge as a Teacher of Mathematicks & he is going to reside near the College. He has now got 38 scholars who are to pay him 10 Dlls. per quarter."[13]

It might have astonished the founders of Harvard if they had been told in the seventeenth century that one day a Catholic priest was to be associated with the faculty of their college, but it caused no stir in academic circles in 1814. President John Thornton Kirkland the year before had shown which way the intellectual winds were blowing when in his Dudleian Lecture he asserted:

> We may therefore naturally abate much of that abhorrence of papists which our fathers felt themselves obliged to maintain and inculcate . . . ; and we may be allowed . . . to admit the possible, nay, more, the presumptive, Christianity of a virtuous and devout Roman Catholic. . . .[14]

Kirkland was much more concerned with shaping the college to the pattern of a university, and with raising the standards of instruction. Good mathematicians were not easy to find, and Brosius came highly recommended by Cheverus whose own reputation for learning was unquestioned. Perhaps it was more than sheer coincidence that a few weeks after the bishop's display of patriotic energy at the Dorchester fortifications Kirkland and the Fellows of Harvard again voted the bishop's friend $100 a month as private instructor to scholars who were excused from regular classes at the college providing they appeared for "Reviews" and final examinations in the subject.[15] Be that as it may, Brosius continued his Harvard connection until the war was over.

Meanwhile, Cheverus had made another friend whose connection with the college proved longer-lived. Early in 1814 the Brattle Street Unitarian Church installed young Edward Everett, a recent graduate of Harvard, as pastor. When the newly created chair of Greek literature was offered him by his Alma Mater Everett determined to go to Europe for further study in that connection and he went off in the spring of 1815 with every proof of Cheverus' affection. Not only did the bishop give him the addresses of all his relatives in Paris, Laval, Ernée, and Mayenne; but he composed as well a graceful testimonial in Latin to recommend Everett to scholarly circles abroad. Cheverus told Everett on April 14:

> I join with all who know you, and all who love *belles lettres* to wish you a happy trip. It could be that in the University of Paris you may find some of my former fellow-students, even perhaps some of my former masters. They could not give me more agreeable proof of their remembrance than to show you friendship's respect. As soon as they know you they will not need my recommendation to feel these sentiments in your regard.

He concluded exuberantly, "Happy voyage, many compliments, farewell!"[16]

While Father Brosius was busy with his pupils in Cambridge, and Everett was acquiring a doctorate in Europe, the Bishop of Boston himself was concerned with educational affairs. It would be pretentious to talk of the foundation of a diocesan seminary during the war years unless a single seminarian makes a school. Yet the arrival of Dennis Ryan in 1814 had its significance, and marked a beginning however modest. When Cheverus mentioned this arrival to Carroll he described the former prisoner of war as a young Irishman of twenty-eight who had studied divinity and philosophy a year at Carlow College in Ireland.

> He is of mild manners, & appears sincerely pious. I have written to Kilkenny for an *Exeat* & if I receive it accompanied with proper testimonies in his favour, after some time I will ordain him. His talents are not brilliant, but I hope he may prove a useful assistant

to my venerable friend particularly when I am from Boston. He was bound to Quebec, was taken by a privateer & brought here last October.[17]

While he was not catechizing or attending the priests during the administration of the sacraments young Ryan continued his studies in the Franklin Street rectory. Perhaps he would prove to be the first priest ordained for Boston. God knew Matignon and Cheverus had cherished enough false hopes in the Kavanagh and Cottrill sons, and the few others who had briefly entertained thoughts of a clerical vocation.[18] When the two Kavanaghs left that spring, after spending the whole winter at Franklin Street, it seemed to Cheverus that all prospects fled with them. Only a miracle could preserve the vocation which Edward's tonsure in Baltimore the year before had seemed to confirm.[19] The advent of Dennis Ryan reminded the little prelate that the ways of divine Providence were in truth inscrutable.

What of the tender heart now beating beneath a bishop's robes? The first five years of Cheverus' reign proved it only more susceptible. Scarcely had he returned from his consecration when sorrow struck in the death of his beloved spiritual daughter, Anne de Neuville Linzee. Fever and infection following on the birth of her little daughter caused the death of Mrs. Linzee after less than two years of marriage. Cheverus had the painful task of burying her on January 29, 1811, and he confessed to Carroll that he was overwhelmed with grief.[20] "We know that you loved and esteemed her; you will mingle your tears with ours," he told the old archbishop who was godfather to Mrs. Linzee's young sister Louisa.[21] It was even more painful to write to the unsuspecting husband who was in Russia, doubtlessly anticipating the return voyage which should reunite him with his young wife and infant daughter.

Archbishop Carroll sympathized with his New England suffragan and sent little Louisa Stoughton a rosary with the instruction that she should use it to pray for her sister. Cheverus replied gratefully, "She and her dear Parents beg to be remembered to you in a most tender and respectful manner. Your kind sympathy for their and *My* loss is certainly a real consolation to our afflicted hearts."[22] Ashamed as he was of his weakness, Cheverus could neither overcome nor disguise his profound grief. In the months that followed he and the Stoughtons drew closer together than ever and his letters to Baltimore carried more frequent references to the consul, Mrs. Stoughton, and Carroll's "dear God-daughter,"

Although he never ceased to mourn the "Angelic daughter" who died so young, Cheverus found in these years a son to whom his expansive affections could cling for the rest of the bishop's life. Like Anne Linzee, the Marquis Jean-Vernou de Bonneuil was a spiritual child indescribably precious to the bishop who explained, "My dear Son, Religion has formed the sacred bonds of our friendship. They will be indissoluble. I will love you on earth to my last sigh, and I hope in God's mercy we shall love each other forever in Heaven."[23] Like Anne, too, Vernou was truly a child of Cheverus in the Church. The young marquis was not a practicing Catholic when the bishop met him, and was convinced that a man of the world had little time for pious devotions when his fortunes lay in ruins about him. During Lent of 1814 Cheverus succeeded in drawing Vernou back to his faith and from that moment on he never abandoned his paternal solicitude for the marquis and his growing family. When little Adé de Bonneuil was born on April 19 Cheverus considered himself a grandfather; as soon as she could toddle Adé had the run of "Nan-pa's" house. Her parents remained "Son" and "Daughter" to Cheverus until he died.

No matter how busy the bishop was, at home or on the mission, he found time to console and to advise these spiritual children. The marquis found his first months back in the fold filled with compunctions and dissatisfactions, and his letters pursued Cheverus to Maine. Cheverus wrote back from Whitefield on August 1:

> Expect inquietude, desolate thoughts, &c. doubts, &c. Do not let that discourage you. Have recourse to Him whose mercy you have experienced and who never abandons those who put their hope in Him. Remember that doubts which are rejected, coldness you experience, are proofs (sometimes meritorious), but not sins. You love God when you are afflicted for not loving him and still serve him faithfully.[24]

Bonneuil was very discouraged about the family's material welfare and talked of going to Guadeloupe to try to recoup some of their fortunes there. Cheverus was most anxious to see his "son" before he sailed and hoped even to travel to Providence with him if he could get back from Maine in time. Meanwhile he exhorted Bonneuil to go to Matignon as he would to Cheverus himself. "I experience with him," he wrote, "always the truth of the Scripture verse: 'A faithful friend is a strong support and he who has found one has found a treasure.' "[25] He enclosed $200 for Bonneuil's voyage.

In spite of his desire to hurry back to Boston the bishop fulfilled his scheduled duties in Newcastle and the other settlements in the Damariscotta Valley. He had to wait for Father Romagné to come over from his Indian mission; if he did not see his colleague in September, it might be another year before they would see each other. He had promised a poor widow that he would find a buyer for her horse, and the bishop kept his promises. Luck was with him in the end. Bonneuil was still in Boston when Cheverus returned with Romagné. It was the autumn of the invasion scare and no man was reckless enough to try to escape to the high seas and the West Indies just then. When the marquis finally embarked in December he had to meet his vessel some miles from shore, but his father in God stood on the shore waving a loving farewell.[26] Bonneuil need have no worries about the family he left behind in Brookline. Cheverus had already made it quite clear that the purse of the Bishop of Boston belonged to his son, his daughter, and his grandchild. Félicie de Bonneuil was scolded for fretting over the money he had already advanced them. "We are rich enough, my dear child, to do without these remittances," he assured her. "You know very well without explanation that the heart, the purse, etc. of your Papa are yours. . . ."[27] He was not rich at all, of course. But with the simple confidence of a heart such as his he accepted without surprise the unexpected arrival shortly afterward of a remittance from his brother Louis of an amount remarkably like that he had given his spiritual son.[28]

While Vernou de Bonneuil was in Guadeloupe the bishop continued his loving supervision of the little family left behind. He saw Félicie and the children safely installed in the Walley home in Brookline, paid off some of their debts, making it appear that the marquis had delegated the bishop to do so, bought "an elegant chaise" for Félicie to give the Walleys as a token of Bonneuil's appreciation toward their hosts, and consoled the separated husband and wife by reassuring notes whenever he could find a minute for quill and ink.[29] On the rare occasions when he could dine in Brookline he went to the Walley house; more often he got his glimpses of little Adé, her mother, and the Walleys at Holy Cross, or across his own dinner table in Franklin Street. There was no more exquisite pleasure than coming home to the crowded room that served all his purposes and finding the darling "grand-daughter" on his bed, waiting for a romp before dinner. If the father could return, Cheverus wrote fondly, "We will all be rich and happy."

His was a faithful heart, as well as a fond one. Mother Seton was never forgotten during the harrowing years of depression and war; Cheverus continued to console and strengthen her as she passed through a succession of almost insurmountable difficulties. After their meeting in 1810 scarcely a letter arrived from Emmitsburg without some plea for advice. Differences of opinion with her superiors, proposals to alter the rules of her community, financial woes, the death of her first-born daughter, finding a place for her eldest son, these and other less painful problems all arrived at the bishop's door. Cheverus had told her when she first went to Emmitsburg that her trials and difficulties were "the stamp of divine favour and protection" upon her community. "Remember St. Theresa, St. Frances Chantal, etc. Like them, I hope you will become saints and mothers of saints."[30] If trials were the mark of favor, she seemed singularly blessed in the years that followed, at least in Cheverus' eyes.

He had heard something of her worries over new rules for the community while he was in Emmitsburg, both from Dubois and from herself. He knew that Benedict Flaget had brought from France together with the bulls for the consecrations a copy of the rules of the Sisters of Charity of St. Vincent de Paul. Mother Seton anticipated that some French sisters would soon follow in the wake of the French rules. Cheverus understood her dismay at the possibility of radical changes so soon after the founding of her group and his first advice was prompted by his sympathy for his "very dear Sister" and respect for John Dubois. In January, 1811, he told her:

> I concur in opinion with Mr. Dubois about the propriety of your establishment remaining independent from the Sisters of Charity, and continuing to be merely a house of education for young females. I believe that you could without any impropriety & without disturbing your peace, express in an humble manner your opinion & wishes to the Most Rev. Archbishop & your other Superiors, particularly if you are authorized to say that you do it with your respectable director's advice. . . . Have another conversation with the Rev. Mr. Dubois on the subject & then do with simplicity what he will prescribe or even wish.[31]

Once the question of rules for her community was settled, and Dubois became the superior of the Emmitsburg community of women delicacy compelled Cheverus to refrain from further comment. "Upon this topic or any other concerning the government of your house," he explained to Mother Seton, "It does not become me, nor indeed am

I able to offer any advice." The Archbishop of Baltimore, the Sulpician superior in Baltimore, and Father Dubois in Emmitsburg were now jointly responsible for her decisions and Cheverus was confident they would extricate her from all her difficulties.[32] His own brotherly recommendations were reserved for more personal distress.

When an anguished note in December, 1811, told him of her fear that her daughter Annina was mortally ill, Cheverus shared Mother Seton's dreadful anxiety, replying at once, "I am every day with you at the bedside of *our* dear Anna. I cry with you, I rejoice with you, I pray with you and the dear child." It was terrible to think that they were so poor in the midst of such sorrow. In 1812 debts seemed to be overwhelming every establishment. He could only say:

> I am much grieved at the troubles you are in, and the more so because I do not see how you will be extricated from them. Yourself to leave your house and travel to make collections, etc. does not appear to me an eligible plan, although it would procure me the happiness of seeing you in Boston.

As things were, a collection would bring in nothing, and a circular letter little more. He would write to Antonio Filicchi at the first opportunity, but communication with Italy was virtually nonexistent. "Did I possess the means," Cheverus explained, "How happy I would be to come to your help!" But those were the years when not a word reached Boston from Louis de Cheverus, and when the bishop could not raise even ten dollars toward expenses for a trip to Baltimore. He marveled at her courage and wrote to Bruté in Baltimore, *"Mère admirable! Fille heureuse!* What an impression must she not make on the young students with the miracles of grace and the sanctity to which she witnesses."[33]

In February when he learned that Annina was entering her last struggle he tried to console Mother Seton. "I bless the God of infinite mercy who has granted her to die the death of saints, and has endowed her dear mother with the faith and courage of the Mother of the Macabees, of St. Symphronicus." He would have been there with them, if he could. He urged Mother Seton to send him all the "details of the delightful things" when she had time, hoping her grief could be assuaged by contemplating the beauty of Annina's death.[34]

This once his words seem to have had little effect for Anna Marie Seton's death on March 12, 1812, was followed by two years during which no letters passed between Emmitsburg and Boston; or, if they were written, they were not preserved. Whether it stemmed from the hazards of wartime correspondence, or was the result of the period of spiritual aridity Mother Seton entered that year of Annina's untimely death, the close bonds between the Bishop of Boston and his beloved "Sister" elude the gaze of history. It can only be said that on April 12, 1814, Cheverus began his letter, "It is an age since I have heard from you," and concluded with the admonition, "I want a speedy reply."[35]

There is no question that the friendship ever altered. Once the correspondence was resumed Cheverus was as deeply involved in her concerns as ever. In November, 1814, Mother Seton asked for news of the Filicchis, hoping she might send them her son William now that the war in Europe was past. Cheverus could only say the Italian brothers had recently published a notice in the American gazettes advising their friends that they were resuming their commercial relations. The notice bore the date of July causing him to believe that both brothers were well and doing well by this time. The bishop had more certain news for her on another subject. A relative by marriage of one of Mother Seton's community had become a fervent convert. "I gave him confirmation & the Blessed Sacrament for the first time the 23d of last October," he wrote. "His dear wife has always been a pattern of amiable piety. They have got nine lovely children. . . . Mr. & Mrs. Walley are our very intimate & dear friends." Could Mother Seton send some news of Mrs. Walley's cousin, and the son who was at Mount Saint Mary's College? Mrs. Walley had never received any reply to her own letter to Mme Guerin. As for the Setons, Cheverus assured her, "Every day I beseech the author of all blessings to continue to bless you & your dear children. Even your dear sons will be preserved in spite of the dangers & temptations of the world. The children of so many prayers & tears cannot perish."[36]

Hope flourished everywhere as 1815 began. For the first time in two years Cheverus had letters from Mayenne and he replied joyfully, "Blessed be the God of Mercy who has given you peace and replaced on the throne the descendant of Saint-Louis, Henry IV, and the brother of the holy martyr, our good King Louis XVI!" Only another Frenchman could understand his satisfaction in learning that the man he had venerated since his school days was now on the throne as Louis XVIII. "Today, more than ever," Cheverus admitted to his brother, "it would be sweet to fly to your arms."[37]

In Baltimore the eighty-year old archbishop forgot for a moment his impatience that official relations with Rome had not yet been re-established and rejoiced for Jesuits everywhere over the recent restoration of their society. He told his faithful correspondent in England, Charles Plowden:

> You, who know Rome, may conceive my sensations, when I read
> . . . of the celebration of Mass by his Holiness himself at the superb
> altar of St. Ignatius at the Gesu, the assemblage of surviving Jesuits
> in the chapel to hear the proclamation of their resurrection, the
> decree for the restitution . . . . of the Novitiate of St. Andrew, its
> most enchanting church, and the lovely monument & chapel of St.
> Stanislaus, which I fondly hope, have escaped the fangs of rapine
> and devastation.[38]

In Emmitsburg, without waiting for verification of the peace between the United States and Britain, Mother Seton resolved to send William to Italy. She was confident Bishop Cheverus would approve when he learned who was to escort her son. On March 9 Father Bruté wrote from Maryland that he was going to France that spring and would take young Seton with him. Cheverus was pleased with all aspects of the trip. He first congratulated Bruté on his appointment as head of St. Mary's College in Baltimore and then continued, "Dear William is very fortunate to have a protector like you." He begged the Sulpician priest to act and speak in Cheverus' name on all occasions when it might help. His heart leaped at the very thought of Bruté's visiting the Cheverus family in any of its branches. He wrote down all the familiar addresses and appended a similar note for Mother Seton.[39] In less than a month Father Bruté and his young charge were aboard the *Tontine* in New York, waiting a favorable wind for France.[40]

Both Louisiana and New York anticipated happier days with the ending of the war. William Dubourg, the administrator of the former diocese, determined to go to Europe to search for recruits for his mission; Father Benedict Fenwick, Kohlmann's successor in New York, resolved to wait no longer for a bishop to fill that see and invited Cheverus to come to dedicate the new cathedral. St. Patrick's was completed save for some minor exterior decoration, and since no Bishop of New York had arrived in the past five years it appeared senseless to delay the ceremonies any longer. The archbishop's age and health had long since necessitated calling upon Cheverus for episcopal services. It was thus on Father Fenwick's invitation and at Archbishop Carroll's command that Bishop Cheverus started for New York.[41]

The ceremonies at St. Patrick's on Ascension Day made quite a stir in New York and the papers reported:

> The ceremony of the dedication, with the solemn service of High Mass was solemn and impressive, the Rt. Rev. consecrator, after the gospel of the day was sung delivered from the altar with his usual sprightly eloquence an appropriate address from the words of the forty-fifth, alias forty-sixth Psalm, eighth verse; "I have loved O Lord the beauty of thy house, and the place where thy glory dwelleth," to his numerous, admiring, and attentive audience.[42]

The cathedral was New York's proudest boast, of course; "no church in the United States . . . can compare with it." It was built in Gothic style after the design of Joseph Mangin, the city's most celebrated architect, and for months crowds of citizens "daily flocked to admire its grandeur and magnificence." It was believed capable of holding 6000 people and on the day of the dedication certainly two thirds of that number were present, including "the best families of New York," the members of the city council, present and former mayors, and many other officers of distinction.[43] The crowd in the street was so dense that Cheverus was forced to omit the aspersion around the walls on the outside.[44]

Inside, six clustered columns divided the church into three naves each crowned with a Gothic arch, and these columns and arches were reproduced in perspective by painting of the walls. The illusion thus created in the viewers a belief that "the altar is placed at only half the length of the church, although it is really at the very end."[45] Three spacious aisles separated the pews with their mahogany armrests, and remarkably large windows provided fine lighting for the ceremonies that May day. It was a pity that Anthony Kohlmann, who had done so much to make this edifice possible, could not be there that Thursday. But Cheverus missed one other presence even more and wrote to his beloved archbishop, "I regret it was not in your power to come. Your presence would have added much to the solemnity and joy of the day." The Bishop of Boston was splendidly enough accompanied during the dedication, having not only the three regular priests of New York, but two visiting Jesuits from Maryland: Father Francis Malevé from Frederick and Father J. B. Pasquet from Bohemia. Cheverus told Archbishop Carroll:

I dedicated the Church in the same manner you did in Boston. We all did our best to make this a truly impressive ceremony. The Fathers desire that all the rites prescribed in the Pontifical may be performed. This I shall go through tomorrow, *privatim et januis clausis.*[46]

Cheverus was deeply impressed by the noble beauty of St. Patrick's and enjoyed following the ritual to the last letter. But after the public and private rites were over he found himself oppressed by the tumult of his thoughts. On the way to New York he had learned of Napoleon's escape from Elba and a thousand doubts crowded his mind. What would happed to Simon Bruté and his young charge? Where were Edward Everett and William Dubourg; would their ships be forced to return? What would now happen to the Cheverus relatives who had rejoiced so few months earlier over the restoration of the Bourbons? And poor Father Romagné! Ever since the defeat of Bonaparte the good Indian missionary had talked longingly of returning to France. Cheverus commented soberly to Carroll:

I know your heart has bled at the late astonishing & terrible event. How uncertain everything which belongs to this world! But in the midst of its frequent & tremendous vicissitudes the truth & the Church of the Lord remain forever. I was on my way here when I heard the astounding news. It overpowered me.[47]

More immediately he was worried by the acute shortage of priests in New York. It was obvious that three priests could not serve the two churches, St. Peter's of Barclay Street and the new cathedral. Unless Father Fenwick got some added assistants he could not stand his responsibilities much longer. As a temporary measure Cheverus prevailed upon Father Malevé to remain for a while, and then distressed by his own meddling he wrote hastily to Malevé's superior in Georgetown, "I have taken upon me to command him in your name to wait here for your orders." He hoped John Grassi would forgive his presumption; the needs of New York and Malevé's health, he admitted, were his only excuses.[48]

At the importunings of Benedict Fenwick, Peter Malou, and Maximilian Rantzau, the three regular priests of the city, Bishop Cheverus agreed to stay on in New York until Whitsunday to confer confirmation, and in the interim Father Fenwick received a letter from Archbishop Carroll that destroyed the last shreds of serenity Cheverus enjoyed. Baltimore had received rumors from Europe that Irish and

French prelates had presumed to interfere in the nomination of bishops for the vacant American sees and that an Irish Dominican was already consecrated for New York. After all the American hierarchy had gone through to decide upon Dubourg and David, after all their confidence that Maréchal was to have New York, it was more than a little irritating. It was of slight import that the meddling prelates were said to be the saintly Archbishop d'Aviau of Bordeaux and Carroll's friend, Archbishop Troy of Dublin. Cheverus wrote heatedly to his old friend in Baltimore:

> It is certainly astonishing that the Prelates in France or Ireland should recommend subjects for the Mission here and be listened to rather than you and those you are pleased to consult. We must only pray that everything may work for good. Had I received the news last week I would never have consented to give confirmation here but . . . Rev. Mr. Fenwick and his Rev. brethren insist on my not disappointing them. Next Tuesday I shall leave for Boston.[49]

He only hoped the new Dominican Bishop of New York duly appreciated the treasure he possessed in the Jesuits who served that city! The Bishop of Boston knew what he thought: "Father Fenwick in particular is the object of universal respect and love. His zeal, piety & talents need not my praise. His praise is in the hearts of all who know him. He is I sincerely believe *dilectus Deo & hominibus.*"

After his arrival in Boston on May 18 Cheverus regretted his outburst of the week before, and tempered the sympathy with which he wrote to Carroll. "I am afraid His Holiness is not sensible of the real state of our missions," he offered. "It is to be expected that the new Bishop of New York will visit you and ask your advice, and I cherish the hope that we shall be affectionate brothers of one mind, and always look upon your Grace as our head and guide."[50] The Bishop of Boston reminded himself that it was unbecoming to a Christian to resent injustice, real or imaginary. They did not know the new bishop nor had they been consulted on his appointment; but they were all brothers in the episcopacy and Cheverus was determined that they should be of one mind and heart once the Bishop of New York arrived. When he mentioned the news to Bishop Plessis of Quebec the same day he said simply, "They expect daily the most Rev. John Connolly consecrated at Rome Bishop of New York last November. He is a Dominican and lived thirty-seven years in Rome."[51]

June brought events whose news soon dispelled the swarm of

anxieties that had plagued Cheverus in May. On a muddy field near Waterloo the 100 Days of Napoleon Bonaparte came to an end, leading that least vindictive of men, Matignon, to exclaim, "If they don't give Bonaparte the place he deserves in the Tower of London between the tigers and lions, at least they will take measures so that his claws and fangs do no more harm!"[52] In June, too, young William Seton passed safely through France on his way to the Filicchis in Leghorn. For Cheverus and the other bishops the best news came from Baltimore with Carroll's announcement that he had at long last received a direct communication from the Holy See; the long years of rupture were over. Lorenzo Cardinal Litta, the Prefect of Propaganda, confirmed the rumors of Bishop Connolly's nomination, it was true; but his letter made clear that the Holy See had never received from Carroll and his suffragans their recommendations of November, 1814. The See of Philadelphia would not be filled without the approval of the Archbishop of Baltimore.[53] With the autumn's news that Dubourg had been consecrated in Rome for the Diocese of Louisiana the most critical years seem to have passed.[54]

CHAPTER XIII

TROUBLED WATERS

On November 20, 1815, the *Blooming Rose* arrived in New York from Bordeaux with Father Bruté and letters from the Bishop of Boston's family in France. Michelle George de la Massonnais, Louis de Cheverus, the Vigeries had all been "enchanted and edified" when Bruté visited them with news of their episcopal brother and cousin in America. Bruté brought, too, very consoling news from Italy, having talked in Bordeaux with the recently consecrated Bishop of Louisiana; Bishop Dubourg had seen William Seton in Leghorn where the Filicchis were very pleased with him; he hinted to Bruté that Philadelphia was soon to have a bishop. When Cheverus wrote to Bruté that December he was hoping that by spring the new Bishop of Philadelphia and Dubourg might arrive in the United States together.

Then he turned to the subject uppermost in all minds that Advent. "What a pity," he wrote sadly, "The crown and glory of our episcopate in the United States is in a state of infirmity. We pray every Sunday and recite every day at the collect of the Mass for our venerable father. Give me news of him. I throw myself at his feet and beg his benedictions."[1] Archbishop Carroll had been eighty years old the last time Cheverus wished him *ad multos annos,* and those who knew him well realized how feeble his health must be to cause Carroll to decline the invitation to speak in July at the dedication of the new monument to George Washington in the national capital. But when Luke Tiernan of Baltimore was in Boston in mid-August he reassured Bishop Cheverus that the archbishop's health was improved.[2] It had been possible to enjoy with lighter heart the visit of Joseph Octavian Plessis.

The Bishop of Quebec was doubly welcome that September, for he had spared Cheverus the necessity of going to Pleasant Point to confirm the Indians there, and in addition had brought with him two other priests, Fathers Boucherville and Gavreau, as traveling companions.[3] There was no lack of conversation during the three and a half days the Canadian clergy remained in Boston. The city itself was enormously interesting to Plessis and he noted in his journal:

> Everything aroused one's curiosity. A vast harbour, bordered by fortified islands; ships from the four quarters of the world at anchor there . . . large, rich shops, three and four stories high, built of brick . . . the State House, whose elevated lantern dominates the town . . . churches of all denominations, each seemingly richer than the next in taste and elegance. The whole sight is imposing to strangers as soon as they see this city, and recalls to them . . . its high place which its commerce and its wealth give it among the cities of the United States.

The friends of the Boston clergy were interesting, too. In Cambridge Plessis was equally impressed by the elegance of the Elbridge Gerry house and the urbanity and uncommon humor of the mathematics teacher who leased it; Father Brosius was persuaded to spend as much time as he could spare with the Canadians until their departure. At the Stoughtons on Wednesday night their hostess struck the visiting bishop as remarkably fervent for a former Protestant native of Hamburg. The jolliest three hours were those in Brookline where Cheverus, Plessis, Brosius, and Boucherville had breakfast Thursday morning with the Walleys, while waiting for Matignon and Gavreau to complete the packing for the trip to New York.[4] Crowding eagerly around the Canadian bishop the numerous Walley children listened rapturously to his tales of the Indian banquet that Father Romagné had taken them to share among the Passamaquoddies in Maine; Cheverus meanwhile reflected gratefully on Plessis' powers of persuasion elsewhere. For Father Matignon had changed his mind, and had agreed to accompany the Canadian clergy on the rest of their journey. At midday he would leave by the mail coach for Worcester, and thence to New York. He could see for himself the splendid new cathedral there.

Cheverus had worried all summer about his beloved friend's health and hoped the roundabout trip that the Canadians intended to take back to Quebec would be not only a pleasant relief to Matignon but a restorative as well. Much of the trip from New York to Albany and northward would be taken by steamboat, and voyages in congenial company were the favorite remedy prescribed by his medical friends in Boston. Plessis' letter from Trois Rivières on September 25 carried happy assurances back to Cheverus, and when Matignon himself arrived in October looking much better and bearing two pairs of stockings from the Bishop of Quebec to his episcopal brother in Boston, Cheverus was delighted on all scores. He wrote gratefully to Plessis, "My venerable friend is enchanted with his trip and penetrated with your goodness."[5]

And then it was his own turn to make a journey. On November 25 John Connolly, O.P., the new Bishop of New York, finally reached his see and, it appeared, desired the presence of the Bishop of Boston at his solemn installation.[6] Cheverus could ill afford either the time or the money to go to New York again that year, but he meant to put into practice his words to Carroll so many months ago, "We shall be affectionate brothers." In the midst of hurried preparations for this departure he received the dolorous news from Baltimore; on Friday, December 8, 1815, Cheverus learned that John Carroll was dead. The feast of the Immaculate Conception was a sadly appropriate day to learn of the passing of the prelate so devoted to the Blessed Virgin, and the little suffragan bishop in Franklin Street was engulfed in mingled emotions — sorrow for his own irreparable loss, and joy at the happiness which must be present in heaven for the remarkably holy death his friend had experienced on December 3. He was grateful to Leonard Neale for the beautiful details even though they increased his grief at having been absent for that last holy benediction.[7]

The *Columbian Centinel* the next day carried a glowing tribute to the founder of the American hierarchy and whether or not Cheverus had a hand in it, the eulogy expressed his sentiments. After summarizing Carroll's career and his part in the war for independence the obituary concluded:

> His talents and learning were eminent; his deportment a model of the clerical character, dignified yet simple, pious but not ascetic. He lived respected and beloved; and has died greatly lamented; particularly by the poor.[8]

On Saturday, December 9, Masses for the repose of the soul of the late archbishop were offered at Holy Cross. On Sunday the Bishop of Boston preached a sermon from his heart, recommending to himself and his flock the pattern of "the venerable Prelate, the loss of whom we so justly and sincerely deplore." He urged his deeply moved congregation to look up to the new archbishop, Leonard Neale, "with perfect and highest respect." To Archbishop Neale he wrote the next day of his grief at the "melancholy tidings," and of his loyalty to the new successor. "I shall leave Boston by the mail tomorrow at 12 o'clock and return here after Christmas."[9]

In New York City Cheverus installed the new bishop with pomp and dignity in the splendid cathedral he had dedicated a few months before. He found Bishop Connolly a man possessed of piety, knowledge, amiability — everything, in fact, except physical strength.[10] Connolly, in turn, found the Bishop of Boston quite to his liking and thought privately that he ought to be the next coadjutor of Baltimore. They talked at length of the Church on both sides of the Atlantic. Cheverus gave Connolly the details of the problems facing the bishops of the United States; Connolly had the latest information concerning the disagreement between the Irish and English prelates, having come to New York by way of Ireland. It seemed that Carroll's old friend, Charles Plowden, was now publishing articles on the subject in England.[11]

When Bishop Connolly learned that the French members of his new congregations were eager to have Cheverus preach a retreat while he was in New York the bishop persuaded Cheverus to stay on till January. In fact, every one wanted to hear Cheverus on every possible occasion. On December 20 he gave the sermon at the services for John Carroll; the next Friday he gave a sermon in French in preparation for the retreat. When the retreat actually began at St. Peter's in Barclay Street Cheverus talked every day at the 8 o'clock Mass and at the 5 o'clock Benediction. He wrote to Bonneuil, "They expect besides that a sermon in English on Sundays and feasts. Here's my task cut out for me! May God give me the grace to do well, and sanctify myself by sanctifying others."[12] With the retreat lasting from the day after Christmas until New Year's Day Cheverus could not expect to leave the city before January 2 at the earliest. He was glad that both Brosius and Romagné had agreed to assist Matignon while he was away from Boston.

The accession of Leonard Neale to the metropolitan see naturally posed the question of a coadjutor bishop, a question which was to hang fire for over a year. Before the matter was settled Cheverus had some very anxious moments, moments he had never anticipated. When Cheverus first learned of Carroll's death he understood that Neale wanted Ambrose Maréchal for his coadjutor, a choice with which the Bishop of Boston concurred perfectly. When Archbishop Neale wrote to Rome in February, 1816, however, he said that the bishops were unanimous in begging the Holy Father to transfer Cheverus to Baltimore. "This is the prayer not only of the bishops, but of all the clergy of Baltimore," he explained, adding that the choice would please Neale for many reasons. Cheverus was a special friend in the first place; further, "he is a prelate of long experience in episcopal functions, and eminent learning, enjoying excellent health and strength, zealous in the care of souls, remarkable for his eloquence, and full of charm and charity." His diocese was still so small it could well be put in charge of a vicar apostolic. If Cheverus could not be transferred, then Neale recommended Maréchal as second choice.[13]

In a reply from Rome that summer Neale was told that Cheverus was acceptable but that the archbishop "should as soon as possible, indicate some one to us who could be appointed to Boston, for it does not seem expedient to leave that diocese, so recently established, without a bishop." Neale's second suggestion of Maréchal was out of the question; Rome had already destined the Sulpician for Philadelphia.[14] Cheverus knew nothing of this exchange. In February the only news of interest from Baltimore was the reading of John Carroll's will, which left to his "much esteemed and respected friend," all of the late archbishop's rights, title, or interest in the property on which the Church of the Holy Cross in Boston was built. Cheverus was moved by this reminder that to the very end his old friend had held Boston in his heart. The will was drawn on November 22, 1815; to have been esteemed by John Carroll in his last hours was an inestimable privilege. Cheverus humbly told the archbishop's nephew, Daniel Brent:

> I am more honoured than I deserve by being mentioned in such terms in the will of such a man as the late Archbishop. May I show myself not altogether unworthy of having been his friend by imitating him.[15]

Then Lent came on with all its duties, and after that followed fifteen April days in Rhode Island. On June 25 he wrote to Bruté in Baltimore, "Nothing new here. I am going to make a mission of two and a half months in Maine and environs." How he prayed for a worthy priest to come and stay with Matignon! Dennis Ryan was still in minor orders and, what was worse, a leg infection kept him so lame it seemed he might never be active in the ministry.[16] There was another reason for wishing to stay in Boston that summer. Vernou de Bonneuil was back from Guadeloupe and the bishop yearned to share

as much of his "dear son's" company as possible. He knew that the
next time Bonneuil left Boston he intended to take the whole family
with him. But a shepherd of flocks could not indulge his private
preferences.

Journeys to the East in 1816 took no more account of episcopal
dignity than had the earlier trips of a youthful *émigré* in 1797. On
June 28 the Bishop of Boston was still in the harbor waiting to
sail for Maine, and trying to dull the edge of his impatience with
a rueful note to Bonneuil. "I have been on board since 11 last night
but we haven't budged yet, and I don't know when we will," he
complained mildly. Once arrived in Wiscasset he was due for another
delay; the stage lost a wheel, and allowed Cheverus another hour and
a half before reaching Newcastle to reflect on the time lost from
Boston. "We would be very happy in this world if we were always
with those we love," he mused. Then characteristically he ignored the
clamorings of his heart and added, "It is harsh, but perhaps salutary,
to be separated. It is good to have some times of penitence and of
privation." As if to take him at his word the weather retorted with
a veritable downpour, not only arousing twinges of rheumatism, but
keeping him from Bath much longer than he had intended.

As he retained his old sensibilities, so too did he still experience the
old ardor for his ministry. Of his aches he said cheerfully, "I consent
with all my heart to the rheumatism. . . . Work is my salvation. May
it be useful and agreeable to God." He marveled at the generous
hospitality of the houses where he dined, remarking the abundance
of raspberries and cream, "the good butter, and sacrifices of lamb
everywhere." The Apostles themselves had not always found so much.
In spite of his preference for a meatless diet he graciously munched
the inevitable mutton that was set before him. He had his rewards,
too. On August 2 he baptized Samuel Bishop, the forty-six year old
lawyer who had been wrestling with doubts for three years. The happy
man wept through the whole ceremony and the bishop who conferred
the sacrament could only hope that the non-Catholic friends of the
catechumen who watched the baptism would soon follow the lawyer's
suit. It was for these moments that a missionary labored. The Sundays
at Newcastle, the week at Waldoborough, the trips to Bath, to Noble-
borough, and to Whitefield, and then as September approached he
headed for Wiscasset once more.[17]

As always, at the port where he might or might not find a ship,
his thoughts leaped ahead to Boston and he wrote gaily to Bonneuil,

"If I go by land I will sleep at home Monday, September 9. If you do not find in Boston that day either my person or a word from me, I will be on the sea." He wondered how he would get along with the deaf-mutes whom he anticipated entertaining at Franklin Street. Laurent Clerc, a pupil of the renowned Abbé Ambroise Sicard, had arrived at Hartford the previous spring to learn English and assist Thomas H. Gallaudet in establishing his own institution for the deaf and dumb. He had arrived with a letter from Sicard for Cheverus and now in September was visiting Boston with some feminine pupils. What matter if the Bishop could not converse in the sign language of *les muettes?* "I doubt not that they will speak to me . . . by more expressive signs, by tender embraces," he reassured himself.[18]

There was an invitation waiting for the bishop when he arrived in Boston; Archbishop Neale wished Cheverus to confer the pallium. On first thought, Cheverus was inclined to refuse. Bishop Connolly of New York was much nearer and could do it more easily. Besides, there were the usual drawbacks: distance, expense, season of the year, and the reluctance to leave Father Matignon alone so much. "There, Most Rev. Sir," he explained to Neale, "is my position." He would make no mention of the invitation so that the Bishop of New York need never know he was second choice.[19]

But Neale would not take "no" for an answer, and a month later Cheverus capitulated, saying that he only awaited the arrival of the pallium to fix the time of his departure. When the symbol of archiepiscopal dignity arrived from Rome with Father Edmund Burke of Halifax, along with the assurance that Burke was to be Vicar Apostolic of Nova Scotia, Cheverus notified Neale that he would leave Boston on November 7, spend the week end in New York, and after stopping in Philadelphia, expected to reach Baltimore by Thursday or Friday with the pallium and briefs.[20]

He actually arrived in Baltimore a day earlier than he had anticipated only to find that Archbishop Neale meant to be invested in Georgetown. It was while he was in Georgetown for the ceremony which took place on the feast of Saint John of the Cross in the parish church of the Potomac town that the Bishop of Boston learned from his archbishop that he had been proposed as coadjutor. He "nearly died of amazement." His second reaction was to seize a quill and write at once to Cardinal Litta. The Church of Boston was his bride; however poor she was, he could not think of leaving her a widow. It was unthinkable that Father Matignon could bear the burdens alone now that his health was far worse than in 1808 when it had been the sole obstacle to his becoming Bishop of Boston; a stranger to the New England scene would work incalculable injury. In any case, there were so many admirable men presently near Baltimore that it would not be hard to find a coadjutor in either Georgetown or Baltimore much more worthy than Cheverus:

> especially among the Fathers of the Society of Jesus there are men whose outstanding talents, religious devotion, zeal and labors . . . can never be sufficiently commended. . . . There are also truly apostolic priests in the Seminary of Baltimore.[21]

Several things are clearly evident in this immediate rejection of the idea of the coadjutorship. One is the selfless love the first bishop bore for the Diocese of Boston. Another is the unqualified veneration Cheverus had for the Jesuits and Sulpicians; for a man who did not belong to a religious community himself he had a remarkable appreciation for the Society of Jesus and the Society of St. Sulpice. But above all the letter presents a man completely devoid of ambition. Cheverus could not help but perceive that Leonard Neale was old and infirm, and so attached to Georgetown that he would not come to Baltimore for the insignia of his office. Cheverus told Plessis, when he later described the events of November, "Our good archbishop is a saint but he is very feeble. He doesn't budge from Georgetown."[22] It would be only a matter of time or title before Cheverus could be either acting archbishop or actual Archbishop of Baltimore, and the second successor of the man he had so loved and admired. Yet without hesitation he rejected the proposal, sending an urgent plea to Mother Seton, "Pray to our Lord to look down on this Diocese and to preserve it and myself from what is intended. The very idea is more than I can bear."[23]

The days that followed in Baltimore were full beyond measure. At St. Mary's, in the charming chapel designed by Maximilian Godefroy, he conferred major and minor orders on November 27, 29, and 30. This was the first time that St. Mary's seminarians were ordained in the seminary chapel, for Carroll had always performed the ceremonies in St. Peter's. On November 29 Cheverus also consecrated the new altar stone for St. Mary's Chapel. On December 1 he gave confirmation at nine in the morning at the parish church; then at eleven, at Fell's Point, he confirmed some more people and dedicated the new bell for Father Moranvillé's church. The next day there were more confirmations, and then, on December 3, the most taxing of all his activities was expected of the Bishop of Boston. At the solemn ceremonies at the cathedral Cheverus officiated and preached on the anniversary of the death of John Carroll, whom he still mourned.[24]

All the clergy of Baltimore were present, of course; and Father Bruté, knowing how Mother Seton would have enjoyed the occasion, wrote to Emmitsburg:

> All hearts still moved by the good de Cheverus. Nothing, my mother, could express to you what he said. You have had the pleasure of hearing him, you know his manner, so mild, so sensible, and the subject! The worthy archbishop would have been charmed himself, and I could see him stretched out at the bottom of his tomb, listening with pleasure and smiling at his second successor, for it appears it shall be so. He will surely be coadjutor and surely one cannot hear it without desiring it. . . . On Monday morning, if he says Mass for you, he could give you the anniversary sermon of the Archbishop, and in the midst of his daughters, hearts so devoted, repeat to you this address so delicious which we have just heard.[25]

Perhaps it was the memory of the first archbishop and a wish to do what he might have advised, or it may have been the contents of a letter he received from Matignon, that led Cheverus to write to Archbishop Neale after the service was over that if he could be allowed to remain as Bishop of Boston he would gladly come to Baltimore to confirm, ordain, and exercise his other episcopal functions as long as Neale lived.[26]

While Cheverus was writing to Georgetown, Bruté was writing to Emmitsburg:

> Bishop Cheverus is going Friday afternoon to be Saturday afternoon at the Mountain and Valley — Sunday to give confirmation at the Sisterhood. . . . Spare his fatigues for he has almost as bad a cold as our venerable archbishop when he was there. Sunday evening he comes back to Uniontown, being obliged to leave Baltimore Tuesday, every moment being strictly calculated, Philadelphia, New York, till Boston before Christmas.

Jean Moranvillé of St. Patrick's Church where Cheverus was so admired gave the news to Mother Seton, saying,

> The amiable and universally beloved Bishop of Boston goes to visit you and your dear family. How welcome he will be to you all! An angel in your holy retirement! He has done a great deal for us here. . . . He consecrated the bell of my church, a ceremony which never took place in this country, but explained and performed by

this heavenly prelate . . . all that he said upon the subject was noble and affecting. How happy, did we whisper to one another, were our metropolitan church blessed with such a pastor![27]

Cheverus was indeed going to Emmitsburg in his episcopal character to confer tonsure at Mount Saint Mary's and for confirmation at St. Joseph's School. He was also going as a friend to console Mother Seton in her latest bereavement, for Rebecca, her youngest child, had died on November 4. Her tragic announcement had arrived in Boston just after he left for Baltimore and did not reach him until after the Georgetown ceremony of November 24. As miserable as he felt with his cold, fatigue, and the anxiety over the Baltimore matter, he determined to go to Emmitsburg if only for a day or two. On the feast of the Immaculate Conception he saw for the last time the religious foundress who held such a special place in his heart.

Elizabeth Seton was emaciated and haggard, and she walked with halting step. Rebecca's last days had been spent almost entirely supported by her mother's arms and knees; Mother Seton was to be lame for months to come. But Cheverus saw only a valiant woman "with her children in heaven and earth," and those two days in Emmitsburg were "treasured up in the memory and affections" of his heart.[28] In spite of all the tribulations her community had faced in the years since his last visit they were now firmly established and the school was an edifying sight with its happy girls and excellent teachers.

Aside from a letter to Antonio Filicchi saying, "Blessed Bishop Cheverus has been again to see us" followed by the wish that he would succeed "our venerated archbishop," there is no way of guessing what was said between the bishop and Mother Seton in the Valley, or between him and Father Dubois on the Mountain; but when Cheverus returned to Baltimore he hurriedly instructed Father Maréchal to inform Archbishop Neale of his most recent thoughts on the coadjutorship. As soon as Cheverus was gone from Paca Street on December 11, Maréchal wrote at length to Georgetown. Cheverus now consented to be coadjutor if he could remain in Boston while Neale's health persisted. He would willingly come to Baltimore when Neale judged it necessary, devoting perhaps three or four months to the Archdiocese of Baltimore. It seemed unnecessary to ask the Holy See yet for a successor at Boston; there would be time enough for that when Cheverus had to leave. In fact, a vicar-general would suffice in Boston for years to come, thus obviating the problem of finding suitable subjects for episcopal sees. Maréchal had already written a few days earlier to Sulpician friends in Bordeaux:

It is M. Cheverus, Bishop of Boston who is destined to be elevated to this post. Every one rejoices and with reason. For one can not see a more apostolic prelate. He is humble, learned, zealous, eloquent, pious and singularly active and vigorous. Indubitably no one, in this country can compare with him. If God grants our wishes, he will be our first pastor and deserves to be.[29]

Cheverus meanwhile was on his way to Philadelphia where he preached on Sunday at St. Mary's Church. For the congregation whose dissensions had hastened Bishop Egan's death the Bishop of Boston chose the text: "Mary of whom was born Jesus who is called Christ," and briefly the peace of the Advent season reigned in the hearts of his "very crowded audience." By December 21 he was home once more in Boston, and the 360 or more Communions on Christmas Day were welcome-home enough for the exhausted little prelate.[30]

He need not have worried, he soon learned. Ironical as it may be, the man most eager to see Cheverus coadjutor, most reluctant to accept episcopacy himself, became coadjutor and the third Archbishop of Baltimore. Ambrose Maréchal in his eagerness to escape the See of Philadelphia and to remain with his beloved seminary in Paca Street was still busy in December enlisting further aid in Europe toward the revocation of his own appointment. He had vigorously resisted the idea of Philadelphia from the very first. He had an unsuspected ally in keeping him in Baltimore, as it turned out. The new Bishop of Louisiana was still in Europe in 1816 and Dubourg strongly urged Rome to name Maréchal as Neale's coadjutor. When Rome reflected on the two recommendations of the Archbishop of Baltimore: Cheverus and Maréchal, and considered Maréchal's petition to be allowed to remain near the seminary, it appeared practical and wise to avoid injury both to the Diocese of Boston and to St. Mary's Seminary by giving Neale his second choice. Maréchal need not go to Philadelphia; he was now coadjutor.[31]

Father Maréchal got the news first through the Sulpician superior in Paris; shortly afterward both he and Cheverus received official notification from Archbishop Neale. Poor Maréchal's chagrin was equalled only by his Boston friend's joy. Cheverus wrote at once to Paca Street:

My very dear Seigneur, I do not congratulate you, certainly; but I do congratulate the clergy and the faithful of the Diocese of Baltimore, and I also congratulate with sincere joy the Bishop of Boston on your nomination. A kind Providence arranges everything for the best; you must submit to it. . . . Father Matignon presents you his respects and congratulates himself.[32]

To Archbishop Neale Cheverus wrote:

I congratulate you and the church on his appointment. . . . I feel a great deal easier than I have done since I left you. I hope now to finish my days in the midst of my dear children here, and I really believe that your diocese is better provided for than by giving it a divorced Bishop. I shall now never consent to part from my dear Spouse, the church of Boston. I felt extremely unhappy ever since I gave even a half and reluctant consent. I shall however always retain a grateful sense of the confidence and friendship with which you have honoured me. You are continually in my prayers and in my heart.[33]

When he wrote to Propaganda on February 7, 1817, he spoke again of the unhappiness he had suffered during the weeks that he had dreaded the fulfillment of Neale's first wish.

But now peace and joy have taken the place of fear and anxiety. . . . I now request, nay, I earnestly supplicate, that I never be ordered to leave my Spouse in Christ, the church of Boston. May I be allowed ever to watch over this flock beloved tho small, and for it to spend and be spent.[34]

When he had some leisure in March he expressed his relief to Father Bruté, to whom he said:

I was in troubled waters until the refreshing news from Rome. The nomination of the dear and worthy Prelate-elect will give new luster and solidity to your holy society, the nourishing mother and model for the clergy. I congratulate you as well as your worthy colleagues. . . . The learned and pious Mr. Maréchal was the object of their first wishes. The nomination to Philadelphia was the sole reason they dreamed of me for a moment. I thank God it was only a dream.[35]

A week later he summarized the whole period of confusion for Bishop Plessis. By this time Cheverus was firmly convinced that he had only been thought of as a last resort and confided in the Bishop of Quebec that he did not believe Neale when the archbishop said that Cheverus had been the unanimous choice of the clergy and faithful. "I am at last delivered from a great anxiety," he said sincerely. "Happily for me, at Rome they revoked the bulls which named Mr. Maréchal for Philadelphia and have expedited others which name him Archbishop *in partibus* and coadjutor of Baltimore. These bulls have not arrived yet, but letters from St. Sulpice in Paris announced the mailing and they are expected here daily."³⁶

April left little time to ponder this felicitous deliverance from the necessity to relinquish the See of Boston, for a very part of the bishop seemed torn from him with the departure of the Bonneuil family. Only three-year-old Adé was left behind to console "Nan-pa," and even that was but temporary respite from total loss; Adé was staying on at the Walleys simply because Dr. Warren argued that taking her to Guadeloupe just then might mean the child's life.³⁷ Cheverus did everything a fond parent could have done to make the departure easy for the Bonneuils; there was no means to ease the aching of his own heart. He saw them off, of course, and the next day removed the remnants of their furniture from the house the marquis had leased. So prompt was he, in fact, that the new tenants were moved in by seven o'clock of the Monday after the ship had sailed.

The following Sunday he used as his text the Gospel verse: "You weep, you groan, but the world rejoices." Thomas Walley told Cheverus after Mass that he had never preached so movingly; "my eyes and heart at least attest to the truth of the text," the bishop wrote sadly to Vernou de Bonneuil." The customary pleasure of finding little Adé on his bed when he came back from Holy Cross was dimmed by her pitiful question, "Grandfather, are you going to *leave Adé all alone?*" He wished he could be as sensible as the child who accepted his fervent reassurance and trotted off to play with a small friend whose world was still intact.³⁸ The bishop's world would never be quite the same again.

On April 30, the Wednesday after the sad parting, Cheverus set out for Rhode Island. On May 1 at Bristol he baptized a baby whose parents wanted the name Napoleon for their son, but Cheverus, still deploring what that name had meant to his beloved country and Church, persuaded them to substitute Nicholas for the name of the fallen emperor. As was his custom when on the mission, he gave a talk before and after the sacrament was administered and one of his listeners was Alexander Viets Griswold, the Protestant Episcopal Bishop of the Eastern District comprising Massachusetts, Rhode Island, and New Hampshire. Griswold stayed to talk with Cheverus afterward and his timidity and embarrassment suggested how much his courtesy cost; his presence at the ceremony alone was very consoling to the Catholic prelate who also loved all men as his brothers.³⁹ On Sunday, May 4, Cheverus offered Mass in the morning for the workers of a coal mine three miles from Bristol, and then in the afternoon returned to Bristol to preach in the court house.[40] Returning to Boston in time for the confirmation ceremonies at Holy Cross on Pentecost, and preparing for the ordination of Dennis Ryan on May 31 left the bishop scarcely a minute for reflection.[41]

Meanwhile in Rome on May 19 the Holy See had put the final seal on the Baltimore matter when the *Acta* recorded that Boston could not be deprived of its bishop simply because there were few Catholics in the diocese; Maréchal's desire to remain near St. Mary's Seminary was approved, and since he was on the scene it was convenient to make him the coadjutor of Baltimore. Cheverus wrote contentedly to Guadeloupe, "They have respected my representations at Rome and I stay decidedly Bishop of Boston. I believe before God that it is better for me and for others."[42]

In June Father Matignon left for a six weeks trip to Canada and it was while he was away that news reached Boston that Archbishop Neale had died in Georgetown on June 18 after an illness of only twenty hours. Father Grassi's letter announcing the news arrived at noon on Sunday, June 22, and at Vespers Cheverus made the announcement to his flock, commenting briefly on the succession in the episcopacy. "When Aaron died on the mountain Eleazar came quickly down to succeed him," he reassured them. He had revered Neale for his deep piety and devotion to the convent of the Visitation in Georgetown. It was a lovely way to die, surrounded by holy virgins. On the following Sunday Bishop Cheverus spoke from the depths of his sincerity at the solemn service for the late prelate:

> The first archbishop showed astonished America the dignity and beauty of the Catholic Church; the second the perfection to which she leads; the third will give ecclesiastical discipline a form most regular. St. Sulpice is a perfect model, and the Prelate-elect one of sacerdotal virtues.[43]

He had already told the prelate-elect how he felt. "I congratulate the Church and if I were near you I would embrace you." Father Matignon wrote to the new archbishop-elect:

> How I thank God for the way things have turned out! I had urged, solicited our good Bishop to surrender to the wishes presented to him, persuaded that you would be forced to accept the see of Philadelphia, and convinced that outside your house no one would prove a more zealous friend and protector of the Seminary of Baltimore than Mgr. Cheverus. What would have become of me if the thing had taken place! God be praised.[44]

If there was one man whom Maréchal could rely upon as an obedient suffragan and loving brother in the episcopacy it was John of Boston. He more than others appreciated the reluctance and dread with which Maréchal approached the office. The humble Sulpician wrote to Rome the very week after Neale died pleading to be relieved of the archbishop's role. "Only the Bishop of Boston could occupy it with advantage to the good of the Church in the United States," he reiterated. "Furthermore, every one demands with great outcry that Monseigneur Cheverus be Metropolitan: Bishops, Priests & the multitude of the faithful."[45] When the bulls did not arrive he told Cheverus, "This delay makes me still hope that instead of being your Metropolitan, I will be quite simply a director of your seminary, which would be so much better for me and the Church in general."[46] Cheverus was not disturbed; he told Bonneuil instead, "He hopes in vain, but I hope to consecrate him in the spring time."[47]

Cheverus was mistaken only in the matter of time. The bulls arrived almost immediately afterward, and when he heard of it he wrote to Maréchal as before, "I do not congratulate you, but I thank God, and rejoice for the Church. Do not delay your consecration, I beg of you."[48] If Cheverus were going to Baltimore, the sooner the better. And, of course, he meant to go. Back in October, thinking of Bishop Dubourg's recent return to the United States, he commented from Newcastle where he was on mission that if the bulls would only arrive too he, Connolly, and Dubourg would see to it that Maréchal was consecrated *in splendoribus*.[49] In fact, he wished Maréchal would have Dubourg do the consecrating. The ceremonies ought to be as elegant as possible and Cheverus cut such a poor figure when contrasted with the tall, handsome Bishop of Louisiana. He begged Maréchal:

> Arrange all for the greatest edification. The right of seniority is a very small thing placed in the scales with so many rights of superiority the worthy Bishop of Louisiana has over me. He said more truly than he knew, the day of my consecration, "Remember, my dear, you are the smallest of Bishops." *Ridendo dicere verum quid vetat?* Give him my tender respects if he is still with you.[50]

But the archbishop-elect had no intention of changing his mind; Cheverus was always his first choice, and certainly William Dubourg, whom Maréchal blamed as the *deus ex machina* in the whole affair, would have been his last choice if a substitute had to be found. He was not at all sorry that the bulls arrived after the Bishop of Louisiana had left Baltimore for his diocese. Cheverus replied resignedly, "I wish they had run after Monseigneur Dubourg. I am at your commands. Let me know them as soon as possible."[51]

On November 17 these commands reached Boston. The consecration was fixed for December 14, and Cheverus made his plans accordingly. He hoped to travel from New York in company with his fellow bishop, John Connolly, but that prelate was not certain he could go. Cheverus told Maréchal, "I would have preferred, to sway the venerable Bishop of New York, you had offered him the role of consecrator. I would have come with the same speed as assistant." Actually, he meant to travel slowly, since he still had a very bad cough, his "faithful companion" since last year's trip to Baltimore. Besides, he would go and come by way of Rhode Island where he had families to visit, stopping a day or two in New York and Philadelphia, and arriving in Baltimore in time to make a retreat if possible. Recollection of the trip a year ago irresistibly carried his thoughts to Emmitsburg. This time, he knew, he could not afford the time or strength to go to see her and he asked Maréchal hopefully, "Couldn't the venerable Mother Seton come to the consecration? Do you think it would be inconvenient?"[52]

It was an arduous journey for the ailing little man who would celebrate his fiftieth birthday in less than two months. The trip from Providence to New York, even by steamboat, took five days. He arrived in New York the night of December 2 and stayed on for two busy days which left him little leisure.[53] Louis DeBarth, the administrator of the Diocese of Philadelphia, insisted that Cheverus preach a charity sermon for the orphans of Philadelphia the Sunday that the Bishop of Boston spent in that city; it was a request Cheverus had no desire to refuse, especially since the orphanage was conducted by Mother Seton's own sisters.[54] But, as he told Maréchal, the charity sermon on December 7 meant "we could scarcely be in Baltimore before Thursday. There's my plan for retreat spoiled."[55] Connolly would not join DeBarth, Hurley, and Cheverus until Monday night, and the four men would travel together from Philadelphia to Baltimore.

On December 14, 1817, assisted by Bishop Connolly and Louis DeBarth, John Cheverus consecrated Ambrose Maréchal the third Archbishop of Baltimore. Anthony Kohlmann, who was now the Jesuit superior at Georgetown, served as deacon; and Michael Hurley from Philadelphia preached the sermon.[56] It was bitterly cold in Baltimore during the week which followed and Cheverus reflected on the perversity of the weather that kept Boston still free from snow and mild as autumn while this southern city shivered in its frigid temperatures; only his archbishop's numerous and perplexing problems could have persuaded him to stay that long.

He was compelled by conscience to stay even longer in Philadelphia, the city that had been bishopless for more than three years, and was still torn with dissensions. It was not simply that DeBarth felt that Cheverus' preaching would do much good at the Christmas season; Maréchal, unable to make visitations immediately, had asked Cheverus to report on the Philadelphia situation. Cheverus preached there on Christmas and the Sunday following; in between times he listened to the many contradictory opinions of the clergy. It left him only time enough for a day and two nights in New York, before he boarded the steamboat again for Rhode Island where he must stop once more at Bristol and Providence. It was January 8 before he was home again at last, to find Boston raging with typhoid fever and mantled in the first snow of the season.[57] It was not the happiest home-coming in the world, especially when Cheverus recalled that it was the birthday of the archbishop he had wished *ad multos annos* for nearly two decades. Yet he was content; at least he was home, and the third archbishop was consecrated beyond the possibility of any further protests against the office the Bishop of Boston had so successfully resisted.

CHAPTER XIV

THE OLD ORDER CHANGES

IT IS almost axiomatic to say that the year 1815 was a turning point in the history of both the United States and France; and, certainly for Cheverus, his second era was characterized by more than the passing of the age of John Carroll in the Church in the United States. Before he died Carroll had predicted that the changes in France would probably cause the loss of some of the French clergy, and it was not long before the Bishop of Boston found that the restoration of Louis XVIII and the principle of legitimacy would indeed deprive him of two priests living in the Diocese of Boston.[1]

The first to go was Francis Xavier Brosius. Impelled by personal longing for his native land and the duty of conducting his family back to France, Brosius left Boston on October 1, 1816. He had never given much assistance to the ministry but his departure meant for Cheverus the loss of an "example of a pure and amiable piety and the pleasing society of a learned confrere."[2] Brosius soon reported from Bordeaux that Archbishop D'Aviau had offered him work in that diocese, and that he was "big and fat" since his return to France.[3] His next letters spoke of joyful plans to rejoin his mother.[4] He was definitely lost to Cambridge and Boston.

With the departure of the Alsatian scholar Cheverus was already dreading the eventual loss of Father Romagné, his Indian missionary. Even before Waterloo, Romagné was dreaming of the day of his return. Although he postponed the date of departure year after year until 1818, on August 22 of that summer he finally sailed for France. He talked of returning to visit Boston, but Cheverus knew that Romagné was permanently lost to the Indian mission where he had done such marvel-

193

ous work for nearly twenty years. Like Brosius, he soon reported having found a place; he eventually became pastor in Sacé, near Cheverus' birthplace, Mayenne, and spent his remaining days there.[5]

It is not to be wondered at that Cheverus and Matignon took an increasing interest in French affairs after Brosius and Romagné had joined Sougé and Tisserant and the other priests who had spent some time in the United States.[6] They would have been interested in any case. The return of the Bourbons was the thing they had ardently wished for all these years. To men of their generation the concept of monarchy was inseparable from the greatest good for the Church in France. Priests educated in colleges and seminaries of the Old Regime thought of the altar and the throne in one phrase. Matignon was voicing this conviction when he wrote to Canada in August, 1815, "I spent a very happy Feast of St. Louis, being in spirit in Paris and Rome at the same time." The restoration of Louis XVIII to Paris and of Pius VII to Rome predicted a return to happier days for the Church in France. Even before Waterloo Matignon had said impatiently, "Things are proceeding very slowly. I do not see that they have yet filled the vacant sees, nor even done anything to improve the lot of the clergy. That of Paris was still vacant on January 20."[7] Mail from France was eagerly awaited.

Cheverus began to receive consoling reports. Nicholas Mac-Carthy, the bishop's "old seminary comrade," wrote from Toulouse in 1816 that he was a priest at last, having been ordained the year of the Restoration. Within two years he was to enter the Jesuit novitiate.

Louis de Cheverus wrote from Mayenne in May of that year. "We are truly enjoying a flourishing recovery under the reign of the most virtuous of kings. Religion is going to flower again under the empire of the Fleur de Lys and morality will be born again with it. M. Sougé, our pastor, has all his wishes fulfilled. Today the missionaries who are so highly praised arrived in his parish. They are traveling all over France, and are making conversions everywhere."[8] From Paris Moreau de la Vigerie was equally enthusiastic, saying, "The missions are performing marvels at Angers, at Nantes, and in all the places the missionaries have reached. God and the King is what they teach. We carry this device around our necks, and, I hope, in our hearts."[9]

The bishop's relatives were excited, as were all hopeful Catholics in France, by the new society called Priests of the Missions of France founded by Jean-Baptiste Rauzan of Bordeaux and having its headquarters in the Rue d'Enfer in Paris. The Priests of the Mission were soon followed by other evangelizing groups and the renewal of spiritual life in France gave bright promise. Cheverus told Bruté in October:

> Today the feast of St. Denis our dear France occupies our thoughts. She is the object of our prayers and affections. Let us hope the missions continue to work miracles and that the worthy Abbé Carron will soon rejoice that his zeal and angelic piety are producing fruits and benedictions.[10]

He may have thought fleetingly of the difference in his own situation if he, like Guy Carron, had declined to leave England during the interregnum.[11] Would he now be back in the Department of Mayenne where even the prefect was one of his own former fellow-students at Louis-le-Grand and highly praised in 1816 by Louis de Cheverus?[12] But the Bishop of Boston was no longer tempted to return; instead, he was impatiently awaiting the arrival from Mayenne of the sacred vessels with which he offered his first Mass on Christmas in 1790. His family were at last resigned to the fact that Boston was his "spouse."[13]

The Boston clergy were even more interested in the changes they anticipated in the relations between Paris and Rome, and French papers like *L'Ami de la Religion et du Roi* and *Moniteur* were impatiently awaited and more avidly scanned for the latest reports of developments. Matignon exclaimed, "How slow they are in terminating with the Pope in France!"[14] Even before the 100 Days negotiations had been started to suppress the Concordat of 1801; now that Napoleon was under British surveillance on Saint Helena and Louis XVIII was re-established on the throne of France, Frenchmen everywhere expected to learn of a new concordat at any moment. While waiting, Boston had to form what conclusions were possible from the reports of Church affairs that arrived by letter, paper, and word of mouth.

These reports were often conflicting. Uncertainty caused even Abbé Sougé to write on occasion that he wished he were back in the United States, and when Charles Nerinckx returned from Europe in 1817 he gave a very distressing account to Baltimore.[15] Cheverus preferred to accept a Paris Sulpician's assertion, "I have the pleasure to repeat to you that every day Religion in France makes marvelous progress."[16]

The postwar situation in Europe augured well in one respect, at least, for the Church in the United States. When Father Nerinckx arrived in Baltimore on July 29, 1817, he had in addition to a dozen or more men for the mission a veritable treasure trove of goods, including a complete set of vestments, several richly textured copes, a bell, an organ, sacred vessels for the altar, twenty chasubles, albs and other linens for the Kentucky seminary, as well as similar gifts for the Dominicans and the Sisters of Charity of Nazareth.[17] Cheverus commented humorously to Maréchal:

> His virtues and zeal are, in spite of the 100 chasubles, the most beautiful ornaments he brings to the Church in America. If the Bishop of N. Orleans returns even better rigged out Europe will fear priests and prelates who come from the U. S.! They will regard them as pious corsairs who only look for booty. They will think they are seeing again the ninth century thieves of relics.[18]

All whimsy aside, Cheverus was quite properly delighted with the success that both Nerinckx and Dubourg had in Europe. Even before the latter's return a token of his success had arrived in the persons of missionaries for Louisiana. The arrival of the *Ranger* from Bordeaux on June 25, 1816, at Fell's Point aroused enormous excitement. Father Bruté conveyed the news to Mother Seton and the Bishop of Boston, and the Sisters of Charity were at once directed to offer their communions and thanksgivings for "the blessed missionaries sent to enlighten our savage land," while Cheverus replied that it made him ashamed to speak of his own diocese. "The arrival of the holy missionaries for Louisiana is a very important event," he prophesied. "There, and in Kentucky, we can hope for good beginnings."[19]

The first band of missionaries sent by Dubourg was in truth a remarkable sight. Three of the priests belonged to the Lazarists, or as they are more commonly called in America, the Vincentians; two more were secular priests; four seminarians and three laymen destined for lay brothers of the Congregation of the Mission rounded out the group. Father Bruté's excitement in greeting them at St. Mary's College in 1816 was amply justified in years to come. Father Felix De Andreis, who was in charge of the band, founded the first establishment of the Congregation of the Mission in the United States, a congregation which eventually furnished the superiors of Mother Seton's community. And one of the group was destined to become Dubourg's successor at New Orleans when the first bishop of that area returned to France in 1826.[20]

When the Bishop of New Orleans himself arrived from Bordeaux in the fall of 1817 he was accompanied by twenty-nine more missionaries including three future bishops. The second group had sailed from Bordeaux on July 1, 1817, aboard the *Caravane* which Louis XVIII had placed at Dubourg's disposal.[21] Again Bruté greeted the new arrivals and once more Cheverus in Boston felt a pang of pleasurable envy when he read that they were going to settle in Upper Louisiana, "as fervent as angels." "I thank God and I hope Religion is going to make rapid progress in the West," he reacted enthusiastically.[22]

Unlike the Dioceses of New Orleans and Bardstown, Boston was not favored with boatloads of priestly re-enforcements. Yet there was some improvement in the number of clergy after the war years. Dennis Ryan gradually recovered from the ulcerated foot which kept him so lame for more than a year and on March 24, 1817, Cheverus wrote to Bruté, "Last Saturday I ordained deacon Mr. Dennis Ryan who has lived with me for two years. I invited the congregation to be present and accompanied the ceremony with explanations; it seemed to make an impression."[23] Two months later, on May 31, Ryan was ordained priest, the first in the Diocese of Boston.[24] A few months later Patrick Byrne arrived from Baltimore to study for the priesthood under Matignon and Cheverus. Like Ryan, Byrne was from Kilkenny, Ireland, and within a few weeks had won the bishop's heart. "He edifies me greatly," Cheverus told Bruté.[25]

The next year proved even better. In the spring Father Philip Lariscy, O.S.A., a thirty-four year old priest from former labors in Newfoundland and Nova Scotia, asked to be allowed to serve in Boston for the summer. He seemed strong and robust, zealous and pious, and delighted the Irish by preaching in their native dialect.[26] For Cheverus' taste the oratory was a trifle too much *in terrorem,* but the preacher himself seemed humble enough and asked nothing except work. Cheverus was so worried over Matignon's health that June that any priest who could relieve the older man was welcomed as a blessing. Before the year was out another recruit from New Brunswick, Paul McQuade, transferred from Canada to the Diocese of Boston, and Patrick Byrne received a companion in his studies with the arrival of a French seminarian, Stephen Cailleaux. Cheverus remarked humorously, "My house is a little seminary. I am superior, professor of theology, etc., etc."[27] Cailleaux who was already in major orders seemed another blessing, since he offered to replace Romagné in Maine as soon as his English improved.

Contrasted with the whole bands of additional clergy entering the other dioceses it was a meager increase, but it was almost more than the diocese could sustain. The bishop confessed in 1816:

Among other obstacles, one which also prevents my doing many other things is the lack of pecuniary means. . . . I would do all I could to procure one or two priests, but I have no resources for their

living. I have received some help from my family, but that is all spent.
I trust in Providence, but I believe that I should not contract debts
which perhaps would never be paid back.[28]

When he reported to Propaganda early in 1817, at the time only
Ryan had been added, he pointed out that the offerings of the faithful
"hardly suffice for food and clothing for this body of clergy." He went
on to describe the situation of the entire diocese:

> The number of those who receive Holy Communion is more than
> 400 in the city, in the surrounding towns and country-side about 100.
> In the Province of Maine . . . 150 persons receive Holy Communion
> there. The largest part of these reside on farms. . . . The priest is
> received hospitably, but hitherto has been given no house of his own
> nor any personal offering. A few acres of land were purchased, which,
> I hope, will in the future, be able to supply a residence and support to
> the priest. The Bishop himself acts as the only missionary in these
> parts, for two or three months in the summer. In the winter these
> people are served by their pastor, the Rev. James René Romagné.
> . . . The government of the State of Massachusetts grants the priest
> an annual stipend of 350 dollars, but whether the same stipend will
> be given a new priest is very uncertain.[29]

Nevertheless, they were not losing ground. Baptisms recorded in
his second era were: 131, 123, 159, and 136 for the years 1815–1818;
marriages numbered: 26, 35, 20, and 21 for the same period. There
were continued encouragements from conversions like that of Samuel
Bishop in Maine, or Mrs. John Seton in Boston. The latter was the
widow of Mother Seton's brother-in-law, John Curson Seton, now
living in Boston with three children by a former marriage. Cheverus
told Bruté in October, 1816, that Mrs. Seton was preparing to embrace
the Catholic religion and was coming to church regularly. Father
Matignon wrote to Emmitsburg on November 10:

> Your sister-in-law was baptized & confirmed on all Saints day,
> & made her first communion the Sunday after, perhaps at the very
> hour that good Rebecca's soul was taking her flight to heaven. Though
> much raptured & rather silent from timidity, she could not help
> telling me a few days after she never was so happy in her life. . . .
> Who knows but she may fall so much in love with you as to leave
> us for Emmitsburg?

> P.S. Mrs. Seton has here a sister (Mrs. Green) with whom she lives,
> & like her a widow and mother of orphans. . . . We have great hopes

she will follow the example of your half sister. She of late frequently attends Mass with her on week-days.[30]

When Cheverus was in Maryland that month he told Mother Seton, "You already know that Mrs. John Seton was baptized and confirmed by me."[31] It was one more bond between them.

The demands of the second era of his episcopate took much greater toll of Cheverus' physical strength since he never spared himself. His health so favorably remarked by Neale in the recommendation to Rome in 1816 had meanwhile noticeably declined. The two trips to Baltimore in 1816 and 1817 were made during months unseasonable for travel and Cheverus began to be plagued with a cough from which he was rarely relieved during the rest of his American days. Popular demand wherever he went compelled him to preach more frequently than ever before; he put such heart and soul into these sermons that he was usually exhausted on his return from prolonged visitations. Mother Seton was very concerned about him when he visited Emmitsburg in December, 1816, and she exacted a promise that he write immediately on his return home to relieve her mind. When he did write on December 30 he explained:

> I arrived safe on the 21st, but could not write sooner. You know how busy I must have been & your goodness will excuse the delay. My cold is a great deal better, & I might have been well, if instead of syrups, &c. I had not been obliged to hear confessions, preach, officiate &c. I am now resting a little. I have no doubt I'll be well shortly.[32]

It was his nature to work doubly hard while he was at home in Boston to spare Father Matignon whom he always left with such an uneasy heart and conscience.

The year 1817 was simply a typical one of the bishop's life. When the heavy duties of Lent and the Easter season were over Cheverus went immediately on mission to Rhode Island. On his return to Boston the confirmation and ordination ceremonies were scarcely over when Matignon went to Canada for his six weeks' absence, and the bishop was left in Boston with its pastoral cares and the task of shaping the first months of Father Ryan's priestly career. It is sentimentally custom-ary to think only of the fresh piety and special blessings that attend the first days of a newly ordained priest's career; but the pastor who bears the responsibility has anxieties as well as pleasure in directing his neophyte. Cheverus had such deep veneration for his vocation, and such elevated standards of clerical perfection, that the direction of this, his first "son in Christ" weighed heavily upon him. For a year after Ryan's ordination the new priest remained in Boston where he could gradually learn prudent judgment, meticulous performance of Church rites, and confidence.[33]

As soon as Father Matignon returned Cheverus went as before to Maine, writing to Archbishop Maréchal from Hope on September 29:

> I have been on Mission for a month. . . . Yesterday and today I celebrated Mass in a particular house and I preached yesterday in a shed to 50 Catholics and more than 200 Protestants. I am 27 miles from the Church. I hope soon to have a regular priest in this district. He would have to love poverty and work.[34]

He was thinking, of course, of Dennis Ryan.[35] Father Ryan would love poverty and work, if his first year's training had counted for anything. In Boston he had been shaped in his bishop's mold.

On the conclusion of the Maine sojourn at the end of October, as we have seen, the bishop found that he must go again to Baltimore for Maréchal's consecration. This was the journey not concluded until after the New Year because of his determination to visit the Catholics of southern New England both going and coming, and his desire to do what he could for Philadelphia. Just as in the previous winter, his return to Boston allowed him no time to mend his own health; this time the city was typhus-ridden and the poor were suffering bitterly from the cold. A prelate who loved the poor and sick was too busy consoling them, and relieving their distress to think of himself. For three weeks he had little peace of mind, for Mrs. Walley, the mother of eleven children of her own and foster-mother to little Adé Bonneuil, lay at death's door.[36]

During all this pastoral work he remained a bishop responsible to Rome, jealous for his charge and of his powers. It was in 1817 that he earnestly solicited permission to remain always in Boston, that he sent the detailed report to Propaganda. In that year, too, he learned from Bishop Connolly of New York that the Dominican possessed dispensing powers relating to matrimony beyond those of his other American brothers in the episcopacy. Cheverus told Maréchal, "The powers ought to be the same for all bishops," and proceeded to request them from Rome.[37] Rome soon complied saying, "What your Amplitude recently requested for the sake of repairing evil and in order to rule well . . . has been sought and benignly obtained from His Holiness, as you will see by the attached document."[38]

Bishop, pastor, teacher, missionary, public citizen, Cheverus was all these things; but he was withal a friend. The year 1818 saw the demands of friendship taxing the fortitude of the gentle bishop almost to the breaking point, involving as they did three of his most beloved friends: Father Bruté, Mother Seton, and Father Matignon. With a nature as loving as his, Cheverus found it easy to identify himself with the problems of others; sympathy welled spontaneously from his warm heart. But he was a man of bedrock principle as well, and he rigorously compelled himself to follow the dictates of his intellect, regardless of the clamoring of his less disciplined organ. This fusion of limitless affection and prudent judgment made his advice as valuable as his love was esteemed.

Simon Gabriel Bruté was visited with vast unrest that year. When illness deprived John Dubois in Emmitsburg of his assistant, Bruté was sent to the Mountain as a temporary substitute and the volatile Frenchman suffered a very real confusion of soul. He loved the Mountain and knew that Dubois needed him. He was by now so closely bound to Mother Seton by spiritual ties that he welcomed a renewal of their director-penitent relationship. But his Sulpician superiors in Baltimore delayed confirming his resignation from St. Mary's College there; there was even talk of suppressing the Emmitsburg college altogether. Bruté saw no happy certainty ahead.

His discontent was further increased by the lingering effects of the missionary bands' arrival in Baltimore in 1817. The sight of all those eager, zealous men setting off for almost virgin fields of endeavor filled him with impatience and he chafed at the routine of academic life. His letters to Félicité and Jean La Mennais carried his discontent to France. In Emmitsburg Bruté talked recklessly of leaving the United States entirely, of going to distant missions in China. Mother Seton tried to warn him against an intemperate zeal which "instead of bedewing the plant" might crush it under foot. She exclaimed:

> Surely you would not leave your Brother *now,* and if God does indeed graciously destine you for China will he not seeing the overflowing of your boiling heart for it, open an evident door?[39]

He was not persuaded. On March 23 he sent a rush of excited, passionate arguments to Franklin Street, begging Cheverus to intercede with the Sulpicians in Baltimore who had such respect for the opinion of the Bishop of Boston. He poured out his discontent and demanded a clear, decisive answer. Cheverus had a presentiment that his reply would weigh heavily with his friend and he dreaded the task. Finally on April 9, 1818, he sat down soberly at his escritoire in the small study-bedroom momentarily empty of visitors and wrote:

> I received eight days ago your letter of March 23. I have reflected before God on its contents & here is the result.
>
> I believe Providence sent you here and it is in the realm of its designs that you stay. I have firm confidence that in spite of trammels, discouragements, &c. your piety, zeal, and knowledge would be very useful to our Church in America. That is what I would tell your superior should I write to him, consequently it is useless for me to do it. . . . Consult him as well as your other brothers. If it is their advice that you leave us, while regretting it, I would pray God to bless your zeal, and if you embark here I don't need to tell you you would be received like a beloved brother.[40]

Bruté did not depart. On June 3, Jean Marie Tessier, his superior in Baltimore, recorded in his diary that Father Bruté was replaced at St. Mary's College in Baltimore and was appointed to assist John Dubois in Emmitsburg.[41] It appeared that Cheverus was right, that it was in the order of Providence that Bruté should stay in the United States. In 1834 he was to be consecrated first Bishop of Vincennes; by the time of his death in 1839 his jurisdiction was well on the way to fathering the future Dioceses of Indianapolis, Fort Wayne, Chicago, Alton, Peoria, and Belleville.

In 1818 the first fruit of Cheverus' advice was Bruté's proximity to Mother Seton in a time of double crisis, a year of trial for a mother whose eldest son was determined to serve in his country's navy and who herself was so near death's door. While Cheverus did what he could to befriend the son in Boston, Bruté brought spiritual consolation to the mother in Emmitsburg.

Mother Seton had dreaded to see William join the postwar scramble for naval careers that attracted so many young men still in college, but she used what influence she had to get him an appointment. Young Seton was assigned to the training ship, *Independence,* lying in the Boston Navy Yard and in February, 1818, in company with a New York friend, Charles Wilkes, he reported to Commodore William Bainbridge and fighting Captain John Downs. Of all the twenty-two midshipmen aboard Seton had less reason to feel discontent, perhaps, than any of the young hopefuls. At the Navy Yard Commodore

Bainbridge spoke at once of having known both Seton's father and grandfather well; Charles Wilkes had lived with the Setons in New York as a boarder and was the son of one of Elizabeth Seton's most loyal supporters during the first years of her widowhood; on shore Seton had Uncle John's widow to visit; and not the least impressive, the Bishop of Boston welcomed him in person, treating Seton like a dear son and sending messages to his mother.[42] William's first letters from the *Independence* assured his mother that he would soon call again on the bishop "whose truly affectionate and tender kindness I shall ever gratefully feel."[43] Cheverus, of course, invited Seton to dine at Franklin Street whenever he could come on shore.

Seton did not have many leaves during his first few months in Boston, but on April 1 he told his mother he had dined with the bishop, Father Matignon, and had seen Mr. and Mrs. Walley there.[44] He also called once on his aunt, Mrs. John Seton. But for the rest, his stay in Boston filled his mother with countless anxieties, particularly where his religious duties were concerned. Cheverus told Bruté after Easter, "Dear William Seton is in good health, but only rarely has liberty to come on shore and could not during our solemnities. They were beautiful and consoling."[45] When she wrote in July Mother Seton told her son worriedly,

> All I judge from is the entire silence of Bishop Cheverus who has never written me once since you are at Boston, and I have had so many full proofs of the kindness of his heart that I am sure if he could have said a word of your approach to God he would have taken time from sleep to tell me.[46]

Cheverus was indeed waiting for some news to give her that would satisfy her hungry heart. When he learned from her that William was transferring to the *Macedonian* in his impatience to put to sea, Cheverus determined to bring the subject up the next time that Seton was on shore. A visit to Franklin Street the first week in August exacted from the young man a promise that he would write to his mother the next day, and moreover, fulfill his religious duties before the *Macedonian* left on her Pacific cruise.

The bishop tried to relieve her mind on other scores. William was always in need of money and besides now needed extra linen and other items before he sailed. Mother Seton had suggested that his Aunt Seton might attend to the latter wants. When Cheverus wrote to her in August, 1818, he explained that Mrs. Seton was unwell and was not in Boston that summer, but he added, "I shall speak to William, indicate to him someone who can see that he has linen and whatever he wants, and I shall most cheerfully advance money for this purpose."

Bishop Cheverus was much less concerned about William than he was about the mother that summer. From her own pen and from Bruté he knew that she was terribly ill and expected never to see her son again. He tried to console her by saying as he had so often in the past, "I have confidence that he will one day be with you in heaven. The child of so many tears and prayers cannot perish." For her own condition he knew no sympathy was necessary; he had perceived her spiritual resources too long to doubt her courage.

> I do not pity you. I envy your situation, running now to the embraces of Him who is love. Dear Sister, pray that I may be endowed with some portion of your faith and resignation. I am weak, very weak. . . . I beg a few lines when your situation permits it. They will be received and preserved as a treasure to the heart of him who in our dear Lord is truly devoted to you. . . . You are most fervently remembered at the altar and will be as long as I shall celebrate the Holy Mysteries. Pray for me here and in heaven.[47]

Young Seton could have repaid Cheverus for the money he borrowed, having received enough from his mother just before sailing on September 18, but he decided against it. "You can very easily repay it in the course of three years," he told his mother carelessly.[48] Yet as scarce as money always was at the bishop's house, Cheverus, if he thought of it at all, would have deemed it a small enough price to pay if it brought any consolation to the little foundress who cared so desperately for her children and nothing for herself. But as the *Macedonian* left Boston harbor that day, "a most beautiful frigate pierced for fifty (carrying forty-eight) guns, more completely and handsomely fitted out than any other ship that ever sailed" in the opinion of one young man aboard, Cheverus had no thoughts for an undutiful son and careless debtor. His beloved Matignon, "dearest of friends," lay dying in the small house where they had lived as one for over twenty years.

Cheverus had known since June that his colleague was failing fast. There was no question of leaving him that summer, and Father Ryan was sent to Newcastle in the bishop's stead. By mid-July Cheverus confided his fear to Archbishop Maréchal pleading pitifully,

> Why are you not here to sustain me? I am menaced by the loss of my excellent friend, my holy colleague, M. Matignon. The doctors

are certain his lungs are ulcerated. He is very feeble. May the Lord have pity on my church and its poor Bishop. *Ora pro nobis.* . . . He asks your prayers. . . . I have more need of them. . . . My heart is broken.[49]

Father Matignon at first insisted on staying out of bed and offering Mass when he was able but soon Cheverus was telling their friends in Montreal, "Our dear sick man is very feeble," and when he wrote to Mother Seton in early August he added, "Our holy sufferer begs your prayers. He perused your letter and bedewed it with tears. It already had been with mine. They flow now and I must finish."[50]

That was the month Father Romagné departed for France. At another time it would have been harsh enough, but now the pain of losing the Indian missionary was swallowed up in the greater sorrow of impending loss. As August wore on Cheverus excused himself from all nonessential courtesies with the words, "Besides my usual duties, I watch an invaluable friend who is dangerously sick. . . . To a man of feeling I need not make any other apology."[51] It is striking proof of his devotion to Mother Seton that Cheverus had William for dinner at such a time; Seton admitted to his mother on August 29, "Dr. Matignon is dying."[52]

Francis A. Matignon was prepared. On August 21 his will was made and he watched death approach with joy and a smile of hope. "He considers it a friend," Cheverus told Plessis, "who will lead him to the bosom of God. Oh, that I had his faith and resignation!"[53] Mrs. John Stoughton was a miracle of kindness during those days when the bishop scarcely knew what was going on outside the sick man's room. Mme Duplessis and her daughter virtually took over the management of the house on Franklin Street.[54]

On Friday night, September 18, just before the two parted for sleep, Father Matignon said to his friend, "My dear Bishop, tomorrow will be the anniversary of my ordination. It will complete forty years that I have been in holy orders. . . . Alas! How many faults and omissions in my ministry."

Cheverus protested swiftly, "And how many good works, my dear friend!"

"Do not speak of them," Matignon muttered painfully. "But God is so good and merciful — that I hope — yes, I hope."

As Cheverus held the emaciated body of his "support, the honor and edification" of his Church, in his arms he could not reply for his own bitter weeping.

Matignon tried to console him. "All that I regret is my separation from you; but we shall one day be reunited."

Then he added quietly, "Pray give me the Blessed Sacrament very early tomorrow morning."

Cheverus slept very little that night and when he entered his friend's room at 5:30 with the Sacrament his hopes rose wildly. In spite of fasting, the invalid's eyes were bright with anticipation and love. After Communion he took even a few spoonsful of coffee. But then he turned ghastly and when Cheverus asked him if he wished to receive Extreme Unction, Matignon could scarcely whisper, "Yes." In a few hours more, without a struggle, he died.[55]

Cheverus told Archbishop Maréchal, when he finally could bring himself to write of it, "Since that moment I have been *tota die moerens et non habens requiem.*" Mourning all day, having no peace, his grief was overpowering. Matignon's virtues were on every tongue, non-Catholic ministers eulogized him from their pulpits, the papers were unstinting in their praise. The whole world seemed to share the bishop's affliction; they knew how the two men had loved each other.[56] But the little bishop left behind yearned only for the day when the tomb would receive him, too, so that the earthly friendship of twenty-two years could be continued in eternity. He wished it had been the bishop rather than their serving woman, Mrs. Gains, who was permitted to die eight days after Matignon.[57] The second era of his episcopal reign was ended; for Cheverus it seemed that life as well was over.

CHAPTER XV

SUNSHINE AND SHADOW

CEREMONIES, eulogies, public and private expressions of sympathy bear bereavement along on a tide painfully appropriate to man's dignity, which more than ever ought to be attested as he leaves this world. But after the tomb at the Old Granary burying ground was closed and the last solemn oratory from Protestant pulpits faded into silence there was the house in Franklin Street with its empty room to face. A poet has said, "Things have a terrible permanence when people die"; everywhere Cheverus turned he saw some reminder of days that were now gone forever.

Yet noble grief does not assuage itself in miserliness, and in the weeks that followed the Bishop of Boston gradually divested himself of many precious mementoes of his beloved friend. In September he gave to the Athenaeum, in whose rooms they had enjoyed reading the latest papers from France, seven works in Latin, French, and English, including a six-volume history of the Peloponnesian Wars by Thucydides; in November nineteen more books followed the first gift. To Matignon's warm friend in Salem, the Reverend William Bentley, on October 20 Cheverus sent a worn little volume with a note:

> I have seen that you cherish his memory. For his sake, I beg of you to accept this small Hebrew psalter. From page 63 to page 84, it is the handwriting of the dear Doctor, as well as the index. It is equal to the beautiful type and *much more precious*. I am sure you will be glad of the loss of the leaves which have been so well replaced. But what can replace the loss I have met with? I am left desolate and forlorn.[1]

The Salem minister had words for such a gift and replied, "The memorial of the Dr. M. is beyond all value. The talent in it is great, and

207

the best of care I have shall preserve it." The Bishop of Boston must know that should he come to Salem, "My house, my friends, my heart is ready for him."[2]

Matignon's room, however, was kept untenanted for a while, and Cheverus when next writing to his "son" in Guadeloupe told Bonneuil he had a room waiting for him if he came to Boston. Time enough to move another priest into the sacred precinct when there were more than two assistants. Counting Françoise, the Negress from Guadeloupe who came to replace Mrs. Gains, and the puttering old fellow who served as both sexton at Holy Cross and general man to the clergy in the rectory, there were only six in the bishop's family.[3]

It was not to be expected that the sense of loss would diminish. Mother Seton told Antonio Filicchi in November, "Our good Bishop Cheverus has been in extreme distress at the death of Dr. Matignon." The bishop's last letter to her had spoken gratefully of that "beautiful Providence" which had supplied him Father Lariscy as an assistant. But Mother Seton knew what her friend in Boston suffered and she re-echoed his sad query, "Who can supply the loss of such a friend?"[4] At first Cheverus was filled with impatient longing to rejoin his departed brother and he wrote somberly to his family:

> My best and best-loved friend is taken from me and a union of twenty-two years is dissolved. But that will, I hope, be only for a time. The same tomb will, perhaps, soon enclose both our mortal remains. May the good Lord deign, despite my unworthiness, to reunite my poor soul to his in heaven.[5]

In Mayenne hope was at once reborn that Cheverus might now be persuaded to return home. Once more letters arriving in Boston carried loving pleas; now that Matignon was gone, what should hold him? But personal woes had never tempted him to abandon his flock in the past and could not now. "The loss of my worthy friend has, in truth, rendered my situation most harsh and sad," he acknowledged to his brother, in 1821, "and I know that in your arms I would find a sweet retreat, but I do not know how to leave this establishment."[6] It was the same answer he had given Louis six years earlier when the Bourbon restoration had been used to coax Cheverus home. "Duty chains me here and it is above all in times of distress that a pastor ought not to leave his flock."[7]

The years following Matignon's death were truly times of distress. The Panic of 1819 was admittedly harder on the West than it was in

Boston, but the eastern seaboard felt its effects severely enough. While speculation in land combined with the government's banking policies brought temporary depression to the frontier, fears of a war with Spain and the discriminatory European commercial restrictions left their wake in Baltimore and Boston. In Maryland "every one rich and poor" seemed to be failing in that time of "trouble of banks and general distress." Mother Seton wrote to her son at sea, "We hear nothing but war, war on all sides. . . . Everything stands just as you left it. Losses a plenty in the money way by our crazy merchants. No new building in such hard times."[8] Albert Gallatin, the American minister to France, reported to Secretary of State John Quincy Adams that in the preceding eighteen months not a single American vessel had arrived in France, while Cheverus in July noted, "The state of commerce is such that in our port there is not one vessel for England."[9]

In the East there was nothing temporary about the depression. In the fall of 1820 Cheverus wrote to Guadeloupe, "Nothing new here except the stagnation of commerce. Money can only be placed at 5%." The following March things were even worse and he reported, "Affairs are so bad that money can not be placed at 5% and the Bank of Massachusetts has just reimbursed its *actionnaires* half of their principal and have paid no interest in the last six months." Although the cost of living was cheap the winter had been long and severe and a time of suffering for his poor.[10] Down in Georgetown the nuns of the Visitation Convent were in such dire straits that Archbishop Maréchal was trying to find them a place in Canada, and as late as 1823 he wrote to Plessis, "You doubtless know, my lord, the hard times that are weighing upon us now in America. I have never seen anything so distressing. The wealthiest families are suffering to a degree I would not have believed possible." In his own poverty it was impossible for the archbishop to help the women who were such a blessing to his diocese.[11]

Nevertheless, Cheverus began a building program in 1819 and the third period of his episcopate became one of outward progress as well as one of inward refinement of spirit. Fewer evidences of the gay humor of the young missionary now flashed from the sober, middle-aged man who passed his fifty-first birthday on January 28, 1819; but the old zeal still gripped his heart. Now, his accomplishments were a twofold tribute to his dear Dr. Matignon; they were built upon foundations the older man had laid, and they were performed in the belief that he was carrying them to fruition as his mentor would have wished.

The first undertaking followed quite naturally upon the Boston pastor's death. The Catholics had never had their own cemetery and Cheverus found it unbearable that the "dear relics" of Matignon should remain in the tomb of John Magner in the Old Granary. On December 21, 1818, his body was removed to a new cemetery purchased in South Boston and the bishop himself composed the epitaph. He liked best the quotation from Ecclesiastes "Beloved of God and men, whose memory is in benediction." But he wanted more. On May 6, 1819, he told Maréchal:

> We are going to try to build a little chapel in the middle of our cemetery a few steps from the tomb of dear Dr. Matignon who will face the door. Our good people have shown great zeal for the acquisition of the cemetery. Father Lariscy, who undertook this good work, has collected about 1500 dollars.[12]

It would be a little Gothic building only thirty-five feet long by twenty feet wide, but in these hard times it was remarkable proof of the devotion of his poor Irish.[13] On Sunday, July 4, at ten o'clock in the morning Cheverus dedicated the attractive chapel to St. Augustine in tribute to the founder of Father Lariscy's order.[14] Small as it was, St. Augustine's now became Boston's second Catholic church and it began to serve the faithful in that part of the city.

At the same time that the South Boston chapel was being built Cheverus was going ahead with changes at Holy Cross. He meant to "completely repair our church and change the vestibule in such a way as to put pews there."[15] It was fortunate that Bulfinch had anticipated expansion, for the church was terribly crowded lately. In spite of his qualms about undertaking expensive projects, and his native horror of indebtedness, the bishop went ahead. The roof was replaced, the seating space enlarged, and the interior was redecorated throughout. In December the workmen were gone and the more than 500 parishioners who went to Communion at the Christmas Mass had one more reason for thanksgiving. Everything was paid for and even though nothing was left in the treasury the bishop felt more confident about his dream of adding a new organ in the future.[16] His health was holding up, too. At least everyone told him he looked well, and the old cough scarcely bothered him at all. "Christmas did not tire me extremely," he assured his anxious friends.

Inwardly all was not quite so serene. The suffering of the poor preyed upon him; they were so numerous. And some dear faces had been missing at Holy Cross that Christmas. He was growing accustomed to the void left by Matignon's death; one learned to live with deprivation, with one half of himself in the neat grave in South Boston. But his other half could still wince at every new dart piercing his loving heart. Adé, the once-gurgling infant on his bed, the toddler of uncertain steps and outstretched arms, Adé Bonneuil was gone, taken home to Guadeloupe that year by her father, to live at Esperance with her family. The lonely "Nan-pa" in Franklin Street wrote fondly on December 27, "The heart of the Bishop often whispers: I want to be at l'Esperance." As full as the Walley pew was at Mass on feast days, to one pair of partial eyes it showed an empty space which only one five-year-old little girl could fill.

The bishop missed, too, the fine old face of Don Juan Stoughton in his Christmas audience. His seventy-five-year-old neighbor was very ill that week, and the whole family was distraught by the tragic news from New York. Just four days before Christmas James Stoughton, the son of the consul's brother, had been assassinated in Broadway at three o'clock in the afternoon, a victim of the horrible revenge of some Baltimore pirates whom he had prosecuted and forced to make restitution. The assassin was seized, of course, and put in prison at once; but Don Juan never lived to learn the outcome of the trial. On January 28 he died; the gracious gentleman who always greeted passersby as if they were princes in disguise would be seen no more in Theater Alley or Franklin Street.[17]

Cheverus could not help worrying about the Duplessis women that winter. The mother and daughter, who had been such a godsend all during Father Matignon's illness and afterward, faced real financial distress in 1820. They tried to conduct a little school but the hard times kept them with very few pupils. Cheverus interested himself in trying to recover for them a legacy to which they believed they were entitled in France, and he wrote to Bruté in January for advice since they were from Rennes, as Bruté was. Father Bruté suggested using his brother's intervention and on April 14 Cheverus told him, "I have forwarded the letter to your dear brother and Mme Duplessis' power of attorney. I have added a word to it. . . . She needs it greatly. She begs you to accept her thanks."[18] It took a long time to accomplish, but finally in the fall of 1822 Cheverus could tell Bonneuil, their mutual friend, that the Duplessis were to get their legacy and meant to return to France.[19] It would mean another painful separation, for Mme Jean Armand Duplessis had been in Boston since 1811; she and her daughter were his "intimate and beloved friends." Painful separations seemed to be the rule of life these later years.

Meanwhile the work of building must go on. The bishop did not deceive himself that the progress being made was due to his own efforts. Father Lariscy was responsible for St. Augustine's, and Matignon's original zeal and subsequent fine management of finances made possible the improvements at Holy Cross. How much more the third building project was due to the dream of a third priest who had served Boston in days gone by. The Ursuline convent school was truthfully a monument to Father John Thayer, the convert priest who had antedated Cheverus' own arrival in 1796.

Father Thayer had lived out his last days in Ireland and after his death in Limerick on January 17, 1815, the Boston Catholics learned that their former pastor had bequeathed to them in Matignon's name his whole estate for the foundation of an Ursuline convent. It had not been a dream easily achieved, for as Cheverus explained to Bruté, "Father Thayer himself was of the opinion it would have to wait until the funds could be increased, for at present, they would not cover the expenses necessary for such an establishment."[20] Father Matignon had invested the legacy with wisdom and at his own death made Cheverus his sole heir to the Ursuline money, adding a third of his own personal estate to Thayer's.[21] Cheverus was determined that the fond hope of the two former pastors should flower as soon as possible.

The winter after Matignon's death he purchased a plot of land next to Holy Cross with the intention of beginning to build in the spring. The lot cost $4,500 and lay adjacent to another one purchased earlier for a school, which like the convent was still only a dream. The two pieces of land together contained about 3,500 square feet and nicely rounded out the properties adjoining the cathedral. In May work on the convent was begun and foundations for the school followed shortly afterward. The little bishop was sometimes aghast at his own daring and he confessed to his archbishop that summer that he was overwhelmed with care and anxieties. There was not an ounce of recklessness in his make-up, and he distrusted his administrative ability at all times. He would gladly have left temporal matters to someone else, as he had happily done when his beloved friend was alive. Now there was no one with Matignon's ability, and he told Maréchal, "I can not prudently rid myself of the temporal care. I have at least the consolation of seeing that all the buildings are started. I owe nothing, and I will have sufficient funds to provide for our Ursulines the first year, and I hope that very soon they will nearly take care of themselves."[22]

The work went along despite the uneasiness of the modest bishop. By the end of the year the convent was ready, and if the weather had been fit for travel Cheverus would have gone to Canada to get the women who were to live in it. How strange were the designs of Providence! If he had had a choice he would have brought Mother Seton's daughters to Boston. He could imagine no greater blessing than having Mother Seton herself. She was still going heroically ahead in spite of the ravages of consumption, and he had no doubt that her prayers brought whatever success he had in his own undertakings in New England. But Thayer's will had been positive; Ursulines it must be.[23] He told Bruté in April, "I am going for the Ursulines at the beginning of June," and asked him to assure Mother Seton that news from Havana announced all well on board the *Macedonian*. He knew her heart where William was concerned.[24]

The women Bishop Cheverus went to fetch from Trois Rivières had been taken there in 1817 by Francis Matignon following their arrival in Boston from Ireland in June. At the time Cheverus had told Bruté, "Someday they will return to Boston to form an establishment."[25] Now, three years later, that day had come. The whole journey was a delight to Cheverus. At Montreal the Sulpician house filled him with limitless admiration. "Like Apostolic times!" He stayed only two and a half days and was busy every minute with preaching and confirmation.[26] He aroused Canadian sympathy for their Sulpician brothers in Baltimore who were victims like everyone else of the hard times prevailing in the United States. By the time he returned to Boston Archbishop Maréchal already had reason to thank the Bishop of Boston for his kind offices. Cheverus disclaimed any credit hastily. "I am ashamed of the thanks you gave me. . . . I deserve neither your gratitude nor that of the Seminary. I have only been the channel of the good deeds of others."[27] But Maréchal knew what a friend St. Sulpice had in Boston. Cheverus never seemed to miss an opportunity to advance either their reputation or their well-being.

By mid-July the Ursulines were installed in the new building in Boston and it was all settled that they should begin teaching in September. In no time at all Cheverus told Maréchal contentedly:

> Our religious here have already contributed to reanimating piety among our young girls. I have been obliged to consent to being their director. Only two have taken vows, the other two will take

theirs on St. Ursula's Day. Since their arrival they have a postulant for *soeur converse*.[28]

Cheverus believed himself scarcely suited to the direction of pious women, especially these who had been trained under the saintly Abbé Calonne in Three Rivers. A year earlier he had been given a fleeting prospect of securing Pierre Babade for the work.[29] Father Babade had been Mother Seton's favorite confessor in her Baltimore days and would have been welcomed in Boston; but he returned to France in August and Cheverus was forced to assume this added responsibility.[30]

His first duty in the Ursulines' behalf was one of intense joy, when on St. Ursula's Day his two novices took solemn vows in Holy Cross before a crowded church and "a great number of Protestants, all attended with tears." The little prelate was never happier than when he could explain to his fellow citizens the significance of the great ceremonies of his faith. Surely the Ursulines would do great good for his diocese. Already their school had more than 100 poor girls, half attending in the morning, the others in the afternoon. They were all day students as yet; but perhaps in another year provisions could be made for boarders as well as externes.[31]

The bright prospects in Boston that Advent were shadowed by news from Emmitsburg. Mother Seton was dying; this time death meant to have his way. Cheverus wrote to Bruté pitifully, "I hope our holy Mother may still be preserved for her children. Our Ursulines have joined me in asking this favor of God."[32] His hand shook unbearably as he wrote to her, "You are every day with me before the Lord, and you know how much I love you in the bowels of Jesus Christ."[33] But with the new year all hope was gone. On January 4, 1821, Cheverus lost the last of the three great friends who had sustained him since the beginning of his episcopacy. John Carroll, then Francis Matignon, and now Elizabeth Seton, all were gone. It was hard to understand why he, the least meritorious of that friendship *à quatre,* should be still spared. He would need all of their intercession, he thought, to continue in the work he did so badly. How strange that he should be the only one left to go to Baltimore for the dedication of the cathedral that they had all so intensely longed to see completed.

Yes, the Baltimore Cathedral whose cornerstone John Carroll had laid in 1806, "for the honor of Almighty God, under the title of Jesus and Mary," was ready at last. When Archbishop Maréchal sent his diocesan report to Rome in 1818 he had announced:

After about eighteen months I will be able to perform the solemn ceremony of the consecration of this Basilica. Without doubt its size and grandeur will far surpass that of any temple built up to this time in the United States of America, whether by the Protestants or by the Catholics. Even the Protestants of Baltimore take pride in it. It is, indeed, the greatest ornament of the city.[34]

He suggested that Rome might contribute to the interior decoration of the magnificent edifice designed by Benjamin Henry Latrobe; statues were particularly needed since "none whatsoever could be found in these regions and there are no workers who could make them." Maréchal had also asked Baron Hyde de Neuville to interest King Louis XVIII of France in the American cathedral and the French minister had agreed with alacrity. He felt sure that he could secure at least a picture and a bell. Maréchal in happy anticipation dreamed of baptizing the "clamorous catechumen," Blanche, in honor of the Duchesse d'Angoulême. The Hyde de Neuvilles, who sailed for France in October, 1819, had been as good as the baron's word. Not only the bell but two paintings were given by the king.[35] It was a pity that Latrobe and Carroll could not have seen the church in all its splendor on the day of consecration.[36]

Cheverus was going to be there, however. His usual winter cold did not leave him that spring and the Lenten schedule had left him so worn and hoarse that his friends were seriously concerned. "They pretend," Cheverus told Bonneuil lightly, "that a voyage is necessary for my health. . . . I am better and apprehend no danger, so don't be uneasy."[37] He acquiesced, nonetheless, to the urgings of his doctor; the death of Mother Seton had left him very depressed and the thought of going to Baltimore and rebuilding his spiritual resources among the virtuous men of the seminary was very appealing. Early in May he sounded out his archbishop on his plan, adding:

I would like to go see you and be present at the dedication of your Metropole. But if the other Bishops are not coming, or are not invited, would they imagine . . . that there is a Gallican conspiracy? Please answer me at once and tell me frankly what you think. Would the dedication really take place the first week in June? I would like to be back here by the end of June.[38]

Maréchal was naturally delighted and the question was swiftly settled. From Montreal the Sulpicians, hearing the news, wrote approvingly, "Monseigneur of Boston, who is our friend, as he is of all St. Sulpice, has just written that he will be at your ceremony. I compliment you. He is a prelate who earns the respect of all."[39]

The trip was a pleasure, needless to say, but it was far from a rest. In addition to the cathedral ceremonies Cheverus was constantly in demand as always. He apologized from Georgetown on June 15 that preaching delayed him there, one Sunday in Washington, the next at Trinity Church in Georgetown. In between time he made a tour with Benedict Fenwick to Alexandria, the Carmelite Convent in Port Tobacco, and St. Thomas Manor. The Visitandines insisted that he offer Mass for Leonard Neale in their chapel where the second archbishop was buried.[40] When Cheverus returned to Baltimore the archbishop could see very little improvement in his small friend's health; Maréchal insisted that he must not resume his heavy duties quite yet and he informed Bishop Plessis in Quebec, "He is a little better but it is thought unwise to return to Boston where he would be overwhelmed by work. Consequently he plans to take a trip to Canada and rejoices at the prospect of seeing you. . . . He can give you a description of our cathedral and the consecration ceremonies."[41] As it happened, Plessis was away on a visitation tour and Cheverus went no further than Montreal where he spent five days and then returned to Boston. From the steamer on Lake Champlain he wrote to Maréchal in a depressed mood, "I am feeble in both body and spirit. Pray for me and find me a good successor."[42] The peace and apostolic life he had seen in the Canadian seminary had made Cheverus long for retirement amid such surroundings. It was a rude awakening to return to the situation he found at Franklin Street; for once in his life the gentle little bishop found he had no patience left.

Bishop Cheverus had left Boston in May confident that he was leaving his diocese with a clergy sufficient in both numbers and zeal. Since the ordination of Dennis Ryan the bishop had been greatly encouraged. Philip Lariscy stayed on in Boston, "an excellent, zealous and pious" man. When Maréchal suggested after Matignon's death that it would be wise if the Bishop of Boston made some recommendation for a vicar-general in case of his own sudden death, Cheverus felt that Lariscy might do. Boston needed some one who "knows more of the world and its affairs," he admitted to the archbishop; but if Maréchal could think of no one more fitted to the task Lariscy's name could be kept on file. "In case of unforeseen accident, good Father Lariscy knows the locality. You would find him docile and I believe without desire for the episcopacy."[43] In 1819 Cheverus would not have asked for more, and he told his brother Louis with a return of his old humor that with two priests, a deacon, and a man in minor orders it was no longer clergy who were lacking but the faithful![44] Young Cailleaux was ordained on the Saturday before Trinity Sunday and Cheverus happily watched him start off with Ryan for the East where his second "son in Christ" seemed eager to follow in Romagné's footsteps among the Indians.

The next year continued the same satisfying advances. Cheverus wrote confidently to Bruté after Easter, "I have three priests with me and two on Mission." Lariscy was the same brave Augustinian, sometimes too lively for his bishop's taste, but devoted to work. "My other two companions are Paul McQuade who goes to Salem the first Sunday of the month and young Patrick Byrne whom I ordained priest the Saturday before the Passion." It was as large a group as Cheverus could employ, and more than his means actually warranted. Involuntarily his thoughts reverted to the days when he and Matignon had cared for the mission alone. "Nothing can replace what I have lost," he added in painful recollection. "Pray for the poor Bishop of Boston."[45]

In 1821 the Diocese of Boston received yet another addition in the person of Father William Taylor, and despite the inauspicious circumstances of his coming, Cheverus believed he had found a competent vicar-general at last. The Bishop of Boston had first heard of Taylor two years earlier when the Irish priest, who was then attached to the Diocese of New York, published *The Christian's Monitor, or Practical Guide to Future Happiness; a new Roman Catholic Prayer Book.* When Archbishop Maréchal consulted the theologians at St. Mary's Seminary they had found some portions of Taylor's book questionable; Cheverus himself felt it a shame that such a work should have been published without advice. He kept the copies Taylor sent to Boston without distributing them and told Maréchal ruefully:

> The prospectus announced a work very different. Doubtless you have written to him, and I hope from his piety that he will follow your advice entirely. . . . If I ever print anything it will be submitted to you as well as to the gentlemen of the Seminary![46]

The author had submitted dutifully, if a bit reluctantly, to the views of Baltimore and his character was cleared on that score as far as Cheverus was concerned.

Taylor meanwhile had become involved in the partisan rivalries within the Diocese of New York, and after making a trip to Rome which did nothing to endear him to his bishop, he returned to find

that Connolly no longer wished to retain him in New York. The Irish
priest expressed a desire to enter the jurisdiction of one of the French
bishops, Plessis of Quebec, or Maréchal, Flaget, or Cheverus in the
United States. He told the Archbishop of Baltimore that he had his
private reasons for not wishing to go to the strife-torn Diocese of
Philadelphia.[47] So with Maréchal's, Connolly's, and Cheverus' consent
the New York priest came to Boston. Boston had on other occasions
sheltered capable priests who were in temporary difficulties. John Thayer
had served there between his periods of service in Kentucky and Ireland; Matthew O'Brien had performed his last priestly functions in
the Diocese of Boston. It was not unusual in those times to find that
men who were *persona non grata* in one diocese could do good work
in another; certainly the shortage of priests who were gifted with
intellect and free from all major failings made it imperative to preserve
for the American Church those virtuous, if occasionally imprudent, men
who arrived from Europe.[48] So Taylor came to Boston.

Father Taylor arrived on Holy Thursday in 1821 and from the
very first the Bishop of Boston found him a decidedly worthy ecclesiastic.[49] Taylor had a charming amiability, a good education, gentle
manners, and his having been a convert made it easy for Cheverus to
accept Taylor's generosity toward Protestants. The bishop did not
doubt his new assistant's orthodoxy or purity of intention; if Taylor
should err on fine points of theology, he showed perfect willingness to
be corrected, to disavow, to retract. Perhaps the Bishop of Boston saw
Taylor's eagerness to unite Catholics and non-Catholics through his
own discriminating eyes which found all men he gazed upon his brothers
but only soundest doctrine soul-satisfying; or perhaps Taylor actually
lost, under the gentle tutelage and example of his new bishop, some
of the tenacity and pride which had brought him difficulties in the past.
One thing is certain, Taylor continued to enjoy the full confidence of
Bishop Cheverus and before he had been in Boston two years the latter
told Archbishop Maréchal he was so content with Taylor that when
the day came for the bishop to retire to a Sulpician retreat or to his
family home in France his new vicar-general would make a good
successor.[50] Taylor had been in Boston only a few months when
Cheverus felt free to take the first prolonged journey since Father
Matignon's death. It was during this absence that Taylor's presence
in Franklin Street provoked beyond endurance the side of Lariscy's
nature which Cheverus had from the first found distasteful, but which
in his charity he had never described to anyone as anything more than

liveliness, the *in terrorem* approach, or lack of grace in human relations.

The bishop was not without warning that things were not as they should be during his absence. His five days among the exemplary Sulpicians in Montreal had been rudely interrupted by letters from Lariscy angrily denouncing the newcomer from New York. Cheverus was quite unprepared, however, for the scene to which the Augustinian submitted the bishop on his return. Cheverus immediately and categorically dismissed Father Lariscy.

Since Philip Lariscy was the only priest ever rejected by Cheverus this seemingly abrupt action in July rouses some curiosity, particularly in the light of Taylor's recent arrival. At first glance, the dismissal of the priest who was Taylor's senior in the diocese seems incompatible with the character of Cheverus as his previous conduct delineates it. He was loyal to his very core and scarcely the man to side with a newcomer in preference to a faithful minister; further, time and again Cheverus during his life brought peace between the most hostile parties. If Lariscy's fault was a simple matter of dissent with a fellow clergyman, it seems incredible that Cheverus should have solved the situation by prompt dismissal. The only direct clues to his action appear in the few references he made to the matter afterward.

On August 17, 1821, Cheverus told Archbishop Maréchal:

> On my return I was obliged to send Father Lariscy away. He had been angry many times during my absence and a scene of passion at my house Sunday, July 22, in the evening gave me an occasion to have done with him. He is still in the city but can, when he wishes it, leave. I will gladly give him an *Exeat* and help him, but he can never be employed here.[51]

He wrote even more tersely to Bishop Plessis on September 6, "I was obliged to withdraw powers from Father Lariscy. He is of a violent and ungovernable nature." Lariscy had been gone for six weeks, by then, and Cheverus presumed he had retired from active service.[52] When he mentioned the matter three weeks later to Maréchal he had learned that the Augustinian had gone to New York where he calumniated his former bishop to anyone who would listen. "God forgive him," he went on:

> I will keep silent, having given him $100 at his departure. They took up a collection of 200 or 300 more. He lodges with Father French and has been received by Msgr. Connolly. He threatens to go to Rome too, but they would be very blind if they did not perceive

how vulgar, coarse, ignorant and hot-tempered he is. Besides, he has left my diocese. Who can force me to take him back?[53]

Writing to Guadeloupe on December 19 Cheverus explained, "I have been obliged to rid myself of Father Lariscy. His coarseness and his rages had become insupportable. He has really tormented me. He is employed in the vicinity of New York. I have in his place an amiable priest, pious and very much admired as a preacher, Mr. Taylor. He has been here since Easter but it was only toward the end of July that I removed Father Lariscy."[54] One of the last references to the affair was made on February 1, 1822, to Father Fenwick whom Cheverus had known ever since the days when the Jesuit was John Carroll's secretary and closest companion. "I live in peace at home since the departure of Mr. Lariscy," he wrote. "Mr. Taylor who succeeds him is admired & loved here & is a pleasant companion as well as a worthy ecclesiastic."[55]

In the final analysis there is no mystery here at all. When the twenty-two years of harmonious life with Father Matignon are recalled, the only wonder is that Cheverus lived in the cramped quarters of his rectory with a man like Lariscy for so long without ever writing one word of real criticism or derogation. Even though he meant to replace the Augustinian if a capable priest could be obtained, he kept him on after Taylor's arrival until the unhappy Lariscy finally provoked his own dismissal. Cheverus still would not send him off empty-handed, as poor as the parish was, nor would he deprive him of his character by refusing him an *Exeat*. Only to Vernou Bonneuil in far-off Guadeloupe did he ever admit that Lariscy had really been a torment to him. The *Laity's Directory* of New York in 1822 reported that Father Lariscy "attends regularly at Staten Island and different other congregations along the Hudson River," but he did not stay long in Connolly's diocese either. He died in Philadelphia on April 6, 1824.[56]

Father Stephen Cailleaux left the diocese the next year, but for a destination and reasons that remain unknown. Fortunately, Patrick Byrne was ordained by then and could be sent to the Indians for at least one month in 1822, and Cailleaux's departure did not permanently decrease the number of priests serving under Cheverus for, although Anthony Kohlmann's suggestion of Samuel S. Cooper did not bear fruit, the ordination of Virgil Barber on December 3, 1822, kept the Boston clergy at five. The stories of both Cooper and Barber are so complex and interesting that they merit attention, but not in these pages.[57] It is enough to say that Cooper in 1822 was between assignments, having left the Diocese of Charleston with an *exeat* from his bishop, and while resting in Philadelphia that summer considered the possibility of entering the Diocese of Boston to offer his services for the Vermont-New Hampshire region. "He enjoys good health, gives solid instructions, and is generally considered a living saint," Kohlmann assured Cheverus. On the other hand, the Jesuits all knew that Virgil Barber, a native of that part of New England, was soon to be ordained and would be very useful in the western section of Cheverus' jurisdiction.[58] As it turned out, Virgil Barber became pastor at Claremont and was scarcely ordained two months when Cheverus reported to Baltimore, "He is going to build a little chapel. This mission shows promise."[59]

When Cheverus was filled with dissatisfaction with his own meager accomplishments he still referred to himself as "a poor missionary bishop *in partibus infidelium* in spite of his title"; more often he was deeply happy contemplating the work of his vicar-general Taylor in Boston, Dennis Ryan serving his two churches in Maine, Father Byrne on his annual Indian missions, Patrick McQuade at Salem, and now Father Barber in Vermont.[60] Baptisms were increasing and so were Communions. In the four years since Matignon's death the former had doubled and Easter Communions exceeded 700.[61] Soon there would be nine churches in a diocese that had begun with one; none of these was very much to boast of except the recently refurbished cathedral in Boston. But from the shabby Indian chapels in Old Town and Point Pleasant to the new brick church going up in Claremont they were a pledge for the future. Even New Bedford had the beginnings of a church, and when the bishop stopped in Vergennes, Vermont, in September of 1822 the number of Communions raised his hopes that soon the needs of that area might produce another small chapel.[62]

Missions were now regularly served at Newburyport, Massachusetts, Portland, Maine, and in Bristol, Newport, and Providence, Rhode Island. Bishop Griswold was no longer constrained by shyness and sent over invitations by his seminarians asking Bishop Cheverus to make use of the Episcopal church in Bristol for his preaching. "The invitation was accepted with characteristic simplicity and courtesy, and the Roman Catholic Bishop preached from Bishop Griswold's pulpit to the great satisfaction of a large congregation."[63] Even the Catholics of Hartford, Connecticut, were talking these days of getting a permanent meeting place; while in New London the Catholic bishop was such "a lion" that both the Episcopal and Congregational churches offered him their pulpits for Sunday afternoon preaching when Cheverus was in the area. In fact, every state in the New England diocese had its nucleus, however small; and each little center had for its shining example the much-traveled small prelate whose principles were so clearly pronounced in the letter he wrote to one such group:

> I am happy to hear that you openly profess your religion. Never be ashamed of it, nor of its practices; and, above all, do honor to it by irreproachable conduct. Be sober, honest, and industrious; serve faithfully those who employ you, and show that a good Catholic is a good member of society, that he feels grateful to those who are kind to strangers, and sincerely loves his brethren of all persuasions, though he strictly adheres to the doctrines of his own church. It is thus, my beloved friends, that you will silence prejudice and win the esteem and favor of all the inhabitants of this hospitable country. Be assured that nothing I can do will be wanting on my part to promote your spiritual welfare. . . . With affectionate and paternal regard, and fervently imploring upon you all the blessings of the Father, the Son, and the Holy Ghost,
>
> I remain your pastor and friend,
John Cheverus, Bishop of Boston.[64]

Perhaps the most notable advance made by the Church during the third era of Cheverus' administration was that implied in a simple sentence at the close of his letter to Bruté of December 17, 1820. The bishop commented, "Catholics, Jews, Moslems now can hold office here."[65] For the first time since the Pilgrims landed two centuries earlier, Catholics in Massachusetts and Maine now possessed full political freedom as their constitutional right. From a larger, national view the admission of Maine as a state to the federal union in 1820 was part of the controversial issue of slavery and the Missouri Compromise; but in the local eyes the new political freedom for Catholics was inseparable from the ardor of a former young missionary to Maine now called John, Bishop of Boston.

In February, 1819, the House of Representatives in Washington entertained a bill for the admission of Missouri to statehood; on August 24 the Governor of Massachusetts issued a proclamation for a constitutional convention in Maine which would lead to a similar petition. When the Maine convention finished its sessions which were held from October 11 to October 29 it had drawn up a state constitution which contained no discrimination whatever against Catholics; there is very little question that Cheverus was a prime influence behind this notable advance in religious freedom.

The men of the convention had at first meant to retain the Massachusetts discriminatory clause, but they received a petition of protest signed by James Kavanagh, Matthew Cottrill, and William Mooney on October 12, a petition whose wording inevitably suggests Bishop Cheverus as the real author. The document, which was actually penned by young Edward Kavanagh, was presented in order that:

> The Constitution which you are about to frame as the fundamental law of this state may contain no clause or provision requiring any man to renounce his religion or become proscribed: to either betray his conscience or be debarred of the privileges and immunities of the citizen.

The petition then explained the objections Catholics made to the antipapal oath demanded in Massachusetts and carefully distinguished between the temporal and spiritual jurisdiction of the pope. It went on to defend the Catholic as a loyal citizen, arguing:

> If the Catholic demean himself as a peaceful citizen, if in his religious worship, he does not disturb the public peace or introduce indecencies or immoralities, tending to the subversion of civil society, if he take up arms and march to the field of battle in the defense of the sepulchres of *our* forefathers and in maintenance of the rights, the honor, the liberties and independence of his country, the undersigned are utterly unable to see why he should not enjoy equal privileges and immunities with his fellow citizens.[66]

The revised constitution was ratified by January and on March 15, 1820, Maine entered statehood without a single political impediment for the religious group whose bishop had once stood before a court facing criminal charges for having presided at a Catholic wedding.

The action taken in Maine soon had its counterpart in her mother state. In Massachusetts, however, the reform seems to have been primarily influenced by Protestant protests in behalf of their Catholic neighbors. Scarcely had the prospect of revising the Massachusetts constitution appeared when an article signed "A Protestant" was published in the *Palladium* of February 18 and 22, 1820. The author was Samuel L. Knapp, the staunch friend and defender of Matignon and Cheverus, and the bishop approved the article so highly that he spent $12.00 for reprints of it. It was a remarkable defense of Catholics and a forthright demand that justice now be done. It favored specifically the abolition of the oath of abjuration which deprived Catholics of active citizenship saying:

> It is a species of persecution. . . . It is absurd in view of the Federal Constitution. . . . It is adverse to the interest of the community. . . . It is not easy to imagine what fair objections can be made to the tenet of the Catholic Church which requires its priests to correspond with a venerable Prelate in another country. . . . Catholics disclaim any temporal authority of the Pope. . . . There is no tenet in the Catholic Church by which Catholics are justified in not keeping faith with those of other denominations or those who differ from them in matters of religion. . . . All these tests are equally vain and fruitless, whether the truth be with the Catholics or not — in the words of Lord Mansfield, "Conscience is not controlable by human laws, nor amenable to human tribunals. Persecution, or attempts to force conscience, will never produce conviction, and are only calculated to make either hypocrites or martyrs."[67]

Knapp's article was nicely timed. The spring session of the legislature authorized a referendum to determine the will of the people on the matter of revising the state constitution. During the summer the *Palladium* thesis was on many tongues. On August 9 the *Columbian Centinel* pursued the matter further, referring to the original argument and adding:

> Let us ponder on the fact that at present no Catholic, if he have all talents and virtues, is capable of holding any office in this Commonwealth. . . . It is most disgraceful to us, that when Catholics are numerous in several parts of the country, when some of them are among the most able and admired citizens of the Union, when our own capital embraces men of that persuasion of the most irreproachable virtue and patriotism, we should obstinately persist in excluding them from rights which the meanest and vilest and worst of all other persuasions enjoy.[68]

On August 16 the referendum approved a constitutional convention and the election of delegates followed. When Boston's votes were tallied it appeared that the Right Reverend John Cheverus had 410 votes of those cast for forty-five delegates! He was not elected, since 855 votes were required; but these votes which were all Protestant contrasted interestingly with the eight cast for Charles Lowell and the three for William Ellery Channing, two of the city's most esteemed Unitarian clergy. It was a handsome tribute to the quiet, gentle bishop of Franklin Street; an even more effective one was the vote of 17,552 to 9,244 by which the oath of abjuration was removed from the Constitution of the Commonwealth. That Cheverus' wishes had been consulted is evident from a reply he made to one member of the convention:

> On my return from Rhode Island last night, I found your kind note sent in this morning. I hope it is not too late to answer it.
>
> The oath of office (by which every *spiritual* jurisdiction of any foreign Prelate is disclaimed) is the only thing to which we object in the Constitution. I send you an address to the legislature printed in the Palladium at the end of the last session which sets the matter in a clear light. . . . The writer is really a Protestant, a gentleman of the law.[69]

Boston had come a long way since John Cheverus was first consecrated bishop a decade ago. When the Reverend John Pierce of Brookline gave the Dudleian Lecture on October 24, 1821, he chose as his subject "The Right of Private Judgment." After treating those Catholic tenets which Protestants did not accept, he concluded:

> We rejoice that, notwithstanding what has now been frankly suggested respecting the faith of the Romish Church, we can retain undiminished affection for its regular and consistent professors and advocates; and that, of this denomination, there are and have been instances of those, in whose friendship we have felt ever-increasing delight, whose talents we profoundly respect, and whose virtue, fidelity, zeal and other accomplishments we can unhesitatingly recommend to the imitation of every preacher, who would earnestly covet the best of gifts.[70]

"The best of gifts." None of his listeners had any doubt as to whom the lecturer referred. Whatever else Cheverus did not accomplish in his career as the first Bishop of Boston, he left a priceless legacy, the incontestable proof that men, however they disagree on matters of most sacred principle, may still dwell together in peace and love.

CHAPTER XVI

MORE DISTANT HORIZONS

ON JANUARY 14, 1823, a Jesuit priest in Georgetown commented to his brother:

> I have lived too long & have seen too much to be a Bishop, especially to desire to be a Bishop in America where trouble only is got by it, where the office is every day more & more vilified, & where if the same progress continue which I have seen made, before many years it will turn out, that he who names a Bishop, names in the same breath, a martyr.[1]

Although these words ring strangely in ears conditioned to the serenity within the Diocese of Boston under the aegis of John Cheverus, they carry an implication for the larger concerns of the Church in the United States which not only interested the Bishop of Boston but which on occasion specifically involved him as a man and as a member of the hierarchy.

The later years of Cheverus in Boston coincided with the hectic nationalistic era upon which the Republic was entering, and his heart was often greatly troubled by the concomitant perplexities which threatened to overwhelm the American bishops during those dreadful years. "Poor church in the United States!" he exclaimed in the midst of these trials. "It would make you shed tears of blood."[2] The Church has since happily emerged from the storm clouds which swirled about the heads of those first prelates; but in the decade following the death of John Carroll the men who braved the menacing elements endured martyrdom of a kind, however bloodless.

One of the chief factors contributing to their difficulties was the unparalleled expansion of the country. Not only was population swelled by reproduction of the native stock and floods of immigration, but there was ceaseless movement of these people into areas formerly either sparsely settled or quite uninhabited by white men. This expansion necessitated the augmentation of clergy and the multiplication of dioceses by an institution perennially handicapped by a shortage of priests and worthy candidates for the episcopacy.

The expansion of the nation had two by-products which held further implications for the bishops. First, the national origins of their flocks were becoming increasingly Irish and less cosmopolitan in point of view. The clergy of John Carroll's time was notably infused by the French *émigrés* who contributed so much to the early history of the Diocese of Baltimore; it was natural that the first bishops should have been predominantly French. But the growing congregations after Carroll's death looked with increasing favor for Irish pastors and began to demand prelates of their own kind. The second result of expansion, an exaggeration of distinct sectional differences, tended to estrange the bishops themselves. The needs of frontier dioceses like Bardstown and New Orleans presented Flaget and Dubourg with problems quite different from those faced by Cheverus in his New England jurisdiction or Maréchal in the southeast. While it has been traditional to admit the Franco-Irish dissensions within the hierarchy during the nationalist period following the War of 1812, it has been less frequently remarked that geographic and economic sectionalism encouraged a vertical alignment of prelates, that the eastern bishops had more in common with Plessis of Quebec than with their own western colleagues.

These cross-purposes fostered by national origins and sectional needs were enhanced by two other factors, one at home, the other abroad, which persisted at that period of Church history. There was lacking, perhaps more than at any other time, an episcopal *esprit de corps*. From the time the first bishops were consecrated in 1810 and held their council until Cheverus returned to France in 1823 there was never again an occasion when all the bishops met together to promulgate further uniformity of policy or action. Cheverus was doubtless justified in resisting such a council during the war years while Carroll was still alive and capable, by force of character and the respect he commanded, of preserving the semblance of a united hierarchy. It is less certain that there was wisdom in his subsequent failure to encourage a council of bishops. When Archbishop Maréchal suggested holding one in 1821 the Bishop of Boston replied, "It would be absolutely impossible for me in the present circumstances to assist other than as Procureur."[3] True, in 1821 it was too late to hope for unanimity among the bishops now including three Irish prelates from Europe. Yet the fact remains, no general convocation of American bishops was held during a period when aggravating problems plagued them all. Instead of acting together, the bishops sent their problems to Rome separately, urging local needs and personal preference to the possible detriment of an area over which another prelate presided.

Although Bishop Cheverus was on no occasion guilty of meddling in the affairs of other dioceses or of trying to enhance his own influence, he certainly wrote to Rome on those occasions when he believed that Archbishop Maréchal's opinions needed reinforcement by the other bishops. He was tempted, fleetingly, in 1817 to go in person, telling the archbishop, "I would like to be able to go there myself. I do not know what fatality [may occur] if they do not understand there the true state of Religion in the United States."[4] But this was at a time when insubordinate priests from other dioceses were going to Rome with complaints against their bishops, and Cheverus felt that Rome "ought to know that at the distance they are it is easy to impose on them." His second thought was to urge Cardinal Litta in 1818 that he or "some other enlightened and impartial prelate" visit the United States to see the true state of affairs.[5]

Cheverus had a profound and abiding respect for authority and love of peace which, combined with his genuine concern for the total welfare of the Church in the United States, made him increasingly anxious to see the Archbishop of Baltimore's position sustained in dignity. He hoped for the day when the pope would add to the archbishop's quality of metropolitan that of papal legate and give him in general the decision in their present and future difficulties.[6] He regretted the independent actions taken by the western bishops and staunchly supported both of Carroll's successors when these actions brought anxiety to Baltimore. Early in 1817 Archbishop Neale had been annoyed to learn from Propaganda that Flaget had addressed an inquiry to Rome regarding the publication in the United States of the Council of Trent's regulations on the subject of matrimony. Neale asked Cheverus' opinion on the matter which he felt Flaget should not have raised "without first consulting." Cheverus agreed perfectly with Neale that it was unwise to publish the regulation. "It would be impossible," he believed, "especially in New England, to conform to the decrees of the Council of Trent on marriage. Flaget's idea is extraordinary." He sent word to Baltimore that he would be glad to write to Cardinal Litta of his complete concurrence with Neale. He was equally as sympathetic when Archbishop Maréchal resented Dubourg's independent actions in recommending candidates for the vacant see of Philadelphia, and Cheverus told the metropolitan, "I regret that Mgr. Dubourg was not frank with you in regard to his ideas for Philadelphia. If he has seen a subject who appears fitted to doing good we would concur with him with all our heart."[7]

Cheverus invariably closed his own letters to Baltimore with sentiments of respect, obedience, and tender friendship; as troubles multiplied Cheverus drew closer in sympathy and support. Yet his counsel, when given, was always founded on charity. When the archbishop was in disagreement with Bishop Connolly over a solution to New York's evils in 1819 Cheverus said, "It seems to me that in your place I would write to the good Bishop of New York. If one has and even manifests prejudices against us, let us reply to this only by frank and friendly conduct."[8] He could not help worrying, nevertheless, as relations among his episcopal brothers continued to deteriorate. "What can be done," he asked dubiously, "if we are not in accord?"[9]

In addition to the lack of rapport among the bishops themselves their relations with the Holy See during this time were, when not downright irritating, most unsatisfactory. The innumerable problems confronting Pius VII and the Roman congregations with the temporal and spiritual restoration of the papacy in 1814–1815 were bound to put American affairs on the periphery. The veto question in England presented a delicate quandary for a pontiff who owed his restoration, in part at least, to the intervention of that nation. The negotiations with the restored Bourbon king for a new concordat and subsequent impediments erected by the French legislature were of major importance. The rehabilitation of the Church in Italy was, of course, a labor of immediate concern. The resurgence of Austria, another great Catholic power, impinging on the very boundaries of the Papal States could not be ignored. It can scarcely be wondered at that the harassments of a handful of bishops in a far-off mission country did not take precedence at Rome.

Rome had not only a secondary interest in, but a primary ignorance of the exact state of the American mission, particularly where geography was concerned. When Cheverus learned in 1819 that the Prefect of Propaganda was considering erecting a see in Virginia he was aghast. Could not John Grassi, the former head of the Jesuits

in the United States, now in Rome, "explain things to the good
Cardinal and show him on the map" that Virginia was at Maréchal's
very door, especially with facilities for travel what they now were?[10]
Cardinal Fontana who had succeeded Litta at Propaganda in 1818 was
even less informed and actually believed that Hartford, Connecticut,
could be made the see city for Virginia![11] When Virginia was in
fact made a separate diocese on July 11, 1820, Cheverus cried, "The
conduct of Propaganda is inconceivable. Our letters, what they ought
to have learned from Father Grassi, our confrere Dubourg, Mgr. de
Quebec, etc., etc. . . . Nothing seems to give them the least idea
of our missions."[12] A few days later he reiterated his amazement to
Maréchal, "The erection of the See of Norfolk is inconceivable. It
seems to me that even the new prelate, if he is what I hope, will
be the first to condemn it."[13] He advised the archbishop to protest
at once. "I will sign your protest without hesitation," he assured him.
It was scanty satisfaction to learn later that Propaganda admitted its
error, the action having been taken while Cardinal Fontana was ill
in Naples.[14] Benedict Fenwick commented ironically, "Wonders will
never cease in this world. . . . Nothing but doing and undoing!"[15]

In Boston and Baltimore it seemed as if the Holy See had equal
difficulty in recognizing bishops suited to the United States. The
Roman belief that well-trained and pious prelates could be assigned
to sees without regard to national boundaries was singularly inappropri-
ate to the American Republic after 1815. However cosmopolitan life
in the new world may have been during an earlier century, the era
following the War of 1812 was one in which the United States was
deliberately nurturing a national character peculiarly her own. European bishops set down unexpectedly in the turbulent parishes of cities
like New York, Philadelphia, and Charleston were handicapped from
the very start, no matter how high-minded their intentions. Although
Cheverus had from the first admired Connolly and remained on
friendly terms with him he was forced to admit by 1819, "The Bishop
of New York does not understand this country."[16] When he learned
that the dissension-ridden city of Philadelphia was at long last to
receive a bishop, but one from Europe, Cheverus commented dis-
approvingly:

> It seems to me that in Dioceses where there are a certain number
> of priests Bishops should be chosen among them. As we are situated
> in this country, a stranger finds himself from the first contradicted,
> etc. and perhaps unable to do any good at all.[17]

His judgment proved unhappily sound. When Bishop Henry Conwell arrived in 1820 he entered a reign of almost uninterrupted schism and difficulties. Cheverus told Plessis sadly in 1821, "The new Bishop of Philadelphia arrived in November and has already experienced disagreements."[18] Although John England, the new Bishop of Charleston, eventually got control of the warring elements in his diocese he at first unfortunately aligned himself with the worst of the dissidents. Cheverus felt that England was a splendid man; but, being a stranger, was at first susceptible to deception. It was not England's fault, but Propaganda's for being deceived about the American scene. "The Congregation will discover her error," Cheverus hoped. "But how repair it? The sole remedies for our evils would be that the Archbishop of Baltimore be made legate of the Holy See and that not one Prelate be named without his approval."[19] The mistakes of the new bishop in Virginia only confirmed his belief. There Patrick Kelly on his arrival gave his support to the trouble-makers in Norfolk in preference to the pastor whom Maréchal had authorized. When Cheverus learned that on his friend's very doorstep a schismatic priest whom Maréchal had deprived of faculties was now rehabilitated by a stranger from Europe he exclaimed in disgust, "I don't want to reflect on it any further. *Oremus pro invicem et pro ecclesia Am.*"[20] Only prayers, it appeared, could deliver them from this tragedy of errors.

It is easy to sympathize with the reactions of Cheverus to the immediate results of naming bishops foreign to the American scene. He and his colleagues had favored at the outset of their own episcopal careers that the Holy See permit nominations "to proceed solely from the Archbishop and Bishops of this ecclesiastical Province."[21] With the exception of Connolly of New York all the bishops previously active in the United States had been recommended from the United States. Cheverus could recall quite clearly John Carroll's own dismay at the appointment of Connolly, a British subject, at a time when England and the United States were at war. The Irish Dominican had taken pains not to arrive in New York before peace was proclaimed, but the first archbishop had gone to his grave saddened by Roman failure to consult the American hierarchy on such an important appointment.[22] Quite apart from the principle advocated by Carroll and his suffragans, the harsh facts of the unfortunate situations attending the arrival of the European prelates were enough to dismay the men who had worked so tirelessly and in such poverty to establish their Church in a non-Catholic environment. The new arrivals could not be blamed for the troubles already existing in Norfolk, Charleston, and Philadelphia; but it was cause for genuine alarm to watch them allying with the trouble-makers before they had an opportunity properly to evaluate their dioceses.

On the other hand, the actions taken in Rome were not without justification from the point of view of the Congregation de Propaganda Fide. Notwithstanding the highly suspect character of their informants, Propaganda had received information from a variety of sources that the growing Irish congregations were not receiving adequate consideration from a hierarchy four-fifths French in its composition. Franco-Irish antagonism dated back to Carroll's time, and had a variety of causes. In 1812, for example, with one exception all the Irish seminarians of St. Mary's in Baltimore had withdrawn because "they took exception to the French mode of training young clerics."[23] About that time, too, acrimony had begun to flare in Charleston, South Carolina, with the appointment by Carroll of Joseph Picot de Clorivière to a congregation torn by the fomentations of an Irish priest, Simon Felix Gallagher. Father Gallagher and a fellow priest, Robert Browne, had chosen to see their misfortunes, not as the products of their own personal defects, but rather as emanating from an over-all conspiracy of the French to keep Irish priests from the American ministry. At the time the charges were first made they were ludicrous since the congregation to which Clorivière was assigned had more French Catholics than any other city in Carroll's jurisdiction.[24] Carroll was himself a descendant of an illustrious Irish family, and Archbishop Neale who retained the French priest at Charleston was likewise of Irish descent. The French Maréchal had come into power only after Rome had entertained accusations by Gallagher and Browne that the American hierarchy favored French priests, together with their plea that Gallagher and Browne be named respectively to Charleston and Savannah.

Needless to say, Cheverus was incensed when he learned that such charges were being listened to in Rome, and he wrote to Cardinal Litta in April, 1817:

> The fact is that the bishops here exercise no undue favoritism. They esteem and even venerate priests who are commendable for piety, zeal, and learning, whatever their nationality; but they are, and always will be opposed to those who are addicted to drink, gaming, or other vices. . . . [Dennis Ryan, a case in point] we have kindly received as a guest and a beloved son into our household and

have supported and taught (and ordained deacon and shall soon promote to the priesthood). . . . Here your Eminence has an example of the method which the French employ to exclude the . . . Irish. With the same charity, not a few who have come from Ireland have . . . been received into the Seminary of Baltimore and at Georgetown. . . . There is no danger that the bishops in this country will overstep the rightful bounds of their authority. The danger lies, as experience has shown, in laymen, nominal Catholics, who are Protestant in spirit, disregarding entirely episcopal authority.[25]

He did not add, as well he might, that all too frequently the nominal Catholics were led in their revolts by Irish clergymen. But he felt strongly that some one "respectable and intelligent" ought to go to Rome to counteract these ridiculous charges. It was a pity Dubourg had not stayed long enough to be present when Browne arrived in Rome with his canards.[26] Cheverus could only hope God would "inspire the two unhappy priests with sentiments of sincere repentance and humble submission" to the third archbishop who *was* French.[27]

It was a forlorn hope, of course. Browne and Gallagher pretended for a time obedience to Maréchal, but it was not long before the old anti-French charges were revived and Cheverus advised the archbishop to write to Rome. "I am going to write on my part," he asserted. Then he went on:

> Do not forget to mention that the two priests who live with you are one an American and the other English, that we already have had three Irish bishops, etc., etc. In a word, that there is no predilection and still less a French faction. . . . As to the language, Father Hurley himself told me that a Frenchman who spoke English had the advantage over an Irishman because of his brogue.[28]

If it was hard to bear the thought of insubordinate priests it was even more painful to feel that the complaints of the laity reached the Holy See as well. Invariably the laymen who protested seemed to "mock the Pope and even Religion," since not one of them approached the sacraments. If someone from Rome could visit the United States, it would soon be evident "on which side there is regularity, piety and zeal." These unjust appeals would soon be seen in their true light, as acts of insubordination by parishioners to their pastors.[29] If Propaganda continued to receive laymen who were Catholics in name only, the consequences would be regrettable, to say the least. Surely the Dioceses of Baltimore, Louisiana, and Bardstown should make it plain that the only ambition of French prelates was "to sacrifice for the salvation of souls, *their* success, the love for their flocks, answering all calumnies without rejoinder."[30]

Archbishop Maréchal did, of course, write to Rome. After an extended visit of his diocese in 1818 he sent a lengthy report of the situation as he saw it. He said bluntly that the Belgian, French, and German priests had proved to be the best missionaries. Worthy Irish priests had always been welcomed with open arms; unfortunately not all the priests who came from Ireland were worthy. It was a lamentable fact that the dissensions now existing, and indeed most of the troubles since the Church was established in North America, were due to priests from Ireland who "were given over to drunkenness or ambition." Their calumny that the French bishops meant to expel Irish priests simply did not agree with the facts. Ten of the clergy now on mission in the Archdiocese of Baltimore were Irish and had received their faculties from Maréchal himself; the greatest part of the clergy studying at St. Mary's Seminary were now Irish; of the fourteen French priests within Maréchal's jurisdiction only six had parish duties, the rest living at the Sulpician seminaries in Baltimore or Emmitsburg.

Maréchal then discussed in detail the precise situations existing in Norfolk and Charleston. He pointed out that although Father Clorivière would be exceedingly valuable in the latter city, it was no longer possible to keep him there as a result of the opposition of Gallagher and his impious adherents. In his place Maréchal had sent two Jesuits, one an American, the other an Irishman; but it was impossible to predict that these new non-French pastors could restore peace. Perhaps the time had come to establish a new diocese in that region. Then he said in strongest terms:

> Perhaps it may seem strange to the Sacred Congregation that I have written to them so often about these dangers. But here we are dealing with a matter of the utmost importance. For if these impious men should again deceive the Sacred Congregation whether by threats or by means of false promises, or if it were to give them the least bit of protection, it would do more harm to religion in these regions than the labor of a thousand missionaries could accomplish for it. The vast multitude of faithful American Catholics is horrified at this impious faction, and is surprised that its messengers going to Rome from our shores have any hope of again deceiving the Sacred Congregation of the Propaganda of the Faith.[31]

Cheverus himself was too weighed down by personal grief at Father Matignon's death that fall, and he told Maréchal, "I do not write to Rome. I have nothing in particular to say. If you wish, make mention of the loss I have suffered." What more could be said than the archbishop's unmistakable warnings? But if the time had come to make another southern see:

> After what has passed at Charleston, and in view of their actual dispositions, their Bishop should not be French. I should like him to be an American. Why should it not be Benedict Fenwick or his brother, if you can make the sacrifice? The Jesuits should not oppose it. Anyway, you know better than I the circumstances and people. Propose whom you will and add with confidence that I am of your opinion.[32]

Benedict Fenwick and James Wallace, the Jesuits whom Maréchal sent to Charleston in 1818, brought peace to that troubled area but the Bishop of Boston soon learned of fresh difficulties in another part of the metropolitan's jurisdiction. The trustees of Norfolk, Virginia, rebelled against their French-born pastor, Father James Lucas, and invited Father Thomas Carbry, an Irish Dominican from Bishop Connolly's diocese, to become their pastor. Without any authorization from the prelate whose jurisdiction he was entering, Carbry went to Norfolk and when Archbishop Maréchal summoned him to appear, or at least to present credentials which could possibly justify such an act, the lay trustees replied that their new pastor was authorized by Cardinal Litta and that they neither recognized Lucas as their lawful pastor nor Maréchal as their lawful bishop.[33] When Cheverus first heard of Carbry's usurpation he was dumfounded. "One would think this unfortunate Father Carbry has lost his reason," he suggested to Maréchal. "Does it seem possible he had from Rome anything which resembles an authorization?"[34] Neither he nor Maréchal suspected, naturally, that on February 25, 1818, the Bishop of New York had recommended Carbry to Rome for Bishop of Norfolk.

Cheverus knew how Maréchal must feel. He had himself had a taste of the kind of man Carbry was proving himself to be. Carbry earlier that year had accused Cheverus, in a letter written to the Bishop of Boston himself, of calling the Dominican priest a drunkard. Carbry had heard it, he claimed, from a Charleston trustee who had visited Cheverus in the fall of 1818. Cheverus replied coolly that he was not much concerned about the Charleston man's tale; there had been twenty other people in the small study-bedroom of Franklin Street at the time Huston called. As for the imputation itself, he continued courteously, "I had not insinuated it, and what is more, I had never thought it."[35] It was distasteful to reflect, however, that a priest whom he had believed he knew on the most gentlemanly level in New York City was now listening to gossip from dissident trustees in one southern city while deliberately stirring up trouble among the same sort of people in Norfolk. Cheverus fervently hoped that Bishop Plessis, who was on his way to Paris and Rome, could convey to Propaganda something of the nature of the American problem.[36]

Meanwhile he watched with anxious eye the next developments in Virginia. On September 28, 1819, Archbishop Maréchal sent a pastoral letter to the Norfolk congregation, extending sixty-three printed pages and outlining the history and teaching of the Church on the jurisdiction of bishops and the rights of congregations.[37] When Cheverus read it he cried, "I adhere heart and soul!" If Carbry did not understand it, after Maréchal's masterly exposition, at least no one except a determined schismatic could recognize the Dominican as pastor of Norfolk. "Your letter is a monument of great significance for the Church in the United States," Cheverus asserted. "It will make for authority in the future and it can be cited with confidence in order to maintain discipline." He urged the archbishop to send it to Rome and to have Father Grassi translate it into Italian or Latin.[38]

Cheverus admired Maréchal intensely and as his respect deepened so did his love. It seemed most timely that the pallium for the third Archbishop of Baltimore should arrive that fall, and when Cheverus learned that Maréchal had asked Anthony Kohlmann to preside at the investment ceremonies he was even more pleased. He wrote affectionately:

> I celebrated with you in spirit at the altar on St. Ambrose, the second Sunday in Advent, and I will celebrate the 4th which will invest you with the Pallium. I am delighted that you asked Father Kohlmann. You could not receive it from holier hands. It is furthermore homage rendered to the Society [of Jesus].

He wanted Maréchal to know how one bishop felt. If troubles ever arose in Boston, he said emphatically, "instead of disputing your jurisdiction I would throw myself on my knees and beg you to interject your authority to which I would submit with all my soul."[39]

No metropolitan ever needed such assurances more. The trustee troubles in Carolina and Virginia were only part of the whole picture. Beyond the mountains Flaget and Dubourg were seeking ways to provide for the growing Catholic populations in their respective dioceses, with energies that sometimes brought each other into conflict and at other times affected the eastern dioceses. Flaget had never deviated from his opposition to David's nomination to Philadelphia and by 1818 Cheverus advised Maréchal that it was futile to continue to think of David for the eastern city.[40] When Flaget consecrated David the next year as his own coadjutor it ended all further hope that the vacant See of Philadelphia would receive either of the two men originally recommended to Rome as Egan's successor.[41]

Bishop Flaget's visions of new dioceses for the Northwest further complicated the question of the eastern sees. While Cheverus and Maréchal were considering Benedict Fenwick a desirable candidate for a see at Charleston, and Demetrius Gallitzin as a possibility for Philadelphia, Flaget's first plans for new dioceses at Vincennes, Detroit, and Cincinnati hinged upon these same men's names. Dubourg, David, and Flaget among themselves discussed Fenwick for Ohio and Gallitzin for Detroit. When Archbishop Maréchal suggested that only one new see at Cincinnati might suffice and that Bishop David could best serve there, Flaget proved adamant. Flaget and Maréchal eventually agreed upon Edward D. Fenwick for the west and Benedict Fenwick for the east, but Flaget's attitude was rather clear in his remark to the archbishop, "It seems to me that it is the duty of each one of us to propose our own views on this matter to Rome."[42] Using the editorial plural the Bishop of Bardstown wrote to Quebec in 1820:

> We have sent the names of several priests to form three or four new bishoprics in the United States. My own diocese ought to help form two others and still leave me enough territory to keep three very zealous bishops busy. If we obtain our requests from the Holy Father we shall lose no time in forming two ecclesiastical provinces and in having two archbishops.[43]

Bishop Dubourg was likewise conceiving plans of his own for Louisiana. Like Flaget he desired a coadjutor, but unlike the Bishop of Bardstown the Bishop of Louisiana could not make up his mind as to the man he preferred for the role. Within two years' time he recommended to Propaganda three different names: Anthony Sedella, Joseph Rosati, and Louis Sibourd.[44] He, too, envisioned a second metropolitan see in the West, but with himself as archbishop. What might result from such an achievement, with a man of Dubourg's changeable nature and enthusiasms, the other bishops could only imagine; but Cheverus admitted to Maréchal, "I have expected for a long time to see Mgr. Dubourg archbishop and I even believed Mgr. David was consecrated to speed this event. If this plan should take place all we can do is to pray that it will contribute to the glory of God and the spread of Religion."[45] Flaget and David had no intention, however, of becoming suffragans of their western colleague and told Baltimore as much; David, writing in Flaget's absence said bluntly, "I have no desire that Mgr. Dubourg be our Metropolitan. Although it will be of advantage to the Church to establish a metropolitan see in the west, it is hardly opportune at the present time."[46]

All this time, while western prelates dreamed of the multiplication of dioceses beyond the Appalachian Mountains, while Maréchal talked of a see at Charleston, and Rome mistakenly believed Virginia should become separated from the Archdiocese of Baltimore, the See of Philadelphia had remained vacant. To Cheverus, who stopped so frequently in the city on the Delaware River on his trips to Baltimore, the question of this diocese had more immediate interest. In reality he had acted for some years as the archbishop's eyes and ears on those visits, and his letters between 1816 and 1820, when a bishop finally arrived for Philadelphia, were full of the subjeect.

In 1817 when it seemed that the troubles were over for a while, the Bishop of Boston believed that Louis DeBarth, the administrator of the diocese since Egan's death, would make a good bishop. DeBarth had re-established the tenuous peace then prevailing and no one appeared more capable of maintaining it. Cheverus was confident from his early acquaintance with Bishop Connolly that if Archbishop Maréchal approached him on the subject, New York would concur. To the other suggestions made by Maréchal, namely, Jean Moranvillé of Fell's Point, and Demetrius Gallitzin, Cheverus saw some objections that year. The former was doing good work where he was; the latter was still in debt. "A saintly bishop may be put in prison," Cheverus said cogently, "but it should not be for debts."[47] On his return from Maréchal's consecration in December of that year Cheverus talked at length to the Philadelphia clergy and then repeated that DeBarth still seemed the best choice. He had found Father Matthew Carr, the Augustinian, evasive on the subject of DeBarth, but unequivocally opposed to Pierre Babade when that Sulpician's name entered the conversations. Father Michael Hurley would continue his work in

Philadelphia if DeBarth were nominated; the congregation of St. Mary's was definitely in favor of the administrator now. "I believe Mr. DeBarth will accept and I believe all will go well," Cheverus reported.[48] Maréchal agreed with Boston's view and said so. Cheverus was content. "Here is the matter decided for dear Mr. DeBarth," he replied. "I hope it will be for the greater glory of God. . . . It is your turn to make bishops!"[49]

But contentment was ephemeral. By the following summer "fermentation" again filled the Pennsylvania city and DeBarth refused to consider an episcopal nomination while part of the people and clergy opposed him. Cheverus said in resignation, "If he refuses I approve. . . . He who begins his episcopate under unhappy auspices of dissensions, etc. is in danger of sacrificing his repose and forfeiting the fruit of his labors."[50] Before the year was over rumors from across the sea indicated that neither the opinions of American bishops nor the preferences of the Philadelphia Catholics mattered, and Cheverus commented dryly, "I fear the clergy of Pennsylvania will view with pain and some indignation that Rome goes to England for their Bishop."[51]

Rumors or not, Archbishop Maréchal continued in his attempt to get his suffragans to agree on a nomination for Philadelphia. But the probability that Charleston was to be erected as a new see served to make concurrence even less likely. The western bishops thought Benedict Fenwick ought to be named for Philadelphia, while Cheverus believed his Jesuit friend ought to be left in Carolina where "he has already worked such wonders as he did at New York." He admitted he had no reason to believe Fenwick wanted to be a bishop of any see, but he suspected Fenwick might be relieved to be extricated from the supervision of his Jesuit superior; Cheverus knew that his friend's relations with Georgetown were not always happy. If Gallitzin were freed from his debts he had all the other qualities required for Philadelphia. "Without those unfortunate debts," he reminded Maréchal, "the venerable Archbishop Carroll would have proposed him after the death of Mgr. Egan."[52] Flaget and David argued, on the other side, that Fenwick, "having all the Jesuit gentlemen at his heels and being so strong by himself, will be a hundred times more capable of restraining those good people and making the best of it, than poor Mr. Gallitzin."[53] Dubourg, too, wanted the Jesuit for Philadelphia but had chosen to forward his views directly to Rome on February 16, 1819. Bishop Connolly of New York was by this time quite estranged from his fellow bishops by sentiment and preoccupation with troubles of his own. Just why he should have succumbed to the myth of a Gallican conspiracy so popular with Gallagher, Browne, and Carbry is not entirely clear; but from 1817 until the new Irish bishops arrived in 1820 he not only refused to concur with the French bishops in regard to Charleston and Philadelphia, but was outspoken in his views to Propaganda regarding the French. In March, 1820, his words to Rome were echoes of his sentiments in 1819:

> The mass of Catholics will never believe French Bishops . . . are able to be impartial in affairs in which their national interests are involved. As to my person, I know that Frenchmen in this country do not respect me much. They know me and they know that I will always be opposed to the system to force the Catholics of this country to be satisfied with French, Swiss, German and Italian Bishops, who do not understand sufficiently the national tongue. They know that I have advocated it many times before the Sacred Congregation.[54]

Oddly enough the quarrels in New York City were due to the very Irish clergy whom Connolly defended. The only French overtones were to be found in the bishop's personal espousal of a priest from Galway who had proved unsatisfactory to Bishop Plessis of Quebec. When Plessis withdrew Father Charles Ffrench's faculties in the summer of 1817, Ffrench had headed for New York where the bishop made him pastor of St. Peter's in Barclay Street. From that time on the little parish where Mother Seton had spent her first years in the Catholic fold was a hotbed of controversy.[55]

Cheverus could not help feeling deep distress at the developments in New York. Even if he could suppress his unhappiness stemming from Connolly's sentiments toward Frenchmen he could not conceal his pain at seeing the fine work of Anthony Kohlmann and Benedict Fenwick being destroyed by quarrels and threats of schism. Cheverus was bound to feel a paternal interest in the Catholics of a diocese which for its first five years had known only his episcopal ministry. He was prone, too, to feel that Connolly had been mistaken in siding with Father Ffrench; Cheverus had respected Plessis much too long to discount lightly the Canadian prelate's opinion of the Irish priest. He could do nothing, of course, except hope that Connolly might allow Archbishop Maréchal to act as an arbiter in the dispute; but this New York was not inclined to do. Cheverus told the archbishop:

As for the church in New York I grieve in silence and that is all I can do. I believe you can no longer do anything else . . . you would only add to the confusion. Besides, I do not understand the state of things except in a confused way. The scandals one priest has given, and his interdiction which occurred in the Diocese of Quebec are not in doubt, but I fear that to make these things public would produce too much rancor. . . . What is unhappily too clear is that this poor church in New York is in a sad state. How all this must afflict good Father Kohlmann under whose regime that church became so edifying and seemed to predict she would cede to none of the churches of the United States![56]

In charity, Cheverus tried to believe that Bishop Connolly did not really perceive the truth of Ffrench's influence.

When Father Taylor, who was at that time still in the Diocese of New York, informed the Bishop of Boston that he was going to Rome and asked for a letter of introduction Cheverus limited himself to saying simply that Taylor was a New York clergyman generally esteemed and asked Taylor to present Boston's homage to Cardinal Litta and to the Holy Father. He plainly told Taylor that he knew nothing and wished to know nothing of the New York controversy. It was not within his province to meddle in the affairs of that diocese.[57]

Like those in Norfolk, Charleston, and Philadelphia, the troubles in New York reached Roman ears and while Bishop Plessis was in Europe during the winter of 1819–1820 he discovered that the French myth was still given serious credence. He was requested to visit the churches in the United States where there were troubles and report his findings to Rome, particularly in respect to the responsibility of the French clergy for these dissensions. On his return Plessis complied and in the summer of 1820 he visited New York, Philadelphia, and the Archdiocese of Baltimore. His subsequent report to Rome stated categorically:

I believe it is my duty to reiterate to your Eminence that the Catholics in the United States have, in general, much respect and affection for their French bishops, and if there are complaints against them they are made by Irish monks, ambitious vagabonds, who to the misfortune of these dioceses, would occupy the first places.[58]

Not long after Plessis penned his report to Propaganda Cheverus was dismayed to learn that in spite of himself he was involved in New York's troubles after all. It happened as a result of Taylor's visit to Europe that year. William Taylor had written earlier from Genoa and Rome that Cardinal Fontana was persuaded that "the French Bishops are remarkable for the tyrannical exercise of their jurisdiction; that they have formed a 'league' with the Jesuits to exclude Irish priests from their mission and that they are in general disliked in the United States."[59] Yet his news that John England was named Bishop of Charleston and Patrick Kelly as Bishop of Richmond had taken precedence over the old accusations against French prelates. In September, however, Cheverus learned from Taylor that the New York priest had written to Rome from Paris on June 6, 1820, suggesting that the Bishop of Boston be made an apostolic visitor to New York saying:

> Cheverus would be the best, since he is near to New York; was there for the consecration of the church and knows the conditions; he is also respected by all people. He is French, to be sure, but he is also father to the Irish who compose almost entirely the Boston diocese and he is known as impartial from all points, especially from the point of nationality. His zeal, prudence, piety are well known over all the country; he would be the best person for such a mission.[60]

The effect of such news was to send Cheverus frantically to his writing desk. On September 26 he forwarded Taylor's letter to Baltimore saying:

> The enclosed will afflict and surprise you. It had the same effect on me. . . . Perhaps Mr. Taylor has written to you, but in any event I think I ought to send you his letter without delay. Before his departure (which he told me had your approbation) he wrote to me and asked for some lines of recommendation. I sent them to him . . . without the slightest idea of the object of his voyage. I sent him the addresses of relatives & friends in Paris and begged him since he was going to Rome to present my homage to Cardinal Litta and to place me at the feet of His Holiness . . . that all I desired was that they give you at Rome [the right to act] as legate or otherwise the most extensive powers which would put an end to these appeals to Rome which have already caused so much trouble. I hope very much that they do not blame me for anything. I have neither the power nor the wish to meddle in these affairs. Besides, whatever the merit of the case, the conduct of Ffrench, etc. what can be done in a Diocese where the bishop, at least half the clergy and a majority of the . . . congregation would be your opponents?[61]

His dread of being compelled to intervene in the New York affair proved needless; the Roman appointment never arrived. Unknown to Cheverus the Congregation de Propaganda Fide decided that another visitor in addition to Plessis was unnecessary, but if one should be sent "it should be neither Boston nor any other French bishop since they are of a spirit of partiality from a national point of view."[62] Although he was unaware of the complete disregard Rome had given to Plessis' opinion, Cheverus said in comic surmise as Advent drew near, "It must be they listened very little to poor Mr. Taylor, and I presume that he will even end by leaving New York."[63] His relief was even greater when he heard from Baltimore that the new Bishop of Philadelphia was reported to be a fine man. "What you tell me of good Bishop Conwell is consoling," he told Maréchal. "I am writing a word of felicitation to the good Bishop of Philadelphia."[64] Since all the new bishops were Irish they might arrive with prejudices against their French colleagues, but he for one was determined that if they came to do good work they would find the Bishop of Boston ready to welcome them.[65] In his heart he pitied the new prelates, especially the bishop named to Virginia. The conditions they would have to face would discourage the bravest man. It was hard enough being a bishop at any time, but the present state of the Church in the United States strained a man's resources to the breaking point and Cheverus confessed to Maréchal, "I would willingly give up my see if they would replace me by a worthy man. I would like to end my days in your Seminary."

If one year in a man's life can be singled out as the worst, the year that began with the death of Mother Seton was for Cheverus his most taxing one. When he sent New Year's greetings to Plessis in 1821 he gave a brief summary of the affairs of the American Church:

> The new Bishop of Philadelphia arrived in November and has already experienced disagreements. Every day the Bishops of Charleston & Norfolk are expected. This last see, as you know, was erected in spite of our worthy archbishop. . . . Things at New York are the same as you left them.[66]

He tried to be optimistic and added, "They tell me our confrere at Philadelphia is a brave man and they say the same thing of the other two prelates." He was heartily glad, nevertheless, to hear from Maréchal a few weeks later that the archbishop was contemplating a trip to Rome. "I bless God for inspiring your resolution," he exclaimed. "Return invested with powers which will put an end to the confusion of our poor church in the United States."[67] It was dreadful to learn that St. Mary's in Philadelphia, the bishop's very cathedral, was on the verge of becoming a schismatic conventicle.[68] It was even worse to discover that the Bishop of Boston himself was being drawn into the disgraceful quarrel Father William Hogan was carrying on with Bishop Conwell.

From a series of three articles published by Father Hogan, Cheverus learned that on March 20, 1821, this insubordinate priest had told his bishop, "Send for the Rt. Rev. Dr. England of Charleston and the Rt. Rev. Dr. Cheverus of Boston, let the plain statement of facts and circumstances be laid before them and let you and me be bound to abide by their decision." It is doubtful whether he knew that the trustees of St. Mary's also demanded that Bishops England and Cheverus be allowed to mediate, writing to Rome in April:

> In this country it is all important to our Holy Religion that we shall have Pastors and Prelates of eminent talents and large resources, men cultivated with moral, physical, and metaphysical science — men trained in eloquence, men capable of preaching revealed truth impressively. Such Pastors only are qualified to establish and diffuse our Holy Religion in this country. Such Pastors only can be the efficient guardians of its welfare. Such a Pastor is the Right Rev. Bishop Cheverus of Boston. . . .

Bishop Conwell quite naturally refused to consider the demands of Hogan, and Cheverus told him approvingly:

> It becomes my duty to explicitly declare that I am persuaded that you had more than sufficient reasons for withdrawing his faculties. My only astonishment is that any one could countenance the writer of "the most abominable pamphlet that had ever disgraced the Church of God in this country," as our worthy Archbishop rightly expresses it.[69]

French or Irish, the bishops all saw eye to eye on the subject of schismatic priests. Both Maréchal and Cheverus could be relied upon to give their brother in Philadelphia every support. They heartily approved Conwell's action of May 27 which excommunicated Hogan as "a putrid member lest any of our flock should be led into schism and error by attending the sacrilegious functions of his ministry."[70]

Up in Quebec Plessis was more than ever concerned about the trials that his American friends were forced to undergo and he tried to offer some solution. He had interested the Vicar Apostolic of the London District, William Poynter, in Baltimore's affairs and the English prelate suggested that a vigilant agent in Rome ought to be authorized to defend the American cause. On April 13 Plessis told Maréchal that Poynter, who himself had the confidence of the Roman Curia, had recommended Robert Gradwell, the rector of the English College in Rome. The Archbishop of Baltimore could address Gradwell through Poynter in London.[71] Plessis' letter was gratefully received and Cheverus commented hopefully that perhaps now "Dr. Gradwell aided by the influence of Dr. Poynter could arrange things according to our desires."[72] If Gradwell would talk to Father Grassi, who was always zealous for their good, things might eventually improve.

This was the year, as we have seen, that the Bishop of Boston went south for the consecration of the Baltimore Cathedral. In poor health and discouraged by recent developments in Philadelphia, he was hardly disposed to hear more bad news. But while he visited the Jesuits in Georgetown two new items reached his ears. Grassi had just written from Rome that Father William Harold, who had caused dissension in Philadelphia in Archbishop Carroll's day, was returning to New York this time as a "patent missionary" subject to no bishop at all! News from the west indicated that again a second metropolitan see was being planned with Badin and Edward Fenwick proposed as bishops under Flaget, information which could only depress the bishop who had cried earlier in the year, "They are making too many bishops!"[73]

The return trip north was painful, too. He stopped only briefly in Philadelphia and New York, but it was long enough to learn in the former city that Bishop Conwell had printed the letters of support that both Maréchal and Cheverus had sent him in the Hogan matter. Cheverus predicted gloomily, "They are to reply to us in the gazettes." In New York there were avid questions about Maréchal's prospect of going to Rome. Cheverus knew the archbishop had hoped the trip need not become public knowledge, but it seemed that Bishop Plessis had made no secret of it. "I regret it," Cheverus wrote to Baltimore, "and fear they have already written to Rome."[74] It was a morose little bishop who finally reached Boston in mid-summer to find his household in turmoil from the rantings of Father Lariscy. July, 1821, marked the nadir of his personal and episcopal resources.

In the depths of his despondency he reread the beautiful and moving description that Simon Bruté had sent him of Mother Seton's death. His thoughts fled back to the days of their first felicitous relationship; it was inevitable that the face of Antonio Filicchi should flash across the screen of recollection. Had anyone ever told the staunch Italian friend that his American foundress had died? Cheverus hastily seized his pen and began copying the Bruté record of her last happy days. In his melancholy he added some lines about his own troubles, his persistent grief over the loss of Francis Matignon, his miserable health, and closed his letter sadly, "I have not forgotten you. I will love you to my last breath."[75] The letter was dated July 31, 1821, a most unhappy feast of St. Ignatius for the bishop who had such admiration for the Society of Jesus.

In August he agreed completely with his archbishop that this was no year to talk of holding a council, and like Maréchal he visualized difficulties that were likely to attend the Roman trip.[76] On September 25 he was disturbed to get a letter from Baltimore asking him to go in Maréchal's place. It did not take him long to reply:

> I have followed your advice and examined the thing before God. I could not leave Boston at least until Mr. Taylor is *plus au fait* and better known. Besides, what could I do? I am French, they would not believe me, and several of our confreres would write in opposition. . . . I doubt even, dear Seigneur, that you could do more than your agent until you are authorized by our other confreres. Besides, the affair is concluded, it would seem, for Mr. Harold, and as to future nominations of Bishops what can be done if we are not in accord? . . . Excuse this letter, it is not in much order, and I swear to you I do not see clearly in our affairs. May the Lord enlighten me and direct me. Pray for me. At least I see very clearly and feel very vividly that I love and venerate you with all my heart.[77]

Archbishop Maréchal understood his friend's refusal, but he was determined that Rome should hear the truth of the American situation before another winter passed. On October 5 he sent a hasty note over to Baron Hyde de Neuville in Washington saying:

> I have long since thought of going to France and of pushing on from there to Rome where the interests of the Church imperiously demand my presence. I do not yet know when it will be possible to start. I am told of a vessel which is to leave at the end of this month from the port of New York for Le Havre. . . . I do not know who is Ambassador of His Most Christian Majesty to the Holy See. A letter of your Excellency in which you ask him to support with all

his influence the representations which I propose to make to His Holiness might be of eminent service to the welfare of our Church here, so ill-treated by Propaganda.

He concluded with a request that Neuville procure a passport from Secretary John Quincy Adams, saying that he needed it by the next Thursday at the latest.[78] Four days later he told Plessis:

> I intend to sail on Monday from New York for Le Havre, whence I shall push on to Rome after having stopped for two or three days in Paris. I regret extremely that my excellent and affectionate friend, Dr. Cheverus, was unable to undertake this mission. But the state of his health and other obstacles would not permit him to leave his diocese and therefore I am obliged to go at once. . . . You know all about the lack of discernment shown by Propaganda. Its members mean well, I know, but they need to be better informed.[79]

When Cheverus himself mentioned Maréchal's departure to Plessis on October 17 he said fervently, "If his efforts could only bring peace to our poor churches!"[80]

Imperceptibly the prospect began to improve after that. True, the letters arriving in Boston continued to bring sporadic recurrences of distress; Plessis informed Bishop Connolly that under no circumstances would he receive Charles Ffrench back in the diocese of Quebec. "For myself," Plessis said coolly, "I am resolved never to employ any of these roving religious who are suited only to bringing trouble in the Churches." Let Philadelphia have him, if it were true that Bishop Conwell would take Ffrench.[81] But Cheverus knew that poor Conwell was ill enough over the Hogan schism and wishing he had never left Ireland. And wherever Father Ffrench went it could do little to help New York, where another priest was now under interdict, this time poor Father Peter A. Malou who had once assisted Cheverus in dedicating St. Patrick's Cathedral.[82]

Within the Diocese of Boston, however, the bishop could regain his equanimity. After Philip Lariscy's departure Cheverus applied himself to the new missal he meant to have printed, "the epistles and Gospels and all the passages of the scripture . . . exactly copies of the Douay Bible, conforming to our resolution in November, 1810, signed by Mgr. Carroll and his suffragans."[83] He was disappointed that Bishop England, who got as far north as New York that fall, did not carry out his intention of coming on to Boston; but Cheverus was glad to see that the Bishop of Charleston was now in agreement with them that

Hogan was in error.[84] The month of Maréchal's departure for Europe found Cheverus on mission in Rhode Island where he worked with a will until All Saints. As the year closed he was consoled by Antonio Filicchi's letter which spoke of his own grief at Mother Seton's death yet reminded the bishop, "Surely she is now the happiest of us all, after so severe a trial as that she experienced all along the course of life in this vale of misery." Cheverus blessed the inspiration which caused his letter of July; it was the first word Filicchi had received of Elizabeth Seton's death. It was comforting, too, to read Filicchi's words, "In the sincerity of my heart I never valued, venerated, and loved a Pastor, a Prelate, as I did, and do, you, in whose welfare I shall ever rejoice above my own, whom I shall always be proud to serve, and obey without reserve."[85]

The next year was infinitely happier and the bishop's letters to his friends in Guadeloupe began to sound as they had formerly, "Nothing new here — my health holds up — the Valnais do not forget you . . ." and happy references to the fourth little Bonneuil now gracing the home of his dear children.[86] In March he told Plessis of his pleasure over the Bishop of Charleston's project of a weekly paper in his diocese devoted "entirely to religion" and costing $3.50 a year.[87] No one had heard anything from Maréchal yet, but that spring rumors were circulating that Bishop Kelly of Richmond was likely to return to Ireland to become Bishop of Waterford and Virginia might once more be part of the archbishop's domain. In June, when still no news of the European traveler was known, Cheverus began hoping that Maréchal might soon arrive to bring it in person. June did bring, however, a copy of Stephen Blyth's new edition of the story of his conversion with its fulsome dedication to the Bishop of Boston. Cheverus reproved Blyth gently, "I am afraid that in your dedication your *Gamaliels* will be looked upon as no compliment to the Canadian clergy or the Seminary at Montreal," but he felt sorry for his convert friend who seemed to need money and was using the book to raise it. The Bishop of Boston would take fifty copies, saying with a flash of his old humor to Father Le Saulnier, "It is necessary to pay for the dedication."[88] He felt very much his old self as he took a boat to Portland, Maine, in mid-June.

It was a happy summer in Maine. Aside from a touch of asthma Cheverus felt very well, and as he visited the multiplying flocks in his eastern mission all the old zeal flowered anew. From Portland he pushed on to the Damariscotta and Sheepscott River Valleys where he visited old friends and dedicated a new church. Father Ryan, who had been pastor there since October, 1818, had built a small, wooden chapel at North Whitefield where the Catholic population now out-distanced those of Newcastle and Damariscotta. On June 30 Bishop Cheverus dedicated it to St. Dennis, in tribute to his first clerical son who "did so much good here and is generally loved and respected."[89]

Even before his Maine labors were half over he wrote vigorously to Bonneuil of his plans to visit two missions in Vermont and New Hampshire and since one of these was on the banks of Lake Champlain he would go on to Quebec. "I count on being back in Boston at the beginning of September," he said, as the busy summer stretched before him. Even in Portland the future looked bright. "The Catholics here have rented a room, erected an altar there, benches, etc. and have made a decent little chapel. I celebrated holy Mass there this morning and will make divine office there tomorrow (Sunday)."[90] He added a little postscript for Félicie with the good news that he and Father Taylor had come into a little legacy from a Marseilles gentlemen who had spent a dozen years in Boston.

Back in Boston in mid-July Cheverus stayed only long enough to arrange an advance in money for the Bonneuils whose commercial affairs were disarranged by the hard times, picked up young Samuel Walley who was to enter the college in Montreal, and started out again on the mission.[91] By July 29 they had reached Windsor, Vermont, where the bishop preached in the courthouse that afternoon.[92] In Montreal Cheverus was as happy as he always was in the company of the Sulpicians and longed to spend some months there. "I would renew there, I hope," he told the director of that holy house, "that priestly spirit which evaporates in the world even in the midst of exercising the holy Ministry."[93] His whole Canadian visit was a joy and he told Plessis, "My visits to Canada filled me with respect for your edifying clergy. There is too much piety for things to go wrong."[94] On the return trip he had the company of a Canadian priest as far as Vergennes, Vermont, and he reported to Le Saulnier from there on September 2, "Yesterday we had four baptisms, 16 Communions, and 2 confirmations. In the afternoon I preached in the *Court House* . . . We leave this morning."[95] His dream of establishing a church at Vergennes had come true; the people were going to get a small chapel and as a token of hope the bishop left the chalice and vestments he had been given at Montreal. On September 21 Father Taylor wrote delightedly to the Kavanaghs, "Dr. Cheverus has returned from Canada in good health and spirits."[96]

Then, at long last, word came from New York; Archbishop Maréchal was home after a fifty-day passage.[97] Inconvenient and expensive as the trip had been he had no slightest regret for having gone. The Roman Curia had overwhelmed him with kindness. Very quickly Boston and Quebec learned the happy tidings:

> The favor I solicited for the good of religion was that Propaganda will write to us and listen to our reasons before it proceeds to nominate men recommended only by intriguing monks at Rome, or by foreign bishops who have no knowledge whatever of our ecclesiastical affairs. Fortunately Propaganda yielded to my representations, and in the future will correspond with us before taking action and will turn a deaf ear to the proposals of men who misled it on more than one occasion.[98]

While he was in Rome in February Maréchal had also succeeded in having Virginia transferred back to his own diocese, and Patrick Kelly who had returned to Ireland to succeed the deceased Bishop of Waterford and Lismore, Robert Walsh, would have no successor in the United States other than the Archbishops of Baltimore for another two decades.[99] It only required the ordination of Virgil Barber at Holy Cross on December 3, 1822, to complete the full happiness of that year of recovery.

CHAPTER XVII

A ROYAL SUMMONS

THE new year, 1823, began pretty much as any other for the Bishop of Boston. He had his usual winter cold, and sometimes was ashamed of his weakness at the end of a full day. He knew that down in Baltimore Archbishop Maréchal was having some difficulties with the Jesuits over property matters, and up in Montreal the Sulpicians were distressed at Archbishop Plessis' action in appointing a bishop unfavorable to their interests; but these were concerns that did not involve anything but Boston's sympathies, which were impartially bestowed. In January Cheverus again vetoed holding a provincial council of the American hierarchy. "We all adhere to the brief concerning Philadelphia," he told Maréchal. "What more could we do? We can not abolish trustees and pews until we agree on this point which we do not."[1] Times were still hard, and in Charleston Bishop England was compelled to suspend publication of the *Miscellany* for lack of money. "He lost considerably," Cheverus informed Plessis. "Nothing new here," he added. "Father Barber is beginning at Claremont and I have some hope of an establishment in the state of Vermont."[2] After Lent and Easter were past the bishop meant to go to Hartford "to gather a little flock there."

In March Father Taylor gave the St. Patrick's Day address, as he had been doing since his arrival, at the banquet of the Irish Charitable Society of Boston. After the *Boston Commercial Gazette* printed it there were some repercussions beyond the diocese, and the theologians in Baltimore were for a second time disturbed by what they believed were evidences of shaky doctrine. But Cheverus would not be disturbed and wrote equally to the archbishop:

The dear and worthy Mr. Taylor read me his discourse. (I had departed when he delivered it) and nothing in it struck me as irreverent. It is not correct theologically, but when one is sure of orthodox faith and pure intention, I don't think it worth the trouble to examine a banquet speech theologically. Mr. Taylor presents his respects and will always be ready to disavow and retract whatever should be inexact.[3]

The collections for the poor taken up after these banquet speeches and turned over to the society by Taylor made much more of an impression on his listeners than his liberal views toward England or his defense of the Church's compatibility with republican institutions.[4]

But in Holy Week news from France arriving in Boston upset not only Cheverus, Father Taylor, and the city but everyone who knew the Bishop of Boston. On March 26, 1823, the Boston journals carried an astounding item. To quote the *Daily Advertiser:*

We understand the name of the Right Rev. Bishop Cheverus appears in the lists of French Bishops; he is nominated to the see of Montauban near Toulouse. Should he accede to the wishes of the French King, our community here will sustain an irreparable loss, in the departure of this amiable, conciliatory, learned and excellent Prelate.[5]

While carrying the same news the *Columbian Centinel* further commented:

When Louis the 14th wished to conciliate his protestant subjects, at Poitou, he sent amongst them the immortal author of Telemachus, and his present successor could not make a more judicious selection than he has done in the person of Bishop Cheverus who possesses the spirit of Fénelon, to secure the affections of the colonists of Montauban. Bishop Cheverus is peculiarly calculated to extract the sting from prejudice by his mild and persuasive spirit, his charitable disposition, and his extensive attainments.[6]

The newspaper accounts were probably based upon a list published in *Moniteur* and other French papers of seventeen new prelates named by Louis XVIII on January 13, 1823. Cheverus himself got the first hint of this astonishing development from his cousin in Paris, Moreau de la Vigerie, and he wrote hastily to Maréchal:

This news surprises and afflicts me and comes most unfortunately at this holy time. I am very upset. I wish to avoid this translation, if it is possible. . . . I hope they refuse at Rome to transfer me to

Montauban. Give me your prayers and advice, My poor head is swimming. The morning papers say they hope I will not abandon Boston.[7]

It was a bolt from the blue, but there was nothing of the quality of rumor about the news. In two weeks he received official confirmation by letter from the Grand Aumonier of the king and from Baron Hyde de Neuville. The former, Gustave-Maximilien-Juste, Prince de Croij, chief royal official of Church affairs in France, writing on January 18, 1823, told Cheverus the king was relying on the Bishop of Boston to comply promptly with this mark of his Majesty's confidence in his piety, zeal, and devotion to Louis' person. Departure for France should take place at once.

The Grand Aumonier explained how the nomination had occurred:

M. le Baron Hyde de Neuville, on his return from the United States, approached me with a very lively interest in your situation. He led me to understand that the climate of the country, little favorable to your health, would perhaps be a motive capable of persuading you to accept a new destination in France. After this flattering hope I proposed to his Majesty that he name you Bishop of Montauban whose re-establishment and circumscription are definitely decreed by the bull of the Holy See of October 10, 1822. Blame me for the reception of this letter and keep me informed as to what you are going to do.[8]

The letter from Hyde de Neuville dated January 24 was an urgent appeal to Cheverus to accept. The king, he said, was thinking of Cheverus' health and the good of the public interest. Montauban was a city of both Catholics and Protestants; who better than Cheverus could maintain peace and fill the people with a spirit of concord? "These labors are not beyond your strength," Hyde de Neuville argued. "It will cost you little to make yourself love and bless our France, which is yours, too. Accept, I beg of you. . . . Bring us your benediction."[9] Cheverus was appalled. This was what came of going south for his health in 1821! The former French minister to the United States had left Washington in 1822 apparently convinced that the Bishop of Boston could not survive in the New England climate. Cheverus wished now that he had never visited the nation's capital and preached there where the baron could reach his own conclusions about episcopal colds.

Cheverus had known the Hyde de Neuvilles since the early days of his episcopacy, of course. There had been those first days of acquaintance while the baron and his lady were exiles in New York in 1810 and making friends with Eliza Sadler. In 1814 Hyde de Neuville returned to France at the first news of the restoration of Louis XVIII arriving in time to flee with the king during the uncertainty of the 100 Days. But in January of 1816 he was named minister plenipotentiary to the United States where his years of exile had furnished him with so many valuable connections. He arrived in late spring that year and was comfortably settled in Washington by the time Cheverus came to Georgetown to confer the pallium on Leonard Neale.[10] The French diplomat could scarcely have avoided noticing how frail the Bishop of Boston seemed that November, for Cheverus already had the nagging cough which he resignedly called his constant companion. Certainly the last time Hyde de Neuville had seen Cheverus in 1821 the bishop's health had been very poor indeed.

When Hyde de Neuville sailed from New York in October, 1819, for a brief visit to France he had several things in mind relating to the Church in the United States. Maréchal had particularly begged him to secure some works of art for his cathedral; but on his own Neuville was determined to mention the Bishop of Boston. When he returned early in 1821 he carried letters from the Cheverus family begging the bishop to return to France. Louis even offered, if money were the obstacle, to pledge support to a successor at Boston. Cheverus had been deeply moved by his brother's generosity, but he had no intention of leaving Boston and told Louis:

> I do not know how to leave this establishment. Unfortunately for both myself and it, I am too necessary to it. This is so true that, although I have three priests with me, I can hardly leave it for a few days. The little Ursuline Convent . . . forms still another bond. . . . I wrote to M. de Neuville to thank him for his attention, but, if I return to France I do not wish *any other title than that of the Former Bishop of Boston.* . . . The noble and generous sacrifice which you wish to make will not be necessary to find me a successor. I assure you that I would like one, but that brings other difficulties.[11]

Neither Cheverus nor Maréchal suspected that when Hyde de Neuville returned to France permanently in July, 1822, he would do anything more about Cheverus' concerns. As far as they knew he was returning to become French minister to Turkey and the only intercession the Bishop of Boston expected was in behalf of old Joseph de Valnais, the septuagenarian consul who really needed honorable retirement in his native France.[12] Certainly when Maréchal was in Paris that summer after his Roman visit nothing was said to disturb his mind on the subject of his most treasured suffragan. The Archbishop of Baltimore had returned full of Hyde de Neuville's courtesies, the amiable welcome given him by the king, "the interesting conversation with his august brother, *Monsieur,* and the touching kindness of the Duchess of Angoulême and the Duchess of Berry."[13] It was probably the news of the re-erection of the Diocese of Montauban in October which spurred the former minister to the United States to broach the subject of the Bishop of Boston's return. By that time, of course, Maréchal was homeward bound. Now, in April, 1823, Cheverus found Hyde de Neuville begging him to make "an act of submission to our King, our Church, and the common good," and asserting that Cheverus dared not refuse this appeal of Louis XVIII.

Cheverus was in a terrible quandary and took the only step he felt possible; he consulted the friends he judged most just and capable of advising him. On April 8 he forwarded the letters of Hyde de Neuville and the Grand Aumonier to Baltimore saying:

> I received these letters Saturday. I want to refuse, but could I do it without going myself to cast myself at the feet of Louis XVIII? Tell me what response to make. God keep me from giving a bad example to my confreres. I am sick and uneasy. . . . Do not communicate these letters to anyone except M. Tessier or others of confidence. . . . I am ashamed of these letters. I am ashamed of the interest I inspire here. I am sick and can scarcely write. . . . Pray for your poor suffragan.[14]

Two days later, after copying both letters again, he wrote to the Sulpicians of Montreal and to Plessis in Quebec asking the same questions. To Father Le Saulnier he added, "If the roads were not so bad I would consult you in person."[15] These men knew him and could tell him what were his duties to the king and to Boston. He would take their advice and act upon it.

The news of his nomination was naturally no secret in Europe. Robert Gradwell, Maréchal's agent in Rome, wrote on April 13, "I have read with concern in the French papers that the Bishop of Boston is nominated to a see in France, and that he is soon expected in his native country."[16] The Sulpician superior in Paris chided Maréchal, "I am astonished that you did not speak to me about the Bishop of Boston, named by the king to the Diocese of Montauban. We doubt here that he will accept. . . . They say he owes his nomination to M. Hyde de Neuville."[17]

In Boston there was more than plaintive protest, and Cheverus wrote to Bonneuil that fear of losing their bishop had put the city in confusion. "They want me painted, engraved, etc. . . . The city wished to present me with an address, etc., etc. All the gazettes are concerned with me,"[18] he added in a postscript to Félicie. Mrs. John Gore insisted that he sit for Gilbert Stuart so that there should be a lasting likeness of the "dear little bishop" after he was gone.[19] The Protestants of the city determined to appeal to his Catholic Majesty of France that their eminent fellow citizen be allowed to remain with them. On April 22 they framed a petition which included the argument:

> The Catholics of this place and of the New England States are generally a description of persons who need not only instructions as to their great duties as Christians, but also advice, consolations, encouragement or correction in their temporal concerns.
>
> To accomplish objects so important to them, and so necessary to the good order of society, the most commanding confidence is indispensable in their ecclesiastical rulers.
>
> It is impossible for us to make known to you by any words how entire, grateful and beneficent is the dominion of Bishop Cheverus over all to whom he ministers in his Apostolic Authority. We hold him to be a blessing and a treasure in our social community which we cannot part with and which, without injustice to any man we may affirm, if withdrawn from us can never be replaced.[20]

Among the 226 signers were the men who represented the city in every capacity, local, state, and federal. Almost every Protestant of note subscribed his name. Included were such men as Elbridge Gerry, the son of the former minister to France and Vice-President of the United States during the War of 1812; Harrison Grey Otis of the Governor's Council, Mayor Josiah Quincy, Judge Daniel Webster, Gardiner Greene, the wealthiest man of the city, John Lowell, Jr., the author of the anti-Catholic letter of fifteen years earlier. There were the names of bank presidents like William Gray of the federal branch bank, Thomas L. Winthrop of the Union Bank; heads of insurance companies like James Hall and Francis J. Oliver; prosperous merchants like Benjamin West, John H. Dexter, and Thomas H. Perkins. Many of these had given money to help build Holy Cross and now believed they had every reason to protect their investments. It was, perhaps, typical that they protested as men of property on grounds of interest in the public order; but that they protested at all is remarkable. When the Canadian superior of St. Sulpice learned of the memorial he exclaimed, "The action of the Boston Protestants in his favor is perhaps a unique thing of this genre!"[21]

Archbishop Maréchal was naturally the person most concerned. To him it was unthinkable that Cheverus should go. He consulted Jean Marie Tessier at St. Sulpice and his vicar-general, James Whitfield, and then wrote hurriedly to Boston that all were agreed that Cheverus should not accept Montauban. If his health demanded it, he might perhaps go for a trip to France and consult some enlightened persons there, but it was their unanimous conviction that he could not be replaced at Boston. "You are regarded, and with reason, as the most suited to maintaining peace and discipline by your example and the general respect you command," Maréchal asserted positively. The king could find some one else for Montauban, and since he was a pious man he would not be offended by Cheverus' refusal.[22]

When the Bishop of Boston read this letter on April 21 he went straight to the foot of the altar and on his knees meditated for an hour; then he replied to his archbishop:

> My health is much better than it was two years ago and does not need a trip to France. I stay here. Send me a letter I can forward to France with my reply and which will support it, and mention in it the advice of venerable Mr. Tessier and dear Mr. Whitfield to whom I offer my gratitude.
>
> My refusal is decided but I will not make it public in Boston until Sunday. Do not make it public previously, but I did not want to delay a moment in reassuring you.
>
> In haste, much agitated, but firmly resolved . . .[23]

While he had pen in hand he wrote to Bonneuil, too.

> The papers of France have perhaps already told you of my nomination by the king to the see of Montauban. I believe I must refuse. It is really impossible to remove me from here, and I could not do it without doing great harm to Religion. Therefore I stay here, and I hope they will pardon me in France where so many others can so well replace me at Montauban. . . . For three weeks I have been agitated but at last my decision is made and I will stay here.[24]

As soon as Maréchal's formal letter of April 24 reached Boston

Cheverus attached it and the protest of the Boston Protestants to
his own letter of April 30 and rushed the packet to Joseph de Valnais
who was returning to France for the last time. Valnais' house, over
which his daughter presided with such grace, had been a pleasant
place for tea these past three years and both Father Taylor and the
bishop would miss the old man. Taylor was to see him off on May 1
and Cheverus knew his letter of refusal was in safe hands. The packet
of the Bishop of Boston included a message, too, for Hyde de
Neuville:

> I am broken-hearted, but I believe I am obliged for the good of
> religion and even for the honor of the French name not to abandon
> my post. If you had seen the struggle I went through, if you knew
> exactly my situation and that of my diocese, you would pardon my
> refusal, I am sure. I have exposed my reasons to the grand aumonier
> for my refusal; I will be uneasy until I know they are found
> sufficient.[25]

With characteristic forthrightness Cheverus had said exactly what
was in his heart, but the letters had not been easy to write. The letter
from the Grand Aumonier had placed him in a terrible position.
"Sentiments compounded of surprise, devotion to the King, love of
country, what I owe to my flock here, to Religion," he explained,
had produced a violent agitation. For days, while waiting for advice,
he had suffered an agonizing indecision being able only to weep and
pray. But Baltimore, Montreal, and Quebec had all agreed: his departure would cause much harm. Maréchal, Roux, and Plessis knew
the truth of his diocese; they had written, "Stay." He had included
the Protestant memorial as further evidence that duty compelled him
to refuse the king's nomination.[26] When Consul de Valnais sailed
on May 1 it should have been the end of the matter. As he had
done twenty years before the obedient little prelate had presumed the
positive decision of his superior to be the voice of God. Maréchal
joyfully spread the news, and Poynter replied from London, "I sincerely rejoice & thank Alm. God that Dr. Cheverus has refused the
See offered to him by the King of France. It would have been a
calamity for his American diocese to have lost such a pastor, so
beloved by his flock."[27]

But nothing was quite the same as that April 29 when the young
priest told Carroll, "Here I stay." Hardly had his refusal left Boston
harbor when he heard from Montreal that Father Roux believed

Cheverus should have gone in person to explain his position.[28] Then letters written in February by his family arrived. They had been composed in eager anticipation; already joyous receptions were being planned. Cheverus could well imagine their terrible disappointment when they learned of his refusal. He tried to make Louis understand his seeming cruelty.

> What can I do? I have no one who does not tell me I must stay. I think if you were here you would say the same. If you won't believe me, at least pity me. I am necessary to religion, the whole city says to society. Surely the French clergy can furnish a worthy shepherd for Montauban. . . . My dear sisters, brother, nephews, nieces, forgive me but love me. If you knew all you would see what a sacrifice I make to duty.[29]

But more than anything else it was the changed situation in France which made 1823 so different from 1803. Two decades earlier only uncertainty prevailed regarding Napoleon's policies for the Church; now, with a Bourbon back on the throne Cheverus believed religion was restored to its former happy position as well. He told Father Le Saulnier quite truthfully when he wrote to Montreal the week after Valnais sailed, "I conformed, but the sacrifice cost me dear. It is done. May the Lord accept it and sustain me. I am still far from tranquil."[30] Father Roux in Montreal knew what a sacrifice it was and told Maréchal, "You must have feared extremely the loss of this admirable prelate and we certainly shared your alarms."[31] Like Maréchal and the Baltimore Sulpicians, however, Montreal felt sure Cheverus could be replaced in Montauban, but never in Boston for all the good he did in America.

Actually, for all the interest the French clergy in North America took in events in France, they still retained an inaccurate knowledge of the needs of the Church there. Something must be said at this point of the French situation which prompted the nomination of Cheverus to Montauban. Plessis, Maréchal, Roux, and Cheverus were quite right in assuming that Louis XVIII's restoration vindicated Chateaubriand's assertion in 1814 that "the throne of St. Louis without the religion of St. Louis is an absurd proposition." The constitutional charter of 1814 had declared Catholicism the state religion and royal ordinances soon after facilitated gifts to ecclesiastical establishments and permitted bishops to open schools in each *département* exempt from control by the state university.

But the reconstruction of a hierarchy and clergy was another matter. In 1816 fifteen episcopal and metropolitan sees were still vacant and the vacancies among the lower clerical positions totaled 16,025 as compared with 35,979 occupied. In the very year before Cheverus was named to Montauban bishops were needed at Orleans, Belley, Carcassonne, Quimper, and Tulle while both Lyon and Besançon lacked archbishops; sixteen other nominations of the king accompanied that of Cheverus on January 13, 1823. Of the three French cardinals of the early years of the reign only Louis-François de Bausset was still living in 1823, Alexandre de Talleyrand and César-Guillaume de la Luzerne having died in 1821.[32] The conferring of the *barette* on Anne-Antoine Clermont-Tonnerre did not occur until the month after Cheverus' nomination.[33] The lower clergy had had to be replenished as well. When Louis XVIII had returned to the throne there were scarcely half as many priests as in 1789 and of those available only four per cent were under forty years of age. Chateaubriand was not the only one to reflect that "if things continue to go on as they are, twenty years from now there will only be enough priests in France to attest that once there were altars."

The problems the Church faced in the first years of the Restoration were complicated by the necessity for restoring amicable relations between Paris and Rome. As early as July 22, 1814, steps had been taken with this in view and Gabriel Cortois de Pressigny, the French Ambassador to Rome, opened these negotiations. The instructions this former Bishop of St. Malo consulted included the demand that changes made since 1800 should be annulled, particularly the Concordat of 1801. Pope Pius VII was not sorry to abrogate the unilateral act of Napoleon which he had accepted in order to prevent outright schism, but he was not inclined to play the role of guilty repentant and the negotiations were proceeding slowly when the 100 Days return of Napoleon interrupted them. In 1816 when conversations were resumed Pierre-Jean, Count de Blacas now represented France and together with Ercole Cardinal Consalvi he reached an agreement which seemed satisfactory to both France and the Holy See. The Concordat of 1801 should cease to have effect, former sees would be re-established, and those erected in 1801 would be assured material independence by government subsidies.

The pope was preparing to issue the bulls needed to promulgate the agreement when French action virtually destroyed the work of the negotiations. First the king insisted on inserting a reservation regarding the liberties of the French Church. After suitable language nuances overcame this obstacle and the pope published bulls for forty-two new dioceses and in consistory confirmed three French cardinals, the French Chambers rebelled, taking exception to the traditional phrasing "the full and free authority" of the pope as impugning the rights of the king; heated argument ensued.[34] Matignon could well exclaim, "How slow they are in reaching an accord with the Pope!" Whatever may be claimed for the government's submission of the concordat to the chamber in the form it did, or in any form at all, the upshot of the debate was that the treaty of 1817 was not put into effect.[35] Pius VII declared that provisionally the old division of fifty dioceses would prevail and the new bishops recently appointed were to refrain from exercising their jurisdiction. Until 1822 this "provisional" state of affairs continued.[36]

The distresses of France during this provisional period show plainly in the address of the hierarchy made to the pope on the feast of Pentecost, 1819. After speaking of their high hopes from the Concordat of 1817 and the subsequent blasting of those hopes when the bulls for the new bishops failed to arrive, the French prelates went on to say:

> The state of the church, far from improving in France, has become and becomes from day to day more deplorable. Not only have we not felt a lightening of our burden of grief, but it presses more heavily upon us; and the time is not far distant when it will be impossible to raise us from our ruins. Ecclesiastical discipline is relaxed, a great number of dioceses are not sufficiently governed, the faithful err like flocks without shepherds, ecclesiastical establishments languish; the priesthood is weakened by losses which are not repaired by the small number of students . . . discouraged by the prospect of the misery and disgusts which attend the exercise of the Holy Ministry.[37]

Pius VII replied on August 19, 1819, that it was his ardent desire to remedy these evils but until the obstacles to the concordat were removed existing bishops must remain in their sees and bishops-elect would continue to refrain from governing. Only vacancies in existing sees would be filled by the king's candidates.[38] Not until September 30, 1822, did the pope officially erect thirty new sees for which the king had little by little secured financial endowments.

What of Montauban, the see to which the Bishop of Boston was then nominated by the king? Since 1819 the Council of Tarn-et-

Garonne had repeatedly voted sums for the support of a bishop and a seminary, but a bishop had been desired for years before that.[39] Although Calvinism had penetrated Montauban in the mid-sixteenth century the city and diocese were still predominantly Catholic. Four-fifths of the city, which numbered scarcely more than the 25,000 inhabitants it boasted during the Revolution, remained true to Rome; in the whole *département* 10,720 of a total of 238,143 were Protestants.[40] The nobility, the merchants, and manufacturers remained loyal to the old faith even if the clothmakers, traders in grain, and working people could be lured away. Even before the Restoration the Catholics had cherished persistent hopes that a bishop would once again preside over the diocese which the Revolution had abolished. When Napoleon and his first Empress Josephine visited the city in July, 1808, the faithful had received the imperial couple with double joy for the French ruler was generally believed responsible for the re-erection of the See of Montauban the previous winter. Certainly his official approval had been later attested by the decree of November 21 ordering the organization of the Département de Tarn-et-Garonne and its episcopal see to take effect on January 1, 1809.[41]

The new diocese was created from segments of Toulouse, Cahors, and Agen and comprised under the Cathedral of the Assumption of Montauban twenty-three cantons, 270 parishes, and sixty-eight auxiliary chapels. But nine years passed without any further progress, and the administration of the diocese was left to a vicar-general, Jean Armand Chaudru de Trélissac, a priest acceptable to the three bishops from whose jurisdictions Montauban had been created. The new concordat negotiated in 1817 which confirmed dioceses existing under Napoleon recognized Montauban and a papal bull of July 26, 1817, specifically re-erected the diocese as a suffragan see of metropolitan Toulouse under the title *Montis-Albani sub invocatione Mariae Virginis.* Louis XVIII had hoped to make Nicolas Mac-Carthy, Cheverus' old classmate, Bishop of Montauban at the time. Unfortunately the failure to execute the Concordat of 1817 and Mac-Carthy's refusal to accept the nomination in any case left the diocese still vacant. True, the king named Jean-Brumauld de Beauregard in Mac-Carthy's place but by the time a working agreement between Rome and Paris was achieved in the fall of 1822 Beauregard was needed to fill the Diocese of Orleans newly vacant after the death of Pierre-Marin Rouph de Varicourt.[42] The royal ordinance which Louis signed on January 13, 1823 thus read: "We have named . . . N. N. of Boston to the Diocese of

Montauban replacing Jean Brumauld de Beauregard, named by ordinance this day to the Diocese of Orleans."[43] It would almost seem that in the government's haste to fill the see it had not even had time to learn the first name of the Bishop of Boston!

With the arrival in Paris of the Chevalier de Valnais in mid-June bearing the refusal of Cheverus there was general chagrin. When the Minister of Foreign Affairs sent the papers over to the Grand Aumonier he said, "These would be very afflicting if the consul, who appears to be a very fine man, did not tell me he knew from Mgr. de Cheverus himself that if the King formally expressed his intention, he would accede."[44] Joseph de Valnais, knowing Cheverus, personally believed that his devotion to Louis XVIII could be used to change the Boston prelate's mind, and when the Grand Aumonier learned this he knew what note to stress in his next letter. Meanwhile, Moreau de la Vigerie who had also seen Valnais, was equally disappointed at his cousin's refusal and the lawyer determined to present his views to the Grand Aumonier, asking his secretary, the Abbé Jacques Besson to arrange an appointment. He told Besson, "He asserts that his health is improved but the Consul of Boston . . . assures me of the contrary. As a close relative . . . I have some information to forward to Monseigneur which the Consul of Boston has promised to give." Vigerie hinted that he could suggest an infallible mode of procedure to "attach to the Church of France a light, a bishop of distinguished merit, rare modesty, and who would be more useful to religion in France than in the United States."[45]

Jacques-Joseph Corbière, as Minister of Interior, was chiefly concerned for Montauban's future since, as he reiterated to the Grand Aumonier:

It is urgent to fill a diocese whose territory has been dismembered for fifteen years in three different dioceses. Grave inconvenience results from so prolonged and precarious a state. I have reminded you of this situation. I believe I might do so again at a time when I have received for the fifth time an appeal from the Département, and at the same time the news that Mgr. de Cheverus will not come.[46]

It is not surprising that the letters which left Paris for Boston that July were therefore very pressing. Vigerie used the arguments he suspected would weigh most heavily with his cousin and accused Cheverus of misleading his family by his talk of ill-health and retirement in France. Vigerie himself had been certain his cousin was all ready to return the previous fall; Louis de Cheverus had nearly died when he heard that his brother was not coming. "Further," Vigerie continued, "M. de Neuville is very upset since he was sure after what you said to him that you meant to return to France. He has been compromised with the Grand Aumonier." Then he summed up his views:

> You must obey the king and respond to his kindness. . . . It is clear that you have been persuaded to stay by the clergy and the people. Your health is a little better, you say, but M. de Valnais says it is not vigorous enough to last long in the fatigues of your apostolate. When you are feeble who will care for you, provide for you? You must leave before a second refusal sorely offends the king, the Grand Aumonier, Neuville and Valnais who are so attached to you. It afflicts us excessively and puts your family in mourning. Montauban is a widow until you arrive.[47]

It was a letter designed to leave the bishop in Boston very little peace of mind. He had, of course, spoken frequently of retiring since Matignon's death in 1818. His letters to Montreal had spoken with longing of his desire to join the Sulpicians in holy retreat from the world; letters to Baltimore had contained the same sort of wishful thinking. His correspondence with his family told of his dreams of spending his last days with them in France. But all of these had been half wistful dreaming and half complimentary expressions of affection for those to whom he confided his private reflections when he was low in physical vigor or uncertain about his length of days. In reality, while Cheverus was able to go about his work he never seriously contemplated immediate retirement. When Maréchal actually suggested that Cheverus come to Baltimore the Bishop of Boston had said emphatically, "My intention is to live and die here; I shall never consent to a translation." He had said as much to Le Saunier as well.[48] No one in Baltimore or Montreal had expected Boston would be deprived of its first bishop just yet. But his relatives across the sea who had known him only by correspondence for thirty years had read those letters with their own desires giving a connotation the writer had scarcely intended.

The accusations now leveled by his cousin Vigerie that Cheverus had caused real grief to his family was hard to bear. But even more painful was the suggestion that he had compromised his friends and offended royalty. To a man of Cheverus' humility and sensibility it was most painful to believe he was the cause for embarrassment to others. It was even worse to think he had given offense to the King of France. Ever since his youthful days as prior of Torbéchet he had cherished a deep devotion to *Monsieur* who was now Louis XVIII, the man he "sorely offended" according to Vigerie.

The letter of the Grand Aumonier doubled his humiliation. The Prince de Croij minced no words. "Doubtless being so far from us," he asserted, "you have no exact idea of our situation, the enfeeblement of our resources after such long trials, the voids which have successively accrued in the clergy, in a word, the penury of subjects suited to high places." It was all very well to furnish protests of Boston Protestants, but their testimony, however touching, could not be placed in comparison with the present situation of the clergy and of religion in France. This was a most critical epoch for the Church, with the necessity for re-establishing so many dioceses. Then the Grand Aumonier added his clinching arguments:

> It was in view of this that I regarded as a sign from Divine Providence the positive assurance of your determination to return to France. . . . I explained these motives for recalling you to the king. He applauded, evidencing full satisfaction. When he learned the contents of your letter he was displeased. The assurance of the will of the king . . . will confirm . . . I do not doubt, all other reasons.[49]

The unhappy little prelate in Franklin Street seemed to have no alternative when he read this letter in late August. On August 30 he hastily replied, "I am covered with confusion. I cast myself at your knees and the feet of his Majesty. I will leave around the first of October." He signed his capitulation, "John, Bishop of Boston, named to the Diocese of Montauban."[50] By now he was so confused he did not truly know what his voyage would bring; he only knew he must go. He sent the cogent part of the Grand Aumonier's summons to Baltimore saying, "I must go. I will sail from here or New York around October 1. If I can get them to let me return I will be here in the spring. If a successor for me is necessary Taylor is always the one I want."[51]

The Archbishop of Baltimore was dealt a mortal blow. As he painfully explained to his Roman agent:

> Mgr. Cheverus is certainly the first bishop of the United States. At any time his loss would be great. In the actual circumstances it could have harmful and incalculable results. . . . How can I govern as a metropolitan, finding myself alone without a single support

among the greater part of my suffragans: Although far distant from me, Mgr. Cheverus was an infinitely precious companion-in-arms in the midst of the struggles which attacked the Church. If he leaves me I fear my post will be untenable.[52]

Perhaps Cheverus sincerely believed he could still return to Boston, but Maréchal could not believe he would.

As for me, I think he will stay in France; he is lost to our America. I know the great sensibility of his soul, and it seems to me that he will not be able to resist the promptings of his family, united to the wishes of the Grand Aumonier, even more, those of M. Hyde de Neuville, who is the author of this nomination.[53]

Father Taylor, too, felt that his bishop was lost to Boston and told their friends in Newcastle, "The bishops of the Gallican Church know his value and are determined to possess him. . . . I hope you will come and condole with us next winter or the latter part of the fall."[54]

Cheverus was so busy in his frantic efforts to make good his promise to leave by October he scarcely had time to ask himself what he hoped. His state of mind is revealed in the reply he made to two letters of protest from Simon Bruté to whom he confessed:

I appreciate the purity of your zeal. I am sick and heartsick. I can not go into details. In May I followed step by step the course our worthy archbishop indicated. I sent the letter to the Grand Aumonier. Instead of accepting my refusal, the King orders that I [be told] in his name, in the name of the country which reclaims me and needs my services, not to displease him too long. The least I can do is throw myself at the feet of his Majesty. I leave broken-hearted, against my will. Blame me, but have pity on me and pray for me.[55]

To the Athenaeum he sent over his last gift of books on September 9 and received Theodore Lyman's grateful acknowledgment:

I could not on the present occasion with propriety and justice to the feelings of the Trustees omit to mention the peculiar obligations this institution is under to you for a great number of valuable books. Indeed you have been one of its greatest as well as earliest benefactors, and this circumstance alone will cause you to be remembered with gratitude and affection by its numerous proprietors.

They were all filled with great and sincere sorrow at the thought of his departure, Lyman wrote: might his voyage to his own country be a prosperous one.[56] Cheverus took time to reply:

The Trustees as well as my other fellow citizens of Boston, are disposed to exaggerate the little that I have been able to do, but they can never rate too high my love and devotedness to them, and nothing but what I believe an imperious duty could ever tear me from them.

I shall be happy in being an agent and correspondent for the Boston Athenaeum and to give some tokens to the proprietors of my affection and remembrance I send with this a fac-simile of the testament of Louis the 16th and his horribly calumniated consort. It will perhaps enhance the value of these interesting documents when my literary friends know that they have often been bedewed with my tears. . . .[57]

It was even more heartrending to reply to the address of his faithful flock who addressed him in fond farewell on September 16:

Dear Father:

Permit your flock, penetrated and subdued by grief, to place before you an humble offering of gratitude and affection. Your departure, which has now become certain, is to us a most afflicting dispensation of Providence; and the event has inflicted a wound, whose anguish time may assuage, but can never heal. The thought of this separation brings with it a thousand recollections which labor for a tongue to reveal themselves; but perhaps it were better they should not be freely spoken; for we know by long experience, that your delicacy would shrink at once from even such a bare recital as the coldest and most careless of us would make in sincerity and truth.

As a religious community, we were connected and consolidated under your auspices; and by your watchings and your prayers we have enjoyed the smiles of an indulgent Heaven; but at this solemn moment of parting, probably forever, the memory of the dead crowds upon us, in the loved form of him, who gathered us as a flock, and who with you walked hand in hand, laboring for our good; but this kind pastor to us, this coadjutor and friend to you, the ever lamented Matignon, has passed to a better world, to receive the reward of the faithful and the just. The living and the dead together possess our hearts.

At this crisis, when the agony of separation is fast coming upon us, we cannot entirely stifle our feelings, and we must, and we will, amidst our tears and lamentations, catch hold of your garments as you turn to leave us, and utter some faint cry of your services and our attachment.

You have fed the hungry and clothed the naked; brought back the wandering; reclaimed the vicious; shared the joys of the happy;

softened the pains of the suffering; held the medicinal cup to the sick and parched lip; and taught the dying that, through faith and repentance, he might repose his hopes on the bosom of redeeming love.

Most spiritual guides go no farther than to instruct in spiritual matters; but you have not stopped there, not there considered your work as finished; for you have come down, as it were, from the altar of God, to the common offices of mankind, to give us council and direction in our temporal concerns. We believe it seldom happens, that one so devoted to things divine, should be so wise in the business of the world; but this wisdom has not been shown by collecting perishable riches for yourself; but in striving to increase intelligence, comfort and respectability, among the people of your charge.

At your approach, discord fled from among us; for in every lecture, in every strain of devotion, you have breathed the mild and holy spirit of the new commandment, to calm the irritations and quiet the heart burnings incident to frail humanity; and we trust in grace that this example, and these instructions, will have a salutary influence on our lives, when you are no longer with us to advise and direct us in the paths of duty, virtue and religion.

You are going, dear father, to a distant country, where honor waits your coming, and where new duties are to thicken upon you; but we entreat you, that even in the joy of beholding your native land, in the transports of embracing kindred and friends, and in the fresh activity of ecclesiastical engagements, that you will remember us, who can never forget you.

May the mild climate of Montauban restore and confirm your health, and awaken your spirits to life and happiness; and may God in his mercy and goodness, continue you for many years, a name and a praise in the Church. And when you shall sleep with your fathers, and be numbered with the great and the good of other times, may our descendants here, learn that your blessings fell upon your first, as on your second love; and that Boston and Montauban were remembered together in your dying benediction.

William Taylor, Rector
T. Walley,
John McNamara,   Committee
John Ward,   of the
William L. Cazneau,   Congregation
Francis McKenna,

Boston, September 16th, 1823.[58]

The tears coursed down his cheeks as he read. Yet his reply was simple and dignified. "My dear Children in Jesus Christ," he began:

Your kind address has been presented to me, and is wet with my tears. How unwilling I am to leave you, I hope you all know, and have seen how cheerfully I refused, last May, the appointment which I *must* now accept.

Since it becomes a necessity, it behoves you and myself to submit.

My services, so gratefully noticed by you, have been at least, prompted by a sincere heart, entirely devoted to your spiritual and even temporal welfare.

It was as it were, at the school of the regretted and sainted Doctor Matignon, that I learned how to love and serve you. Remember him always as the founder of this church.

I expected my mortal remains to be deposited with his, and never can you honor or gratify me more than by uniting our names in your blessing and remembrance.

Remembered and cherished you will be, as long as I breathe. Never shall I cease to watch over my dear flock with paternal anxiety. Happy if I can at any time do any thing for you. Excuse my faults in the exercise of my ministry; pray that they may be forgiven by the Supreme Pastor. I feel consolation in leaving you under the direction of the Rev. William Taylor, Rector of this Church, whose talents and piety are already known to you, and who has been for more than two years my faithful cooperator.

My beloved children, I press you all to my paternal bosom. I wish, and still have some hopes, to come to you again, and indulge the comforting hope that we shall be united in the kingdom of our Heavenly Father.

John Cheverus.[59]

On September 26, 1823, Bishop Cheverus left Boston for the last time. He was to sail from New York on the *Paris* on October 1. His good friend Samuel Knapp said of that Friday morning:

The parting scene I shall never forget. At a very early hour in the morning the vestry was filled with Protestants and Catholics, dissolved in tears to think they should never see him again. It required all his firmness to support himself in bidding them farewell. As he left the house for the carriage, lisping infancy and silver-haired age rushed forward to pluck his gown and share the good man's smile; and the last accents of his blessing were mingled with moans of grief at his departure.[60]

What the future held for the fifty-five-year-old prelate he had no desire to anticipate; his thoughts were only of Boston and the grave facing the door of St. Augustine's where he had once hoped to be placed beside his dear Matignon. He was oppressed by the thought of his distracted people, his "widowed spouse." Twenty-seven of his thirty-three years in the priesthood had been spent in Boston, and while he lived no flock would ever be dearer. In Boston he had been greatly loved. As the *Commercial Gazette* remarked prior to his departure:

> The amenity of his manners as a gentleman, his accomplishments as a scholar, his tolerant disposition as a religious teacher, and his pure and apostolic life, have been our theme of praise ever since we have known him.[61]

And after he was gone, on September 27, 1823, the *Columbian Centinel* commented sorrowfully, "Our community indeed sustains a heavy loss in his departure. . . . Without hesitancy we say that the labors of no individual have produced more good than his. The best wishes of our community follow him."

CHAPTER XVIII

PRELATE IN WAITING

CHEVERUS was not sailing to France alone; three of his warm friends were booked for the *Paris* that fall. Mme Duplessis and her daughter from Boston were at last returning to France after several changes of plans. After the bishop's decision to remain in Boston in the spring of the year the devoted women had found it impossible to leave their beloved friend; they, too, would stay in Boston. But with his change of plans in September they had determined to follow him home. They talked happily of settling the business of their properties in Rennes, and of going to Montauban where they could continue to live under his paternal wing. Father Jean Moranvillé from Fell's Point was returning to France on the *Paris,* too, whether by sheer coincidence or by design to travel in the company of his much revered compatriot is not clear. The four French travelers who had spent so many years in the United States were grateful for each other's company.

The passage from New York destined for Havre began pleasantly enough and Captain Henry Robinson anticipated a short run. The passengers almost forgot they were on board a vessel, finding themselves "as it were in the hospitable house of a kind friend, anxious to make them comfortable and to anticipate all their wishes."[1] Cheverus had leisure to think of the rush of events of the past months, and to reassess his action. What the future held for himself, for Boston, or for the Church in general he could not imagine. It was idle to speculate about his arrival in France; time enough for that when he landed. He only knew that the Grand Aumonier had assured him that when he arrived his demission would be regularized and his new brief secured through the papal nuncio in Paris.[2]

There was no way, either, of predicting what the reign of the new pope would mean for the Church. Pius VII, who had died on August 20 after a reign of almost a quarter-century, had been a remarkable pontiff. What a contrast in the situation of the Church in 1823 with that harassed institution when he had ascended his throne in 1799. The late pope's apostolic virtues, his moral and spiritual radiance through all his heavy trials, had impressed the whole western world. His eminent Secretary of State, Ercole Consalvi, had brought to Church diplomacy a spirit of realism, a suppleness of method, and a fresh point of view which had promised a new era. The outcome of the conclave which opened that September to elect a successor to Pius VII would be known to Cheverus only on his arrival in France.

There was more profit in thinking of Boston, painful as it might be. Cheverus was confident that his vicar-general would continue the good work there. The bishop wondered if even now he would be sailing toward Havre if he were not so sure of Taylor's capacities. But for more than a year he had visualized William Taylor as his eventual successor and if the diocese had not been so small he would have liked to make him coadjutor.[3] The day of French bishops was waning and men like Taylor ought to receive the future episcopal nominations. Perhaps he was a little imprudent in his zeal at times, but Taylor had other qualities a bishop in Boston needed. He was intelligent, well educated and well bred, virtuous and charming. Cheverus had no doubt that the faithful of Boston would follow his leadership and already, in spite of his short stay in the city, men of other religious affiliations had come to respect him. Cheverus fervently hoped a new bishop for Boston would not be named without consulting the first one.[4] Pius VII, of course, was still reigning when Maréchal had assured Cheverus, "If you ask the Holy Father for Mr. Taylor at once, you will obtain him."[5] If Montauban must be his next destination, Cheverus was determined to express his own views on the vacant see of Boston as quickly as possible to the new pontiff.

Cheverus did not deceive himself that Bishop Connolly of New York would favor Taylor after the latter's imprudent Roman trip; but Bishop England of Charleston was very friendly to the Boston vicar-general and Maréchal, of course, shared Cheverus' own estimation of Taylor in most respects. Cheverus still hoped for the day when no episcopal nominations for sees in the United States would be made without consulting the Archbishop of Baltimore. The assurances Maréchal had been given in Rome the year before nurtured this hope.

Cheverus had time to re-live his last moments in Boston with the innumerable expressions of affection shown him on his departure. None was more indelibly engraved on his heart than the heroic generosity of John McNamara, the struggling grocer who had offered his departing bishop his tiny fortune. "I was on the point of leaving you," Cheverus wrote to him, "I could not have blamed you, if you had felt half displeased with me. But your generous soul is a stranger to mean feelings & at a moment when I could no longer be of service to you, you offered me a portion of your property for my own private comfort." Cheverus had not accepted, of course; he did not need much for his simple tastes. But he would never forget McNamara.[6]

Thus, reflecting with both hope and grateful love on the city left behind, Cheverus spent the first three weeks of the voyage. Then on October 18 the wind began rising and the weather became thick and rainy. The crew had to carry a press of sail to keep clear of the English coast and when mid-Channel was reached the gale had become so strong it was difficult to reef the sails. On the morning of October 30 the mizzen-topsail sheets were carried away in the hurricane velocity of the wind and when the weather cleared a trifle at noon the Island of Alderney was sighted on the leeward. Although they were only forty miles from Havre at midnight, there was now little hope of reaching their original destination. The women were terribly frightened and both Cheverus and Moranvillé moved among them trying to calm them. Captain Robinson later remarked:

> The scene among my passengers can be better conceived than described. To those who desponded, that truly great and good man, Bishop Cheverus, administered consolation and recalled confidence, being himself at the most trying period perfectly calm and undaunted.[7]

The little bishop was indeed calm; they were in the hands of God as always, whether in Boston or on the sea. His letter to Bonneuil that night of October 30 made no reference to the storm whatever, but rather spoke of Boston and his own qualms about going to Montauban. "I fear, my dear son, that the good 'Papa' of Boston will make a miserable Bishop of France," he wrote. And as he recalled the happy days when the Bonneuils were still with him he added, "You know, my dear son, that an adopted family may become even dearer than the one to which we are united by blood."[8] His warm heart was too preoccupied with love to have room for fear.

Captain Robinson's only hope was to make for the Passage du Singe, a narrow intricate channel among rocks and mountainous breakers. The sea was the worst he had ever navigated. Unless he could run the ship on shore before nightfall they were doomed. At 5:30 he gave orders to carry all sail the crippled *Paris* could manage and after beating over the reef she ran high up among the rocks. His plan had succeeded; when the tide fell the passengers and all hands got safely ashore.[9] Father Moranvillé told friends afterward, "I lost no time with the bishop and some others in leaving the wreck of our ship and . . . walking in water and mud for an hour and a half."[10] November 1, the feast of *Toussaint!* It was an odd way for a bishop to begin his fourteenth year in the episcopacy, clambering at midnight over the side of a shattered ship stranded high on the rocks six leagues from Cherbourg. Nothing was left of their baggage except some insignificant articles, but when they considered how many ships went down in that storm, how many people perished, it seemed a miracle of divine Providence that not one was lost aboard the *Paris,* the only ship to survive.[11] If the ship had run in one hundred yards to either side of the spot she did, all aboard would have been lost. Instead, by midnight all had been rescued and the next day, when the waters receded, even some of the cargo was saved.

The good people of Auderville welcomed the victims of the shipwreck and Father François Maijer, the pastor of the parish, offered shelter to Captain Robinson, Bishop Cheverus, and Father Moranvillé. On Sunday everyone went to the parish church to offer thanks for this marvelous preservation and Cheverus gave "a most excellent and affecting discourse in French and English."[12] To the intense embarrassment of Bishop Cheverus he was now the center of great excitement. The two days he stayed in Auderville and his subsequent journey to Paris were reported in the Paris journals and reprinted in papers elsewhere. All of France, and eventually Boston, learned that while he was with Father Maijer the clergy from the surrounding places had come to pay their respects, that at Beaumont he had received marks of veneration and found among the theological conference in progress there fifteen priests who had been in English exile with him, that at Cherbourg he had been equally honored, that the Bishop of Montauban "in spite of the brevity of his stay, left in that region a memory of most touching virtues."[13] From Cherbourg on the evening of November 4 the tired little bishop wrote longingly to Bonneuil, "They cover me with honors, but Boston. . . ."[14]

If Cheverus felt any deep joy at being once again in France, it was quickly invaded by sorrow. On November 6, 1823, Michelle George de la Massonnais, his widowed sister, died leaving her children orphans.[15] Eighteen-year-old Jean Baptiste-Amadée had been studying with the Jesuits of Sainte-Anne d'Auray and was destined for the priesthood; Cheverus immediately resolved that his nephew should have his protection.[16] As for Fanny and Louis Able, who meant to become a doctor, they too would always be welcome to spend as much time at Montauban as they wished. Meanwhile, the bishop-elect's first duty was to report to Paris, and on the second Wednesday after the precarious debarkation at Auderville the exile of thirty years entered the city from which he had fled in 1792.[17] He went to his cousin's house in Cul de Sac Ferou near Saint-Sulpice and was welcomed by the Councilor of the Cour Royal who had been so insistent that Cheverus return to France. For the next eight months nothing seemed quite certain and Cheverus could have wondered often, as the weeks dragged by, whether it was indeed the will of divine Providence that he go to Montauban.

His meeting with the Grand Aumonier confirmed what he had been told in their correspondence: Montauban needed him badly, the king definitely wished Cheverus to remain in France. But Cheverus now learned for the first time that the papal nuncio at Paris, Vincenzo Macchi, Bishop of Nisibi, was equally concerned for the needs of Boston and did not favor Cheverus' transfer. The letters that left Paris for Rome in November, 1823, presented conflicting views. Cheverus himself, on the advice of Croij, wrote on November 22 that the state of religion in France and the particular circumstances at Montauban impelled him to favor his transfer, and if this should be effected he wished as his successor at Boston William Taylor.[18] The nuncio reporting Cheverus' request for translation the next day commented, "A prelate so distinguished will doubtless be an acquisition for the church of Montauban but therefore a true loss for that of Boston where his indefatigable zeal worked so much good for the Catholic religion." Two days later, commenting on Taylor, the nuncio recommended, however, that Cheverus ought to be consulted since he knew the needs and the circumstances of the area and people.[19]

Cheverus was in an unenviable position. As he told Taylor on November 24, "I fear I can not return, although it is desired at Rome, and I have told the Nuncio I am ready to do it."[20] It was difficult trying to submit to the wishes of both the king's Grand Aumonier and the pope's nuncio when they did not agree where his real duty lay. The only thing Cheverus could do was to wait submissively for the will of God to be shown more clearly. His distress was only partially alleviated by the pleasure of seeing Father Stephen Badin from Kentucky; their conversations of the United States simply exaggerated his uncertainty. He assured Badin that in his letter to Rome he had stressed his belief that episcopal appointments to the United States ought to have Maréchal's consent, but of his own case he had no assurance to give. He had shown the nuncio Maréchal's letter discussing Taylor, but Cheverus had no more idea than Badin who would be the Bishop of Boston in the end.[21]

After seeing Father Moranvillé on his way to Amiens Cheverus decided that while he waited for the outcome of Franco-Roman accord to materialize he might as well visit his family in Mayenne. In Paris he was constantly in demand for public and private preaching and after the harrowing voyage he needed some respite. He had already been welcomed by his former comrades at Louis-le-Grand, preached at Saint-Nicolas Seminary, the Seminary of Issy, and many churches.[22] The Sunday before he left for Mayenne he visited the Association of St. Joseph where he was welcomed by the Abbé Rauzan and his famous missionaries. Cheverus celebrated high Mass and preached and when *l'Ami de la Religion* reported this occasion in detail it commented, "The piety of the Prelate, the sweetness of his words, his affectionate tone of voice, his appropriate counsel, all deeply affected his audience."[23] But the bishop was tired and on Monday, November 24, he started south toward Mayenne.

If Cheverus hoped to arrive inconspicuously in the city where he had first been made a pastor, he was doomed to disappointment. "As soon as he set foot in the city the news spread, bells rang, and people with *flambeaux* and mad with joy escorted him to his brother's house."[24] The next morning the clergy went in procession to the home of Louis de Cheverus to welcome his illustrious brother from Boston. For a second time sorrow intruded, for Jean Sougé, the pastor of Notre Dame who would have spoken the formal words of welcome, had been buried less than a week; the friend and relative who had been Cheverus' companion-in-arms in distant places had died on November 21 while Cheverus was detained in Paris. It was to the first assistant of Notre Dame de Mayenne that the bishop "replied with much elegance and facility" before proceeding to the church to officiate in *pontificalia*.[25] The rest of the day was filled with visits from the officials of the city whose joy, to quote the *Ami de la Religion* whose journalistic eye followed the American bishop even to Mayenne, "was only dimmed by the prospect of his departure to superintend a distant flock who anxiously await his arrival."

It was an incredible contrast to the forced departure of three decades ago. It was most heartening to see that the desolation caused by the revolutionary eruption and the boundless ambition of the late Napoleonic regime was every day diminishing. Certainly in Mayenne the clergy of the French church were edifying in their zeal, and the people were truly pious.[26]

As Advent progressed Cheverus remained in doubt as to his own position and the day after Christmas when he wrote to Father Taylor he said:

> There is still a feeble glimmering of hope that I may return to Boston. The Pope's nuncio, a venerable prelate, wishes it much. It will be seen at least, that if I do not return, it is no fault of mine. I quitted Paris and left everything in the hands of the Nuncio. I expect a letter from him and will immediately return to Paris.[27]

To the nuncio that same week Cheverus reported uneasily, "I am here in my natal country in the midst of my relatives, but I desire to be in Paris when the replies from Rome arrive." He enclosed recent letters from Boston expressing the unanimous desire of the laity and clergy that Taylor be their next bishop.[28] The letter which actually summoned him to Paris was not from the nuncio but, instead, a most urgent one from the Grand Aumonier. Written on the same day that Cheverus had expressed his anxiety to Nuncio Macchi, the letter of the king's Aumonier who was now Archbishop of Rouen as well as Prince of Croij said:

> An affair of greatest importance requires your presence in Paris. I beg you, Monseigneur, to start as soon as you receive this. I am truly sorry to trouble the repose which you need so much after so many dangers and fatigues; but you will judge for yourself when you learn the gravity of the question I have to propose to you that it is absolutely impossible to spare you the hardships of travel.[29]

The letter arrived in Mayenne the day after New Year's and Cheverus tried immediately to secure a seat on the mail coach for Paris that night. He scratched a hasty note to the archbishop saying, "I hope to present myself to your Highness Sunday after Mass, or in the evening." His health was not good, the constant companion of his Boston winters having accompanied him to France, but nothing would prevent him from speedily obeying such orders or from conforming to all the king's intentions. He did not add that anything was preferable to this agony of uncertainty.[30]

The truth was that the Grand Aumonier wanted to see Cheverus before the nuncio had an opportunity to inform him that the latest instructions from Rome were unfavorable to the king's intentions. Propaganda had been busy during the past month in regard to Cheverus' case. On December 7 a conference was held to consider Maréchal's protests against the translation of the Bishop of Boston. Two days later Propaganda notified Guilio Cardinal della Somaglia that the pope had been given Maréchal's memorial. On December 10, Somaglia had notified Cardinal Decamo that tomorrow's post would dispatch to Paris the papal recommendation that Cheverus should not go to Montauban. Bishop Macchi, the nuncio, was to relay this to both Cheverus and the Archbishop of Rouen; a letter to Cheverus dated December 20 was included in the packet addressed to Macchi.[31] It was quite clear that the same arguments Maréchal had given Robert Gradwell in September had convinced Rome that Cheverus was indispensable to Boston. But Paris was not going to surrender without a last valiant effort.

When Cheverus met with the king's chief official in these affairs at 8:00 o'clock on Sunday, January 4, he did not seem to realize what a game of rival pressures was being played with himself as the innocent pawn. He told his brother the next day that all the Grand Aumonier had desired was that Cheverus express a desire to go to Montauban. "This could have been done by writing and saved both money and trouble," he wrote ruefully. It had been a wild goose chase, as far as he could see, and his only satisfaction came from seeing his nephews, Louis de Cheverus and Abel George de la Massonnais, who insisted on escorting him to the Vigerie house.[32]

But there was method behind the Archbishop of Rouen's precipitancy. During the interview with Cheverus on Sunday he exacted a promise that Cheverus would personally call upon the nuncio and give him his assurance that he sincerely preferred to go to Montauban. On Monday and Tuesday Cheverus was not well and he remained at home with his cousins, reading letters from Montauban which told him the Duplessis women had arrived there before Christmas and that the diocese sorely needed more priests as well as a bishop. The mad dash from Mayenne to Paris had taxed him sorely and in the reaction after Sunday's seemingly needless interview Cheverus was too sick to go out just to confirm what the nuncio already knew, that he had come to France at the king's urging and meant to accept, if it was God's will, a see in France that needed him.

On Wednesday, however, he kept his promise and called on the nuncio with his reasons for wishing to remain in France neatly listed according to the Aumonier's recommendation. But the wording was that of John Cheverus; the little man could never express himself other than frankly and simply, and the paper he left with Macchi said precisely what Cheverus felt that first week in 1824. "At this moment," he began, "I cannot return to the United States." First, because of means. He had dispossessed himself of all he had when he left Boston, in favor of the church, the Ursuline nuns, and the clergy. He had no patrimony of his own and was still indebted for his voyage to France. Secondly, his health at present was feeble. "I doubt that I could survive a voyage to America," he said sincerely. Further, having reflected before God, he felt he could not go back on his word, "I might even say the commands, of the king." He hoped that in France he could contribute to upholding the altar and legitimate monarchy, "sacred causes to which I have devoted my whole life." If one wishes to know the real reasons for Cheverus' decision to remain in France, they are here in this list he gave the Bishop of Nisibi on January 7, 1824. It was typical of his concern for honor in financial affairs that he listed first the practical difficulties of a voyage back to Boston. It was natural in the depths of his distress and illness following the recent trip to Paris that he should list health as a second factor. But the reason that went beyond coincidence of time and weather was his conclusion. It is beyond refutation that in the heart of the former Bishop of Boston there had always remained, after his love for the Church, an unalterable devotion to France and her legitimate rulers.

Speaking with the nuncio in person, of course, he said other things as well. He spoke of his genuine sorrow at leaving his flock in the United States, of his confidence that under Taylor all would go well, of the impatience of Montauban for a bishop, of his willingness to go to Rome at any time to report on conditions in the United States, adding that in all truth he did not believe his return to the United Sates could remedy the troubled conditions there. After this second interview Cheverus reported it to the Grand Aumonier and gave him a copy of the list of reasons he had left with Macchi.

I saw Mgr. the nuncio at noon. He informed me of His Holiness' desire that I return to America where he believed I was needed, but he added that the Sovereign Pontiff did not wish to displease the King. He told me all that was required of me was to remain neutral and conform to whatever was decided between your Highness and himself in the name of His Holiness and our august Monarch. I promised with all my heart.[33]

It is impossible not to admire Cheverus for his honor and his earnest desire to deceive no one, least of all himself. He remained in Paris for a while at the suggestion of the Archbishop of Rouen and wrote to Rome on January 13 the same reasons which he had given the nuncio. He tried to give Taylor in Boston as clear a view of affairs as was possible that month, writing from Mayenne on the 24th:

> In Rome they desire me return to America, but in Paris the government, and of course my family here, do not want to hear it mentioned. I have been obliged to write to Rome according to the intentions of the government and I presume I will have to stay in France. If the Holy Father recovers his health, the thing will be decided in six weeks. Then you will receive a letter for my dear flock of Boston who, I have reason to hope, will have you for Pastor. I have spoken to the Nuncio and written strongly on the subject.
>
> Although I am convinced today that I can render Religion more important services here than in America, I believe that if I had *foreseen all,* I would still be in Boston. But I am here and my feeble health tells me to stay here, at least until they give me a contrary duty.[34]

The Grand Aumonier's reasoning had been sound; when Rome received the nuncio's report and its recommendations that Cheverus' reasons be given consideration, the affair was resolved in France's favor. On February 14 Cardinal Somaglia notified Propaganda that Cheverus was to go to Montauban, citing health as the decisive factor. A week later Propaganda notified Cheverus that Pope Leo XII had been satisfied with his reasons for not returning to Boston. On February 21 letters went to the United States asking for opinions on Father Taylor as a possible successor to the bishop who was now definitely destined for Montauban.[35]

The nuncio in Paris was delighted to receive the news. Knowing Cheverus as he now did he told Rome frankly that it was impossible to evaluate all the spiritual advantages Montauban would enjoy from a prelate so worthy, so full of religion and zeal.[36] The die was cast. Jean Lefebvre de Cheverus was now Jean VI of Montauban and in vain was Maréchal's cry of January 8, "God give him the grace to refuse the see offered to him and return to his post for the consolation of his flock, myself and all who know him."[37] The Sulpician superior in Paris told the Archbishop of Baltimore:

> Rome's first refusal to agree to the transfer was without success. The French government continued to insist and the Pope could not refuse their demands. If Mgr. de Cheverus had wanted to resist I believe they could not have forced him; but it seems that after the advances had been made he decided not to return to Boston, protesting the derangement of his finances and his health. Now everything is settled. . . . Thus America must sacrifice in favor of France where he is singularly beloved and where he will do great good.[38]

Up in Amiens, Jean Moranvillé blamed the whole affair on Hyde de Neuville, and when he wrote to Maréchal of Cheverus' proposal that Taylor should be the next Bishop of Boston he reflected dubiously, "He is still young for so eminent a post. God grant, if he is elected, that he may be able to replace his predecessor worthily."[39]

As for Cheverus himself, the news from Rome brought no sense of victory or exultation, least of all contented conviction that he had really done God's will. He had come to France at the king's command; once there, he had had sincerely tried to follow the nuncio's command that he remain neutral and conform to whatever was decided between the French government and the Holy See. At the urgings of the Grand Aumonier in January he had expressed a desire to go to Montauban in accordance with the king's wishes, using the arguments Croij had felt would carry most weight in Rome. The nuncio's support of those arguments had led to Roman approval of the appointment to Montauban.

But now that the decision of Rome was given and there was general satisfaction in Paris that so fine a bishop had been obtained for France, the humble man who had been the object of the negotiations could think only of Boston, of Baltimore, and of his former colleagues struggling against such odds in the United States. Could Maréchal ever pardon him for his desertion? To Bruté, who was in Paris that spring, Cheverus confessed:

> My poor heart has experienced cruel anguish. I found myself here in a position allowing no escape. Another with more force and virtue could have succeeded. If you believe it, have pity on my weakness and forgive it. I will give all the details to our worthy Archbishop. If they blame me I hope at least they will be charitable enough to pardon me and pray for me. I beg you to do so. I shall never have

a sweeter consolation than the power of doing something for our church in America. My eyes and my heart will always turn toward her.[40]

It never occurred to him to be flattered that he was desired on both sides of the Atlantic, or that in his case Rome found one French bishop whose American career was so valuable to the Church in the United States the Holy See had to be persuaded to let him leave. Nor did he take any consolation from the thought that no matter how Rome had decided, his acquiescence would have given dissatisfaction to the nation which lost him. He only knew that he was unhappy to have hurt anyone and in his unhappiness he believed his own defects in character, his own weakness and lack of virtue were to blame.

The months that followed did nothing to lessen his misery. Instead of being able to go at once to Montauban where he could plunge into the ministry which he loved, he was forced to wait interminably in Paris. Leo XII was so ill that no papal action could be taken until May, not even an encyclical appeared to outline the program of the new pontiff who had been elected the preceding September. When the *Journal de Tarn-et-Garonne* on March 13 published extracts from the Boston *Gazette of Commerce* of the letter of the congregation of Boston to Cheverus, and the bishop's reply, it prefaced the American items with the remark:

> While waiting for the transmission of the bulls for Mgr. de Cheverus, Bishop of Montauban, delayed by the illness of the Holy Father, to allow this prelate to come to his diocese, where the renown of his evangelical virtues has preceded him and where his presence is so intensely desired, we believe it would give real pleasure to the inhabitants of the departement to publish the following documents.

April came and the bulls did not arrive. Cheverus wrote to Taylor on April 26 that he was still in Paris, hoping for the bulls with every courier.[41] Moranvillé, writing to Baltimore from Amiens, commented, "Everything is prepared for his reception in his new diocese. However, it is astonishing that he is still waiting for the bulls."[42] It was only on May 3 that Cheverus was finally officially confirmed at Rome.

One more delay was in store for Cheverus. For reasons not apparent the news of the official confirmation of the Bishop of Montauban was immediately followed by a discussion in the Council of State in which some members argued that his residence in the United States for twenty-seven years deprived Cheverus of French citizenship and the right to the emoluments of his new office. The heartsick prelate waiting restlessly on the Left Bank now saw his name once again occupying the Paris journals, this time in fevered debate which was only terminated by the king's ordinance of June 12 by which he specifically reinstated Cheverus in his quality and rights as a citizen of France. A fortnight later Louis XVIII ordered the publication of the bulls for the canonical institution of the prelate he had nominated a year and a half earlier.[43]

The king's government did not intend, of course, that Cheverus should suffer from this prolonged delay. On June 23 the Minister of Interior proposed that in addition to the usual 10,000 francs bishops received for the expenses of establishing themselves in new sees Cheverus be granted 5000 more. Corbière pointed out that the other bishops named in January, 1823, had all been installed a year or more ago; it was not the fault of Cheverus that his installation had been delayed. In addition, there was the matter of the expense of his voyage from Boston to consider. Needless to say, the measure received the king's signature.[44]

After the long years in New England when Cheverus had scarcely ever had a moment to relax, the days of waiting in Paris were a torment. He was kept busy enough, of course, with invitations to preach and assist at religious functions. His sermons at Saint-Sulpice were heard by large crowds including on occasion Peers of France, other prelates, and the Grand Aumonier himself.[45] In May Cheverus, assisted by a numerous body of clergy, presided at the installation of his former preceptor, now the Reverend Dr. Augé, the new president of the College of St. Stanislaus, and after the Gospel Cheverus gave a fine exhortation to the students.[46] On June 6 he assisted the Archbishop of Rouen at the consecration of Charles-Auguste Forbin-Janson for the Diocese of Nancy.[47] But none of these elegant occasions could substitute for the work nearest his heart.

Yet while he longed to enter upon the pastoral career for which he was destined he suffered grave misgivings about his ability to accomplish the good expected of him. His deficiencies loomed large when he contemplated "the difficulties he would have to encounter in raising his church from its ruins and re-establishing the discipline which the relaxation consequent on the revolutionary storm had almost destroyed."[48] When he went to Saint-Cloud on Thursday, July 8, to take the oath at the hands of Louis XVIII, the king told him that "knowing many Protestants to be in his diocese, he should imitate the example of the Good Shepherd who leaves the ninety-nine to seek that which was lost."[49] The papal nuncio wrote to Rome that this royal admonition proved "how great is the heart of his Majesty for the propagation of the Catholic religion and how great his desire to see returned to the fold those of his subjects who had remained so long away"; but Cheverus received the admonition with private, personal foreboding and told his brother, "I am sad and uneasy about taking charge of my diocese. May God sustain me. If I do not succeed I will cast myself in your arms which are always open to me."[50]

While waiting for Corbière to obtain the money for the trip to Montauban Cheverus was kept busy. He was invited on July 11 to preach at Sainte-Geneviève but did not feel *en verve* and offered his Mass instead at the minor seminary in Rue du Regard. He had already preached on Wednesday at the Communauté des Oiseaux where he was delighted with the religious and their boarders.[51] He wrote to the two priests he meant to take from Mayenne, to augment the clergy of Montauban which Vicar-General Trélissac had warned the new bishop was sadly inadequate, that he hoped to leave Paris on Monday, July 19; the priests could start at once, or wait until he had arrived in Montauban, as they preferred.[52] He enjoyed last minute visits from his nephews Louis de Cheverus and Abel George de la Massonnais. Finally, on Wednesday, July 21, 1824, Cheverus set out from Paris for his new see. After ten months of belonging nowhere it would be good to have his own flock again. His thoughts were once more in Boston with the sheep that used to crowd around him Sunday mornings after the Mass at Holy Cross, and from Bordeaux on July 26 he wrote, "A particular & affectionate remembrance to all in the sacristy on Sundays. How often my poor heart is there with you."[53] What awaited him in Montauban only Heaven knew, but in the years left to him by word and example, as much as his strength allowed, he meant to preach "love for religion and for the best of kings."[54] From now on he was to be "Monseigneur l'Évêque de Montauban" and must sign himself "Jean."

CHAPTER XIX

CITIZEN OF TWO WORLDS

MONTAUBAN, the chief city of the Département de Tarn-et-Garonne, spread out in the July sunshine on either side of the Tarn River flowing peacefully below the fine high arches of the bridge which made east and west one. The bridge was one of the most splendid monuments of the city, as a matter of fact. Dating from the early fourteenth century, it was built to withstand both the ravages of the river and the projectiles of the enemy in a day when the city had been an outpost of royal power. In 1701 the towers guarding the entrance to the bridge had been converted into an enormous *porte* or arch of triumph in memory of the Peace of Ryswick and until the Revolution had always been guarded by the king's men. In the middle of the bridge, on one side was a chapel dedicated to Sainte-Catherine, on the other a cage for enclosing blasphemers or plunging erring women into the water far below. Both the arch of triumph and the chapel were still very much in evidence the year that Jean de Cheverus entered the city to take possession of his see.[1]

From the Porte du Pont the streets sloped down and disappeared among the houses that made Saint-Orens Parish in Ville-Bourbon. From the other end of the bridge they rose swiftly to the upper city where the single rosy spire of Saint-Jacques proudly recalled the days when the cathedral chapter had occupied its ancient choir, and the classic façade of the Cathedral of the Assumption raised its two companiles against the bright blue sky. Although the cathedral was thirty years older than the bishop who arrived that morning in July, it still stood out as new and different by reason of its stone walls and pillars in a city almost entirely built of brick.[2]

The city on the hill had ancient origins, having been "peopled by the Celts, cleared for habitation by the Greeks, civilized by the Romans, and conquered by the Goths" before modern French history began. The scandalous conduct of Bishop Jean de Lettes had opened its doors to Calvinism in the sixteenth century, and after the wars of religion which were exceptionally bitter in Montauban the Calvinists had regarded themselves as masters of the city.[3] At the time the Revolution broke out there were some 6000 Protestants ready to respond to the incitements of the National Assembly against the Church. In 1790 their club, the Friends of the Constitution, was founded and became in the months that followed a foyer of fanaticism and patriotism.[4] On May 10, 1790, violence had erupted in the square in front of the cathedral and near the homes of the mayor and the commander of the National Guard. Five deaths and several hours of rioting followed, but compared with the disorders at Nimes the trouble at Montauban was negligible.[5]

The real victory of the anticlerical forces of Montauban came with the suppression of the diocese, and in the years that ensued priests were deported, the bell towers of the churches were demolished to make way for statues of liberty, and the Goddess of Reason was honored at altars where the Divine Sacrifice had formerly been offered. But the Terror had been everywhere in those days, and in Montauban was much less Protestant than anti-monarchical. "There is no indication that the patriots . . . at Montauban . . . considered themselves the defenders of the Protestant religion against the machinations of their 'born enemies.' " During the crisis of dechristianization, 1793–1794, ministers had abdicated in such large numbers, that Protestantism became "a church deserted by its pastors and forgotten by the faithful." The recognition granted Protestantism by the law of 18 germinal of Napoleon did not measurably modify the listlessness of the Protestant population of France, and the proportion at Montauban had not noticeably increased during the suppression of the diocese.[6] The arrival of a bishop in 1824 was an event long and anxiously awaited by the great majority of the citizens, and the city was seething with excitement bright and early on the morning of July 28, 1824.

Nine days earlier, on Sunday, Vicar-General de Trélissac, who had been administering the diocese ever since its re-erection by Napoleon, took possession of the episcopal see in the name of Bishop de Cheverus from the great altar of the cathedral. On that occasion he had spoken joyfully of the virtues of the new shepherd with whom he had already had an edifying correspondence. The functionaries and the faithful present had joined in a *Te Deum* which fittingly ended the portentous ceremony. Now the bishop himself was to take possession in person.[7]

Six days after Jean de Cheverus left Paris he first set foot on the soil of his diocese at Lamagistère. From that moment on his progress was a triumphal procession. People knelt in the streets to receive the blessings of the prelate whose reputation had preceded him. In the towns through which he passed, Golfech, Valence, and Moissac, he insisted on going into the parish churches to bless his flock and to acknowledge the warm welcomes that touched his gentle heart. The night before he was to enter Montauban he stayed in Moissac; then, rising at 5:00 o'clock, he celebrated Mass and set out for his episcopal city.[8]

In the tree-lined Promenade du Cours high above the river all was in readiness. The milling, excited crowd presented a sharp contrast to the municipal corps standing proudly erect in bright uniform and the patient clergy waiting in more sober dress. The prefect of the *département*, M. de Limairac, silently rehearsed his words of greeting and M. le Duc de la Force, the commandant of the military, displayed all the decorations which the Restoration government had seen fit to confer upon him.[9] The deputations of the religious communities and city corporations jostled each other piously under the tents prepared for the reception. And then, about 8:30, the bishop's carriage was sighted on the Avenue de Montauban. Jean Lefebvre de Cheverus had arrived.

As the slight, almost diffident figure of the bishop stepped down from the carriage a salvo of artillery went off. The Chevalier Dumoulinet de Graves, mayor of the city, spoke for them all:

> In Boston all grieve over your absence. Here you will find the same affection. . . . Happy the city which possesses in its midst a prelate whose every thought is a generous sentiment, whose every deed is an act of beauty, and who, in speaking of religion like a Bossuet, makes it loved like a Fénelon![10]

Then Jean de Trélissac, who more than other men rejoiced at the bishop's arrival, spoke for the clergy in a voice shaken by emotion. The heavy summer foliage of the trees that lined the open field hung motionless in the clear air. Down below the steep quays which bordered the river from the Cours to the bridge the Tarn gently eddied on its way. The troops stood stiffly at attention. All eyes were fixed upon the humble man who had spent so many years far from his native land. The bishop's eyes were filled with tears and it was with difficulty that he replied to the gracious words of the mayor and Father de Trélissac.

After resting briefly in the pavilion prepared for his use he donned pontifical vestments and amid fresh salvoes of artillery the Bishop of Montauban started for his cathedral. Four of the clergy accompanied him with a canopy, and surrounded by the civil and military officials they began to move toward the heart of the city. Laymen with banners and religious women garbed in white formed a procession behind him and the garrison troops formed an aisle in the streets to let the solemn procession pass while the National Guard struck up a joyful march. Up past the bridge they surged, sacred hymns alternating with the martial music, mounting Rue des Bains and Rue Lacaze, into the Place d'Armes in front of the cathedral. At the great door the pastor of the church presented the bishop with the keys and Cheverus moved inside to pray at the foot of the altar. Then he mounted the pulpit and spoke to them all.

> My dear children in Jesus Christ, at last I have arrived among you. . . . You are all in my heart; and it is large enough to contain you all. Father of this great family, you are my children, and with pleasure I will give my life for your happiness and safety. There is an interesting part of the dwellers in this diocese who, although strangers to our communion, have an equal place in my affections. For them, too, I hope to be a father. Happy the day which may unite us in faith as we are now united in love.[11]

As he had been in Boston, so would he be in Montauban from the day of his arrival; and the legend of his devotion to Christians of all diversities remains to this day. A prelate of gentle piety, whose charity, evangelical simplicity, and tolerance were summed up in his people's comment, "He wants us to love Protestants." Indeed, he wanted them to love all men.[12]

The brilliant ceremony of the July morning was concluded with a *Te Deum* and, in honor of Louis XVIII, the *Domine Salvum fac Regem*. The rest of the day was spent in receiving visits of the officials of Church and State at the Hotel de la Prefecture where the bishop was to stay temporarily. The *Journal de Tarn-et-Garonne* reported that day as one of fête with the joy of the people showing in their faces. "He had already conquered the hearts of his new flock as those of his former, and he was to receive as the price of his paternal care their filial devotion."[13]

But the days of fête and brilliant ceremony are fleeting and the simplicity of high emotion disappears in the complexity of aftermath. Jean de Cheverus would remain for many months to come a citizen of two worlds; and for a heart of such sensibility his eagerness to enter without reservations into this new milieu in no way canceled old loyalties or obliterated former affections. He was a man of sense as well as sensibility and he did not underestimate the task which lay before him. It was the great mark of Cheverus, however, that while gentleness of heart and humility of spirit made him perceive more vividly than many men the difficulties ahead, his steadfast, patient, and daily fortitude found him ready to go ahead without delay. As the aching of his youthful heart in English exile did not prevent the founding of Tottenham Chapel, as the rigors of mission life in Maine and the harsh winters of Boston produced no faltering of his steady footsteps, so, too, the problems presented by a resurrected diocese in southern France would not dismay him. Montauban was to receive the best Jean de Cheverus had to offer.

It was natural that the first time the new bishop preached at Saint-Jacques, eight days after his arrival, he should openly address himself to the heart of the matter and speak on respect for the Church. He was quite aware that there were Protestants in his audience, as there had been in the cathedral the day of his arrival; he was even more conscious of the fact that the Revolutionary era had leveled criticisms against the magnificence of the Church and the pomp of her ceremonies. Much of the material magnificence had been destroyed, never to be recreated. Cheverus himself was the simplest of men both in taste and in habit. But the Church was the creation of God and the glories of her liturgy were small enough homage to her Creator. His eloquence would never cease to defend the beauty with which worship ought to be clothed. His sermon that day in the old brick church whose remarkable bell tower dated back to the mid-fourteenth century was profoundly moving.

"Raising his church from its ruins," as he had put it when writing to Father Taylor, meant taking immediate steps to re-establish those essential supports of episcopal government and in September the cathedral chapter was organized. The reconstituted chapter of the Cathedral of the Assumption was composed of eleven members in addition to the rector of the cathedral: nine canons and two vicars-general. After the royal approbation was given, the new chapter was solemnly installed in September with Bishop Charles-André de Ramond-Lalande of Rodez assisting Bishop de Cheverus.[14] The finest insurance for the future, however, would be the establishment of a diocesan major seminary. His first pastoral letter discussed the subject at length. He did not doubt that the government would aid them in securing a site and buildings, but the responsibility of furnishing students and sustaining them was a task they must all share. "This labor alone can perpetuate religion among us," he concluded, signing himself "Your bishop, your brother, and your friend."[15] Within a few months donations, pledges, and legacies predicted the success of the seminary.

For directors of the seminary the bishop had first tried to enlist the Society of Saint-Sulpice whose seminaries in the New World had always filled him with such wondering admiration, but he was compelled in the end to entrust the work to the Lazarists.[16] A former Capuchin convent now belonging to Pierre Garrison was offered for sale as a seminary site in November, but some time elapsed before the necessary authorization for the purchase was granted by the prefect and Cheverus could not announce the happy completion of the purchase until August, 1825.[17] At last the Catholics could pass the Protestant seminary with fewer misgivings. The Calvinists had been preparing their clergy in Montauban since the decree of September 17, 1808, permitted the establishment of such an institution. Cheverus commented to an American friend, "The principles are those of Andover. They have visited me and have met ... with a friendly reception. This theological institution is the only one of the kind in France."[18]

Meanwhile the Bishop of Montauban was getting to know his flock. The Département de Tarn-et-Garonne whose boundaries were also those of the Diocese of Montauban derived its prosperity from small industrial enterprises in cloth-making, silk thread, tanning, ceramics, and printing for the most part. Montauban was the cradle of the silk gauze used in flour-milling, and the Duplessis women soon after their arrival in the city became engrossed in their attempts to raise silk worms. Cheverus humorously reported to Bonneuil that the worms were a great success, but the expenses the ladies incurred in nurturing their elegant specimens left them little profit.[19] But the Duplessis were newcomers, of course; native Montalbanese found silk more profitable. The potteries of the area were another industry for which his diocese was noted, and although they were less flourishing than a decade earlier, Cheverus learned the names of such eminent families as the Lestrades, the Lapierres and Garrigues whose forebears in the eighteenth century were synonymous with the production of the yellow, red, and black pottery peculiar to Montauban. Four fifths of the ceramics were sold in Bordeaux, Toulouse, and Cahors or in the surrounding localities.[20]

Although the French workers were not too different in their relations with their bishop from what the Irish people of Boston had been, Cheverus found that the upper classes of society were firmly rooted in traditions that made life in Montauban quite different and he wrote to a former parishioner in Boston, "I am bound by a certain etiquette and no longer enjoy the sweet and unceremonious freedom which was so pleasing between friends."[21] He missed the social simplicity which suited him so well. He tried to adapt himself to the protocol surrounding his office, but in matters of religion he could not, and never wished to, eradicate the methods he had used in Boston. Ignorance and intolerance were rife here, even among the pious, and his first months in Montauban were used to give the simplest instructions. In the end he openly admitted that he had been teaching the catechism. "Learn, then," he said at the parish Mass, "that the Catechism is the book of the old as well as of the young, of savants as well as the ignorant. All may find in it something to instruct, to admire, to meditate upon. Only absurd prejudice regards the Catechism with disdain."[22]

His new flock may have found him a trifle too American at first. Certainly the anecdotes of his simplicity are legion. One day he encountered his sacristan very much upset at not finding a priest free to administer to a parishioner seriously ill. Cheverus inquired reprovingly, "And I, am I not a priest?" On another occasion a common soldier was being punished for what seemed to Cheverus a minor infraction and when the bishop's pleading failed to move the captain to leniency, Cheverus shrugged and said, "Well then, I shall stay in prison with this soldier and will emerge only when he does."[23] The captain conceded in some bewilderment. In spite of this insouciance, which seemed to have more of the American than the French about it, the bishop was loved; his was the eccentricity of limitless charity.

The old days lived on in other ways, too. A note from Bruté from Paris that fall brought a pang. "My heart followed you," Cheverus wrote to the departing Sulpician. "I am waiting for the nomination of my successor to write to our holy and so dear archbishop."[24] A whole year was to pass before that successor was named but the Bishop of Montauban could not remain disinterested while his friend and former vicar was still in Boston. By September, 1825, William Taylor knew his chances were gone and began talking of following Cheverus to France. "I desire my ashes to repose near those of the Fénelon who took the place of father and friend," he told Maréchal.[25] When Cheverus learned of Rome's decision for Boston he accepted it without rancour. To his family he commented simply, "My vicar-general of Boston, Mr.

Taylor is not named bishop. I know the one who was named. He is a worthy prelate and one of my former friends."[26] To Benedict Fenwick, the new Bishop of Boston, whom Cheverus had admired without qualification for many years, his predecessor wrote with his habitual candor that although he had recommended Taylor he was quite content.[27] He could congratulate the Jesuit quite sincerely. He had known for a long time that Taylor's nomination was opposed in Rome and had explained this to his friend[28] but he could sympathize with Taylor, assuring him as he had earlier that year, "You know well you have, in my present diocese, any appointment it is in my power to bestow."[29]

While Father Taylor's arrival in France continued to remain only a prospect the Bishop of Montauban had more immediate reminders of his earlier American missionary career. He renewed the old friendship with Father Romagné, sending gifts at Christmas by way of Sougette de Cheverus with a note, "I will send his name tomorrow to the ministry for the King's approbation . . . the nomination belongs to me and is a matter of form."[30] He hoped to have the former missionary to Maine with him in Montauban, and although Romagné accepted the parish church of Sacé at the beginning of 1825 Cheverus made his old friend an honorary canon at the cathedral in Montauban, explaining to his brother, "This in no way obligates him. But if he comes here, as I hope he will, he will have a place in the choir and can appear there in hood and surplice." He envied Romagné and would willingly have changed places with him. He would have preferred to be a simple pastor, or rather nothing at all. "It is a terrible thing to be a bishop in France," he told Louis. "It is not that they don't admire me, applaud me, or even say they love me. But all that is neither tranquillity nor happiness."[31]

Another reminder of his Boston days arrived in Montauban in the summer of 1825 when Vernou de Bonneuil arrived with Adé, now a slim, pretty girl of eleven. Adé was to go to school in France and what better place than in the city where "Grandfather" was now the bishop? She could live with the Duplessis ladies and attend classes conducted by the Dames Noires. Cheverus could hardly contain his joy at the reunion with his beloved son and the wide-eyed child who inquired in awe if Grandfather were as great as the King of France. Vernou spent two weeks in Montauban when he brought Adé and meant to return there after transacting business in Paris. "Who would have said in Boston we would see each other here!" Cheverus exclaimed. By the time Vernou returned from Paris the bishop hoped to be settled in his new quarters and assured him, as he had so often from Boston, "Your room is ready to receive you."[32] While Bonneuil remained in France the bishop's schedule would wait upon him and Cheverus wrote to him on September 27, "If you could pass a few days here in October I will write to the provinces where I am expected and instead of the 7th I would go there the 14th." The invitation was irresistible, naturally, and Bonneuil left Montauban the second time on October 12, returning to Guadeloupe from Bordeaux with all sorts of news for Félicie about the bishop's household in Montauban and his relatives in Paris and Mayenne.[33]

American simplicity and loyalty to former American connections did not alter the fact that the new Bishop of Montauban had to adjust to a very different type of ecclesiastical administration. Church and State were united in Restoration France and Cheverus stood between his 350 priests and the government's Ministry of Ecclesiastical Affairs. He had innumerable matters to regulate in concert with the king's ministers and he confessed, "I am quite a novice at this kind of thing."[34] The matter of creating his cathedral chapter, for example, all had to go through the state, and nominations required the consent of royal ordinance. On July 20 and August 13, 1824, the king had signed the ordinances confirming the bishop's own nominations for two vicars-general and six canons but Cheverus was left uncertain about the remaining three. He had been told that two were named in Paris but he did not know how to list them or their salaries. On September 23 he wrote to Paris, "I have not yet received official notice of the ordinances naming the canons. . . . I don't know how to list their salaries. Do they begin the date of installation?"[35] The ministry replied that the two canons had been effectively appointed the day Cheverus took his oath at St. Cloud, July 8. The king was privileged to name one in the category of "joyous event" and the other as the gage of the bishop's oath of fidelity. Their salaries began on the day of installation.[36] On the same day Cheverus had inquired, the king had named Jean-Baptiste-Louis Boutang the ninth canon for Montauban, thus filling out the bishop's chapter.[37]

The bishop's salary and residence were a matter of civil regulation as well. Although Cheverus was named Bishop of Montauban the first month of 1823, his remuneration hung fire months after his arrival there in the summer of 1824. As we saw earlier, Corbière had proposed measures covering the costs of installation and an additional subsidy and had secured the king's approval in July, 1824; but a good month after Cheverus' arrival in his see city his full name and birth date were just being forwarded to the Minister of Finances and it was still later before Villèle reported back to the Minister of Ecclesiastical Affairs and Public Instruction that the Bishop of Montauban was not inscribed in the book of pensions of the national treasury.[38] In the end, of course, the new bishop received his just salary, and more. The General Council of the Département de Tarn-et-Garonne in 1825 voted their beloved prelate an additional 5,000 francs to enable him to live "as a bishop should and could not do in dignity on the 15,000 allowed by the state." The council went further and doubled the amount proposed for the first expenses of establishing an episcopal see.[39]

The matter of an episcopal residence tells much the same story of red tape and local generosity. The grand palace on the bank of the Tarn which had been the episcopal residence in the days of the Old Regime when bishops were princes in every sense of the word had, with the abolition of the see, long since been perverted to civilian uses. Today, its noble beauty serves as an exquisite setting for the treasures of the Ingrès Museum. Cheverus took up his temporary residence in the Hotel of the Prefecture when he first arrived, but the happy citizens meant to procure for the new bishop a home suited to their respect. In October the prefect reported to Paris that the General Council had held several sessions to discuss the matter.[40] In 1825 the council, "in spite of considerable sacrifice already made," had increased the proposed allotment from 6,000 to 10,000 francs.[41] The house they meant to purchase had first belonged to Paul-Antoine d'Alies and had since passed to the Marquise de Bellissen, his granddaughter. It was not until Saturday, September 17, that Cheverus moved into his permanent home; but again, once the furnishing began, the place was so far beyond his hopes that he told Sougette he wished she could come to act as mistress of it.[42]

It proved to be a very happy house. Not only was Cheverus able to entertain Vernou de Bonneuil there in October but in the months to come all sorts of loved and respected faces would smile at the bishop across his table. The Duplessis ladies with Adé and her little friends were regular visitors, and when an episcopal guest was present as well, young Adé was enchanted.[43] Amadée, his nephew studying for the priesthood, spent his vacations there and a veritable procession of relatives from Mayenne, Paris, and Ernée invaded the bishop's domicile during the late summer and early fall. Cheverus loved nothing better than gathering those he loved about him and it was wonderful to be able, at last, to return some of the loving generosity they had all shown him in the days when he was the poverty-stricken Bishop of Boston. And when the different groups of relatives had departed for their respective homes he had always his priests, Trélissac, Guilleux, Carle, and the others who lived with him or came to dine. The dear days in Boston did not dim in his memory; but since his heart knew no bounds they were augmented by precious days in the midst of his new children. When he wrote to Josiah Quincy he explained:

> If, as you have the goodness to assure me, I am not forgotten in Boston, I can say, with truth, I do not forget Boston. So dear and familiar is the name of the beloved city, that even in conversation I say Boston instead of Montauban, and this often; and I am then told, "You love Boston better than Montauban, but we defy the Bostonians to love you more than we do." I must acknowledge that here, as well as in America, love and respect are given me much beyond my deserts.[44]

CHAPTER XX

JEAN VI OF MONTAUBAN

WHILE the new Bishop of Montauban was settling down in his diocese the king who had recalled him to France lay dying. Louis XVIII could not win the agonizing struggle against the gangrene creeping inexorably through his limbs, but he could preserve both his dignity and his wit to the end. He would die like a gentleman and a Christian. On September 13, 1824, he received the last sacraments.[1]

Jean de Cheverus was not at home when the news reached Tarn-et-Garonne. His metropolitan, the Archbishop of Toulouse, while visiting Montauban to welcome the former American prelate a month earlier, had invited him to preach at the dedication of the outdoor Stations of the Cross recently erected by the Récollets. Cheverus had gladly consented, not for any honor implicit in Anne, Cardinal Clermont-Tonnerre's invitation, but for love of the feast day itself. The feast of the Exaltation of the Holy Cross would always remind him of his cathedral in Boston, and no feast would ever be dearer to his heart.

He spoke very forcefully on September 14 inside the church of the Récollets, but it was his improvisations at each of the stations which moved his listeners most. He seemed to be meditating aloud, and his words went straight to the heart. The cardinal in particular was touched, and he asked Cheverus to give them all his blessing. Cheverus demurred. "It is not my place to bless your people in your Eminence's presence," he explained. But the cardinal's finesse was equal to his suffragan's humility. He gave the kneeling Cheverus a blessing which he insisted must be passed on to the people.[2] It was all very graceful and gracious. Cheverus stayed on in Toulouse to preside at the investiture at the Convent of Notre Dame. It was there that the news of his king's last illness reached him.

Hurrying back to Montauban Cheverus entered anxiously into the Forty Hours of prayer for the dying monarch. But prayers could not save this Bourbon who was the last French king to die on his throne. At four o'clock in the morning of September 16 Louis XVIII expired. The couriers bearing the news arrived a few days later, and on September 19 Cheverus issued his pastoral prescribing the necessary and proper services of mourning.[3] At the Cathedral of the Assumption, of course, Cheverus himself presided on September 22. The eulogy which the recent Bishop of Boston pronounced that morning was judged by Frenchmen one of the "most worthy monuments raised in memory of that good King."[4]

Cheverus began by tracing the great virtues of the late king, both in English exile and on his French throne. Louis XVIII was compared to St. Louis in piety and wisdom, to Louis XII in justice, and to the great Henry IV in magnanimity. Then passing on to the monarch's devotion to his subjects Cheverus demanded to know how anyone could fail to mourn a king so Christian, a ruler so benign. Looking directly at the public officials assembled down front, he said feelingly, "You are too good Frenchmen, too devoted to legitimate monarchy not to shed tears at the death of this tender, august father." To the military he cried, "I speak also to you, brave soldiers that you are, who have served with glory your prince and fatherland. You have hearts too sensitive not to mourn at the tomb of this best of kings!" Then pausing in noticeable emotion, his eyes glistening, he concluded, "I have tears for such an event; I have no words."[5]

Although a funeral oration need not present the ultimate judgment of history on the subject of the speech, this eulogy delivered with more than usual fervor does reveal something of the speaker. Thirty years away from France had done nothing to alter the ardor of his devotion. First and always the universal Church, then France his fatherland, then legitimate monarchy: these were the objects of his loyal service. God, country, and king — generations of French prelates had served this triumvirate with varying degrees of emphasis. Yet Jean de Cheverus, who scarcely a year before had sailed from New York, who less than two months ago had arrived in Montauban, spoke as a French bishop among French prelates. And if there was any diminution of devotion to the House of Bourbon in the years that followed, history has left no record of it. His first Lenten charge to the Diocese of Montauban drew its illustrations from the example of Louis XVI in prison, smilingly content with a piece of bread dipped in wine, his sister Madame Elizabeth who passed an entire Lent with only bread and coffee for nourishment. "As Christians and as Frenchmen let us thank the God of Saint Louis," he urged, "who gives us both in their lives and in their deaths this august, dear family of Bourbons as such sublime models of faith and piety. As Christians and Frenchmen let us make it our duty and our glory to imitate them."[6]

Charles X, the new king who entered Paris in the midst of a steady rain on September 27, 1824, was given a warm welcome there. The sixty-seven-year-old monarch had all the dignity of the Bourbons and more than their usual ease of manner and charm. He would inspire among his intimates a devotion sentimental almost to the point of being feudal. Less intellectual than Louis XVIII, nevertheless he had a high sense of duty to the State, a real desire to assure the greatness of France and the welfare of his people. Simple in his own tastes, he was almost excessively generous to others when it was a question of aiding them. Since the death of his last mistress in 1804 he had scrupulously adhered to his oath to remain faithful to God. However narrow and formalistic his own devotion may have been in the quarter century which followed, he never frowned at those who did not share his religious austerity.[7] Even if he had not proved so generous to Jean de Cheverus, the Bishop of Montauban would loyally and lovingly have served such a man as the new king.

On the feast of St. Charles, Cheverus, who happened to be at Moissac, pontificated at St. Peter's Church to beg divine Providence to preserve the king, and his sermon naturally took as its subject the Bourbon monarchy. On May 10, 1825, the Bishop of Montauban announced that the consecration of the king would take place on Trinity Sunday, the twenty-ninth of that month. "God in his mercy has given us a king after His own heart, and dear to the heart of all Frenchmen," he wrote in his pastoral. The king desired their prayers, and to that end each priest should say every day until his consecration the collect, secret, and post-communion prayers *Pro rege.* On the day of the event itself all the churches of the diocese would sing the *Veni Creator* before the high Mass, after the Mass the *Exaudeat,* and at Vespers both the *Domine Salvum fac Regem* and the *Te Deum.* Following the consecration Charles X requested more prayer and Cheverus on June 5 fixed a week from that day for a solemn ceremony at the cathedral. At Vespers that day he spoke on the sacred character of the king's consecration and of the happy future they would all enjoy, of the grandeur and antiquity of the dynasty, and of the love they all had for it as Frenchmen.[8]

Although the first year that followed the consecration of Charles X found Cheverus on the periphery of politics of the new reign, owing to the remoteness of his diocese from Paris and the spiritual needs of his flock, he did adhere to the declaration of the French hierarchy of April 3, 1826. The declaration was, in a sense, a retort to Félicité de Lamennais, one of Father Bruté's dearest friends in France. Lamennais, who had been a member of the clergy since 1815, had published what was considered a diatribe against the Gallicanism of the French bishops and Denis Frayssinous, the Minister of Ecclesiastical Affairs, in particular. In a publication called *On Religion Considered in its Relations with the Political and Civil Order* in 1825 Lamennais had deplored what he visualized as an attempt to introduce democracy into the Church, a subjection of the spiritual power to the political, a threat to the divine constitution of the Church which could lead to heresy and schism.[9]

In February of 1826 a different sort of pamphlet emanated from the pen of the Count de Montlosier, to the astonishment of those who knew him to be a pillar of the reactionary nobility. The pamphlet was entitled *Mémoire à consulter sur un système religieux et politique tendant à renverser la religion, la societé, et le trône,* and it was as interminable as its title was incoherent. Ancient elements of anticlericalism were all there: the danger from the Jesuits, ultramontanism, clerical usurpation, a secret movement to overthrow the Constitution in favor of a theocratic state. It had its hour, and Montlosier was hailed as the "Torch of France."[10]

To refute such contradictions, that they were working to make the Church dependent upon the government, that they were intent upon subverting the Constitution in favor of theocracy, the French prelates addressed their letter to Charles X on April 3, asserting:

> We remain inviolably attached to the doctrine our predecessors transmitted to us on the rights of Kings and their full and absolute independence in the temporal order of authority direct or indirect of all ecclesiastical power. But we also condemn with all Catholics those who, under the pretext of liberty, impugn the primacy of Saint Peter and the Roman pontiffs.

At the invitation of Frayssinous, Cheverus adhered, as did the Cardinal Archbishop of Toulouse. In fact, all the bishops with the exception of four agreed to the statement which was chiefly aimed at Lamennais. The work which had provoked the opposition of the hierarchy was subsequently suppressed.[11] Cheverus must have wondered at the evolution of Lamennais' thinking since the days when he had known it from Bruté as being ultra-royalist at the time of the Restoration. Now Lamennais seemed to defend a separation of altar and throne. But the Bishop of Montauban had more immediate concerns within his diocese.

For the most part the rest of Cheverus' stay in Montauban was preoccupied with local episcopal duties, the further reorganization of the diocese, pastoral visits, instructions to converts, and the minutiae of his own see city. Other priests and bishops enjoyed calling on him at the episcopal palace; Cardinal Clermont-Tonnerre continued to stop in Montauban on his trips to and from Normandy; Bishop Raymond-Lalande did not require public functions alone to draw him to the welcoming gates of the courtyard on Rue des Bains. The ordinary clergy knew that Cheverus considered his house open to all and there was always a clatter of hoofs in the street sloping up from the bridge when the bishop was in residence.[12]

Episcopal visitations were, of course, a very important part of the work of revitalizing an area so long deprived of a regular bishop. Cheverus began on October 2, 1824, by going to Monclar in the company of his vicar-general Trélissac whom he had loved from the very start. This parish had prepared for their bishop's arrival by having a mission and Bishop de Cheverus was greeted not only by the pastor and mayor, but by the mission preacher as well.[13] On Sunday the prelate administered confirmation and the Eucharist to about 800 people. On Monday all the parishes of the canton came in procession to receive those sacraments. Cheverus then shared a retreat with the clergy and on Saturday left for Beaumont. After five days in the latter place he returned to Montauban where he was happily delayed a while by the return visit of Vernou de Bonneuil. After Bonneuil left for Bordeaux, Cheverus set off again on October 30 for Moissac.

And so the days went by. On his return from Moissac he presided at the Ursuline Convent for the clothing of four nuns, an occasion which forcibly reminded him of the first such ceremony he had witnessed in Boston. Three days later he installed the new pastor in Saint-Étienne's Church of Tescou. Then to the canton of Caussade northeast of Montauban. In December, after a tour of the parish of Monbeton in the southwest, he enjoyed at home the company of Clermont-Tonnerre and prepared for the ordination ceremonies in his cathedral on December 18. Montauban had not seen such a ceremony for thirty-six years and for the bishop it was a memorable day for other reasons as well. Thirty-four years before on that very day he himself had received holy orders in Paris. His thoughts were myriad; but his dominating emotion was his sense of terrible unworthiness and he begged his people to pray for him that God would forgive him for all his faults and negligences.[14] It was with renewed fervor that Cheverus returned to Moissac the next day.

Back in 1808 a new bridge had been begun to span the river at Moissac. The fall of Napoleon had suspended work on the project until 1820, but now on December 19, 1824, the last stone was to be fitted formally into place in the midst of elaborate ceremony. It was only fitting that the new bishop, whose carriage had been the first to cross it a few weeks earlier, should now give the bridge his blessing. Again accompanied by faithful Trélissac, Cheverus went to join the civil authorities of Moissac, Castelsarrasin, and the Département de Tarn-et-Garonne together with the engineers whose ingenuity had produced the work. Since it was the birthday of the dauphine the bridge was dedicated to Marie-Thérèse and all the dignitaries present received a medal struck for the occasion.[15]

And then, all too soon, it was Christmas, the first Cheverus spent among his new flock. In his pleasure at being among his own countrymen and in his ardent desire to give the holy season every liturgical dignity it deserved, Cheverus himself presided at every ceremony of the night and day. He knew no fatigue, only a compulsion to share with his people the mounting joy the feast always brought. He almost envied Canon Cavalié who had died just as he left the sacristy to celebrate Mass. It was a lovely season in which to be called home.[16]

The new year found the bishop back at his visitations. It would serve no purpose to list them all here.[17] It is enough to say that he was indefatigable, that he never cared how he traveled: horse, simple buggy, public carriage, it mattered not at all. There was always something of the missionary, the apostle, and the tender father in his episcopal character. He tried to reconcile pastors who quarreled with the mayors of their cities; he brought peace to congregations who quarreled with their pastors. Always and everywhere his greatest joy was to relieve misery, and the anecdotes surrounding his visits are many.[18]

The receptions he received everywhere seem to have been unanimously cordial, but to the town of Lauzerte must go first place for devising a welcome that virtually killed their beloved prelate. Cheverus was expected in June and the zealous townspeople were determined to receive him with the greatest eclat. At the entrance of the city they erected an arch of triumph thirty-five feet high at the top of which perched the ablest musicians and singers of the region. All was in readiness. But at the very moment that the little prelate knelt beneath the arch and the symphony burst into harmonious welcome, a most unmusical creaking and cracking was heard. The whole arch gave way, and the episcopal guest was almost inundated in the chaotic descent of flowers, instruments, and performers. "The panic was indescribable!" When the first rumors of the disaster reached Montauban the see city was momentarily uncertain that they still possessed a bishop at all. But Cheverus, who had survived the Terror and shipwreck, was not the man to be dismayed by the collapse of a verdant arch of triumph. In truth, he was much too busy consoling his devotees who had been wounded in either their sensibilities or their persons by the unceremonious disintegration of their grandiose welcoming. Since none of the legends of the Montauban era suggest that Cheverus had lost his sense of humor, it is quite probable that this once the little bishop consoled the suffering with a twinkle in his eye.[19]

As the year 1825 came to its close a more serious calamity struck. Two days before Christmas the waters of the Tarn began to rise with alarming speed and the merrymaking of the dwellers of the riverside houses was cut short by frantic efforts to resist the ravaging and swirling waters. Then on January 5 torrential rains brought a second even higher flood tide. Not since November 18, 1766, had the river risen so high and on January 6 the suburbs of Sapiac and a large part of Ville-Bourbon were inundated and the people fleeing from their homes. All of the Montauban officials rushed into the frantic rescue work with the Duc de la Force side by side with Cheverus. It was the bishop, however, who received the highest praise from the French press:

> We can not recall, without tenderness and admiration, how after having taken into his episcopal palace several hundreds of inhabitants who had lost everything, how our worthy prelate protected them, fed them, slept them, and warmed them for many days; how he scarcely left them, spending a great part of his time serving them, consoling them and praying with them; and how finally he would not allow them to re-enter their homes until they could return without danger and further help had been assured.[20]

The news spread over the nation and on February 2 the Minister of Ecclesiastical Affairs wrote a long report of the affair to Charles X.

After describing the floods and desolation he reminded the king of the large number of Protestants in Montauban. "But your Majesty also knows what can be the extent of charity and devotion of a true minister of Jesus Christ, when it is a question of relieving fatal misfortunes." He continued:

> Your Majesty will not be surprised, therefore, to learn that on this occasion the venerable Bishop of Montauban was found at the places most dangerously threatened, bareheaded, in water up to his knees, encouraging the workers by his advice and his example, helping the victims save their furnishings, receiving the unfortunates (Catholic and Protestant without distinction) in his episcopal palace where he lodged and fed them eating with them himself and assuaging their misery as much as lay in his power.

Frayssinous then commented that Cheverus had consulted his heart rather than his means. The Bishop of Montauban had no personal fortune as did most French prelates. He had left Boston with nothing, arriving in Montauban with scarcely enough to pay for his journey. Could not an extraordinary indemnity be granted?[21]

When Cheverus wrote to Bonneuil on March 9, 1826, he said:

> The gazettes will inform you that we have had here an inundation of the Tarn. Happily no one perished. . . . They have greatly exaggerated in the public papers the little I had the good fortune to do & the King himself being informed has given me . . . 5000 francs as reparation, and adding the gracious words, "To give to the Bishop of Montauban is to give to the unfortunate."[22]

He might have added that he had immediately distributed the royal gift among the poor.[23] Instead, he concluded, "We opened the Jubilee Sunday the 5th. I am really very busy."

A pastoral of February 27 promulgated the papal bull, *Exultet spiritus noster,* which accorded the second jubilee since the beginning of the nineteenth century. The events which had turned Europe topsy-turvy had prevented Pius VII from granting such an occasion for spiritual blessings; but his successor, in spite of opposition from the chancelleries of the continent, was determined that a jubilee should mark the opening of his reign.[24] His illness had delayed the announcement until May, 1824, and the situation in the Diocese of Montauban had delayed it even longer in Cheverus' jurisdiction. But Cheverus, like Leo XII himself, saw in the days of the jubilee a wonderful opportunity to lead souls back to the Church and he entered into the specially privileged six months with all his strength. Father Guilleux, one of the priests who had followed him from Mayenne, worried for fear his bishop was going even beyond his strength and wrote of his concern to the Cheverus family. Guilleux said he hated to alarm them with an account of what Cheverus had undertaken for Lent that year, but everyone was anxious about his health, even though it appeared that God was visibly sustaining him.

The Jubilee which we entered the fourth Sunday of Lent, and especially the sermons of Mgr. have done, and do daily, enormous good. No one can resist him. He moves, he persuades, he captivates everyone.[25]

The whole city had outdone itself in the procession opening the jubilee in the course of which Cheverus had exhorted them to listen to the voice of Leo XII as an echo of St. Peter; but for many of the grateful citizens it was the voice of Jean, their bishop, which impelled them. Everyone was determined to give this procession an elegance unequaled in the history of Montauban. Prefect de Limairac, the Duc de la Force, the entire regiment, the tribunal in a body, all in most formal dress were zealous rivals in the affair. At the head of the procession more than a thousand maidens and small girls dressed in white moved in beautiful order and perfect silence. After them came the widows in black, then the men: students of the minor and major seminaries, all the parish clergy, and last the civilian and military authorities. Half a league long, the line moved with banners flying. Describing the occasion Father Guilleux said, "He spoke only a few words yet never made so many cry. How he is loved!"[26]

However mixed the motives of his flock may have been, those of the bishop were clear; the six months of the jubilee were ones of extreme striving to outdo himself in zeal for the Lord. All during Lent he had been preaching every Sunday, Wednesday, and Friday; on April 2 he told Bonneuil that he was now preaching every day for a retreat at the cathedral.[27] He pursued the sinner or the indifferent Christian to his very household. He brought back a priest who had fallen away more than three decades earlier during the Terror. His most outstanding success was, however, the work he accomplished among the soldiers of the Montauban garrison.

Although the military took part in processions and formal occasions the bishop was aware that the spiritual benefits of the jubilee were passing them by; they seldom frequented the churches. Cheverus decided to give them a retreat himself. His ardor was irresistible. Soon the men began going to confession to their bishop and it was not long before they were all willing to follow him to the various churches of the city, old Saint-Jacques, Saint-Orens across the river, the cathedral, to make the stations of the jubilee. In a way it was a much more moving procession, this smaller one, led by the short man in episcopal robes and composed of stalwart men in military dress marching gravely through the city, murmuring prayers as they went. This time they marched not by order of their commandant, but from compulsion of their hearts, hearts that were drawn at last to the true meaning of the jubilee.[28]

The year 1826 seemed destined to be a wondrous year for the Church in Montauban. Back in New York William Taylor was talking again of coming to join his "father and best earthly friend" in the city where Cheverus had named him an honorary canon.[29] In March the king approved five whole *bourses* or scholarships for the diocesan seminary and the same month the city council, to show their respect for Cheverus, named his vicar-general Trélissac to their ranks.[30] The new mayor of the city, the Vicomte de Gironde, in his inaugural address said plainly that it was "his most ardent wish" to follow in the footsteps of the city's prelate whose "paternal administration had made this city a city of brothers."[31] In April four *succursales* or auxiliary chapels were approved for the cantons of Castelsarrasin, Saint-Antonin, Lauzerte-et-Molières, and Lavit.[32] The May report on *bourses* throughout the kingdom showed that Montauban had fourteen of the 675 in France, no diocese having more and Paris having two less than that number.[33]

The bishop's personal life was extremely joyous, too. Adé de Bonneuil was growing very tall these days and with the arrival of fine weather came over almost every evening. In May the Moreau de la Vigeries arrived from Paris with Fanny George de la Massonnais, Nanette Le Jariel, and their own daughter Clotilde. Fanny stayed on after the others left to enjoy the company of her brothers Amadée and Abel when their vacations began. Amadée was doing so well at Saint-Sulpice the bishop's heart pulsed with pride. It was wonderful to be among his family again and to share in all their concerns. His brother Louis and his family were expected in September and intended to stay until *la Toussaint*.[34]

Then in July, while Cheverus was listening fondly to Adé's excited accounts of the role she was to play in a little drama composed for the feast of Sainte-Anne, an event in Bordeaux brought rumors to Montauban which filled the latter city with uneasiness and its bishop with pain. On July 11, 1826, Archbishop d'Aviau du Bois de Sanzay of Bordeaux died. The *Moniteur* in a necrology printed five days later summarized the remarkable virtues of the late prelate and suggested that he would be a most difficult man to replace.[35] The same day the king granted permission for the burial of Aviau in Saint-André Cathedral in Bordeaux, but his thoughts were already busy with the problem of naming a successor. In reality it was no problem at all. Charles X knew only one prelate whose virtues rivaled those of the late archbishop; his name was Jean Lefebvre de Cheverus. He scarcely needed the recommendation of his Minister of Ecclesiastical Affairs to decide the matter. On July 30 he approved the names of three vicars-general to administer the see during its vacancy but the very next day he named Cheverus to Bordeaux.[36] On August 2 the *Moniteur* carried the news of the nomination.

When Frayssinous notified Cheverus he tried to forestall the objections he knew would be forthcoming. "I appreciate very well your distress and the affliction of the city of Montauban," he wrote. "But you are the man for the thing, and the king has judged it necessary to impose such a sacrifice on the Diocese of Montauban and on you."[37] There was complete consternation in Montauban. The mayor wrote to the ministry; the citizens addressed letters to the king and to the dauphine.[38] Cheverus himself wrote to Frayssinous on August 4:

> The noise of my nomination has spread here. I am tormented by everyone and I can not reassure them. It seems very important to me that if his Majesty absolutely wishes me translated to Bordeaux my successor be named immediately. . . . I am in a more distressing situation than I can describe. Clergy, faithful . . . all tell me in tears: don't abandon us. And I can promise nothing. . . . Have pity on them; have pity on me.[39]

He added dutifully that he had the necessary strength and good sense to make the sacrifice for religion and the king; he was most anxious, however, that his successor should spend some time with him before he left so that he could make the people want him and appreciate him. His first concern was for his diocese, but he confided in Bonneuil, "Neither my protests nor those of my diocesans could deliver me from this terrifying dignity. I have been very afflicted by it and sick."[40]

If any circumstance could make Cheverus willing to leave Montauban it was the thought that his successor would probably be William Valentine Dubourg, his former fellow bishop in the United States and the man he had so many reasons to admire. It was now twenty years since the two French *émigrés* had discussed the future of Mother Seton in the small study on Franklin Street; for over half of that time Dubourg had been Bishop of Louisiana. Now he was in France, perhaps on his way to Rome, and in more than one quarter there was speculation that Dubourg was to have at last some respite from the hardships of his American mission. The Roman agent of Bordeaux commented, "We expect the nomination of Mgr. Dubourg to Montauban. It must be said that it is high time that venerable pastor had a rest from the rigorous work he has had for so long."[41] On August 13 a royal ordinance confirmed these hopes, on September 7 the nomination reached Rome, and on October 2 a consistory held at the Vatican confirmed Cheverus for Bordeaux and Dubourg for Montauban.[42]

Meanwhile, as soon as Cheverus learned of the king's choice he wrote to his old friend, welcoming him to Montauban. Dubourg replied, "I was not listened to any more than you were. In the end I am nominated. . . . Now, for the love of your flock, who are to be mine, prepare the way, my dear Sir. Yes, you well may promise them that I will love them tenderly and without distinction. They have won my heart by the regrets they have for you."[43] It was a charge Cheverus had only been waiting to fulfill and now, whenever his departure was decried, he replied with praise for Dubourg, for his superior talent in the pulpit, his edifying piety, his exemplary zeal, and above all his charity and tolerance.[44] The bishop-elect knew that it would take all his talents and virtues to follow in Cheverus' steps and he told a friend back in New Orleans, "The consummate wisdom, the gift of persuasion which enchants all souls, that fine talent for speech and profound learning which distinguish Mgr. de Cheverus will always leave a void which they ought not hope to see filled by his successor."[45] When Antoine Garnier in Paris reported the changes to Maréchal in Baltimore he ventured the opinion. "It will not be easy to succeed Mgr. de Cheverus who is regretted by all. This latter prelate is highly praised in public opinion."[46]

If Dubourg had qualms about succeeding Cheverus at Montauban, the latter had even greater misgivings about going to Bordeaux. As he told the vicars-general of that city on August 29,

Only obedience could separate me from my dear diocesans. Their regrets pierce my heart and my tears fall with theirs. But once the sacrifice is made I will do all in my power . . . not to replace the holy Archbishop you mourn (I could never presume to do that) but to do the least harm that I can. . . . I know how honored I have been to be placed at Bordeaux, but I am also aware of my weakness, and such an unmerited honor only frightens me.[47]

The vicars at Bordeaux may have thought these words were mock humility before they learned to know their new archbishop but Félicie de Bonneuil who had known him for a dozen years knew what he suffered when he wrote to her, "If we were only all together again in Boston. There, no grandeurs. They overcome me. I did my best, I could not escape."[48] The brief happy days in Montauban were over. Now Louis, Sougette, and young Louis de Cheverus would be deprived of their visit to his first palace in France. Luckily Augustin Le Jariel had come down with Amadée and Abel when they joined their sister in late summer.

The thought of young Adé pressed upon him. She would spend the winter with the Dames Noires, but after that he did not know what to anticipate. Father Carle, who was as fond of her as the bishop, was going to Bordeaux; he, Guilleux, and Trélissac found it unthinkable that they should be separated from Cheverus and were delighted that the bishop wanted them with him in his new see. Amadée would be in Saint-Sulpice another year and vacations could as easily be spent in Bordeaux; Abel was in medical school and Fanny would be left at Saint-Denys.[49] But Adé was still so young, and Cheverus knew she was only in Montauban because Vernou relied on the bishop to protect her welfare. There were days when Cheverus did not quite see, in spite of the king, how he could ever leave.

On October 5 the French chargé d'affaires at Rome notified Bordeaux that Cheverus had been preconized by His Holiness in the consistory of October 2. "The bulls have been sent to Paris where the Pallium destined for this prelate has already been forwarded."[50] Dubourg was already in the capital and on October 15 the *Moniteur* reported that "Mgr. de Cheverus must leave Montauban on the 20th of this month to go to Paris to take the oath at the hands of the King. The prelate will then go to spend some time with his family."[51]

So all was resolved. Cheverus delegated Vivien Soulan to ship his table silver and sacred vessels to Bordeaux.[52] He hurriedly set off on a pastoral visit he had scheduled for late September in Lavit where "he administered the sacrament of confirmation . . . to a crowd of young children who seemed, like their parents and pastor, to gather around this angel of peace snatched too soon from the homage of his flock."[53] He would work for them until the last minute and told Bonneuil, "To avoid a painful scene I will leave Montauban at night and will keep the time of my departure a secret."[54] He could never again face the anguish of a parting like that from Boston. In company with two of his most valued priests he quietly left the city under cover of darkness. The silent trees still stood in ranks along the Promenade du Cours; the Tarn once more flowed peacefully down below in the dark. But even if it had been light as day the little prelate crouched behind the curtains of his carriage would not have seen; his eyes were full of tears.

CHAPTER XXI

ARCHBISHOP OF BORDEAUX

ONCE again in the month of November Jean Lefebvre de Cheverus found himself in Paris awaiting the arrival of papal bulls that would canonically institute him in a new see city. But the contrast between this time of waiting and the one of three years before was sharp, and for Cheverus most distressing. On November 6 the *Moniteur's* front page carried the notice that Charles, by the grace of God King of France and of Navarre, had the day before elevated Comte de Cheverus, the Archbishop of Bordeaux, to the dignity of peer of the realm.[1] His protests against this latest honor were no more effective than the ones against his translation to Bordeaux and he began to feel like a drowning man. What a far cry from the sweet simplicity of those Boston days were the days to come. He wrote dolorously to Bonneuil, "Your poor Papa, my dear son, scarcely gets accustomed to grandeur. The obscure but so sweet haven of filial piety became him much better."[2]

The delay was much shorter this time, too. On November 10, 1826, at Fontainebleau the king signed the ordinance for the publication of the bulls given in Rome a month earlier: Cheverus for Bordeaux, Dubourg for Montauban, and Simon Garnier for Vannes.[3] On the same day Frayssinous applied for the indemnity attached to the title of Archbishop of Bordeaux; before the week was over Charles X had also confirmed the request of Cheverus that his Montauban friends, Trélissac and Carle, be made vicars-general of Bordeaux.[4] In the meantime Cheverus had gone to take the oath at the hands of the king on November 13. The only impediment this November was the prelate's own reluctance.

At least he had escaped one further responsibility. When the question had arisen for a new preceptor for the Duc de Bordeaux who was in line of succession to the French throne Comte Roy and Chateaubriand had suggested Cheverus for that difficult and delicate honor. Charles X replied, "The choice would be excellent. I am annoyed not to have thought of it two hours earlier. It would have been done. But now it is too late." Another had already been officially named.[5] Cheverus could only rejoice at this fortuitous delivery. He left his cousins Vigerie and began his journey to Mayenne for some time with his family.

His thoughts on leaving Paris were less gloomy than on his arrival from Montauban. The reassurances that he had been given on every side in Paris were meant to convince him that his king and his country demanded his sacrifice in leaving Montauban. Seeing Dubourg again (the new Bishop of Montauban was staying at Saint-Sulpice, a mere stone's throw from the Vigerie house) had reminded the modest Cheverus all over again how many superior talents the former Bishop of New Orleans possessed. Montauban would be much better under this tall, handsome, and polished prelate. Montauban was to have another American missioner, too, in the person of Father Louis Sibourd whom the king had confirmed for the first vacancy in the cathedral chapter.[6] Sibourd had been vicar-general for Dubourg in Louisiana but Cheverus was more prone to remember him as the zealous pastor who had tried to restore regularity and discipline to St. Peter's of New York in the days when Elizabeth Seton was Sibourd's friend and parishioner. How strangely hearts were united in this world. All three French priests had loved the Church in America and served it well; all three had known Mother Seton and had helped to shape her career. Now, five years after her death in the hills of Maryland, all three were to be united by a common love for a small city in the hills of southern France. Time and distance had not altered Cheverus' earlier affections and could not alter these more recent ones. He was almost reconciled to leaving Montauban at last.

Mayenne was even more excited over this second sojourn of the city's most illustrious son, and requests poured in from all sides that the archbishop honor the local institutions by his presence. He preached, of course, at Notre Dame de Mayenne; he spoke at the Convent of the Visitation; he gave his blessing to the inmates of prisons and to the suffering patients in the hospitals. In spite of a severe cold and fatigue he could not refuse. And then it was time to go to Le Mans for the conferring of the pallium by Bishop Claude de la Myre-Mory in the chapel of the major seminary. It was quite fitting that Cheverus should receive the symbol of his metropolitan dignity at the hands of the Bishop of Le Mans, a successor of that deported prelate to whom the young nonjuring priest had remained so loyal and whose interest had secured the scholarship which the boy Cheverus enjoyed at Louis-le-Grand. Jouffroy de Gonssans had said so long ago, "Little Abbé de Cheverus will be one day the first subject of this diocese." Now Cheverus was one of the first prelates of France and, although his simplicity preferred the quiet chapel of the seminary for the ceremony, the city itself should have the honor of the event.[7]

That night he went to the cathedral to be present at a mission being conducted there. His throat was so sore he could scarcely speak, but Le Mans would hear him. Ignoring the archbishop's protests the mission preacher insisted on calling on Cheverus for a few words. Hoarse and muffled as it was, it was still the voice that had reconciled so many sinners and brought peace to so many souls. The zeal of his ardent heart once more triumphed over his physical distress and Le Mans could boast that she, too, had heard the most beloved prelate in France. The next day Archbishop de Cheverus departed for Bordeaux.[8]

In Bordeaux, naturally, the arrival of the new archbishop had been the subject for weeks. Cheverus had written from Paris on November 13 after the publication of his bull authorizing his first vicar-general to take possession of the see. Trélissac and Carle were to be second and third vicars-general since Cheverus meant to retain an experienced man of the archdiocese in first place. Carle was still in Montauban winding up affairs there and one of the vicars-general acting during the vacancy of the see, Barthelmy Morel, would act in Carle's place temporarily. Good Trélissac had gone on to Bordeaux to be there when his friend and archbishop arrived. Guilleux, who was to be the archbishop's secretary, probably accompanied Cheverus.[9] But Vicar-General Pierre Barrès was really in command for the Archbishop of Bordeaux and on November 22 took formal possession of the see in Cheverus' name. In the cathedral chapter Barrès read all the formal documents: Cheverus' authorization of November 13, the papal bull of October 2, the declaration of the Grand Aumonier that Cheverus had taken the oath of fidelity to Charles X, Cheverus' letter of November 16 conferring special powers on Barrès. The chapter then went from the episcopal palace across the street to Saint-André Cathedral where the *Veni Sancti Spiritus* was sung at the foot of the great altar. The documents were all read again in a loud voice by the presiding canon and then Barrès was conducted to the thrones in the sanctuary and choir. The vacancy of the See of Bordeaux was officially ended.[10] The following day Barrès notified all the clergy of the fact saying:

> Mgr. will make his solemn entrance into Bordeaux Thursday, December 14. . . . Soon we can see at hand this touching goodness and affectionate piety, this zeal in two worlds, and this tender attachment to his clergy, which so eminently distinguish our venerable prelate.[11]

The civilian officials immediately went into action. On November 24 the Prefect of the Gironde, Baron d'Haussez, after congratulating Barrès on his appointment as first vicar-general said, "I would like to have a conference with you on the subject of the *Entrée* of December 14. I am eager to present my respects to him. His high virtues and the nobility and holiness of his character make him doubly precious to me."[12] By December 6 the prefecture had its part all organized and a copy of their printed program for the reception of Cheverus was in Barrès' hands; every one of the civilian authorities, Haussez assured him, was determined to participate.

The military were not to be outdone and the commandant of the 11th Military Division informed Barrès that he had taken "all the necessary measures to carry out our part." The Cour Royal of Bordeaux had already selected a special deputation to call upon the archbishop at his palace, but all the members meant to take advantage of the invitation to assist at the cathedral ceremonies. They would, of course, wear full regalia.[13] The greatest excitement prevailed among the more youthful members of the great city's population. None of them had ever seen an archbishop's *entrée,* the late Aviau having entered Bordeaux a quarter of a century earlier. They meant to be up bright and early on the morning of December 14.

The first entrance Archbishop de Cheverus made upon the soil of the jurisdiction where he was destined to spend the last decade of his life was made from Angoulême on December 13. In distant Bordeaux all the bells in the city had rung at five in the evening, announcing the event. Barrès, Trélissac, and Morel, his vicars-general had already left earlier in the day to go meet him. The cantons of Saint-Savin and Saint-André de Cubzac were the first to welcome the new prelate in pontifical style. Cheverus then spent the night, as became a peer of France, at the Castle of Cubzac with the Comte de Montbadon, peer of France.[14]

At seven the next morning the bells of Bordeaux began their tumult again and would not stop until Cheverus entered Saint-André Cathedral. A crowd of impatient young people went out to Carbon-Blanc to be the first to see the famous man, pushing about his carriage as it moved toward Bordeaux and at last clattered across the Garonne. Cheverus got down at the end of the bridge near Place de Bourgogne where, in charge of the master of ceremonies of the Sulpician seminary, the cathedral chapter and the clergy of the diocese were waiting to receive him. Marching in two columns ahead of the archbishop the canons bore his insignia, the choirs began intoning the litany of the Blessed Virgin, and the procession began to move along the *fossés,* up Rue du Hâ, to Place Rohan in front of the magnificent palace which had formerly housed the archbishops of Bordeaux.[15]

It was almost the middle of December and Cheverus was physically exhausted by the rigors of travel and the effects of his cold, but as the procession moved toward Saint-André his heart began to soar at the sight of his cathedral, that "old vessel eternally at anchor on the bank of the river." Even today, amid the bustle and din of a twentieth-century metropolis, Saint-André still dominates the city and gives exquisite pleasure to those who love the old cathedral; but a century ago it was even more the very core, the soul of the city. The tired little man being carried along on waves of adulation and song, whose cathedrals had formerly been the simple one in Boston and the stiffly classic one of Montauban, was overwhelmed as he gazed at the towering spires, the unique enormity of the Gothic nave so powerfully symbolizing the solidity of the faith in the plenitude of charity, and the aged elegance of the apse.[16]

At the entrance of Saint-André Barrès welcomed Cheverus in the name of all the clergy, and Cheverus responded with words from the fourth Council of Carthage, *"Episcopus in ecclesiam sublimior sedeat; intra domum vero collegam se presbyterorum esse cognoscat."* In the government of the Church a bishop must be above his priests, but within his house he must be their colleague. Authority and forcefulness were necessary to government, but in common intercourse only friendship and cordiality should prevail. "I need you for my friends," he said simply. The immense crowd which had followed him up to the door knew that the late Archbishop d'Aviau whom they had so recently mourned had a truly worthy successor and shouts of *"Vive Mon-*

seigneur!" "Vive le père des pauvres!" came from all sides.[17] His reputation as a father to the poor had preceded him, but now they saw for themselves his sweet simplicity, and their enthusiasm knew no bounds.

Then in through the great door the procession passed, under the great organ which would soon thunder from its noble loft, down the long aisles where the notables sat in their reserved seats, to the foot of the great altar. Thus, for the first time in his last cathedral, Jean Lefebvre de Cheverus, Archbishop of Bordeaux, Count and Peer of France, intoned the *Te Deum* and the cathedral choir answered with a resounding burst of praise. Mounting to the throne Cheverus gave his solemn benediction and announced the indulgences attending the ceremony.

Later, at his temporary episcopal palace, the Hôtel du Doyenné at the corner of Rue Sainte-Hélène and Place de l'Archevêché, the archbishop received the delegations of all the civil, military, and judicial authorities who came to pay their respects.[18] With the gentle tact which was inherent Cheverus replied to each address of greeting with disarming skill. When the president of the Royal Court said, "The presence and virtues of your Eminence are the only things that could console us for the immense loss the diocese has suffered," the archbishop replied, "You render justice in the name of the God of Justice, we preach peace in the name of the God of Mercy; thus are we brothers. We must sustain and love each other as such. Religion and justice are sisters who must never be separated."[19] It was an auspicious beginning and when William Taylor arrived in Bordeaux a few weeks later he reported to Cheverus' friends in Boston:

> He is totally occupied in replying to addresses and attending civic entertainments. He is decidedly the most popular prelate in the Gallican church. . . . He possesses an astonishing facility of communicating his ideas, and in doing so, he, without any labored effect, selects the most precise, chaste and beautiful epithets in his native tongue. . . . Already he is here revered and admired.[20]

The milieu in which Father Taylor found his former American bishop was strikingly different from the life they had shared in Boston. Bordeaux in 1826 was the most thriving port of France with a population numbering well over 93,000. The Gironde, of which it was the capital and whose limits marked Cheverus' jurisdiction, contained more than half a million people.[21] Although the people of the outlying districts still spoke in dialects and in some suburbs did not even know French, within the city there was a brilliant social life and a flourishing intellectual activity.[22] The Academy of Sciences, Belles-Lettres and Arts of Bordeaux which had been founded in the reign of Louis XIV had survived the ravages of the Revolution and within two years of Cheverus' arrival was to receive from Charles X the full restoration of its former titles and statutes.[23]

The civic leaders with whom Cheverus mingled were of families eminent for their ties with Church and the monarchy. Bordeaux had been the advance guard of the Restoration when on March 12, 1814, it opened its gates to the Duc d'Angoulême and the supporting British arriving from Spain. Bordelais had hoisted the *cocarde blanche* and proclaimed the restoration of Louis XVIII. From Hartwell Louis had congratulated the mayor, "To use the language of the good Henry, my hour has begun."[24] The present mayor of Bordeaux, André-Guy-Victor du Hamel, had been one of the first after the Duc d'Angoulême to take part in those events of March, 1814.[25]

Camille, comte de Tournon, a colleague of Cheverus in the Chamber of Peers, had worked energetically under Cheverus' predecessor Aviau to restore religion in the city and the Gironde while he was prefect. Urgently needed repairs on 360 churches were undertaken; Saint-André, which had suffered severe damages to its façade during a storm in 1820, was only one of many beneficiaries. When Tournon left the prefecture to become Peer of France in 1823 plans for a general restoration of the cathedral's nave, spires, and vaulting were complete. Other churches within the city: Saint-Louis, old Saint-Seurin, Saint-Michel, and the Chartreuse were all part of Tournon's projects of restoration. During his prefecture the count had worked indefatigably as well for subsistence for the clergy; fifty-four rectories were acquired and twelve others were purchased later as a result of his efforts. Tournon was less successful in his attempt to rehabilitate Catholic cemeteries, but his support of the archbishop's plans for a new seminary at Bazas had happier results. Although Cheverus and Tournon met more often in Paris than in Bordeaux, they shared similar views on the subject of religion in the latter city. Both were firm believers in religious toleration in a city containing so many Protestants; both advocated firmest authority and obedience to law on the part of ministers of religion; both strove assiduously for the amelioration of the lot of the clergy.[26] Camille de Tournon was never as devout a man as Jean Lefebvre de Cheverus, but he was always a practicing Catholic. His talents lay in statecraft; the arch-bishop's were demonstrated in the spiritual domain. But each in his turn left a permanent mark on the Church in Bordeaux.[27]

Another statesman from Bordeaux with whom Cheverus shared friendship, if not always his reactionary policies, was Charles-Ignace de Peyronnet. The year that Cheverus came to Bordeaux Peyronnet was Keeper of the Seals in the first ministry of Charles X. Two years later Peyronnet was made Councilor of State and Peer of France and for the rest of the reign Peyronnet and Cheverus were colleagues from the Gironde in the high chamber. More than once during those years Peyronnet opened his heart to Cheverus in confidence and friend-ship; unfailingly he found tender interest, sound advice, and consola-tions for his difficulties.[28] On May 16, 1830, Peyronnet became Minis-ter of Interior in the last ministry of Charles X. This ministry of Jules de Polignac included as well Baron d'Haussez, the prefect who had so warmly welcomed Cheverus on the occasion of his *entrée* in 1826 and who continued to work on most cordial terms with the arch-bishop in Bordeaux until 1829.[29]

If the civic circles in which Cheverus was now expected to move were more studiedly aristocratic than those he had known in Boston, so, too, was the outward form of his spiritual domain. The Archbishop of Bordeaux had as suffragan bishops the prelates of Agen, Angoulême, Poitiers, Perigueux, La Rochelle, and Luçon.[30] His cathedral chapter was one of most ancient and noble traditions with a coat of arms more brilliant than Cheverus' own.[31] As much as the archbishop the canons were the very heart of Saint-André, and during a vacancy of the see were administrators of the archdiocese as well. Prelates might come and pass away; the cathedral chapter went on forever. When Father Taylor was made an honorary canon he was chiefly impressed at having a stall in the choir and the privilege of wearing purple, but Archbishop Cheverus more fully realized the high honor he had conferred on his American friend.[32]

The matter of an episcopal palace was another symbol of the changes Cheverus had to face. When the vicars-general who administered the see during the interregnum of 1826 learned that Cheverus was to be their new archbishop they dreamed of establishing him in the most elegant palace in the city. What could be more appropriate than the former archiepiscopal palace of the Old Regime, Le Palais Rohan behind the cathedral built by Prince Ferdinand de Rohan-Mériadec when he was Archbishop of Bordeaux and entertained kings and princes of the blood? But when Cheverus heard of this proposal he objected categorically. "It is not fitting," he said, "that a poor bishop like myself should live in such an elegant palace. The humble refuge of my saintly predecessor will be too good for me. Besides, I would be unhappy to deprive our beloved princes of the least part of the palace destined for them when they come to visit us."[33]

But Bordeaux was determined that he should live grandly as befitted an archbishop and peer of the realm. Prefect d'Haussez was authorized by the king to buy in the name of the nation for 220,000 francs the fine mansion and its dependencies which was near Saint-André in Rue Judaïque and Cheverus told the Bonneuils that the site at least was satisfying since it was next door to the Dames de la Foi where young Adé was now going to school.[34] The Duplessis ladies and their young charge had arrived the month before and the old archbishop was consoled by the thought that if he must live in style it would be near his "granddaughter."[35] He envied his vicar-general Carle who was living simply in a house he had rented, with one half of it occupied by Mme Duplessis, her daughter, and Adé de Bonneuil.[36]

To a man less modest in his tastes the new archiepiscopal palace would have been a joy, for it was a truly lovely house with its magnificent winding staircase adorned with a railing of unrivaled wrought metal, its mellow parquet floors, its paneled walls inlaid with oil paintings, its crystal chandeliers, and exquisitely formal little garden in the rear. Yet Cheverus was oppressed by the necessity of going to live in the Hôtel des Lahens and confessed to Vernou, "It will not be as valuable to me as my house in Boston when I used to receive my dear children there." He moved into his new home in October, 1828, with heavy heart, and on November 20 commented in his letter to Guadeloupe that although it was indeed a very beautiful house he could only view it with indifference. "I would much prefer to be still Bishop of Boston," he mused sadly. He tried to believe that Providence willed him these burdens of magnificence. "They must be borne."[37]

Yet if he lived within the walls of the fine mansion he never shared its splendor. He would live always as he had done in Boston. He chose for himself the least impressive room in the house where a small table and chair were his only furnishings besides the folding bed with its thin mattress. He kept only two servants, a cook and a man-of-all-work; he had always believed in doing himself whatever he was able and now, archbishop, peer of France, councilor of state, and later cardinal, the little man who had sawed wood for his parishioners in

Boston still carried wood to his own fireplace in this palace in Bordeaux.[38] His hospitality, too, remained unchanged. Besides the regular inmates of the palace: Trélissac, Guilleux, and his chief vicar Barrès, there were always guests. While he remained at the Doyenné his first years in Bordeaux friends and relatives had enjoyed that simpler residence, of course. When Taylor arrived in Bordeaux the month of Cheverus' *entrée* he had gone to a hotel, expecting to call upon the Archbishop of Bordeaux with the formality his new rank demanded. But before he could settle himself a carriage had driven up to carry Taylor to the Doyenné. Cheverus met him in tears. "We shall live as in Boston," he protested.[39] Louis de Cheverus, who had been deprived of his visit to Montauban in the fall of 1826, came at once to Bordeaux with Sougette and young Louis. His sister Le Jariel, with Clotilde and Augustin, arrived in the summer of 1827; the George-Massonnais children were there, too, that summer except for Abel who was newly married.[40]

Needless to say, the larger palace was kept even busier with guests, not the least cherished of whom were Adé and her school friends. Once Amadée was ordained he came to be a permanent part of the archbishop's household. Although Father Taylor did not live to see Cheverus established in Rue Judaïque many another American did visit there. All in all, Cheverus was well served by the size of his residence, however he may have deplored its magnificence. Yet the gentle host who presided over the expanding table was very little changed, if the weight which comes with age may be discounted, from the unpretentious missionary bishop of an earlier decade. In his heart he resisted magnificence to the very end of his days in Rue Judaïque and his letters to friends outside of France never ceased to reiterate the sentiment voiced to Félicie de Bonneuil in 1829, "I can say in the midst of grandeurs I need resignation to the will of God. My will would be the simple life of Boston. . . . "[41]

While his private tastes remained simple his public life was perforce greatly changed. It was characteristic of Cheverus, however, that he adjusted to his larger responsibilities with a minimum of strain on those about him. The first months of his reign at Bordeaux were marked by three principles which were wise as well as typical. The first stemmed quite naturally from his old habit of treating everyone alike with courtesy and love. The Protestants of Bordeaux received the same respect that Cheverus accorded those of Boston or Montauban, and they reciprocated in kind. With the Jews, a religious people whom

Cheverus was meeting for the first time in any numbers, he was on equally good terms. On his arrival Rabbi Abraham Andrade had courteously called to present his respects, likening himself to the Queen of Sheba who had come to admire the wisdom of Solomon. If the words were in 1826 mere polite formality, they came in the years that followed to be quite sincere. The Jews of Bordeaux held Cheverus in high esteem and stood in respect whenever he passd through their quarter. Rabbi Andrade himself shared his private griefs with the archbishop and when his beloved daughter died he told Cheverus simply, "I come to seek consolation from the representative of Jesus Christ, who wept at the grave of Lazarus."[42]

The second principle, born of humility, was his resolve to follow without deviation the policies of the late Archbishop d'Aviau whose sagacity and virtues Cheverus could not imagine himself surpassing. His first letter to his clergy in the new year, 1827, was devoted to the *Petites Communautés* so dear to Aviau's heart, and Cheverus' recommendations were largely taken from his predecessor's writings.[43] His first Lenten pastoral, too, was patterned on that of Aviau's for the year previous.[44] This policy, of course, served the new prelate well for old loyalties were in no way offended and the past rather easily and painlessly became the present. By the time Cheverus began to promulgate his own plans for Bordeaux his people were as devoted to him as if he had always been one of themselves. Had he not shared their reverence for Aviau and sympathized with their grief? His eulogy of the late prelate on the first anniversary of Aviau's death was more than convincing testimony.[45]

The third rule of the new administration was the product of past experience and the inherent good sense of the man. Cheverus never went rashly ahead to establish new institutions without first evaluating the people, the places, and the circumstances involved. Consummate patience may account for the fact that all of the beginnings he made — in England, in Maine, in Boston, and in Montauban — became an enduring part of the stream of later history. And this patience was accompanied by an exemplary administrative efficiency. Once a program was undertaken, Cheverus worked with phenomenal speed and demanded from his subordinates an equally efficient energy. When the first months of his reign went by and he found that some of the clergy were not complying with his first recommendations in regard to the *Petites Communautés* he wrote to them again more vigorously:

They form the first degree of ecclesiastical education in the Diocese. They can not, by their nature, share in the government funds. To facilitate gifts it became a principle that you could apply the offering of an intention of the Mass once a month. Some have forgotten it. At the end of the year it has resulted in a great shortage. I again recommend it to your religious zeal. . . . I wrote to you last January 23.[46]

It was reasonable but it was authoritative.

Men in the Church liked to work under him, and men in state affairs enjoyed collaborating with Cheverus. Before he was in Bordeaux a month another canon from Montauban, Ferdinand Gasc, had followed him to his new see.[47] In Paris the Minister of Ecclesiastical Affairs found that Cheverus' reports always came in among the first.[48] He handled an enormous correspondence with amazing promptness and could easily separate the wheat from the chaff; he could be very terse while politely refusing to act outside his proper sphere.[49] At the same time he was never obsequious in his equal courtesy to high dignitaries whose requests demanded his attention.

The truth is that from the day of his arrival Jean de Cheverus was very much Archbishop of Bordeaux. While he was still in Paris in 1826 he had directed Barrès to check on the exact state of the jubilee in Bordeaux. Tables in duplicate were sent to all the pastors to be filled out with exactitude.[50] Early in February of his first year he visited the minor seminary at Bazas and gave confirmation in the church there.[51] Upon his return to Bordeaux he assumed the task always nearest his heart, making it easier for the poor to live as good Christians. Ever since March 25, 1817, legal marriages among the poor had sharply declined because the expense of furnishing the records exacted by the civil authorities was beyond their means. A charitable society which had formerly tried to promote the proper celebration of both the civil and religious ceremonies had grown discouraged and was no longer able to prevent scandals. Cheverus wrote to Peyronnet asking if it could not be possible to revive the former custom *Pro Deo* which existed under the old law. "I hope you will . . . realize that I have only the interests of religion and the poor at heart," he explained.[52]

Meanwhile Lent had begun and Cheverus as usual set an example for his people of a prelate who put first things first. In between his self-imposed and rigorous devotions he continued to bring himself up to date on diocesan needs. "My health holds up," he reassured the Bonneuils, "and Lent did not distress me. I have already made some diocesan visits and I preach every Sunday at the Metropole."[53] He did not add that he had already undertaken a new printing of the *Processional,* authorizing printer Henry Faye to handle the work.[54] Nor did he mention that Leo XII had been approached for indulgences for the Bordeaux confraternities of the Blessed Sacrament with immediate success.[55]

The real need, as Cheverus perceived, was for a resurgence of spiritual vigor among his clergy. He made his plans carefully and with tact. He would revive pastoral retreats which for some years had been discontinued. When he learned that d'Aviau had intended having the vicar-general of Tours conduct such exercises he immediately invited the Abbé Ferdinand-François Donnet to Bordeaux for the retreat. On July 19, 1827, Cheverus told his priests, "I inform you with lively satisfaction that the pastoral retreat . . . will be given next month. It will open August 17 at 5 P.M. and end the 24th in the morning." He had undertaken necessary precautions for handling the needs of each canton during the absence of its pastor and admonished the clergy, "As the interests of your parishes could be the only motive which could keep you there I do not presume that any but very special reasons will dispense you from accepting my invitation."[56]

The feast of the Assumption on August 15 which occurred just before the retreat opened was an occasion for what appeared to Cheverus to be scandalous violations of a holy day in a Christian nation. During the retreat he mulled the matter over in his mind and at the close of the retreat he was determined to bring the matter before the prefect of the Gironde and the mayor of Bordeaux. Their response was immediate and heartening. Mayor du Hamel said that the city council was much concerned and had, in fact, been on record annually against the law of November, 1814, which was not rigorous enough for populous cities like Bordeaux. The city council was hopeful that soon the king's government would attack a matter of such importance but meanwhile, Hamel assured Cheverus, "I will recommend to all agents under my orders to double the surveillance to prevent the growth of the evil." Baron d'Haussez was similarly sympathetic and Cheverus thanked both the mayor and prefect for their solicitude. In spite of weak legislation, if all three were of the same mind perhaps violations would decrease even though they did not completely disappear.[57]

Cheverus had to accustom himself in those first years to the public occasions traditional to Bordeaux and requiring the archbishop's services. March 12, for example, meant a solemn ceremony commemorating the events of 1814 to which all the authorities, religious, civil, and military must be invited.[58] The annual Mass voted by the municipal corps for the preservation of the Duc de Bordeaux was celebrated at Saint-Michel on September 29, and the archbishop was expected to attend and extend the invitation to the cathedral chapter and pastors.[59] In 1827, too, the coinciding of the solemnity of St. Charles with a Sunday gave an opportunity for celebrating the king's patronal feast with extra pomp and Cheverus told his clergy, "I remind you with great pleasure of this happy anniversary on which we can highly manifest by our prayers and our wishes the sentiments we have in our hearts for our God and our King."[60] Then November included the custom established by Aviau in 1824 of processions throughout the diocese to the Catholic cemeteries. In the parishes these might be held on either Friday or on Sunday following the king's feast day, but in Bordeaux the procession took place on Friday, November 9. Leaving Saint-André at ten sharp it proceeded to St. Bruno's across from the cemetery where Cheverus celebrated a Mass of requiem and gave a sermon. The ceremonies concluded with a general absolution.[61]

Before the archbishop could believe it Advent was upon him and with it the anniversary of his entrance a year ago. It had been a year of adjustment more than one of new beginnings. He had not made any serious mistakes, he reflected. The good will and affection he found on all sides indicated as much and when he contemplated his blessings he wondered if the Lord might not say to him one day, "You have received your recompense in this world."[62] But he had done scarcely more than fill the void left by the death of Aviau. When he had given that good man's eulogy on July 11 he had been only too forcibly reminded how inadequate he, Cheverus, was to the task. It had been very painful to hear well-meaning enthusiasts compare him to his saintly predecessor and he recalled with shame his sharp reproof on one such occasion when he had cut off the orator of the day in sudden, unbearable rebellion.

"To compare me with my saintly predecessor is outrageous, because it makes plain to all eyes my insufficiency. I will not suffer such an outrage in public," he had cried.[63]

Comparisons voiced in his presence had ceased after that. But deep within himself Cheverus continued to be very conscious of the meagerness of his own contribution. His good vicars-general, faithful Trélissac and Carle, Pierre Barrès who knew the diocese so well, could have done as much, he thought. He was out of place in such a jurisdiction, and as the year closed he wrote to Félicie of his regret for the days when he could wish her a happy new year in person. "I still do so with as much tenderness," he asserted. "But then I had more tranquillity and true happiness than with all my dignities."[64] With the new year his diocese would in fact be entrusted to his vicars, for Paris was insisting that Comte de Cheverus, Peer of France, fulfill his duties to his nation as well as to his Church. "The session will be stormy," he told Vernou. "I hope God will have pity on France & bless her good King."[65] As for the Archbishop of Bordeaux, he already found his duties greater than his capabilities.[66]

CHAPTER XXII

PEER OF FRANCE

Shortly before leaving Montauban in 1826 Cheverus had written back to Boston, "I must now begin a new work & an arduous one. Dignities you know have no charms for me, but I cannot escape them. . . . Pray for me that I may not sink under the heavy burden of high honours and painful duties."[1] He had been thinking only of the position of Archbishop of Bordeaux but he spoke more truly than he knew when he said he could not escape dignities. Three other honors were to be conferred by Charles X before the Bourbon monarch lost his throne. As we have seen, in November, 1826, Cheverus was elevated to the peerage; two years later the king named him Councilor of State, and in 1830 the Archbishop of Bordeaux was made Commander of the Order of the Holy Ghost. Although Cheverus accepted each of these honors reluctantly, the last two suggest that in politics he was always devoted to the royalist cause. His career in the Chamber of Peers from 1827 to 1830 further confirms his consistent adherence to the *politique* of Charles X.

The French Chamber of Peers in the days during which Cheverus attended was from one point of view an essential part of the legislative power. Parisians who loved notables were quite willing to fête the peers publicly when they rejected laws contrary to the public wishes. Although nobility had been struck harsh blows by the Revolution, the upper chamber was a symbol that all aristocratic participation in government was not lost. True, the peers rarely took the ascendant in shaping policy or molding public opinion; but they did comprise a conscientious, and occasionally sage, opposition. Brilliant oratory, intellect, and experience were theirs; and in the words of one French historian, "One might say, in truth, in reading the fine discourses pronounced there from 1820 to 1830, that France knew in those years the Golden Age of her parliamentary regime."[2]

From another point of view the peers were an emanation of executive power. Nomination was by the king, who could not only determine their number but their nature, changing their dignity, naming them for life, or even rendering the title hereditary, as he chose. On more than one occasion the Bourbons of the Restoration created several dozens of peers at one time for clearly political reasons.[3] The single elevation of Cheverus in the fall of 1826 was in recognition of his personal worth rather than from reasons of state. Members of the royal family and princes of blood were peers by right and took the first benches while ecclesiastics like Cheverus took first place thereafter.[4] The peers, who numbered at the time of the July Revolution of 1830 close to 400, all held office at the king's pleasure and were doubly dependent upon him for the pensions attached to their titles.[5] Most peers, of course, had independent fortunes of their own but in the case of Cheverus the royal pension was essential. As he remarked to the Bonneuils:

> The peerage with which the king has honored me is accompanied by a pension of 12,000 francs but it produces an excess of expenses & although my revenues here mount to 40,000 I am less well off than at Montauban. Also I was more free there in every way, less obliged to etiquette, etc. In a word, my dignities are only an increase of expenses and burdens. I had no ambition for them. They pushed me into them by force, believing I would do more good. God grant it. . . . Alas, I scarcely dreamed & scarcely like being a legislator.[6]

The Chamber of Peers was far from a homogeneous body in 1827. During the Restoration era it included such disparate elements as liberals, ultra-royalists, former imperial senators of Napoleonic days, "invalids" from discredited ministries, and those like Cheverus who were recipients of rewards for meritorious service in non-political fields. In the years that Cheverus and Comte de Tournon sat in the chamber there were at least three fairly clear divisions of opinion on political matters, while the members of the hierarchy who attended disagreed over such ecclesiastical questions as the liberties of the Gallican Church, the Jesuits, or the congregations.[7]

Sessions of the legislature began with pomp and circumstance. Each peer was summoned by *lettre close du Roi* countersigned by the chancellor, who was regularly the presiding officer of the upper house. Members of both houses went in full regalia to the Mosaic Room of the Louvre to await the arrival of the king. He was met at the foot of the staircase of honor by the ministry, the members of the royal household, twelve peers, and twenty-five deputies all of whom accompanied him to the throne. After the monarch had commanded the peers to sit and had granted permission to the deputies to do the same, he pronounced the royal discourse. Then the new peers created since the last session approached him one by one, placed their hands between those of the king, and said, "I swear to be faithful to the king, to obey the constitution, and to conduct myself at all times as becomes a good and loyal Peer of France."[8]

Comte Lefebvre de Cheverus was admitted to the Chamber of Peers on Tuesday, May 15, 1827, and since the house had been in session for some time the proceedings recorded a simpler ceremony.

> The President proposed that he be admitted to take the oath. The Chamber adopted the proposal. They proceeded to receive the new peer according to Article 78 of the rules. Two members, Comte de Sèze and Comte de Marcellus, went before him and reentered the room with him preceded by two ushers. The new peer stopped in the middle of the parquet and stood facing the tribunal and took the oath in the form indicated by the President. This oath taken, he was admitted to take part in the session.[9]

His sponsors were both men of importance. Marie-Louis Demartin du Tyrac, comte de Marcellus, was a man of taste, Greek scholarship, and diplomatic experience in Constantinople, London, Madrid, and Lucca. Raymond, comte de Sèze, had been an adviser to Marie Antoinette, had defended Louis XVI before the Convention, and was venerated by all royalists in France.

Cheverus had dined the evening before in company with the Duc de Bordeaux, the king's grandson whom he found charming and most courteous, and his letter to Louis the day following the admission to the Chamber of Peers contained more social news than political comment. Of the Tuesday ceremony he said only, "It was required that I put in an appearance. . . . I took the oath and was seated yesterday. The comtes de Sèze and de Marcellus were my sponsors."[10] He was in Paris scarcely a month and probably did not notice how much irritation and general unrest attended the closing of the parliamentary session.[11] He was much more interested in the retreat for his clergy which he was planning that summer.

By the close of 1827, however, even to a man as unpolitically minded as Cheverus it was evident that conditions would require every man loyal to his king to attend future sessions of the legislature. Opposition to the ministry of Joseph Villèle could not be denied. The *Moniteur* of November 6 announced the creation of seventy-six new peers and the dissolution of the deputies with elections scheduled for later in the month. Cheverus commented to Bonneuil anxiously, "We are at a critical epoch."[12] When the elections returned an even larger proportion of liberals than ever it became necessary to form a new ministry and some of the papers even suggested that Cheverus was to be included. "Happily it is only so in the Gazettes," he told Bonneuil. Although the new ministry heralded by the *Moniteur* on January 5, 1828, substituted Jean-Baptiste de Martignac for Villèle as chief there was no indication that Charles X expected his policies to be modified by this former lawyer from Bordeaux. Cheverus confessed to Félicie, "I fear I will have to go to Paris next month. I would get out of it if I could."[13]

Unfortunately for his biographers, the precise career of Cheverus in the legislature remains only dimly suggested. Since sessions of his day were not public the *Moniteur* printed only cursory résumés which offer few clues. The proceedings of the Chamber of Peers published a half-century later make no reference to Cheverus after his admission in 1827. The biographical sketches of the peers published in 1829 merely commented, "We do not know the vote of this worthy prelate in the high chamber; but, whatever it is, it could only be the result of sincere conviction."[14] The letters Cheverus wrote from Paris during his attendance show chiefly his anxiety to return to Bordeaux as soon as he were "allowed." He told Bonneuil, "My functions as archbishop & my duties as peer are scarcely compatible. I do my best but the task is difficult."[15] His stays in the capital filled him with "ennui, chagrin, and anxiety." But he tried to believe that affairs were not so bad "as they seem to certain spirits." He never deviated from his position in 1828 when he asserted, "I am for moderation & submission to the government."[16] It was thirty long years since he had told Bishop Carroll of Baltimore, "Everywhere I shall seek the peace of the country in which the Lord will have me dwell"; Archbishop of Bordeaux or missionary to Maine, Cheverus did not change. If present day political theorists choose to discriminate between liberal republicanism and reactionary monarchy as the point at issue, they must miss the simpler truth that Cheverus was profoundly consistent in principle. Had the Bourbons given him no honors at all, while he lived under their regime he could not have been other than loyal. To have been otherwise would have violated his very nature, for the standards by which he gauged his conduct were never political but spiritual. When the man himself is rightly seen there can be no paradox in the assertion that the little bishop who was called the first citizen of Boston was the most obedient subject of his Majesty the King of France.

The three particular matters which demonstrate the part Cheverus played in the legislative concerns of 1828 are all compatible with his character. On January 12, 1828, he addressed a letter to all of his pastors saying, "I have to present at the next session of the Chamber an important work on Catholic primary schools. I want a report from you. Please do not lose a moment in making these reports."[17] He enclosed carefully prepared forms or tables to be filled out and returned. When the tabulations trickled in more slowly than the efficient archbishop desired he wrote again on January 16 with greater urgency. Although the effect of Cheverus' report cannot be estimated the royal ordinance of April 21 was certainly consistent with his desires. The government decreed that since primary instruction must rest upon religion as its natural base, no one could teach without a certificate of religious instruction from either the bishop or the pastors of the parishes involved; bishops had the right to visit the schools in person or by delegate in order to exercise permanent supervision; bishops were further to have the right to name the president and two members of the local committees on education.[18]

Minister of Public Instruction Antoine-François Lefebvre de Vatimesnil notified Cheverus in May,

> The committee heads should be men of sincere zeal, perfect moderation, and exact impartiality. The wise and good men you know how to select, with the discernment which colors all your own acts, will contribute powerfully to give birth to and maintain good spirit in the committees. The visits to the schools you deem necessary will produce favorable results, and the head of the teaching staff will be lucky to have you. . . .[19]

While Cheverus was in Paris for the session of peers of March 7 to May 12, 1828, he was informed that Charles X had named him to preside at the meeting of the electoral college of the third district of the Département de Mayenne convoked for April 21 to elect a deputy to the lower chamber.[20] For Cheverus it was a very delicate situation. This special election was necessitated by the fact that Hyde de Neuville who had been elected deputy the preceding November 18 from that district had since sat for the Département de Nièvre and then had accepted the ministry of marine and had to be replaced. The king was naturally eager to have a deputy equally devoted to the throne elected. The journals of the opposition were attacking Prefect A. de Freslon for alleged irregularities in closing the lists of electors to the radicals, and Cheverus' brother Louis, who had tied for secretary of the electoral college of the third district, had lost out because his opponent was older.[21] The Prefect of Mayenne anticipated disorders and requested the Minister of the Interior to augment the local police for the coming election.[22]

Cheverus was loath to become involved and he wrote to the Minister of the Interior:

> This mark of confidence of his Majesty is an honor which I appreciate and I will make every effort to respond, but in the midst of my family & of my fellow citizens, and in the particular circumstances, my situation will be delicate & difficult. I wish therefore, if it is still possible, that another be designated; but in any event, the will of the King will be sacred to me & I will always be disposed to make every sacrifice to obey as a faithful subject.[23]

His private preference was ignored and at 8:00 o'clock on the morning of April 21 he opened the meeting of the electors in the city where he had been so briefly a pastor thirty-six years ago. After reading the decree of March 6 convoking the college, and that of April 6 which named himself president, Cheverus gave a discourse praising the king and asking that a deputy devoted to his interests be chosen. He said:

> I do not pretend to prescribe what ought to be your choice; I am here only to learn it and proclaim it. But I would do myself violence and you an injustice if I did not say I expect from you the choice of a deputy who is a friend of religion, of legitimacy, of monarchy, of the king and his august family, of a deputy quite persuaded that the charter and our institutions need above all an authority powerful, paternal and protective which can maintain and protect us from license; of a deputy finally whose heart truly loyal thrills with ours at the name of our beloved Charles X.[24]

The electors responded to the personal fervor of Archbishop de Cheverus with repeated cries of "Long live the King!" But to the king's request for a sympathetic deputy they replied by electing Prospero Delaunay by a wide margin on the following day.[25] Cheverus had failed.

Afterward Charles X read the discourse to the electors of Mayenne with close attention and found no fault with it. He told Cheverus so at the Tuileries on the archbishop's return to Paris. The Dauphin said, "Your discourse was perfect." The ladies of the royal household tried to console him; but Cheverus was sad and uneasy. "I truly do not know where we are," he told his brother. "If they decide my presence is necessary or even useful in Paris, I will stay." But his heart was not in statecraft. "Here it is time for the Chamber of Peers. I must go. Your poor brother is little suited to being a legislator. . . . How I wish I could be tranquil and ignored."[26] His letter to Bonneuil that May spoke of the three week Mayenne trip as a wild goose chase whose only benefit was that Cheverus had a chance to see his family. "Amadée will be ordained Deacon on May 31," he added with more pleasure.[27]

An issue of much greater importance than the election of a single deputy from his boyhood home was coming to a crisis that spring. The anticlerical storm precipitated by Montlosier's pamphlet in 1826 was gathering full force above the heads of the Jesuits and seemed about to fall. Both chambers had seized upon the subject in 1827 and it had contributed to the fall of Villèle. Since then the attacks in public print against the Jesuits had mounted.

The Jesuits of France during the Restoration were undeniably monarchist, believing like Cheverus that legitimate royalty was the guarantee of a Christian tradition in France as opposed to Voltairean impiety and Revolutionary atheism. Their clientele, in the schools especially, was fervently monarchist including as it did the sons of the former nobility and families most devoted to the Restoration. When Comte de Sèze visited Saint-Acheul he was received with veneration as the illustrious lawyer who had defended the king before the Convention. From the very beginning of the Restoration there had been, of course, antimonarchical agitation and it suited the liberals to make war on both the throne and the altar while pretending to defend both. With hypocrisy everywhere the Jesuits became a natural target for attack.[28]

The threat of the Jesuits to freedom and safety in France was, of course, chimerical. In 1828 there were only 234 Jesuit priests, 140 brothers, and 182 scholastics. Armand Carrel writing of the actual situation four years later said:

One knew very well that the Society of Jesus properly speaking offered no great dangers. There was only a grudge against the Jesuit spirit, the spirit of devotion, the spirit Tartuffe, the spirit of the reigning dynasty. It was marvelous what the word Jesuit connoted: it was synonymous with devotion to legitimacy. In those days the word Jesuit meant royalist.[29]

The Society of Jesus knew that hostility directed at themselves was only a symbol of the larger attack launched against the Church and monarchy; the new ministry felt, too, that the press crusade against the Jesuits threatened the throne. From the very outset the ministry of Martignac felt compelled to make concessions, and a commission headed by Hyacinth-Louis de Quelen, Archbishop of Paris, was instructed to make an investigation of the minor seminaries where the Jesuits were admitted to have some influence.[30] The report of this commission, which appeared in the *Moniteur* on June 21, affirmed that bishops had not exceeded their rights in confiding minor seminaries to Jesuits and that "the situation of the secondary ecclesiastical schools directed by those priests did not appear contrary to the laws of the realm." The report offered no measures to be executed against them.[31]

But the ministry had already recommended to Charles X that the seminaries under Jesuit supervision be closed. The king hesitated for some time before giving his signature to ordinances including such a stricture. His first *aumonier*, Denis Frayssinous, declared himself adamantly opposed to the ordinances unless extreme necessity demanded them. Frayssinous preferred to resign as Minister of Ecclesiastical Affairs rather than be a party to such measures. His portfolio was offered to Cheverus, but the Archbishop of Bordeaux refused it and the Bishop of Beauvais, Jean-François-Hyacinthe Feutrier, on becoming the new minister agreed that measures against the Jesuits could not be averted.[32]

Charles X was in a real quandary. Frayssinous had argued emphatically that the ordinances could only harm the episcopacy and have tragic consequences for the Church and all friends of religion. Monarchy would suffer as well. On the other hand, *Salus populi suprema lex;* the general welfare, or reason of state, demanded some solution to the crisis. The king in an agony of indecision appointed a commission composed of Frayssinous, Cheverus, Quelen, and Quelen's vicar-general, the Abbé Desjardins, to examine the question as moral theologians and render an opinion.

It was now Cheverus' turn to face a dilemma. There was no doubt in his mind as to the injustice of the attack on the Jesuits whom he both admired and loved. During his episcopacy in Boston he had held the Jesuits in unqualified respect. Of their work in New York he had said, "I hope the Bishop of this Diocese will duly appreciate the treasure he possesses in the Fathers of the Society."[33] On the occasion of the official restoration of the society in 1815 he had congratulated the Jesuit superior in Georgetown saying, "The existence of the Society in this country was to me always a subject of thankful joy even previous to its solemn and so much desired re-establishment."[34] The minor seminary of Bordeaux was in Jesuit hands and Cheverus was very grateful for the fine work being accomplished there. That such clergy could be a danger to France was unthinkable. Their whole number in 1828 did not exceed 300 and the rumors of 50,000 armed men at the Montrouge novitiate ready to march on the Tuileries would have been laughable if they were not such a tragic indication of the prevalent animosity.[35]

But the commission was asked only to pronounce as theologians. Together with his fellow members Cheverus stated that the ill consequences could never be compensated for by the advantages; that none of them would ever countersign an ordinance decreeing such an attack. But there remained a third matter to resolve: suppose reason of state demanded such concessions, could they be permitted? Here the commission could in conscience give only one answer, an affirmative. They were unanimous in stating that, presuming necessity demanded the measures, they could not condemn them.[36]

When the decision of the commission was made public in Paris the outcry of the Catholic population was frenzied. Archbishop de Quelen hurriedly retracted, writing to the king that he could not be a party to the third article of their decision. "It would be impossible, Sire, to allow to fall upon me a suspicion so injurious to a bishop of having weakened truth in the eyes of the king and of having advised him weakness."[37] The others stuck to their guns and Frayssinous told Quelen:

> We were not convened as councilors of the Crown charged with deliberating what might be required by *haute politique* for the good of the realm. We were consulted as moral theologians. As a matter of conscience we did not have the right of imposing our political views on the King; we were required to recognize him as the judge of

things of that nature in his capacity as chief of state. The more I reflect on my decision, the more I find it exact, so much so that to have decided otherwise would have been criminal.[38]

As for Charles X, reassured by the verdict of the commission, he proceeded to sign on June 16, 1828, the controversial measures. The first submitted to the control of the University of France the eight colleges directed by the Jesuits, and required a written assurance from all those engaged in instruction that they were not members of an unauthorized religious community. The second ordinance placed minor seminaries under government control, limited the total enrollment of such schools to 20,000, and required that all students wear the ecclesiastical garb after two years in such schools.[39]

The ultra-royalists reacted violently, comparing the ministry to Marat, Diocletian, Julian the Apostate. When Feutrier gave a dinner for the bishops they declined. Clermont-Tonnerre of Toulouse, who had formerly enjoyed visiting Cheverus in Montauban, published in his diocesan paper his strong opposition to the ordinances. Led by Quelen seven prelates drew up a formal protest to which seventy members of the hierarchy adhered. Like the apostles, they avowed, they would obey God, not man; they righteously proclaimed that they would content themselves with a simple *non possumus*. Cheverus, of course, did not adhere. He believed that it was imprudent for the episcopacy to take such a public stand since their subsequent conduct would force them to contradict their words. The bishops would have to submit or see the annihilation of the priesthood by the closing of their seminaries. A *non possumus* ought to be reserved for occasions which offered no alternative save martyrdom. "I would rather have effaced the *non possumus* with my blood," he said emerging from the meeting. "I begged, I conjured them to retract. . . . It would certainly have been easier to add my name to those of my colleagues. . . . But duty comes before *what will people say."*

Actually he was not alone. The eminent Archbishop of Albi, Charles Brault, refused to adhere and so did the Bishops of Arras, Troyes, Poitiers, Tarbes, Vannes, and Dijon. The papal nuncio at Paris, Luigi Lambruschini, wrote to Cardinal Bernetti in Rome of the episcopal protest:

These prelates have ruined their cause in an irreparable manner. If, before presenting their work, they had informed me of it . . . I would equally have begged them not to pronounce the terrible *non possumus,* in order to avoid placing themselves in a false position from which they can not extricate themselves without compromising their honor.[40]

When Charles X had first sounded out Rome on the matter of the ordinances his secret emissary had been assured by Cardinal Bernetti that "His Holiness, confident on the one hand of the piety of the elder son of the Church, and on the other of the devotion of the bishops to their king and of their love for the true interests of religion, would never be compelled to speak. . . ."[41] When Leo XII finally broke his silence he vindicated Cheverus' position. The protesting prelates were told that the June ordinances did not violate their episcopal rights, that they must rely upon the great piety and wisdom of the king, and that they must go in accord with the throne.[42]

It was small consolation to Cheverus. His heart and his mind were at odds. Intellect and will bade him respect authority, both of his king and of his vicar in Rome. But his heart was with the students of Bordeaux, those "former students of *petites séminaires* confided to the Jesuits" whose formal protest of July 8, 1828, everyone could read in *l'Ami de la Religion.*[43] There were no hard feelings in his minor seminary, he knew. When the Duchesse de Berry visited there a week later the Jesuits received her with poems, songs, and orations as in the old days. Not one word of complaint was uttered against the king; it was understood that their devotion to his person and family had not changed even if circumstances had forced him to sign the ordinances.[44] Least of all was there any resentment against Cheverus. When the Jesuits left Bordeaux their superior bade the archbishop such a farewell before the congregation of Saint-André Cathedral that his words of praise brought scalding tears to the prelate's eyes.[45] It was a painful thing to share in statecraft in such a year as 1828, and Cheverus wrote to Guadeloupe that fall, "I say nothing of our political situation. I am far from seeing things clearly. I have in principle the duty of submitting to the ordinances of June 16. I don't know what faces us in the next session."[46]

It was no consolation, either, to receive another sign of the king's favor that November. "I feel very uneasy in the midst of my dignities," he told Félicie on December 12. "The king has just, to my great surprise, further named me Councilor of State. I would be very embarrassed to give advice."[47] The Council of State, which was abolished in 1791, reconstituted in the Year VIII, and reduced to a rather modest role during the Restoration, had two kinds of service: ordinary and extraordinary. The *Almanach Royal* for 1828–30 listed Cheverus as "councilor of state in extraordinary service, participant in the work of the committees and in the deliberations of the council." Extraordinary service actually implied two types of members, those who shared in the work of the council and those who received only the title. Like the Chamber of Peers the council comprised many varied elements. Some had been members of Napoleon's council, some were men of talent of the Restoration, others were magistrates of note or men prominent in other fields of public endeavor.[48] There is no record of Cheverus' participation in the work of the council and it seems probable that his appointment was chiefly due to the king's appreciation of the painful and unsuccessful efforts of the Archbishop of Bordeaux to consolidate his monarch's position. With the July Revolution and the exile of Charles X Cheverus was deprived of his place when the Duc de Broglie, head of Public Instruction and Religion for the new regime and president of the Council of State, wrote tersely to Cheverus:

> Experience having shown that your episcopal functions do not allow you to take part in the work of the Council of State, I have the honor to inform you that the King has revoked the ordinance which authorized you to assist at the deliberations of the Council of State.[49]

With the opening of the legislature in 1829 Cheverus went again to Paris for two months but this session was less harrowing for the gentle archbishop. The peers discussed the organization of military tribunals, postal charges on foreign mail, Chateaubriand's report on foreign affairs, and budgetary reforms. When Bordeaux's local interests were concerned the Comte de Tournon acted as chief spokesman on such subjects as prison reform or better quarters for the police.[50] Cheverus returned to Bordeaux in time for Easter and did not return to the capital that year.[51]

The last session of the Chamber of Peers to include members created by Charles X, which opened on March 2, 1830, was not attended by the Archbishop of Bordeaux as far as any evidence would indicate. True, shortly after the king's ordinance of January 6 summoning the legislature reached Bordeaux, Cheverus told the Bonneuils, "I fear having to go soon to Paris. The political horizon is sombre."[52] But ecclesiastical duties kept him in Bordeaux all through the spring and by the time summer was over Charles X was no longer king and the peers he had created were no more.

The old Doyenné of Bordeaux, Cheverus'
first episcopal palace. Water color by
J. de Verneilh, 1881.

Episcopal palace of Bordeaux. Staircase
of honor.

Episcopal palace of Bordeaux in time of
Cheverus. Exterior and garden.

MARCO PILLOT

Cheverus' tomb, Saint-Andre Cathedral, Bordeaux.

The porch of the Cathedral, Bordeaux.

The new government of Louis Philippe claimed that "the interests of the double restoration of 1814–1815 are directly opposite to those of the regeneration of 1830 and it is therefore necessary to combat and destroy, at the heart of the power, these early interests to fortify and serve the latter."[53] *Le Temp* explained, "France and the Peerage must understand that a new government, a new Constitution, a new dynasty call for new powers; that it is impossible to suppose promotions founded on a spirit which dominated for fifteen years would be sympathetic to the new order which has arisen."[54] Cheverus, the fifth peer created by Charles X, was only one of four from the Gironde who were eliminated by virtue of Article 68 of the new charter.[55]

Several members of the new regime hoped to associate Cheverus with their government and the deputies from the Gironde tried to force his reinstatement. But Cheverus was only too glad to be free from legislative duties which he had never relished and he cut off such attempts by making a public announcement of his wishes.

> Without approving the exclusion pronounced against the peers created by King Charles X, I rejoice to find myself beyond a political career. I have taken a firm resolve not to enter one, to accept no place, no function. I desire to stay in the midst of my flock, and to continue to exercise a ministry of charity, peace, and unity. . . . I feel more and more attached to the people of Bordeaux; I thank them for the friendship they evidence. The wish of my heart is to live and die among them, but without any other title than that of their archbishop and friend.[56]

He sent a copy of the news item to Guadeloupe saying, "Fatigued with seeing myself extolled and thrust in the foreground in the public papers I believed I must publish the enclosed declaration. It produced a good effect within & beyond my diocese."[57] His career in government was over.

So, too, with the July upheaval vanished the very last honor accorded him by the Bourbon dynasty. In the last months of the reign of Charles X the king had named both Quelen and Cheverus Commanders of the Order of the Holy Ghost.[58] This select and honorable body dated back to the sixteenth century when it was founded by Henry III. It was composed of princes of the blood, the royal family, prelates of note, and chevaliers. The monarch himself was grand master of the order and his *Grand Aumonier* was always a member. Portraits of Cheverus made during the Bordeaux period of his life sometimes show him wearing the decoration of the order, a Malta cross with a dove on both sides, which prelates were entitled to wear on a blue ribbon as a collar or necklace, bearing the motto *Duce et Auspice.*[59]

When Peyronnet, the Minister of the Interior, notified Cheverus of this last honor he said, "The blue ribbon will add nothing to your virtues and your merit; but it will prove that the King knows them, loves them, and takes pleasure in honoring them."[60] Like his other honors, count and peer of France, councilor of state, the title of commander was destroyed in 1830 for after that the Order of the Holy Ghost was discontinued. In spite of the portraits, it is very doubtful that Cheverus wore his blue ribbon and cross for long.

Jean Lefebvre de Cheverus was well along in his sixty-third year when the last of the Bourbons was overthrown. For seven years he had loyally obeyed the behests of the two kings of the Restoration. The service had cost him dear in heartaches and uneasiness; but he had been amply rewarded in honors and royal friendship. Now those honors and those kings were no more. *Sic transit gloria mundi.* Yet in spite of his sorrow over the passing of the old order, the Archbishop of Bordeaux felt only an overwhelming relief that at last he could follow once again the only path he had yearned to tread, fill the only office he had ever craved, that of father to his children in Christ and friend to his neighbors at home.

CHAPTER XXIII

PASTOR BONUS

A BIOGRAPHER may, under the pretext of unity, cut across the years to reflect on the political involvements of a prelate, but the chronological truth of history may not be denied. It goes without saying that during the years Cheverus served as a peer of France in Paris he was still archbishop and shepherd at Bordeaux; and, however barren his legislative actions may have proved, his pastoral efforts during these years bore abundant fruit. It was during the last two years of the reign of Charles X that the clear mark of Cheverus appeared in the development of religious life in the Gironde. In education, in liturgical practice, in administration, the executive genius of Cheverus achieved striking gains. Yet always the infinite charity of the man covered all with a mantle of love.

As the year 1828 began, the economic plight of his people was the chief concern of the Archbishop of Bordeaux. High prices and a scarcity of food led him to lighten the rigors of strict Lenten observance, and his pastoral of February 2 urged his flock to make up in alms and good works what had been ceded "because of the gravity of the circumstances."[1] Mayor du Hamel, who was likewise concerned over the decline in commerce and rising prices in the port city, assured Cheverus that "the gratitude of the people will bless this indulgent concession."[2] Bordeaux was no stranger to poverty, and Prefect d'Haussez had already established a relief depot with the co-operation of the archbishop.[3] It is easy to understand the reluctance of Cheverus to leave his people for the session of peers that February; he was still the same man who had said in Boston in 1815, "It is above all in times of distress a pastor ought not to leave his flock."

While he was in Paris and Mayenne that spring he assiduously performed as many priestly functions as he could fit in between the legislative sessions. On Good Friday he was invited to preach at l'École Polytechnique, an invitation which might have filled him with trepidation for only the year before when the Archbishop of Besançon, the famous Rohan-Chabot, had tried to preach there the tumult of the student audience had forced him from the pulpit.[4] But Cheverus possessed an insinuating charm and he began his sermon:

> If it were my intention to speak of human science, I should first come to take lessons in this learned school, and from yourselves, Gentlemen; but I am to treat this day of the science of the Cross; this is my peculiar science, the science which I have studied and preached for forty years, among civilized nations, as well as among savage people, because it equally concerns all; you will permit an old bishop to communicate to you the result of his long studies.[5]

He then took his text from Saint Paul: "I am determined to know nothing among you save Christ Jesus, and Him crucified." Not a restless move stirred his young listeners as the Archbishop of Bordeaux preached one of his finest sermons.

On May 16 he preached at the Irish College and encouraged Father Taylor, who had accompanied him to Paris, to give a retreat there.[6] Cheverus' own sermon was the first he had given in English since his return to France in 1823, and the king complimented him on his facility. "Sire, I have very little reason to merit your praise," Cheverus said diffidently, "for English, I am ashamed to say before the King of France, is more familiar to me than French."[7] Yet he preached with equal grace in French, as the king had reason to know. The Dauphine and the Duchesse de Berry both heard Cheverus speaking that same spring in behalf of the war victims of the Vendée, and the royal ladies had described his stirring appeal in a glowing report to Charles X.[8] At Saint-Nicolas Seminary in Conflans Cheverus gave in one day seventeen exquisite little discourses in the process of blessing as many statues of the Greek and Latin Church fathers. His knowledge of history, and his elegance of expression amazed his listeners.[9]

While he was compelled to remain away from his archdiocese he was determined to live in a manner becoming to the father of the poor, rather than as peer of the realm; he stayed as always with the Vigeries in Cul de Sac Ferou. When Samuel Topliffe of Boston called on Cheverus in March, 1829, he found "this third dignitary of the king-

dom in a small room of a house in the third story, situated in an obscure passage, and dressed in a very plain and simple manner." Cheverus
apologized for not being able to entertain Topliffe in the manner the
latter deserved. "But if I can be of any service to you," he said warmly,
"to further your views in any way, I shall be most happy to do so."[10]

Topliffe was delighted to find Cheverus so completely unchanged except, as he reported back to Boston, "his health, under a milder climate,
was better than in Boston, where the severity of our winters began to
undermine his constitution before he left." Cheverus had never looked
better, Topliffe thought, and still had the delightful humor that had
endeared him to New England. "I would give you my Peer's ticket,"
Cheverus said with a twinkle in his eye, "as it is probable you would
not be known otherwise than as a Peer, if you spoke French! But if
you should open your mouth, the cat would be let out of the bag."
Cheverus did, however, escort Topliffe through the Chamber, through
the Palace of Luxembourg, and offered the Bostonian a coach to carry
him wherever else he wished to go. In his letters home Topliffe asserted elatedly, "The walls of Paris do not enclose two characters of
more exalted worth than General Lafayette and Bishop Cheverus."

Topliffe's stay in Paris was a bitter-sweet experience for Cheverus.
He loved to be of service, and he secured permission for his American
friend to visit the Royal Porcelain works at Sèvres.[11] He called on
Topliffe at the latter's lodging and received Topliffe again in Cul de
Sac Ferou, "equally social, playful, and humorous as at the first" visit.
But the old days came rushing back, and he confessed to his visitor
that it had been the wish of his heart to live and die in Boston. Only
a sense of duty had compelled him to obey the call of the king. "I am
not so happy as in Boston," he said simply. He was full of inquiries
"respecting Boston and its inhabitants," speaking of Josiah Quincy's
exchanging the mayoralty for the presidency of Harvard, of Harrison
Gray Otis' becoming Mayor of Boston, in short, "taking a lively interest
in everything connected with Boston." It pleased Topliffe to hear
Cheverus refer to himself as an old American citizen who had passed
many happy days among them. For it was clear to the Bostonian that
Cheverus was highly esteemed in France. Topliffe attended some of the
functions at which Cheverus preached in Paris, and he wrote home,
"As far as I can learn there is not so popular a man in the Gallic Church,
as the Archbishop of Bordeaux."[12]

There were other Americans who found the little archbishop and
peer from Bordeaux eager to enhance their visits to Paris and to recall

the former happy times. One charming story is told of the Irish chambermaid who accompanied her mistress to Paris, and, upon reading in the papers that the Archbishop of Bordeaux had arrived for the session of peers, determined to see her former pastor. Her mistress scoffed at the idea, saying that such a high dignitary would not receive so lowly a person; but the girl retorted, "I know Father Cheverus better than that." So she went to Cul de Sac Ferou, only to be told that Cheverus was then in audience with the king. Her mistress laughed at the girl's discomfiture. But her laughter was of short duration. As soon as Cheverus learned of his former parishioner's presence in the city he came in person to call upon her, and give her his benediction.[13]

No commission of courtesy or kindness was beneath this peer and archbishop. It was equally characteristic of Cheverus that while he stayed in Paris he made his confessions at the chapel of the *Grand Penitencier,* the confessor whose powers of absolution were usually required in cases where some censure was added to the sin, *cas réservés.* The humble little prelate, the enemy of distinction in all things, took his place among the faithful, seeing himself as the least deserving of men.[14] "No pomp, parade, or outward show of pride," was the way Topliffe described him; alone, on foot, and wrapped in a plain dark cloak was the way in which he appeared at the chambermaid's door; unobtrusively seeking absolution among the most serious sinners was his approach to his confessor. Not all the honors in France could alter Jean Lefebvre de Cheverus.

It was just as characteristic that in the summer of 1828, when Cheverus would have preferred to be in Bordeaux to extend the courtesy deserved by the Duchesse de Berry on her visit to his city, he stayed on in Paris out of a sense of duty to the government. In May, when she had told Cheverus of her desire to visit Bordeaux, he had said hopefully to his brother, "Her journey which seems nearly decided would furnish me a pretext in which I would rejoice for returning there."[15] But when July came and the peers were still sitting, the Archbishop of Bordeaux remained in Paris; Barrès presided over the Mass at Saint-André the day of her arrival, while a *préfet par interim* substituted for Baron d'Haussez who was likewise detained in the Chamber of Deputies in the capital. Baron Janin of the military and Mayor du Hamel were lucky enough to perform their usual offices of welcome and the duchess listened gravely to the speech of the one and opened the ball in the Jardin-Public with the other. But Cheverus was not there while the lady went on her rounds to Saint-Michel, the seminaries, foundling homes, the manufacturing plants of Bordeaux, and the exposition at Vaux-Hall where the products of the Gironde were proudly displayed.[16] Nor could he know what she privately thought of the public acts of vaudeville presented in her honor and entitled, *"Déliberation inutile,"* and *"Buste d'Henri IV."* With her cortège she departed at seven in the morning of July 18, a full week before the Archbishop of Bordeaux returned.[17]

There was another reason why Cheverus was not present for the visit of such a noble lady, and it had to do with old loyalties and affections quite unrelated to things French. William Taylor, his former vicar in Boston, was mortally ill in Paris that July. Very little evidence remains of the last years of Father Taylor which he spent, as he had wished, near the "Fénelon" of his heart. Aside from the honorary position of canon of Saint-André there is no record of his exercising a regular pastoral career in France. Soon after his arrival he had written to Father Byrne in Boston, "I have access to a good library and the dear Bishop would instantly give me a permanent and lucrative situation did he not apprehend exciting jealousy of some panting expectants. Whatever situation I may occupy I am to reside in his Palace."[18] Cheverus himself made very few references to Taylor in the correspondence which still exists. Perhaps he had learned, as it seems most likely, of his friend's ill-advised and discourteous sermon on the occasion of the consecration of John Dubois as Bishop of New York in November, 1826.[19] It was not Cheverus' way to write uncharitable criticisms of his friends in private letters, but if he knew the details of Taylor's behavior before leaving New York for France he must have been shocked at the reports of his former vicar's attack on Cheverus' friend Dubois. If the knowledge influenced the Archbishop of Bordeaux in regard to securing a permanent place for Father Taylor in France, it never altered his friendship. When Cheverus left Bordeaux for Paris, Taylor went with him. The Cheverus family in Mayenne always extended invitations to Taylor to visit them there. And when Taylor died on August 1, 1828, the archbishop was deeply grieved. He told Vernou de Bonneuil:

> Dear Mr. Taylor, who came to join me at Paris, died there on August 1, aged thirty-nine. He succumbed to a hydropsie & a general exhaustion. I regret him very much. He was very devoted to me.[20]

"A worthy man and a good friend." It was all that was required to touch the heart of Cheverus.[21]

On his return to Bordeaux that summer, the archbishop devoted himself at once to the problems presented by the new educational measures. As early as June the rector of the Bordeaux Academy had asked Cheverus to express his wishes in regard to the new committees to supervise primary education in the Gironde, but Cheverus had been busy in Peers. Now, in August, he speedily approached Dauzet suggesting an opportunity for discussing the matter with him. "I need to talk to you about the different points which are raised by the new measures," he said.[22] Within the week he had nominated his own quota to the committee, sending his list to both Rector Dauzet and Prefect d'Haussez who reciprocated with their respective nominations.[23] Cheverus and Dauzet also consulted that month on the matter of inspection of girls' schools, and the rector was more than ordinarily moved to co-operate with the prelate who showed such deference. If Cheverus had any lingering doubts over the proper interpretation of the regulations, Dauzet assured him, the rector would hasten to seek further clarification from the Ministry of Public Instruction.[24]

But these were relatively minor matters. The changes necessitated by the anti-Jesuit decrees were something else, requiring not only haste but wisdom as well. The ordinance of June 16 had fixed October 1 as the date when the Jesuits must vacate the secondary schools. Their institution in Bordeaux concluded its scholastic year on August 16, and the "Fathers of the Faith" who had conducted it since its origin in 1814 were prepared to leave quietly and without rancor.[25] But Cheverus was troubled by more than keen regret over the departure of the men he loved and admired. The fact was that the building which housed the school might be lost to the archdiocese if he did not act promptly.

At the time his predecessor Aviau had inaugurated the minor seminary, the general council of the Gironde had granted him the Dépôt de Mendicité building for his school with the stipulation that should the original purposes of the institution ever be perverted the depot would revert to the *département*. Owing to the excellence of the school under Jesuit direction many secular students had applied for admission over the years, and the Archdiocese of Bordeaux had felt it necessary to found a second minor seminary at Bazas in 1819.[26] Now in 1828 the royal ordinances forbade more than one minor seminary in a diocese and limited the number of candidates to 300. The report required by the Commission of Secondary Ecclesiastical Schools, compiled prior to the ordinances, showed that Bazas alone had 236 paying students and two dozen free seminarians.[27] If Cheverus were to maintain his one seminary at Bazas he could not retain the seminary building in Bordeaux.

He saw only one solution: Bazas seminary must move to Bordeaux and continue in the Dépôt de Mendicité under secular priests of the diocese, while Bazas should be conducted in the future as a secular secondary school. In September he sent Father Jean-Baptiste Lacombe to Paris to make representations accordingly to the government. The king quickly approved the change and the transfer of some 250 seminarians began. On October 1 the Minister of Ecclesiastical Affairs proposed to Charles X that Cheverus be granted an indemnity of 3,000 francs to help defray the costs of the transfer.[28] To show further approval for Cheverus' solution, the government by the end of the year increased the number of *bourses* or ecclesiastical scholarships by 100 over and above the number already granted by the June ordinances to the Archdiocese of Bordeaux.

The task of moving the Bazas Seminary to Bordeaux was principally a physical one and, aside from the criticisms of those who did not understand the June decrees, was not too difficult for the archbishop to effect; but the establishment of a school for seculars at Bazas entailed more consideration. While Lacombe was in Paris in September he consulted Antoine Garnier, the superior of the Society of Saint-Sulpice, regarding the nature of the prospective school. The Sulpician recommended a simple institute rather than a college for Bazas.[29] Cheverus meanwhile recommended to the Minister of Public Instruction, Vatismesnil, that the superior of the Little Community of Clerks of the Holy Cross be appointed head at Bazas. Jean-Marie La Croix had long been associated with the education of the young, and he seemed like a wise choice; on September 23 the choice was confirmed in Paris and by the beginning of October Cheverus had received the news.[30]

Coming so soon after the death of Father Taylor, the criticism directed against the archbishop for his actions in solving the minor seminary problem saddened Cheverus. In June when he had been harshly criticized for his opinion as a theologian on the anti-Jesuit ordinances he had written calmly to his vicars-general, "In the course of my life I have been praised so much beyond my deserts, I ought not to complain if I am now blamed. If I need to be humbled, I will bless the Lord for it." But in the fall of the year criticism was harder to bear because it stemmed from bitter disappointment which Cheverus could not only understand but share. The loss of the Jesuits was a severe one and his efforts to retain the Dépôt of Mendicité were made partly in the hope that one day the Jesuits might return there.[31] But he could sympathize with the young men who were forced to make the transfer. In an effort to take the edge off their distress, and because Bordeaux was entitled to more than the 250 seminarians transferred, he decreed that those few who wished to prepare for ecclesiastical studies at Bazas would be admitted to the major seminary of Bordeaux on equal terms with those from the Dépôt de Mendicité seminary. When he visited the minor seminary in November to confer tonsure he showed his appreciation of Lacombe's efforts by making him an honorary vicar-general. It was by no means a perfect solution, but it was the best possible while trying to satisfy the requirements of the law, the needs of his archdiocese, and the sensibilities of all involved. "I strive to believe that Providence wanted me here," he told Bonneuil, "amid these troubles and perplexities. It is necessary to submit to them . . . the attributes of grandeurs."[32] It was the old lesson to be learned and relearned: submission to a will higher than his own.

With the questions of secondary education answered for the moment, Cheverus turned his thoughts to a matter which had plagued him ever since his arrival in Bordeaux — the appalling lack of uniformity throughout his large jurisdiction. It was scarcely to be wondered at, when he considered the changes the clergy had been compelled to undergo during the Napoleonic era. Some had complied with good grace and obeyed the decrees by which Aviau had attempted to make the necessary adjustments to the new order; others, through mistaken principle, or the simple stubbornness of the aging, had persisted in the old practices. There was the matter of the suppressed feasts, for example. An apostolic indult in 1802 had placed on Sundays the feasts of Epiphany, the Blessed Sacrament, the Apostles Peter and Paul, and all parish patrons. Other feasts which could not properly be moved to a Sunday had also been suppressed as holidays for general festivity and cessation of work. Aviau had tried to promulgate uniformity by special pastoral letters on three different occasions, but in many parishes pastors were still acceding to local pressure and continued to celebrate the feasts on the days on which they fell.[33] The cessation of ordinary work and the abuses for which feast days served as a pretext caused an outcry from employers and law-enforcement officials alike, and these criticisms threatened the relations which ought to exist between the clergy and their fellow citizens.

On December 14, 1828, Cheverus therefore reminded his pastors of their obligations. His motives went beyond a mere desire for uniformity; his own high sense of obedience to lawful authority and his love for the universal Church, made it inevitable that he should regard with disapproval any pandering to local preference where the laws of the Church were concerned. He had witnessed too long in Protestant America the bewildering diversity which individual interpretations of either divine or ecclesiastical law could produce. The suppression of the feasts had been pronounced by Rome; as archbishop it was his duty to recall his pastors to their duty. Furthermore, the second decade of the nineteenth century was witnessing changes which demanded the clergy's recognition of the rights of employers in a society which was no longer purely agrarian.[34] The rise of industry and the expansion of commerce were revolutionizing concepts of work days and work weeks. It was not that Cheverus loved the liturgical cycle the less. He admonished the clergy to celebrate divine service on the actual day of the feast; but low Masses would suffice. "Conforming to the wish expressed by the sovereign Pontiff, pastors would exhort those not obliged to live by the work of their hands to assist at the sacrifice of the Mass." At the same time, however, the faithful must be reminded that not only was work permitted on those days, it was "an obligation for all those who are responsible to masters." He did not mean to be arbitrary; if particular circumstances made it seem necessary to celebrate patronal feasts on the actual days, and if justice were not violated, pastors could present their reasons for a dispensation. "I would see that it took place accordingly," the archbishop assured them.[35]

In May of the next year he amplified his instructions to make it clear that the suppressed feasts which could not be celebrated on a Sunday might be celebrated by Mass with chant if the service were fixed early enough in the day. "Toward evening an instruction and Benediction of the Blessed Sacrament could be given." He knew the feelings of the faithful, and he added, "If you think that these measures . . . would occasion some discontent among your parishioners, read the present letter from the pulpit and have them note it is not in your power to evade a rule which ought to have been followed previously in all the parishes of the diocese."[36] From that time on he had no occasion to admonish his pastors on the subject again.

Cheverus was actually very sympathetic to local custom when it did not conflict with papal injunctions or the general good of the archdiocese. He was prompt enough in approaching the civil authorities when it was a matter of securing little privileges for the numerous societies which delighted in their respective insignia and processions. When the Confraternity of St. James were fearful of losing their traditional funeral ceremonies because the disorderly conduct of some assemblies of country folk had roused the ire of the city officials, Cheverus wrote to Mayor du Hamel begging an exception. Hamel replied promptly that the confraternity, "has never excited complaint from anyone. . . . I see no reason therefore why they can not be authorized to carry the insignia which distinguishes them."[37] At the next funeral of one of their members they marched proudly to the cemetery in full regalia, grateful to the archbishop who had retained for them their privileges. They were quick to appreciate that if they had a strict father they had an understanding one as well.

The year 1829 saw the death of Pope Leo XII, after a short reign of six years, and the election of his successor. Many members of the French hierarchy had found the late pontiff's anti-Gallicanism suspect and were not, to say the least, submerged in grief at his passing on February 10 in the sixty-ninth year of his life. Although the conclave opened in Rome on February 23, the French cardinals Clermont-Tonnerre and Croij did not arrive until a month later and consequently from the French point of view the first deliberations were "purely formal."[38] On March 31 Cheverus' Roman agent wrote to Bordeaux, "The canon of Chateau St. Ange announces the election of the new Pontiff. Cardinal Castiglione has been proclaimed this morning. He has taken the name Pius VIII."[39] Francesco Castiglione was an eminent jurist and had been a cardinal since 1821. His first encyclical, which was strong and perspicacious, did little to assuage the French Gallicans. It began by asserting his authority not only over his flock, the faithful, but included specific references to bishops. In Paris and Toulouse this could scarcely be received with joy. But in Bordeaux there was only rejoicing that a new pontiff had ascended the chair of St. Peter.

Bordeaux had ceremoniously mourned the passing of Leo XII with a solemn service at Saint-André on March 7 in the presence of all the civil and ecclesiastical authorities. Local churches had held their special services on March 9, and the religious houses had followed suit the next day. For nine days after these solemn rites the former pope was the subject of their prayers. From that time on until March 31 all Masses had included prayers *pro elegendo summo pontifice* for the choice of his successor.[40] In June Bordeaux received the papal announcement of the jubilee on the occasion of the exaltation of Pius VIII, and on October 20 Cheverus issued a decree to the effect that the jubilee would open in Bordeaux on the first Sunday of Advent, November 29, to last two weeks.[41] The evening before, all the bells of the diocese announced the happy occasion and repeated their joyous caroling at six o'clock the next morning. Cheverus presided at a pontifical Mass at Saint-André and the two weeks of special devotions and benefits began. It was a particularly happy time for the archbishop, for the special preacher that Advent was his old schoolmate, Nicolas Mac-Carthy, now a Jesuit and the most celebrated preacher in France.[42] The old days at Saint-Magloire were re-lived, and the intervening years were reviewed; it was as if the time between had never existed, and Cheverus was as free with his criticisms of Mac-Carthy's sermons as they had ever been of each other's model discourses in another day.

Advent that year was a season for fewer misgivings for the little man in the large palace in Rue Judaïque. In Rome the new sovereign pontiff was showing himself a man of wisdom and moderation. In Bordeaux the laity were being marshaled to the support of their faith by excellent Barrès who handled the details of the National Association for the Defense of the Catholic Religion.[43] The clergy, taking heart from the admonitions of their archbishop at the pastoral retreat in September, were displaying new vigor. On September 13, 1829, the new ritual had been promulgated when Cheverus had urged with more than his accustomed earnestness:

> Considering that the absence of good regulation, leaving too much to chance, necessarily leads to abuses and a bizarre melange of various usages which ill become the beauty of the Church which its divine author meant to be perfectly one . . . and particularly considering the profound ignorance of either the most elementary truths or the mysteries which are the object of our solemnities, the best way to remedy so great an evil is to instruct the people by frequent reading of the Prone . . . and above all developing each Sunday by familiar instruction — clear, simple, and without vulgarity — some part of the authentic doctrine of the Church.[44]

It was a deaf ear, indeed, that would not hear the concern of the shepherd for his flock in this exhortation, and Cheverus felt a deep satisfaction with the improvement in preaching that had followed his appeal.

In a private way, too, the closing of the year brought the archbishop happiness, for Amadée was now a priest and since All Saints was a permanent addition to the household. "He is an assistant at the cathedral," Cheverus told Bonneuil proudly. "They love him and admire him. He merits both."[45] Cheverus was determined not to show any partiality toward the fervent young priest, but in his heart there was no reservation. Amadée bore all the marks of a vocation shaped by Saint-Sulpice, that society *par excellence* in the education of the clergy. The nephew bore as well a remarkable likeness to his uncle both in appearance and in ingratiating charm. The older priests, Barrès, Trélissac, and Guilleux, rivaled Cheverus in fond doting; the archbishop found he needed a disciplined heart to resist its own promptings and the urgings of his vicars-general in the matter of advancing Father George de la Massonnais too rapidly. But there was no denying that a new and lasting joyousness pervaded the palace now that this beloved nephew and foster son had come to stay.

The clergy of the Archdiocese of Bordeaux had their reasons, too, for remembering 1829 as a good year. Like the faithful, they came to appreciate that their archbishop was both severe and generous. Pastors were required to be prompt and accurate not only with Cheverus but in their dealings with the government as well. When Cheverus learned that the city accounts had been held up by failure of one of his pastors to apply for his salary the recalcitrant was speedily dealt with.[46] On another occasion pastors were notified:

> After my request to the government on the subject of supplementary salaries for pastors . . . it has been decided by his excellency, the Minister of Interior, that a supplement of 250 francs will be allowed. . . . Do not make requests to the administrative authorities. I will always be disposed to receive your just requests and forward them with my favorable support.[47]

Yet, exacting as he was in these business matters, Cheverus had only their interests at heart, and the clergy knew it. For 1829 was also the year when the priests of Bordeaux were given for the first time the assurance that their old age would no longer be a period of insecurity and distress; it was in that year that the archbishop announced his plans for a retirement fund for the clergy. On October 20 they were notified of the details of a plan Cheverus had been working on for some time. It was only for their examination, he explained. "I want it to be voluntary." But the care with which he had drawn up the proposals left little room for dissatisfaction. Everyone knew the painful and afflicting situation of priests whose age or infirmity no longer allowed them to perform their duties. The aid allotted by the government was woefully inadequate.

The plan Cheverus submitted would encompass the whole Archdiocese of Bordeaux. Priests entitled to the pension would present the testimony of the local notary public verifying that the applicant was either aged seventy or infirm. The pension fund was to be made up from the annual offerings of each priest, the contributions of parish societies, and offerings from the faithful. A table of proportionate clerical contributions then followed, varying from 1000 francs for the archbishop to as little as ten francs from ordinary priests of the parishes. For the first year contributions were to be made in two installments, but thereafter in four. Any one could subscribe more, if he could afford it and wished to do so.

The administration of the fund was to be in the hands of a committee appointed by the archbishop and would include one vicar-general, one canon, a pastor, a *desservant,* and a curate or assistant. A quarterly examination of the fund would be made in the presence of the archbishop, and the three keys to the fund would be held by a vicar-general, a pastor, and a *desservant.* Pensions paid from the fund would depend upon years of active service and ranged from 300 to 1,000 francs. In cases of grave infirmity the pensions would be increased, and the archdiocesan pension would in no way prejudice the government pension, if one were enjoyed. Pension payments were to be on a quarterly basis paid in advance. An annual report of the pension system would be printed and sent to any priest interested.[48]

The plan was greeted with an almost unanimous enthusiasm, and it was put into effect immediately with the added provision that newly ordained priests could enroll in the year of their ordination. The first supervisory committee was composed of Vicar-General Barrès, Canon Marginier, the pastor of Notre Dame Parish, the *desservant* of Saint-Martial, and the assistant at Saint-Paul.[49] The pension system was a success from the moment of its inauguration, and on September 8, 1830, Cheverus could report to his clergy that already the fund justified their confidence in establishing it. Before the system was two years old the number of pensions being enjoyed had notably increased, and yet the resources of the fund had not diminished.[50]

Cheverus imputed the success of the pension plan to the co-operation and speed with which the clergy renewed their subscriptions each year, but the archbishop himself was the real reason for its phenomenal success. He not only put in his regular share each year but went further and invested 20,000 francs in the name of the fund so that it would not fail after his death. Whatever money he could divert to the system without prejudice to his regular charities he always used for pensions, on one occasion turning over 10,000 francs which had been given him for his own use. "I do not know any charity better bestowed," he argued, "than that which affords assistance to a priest who has grown gray in the work of his ministry, and who is poor because he has been charitable."[51]

The nineteenth century was to see a remarkable advance in social consciousness of the needs of the aged and infirm; statesmen like Bismarck would come to demand social insurance. It would be a mistake, however, to view the retirement system devised by the Archbishop of Bordeaux as a precursor of later programs emanating from either Marxian or egalitarian inspiration. Nor was Cheverus' thinking akin to the contemporary socialism of a Saint-Simon. The Archbishop of Bordeaux distrusted the rising ambitions of the proletariat as a scourge of modern society. Restlessness and revolution, he felt, must go hand in hand. "Every condition is honorable, when it is well filled," he reminded his people. "Happiness is found everywhere when we are virtuous." He preferred to visualize society as another Jacob's ladder, with angels descending as well ascending. "The angel on the step nearest earth was no less great, no less happy, and no less honorable, than he who was on the round nearest heaven."[52]

Like the other prelates of the Restoration, the Archbishop of Bordeaux was too busy with his first duty, that of restoring the heart and soul of the Church in France, to wage war on the evils of capitalism. As a matter of fact, industry did not make notable progress in France until after 1830; the "social question" was not born until the reign of Louis-Philippe. By the time any real economic transformation began in the 1840's and the problem was precisely posed for the French prelates, Cheverus was dead.[53] The only sense in which his *Caisse des Retraites* may properly be considered avant-garde is that of the precedent he set, which other French dioceses were soon to follow, of safeguarding the clergy in their twilight years. In this he was much closer to apostolic times and the Petrine injunction: "Be shepherds to the flock God has given you. Carry out your charge as God would have done."[54]

Slowly but surely Cheverus was drawing together, with his gentle, firm hands, the strands of the spiritual life of the Gironde. Integration based on regularity throughout the archdiocese imperceptibly healed the wounds the Church had suffered in the decades preceding his arrival. The clergy, convinced of authority and reassured by paternal solicitude, were coming to form a disciplined corps whose morale was high and whose piety had deeper roots. The new reinforcements to the ranks, "those new children of his sacerdotal family," emerging from the seminaries knew their archbishop as a friend. His frequent visits to the seminaries kept his example ever before their eyes in those days when mind and heart were most susceptible to remarkable evidences of prudence, charity, and zeal. The retreats he shared with them prior to ordinations were a portent of the happy rapport they would enjoy with a superior who signed himself "Your devoted and affectionate servant." The directors of the seminaries, too, worked with added zest, possessing as they did the unqualified esteem of Cheverus. They knew the mind of their archbishop and his confidence in the Society of Saint-Sulpice. He never meddled in seminary affairs, convinced as he was that "unity is essential to every government and similarity of views to every administration."[55]

The laity were becoming a more cohesive family in Christ. The work of distributing good books, which was begun under Aviau, was constantly encouraged by Cheverus. Six hundred volumes were distributed by the archbishop himself, new indulgences were obtained from the Holy See for the work, and Cheverus preached often on the subject wherever he went. He presided at the meetings of the promoters which were held in his palace, and he organized a committee to evaluate the books proposed for circulation.[56]

Meanwhile, those charitable works nearest his heart were given every aid at Cheverus' disposal. The Daughters of Charity had scarcely had such an ardent supporter since Saint Vincent de Paul. The memory of Elizabeth Seton often tinged his thoughts when he contemplated the marvels effected by the French sisters. He liked to recall that when some American Protestants had protested against her daughters' operating a hospital they had been rebuked by the retort, "When your own workers form such angels as these your complaints will be heard."[57] Cheverus could refuse the French Sisters nothing. "They are the highest glory of religion," he maintained, "the best manifestation of grace, the most striking proof of the divinity of Catholicism." He loved to visit their orderly hospitals, to pass through the wards where suffering and disease were alleviated by the women he esteemed so highly. "How full of blessings must be those hands which are employed only in acts of charity," he reflected.

The Bordeaux House of Retreat and Mercy had his unfailing patronage. He sometimes felt that those 300 penitent women might be the true marvel of his diocese, for these were souls who had voluntarily retired from the world and sin to lead lives of hard labor and self-denial. Visitors to Bordeaux were inevitably led there by Cheverus who saw in the House of Mercy the hand of God. His will at his death proved his devotion; he left the principal part of his property to the establishment. While he lived the saintly woman who headed the house had his unfailing support.[58]

The archbishop's protection of charitable institutions did not detract from his equal interest in schools. He never tired of attending their exercises, distributing prizes, and listening patiently to the memorized selections rendered by voices made more breathless by the archbishop's presence. The *Dames Noires* came first under his paternal gaze, naturally, by reason of their location which adjoined his palace and because Adé de Bonneuil was growing into a graceful young woman under their careful tutelage. But any community of religious women or men devoted to the education of youth could rely on the archbishop's favor. The *Frères des Écoles Chrétiennes* knew Cheverus called them his co-workers in the ministry. "If Bordeaux should lose these good brothers," he told the government, "it would be an unspeakable misfortune. In their school is learned love of good order, submission to law, respect for authority, because they always preach it in the name of religion, the only solid foundation for social felicity."[59]

Thus, with the time-honored instruments at his disposal, but with a genius for integration peculiarly his own, Cheverus strengthened his flock against the day of ordeal. And that day was fast approaching. The year 1830 was to see the overthrow of the Bourbon government which had been so sympathetic to the Church and so generous to Bordeaux. In many another diocese the July Revolution would leave in its train divided loyalties and social schism, but the Gironde and the Archdiocese of Bordeaux would suffer remarkably few upheavals during the transition. A sympathetic biographer has no difficulty in attributing a cause: the good shepherd at Saint-André had done his work well. His flock would know his voice; they would not be dispersed.

CHAPTER XXIV

REVOLUTION IN JULY

THE *Mémorial Bordelais* on January 1, 1830, began the new year with a traditional greeting to its subscribers. "Our first wishes," it asserted respectfully, "are for the King. May he always be happy. May he cast a backward glance of satisfaction on the past, on fifteen years of peace and happiness which France owes to the return of his august family." It is doubtful that its readers saw anything ominous in the conclusion of the salute which added, "But the true glory of the King is the happiness of his people." The subjects of Charles X throughout France were, indeed, unhappy that January; but their distresses were not political. It was a matter of weather.

The preceding issue of the *Mémorial* had commented:

> For three days our river and its banks have presented the aspect of the Neva. Masses of ice covered with snow are piling up and descending the whole course of the Garonne. All the ships which were anchored in the harbor having been beached on shore, the eye encompasses the entire extent of the river half-frozen over. An immense crowd gathers every day on the bridge and on the neighboring banks, about mid-day, in spite of the rigors of the excessive cold, to see this novel spectacle.[1]

The winter of 1829–1830 was to go down in history as the *grand hiver,* and Cheverus wrote to Bonneuil, "Since Christmas we have had a Boston cold!"[2] Huge quantities of snow fell over all France; roads were vast glaciers; even wine froze in its bottles, and everyone agreed that never in man's memory had France seen so cruel a winter. In Paris the poor were freezing, in Toulouse the temperature was reported six degrees below zero, and in Bordeaux the Sisters of

Charity crept precariously along the icy streets in temperatures which fell as low as fifteen degrees below zero.[3] The gazettes of Bordeaux announced, "As during the years 1812 and 1816, the administration counts upon the sentiments of humanitarianism which have always characterized the citizens of this city." Gifts for relief would be received at the Hôtel de Ville in Rue du Temple, by the justice of the peace, or by the pastor of Saint-Martial. Mayor du Hamel decreed that beginning on January 2 and lasting during the rigorous cold all indigent men over sixteen years of age would be granted daily pay upon reporting to the bureaus of charity.[4]

It was an emergency that the talents of Archbishop de Cheverus were best suited to meeting. He was never more energetic than when he could exert himself for his suffering fellow men. Hamel said later that it was the archbishop's solicitude and active charity which gave "the example and the impulse for relief almost equal to the need."[5] To comfort his people living distances from the city Cheverus went in the bitter cold to coastal settlements like Landes, where one simple woman cried out, "What a miracle to see a man like that, in a country like this, in weather like this!" The archbishop believed in suiting his schedule to the needs of the poor. They could not wait for warmer weather.[6] His preaching would not be missed in Bordeaux, for Nicolas Mac-Carthy was back giving a fine series of sermons in the Church of Notre Dame.[7]

When the middle of January came with no relief from the cold, Hamel asked Cheverus if he would authorize public prayers for its cessation and the archbishop immediately ordained that the prayers in time of calamity would continue as long as the crisis prevailed.[8] When the mayor inquired about the Lenten regulations Cheverus replied, "The strongest proof I can give of my interest is to send you the Lenten decree I have just published."[9] It was a decree quite typical of Cheverus:

> It is almost with fear that I come again to announce the penances of the holy season of Lent. . . . You have borne with resignation and a spirit of penance the privations and suffering resulting from the cold and ice which a just God has sent us . . . to remind us that no one can resist His power nor escape the effects of His wrath.

He then went on to tell them how concerned the civil authorities were for their welfare, and listed the relaxations permitted. The spirit of the season must not be diminished one iota, he warned. "Make up for these modifications which we willingly grant for this year of distress and calamity by a spirit of penance." According to their means they should give what alms they could to the seminaries this year.[10]

Such was the heart of Cheverus that major calamities produced in him simultaneously an immediate and vigorous activity for the relief of his people, and the reflection that the clergy, more than ever, must perfect themselves in order to lead their flocks safely through such disasters. On the same day that his Lenten decree recommended the seminaries to the laity's generosity he sent to all his pastors a notable letter on ecclesiastical conferences. The time had come to institute a regular system which would foster uniformity of conduct, love of study, a taste for ecclesiastical science, and a growth in charity and union of hearts. He outlined the order of procedure to be followed in each district: first, a short exhortation on the virtues and duties of the clergy must be given, preferably modeled on those of Saint Vincent de Paul or Jean-Jacques Olier; second, some explanation of Holy Scripture should follow, "since it ought to be the first and habitual study of the priest"; third, questions of dogma were to be discussed "because in these bad times impious works have been disseminated profusely among all classes of society and all priests have to listen to the objections of unbelievers and *must* know how to answer these objections precisely"; and, finally, attention must be given to the treatment of human conduct "which is the foundation of all morality."

It was a project he had thought about for some time. During pastoral retreats or episcopal visitations the matter had been broached more than once, and he now presented the program for regular conferences of the clergy as if he were only the instrument of their own wishes. "As always," he said, "since the clergy took the initiative, they ought to have the glory of executing it freely and spontaneously." But the formulation of the plan bears the unmistakable mark of the archbishop. Nothing was left to chance; each conference would send a *procès-verbal* to provide Cheverus with a record of each district's meeting. He meant to compare these reports and then offer his own reflections. "These are the means by which I thought I ought to second the laudable zeal of a great number of my priests," he concluded, as he gave sixteen exact rules to govern each conference.[11] Perhaps the bitter winds which swirled up from the ice-bound river and past the episcopal palace in Rue Judaïque might blow some good after all.

On January 6, 1830, Charles X decreed that the legislature would convene on March 2, but Comte de Cheverus did not plan to attend. It would be marvelous to witness the ceremony in Paris for the translation of the body of St. Vincent de Paul, to which Archbishop de Quelen invited him; but Archbishop de Cheverus was much too pre-occupied with the needs of the Gironde.[12] He had never been completely satisfied about the exact operation of the Ordinances of 1828 in the area of primary education, and the answer furnished by the Rector Dauzet had been filed away with the notation, "Presents some difficulty." Cheverus sought further clarification from the Minister of Public Instruction. On February 9, 1830, Martial, comte de Guernon-Ranville replied saying that the girls' schools run by religious women were not covered by the rules of Article 21 of the 1828 decree; they would continue to be supervised by ecclesiastical authorities. "I have informed the Rectors of the Academies and told them to inform the free com-mittees of primary instruction that their supervision does not extend to girls' schools conducted by religious."[13] It was the reply Cheverus had hoped to receive, and he wrote to Paris,

> Accept my thanks for this decision which you did so much to evoke and which tends to favor the schools so indispensable to the poor, especially in cities of large population which could not main-tain them if they had to be submitted to the same regime. . . .[14]

Further improvement in primary education seemed predicted by the royal ordinance of February 14, 1830. Although the Restoration monarchs had issued new ordinances every four years since the decree of February 29, 1816, many communes still had no schools and others, for lack of means, were in danger of losing those they had. The new decree asked the communes to act immediately in their May sessions. Besides additional primary schools, model schools for teacher-training should be established in each departement. The national budget would include appropriations for the specific purposes of aiding the poorer communes, distributing elementary textbooks, and encouraging teachers distinguished by their "zeal, ability, and good conduct."[15] When Guernon-Ranville forwarded the ordinance to Bordeaux, he commented, "I am confident that you will do all you can to promote the King's wishes. The circumstances which made some bishops hesitate to carry out the Ordinance of April 21, 1828, no longer exist. Let not the clergy themselves surrender the rights which this ordinance gives them."[16]

It was an admonition the Archbishop of Bordeaux scarcely needed. The clergy of the Gironde were already quite familiar with their superior's views on complying with the exact letter of the law. Cheverus replied, "The interests of Religion and society are too attached to the instruction of youth not to require me to do my duty and co-operate with the wise and pious intentions of the King."[17] Neither he nor the Minister of Public Instruction could foresee that before the budgetary provisions could go into effect the government which advocated them would be swept away. For Cheverus, the February reform was one more proof of the solicitude of his king for France. He celebrated with his usual fervor the solemn Mass at Saint-André on March 12, in commemoration of the return of the Bourbons.[18]

Spring came on with April weather and mingled emotions. His "beloved friend and pupil," Father Patrick Byrne, brought back old memories with his visit and a copy of Josiah Quincy's address on leaving the office of Mayor of Boston. Cheverus sent back by the same bearer his congratulations to the President of Harvard:

I am honored to be remembered by the honorable Josiah Quincy. I have not forgotten his eloquence in Congress, his zeal and services as mayor, and I see from afar his new and successful exertions as the Chief of the University. . . . May Harvard long flourish under your direction and auspices.[19]

Byrne could give Quincy all the details of the French situation, attended with so many difficulties and anxieties; but Cheverus would reiterate himself, "I miss the peaceable abode and ministry in dear Boston."

Across the city of Bordeaux ancient Saint-Seurin was presenting a new western façade to the children who gaped up in wonder at the sculptors working on the cornices and capitals. Maggesi, the finest sculptor of them all, was perfecting a great bas-relief of Saint-Armand giving the insignia to Saint-Seurin.[20] On April 24 the Bordeaux papers carried the *Moniteur's* version of the government manifesto announcing an expedition to be taken against Algiers.[21] It appeared to be a season of new beginnings and progress everywhere.

In opening the chambers in Paris on March 2, 1830, the king announced the end of the war in Greece and promised that the insult to the French consul in Algiers would not go long unpunished, but the origins of the conflict with the African power were remote and complex. Cheverus had still been in Boston when Jefferson's government had been goaded into war by piracy which had imperiled France as well as other sea-going powers. Since 1819 financial dealings between Algiers and France had brought a new cause for friction, and the striking of the French consul by the Algerian Dey in a formal encounter was only one pretext. French vessels were dispatched to reinforce the demand for reparations for this insult, of course, and relations had rapidly deteriorated after that.

A meeting of the Council of Ministers held on January 31, 1830, favored the principle of direct intervention, and preparations were begun. The British government tried to exact a promise that the intervention would not lead to permanent French control of the African coast, but the Polignac ministry adroitly evaded committing itself on the subject of future French policy. Some Frenchmen opposed the expedition on grounds of unpreparedness, but Baron d'Haussez, who had exchanged the prefecture of Bordeaux for a place in the ministry, worked wonders with both men and materials.[22]

On May 17, 1830, Charles X made known to the Church in France what he expected from the faithful, and Cheverus received a letter which read:

My Archbishop,

At the moment that the French flag goes to punish the insult of a barbarian power we like to recall to you the pious examples of the Kings our Ancestors, who always placed their military undertakings under Divine protections. . . . Our intention is, therefore, that you ordain public prayers in all the churches of your diocese to ask that the God of armies always may protect the banner of the lilies, that He give victory which already seems promised by the justice of our cause and the valor of our soldiers.[23]

Cheverus speedily decreed on May 24:

An important expedition calls our soldiers to a foreign soil to defend the honor of France and end the long vexations of a people hostile to the name of Christian. The King desires our prayers to be united to draw God's blessings on the army. . . . For three Sundays after receiving this decree sing at the beginning of Vespers *Deus noster, refugium et virtus,* the Litanies of the Blessed Virgin, and the Psalm *Exaudiat.* . . .

All the clergy of the Gironde would say for three weeks the prayers *pro tempore belli.*[24]

The French expedition, as history records it, was victorious and on July 10 Charles X addressed the prelates a second time. "Heaven has blessed our arms," he announced. "Justice, religion, and humanity have triumphed. Algiers has fallen. . . . The first need of our heart is to carry to the foot of the holy altars, amid acclamations of public joy, the solemn expressions of our gratitude." *Te Deums* were to rise again all over France in the presence of the ecclesiastical, the civil, and the military authorities. Cheverus published the king's letter in his own decrée of July 16 with the words, "Listen with respect and tenderness to the paternal voice. The heart which could listen coldly is neither French nor Christian. Ours are both and beat with love at the name of Charles X, the well-beloved."[25] Cheverus, of course, presided at Saint-André when the *Te Deum* was sung the following Sunday, little dreaming that it was the last time he would publicly mount the pulpit to praise the "well-beloved Charles." Yet at that very moment, while patriots in Bordeaux rejoiced over the victorious French arms, discussions in Paris were taking place that soon would effect the downfall of the king who had sent them forth to battle.

Perhaps Cheverus, like the papal nuncio in Paris, Luigi Lambruschini, was too sympathetic to the ultra-royalist views to foresee anything but triumph for the king over his most recent opposition on the subject of domestic reform. Lambruschini as late as July 28 still insisted to Rome that "the excellent king" would be successful at home as he had been abroad.[26] But Pius VIII had had presentiments for some time that a storm was gathering in France. Lambruschini had also predicted favorable election returns in March and had been quite mistaken.

The chambers which opened on March 2 had heard an address by the king delivered in a tone that fell upon liberal ears as nothing short of menacing. "The Constitution has placed the public liberties under the protection of the rights of my Crown," Charles asserted coldly. "If blameworthy manœuvres place obstacles in the way of my government, ... I will find the force to surmount them in my determination to maintain the public peace." The reaction of the Peers was generally moderate, but in the reply the Deputies addressed to the King they demanded a change in his ministers if concord were to prevail. Charles then issued the ordinance of March 19 which dissolved the legislature and called for new elections.[27]

The French prelates were expected to use their influence to secure the election of deputies favorable to the ministry, as the Minister of Ecclesiastical Affairs and Public Instruction made quite clear. On June 15 Guernon-Ranville sent the hierarchy a pointed rebuke:

> I thought that by the organ of the cooperators of your zeal the august words from the throne would be understood sooner and with more effect among the faithful population of our countryside. I pray you therefore, Monseigneur, to transmit *immediately* a copy of the royal proclamation to each pastor and *desservant* of your diocese, giving them an instruction needed to make understood by all his subjects the noble language of our beloved monarch.[28]

Cheverus dutifully passed this message on to his pastors with the words:

> I hasten to transmit to you the Proclamation of the King which I have just received. He desires all Frenchmen to hear his voice. They ought to listen to him with filial love, profound respect, and entire confidence. His royal and paternal words should be engraved in their hearts and be the rule of their conduct.[29]

The next day Bordeaux informed Paris that the mandate had been heeded, but Cheverus added that he needed extra copies of the royal proclamation. "Since the number was unequal to the parishes of the diocese," he explained, "I gave preference to the pastors less likely to have had knowledge of this royal act."[30]

The civil officials at Bordeaux, too, supported the king's desire to secure favorable elections, and on June 18 Vicomte de Curzay, Haussez' successor at the prefecture, announced that the Bordelais were forbidden to gather in the streets where the elections were scheduled to take place. This was something quite new in the experience of the Gironde and was regarded by the people as sheer insolence. Curzay may have been acting solely in the interests of the public order, but the man in the street impatiently awaiting election returns was loath to believe it, especially when Curzay followed up his first decree by removing two mayors of the Gironde because they openly refused to support the government's candidates. The Mayor of Bordeaux was just as high-handed and discharged a lawyer from the city council for similar reasons. Neither the admonitions of the clergy nor the pressure of the public officials swayed the elections of Bordeaux, however; only one of the ministry's candidates was elected.[31]

Cheverus had only recently received the cross of the Order of the Holy Ghost but he said to those about him, "We are in such unhappy times, society is in such a terrible crisis, that one would have to be devoid of every feeling of charity to think of his own personal interests. Only the public misfortunes touch us."[32] Publicly he gave no sign of his private reactions to the political bitterness rising in the city that July, and went calmly ahead with his plans for the pastoral retreat he had scheduled for the end of the month.

The archbishop meant to conduct the retreat jointly with Father André Hamon, the director of the major seminary. Pastors were told not to worry about services in their parishes; even if some of the congregations were deprived, the faithful could be assured the preceding Sunday that Mass was not an obligation for those who might find too great hardship in attending. The clergy were to make the retreat in its entirety. "Let nothing prevent accepting this invitation," he said sternly.[33] He was not blind to the needs of the laity, and worried incessantly over the rain which threatened all the crops. After the disastrous cold of the previous winter his people of the agricultural communes direly needed a good harvest in 1830. On July 5 Cheverus ordered all pastors to use the prayers prescribed for petitioning good weather.[34]

And so July went on. William Dubourg sent over from Montauban his new *Concordance for the Four Gospels* for Cheverus' approval.[35] Bishop Jean Jacoupy of Agen wrote of his gratitude for Cheverus' assistance in solving the shortage of priests in his diocese.[36] On Wednesday, July 21, at five o'clock in the afternoon Cheverus and his clergy opened the retreat. When he was not giving conferences the archbishop attended to his other duties and the *Mémorial Bordelais* reported on Monday:

> A pious and touching ceremony took place yesterday at 8 A.M. in the chapel of the royal college of this city. Mgr. the archbishop pontificated and a large number of boarders and externes received from his hands the Sacrament of Confirmation. By a short fatherly exhortation Mgr. highly praised the religious instruction given to the young, the instruction of this University establishment, and by his eloquent and persuasive words he caused among all the faithful who heard him a most lively and profound emotion.[37]

The college ceremony took place on Sunday, July 25, a day not soon to be forgotten in France; for, far to the north at Saint-Cloud, directly after Mass, Charles X summoned his ministers, and after consultation took the fatal decision in favor of the July Ordinances.

The repressive measures promulgated that day suppressed freedom of the press, dissolved the newly elected Chamber of Deputies, reorganized the electoral system, and called for new elections in September. The *Moniteur* came out later than usual in Paris that Monday, July 26. As news of the ordinances spread through the city the rumbling of revolution began. At the Bourse interest rates began to drop. Students and workers of the printing trades began to congregate, and cries were heard of "Long live the Constitution! Down with the ministry!" The night seemed calm enough, but the next day barricades began to appear and the government declared Paris to be in a state of siege. After that the tempo of events accelerated.[38]

On Wednesday morning in Bordeaux the clergy emerging from their retreat at nine o'clock, after the renewal of their clerical vows, found the city alive with rumors. Although the news of the ordinances had not yet arrived, everyone knew something was in the wind. Earlier in the week the *Mémorial Bordelais* had reported ominously:

> Rumors of a coup d'état are renewed with more vivacity than ever. One is astonished to see that M. d'Haussez, who is certainly not a fool, is exposing himself voluntarily to new defeats in the electoral college where he really has not a chance. Persons who know M. d'Haussez explain the singularity by the desire of the Minister of Marine to become Peer of France. It seems a peerage has been promised him.[39]

Sardonic comments on their former prefect's futile ambitions were succeeded the following day by Prefect de Curzay's announcement that he had received a telegraphic despatch confirming the dissolution of the Chamber of Deputies, and the *Mémorial* described it as "news afflicting to all sincere friends of the constitutional monarchy."[40] By Wednesday night, priests who had not yet left Bordeaux to resume their pastoral cares saw placards announcing the complete text of the four fatal ordinances which were to be inserted in the papers the next day, and decrees of the mayor limiting public meetings. On July 29 the *Mémorial*, the *Indicateur*, and *Défenseur* printed the texts but with bitter comments on freedom of the press. Scarcely had the editions appeared than the police seized all copies, sealed the presses, and hinted loudly that legal action against the printers was soon to follow. The *Mémorial* later courteously remarked, "It is only just to say that they did it politely and moderately."[41]

The populace proved less restrained, and the Bordelais received the ordinances with "grief and indignation." News filtering through from Paris, in spite of the censorship, described the insurrections already forming in the capital. Bordeaux was as opposed to ministerial tyranny as any French city, sober citizens murmured. The curious man in the street noted unusual activity among the officials close to the mayor and the prefect. Everyone knew that the telegraph, that aerial marvel of Claude Chappe's invention, whose great, grating arms relayed the news from tower and steeple, was incessantly busy. Unfortunately, the proprietors of workshops and dockyards had closed their places of business as soon as the Wednesday placards appeared, and the idle masses now had nothing to do but feed the fires of their own unrest. When a courier got through from Paris at four o'clock on Friday afternoon, with news of violence against the royal guard, those fires leaped out of control.[42]

The first rush of the inflamed mob was to the home of the editor of the *Défenseur,* where they destroyed his books and ruined his press. Moving on the prefecture they disarmed the guard, broke down the doors, and surged into Curzay's apartment. Hoarsely they demanded that he inform them at once of all he knew regarding events in Paris, and of his intentions in Bordeaux. The prefect proudly refused all explanation and the mob then seized his furniture and threw it from the windows. Amid a hail of stones and furniture Curzay fled.[43]

The prefect had anticipated disorders, of course, and had conceived the precautionary measure of augmenting the Bordeaux garrison by a squadron of cavalry from Libourne. Unhappily for Curzay, the cavalry did not arrive until the following day, and he was compelled to continue his flight after being forced from his home. He sought refuge first in the Grand Theater, but in reaching the opera house he wounded a citizen with his drawn sword, and from that moment the popular fury knew no bounds. The prefect's clothes were ripped, his head wounded, and thus covered with blood and dirt he was dragged first toward the Maison Gobineau, then toward Notre Dame, then toward the Cours de l'Intendance. He was very nearly dead when he was finally rescued and taken into hiding. When the garrison troops finally emerged with drums beating, flags flying, and guns on their arms, it was too late. The Hôtel de la Prefecture was empty.[44]

All that night the mob continued pillaging. They seized the city records and tax registers and burned them in the squares or at the gates of the city. By morning the more sober citizens determined to bring order to Bordeaux in one way or another, and after requesting the mayor to order out the National Guard they armed themselves as auxiliaries. Soon most troublesome sections found regular and provisional guards stationed nearby, and in this way the rioting was eventually quelled. Not without incident, however. During the morning of July 31 in the absence of Curzay the prefecture was taken over by a member of the city council. This official issued a proclamation which indiscreetly began, "A horrible murderous assault was committed yesterday on the person of the First Magistrate." When the reading of the proclamation was attempted at Place du Palais the people whistled and jeered so wildly the reader had to retire. His persecutors pursued him to the Hôtel de Ville where the guard fired upon them. One man was killed and two women were fatally wounded. It took the National Guard's intervention to disperse the people. By evening, however, the security of the city seemed assured, and that night perfect calm reigned.

Under cover of the darkness Curzay was helped out of the city. He remained hidden at a friend's house in Audenge until his wounds healed, and then he retired to his estate in Poitiers. After that the people felt more confident that their liberties were assured. General Janin of the military announced that the troops would not act against them, and the mayor, although clearly not sympathetic to popular feeling, tried to give the impression of consulting their interests. He called a meeting of the city's leaders at which it was decided that all news coming from Paris would in the future be made public immediately, couriers would no longer be intercepted at Dordogne, newspapers would operate again, and the city council would appoint six members of the National Guard to administer the city until a new regime could be installed.

And so it was that when the *Moniteur* of July 29, with the news that Paris had successfully revolted, reached Bordeaux the worst of the violence in the southern city was already over. Baron Janin wisely notified the people in advance of the telegraphic message foretelling the arrival of the courier from Paris, and a group of chasseurs was ready to escort him into the city on his arrival at four o'clock. People read in great excitement Talleyrand's remark, "At five minutes past noon the older branch of the Bourbons ceased to reign," and the king's comment, "Here I am in the same unhappy situation as that of my brother in 1789." But by nine o'clock the clamor had subsided and Bordelais slowly circulated through the streets crossed in silence by inoffensive patrols. True, the next day one isolated group of the more stubborn rabble upset the pyramid erected in honor of the entrance of the Duc d'Angoulême in 1814, but by August 3 the electoral college of Bordeaux met spontaneously at the Hôtel de Ville to set up a government for the city. The mayor was replaced by a provisional committee of twelve men acceptable to the people. The National Guard adopted the tri-color, and when the cavalry from Libourne tried to intervene they were ordered out of Bordeaux. As soon as it was learned that Louis-Philippe had been proclaimed king the municipal committee sent a delegation to Paris to attest their loyalty. On August 16 the provisional committee ceased to function with the installation of a new mayor and council elected according to law.[45]

It is natural to inquire why the revolution in Bordeaux was so limited. One reason, apparently, was the wisdom of Baron Janin of whom the *Mémorial* of August 2 commented:

> During the three days the conduct of General Baron Janin has been as noble and pure as his life. Faithful to his duties toward the State and the country, he knew how to give his troops a firm, moderate attitude, and if during the day of the 31st a hand maddened by fury caused him wounds, which happily do not hazard his life, all the inhabitants regret it and give sincere wishes for his health.

The city later voted him a sword of honor in gratitude.[46]

But something more remains to be said. The July Revolution was not only a political event involving a conflict for power between the aristocracy and bourgeoisie, with the common man briefly providing the street scenes and sound effects; it was, in addition markedly anticlerical, as most historians agree. Once the close union between the altar and the throne of Restoration France is admitted, the anticlerical character of the insurrection offers no enigma. As in 1789, the Church had to pay for this union. In Paris the crowds sacked the episcopal palace of Hyacinthe de Quelen and the archbishop escaped only through the intervention of a medical friend; the sacristies of Notre Dame were profaned; houses of the missionaries and Jesuits were ransacked; almost everywhere Stations of the Cross were destroyed. Priests who dared to wear the soutane in the streets were molested, and churches had to be kept locked during the week. At Reims and Besançon the Cardinal Archbishops Latil and Rohan were so menaced that they fled the country, as did Bishop Forbin-Janson of Nancy. Even in the country parishes priests were insulted and chased from their rectories, while the press and theater almost universally denounced *"Les hommes noirs."*[47] The July Revolution seemed to proclaim, as Heinrich Heine remarked, "The old religion is dead; the majority of the French do not wish to hear the corpse mentioned and hold a handkerchief to their noses when it is a question of the Church"; or as Jules Janin put it, "This religion was very ill ever since the great blow of 1789; the July Revolution killed it completely."[48]

In Bordeaux, a city which had a substantial Protestant population and a rising mercantile class and therefore might be expected to be as anticlerical as it had been in the great Revolution, something was oddly different. The *Mémorial* of August 5 carried a small item on its third page which read, "Mgr. the archbishop and his clergy are peaceful spectators of the great movement. As vacations are near the young seminarians may go home." The serenity of this commonplace is significant; not only does it lack the acerbity in regard to the clergy prevalent in other places, but it seems to imply an affectionate concern for the priests-to-be. On August 8 Cheverus sent a little note to the Bonneuils saying, "Do not be uneasy about Adèle and also in reference to me. They love me and do not trouble me. Let us pray for one another."[49] This may have been simply meant to reassure anxious parents, of course. But on August 14 the *Mémorial* gave even clearer evidence of the local attitude when it editorialized:

> Ordinarily in this city a general procession, at which all the civil and military authorities assisted, took place, as in all France, on August 15, the day of the feast of the Assumption. This year, one says, because of fear of disorder the procession will not take place. It seems to us these alarms are ill-founded and that the Catholic religion is too deeply engraved in the hearts of the Bordelais for them even to be troubled by the exterior acts of the religion they profess. The procession ought to be held as usual.

As we have seen in an earlier chapter, August was also the month in which the deputies from the Gironde protested the exclusion of their archbishop from the Chamber of Peers. In the light of the riotous events which preceded Cheverus' words of August 19 making public his desire to be free from political office, his declaration takes on more significance. "I feel more and more attached to the inhabitants of Bordeaux," he said. "I thank them for the friendship they have testified toward me." When he mailed Bonneuil a copy of his declaration he added, "My personal safety, nor that of my clergy, has not been compromised here. The authorities have shown me respect and attentions." And Adé, who was standing by his arm as he wrote, added, "I dined with our good grandpapa today." Life in Rue Judaïque had not changed at all.[50]

Another indication of the attitude of Bordeaux toward the Church is found in the *Mémorial* of September 3:

Cheverus in 1830, wearing the decorations of the
Order of the Holy Ghost.

Painting of Cheverus receiving la barette *from Louis-Philippe in the chapel of the Tuileries.*

In this regeneration of France signalled by the fall of an ancient throne of long veneration, and by the sudden elevation of a new dynasty, the clergy of France are plunged by the nature of their august functions, in grave and profound meditation on these events of the last month and on the incalculable consequences . . .

But today all the priests of this diocese, enlightened in their duties toward the King and country by the new Fénelon Providence has given us for our supreme pastor, have rallied in silence to the new order of things; and by this evangelical submission they calm the passions and hates raised by the wicked who are the enemies of the Catholic religion.

The most striking proof, however, of the role played by Cheverus is contained in a letter of the new Prefect of the Gironde to the Minister of Public Instruction. On September 20 Paris requested that prefects send in confidential reports on the relations between the new civil governments and the diocesan authorities. The prefect's reply deserves scrutiny:

I am going to reply successively to the questions you addressed to me.

1. I congratulate myself daily on my relations with the Archbishop of Bordeaux. It is not just today that I am in a position to appreciate the character and virtue of the respectable Mgr. de Cheverus; I had the honor of knowing him when he was Bishop of Montauban, and I consider myself lucky to have him at the head of the Catholic clergy of the Département de la Gironde. No other prelate seems so worthy of the confidence of the government.

2. M. the Archbishop wrote on August 20 to all the pastors of the department to have them sing in their churches the *Domine Salvum fac regem.*

3. Only a small number of complaints have yet reached me of the conduct of the clergy of the diocese, who generally show themselves submissive to the laws. These complaints are directed against young priests; I have sent them to M. the Archbishop, begging him to take as promptly as possible measures which prudence suggests. The old pastors seem tolerant and submissive.

4. M. the Archbishop has invited all the pastors of the cantons to bless the flags of the national guard every time the request should be made.

5. He does not believe he ought to address, to the clergy of his diocese, instructions or rules of conduct; he thinks that this measure would have a political nature which ministers of religion ought meticulously to avoid. He has given them an example of submission,

and he is determined to remind them, if any of them forget it, that affairs of government are not in their province.

I second, Monsieur le Duc, with all my power, these sage dispositions.[51]

The character of Cheverus shows in sharp relief. In practice he adhered strictly to the principle of the Church throughout the ages, that of respecting the government under which he lived; in general, because he believed that religion and state suffered from reciprocal antagonism and benefited from mutual respect, but in this particular case because, as he told Bonneuil, "It is greatly to be wished that the present government acquire power, for . . . anarchy . . . threatens us."[52] Bishops were meant to be the father and friend of all their people, and consequently must forego academic debates over the best form of government. For twenty-seven years he had worked happily under the enlightened republican form of the United States and his fellow citizens had found him a patriot of undeviating loyalty. For the six years since his return to France he had been the devoted servant of a legitimate king. For the rest of his life, if the good of religion required it, he would offer an equal loyalty to the Citizen King, Louis-Philippe. He admonished his clergy that they must keep themselves free from all political party spirit that they might better fulfill their missions of peace and love, under any form of government whatever. "We ought not to give occasion to any existing party to regard us as enemies, since we are called to save men of all parties."[53]

But what of the heart of Cheverus? It was a very loyal heart, and now in the fall of 1830 it was very heavy. As he told the civil authorities of Bordeaux, "I should be unworthy of your esteem if I should conceal from you my affection for the fallen family; you would despise me as an ungrateful man, for Charles X loaded me with kindnesses."[54] He had enjoyed close relations with the whole royal family and more than once the king had sought him out for those conversations which only friends exchange. As Cheverus put away the ribbon of the Order of the Holy Ghost which would never be worn again he could only reflect sadly on this last token of the fallen monarch's generosity. In sending the decoration Peyronnet had spoken of the king's appreciation of, and pleasure in rewarding, the virtues of the Archbishop of Bordeaux. Now Charles was doomed to exile, and Lulworth Castle in England was once more playing host to a French *émigré*, this time of royal blood. Poor Peyronnet had been arrested while trying to reach Bordeaux from Tours, disguised in wig, woolen stockings, and heavy shoes.[55] Baron d'Haussez had managed to reach foreign soil but the other ministers who were not so fortunate were held for trial, and by the end of the year Peyronnet, Guernon-Ranville, Polignac, and Chantelauze would be confined in the fortress of Ham.[56]

The old order had passed, never to return. There was no regret in the archbishop's heart for the lost honors he had never sought nor enjoyed. Unlike the king and his ministers, Cheverus was neither in exile nor in prison, but free to exercise the only functions he had ever desired. He tried to keep uppermost in his mind the workings of divine Providence which had restored tranquillity to Bordeaux and spared its archbishop so much as even a harsh word. On Christmas Eve he wrote to Bonneuil, "No one has troubled me. . . . We are in the hands of God."[57] He would conform to the new regime, carefully guarding his words and actions; but he was speaking more for himself than to his clergy when he said, "We are permitted to regret; we are obliged to give an account of our affections only to God, and the heart is a sanctuary into which men have no right to look."[58]

Although he meant to submit to the July monarchy, it was not easy. No longer did the writing of his Lenten decrees evoke the former rush of praise for the virtues and pious example of legitimate rulers. For a while public announcements of prayers in honor of the new king's feast day were terse and said no more than protocol required. Until the day in 1836 when he went to Paris to receive the cardinal's hat, Cheverus never saw Louis-Philippe in person. Yet, so valiant a battle did the little man in Rue Judaïque wage against his own private feelings that on no single occasion did he ever privately or publicly voice the slightest antagonism toward the Orleans regime.

On the contrary, he quickly came to be regarded as the most valuable support the French government possessed in the hierarchy. In Bordeaux, the new authorities sought his counsels and asserted that they would never make decisions without consulting his advice; "by 1831 the union was perfect."[59] In May of that year Cheverus told Bonneuil that they never stopped showing him consideration. "The Council of the Department has allowed me the supplement of 8,000 francs as in preceding years," he added as proof.[60] Less than two years after the fall of the Bourbons the prefecture at Laval suggested to Paris that one of Cheverus' pastorals might prove a valuable antidote to the "very different spirit" of the Bishop of Le Mans. The report explained:

The clergy of Mayenne are generally animated by a very bad spirit. The pronouncements from the pulpit which daily resound against the principles of our late revolution demonstrate this only too clearly. A writing in which the lessons of Christian doctrine were associated with wise maxims on government policy would, in the present circumstances, present a useful counterweight to the rash preaching. I think I have found it in the pastoral letter of the Archbishop of Bordeaux. . . . I do not doubt that his pastoral letter, already known in the journals, would produce an excellent effect in the rural area, if it were circulated.[61]

Whatever official divorce there may have been in Paris between the public officials and religious ceremonies, in Bordeaux customs did not radically change. The *Mémorial* of May 2, 1833, in reporting the ceremonies at Saint-André on the king's feast day, quoted the archbishop's compliment as he paused before the civil and military authorities:

Permit me to express my joy and appreciation at seeing you here. The law does not call you here, but your hearts lead you here. I join my heart to your intentions which you make for the prosperity of France and her chief. I congratulate myself on living in a city governed by such authorities.

By 1834 the Prefect of the Gironde reported to Paris, in reply to a request for a confidential report on the clergy:

M. the Archbishop is beyond all praise. He is charity, simplicity, tolerance in person. Having passed thirty years of his life in the United States, he acquired there the conviction that no form of government is incompatible with religious liberty, even with a high degree of influence for ecclesiastics. This conviction has for long years made him the prelate in France the most favorable to political freedom. On several solemn occasions he has highly manifested his ideas of peace, his respect for the government is established in a way completely satisfying to the servants and the friends of this government. On the last feast day of the King he addressed to those present a short sermon full of unction, charity, and veritable patriotism in which he even eulogized the King, speaking of his efforts to insure the welfare of France. . . .[62]

In the conflict between emotion and will, the archbishop's will had won out. As it turned out, his personal victory was to bear fruit which both the Church and the government of France could savor. But that is another chapter; it is enough to say here that the victory cost him dear. His whole life in France had been lived under three Bourbon brothers whom he had profoundly revered. Two had suffered exile and one a violent death. In all their sufferings, either of body or spirit, the sensitive heart of Jean de Cheverus had shared. He had returned to France in 1823 primarily to lend what support he might to the Church in France and to legitimacy, those sacred causes to which, as he said, "I have devoted my life." With the overthrow of the last brother, Cheverus turned with renewed fervor to the service of the Church. But the artists whose pens and brushes put the Archbishop of Bordeaux on paper or on canvas after 1830 all found traces of gentle sadness on the face of their subject. The will may command the limb, the thought, the tongue; the face is in service to the heart.

CHAPTER XXV

THE PRISONER OF BLAYE

It was all very well for Casimir Perier, who quickly became chief minister of the new regime, to say, "The trouble with this country is that many people imagine there has been a revolution in France. No, Monsieur, there has been no revolution; there has simply been a change in the person of the chief of State."[1] For the clergy of France it had marked the end of a system. Not only was the new order to be guided by the will of the people under a ruler known as "King of the French people"; the triumph of the bourgeoisie ushered in an era when religion, when not treated with open hostility, met at best reluctant respect. Louis-Philippe and his family attended Mass, but officially the monarchy was no longer Catholic. Article 6 of the Constitution now recognized only that Catholicism was the religion of the majority. No religious ceremony attended the coronation of the king, and the name of God disappeared from official discourses. The budget for religion was constantly decreased by the Deputies until 1835; army chaplains were abolished; and the strictest religious orders, one of the most fruitful sources of spirituality in the Church, were expelled.[2]

The most immediate question facing the clergy was that of their obligations to a government which had not yet been officially recognized by the Holy See. In August several of the hierarchy wrote individually to Rome. Should the clergy pray publicly for the King? Should they sing the *Te Deum* commanded by the government for the "glorious July days"?[3] Cheverus' suffragan, Jean Jacoupy, was concerned over the royal rights in the matter of nominating canons, vicars-general, and pastors. Were the former Franco-Roman concordats now null and void?[4] The prelate most interested was Archbishop de Quelen of Paris. He was still a Peer of France, and a law of August 31, 1830, declared that all functionaries must take an oath of allegiance to the king of the French and swear obedience to the Constitution and law of the land. Anticipating the passage of the law, Quelen in mid-August sent letters to Rome requesting authorization for bishops to take an oath of allegiance to the new regime.[5]

Before replying to any questions involving the obligations of the clergy to the government, Pius VIII faced a prior decision. What official position should the Holy See adopt in regard to the king himself? On August 31 a confidential letter was addressed to the papal nuncios at Madrid, Vienna, Naples, Florence, Turin, and Brussels asking them to sound out the dispositions of the governments at those capitals. Then on September 12 a meeting was held of the Congregation of Extraordinary Ecclesiastical Affairs in Rome to discuss the subject of recognition. The general opinion of the princes of the Church was that recognition was not immediately desirable. But Pius VIII acted independently. On September 25 he addressed letters to "Louis-Philippe, most Christian King of the French." Not only was the Orleans monarchy recognized, but the phrase *Regi Christianissimo* was the same formerly accorded the Bourbons. To the French chargé d'affaires at Rome the pope said simply that he was eager to preserve the cordial relations which had formerly existed between his kingdom and the Holy See.[6] As it proved, the pope in ignoring the advice of the cardinals was more clairvoyant than his contemporaries perceived. "By freeing the Church in France from all official attachment to legitimacy he had shifted it to a road of independence with regard to regimes which permitted, once violence abated, a purely spiritual role."[7]

Rome was then ready to consider the issues of concordats and the oath. On September 22 the congregation reconvened to discuss the doubts raised by the French prelates. Opinion was divided and the debate prolonged, but in the end it was agreed that there was no incompatibility between the new French Constitution and existing treaties, and that the oath could be taken according to the formula of 1801. On September 29 the Holy See addressed to the uneasy bishops of France a brief which cleared their consciences in regard to the oath and the prayers for the king.[8] The brief did not reach Paris for a month and a half, but on November 16 Archbishop de Quelen forwarded a copy to Bordeaux saying:

The need for enlightenment which I had in the difficult circumstances in which the recent events placed us, the desire to see reign among us a uniformity of sentiments and of conduct equally necessary for public peace and the repose of consciences, made me send as quickly as possible to the Holy See on the subject of the most delicate questions which could involve the clergy and the faithful of the Church in France. The delay probably renders it useless for many persons, but I thought it would be agreeable to the bishops to know about it. I send it *confidentially.* Your wisdom, Monseigneur, will know how to regulate the use to which it can be put. . . .[9]

The Archbishop of Paris, invoking reasons of religion, had refused to take the oath earlier. Now Rome reminded him that the form used was nothing new. The faithful who had formerly taken such an oath under the Bourbons, the Holy See pointed out, "could take the oath to the new king of the French people who, tranquillity having been restored, actually occupies the throne." The pope urged Quelen personally to become "the immediate interpreter of our wishes to the French clergy, exhorting them in our name . . . to submit and obey."[10] The time fixed for the taking of the oath, if Quelen was to have entered the Chamber of Peers that fall, had unfortunately elapsed. The Archbishop of Paris, however, on December 2 requested an audience with the king so that he might explain his failure to take the oath and discuss the possibility of resuming his official functions; on January 16 he went to the Palais Royal to present his respects.[11]

Cheverus, having been deprived of his seat in the Chamber of Peers, had no such problems. In his private bout with conscience he had already attuned his mind to the mind of Rome and had ordered public prayers for the king two months before the papal brief arrived in Bordeaux.[12] The only protest he chose to make had already been effective. When the question of the oath was first debated a deputy had proposed that since the clergy received their salaries from the government each priest should be compelled to take the oath. Cheverus wrote immediately to Élie, duc Decazes, "I will be answerable for my clergy if the oath is not demanded; but if it is, I will answer for nothing." The government was not impervious to Cheverus' reasoning which suggested that the proposal was both impolitic and imminently disastrous. There well might be repeated the fatal division of juring and nonjuring clergy as in the great Revolution, which Cheverus had such painful reasons for recalling. It could only embarrass the new government, agitate the clergy, and alarm the people. The Chamber of Deputies, urged to defeat the proposal, rejected the clause on

August 19, and consequently the law of August 31 did not contain the stipulation Cheverus believed so dangerous.[13]

In December, while Quelen of Paris waited for an answer to his request for an audience with Louis-Philippe, Cheverus of Bordeaux was immersed in private grief. His beloved sister Anne Le Jariel died unexpectedly from a stroke of apoplexy the second week of Advent. "She was (and is, I hope) a Saint," Cheverus told Bonneuil in reporting the sad news. Her son Augustin came to Rue Judaïque with Cheverus after the funeral.[14] To his weight of personal sorrow was added the knowledge that the whole Christian world had suffered a loss as well. Pius VIII was dead.

The Roman agent of Bordeaux wrote on December 1, 1830, "It is with regret that I perform the sad duty of informing you that the Sovereign Pontiff died last night at nine o'clock because of a malady of the chest."[15] The news came at a time when French influence at Rome was most precarious. When the conclave opened on December 14, of the four living French cardinals Latil and Rohan had fled the country, and only Isoard was actually present in his French diocese, and in a position to carry whatever instructions the new government of France might decide to issue. But Joachim Cardinal d'Isoard wrote to Cheverus from Auch on December 17, "Tomorrow, as soon as possible after the ordinations, I will take coach for the conclave. Who knows whether I shall arrive too late?"[16] In Rome, the French chargé d'affaires was most uneasy because rumor was rife that his nation had either lost, or was disdaining to exercise, her right to take part in the election.[17] Cheverus issued a pastoral to his clergy ordering prayers for the deceased pontiff and a second novena for the election of his successor. "May the union and fervor of our prayers secure a new shepherd who will prove a worthy successor of him whose loss we mourn," he concluded.[18] Then, just as the year ended, the *Mémorial* reported news from Rome dated December 12 to the effect that the Cardinal Prince de Rohan had arrived on December 9 and was settled at the Hôtel de Cerny. He had announced that he desired to enter the conclave for the French nation and would receive with pleasure all instructions his government might send, "if they were not opposed to his character and conscience." Prince de Croij, the Cardinal-Archbishop of Rouen, was also expected at any moment.[19] In the end Isoard arrived in time to use his influence; and while Spain did its best to ruin the chances of Giustiani, France did as much for the prospects of Vincenzo Macchi, who had been nuncio in Paris the year of Cheverus' return to France. By February 2 Mauro Cappellari had the necessary votes to be proclaimed, taking the name of Gregory XVI.[20]

Bordeaux soon learned the details of the new pope's reaction to his election. Cardinal de Rohan, who had the room next to the former Cardinal Cappellari, enjoyed passing them on. During the fifteen days of the debate he had been calm enough, until it began to appear that he would be elected. Then he grew troubled and sad. "As soon as the election was pronounced he cried for an hour and a half, and when the cardinals all came to kiss his feet and hands, he took their hands and kissed them with humble and touching emotion. . . . He said to Mgr. Rohan, 'Recommend me to our Lord.' "[21]

From all sides came praises for the "good Pope," who was consecrated on February 6, 1831. The French government officially notified the clergy of the election, as did Nuncio Lambruschini, and on February 24 Cheverus decreed that the prayers *pro gratiarum actione* and *pro summo pontifice* express the general joy of the Catholics throughout the Archdiocese of Bordeaux.[22]

In the months which immediately followed, the larger joy of the Archbishop of Bordeaux was overshadowed by a succession of minor local irritations and personal perplexities. While the anticlericalism of the July Revolution was spending its force in 1831 several traditions dear to the hearts of the Bordelais were sacrificed on the altar of bourgeois evolution. Mission crosses were the first to go. Although there was no governmental decree against these sacramentals, in many cities they had provoked outbursts of bigotry. The prudence which was such a persistent trait of the archbishop's nature led Cheverus to request, "In parishes where it is deemed necessary to remove mission crosses the pastors will let the civil authorities act, as we did in Bordeaux, to use their influence to prevent this action from becoming an occasion for trouble."[23] It had been hard enough to see removed the gigantic cross from Place Pey-Berland, that impressive symbol of regeneration erected with the acclamations of the whole city reconciled to God in the happy reign of Louis XVIII.[24] Cheverus wanted no pretext for desecrations left in other parishes if he could avoid it. Prefect de Preissac, too, sent a circular to the mayors of the cantons urging prudence in this regard.

Scarcely had this matter been attended when Cheverus received from the prefect a circular from Paris ordering the removal of the *fleurs de lys* from all public places and monuments. The July monarchy feared, it seemed, that the former Bourbon symbol would "stir up agitation of spirit" in those Frenchmen who had fond memories of earlier days. "I invite you," the circular said with superb indirection, "to co-operate with the ecclesiastical authorities in your department to have all *fleurs de lys* removed from monuments and objects sacred to religion." The prefect commented wryly, "No doubt you will persuade your pastors to concur in the execution of this request."[25]

In May, the month of the Blessed Virgin, the archbishop was further depressed by the scandalous disorders in the streets of his episcopal city. It was small comfort to be assured, as the *Mémorial* so courteously attempted, that the violent behavior in the city was not really political or religious, that these disorders were "the result of the profound misery which torments the indigent classes," that the "authors of these troubles are strangers to our department."[26] Things were really much better in Bordeaux than in some places, and Cheverus told Bonneuil, "The services, the preaching, the processions as usual."[27] But the poor and the unfortunate overwhelmed him with their needs, and the sporadic disturbances preyed upon his mind. Disturbances would only provoke further restrictions of religious practices, restrictions which once pronounced he must in conscience promulgate. Even though the Corpus Christi procession took place as usual in Bordeaux that year, on July 30 the Minister of Public Instruction and Religion notified the prelates of France that the processions on the feast of the Assumption must be stopped.[28]

The suppression of the Feu de la Saint-Jean might seem a small thing beyond France, but to Cheverus who had insisted on the ceremony even when he was in the wilderness of Maine with Indians who fired their guns in joyous celebration it was one more deprivation. How could Frenchmen who on the eve of June 23 had been accustomed to ushering in the summer season with leaping fires now content themselves with a simple blessing of the crosses destined for places above the doors of their houses?[29] Nevertheless, authority must be obeyed, and when the order came regarding the great August feast in honor of the Blessed Virgin he informed his pastors that they must forego the processions and prayers which had been a tradition since the Vow of Louis XIII. "You could," he suggested, "before Benediction of the Blessed Sacrament, chant the Litanies of the Blessed Virgin with the prayer *Concede nos*. For the rest, the feast of the Assumption is to be celebrated with the same solemnity as other great feasts of the year."[30] The Bishop of Marseilles, who was not so compliant, had cause to regret it. He later admitted his mistake and told his own clergy, "We had reason to hope that our rights as Catholics would be respected, that a cortège so uniquely religious could advance peacefully in the streets of a city known for its Catholicism." Now he urged his pastors, too, in the spirit of peace to be calm and submit, to forego future processions in their parishes.[31]

And so, one by one, the old and beloved customs disappeared. In 1831 the procession of Saint-Lazare was discontinued; by 1833 the procession in honor of Saint-Jean was no more. Even the very core of a French Christmas, the midnight Mass, disappeared save from the chapels of the religious communities where none of the laity could participate. In 1835, the last Christmas that Cheverus would know in Bordeaux, the mayor offered to take police measures if the archbishop meant to resume the service which had been discontinued because of "the scandal of the presence of ill-intentioned people," but Cheverus thanked him for his zeal and declined. Mass would be at five in the morning; "there is no need to fear opening the churches at that hour," he said with unintentional irony.[32] Churches had long since ceased to remain open except when in use.

Almost from the beginning of the reign of Louis-Philippe churches were visited by thieves and terrible profanations. Paris, of course, suffered the worst depredations; and the sack of Saint-Germain-l'Auxerrois and the pillaging of Notre Dame and the episcopal palace of Quelen in February, 1831, put an abrupt end to the conciliatory gestures of the Archbishop of Paris. It was one thing to endure the ravages committed during the revolutionary days of 1830; it was quite another to forgive an organized government for permitting such outrages in 1831. Except for a brief reconciliation following the attempt on the king's life in 1835, Hyacinthe de Quelen resolutely refused to compromise with the Orleanist monarchy.[33] In the Gironde thefts continued to distress the Archbishop of Bordeaux, in spite of strictest admonitions to the clergy. Instead of blaming the civil authorities, however, Cheverus put the problem squarely in the province of his pastors; sacred vessels and other objects of value were to be kept in the rectory. "With prudent measures the malefactors will grow discouraged," he assured them. It was the clergy's duty not to expose criminals to the hope of success.[34] The poor could not be blamed for the terrible misery. "What will this winter be!" Cheverus exclaimed to Bonneuil. "Commerce does not exist, business failures without number. Let us have faith in Providence."[35] They were in the hands of God, not the civil authorities from whom "neither the clergy nor the religious communities have experienced anything annoying."

His own situation was financially much more difficult. His revenues were reduced by more than a third since the loss of his other titles. Yet because the Council of the Gironde granted him his customary supplement of 8,000 francs he was expected to maintain the same kind of house as before. Meanwhile the needs of the poor had increased.[36] Writing to Boston in those years after 1830 he confessed:

> Since the events of July, 1830, my situation is altered. Some of my honors and titles gone, my income reduced over half, etc., etc. These, I am sure, have not caused me a moment of regret but my charge has borne heavier, my ministry is arduous & surmounted by many difficulties.

Then he added, "I cannot complain. I am still loved & respected as in Boston, more than I deserve."[37]

It was quite true, that he was loved and respected; but it was because he deserved to be. His acquiescence in the exigencies of the changed situation was not dictated by expediency, cowardice, or ambition. He accepted the curtailment of the accessories of worship in order to preserve the right to worship and to prevent the profanation of holy things. He never ceded an inch on matters of principle. When the mayor tried to prevail upon him to accord Christian rites to a man killed in a duel, Cheverus replied bluntly:

> I deplore with you the fatal duel. . . . The respectable pastor of Notre Dame shares these sentiments. But the clear and precise laws of the Church permit neither him, nor me, nor any other Catholic priest to celebrate a religious ceremony. . . . I hear threats are made. As for you, it suffices to inform you in order to prevent disturbing the peace or violating the rights of religious freedom.[38]

Again, when the mayor arrogantly demanded action against a priest who allegedly offended a member of the National Guard during a public religious ceremony, Cheverus replied briefly but equably, "I saw Roche the day after the procession and made some observations to him on this act of vivacity. I have his assurance that a similar misdemeanor will not happen again."[39] He had no intention of being provoked. He was still the same man who could parry an insolent criticism in the old days with the calm rejoinder, "I thank God, Sir, that He has given me the grace not to reply to you in the tone in which you have spoken to me."[40]

Cheverus made no effort, either, to disguise the sympathy he felt as a man and priest for the unfortunate Duchesse de Berry while she was imprisoned at Blaye during the winter of 1832–1833. Her presence in the Gironde certainly resurrected political animosities. Although the announcement to the Chambers of Charles X's abdication on August 3, 1830, made no mention of the Duc de Bordeaux, it was no secret that Charles had briefly hoped to abdicate in favor of the son of the Duchesse de Berry. The whereabouts of the duchess herself kept alive rumors of Carlist risings and the conduct of that lady during the year following the July upheaval was a subject fraught with implications both political and social.

The Duchesse de Berry had gone to England with the royal family but she had not remained there. In accordance with a plan devised at Bath, she left London for the continent in June, 1831, and spent the following winter in Italy.[41] A French priest in Rome who was devoted to the duchess later claimed that Cardinal de Rohan told him on January 12 that the duchess had secretly married an Italian Comte Hector Luchesi-Palli. At the time the Abbé Germain Sabatier attached little importance to the news; he was more interested in the possibility that the plot to restore the Bourbons might fail.[42] And fail it did. After hurriedly passing through Toulouse, Agen, Bergerac, Libourne, and Blaye, she reached Lege in late May. With the collapse of the rising she took refuge in Nantes where she was finally betrayed to the Prefect of Loire-Interieure by a former member of her suite on November 6, 1832.[43] From the moment the news of her capture appeared in the Saturday issue of the *Indicateur* on November 10 the excitement in Bordeaux knew no bounds. The *Mémorial* was a day late with the "Capture de Caroline Berry et autres conspirateurs legitimistes" but in succeeding issues talked of little else.

A veritable war of gazettes then ensued. The *Indicateur* of November 11 editorialized on the capture:

> The legitimists of all countries will see in it the end of their bellicose dreams and chimerical hopes; all of France sees in it the gage of her future tranquillity and the prelude of the union and concord which must assure her prosperity. Let us congratulate ourselves, in the name of humanity, on the end of the cruel as well as useless war which, for two years, the July Revolution has had the patience and long-suffering to allow to be made by the incorrigible partisans of the fallen dynasty.

The *Mémorial* two days later, on printing the news that the Duchesse de Berry was to be imprisoned at Blaye, deplored the choice as a great triumph for the *Indicateur*. *La Guienne,* the flagrantly legitimist paper, taunted the *Mémorial* with apostasy and quoted their praises of the Duchesse on the occasion of her visit in 1828. The *Mémorial* replied: "The difference in the character and conduct of the princess necessarily leads us to a difference in sentiments and language. . . . Our country first, persons next!"[44] When rumors of the duchess' pregnancy began to circulate, the *Guienne* became so incendiary that its issue of November 26 was seized by the civil authorities.

The ordinary Bordelais read the latest descriptions with avidity, especially after the duchess was known to be arriving at Blaye. The citadel was located on the right bank of the Gironde River some thirty-six kilometers from Bordeaux. It had been built by Vauban, the noted engineer of Louis XIV, and at the summit there was an old Gothic castle still standing. The citadel itself was a military colony at the time the duchess arrived, with two battalions of infantry, the 48th and 164th, a detachment of cavalry, and two batteries of artillery in addition to several brigades of gendarmes. The effective force numbered about 900 men; at the foot of the citadel a naval station guarded the approaches.[45] On November 13 Prefect de Preissac inspected the fortification, where General Baron Janin who had once opened a ball with the duchess in Bordeaux was now busy transforming the place into a prison for the royal lady.[46]

The Duchesse de Berry left Nantes on board the *Capricieuse* two days after her capture and at the entrance to the Gironde was transferred to a steamboat, the *Bordelais.* She refused to be parted from her little dog "Brévis" and the *Mémorial* described her arrival at Blaye down to the last detail, including the tiny hat of violet velours, green coat, and white shawl. Baron Janin was reported to have gallantly offered his arm with the words, "Madame, I offer you the protection due to misfortune."[47] Once she had arrived in mid-November, the legitimists of the Gironde offered themselves as hostages in her place, or begged to share her captivity. "If access to Blaye had not been rigorously forbidden, the court would have been more brilliant than the Tuileries."[48] Among those who asked to call upon the duchess was the Archbishop of Bordeaux whose disappointment was relayed to Guadeloupe in the brief sentence, "You must have seen in the gazettes that I was not permitted to see her; she desired me to be admitted."[49]

Although Cheverus was not permitted to go to Blaye himself, the spiritual needs of the royal prisoner were not neglected. Élie Descrambes, the pastor of Blaye, was delegated to attend to those matters, and on November 20 went to the citadel to bless the sacred ornaments sent by the Archbishop of Bordeaux so that the salon of the duchess could serve as a chapel. Lieutenant Ferdinand Petitpierre thought them a handsome present, but Cheverus said of their pitiful simplicity, "Alas, they were thought to be good enough for a prisoner." They were a far cry from the splendor to which she had been accustomed in the old days in Paris, but even in this he tried to comply with the wishes of the government.[50] Adolphe Thiers, the Minister of Interior, had directed on November 18 that everything coming to Blaye from Bordeaux must be examined scrupulously.[51] Cheverus took what comfort he could from the reports that Colonel Chousserie who was in command of the fortress was very gallant in his conduct toward his prisoner.

Early in December the Abbé Sabatier arrived in Bordeaux, and when the archbishop inquired why he was there Sabatier replied, "I arrive in Bordeaux, Monseigneur, because the Duchesse de Berry, whose chaplain I have been in exile, and whose sterile projects I have seconded, is at Blaye. It seemed my duty to share her captivity." Cheverus could not help admiring his forthrightness and told the fine-looking priest, "I praise, I respect your devotion, and I will do my best to forward your desires."[52] For the time, however, the duchess was quite content with the Abbé Descrambes. The first excitement over her arrival was waning in Bordeaux, and in December the *Mémorial* devoted its pages to other matters.

The new year brought a renewed interest in Blaye, however. When Thiers was replaced in the Interior by Apollinaire, comte d'Argout, in January, the latter appointed General Thomas Bugeaud to command the citadel. The arrival of Bugeaud the first week in February caused a frenzy of speculation. If the foremost military man in France was to guard the duchess some new political importance must be attached to the prisoner of Blaye.[53] Coming so soon after the removal of Comte de Preissac as Prefect of the Gironde, Bugeaud's appointment to the citadel was doubly interesting. When Cheverus wrote to Bonneuil on Saint-Blaise's feast he commented:

They have just removed our Prefect. He is generally regretted & by no one more than me, who found in him a very precious support in the actual circumstances. His successor has not yet arrived. All is tranquil at Bordeaux & even at Blaye. The health of the Princess no longer causes any anxiety.[54]

But that was only the archbishop's opinion. When the noted Doctor Menière arrived in Bordeaux on February 17, en route to Blaye, gossip blazed even more wildly.

Meanwhile, Bugeaud suspected that the Abbé Descrambes was conniving with a servant within the fortress to get messages from the duchess to her legitimist friends in the Gironde, and the general complained to Paris. Argout replied on February 8:

> You will have learned, without doubt, that there is a question of giving him a successor. But the thing is more desirable than easy. Agreed upon on the nomination of the Archbishop of Bordeaux, after excellent recommendation, this ecclesiastic has not shown all the reserve becoming to his role. . . . But if it were actually a question of changing him, the princess would not fail to cry tyranny and restraint. She has already declared that she would forego Mass rather than receive a new priest. Nevertheless, if a change should appear indispensable, if it must be effected, it could only be through the medium of the Archbishop of Bordeaux. . . .[55]

All thoughts of Descrambes were thrust in the background when on February 22 the Duchesse de Berry gave General Bugeaud a declaration for publication. On February 26 the *Moniteur* in Paris carried the astounding item:

> Pressed by circumstances and by measures ordained by the government, although I had motives the most grave to keep my marriage a secret, I believe I ought, for myself and for my children, to declare that I was secretly married during my stay in Italy.

When the *Mémorial* printed the declaration on March 1 in Bordeaux it commented, "It is the death blow to the legitimist party; they can never recover from the terrible blow their heroine has just delivered." Her public admission that the arrival of doctors at Blaye had only one meaning ended her political importance forever. Comte de Marcellus could declare as loudly as he liked that he would never believe it until he saw it for himself, the *Mémorial* delightedly announced on March 10 that Doctor Antoine Dubois was joining the other doctors at Blaye for the express purpose of delivering the duchess.[56]

There was no question any longer of detaining the duchess in

France. The *Gazette de France* was quoted in Bordeaux as saying "Liberty has been promised to the Duchesse who announces that she wishes to retire to Naples." On May 10 Bugeaud notified the Prefect of the Gironde, "The Duchesse de Berry was delivered of a daughter this morning at 3:30." The little girl was baptized by Descrambes "Anne-Marie-Rosalie" and her birth was recorded in the Parish of Blaye three days later. When the ship *Agathe* arrived at the naval station the *Mémorial* remarked, "One knows it is meant to take Comtesse de Luchesi-Palli to Sicily." Rumors around the city claimed that Hector Luchesi-Palli was then in Paris, requesting authorization to come to his wife in Blaye.[57]

On May 31 the prefect received a telegraphic dispatch from Argout instructing him to ask Cheverus to suggest a chaplain for the duchess on her voyage. It was known in Paris that General Bugeaud hoped to have a relative of his own appointed, but the government preferred to consult the Archbishop of Bordeaux. The time had come at last for Cheverus to keep his promise to Sabatier. The next day while the archbishop was at the major seminary for ordinations he sat next to Sabatier in the refectory and said to him, "I am charged with designating a priest to go with Madame la Duchesse; if you still persist in your resolution, you are named." Together they went after dinner to the prefecture, and the prefect sent a dispatch to Blaye notifying Bugeaud that Sabatier was to sail on the *Agathe*.[58] The captain of the ship had already received notice from the Minister of Marine, "On the request of the Archbishop of Bordeaux the government authorizes the embarkation of an ecclesiastic on board the *Agathe* to accompany the Duchesse de Berry."[59] Bugeaud was not very happy about the affair, but Cheverus was content that this Bourbon lady should leave France attended by a priest devoted to her interests. It was the least he could do for a member of the family which had done so much for him.

On June 4 Sabatier reported to Cheverus his arrival in Blaye and the archbishop wrote back:

> I received your letter with great pleasure. . . . Providence seems to have destined you for the ministry you are going to fill and it has already placed in your soul everything needed to render it useful and agreeable to Madame. I unite with you from my heart for a happy voyage and for the peace, health, and good fortune of her whom you are to accompany. I would receive with gratitude a small word from you before your departure. I hope nothing will delay it.[60]

On June 8 the *Agathe* sailed for Palermo and the next day the *Mémorial* described the departure, closing with the comment, "The coldest calm presided over this ceremony, and the indifference of yesterday is today oblivion. May heaven conduct her to a good port."

The archbishop's good offices in securing a friendly chaplain for the duchess produced a brief flurry of hostility in some quarters. The *Guienne* imprudently announced the choice of Sabatier in a triumphant tone certain to provoke the rival gazettes.

> Her royal highness has chosen, to accompany her as chaplain, M. l'Abbé Sabatier, and he left yesterday morning for Blaye. This choice, due entirely to the wish of the illustrious prisoner is, without doubt, the recompense for the zeal this ecclesiastic has always shown in defending the unfortunate. One more friend surrounds Madame. May the royalists find here proof that Madame's misfortunes are coming to an end.

The resulting outcry reached the ears of the government in Paris and the Prefect of the Gironde received a telegraphic dispatch questioning the wisdom of the appointment. Cheverus gave Sabatier an account of the matter later, saying:

> Do not let your good heart feel any pain or anxiety. I experienced no unpleasantness in your regard. Some hours after your departure a telegraphic despatch ordered M. le Préfet not to let you embark. This despatch gave a description of you, designated you as being compromised in the plots of the partisans of the Duchesse de Berry, their emissary in Italy, their agent in Marseilles, etc. For fear that the prefect might experience some unpleasantness, as soon as he had communicated this despatch to me, I wrote to the Ministry and took upon myself all responsibility.
>
> I told them that I believed I had complied with the benevolent intentions of the Government in giving the Princess as chaplain a person I knew to be agreeable to her; that I was ignorant of what you might have done in Italy or in Marseilles, but that I believed I could certify that, during the seven months of your residence in Bordeaux, you have been completely foreign to all political intrigue, and that you had limited yourself to exercising your ministry with enlightened zeal and prudence.
>
> Since my letter, neither the prefect nor I have heard anything more said of the affair. Be tranquil, therefore, on this matter and be assured that I have for you the same esteem and that I will always see you with pleasure.[61]

This last loyal gesture on the part of the Archbishop of Bordeaux actually did very little to modify the esteem in which he was generally held. The events of the preceding months had shown the local authorities only too clearly how much the city owed to the integrity and courage of their prelate. The peripheral excitement which briefly focused on Blaye could not destroy the permanent memory of the dreadful months in 1832 when the whole city had faced cholera-morbus together. The *grande peste* which swept over western Europe in the wake of the July Revolution had begun in Russia in 1831. By March of 1832 Paris began to feel its inroads, and Archbishop de Quelen immediately ordered a novena of prayers. Before April was two weeks old he was compelled to notify his clergy that since the epidemic made it difficult "to present all the bodies of the victims to the church," once or twice a week a Mass of requiem should be celebrated for the repose of all who died of cholera.[62] Bordeaux was not yet struck by the plague but Cheverus was already preparing his priests to emulate "the heroic devotion of the worthy Archbishop of Paris and his pious clergy." In a fine pastoral he urged:

> Prayer is the wisest precaution, the most powerful preservative. It places us in the hands of the greatest Physician who alone has power over life and death. . . . Show your flock that fear is unworthy of a Christian. Fear is dangerous — itself a sickness. . . . Remind your parishioners that it is Jesus Christ who is sick in the persons of our brothers who claim our help.

Of course, they were to be practical, as well. God meant them to consult doctors, to obey the sanitary regulations, and to put their temporal as well as spiritual affairs in order. Moderation and sobriety, two sources of virtue at all times, were now recommended above all.[63]

The mayor, too, was busy with preparations. The gutters of the streets were repaired to facilitate drainage; the interior of prisons, hospitals, and public buildings were newly whitewashed. Even the outside of buildings where crowds were apt to gather were whitened. In a general meeting of civic leaders at the Hôtel de Ville plans were carefully made to collect and distribute money, food, clothing, and medicine to the needy. Ten aid stations or *ambulances sanitaires* were prepared in different sections of the city to which the cholera victims should be brought, as soon as the first signs of the epidemic appeared. When Cheverus found that the mayor was in a quandary for a station in Rue Judaïque he immediately offered the episcopal palace, and beds were quickly set up. *Maison de secours* read the sign over the door.[64]

Cheverus had anticipated that fear would be one of the worst aspects of the epidemic, but even he could not suspect the extremes to which it would go. "The houses of succour are houses of contagion and death," people were muttering in panic. "A funeral lamp announces their sad destination. The sick are to be snatched from the bosom of their families. Murderous remedies and coffins await them!" Such rumors, as horrible as they were absurd, could destroy the efficacy of the measures by which the administration hoped to limit the ravages of the disease. Devilish malice seemed to swell the hysteria which "folly and fear — or ignorance and stupidity" engendered. The city officials, apprehensive that an insurrection was brewing, begged the archbishop, "The poor are accustomed to listen to you. We need your voice to help us."[65] Cheverus at once dispatched a strong letter to his pastors which was to be read at all the Masses. Speaking himself from the pulpit of Sainte-Eulalie, Archbishop de Cheverus made one of the most ardent appeals of his career. "Scotch these calumnies," he cried, "Listen to the truth!"

In cholera-morbus immediate aid is of the utmost importance. In each district, day and night, doctors and nurses are ready in these houses of succour to assist the sick brought to them, or to fly, at once, to those homes which call them.

All those who *want* to stay with their families will stay there. But those who *are* deprived of the cares of their fathers and mothers will find aid in the houses of succour. Can a mother, a sister, for example, be more tender or attentive than a Sister of Charity (it is a well-chosen name)? It has been said that these earthly angels distribute poisoned medicine. Holy daughters, pray for your accusers!

Bring me the food, the beverages said to be poisoned. I will share them with you. I will bless with you the charitable hands which furnish them.

When you are uneasy, your eyes filled with tears, your heart saddened, go in the dark night to ask aid for a loved one, or take her to our asylums of charity. The lamp which is distinguished for you by its particular color will no longer be for you a frightening fire, but a star of safety in the midst of storm. It shows you the port where you will find refuge, where you will find a bed of repose and not a coffin.

Have confidence in the administration. It deserves your confidence. Your archbishop and his clergy have had its respect. Your archbishop and all his pastors are members of the general commission by their invitation. Of the six bureaus of the district, one is presided over by the archbishop and three by pastors, and I must particularly express with truth and gratitude that all the authorities, both civil and military, have never ceased and do not cease to show me every mark of friendship and respect.

Let us banish then, distrust, calumny, and hatred. Let us love one another as Jesus Christ has loved us. Let the bonds of love be strengthened in time of calamity![66]

The hysteria in the city streets faded. Inside the poorhouse, where violence of the disease had maddened the survivors to the point of mutiny, Cheverus brought his message of reassurance and consolation in person; again insurrection was prevented. Again, the administration which had invoked the archbishop's intervention was relieved.

Cheverus had written to Bonneuil on May 7, 1832:

Long before you receive this you will know of the ravages of cholera-morbus in Paris & in the provinces where, however, they are less than in Paris. Until now we are exempt at Bordeaux & I hope it will not attack us. Nevertheless, we are taking precautions to prevent the plague, or at least to moderate it. . . . I have hopes that in a few months France will be delivered from this dreadful disease. . . . I have no more fear for myself than I did for the yellow fever in 1798 at Boston & although constantly with the sick (as it would be my duty to be) I was not attacked & I believe I will not be by cholera. Do not be anxious. My health at this moment is excellent.[67]

All of his predictions of the spring were fulfilled by autumn and the archbishop's pastoral letter in November asserted, "We ought to be grateful to the zeal of an enlightened and vigilant administration. But what could these precautions and cares have availed without the protection of Him who is the sovereign Administrator of our lives!"[68] Over in the Hôtel de Ville the city officials wished to add, "or without His earthly representative in Bordeaux!"

Although the ravages of cholera were not so great in Bordeaux as they might have been, the common peril had cleared the air of a more virulent germ, the infectious distrust which had threatened the social health of the city since the fall of Charles X. The ringing words of the archbishop's pastoral in May had been heard in every corner of the Gironde. "Let us banish then distrust, calumny, and hatred! Let us love one another as Jesus Christ has loved us!" Royal prisoners might come and go at Blaye; in Bordeaux, they knew their prelate. The time of calamity, in truth, had strengthened bonds of love.

CHAPTER XXVI

LONG LIVE THE KING

As THE *Agathe* sailed toward Sicily, bearing the lady who had dispelled the forlorn hopes of the legitimists of the Gironde, in the episcopal palace in Rue Judaïque plans for a wedding were rapidly maturing. Ever since January the archbishop had anticipated the marriage of his nephew, Louis de Cheverus, and not always with perfect contentment. The match, which had been encouraged by a local priest of Soussac, involved a young lady of twenty-five whose fortune far surpassed her reputation for beauty, and Cheverus confessed to Bonneuil that although Louis's parents seemed satisfied the archbishop suspected that the young man sighed after the fortune of this only child.[1] By the time the Abbé Sabatier departed for Blaye in June the plans for the wedding were completed, and the Cheverus family together with Fanny George de la Massonnais were already at the archbishop's residence. "The marriage of my nephew Louis seems fixed for the beginning of July," he wrote to Guadeloupe.[2]

The ceremony took place on July 7 in the archbishop's chapel, and Cheverus was pleased to discover that in addition to her prospects of inheriting an estate worth 400,000 francs the bride was a fine figure of young womanhood and graced with charm. The young newlyweds spent most of July in Bordeaux and by the time they departed for Eaux des Pyrénnées their uncle had no qualms left about the match.[3] Indeed, the house seemed desolate when all the relatives were finally gone.

Cheverus was beginning to feel his age. With Louis married, and Adé de Bonneuil old enough to consider a similar step, the archbishop was very conscious of his sixty-six years. The loss of Adé depressed him as much that summer as when Vernou had taken her home ten months earlier. She was eighteen the year of the cholera, and it was natural that she should rejoin her own family now that she had completed her education and was of marriageable age. But Mme Duplessis, who had been a second mother to the girl, and Cheverus who had befriended her since her infancy, were inconsolable. Vernou's short visit in September, 1832, was a dream with a rude awakening.[4] Mme Duplessis had gone off to Auch to visit old friends in an effort to forget her sorrow and loneliness, but the archbishop knew he would never find a remedy for his own heartache. "I cannot tell you how I miss Adèle," he told her mother in January. "It was the 26th of September in 1823 that I was torn from my friends of Boston & it was the 26th of September that Vernou & Adèle had to tear themselves from my paternal arms. I have no friends like you left."[5] When the news arrived less than two years later that Adé was to be married he exclaimed, like any fond grandparent, "May she have a husband worthy of her, who knows how to appreciate her!"[6]

It was pleasant, however, to know that another Bonneuil would still be in and out of the episcopal palace for some time to come. Vernou had brought his young son Maxime to France to be educated, and the boy was placed in the college at Bazas where he could be under the guidance of the good Abbé La Croix. His holidays were to be spent with Cheverus, of course, and the archbishop told Félicie not to worry. "*Mama* Bishop watches over him as over his child at Brookline."[7] Maxime and his friends would be as welcome as Adé and hers had been in days past. After the Cheverus wedding party had all departed the archbishop's visitations took him to Bazas, and by the time he left it was all arranged that Maxime and his companions, Charles and Paul Sarrogot, would come in September for a fortnight.[8]

The older he grew, the more he loved his foster family in Guadeloupe; his letters carried repeated assurances that "neither time, nor distance, nor age have cooled my heart."[9] But in one respect he no longer allowed his heart a hearing. With the departure of the Duchesse de Berry from Blaye in 1833 a door closed; and when the Abbé Sabatier returned to Bordeaux early in 1834, although there was lively interest around the table as the erstwhile chaplain gave an account of the voyage to Palermo, Cheverus advised the young priest to forget the lost cause. "My dear friend," he explained, "this government will endure; and if it should fall, it would not be replaced, you may be sure, by the one you desire."[10] Sabatier was young, energetic, and notably endowed; he could do far more good as a professor of sacred eloquence on the Faculty of Theology of Bordeaux. "Now that there are no captive princesses to accompany," Cheverus said with a twinkle, "I hope that you will be seriously ours."[11]

The archbishop had only to look at his nephew, Amadée, to know what good a zealous young priest could bring in these difficult years of change. "We are destined to live in times of incertitude & danger," Cheverus mused. "But the good Lord watches over us & protects us. No revolution can make us lose Heaven."[12] Amadée was a very constant reminder. The young Abbé George was now chaplain at the royal college of Bordeaux. Although the Catholic chaplain still served a majority of the students, the Orleanist government paid the salaries of Protestant chaplains at Bordeaux, Rouen, Toulouse, and Nantes; Amadée's post was not easy, but he was doing well and had no desire to quit.[13]

Cheverus did everything he could to strengthen the ardor and constancy of his young relative in his efforts to maintain religion in its proper place at the college. Students were welcomed to his country place, where they enjoyed games, refreshments, and the delightful company of their archbishop. Every year Cheverus celebrated the feast day of the patron saint of the school, and officiated at the first Communions of the students. "The Royal College of Bordeaux became a house of edification, a school where religion was not only honored but practiced."[14] The Archbishop of Bordeaux was not a protagonist in the growing liberal Catholic movement which, after his death, was to train its guns on the state's monopoly of higher learning and on the atheism which critics like Louis Veuillot castigated in the University; but while he lived, Cheverus was determined to preserve religion in the college of his own city.[15]

Primary education presented less pressing problems. From the beginning of Louis-Philippe's rule Guizot had organized a system more satisfactory to the Church. The liberal bourgeoisie seemed unopposed to the influence of the Church among the masses. As Tocqueville said in 1834, "All recognized the practical utility of religion."[16] A law of December 14, 1832, dealing with the primary normal schools of Nimes, Bordeaux, Montauban, Strasbourg, Colmar, Versailles, and Mende clearly preserved the influence of religion. Another law of June 28, 1833, permitted the clergy to serve again on school committees, and the Bishop of Versailles urged his clergy to assist assiduously at the monthly meetings. "Zeal is necessary," he reminded them, "and we

must not neglect using all the authority which is in our hands."
Cheverus adopted this pastoral letter of Versailles and circulated it
among his own clergy with the comment:

> I wish to add that the Prefect has indicated to me a desire to
> have pastors use their influence so that the instruction of the young
> may be truly moral and religious. He is confident, as I am, that the
> mayors, the members of the committee, and the instructors, in ac-
> cordance with the clear intentions of the government will be disposed
> to second the clergy in forming true Christians and consequently
> good citizens.[17]

The situation of the minor seminaries was less consoling. The education of the clergy provoked acrid comment in the Chamber of Deputies
where members went on record that the Church must become reconciled
to the century. "The light of our times should penetrate into our seminaries," sarcastically asserted Saint-Marc-Giradin from Haute-Vienne.[18]
The state *bourses,* which under Charles X exceeded a million francs,
were suppressed in 1831 and the ministry took no alternate measures
in regard to the seminaries. At Bazas, La Croix begged to be relieved
of his burden as director of the college and the seminarians. Cheverus
was disturbed, and he wondered how much the financial difficulties of
the school had to do with La Croix's request. La Croix assured him,
"The only reason which determined my request was the conviction of
my inadequacy. . . . It is a matter of conscience for me that I leave."[19]
Cheverus explained the change at Bazas to Maxime's father saying,
"M. La Croix has wanted to leave Bazas for more than two years, and
I have had to replace him. I have found an excellent successor in the
Abbé Martial and you can rest easy." He meant to install Jean-Baptiste
Martial on the day of the distribution of prizes during the fall term of
1834.[20]

By December the archbishop could assure Bonneuil that all was
going well at Bazas under Martial; but it was not a perfect solution.
Martial's educational credentials did not meet the legal requirements,
and Guizot would grant only provisional authorization to the new head
of the school.[21] Vernou de Bonneuil began to question whether the
Bazas institution was the best place for his son. Cheverus replied that
for its culture, religion, and the care it offered the boy he could not do
better. He recommended that Maxime be left there at least until he
made his first Communion.[22] So young Bonneuil stayed on, and on
July 8, 1835, the archbishop told his father:

Last Thursday July 2 I was at Bazas where I went expressly to give first Communion to our dear Maxime & to confirm him. . . . He came to see me the evening before to ask me to give him my blessing and yours, since I represented you to him. . . . I embraced him and burst into tears.[23]

While the government did not restore financial aid to the seminaries it did prevent some other measures which could have harmed the Church. The seminaries at least were not compelled to pay the tax, as some deputies in Paris would have preferred; and the bishops were still in control.[24] The ministry prevented an even more dangerous economy in the budget appropriations for religion, an economy which could have worked irreparable harm to the Church in France. In 1832 when the budget for the coming year was discussed the hierarchy were appalled to learn that there was talk of suppressing thirty dioceses. The constitutional argument ran that these thirty had not been part of the Concordat of 1801; the economic argument, of course, was the reduction in expenditures for religion. Fortunately, from the Church's view, Louis-Philippe and his ministers opposed the idea from the start.

The immediate concern, in Paris and Rome, was for the Dioceses of Beauvais, Langres, and Verdun where vacancies existed. But Cheverus thought primarily of Montauban, his former see, where Dubourg was bishop. Montauban was one of those created by Pius VII in 1822, and Cheverus could still recall the joy of the people in 1824 at having a bishop once more. It was fortunate that William Dubourg was a friend of the king's, and that the friendship dated back to the days when Dubourg was in Louisiana. Dubourg loved Montauban as much as Cheverus did; and when the king offered him the See of Besançon, Dubourg refused to accept until he was assured that Montauban would have a worthy bishop.[25]

It was then Cheverus' turn to act. He presented the name of his venerable vicar-general, Jean de Trélissac, to Louis-Philippe, strongly recommending his nomination. On March 5, 1833, the Minister of the Interior announced the will of the king. Poor Trélissac did his best to evade the appointment. He had come to Bordeaux with Cheverus, hoping to end his days with the saintly archbishop; he was too old, he argued, to take up again the reins of administration at Montauban. But his objections were in vain. If the See of Montauban were still vacant when the Chambers reconvened, there would be danger of suppression, and the ministry replied firmly on May 27, "The king, persuaded that the good of religion calls you to head this diocese, believes that he must reject the excuses you asked me to submit to him."[26] Cheverus explained to Bonneuil in June:

> The dear Abbé Trélissac who refused the See of Montauban has been obliged to accept to prevent the immediate suppression of the See. . . . I will consecrate him here & accompany him to Montauban. Before it is all finished it will take three months. It is a very devoted friend who is being taken from me.[27]

It would mean a painful readjustment in Rue Judaïque. The old friends who had followed Cheverus from Montauban were going, one by one. The dear Abbé Gasc had died that spring, and Guilleux was now canon in his place. Carle was seventy-nine that summer and was very feeble. People might wonder why the archbishop did not move his nephew into one of the vacancies but Cheverus told Bonneuil:

> Amadée is still at the College. His appointements are 2000 francs. That and his patrimony make him rich and he prefers waiting before being canon or vicar-general. I have appointed M. Guilleux who has been devoted to me for ten years & who in case of accident, would find himself without a place or any resources.[28]

The secretary of the archdiocese, Gignoux, would replace Trélissac as vicar-general.[29]

No one could really replace Trélissac in the archbishop's estimation. Only Cheverus could know what the loss of his friend would mean. Since the death of Francis Matignon in Boston no deprivation would press so sorely. Trélissac had been the confidant of his every thought, the depository of his difficulties, his alter-ego. "It is a harsh separation," he told Vernou who knew Trélissac and the place he held. "But I have experienced the most cruel of them & it is necessary to be resigned to it."[30] Only for Montauban could such a sacrifice be tolerated. People must wonder at the good sense of an archbishop who sent from his house the best support and friend he had, while taking in and sheltering an odd and aged priest from America who seemed nothing but a burden. With Trélissac gone to Montauban, the regular members of the Cheverus household would include only Amadée George, Jean Guilleux, and Samuel Sutherland Cooper.

There is no way of accounting for the arrival of Father Cooper in Bordeaux, or for his decision to live out his days in the French port. His life previous to his arrival had been erratic enough to cause little surprise in regard to this last decision. Born in Norfolk, Virginia, he had become a prosperous merchant of Philadelphia by the time

Cheverus learned anything of him. Cooper had entered the Catholic Church in 1807 and a year later entered the Sulpician Seminary in Baltimore. While in Baltimore it had been Cooper's money and expressed wishes that led to Mother Seton's location in Emmitsburg. Cooper was almost fifty years old by the time he was ordained and assigned to Emmitsburg in the fall of 1818. He and Father Bruté had formed with Mother Seton a trio of fervent friendship during Cooper's brief stay in Emmitsburg.

His peculiar fervor and uncertain health led to an existence of frequent change. After serving for a while in Georgia he returned to Philadelphia from which city he talked of going to Boston in 1822. After Cheverus returned to France, Cooper made a journey to the Holy Land, and on his return Archbishop Maréchal assigned him to Virginia; but his health broke down and Cooper returned to Philadelphia, once more. It was after the July Revolution had reduced Cheverus' income that Cooper turned up in Bordeaux, but he was welcomed to Rue Judaïque. "Of all the virtues Saint Paul demands of a bishop," Cheverus used to say, "I have only one: *Oportet episcopum esse hospitalem. At least I can practice hospitality." But Cooper was scarcely a substitute for Trélissac.[31]

The consecration of the new Bishop of Montauban must be as elegant, as majestic, as possible. Old Saint-André was gotten in readiness. Grandstands to accommodate the crowds were erected along the walls, and a platform was raised in the nave so that the two altars used in the consecration might be clearly visible. Cheverus wrote in anticipation:

> I am to consecrate Sunday dear M. Trélissac and Tuesday M. Double, pastor of Montauban, brother of the famous doctor and named to the See of Tarbes. I expect tomorrow & the day after the bishops of La Rochelle, of Périgueux, and Angoulême who will assist me in the ceremonies. When they are over we will find ourselves seven bishops at my table, and perhaps eight, for they announce to me another prelate. I do not know what we will do with the crowd which will encumber the cathedral.[32]

In addition to Trélissac and Pierre-Michel-Marie Double there was, as it turned out, a third bishop consecrated that week. Jean-Pierre Cadalen, the bishop named to Saint-Flour in June, asked Cheverus to include him in the succession of ceremonies, and on November 26, 1833, a third ceremony filled the cathedral.[33]

As the Archbishop of Bordeaux looked out over the crowd cramming the huge church on the day of Trélissac's consecration his own sense of loss was swallowed up in a rush of joy. So it was that Holy Mother Church went on her glorious way. His loyal old friend, waiting in humility, was the eternal symbol, "the victim who sacrifices his affections and his repugnance to the glory of religion." The color, the richness of all the episcopal trappings were only proper. To the sea of faces stretching out to the Great Door he said, "If he appears to you today decorated with these noble insignia of the episcopate, understand that the more the victim is ornamented, the more he is destined for a great sacrifice." As he turned to begin the ceremonies, Cheverus could feel in all sincerity that this was the happiest day of his reign in Bordeaux.[34]

As the last straggler left Saint-André the dignitaries gathered at the episcopal palace. The eight prelates mingled with the civil authorities, and in the dominant spirit of religion and faith political differences were put aside. Lostanges, the Bishop of Périgueux, could not conceal the joy he felt and exclaimed to Cheverus, "Oh, my good father, I truly savor what the Holy Spirit says: Nothing is so good, nothing so delightful, as the reunion of brothers — *Ecce quam bonum et quam jucundum habitare fratres in unum!*"[35] What were the thoughts of the tired but happy host? Perhaps he was recalling a smaller table in Montauban which he and Trélissac had shared, when the sight of three bishops dining together had amazed and delighted Adé de Bonneuil. Or did his thoughts leap the hurdle of twenty-three years to summon up the occasion of three other consecrations in one week when Flaget, Egan, and a reluctant New England missionary had received their powers from the venerable hands of the first Archbishop of Baltimore? No one knows.

But when the days of rejoicing were over, and the bishops had all returned to their dioceses, Cheverus set out for Montauban to install his old friend in the cathedral the archbishop had not seen for seven years. From the moment his foot touched the soil of the diocese their progress was triumphal. At Moissac, the second largest city, the old days were relived and the throngs in the streets swept eagerly about their beloved former bishop. Cheverus had planned to arrive in Montauban itself at night, yet in spite of the darkness and the falling rain the avid citizens kept watch in the streets and at the gates of the palace. His appearance was greeted with an explosion of joy. By morning the crowds presented an unbroken line from the palace to the doors of the cathedral, jostling and vying with each other for a chance to kiss his hand, to touch his robes, even kneeling on the hard stones to kiss the hem of his cassock as he passed.[36]

That night at Vespers Cheverus took his text from the Gospel: "A new commandment I give you that you love one another." With the testimony of their affection filling the cathedral he could not resist adding, "If I were not afraid of blaspheming, I would revise my text and say, 'Love one another as you have had the goodness to love me.' "[37] On his return to Bordeaux he reported to Guadeloupe, "We were received at Montauban with an enthusiasm difficult to describe. Every one asked for dear Adelaide. There, as everywhere after seven years of absence, deaths, marriages, etc."[38] Affection had changed not at all.

Trélissac's return to Montauban was clearly a blessing. Archbishop Dubourg lived scarcely a month in his new see, dying on December 12, after having officiated only once at Besançon.[39] Bishop Trélissac, in spite of his age, labored for a decade to bring new benefits to Tarn-et-Garonne, not the least of which was Cheverus' system of retirement pensions for the clergy. "The Bishop of Montauban is getting used to it there," Cheverus told Bonneuil wistfully. "I must get used to his being away!"[40]

On January 28, 1834, the Archbishop of Bordeaux noted, "Today the old *Papa* of Boston enters his 67th year. . . . The winter of years has not cooled my heart. . . ."[41] It was the birthday of Mme Duplessis, too, and she was to celebrate her sixtieth by dining with Cheverus. They would talk of the old days and briefly forget how horrible the winter was for those who earned their living on the sea. Although there was still no ice, the storms were so tempestuous that no boats arrived or departed from Bordeaux. There was something eerie about such warm and humid weather in January.[42] Perhaps the climate was responsible for the fresh disturbances at Blaye.

Élie Descrambes had not long survived the departure of his noble penitent and when Cheverus sent his nomination for a pastor at Blaye to Decazes on February 6 he added:

> The choice has embarrassed me & I have sought a man against whom no false political opinions could be imputed. I have named M. l'abbé Fortin . . . a wise man, moderate, of agreeable and distinguished form. I hope he will be an angel of peace in the midst of people arrayed one against another. It is proper that the government make inquiries, but as I have no doubt they will be favorable

I desire for the good of peace and tranquillity that the installation take place as soon as possible.[43]

Another appointment made that spring was easier to decide. The reasons for it all appear in a letter Cheverus wrote on April 12 to Adé de Bonneuil.

> I have to tell you of the death of good & beloved Abbé Carle. He died Easter day without any other illness than feebleness. He was in church Holy Friday & Saturday & was beginning to robe for Mass on Easter day when he felt distressed, returned home, and expired sweetly at 11:30. I have named Abbé George to replace him as vicar-general. All applauded my nomination. Saturday evening April 6 after an excess of coughing, being alone in our little salon after evening prayers, I lost consciousness and fell on the rug. I awakened soon with some contusions on the face. They bled me & applied leeches & I am, thank God, as usual. You can be without anxiety.[44]

Adé had known and loved Carle and the letter was written to tell her of his passing. Cheverus made light of his own attack both to the daughter and to her father later that month when he told Vernou humorously, "The contusions on my face have all disappeared and I am as pretty a boy as I ordinarily am. . . . I am really as well as ever."[45]

He was not as well as ever, of course, and his final capitulation on the subject of advancing Amadée was an admission of the archbishop's condition. "I know old age has its illusions," he told his nephew. "The more the faculties decline the more we disguise our impotence. We always believe ourselves capable, even when it is evident that we no longer are." He did not want Bordeaux to suffer if the day should come when he could not properly fulfill his duties. "In associating you with my administration," he said sternly, "I charge you with the duty in conscience of informing me of it."[46] Until Amadée should tell him that he was being a stubborn old mule, however, the Archbishop of Bordeaux meant to keep his usual schedule. As the months passed with only one mild recurrence of the April attack Cheverus refused to worry. "I do not have & could not have the strength of a young man," he said cheerfully. "But on the whole I am well & I manage."[47]

There were other things than the inexorability of age to occupy his thoughts in 1834. On May 6, that year, his friend Bruté was made a bishop in America. The west was filling up rapidly and Indiana was to have a see city at Vincennes. There would be no one left in Emmitsburg of the trio Cheverus had loved there in the old days; but what a blessing that Bruté had remained in the United States. Cheverus had always believed that Providence meant his friend to stay.[48] It was not so clear what Providence intended for Bruté's French friend, Félicité de Lamennais, whose name was the chief topic of episcopal speculation that year.

Although Cheverus did not take any active part in the Lamennais affair, he could not have remained deaf to the clamor in Paris, however faint its echoes in Bordeaux. At the time Lamennais and his associates had instituted the General Agency for the Defense of Religious Liberty, Cheverus had been asked for his paternal approbation as were the other members of the hierarchy. In January of 1831 there seemed little to disapprove in an agency which announced in its prospectus that it had as its principal objects: the redress of governmental infringements of religious liberty; the defense of all primary, secondary, and higher education; the maintenance of the right belonging to all French people to unite to pray, study, and promote the civilization of the country.[49] But the agency founded on December 18, 1830, did not remain purely national; in less than a year it announced its intention of uniting into a vast international federation the liberal Catholics of the western world.[50] The government was embarrassed by protests from England and Austria against this stimulation to Irish, Italian, and Polish dissidence within their respective empires; Rome was visited with complaints; and the prelates of France became increasingly incensed at the ferment provoked in their dioceses.

As a matter of fact, even before the *Agence Générale* was organized, Lamennais had been obnoxious to both the king and the Gallican prelates for his fulminations in *l'Avenir*, a journal launched on October 16, 1830. Louis-Philippe was antagonized by the criticisms of his first episcopal nominations; the bishops were furious at the undermining of episcopal authority for which they blamed Lamennais, and fearful of the schism which they believed his attacks would create.[51] Condemnation of *l'Avenir* by individual bishops led to the decline of subscriptions and to the suspension of publication by the end of 1831; but the hierarchy did not pause with this success. On April 23, 1832, thirteen prelates addressed a petition of censure to the pope, listing fifty-six causes or propositions. Among the thirteen original signers were Dubourg of Montauban and Cheverus' suffragan, Alexandre de Lostanges of Périgueux.[52] Archbishop Paul-Thérèse-David d'Astros was anxious to get Cheverus himself to adhere and wrote on July 17, "You have doubtless more than once wished to see an end to the false doctrines which divide the clergy. . . . It is to be hoped that you will send as soon as possible to the Holy Father your adherence to the censure or your judgment of it."[53] The original censure had already gone to Rome two days earlier, Astros explained.

The Archbishop of Bordeaux was entering the pastoral retreat at the seminary the Thursday that the Archbishop of Toulouse was penning his appeal, and he requested the Sulpician theologians to prepare their opinions on the propositions of Lamennais which were under question. The Bordeaux Sulpicians rendered their opinion on August 15, 1832. That day Archbishop d'Astros wrote from Toulouse, "Today I have received replies from twenty-six colleagues. . . . Twenty-one completely adhere. Three write that they are examining and show themselves opposed to the new doctrines."[54] But it was, in addition, that same day that Gregory XVI issued the encyclical *Mirari vos* which, although not naming Lamennais, condemned the doctrines at issue.[55]

When Lamennais submitted in September, and together with his associates announced the suppression of both *l'Avenir* and the Agency, the matter seemed closed, as far as Cheverus was concerned.[56] But it was not over. In the spring of 1834 *Les Paroles d'un Croyant* was published by Lamennais, and the nuncio at Paris sent hurried reports to Rome during the first week of May. Except for a special grace from God, Lamennais was lost forever.[57] On June 24 the papal encyclical *Singulari nos* solemnly condemned the *Paroles,* and classified its author with the Wyclifists, Hussites, and other heretics.

When the Cardinal Prince de Croij notified the clergy of the Archdiocese of Rouen of the condemnation on July 25 he summarized the developments in *l'affaire Lamennais*. The former Grand Aumonier of the Bourbons explained that the papal encyclical accused Lamennais of presenting temporal princes as contrary to Divine law, even the work of sin and the devil, of describing bishops and kings in criminal alliance against the rights of the people.[58] When Archbishop de Quelen informed the clergy of Paris he said:

> Before knowing the encyclical letter of our Holy Father the Pope relative to the work entitled *Paroles d'un Croyant,* I had had occasion to manifest my sentiment on a book which I saw appear with grief. . . . The judgment of the Doctor of Doctors leaves hereafter no hesitation, no subterfuge. . . . May the voice of the common father and supreme pastor restrain on the edge of the abyss the sheep which strays, lead him back to the fold, or at least preserve from danger all those who would have the folly to follow him. . . .[59]

But when Cheverus received his copy of the encyclical he transmitted it to his suffragans with the simple comment, "I have the honor to transmit the enclosed encyclical letter of the Pope by which he condemns the publication in France of *Paroles d'un Croyant.* This encyclical was addressed by the chargé d'affaires of the Holy See at Paris with the request that it be sent to all the bishops of the Province of Bordeaux." To Paris he wrote as briefly, "I have received your letter of the 14th of this month. I have sent copies of the encyclical to the bishops."[60]

Perhaps he needed time to assess his own reactions; or possibly his fellow prelates urged him to take a definite position in the sad affair. In any case, on September 15, 1834, he did send a pastoral letter to his clergy saying:

> The dissensions prevalent on the subject of the works of M. l'Abbé de La Mennais have, thank God, been foreign to this peaceful diocese and its pious clergy. I have every reason to believe that the last writing, *Les Paroles d'un Croyant,* which we saw appear with sad astonishment, is known only in name by the majority of my colleagues. On the other hand, the encyclical of our Holy Father the Pope, which condemns this unhappy work and the new systems of philosophy, being generally known I thought it needless to address a copy to you officially. However, to imitate my brothers in the hierarchy, and to declare like them that I adhere to this encyclical, and that I receive with respect and love the decision of the sovereign pontiff, I send you this apostolic letter that it may be your rule as well as mine.[61]

As far as existing evidence can prove, Cheverus never touched on the subject again.[62]

It is fruitless to attempt to reach any definite conclusions regarding Cheverus' private convictions in regard to the Lamennais controversy; it is even less easy to suggest that the king's attitude toward Lamennais led to any rapprochement with the Gallican clergy. It is much easier to see in two other developments of 1834 a diminution of the gulf which first separated the July monarchy from the French hierarchy. The first of these was implied in a circular of July 1, marked "Very Confidential," which the Ministry of Justice and Religion sent to the prelates on the subject of episcopal nominations. Before he died Dubourg had suggested the wisdom of keeping in readiness a list of fourteen names to propose, with the approval of the suffragans, for the fourteen metropolitan sees of France. The government now notified the hierarchy that it was most solicitous that worthy subjects for the episcopacy be chosen. "The best means would be to have the bishops themselves notify the Minister of Religion of the ecclesiastics of their dioceses or of any other who seem to combine the highest degree of piety, education, spirit of wise tolerance, and the other eminent qualities which the episcopal dignity requires." The ostensible reason was the avoidance of delays in filling vacancies; but, to the prelates reading this letter, it seemed as well an admirable way of preventing the former complications presented by the first ill-advised nominations of the July monarchy. Whatever the motive, the policy of 1834 was in effect a return to the methods of the preceding Bourbon regimes.[63]

The second cause for an amelioration in Church-State relations was partially the result of Cheverus' own intervention. A royal ordinance of December 25, 1830, had prescribed rigorous qualifications for all pastors of chief cities, canons, vicars-general, and bishops, a law which would have infringed upon episcopal rights. It had, however, remained in abeyance until the year of Lamennais' condemnation; then on December 24, 1834, the Minister of Religion informed the hierarchy that beginning with January 1, 1835, the law would be rigorously enforced. Archbishop de Quelen, on March 1, protested in a *mémoire* to the ministry but his protest began with the argument that the ordinance was unconstitutional, infringing upon freedom of religion guaranteed under the Concordat. The minister replied on March 6 that he would take Quelen's other arguments under consideration but that his observations on religious freedom and ecclesiastical jurisdiction were not convincing.[64]

The Archbishop of Bordeaux made an equally spirited protest, but his *mémoire* went straight to the heart of the matter: the practical effects of trying to enforce this infringement of ecclesiastical jurisdiction. His note to Paris, like Quelen's, had three categories of objections; unlike the note from the Archbishop of Paris, Cheverus' spoke in concrete terms of what the requirements would mean in Bordeaux. After pointing out that bishops alone possessed the responsibility for theological instruction and the right to judge the capacity of their subjects for spiritual functions, he went on to emphasize the impossibility of enforcing the law in the Gironde.

During the three years of seminary, candidates for the priesthood were entirely too preoccupied to have the leisure to prepare for university grades; on leaving the seminary they were too busy with the ministry. Again, it would be impossible to have all seminarians come to Bordeaux to take their grades; travel, living in public lodging, the expenses involved, were all repugnant to the sacerdotal character. And it was all so unnecessary. The bishop already carefully supervised the progress of each student through the system of examinations in use at the seminary. It was ridiculous to say that a thirty-year old man was competent to sit in the Chamber of Deputies but require that a pastor be forty before he could govern a parish! And what was to happen if a bishop's best subjects, either through modesty or from economic impossibility, were barred from advancement because they lacked the university grade? What of the self-sacrificing men who labored in the hospitals, the prisons, the orphanages? Cheverus begged the ministry to forget the ordinance. They might even find themselves embarrassed for episcopal candidates if they insisted on promulgating a measure which was not only a mare's nest of impossibilities but a source of discord as well between the government and the hierarchy.[65] The ordinance was not heard of thereafter.

Cheverus began Lent that year "with courage," and on April 11 wrote to Vernou, "Here it is Holy Week. I am very busy. I am to preach a charity sermon tomorrow and on Easter Monday I leave Bordeaux for fifteen days." In May Trélissac came up from Montauban to spend a fortnight at Rue Judaïque; the seventy-six year old bishop seemed remarkably well and Cheverus was cheered by his visit. A present from Adé and her new husband reminded him that he was not forgotten in Guadeloupe. He resumed the visitations of his jurisdiction with renewed vigor.[66]

Imperceptibly the wounds inflicted by the July Revolution healed, and just as gradually something of the old fervor for national fêtes returned to Bordeaux. In 1834, when the time came to commemorate the victims of July, 1830, Mayor Brun said to Cheverus, "The band of the artillery company of the National Guard want to assist at the service to be held in the cathedral on July 28. They think it would add a little pomp to the ceremony."[67] By April of 1835 the plans for the king's feast day drawn up by Baron Janin, who was now back commanding the 11th Military District, Prefect de La Coste, and Cheverus, were as gala as in the days of the Bourbons. May 1, the feast of St. Philip, was greeted by bells and salvoes of the artillery. Flags flew from all the public buildings, and at 11:00 the services in Saint-André Cathedral commemorated the patronal day. In the afternoon the National Guard passed in review before the assembled authorities, and the gaiety mounted as the hours passed. Soldiers were given extra rations and wine; the poor and the inmates of the prisons were given alms. In the evening all the public buildings added the glow of their illuminations to the fireworks which were set off at 9:00 at Place Louis-Philippe, while orchestras fought to be heard over the laughter and exclamations of wonder as each new burst of flaming particles cascaded across the soft night sky of May. The *Mémorial* had dutifully announced the program with the assertion, "The Bordelais have never ceased giving proofs of good spirit and their attachment for the head of the institutions which govern us." But the celebration that year went beyond mere courtesy.

And so it was that in July the horrible news of an attempt on the life of their monarch, arriving just as the review of troops in honor of the July victims ended in Bordeaux, filled the Bordelais with consternation. The prefect received a telegraphic despatch which had been sent from Paris at 2:00 that afternoon:

A horrible crime was attempted this A.M. during the review. The King of France was not killed although his horse was wounded. . . . The Duc de Trevise was killed . . . the crime was committed by an infernal machine placed behind a window. The people threw themselves in the path of the King and accompanied him to the Chancellery.[68]

La Coste spread the news at the Grand Theatre and Mayor Brun at once suspended all the signs of rejoicing which had been prepared for the solemnity of the day. By 9:30 all festivities had ceased and only muted questions which could not be answered passed from one tense knot of citizens to another.

On July 31 the city received the full details in the gazettes. The list of casualties began to enlarge; in addition to Trevise, a captain and lieutenant-colonel as well as three grenadiers had been killed. The *Mémorial* listed an unknown woman and baby in its account. The king had continued the review with courage and then returned to the Tuileries at 5:00, surrounded by indignant citizens loyally defending him from further outrages.

The assassin had been immediately arrested. It began to appear that he had rented a house at Number 50, Boulevarde du Temple, where for three months in the third floor he had plotted to construct a machine that would discharge twenty-five gun shots through a window facing on the boulevarde. In the explosions he was wounded himself on the forehead and neck. Caught as he was trying to escape by a rope let down from a rear window, he confessed his crime. His name was Joseph Fieschi, but he was known in Paris as Jacques Girard, which was only one of his aliases. The fact that he was a husband and father did nothing to diminish the anger felt throughout the nation at the death of one of their most illustrious generals. Everywhere loyalty to the king, to country, and liberty was fervently proclaimed.[69]

Later reports of the Fieschi attempt on the life of Louis-Philippe added to the lists of both accused and victims. Altogether, on July 28 eleven died as a result of the plot. By September seven more had succumbed. The wounded still surviving numbered twenty-two. To the name of Girard or Fieschi were added those of Pierre Morey and Pierre-Theodore Pepin among those responsible for the tragedy. Subsequent issues of the *Mémorial* were ghoulishly graphic in their descriptions of the infernal machine, and the love affairs of the Corsican criminal whose mind had devised the machine.[70]

Meanwhile, Louis-Philippe wrote to the bishops of France:

> Providence turned aside the blows meant for me and my sons, but if we ought to thank God for protecting us and disconcerting the assassins' designs, what regrets, what tears do we not owe to that illustrious marshal, to his noble companions in arms, and the generous citizens who surrounded us to death.

He claimed the prayers of the Church accorded to all who die in her bosom. Cheverus relayed the king's message to his clergy with the note, "The life so precious to France . . . has been saved. Divine Providence has saved the king and his family." He then set August 8 and 13 as days when funeral services for the victims should be held. The Sunday following would be devoted to special prayers of thanksgiving for the preservation of Louis-Philippe.[71]

The funeral service held in Paris was "a great success." *Moniteur* reported the astounding news that the king had received the Archbishop of Paris and his vicar-general. Nuncio Garibaldi reported to Rome, "Behold Monseigneur the archbishop reconciled to the king and his government. Behold the king for the first time making a public religious act!"[72] A Paris correspondent to Bordeaux exclaimed, "Louis-Philippe has gone to Notre Dame; now we have a complete restoration!" Dissident bishops like those of Meaux, Versailles, Rouen, and Orleans were reconciled to the throne. The *Mémorial* editorialized:

> After the Revolution of 1830 a part of the high clergy stayed attached by sympathy and a just sense of gratitude to a family whose faults sent it into exile. But public displays of such sympathies could

provoke divisions in the heart of the family. To these considerations, so powerful over the ministers of the Gospel, are now joined those of the evident protection of Providence in the affair of July 28. . . .[73]

It seemed that Providence had at last intervened to win over the last reluctant heart.

In Bordeaux, the effects of the *attentat* were such as to remove the last vestige of coolness in the heart of the archbishop. The king was France. An attack on his life struck at the very foundations of all those things the French held dear in common. Mayor Brun was so delighted with Cheverus' letter to the clergy that he asked for permission to publish it. "It would result in great good to the public," he said warmly.[74] Already Bordeaux's deputies were on their way to Paris; the address of the Royal Court to the king was "full of energy and moderation at the same time"; the Municipal Corps prepared an address to Louis-Philippe deploring this attack on constitutional monarchy and liberty, attesting their loyalty and love.[75] The culmination of these sentiments was reached in the funeral service for Maréchal Mortier and the other victims, and the address of Cheverus at Saint-André on August 8 left very few dry eyes.

"Great griefs have no expression," he began, "tears and sobs are the only worthy signs." Then he went on to eulogize the fallen hero, recapturing in words the dreadful scene of the July day. Then his thoughts turned to his monarch, and what the event must mean for them all.

My brothers, my friends, let us shed our tears over these graves. Religion invites us to sacrifice as well our dissensions and hatreds. Let us foreswear all party spirit and be hereafter united together, let us form only one family. I cannot prevent deep emotion, when I think of that heart-rending scene of an august Queen, a model of wives and mothers, receiving in her arms him who is also a model of husband and father, whom Providence has saved from death. . . . Unite, my brothers, unite your tears to those august and royal ones, and pray all together, as I have just prayed during the holy sacrifice, for these noble and unfortunate victims to whom France and humanity owe eternal regrets.

The *Mémorial* the next day printed the complete text of the address commenting, "How at that moment, at the foot of the altar, in the words of the prelate, in the face of a united people, how the King of France was avenged for the outrages which for five years his devotion to the interests of the nation exposed him!" The article went on to say of the whole ceremony, "If it was less remarkable for pomp than that of which the Paris papers gives us the details, it cedes nothing in respect to considered patriotism and sincere devotion which is the gage for the July monarchy."[76]

Considered patriotism and sincere devotion, these were indeed what the Archbishop of Bordeaux had always offered his nation; but for Cheverus, with that particular heart which beat so sensitively beneath his episcopal vestments, one thing more was required: to love his king as well. Now, in August of 1835 he could at last surrender. The sermon that morning at Saint-André bore all the marks of his eulogy of Louis XVIII delivered with such affection a decade earlier at the Cathedral of the Assumption in Montauban. His conscience had won its victory in 1830; but now his heart was full.

It was ironic that this last capitulation, which unlike Quelen's in Paris was to be permanent, aroused for the first time a public demonstration against the archbishop which nearly broke his heart. The lingering legitimist sentiments in Bordeaux deplored his plea for peace and when the *Mémorial* was distributed the next day copies of the speech were openly ground into the mud. Without ever intending to wound the people who had once been his noblest friends, he had uttered words which seemed destined to alienate one of the most worthy divisions of his flock. He burst into tears several times during the rest of the day, and those closest to him noticed a profound sadness in the little prelate which followed him to his grave.[77]

It was characteristic that his letter to Guadeloupe in September made no mention of his grief. He spoke of Guilleux's vacation in Mayenne. "Maxime is with me and will spend his vacation here with the two Sarragots. I have taken a Mathematics teacher for them who comes every day and reviews their studies of the year. . . . They are no trouble," he assured the Bonneuils.[78] The patterns of loving kindness of a life time did not vary. Nor did a conviction reached in mature reflection. Providence, in saving the life of Louis-Philippe, had saved France and in that salvation had pointed the way. It was painful to be detested and reviled, especially when one's nature craved affection and peaceful unity. But in the time left to him to serve his native land, the Archbishop of Bordeaux must cry, "Long live the King!"

CHAPTER XXVII

JEAN CARDINAL DE CHEVERUS

In the month which came between the *Fête du Roi* and the Fieschi attempt on the life of Louis-Philippe in 1835, Charles Dupin had risen in the Chamber of Deputies in Paris to propose "that the government name as cardinal an illustrious Cheverus, such a choice as would honor at the same time France and Christendom."[1] Cheverus wrote in dismay to Vernou, "They talk of making this poor little Bishop of Boston a cardinal but I hope nothing will come of it. Honors have always pained me & would pain me more than ever. The title of your Papa is much dearer to my heart than that of Eminence."[2]

This may have been the first time the Deputies and the Archbishop of Bordeaux had to consider such a proposal, but the government had been hoping to secure the honor for France for many years. Even before the July Revolution Charles X had intended to nominate his loyal little friend. As one of his ministers told Cheverus on February 25, 1836:

> I regret, for the sake of those who now have and will ever possess my affection, that you were not made a Cardinal seven years ago. I wish you, at least, to know that such was the intention of the Prince, who honored me with his confidence, and, I need not add, it was also that of his ministers.[3]

The Orleanist regime had been of the same mind ever since the conclave of 1831, for the situation in regard to French influence at the time of the election of Gregory XVI had been grave. Although France had four cardinals, only two — Isoard and Croij — could be thought of as loyal to her interests since Latil and Rohan had fled after the fall of Charles X. The Minister of Justice and Religion, summarizing the situation later, said bluntly that it was extremely important to reinforce that position. "A prelate, of eminent virtues, acceptable to all parties and opinions, called for this high reward, furthermore, by his long service in the Church in two worlds." Cheverus was obviously the man, and he was proposed for the purple in 1831.[4]

Circumstances were not favorable for such negotiations between Paris and Rome, however, owing to the French policy in regard to the Papal States. The day following Gregory's election insurrection had broken out in Modena and the great powers had intervened with a demand for indispensable reforms in the Italian possessions of the pope. The conference at Rome which found France and England aligned against the Austrians, Prussians, and Russians took place without papal participation; Gregory XVI replied to the demand for reforms by pointing out that such reforms could only be initiated by the pontiff freely exercising all the prerogatives of an independent prince. The crisis was complicated by Austrian action against Ancona in March, and the seeming French failure to dominate the Roman conference in May. When the Chamber of Deputies debated the affair subsequently explosive protests were directed against the Perier ministry and its desertion of liberty and abdication before Austrian power. The king felt compelled to demand that Gregory expel his Austrian "protectors" under threat of French occupation of Civita Vecchia and Ancona. When France did in fact occupy Ancona, the strained relations between Paris and Rome were scarcely conducive to securing a new French cardinal in 1831, or immediately thereafter.[5]

The situation of French influence in the College of Cardinals seemed to improve early in the spring of 1832 with the rumor that Cardinal de Rohan meant to return to his see. The French Ambassador in Rome reported on March 30 that Rohan was disposed to return to Besançon.[6] Perhaps it was a desire to be with his flock during the dreadful days of the cholera; in any case, the Prefect of Doubs reported to Paris on May 24 that the cardinal had arrived that morning in his episcopal city. But this prelate of the Old Regime had less than a year to live. He died the evening of February 8, 1833, in his forty-fifth year; his passing "caused a certain amount of emotion but no special agitation."[7] Meanwhile Latil remained with the fallen Bourbon king, preferring to resign his see rather than return to Rheims, and by 1834 it was increasingly evident that France must act. Gregory XVI was entering his seventy-fifth year, Cardinal Isoard was very sickly and would probably not survive another conclave. Never had French representation in the Sacred College been so precarious.

French strength in the college had varied greatly, of course. At one time she had as many as ten, although prior to the great Revolution seven had been rather customary. In 1791 there were five; but Napoleon had later asserted that France ought to have one third of the total number! Actually, during the Empire the number had never exceeded five; and during the Restoration only once was that number attained, when Isoard was elevated.[8] Gregory XVI had held consistories every year since his election, but of the twenty-three cardinals proclaimed not one had been a non-Italian. It was unthinkable that at the next conclave France should have, perhaps, only one representative. The report of the Minister of Justice and Religion of July 21, 1834 stated, "In such a position the admission of Mgr. de Cheverus to the sacred college is heartily to be desired. The veneration which this prelate inspires would permit him to exercise in conclave an influence no less happy than that of Mgr. d'Isoard." He then gave what appeared to be the major obstacle, "the suppression of the subsidy for cardinals and their expenses of installation." The necessity of new promotions to the cardinalate was incontestable; it inevitably followed that the budget of the nation must restore both the subsidy and the indemnity for installation.[9]

There was the crux of the matter. An ordinance of October 21, 1830, passed in the first fervor of anticlerical economizing, had abolished both the subsidy and the indemnity customary since 1803. The First Consul had ordered that each cardinal be given 45,000 francs to defray the costs of installation, and 30,000 francs every year to keep him in the dignity proper to his high station. The costs of installation for more than two decades were actually paid for by the Department of Foreign Affairs until, at the time of d'Isoard's nomination, the secretary of that office said that since cardinals were ecclesiastical dignitaries the payments should be made by the funds for the clergy. Immediately following the July Revolution the question of these costs was fiercely debated by the bourgeois anticlericals. In reasoning satisfactory to themselves, they argued that the payments were made for dignity, not for any function performed for the nation. Cardinals had fortunes of their own. Furthermore, the salary had never been automatic; a particular ordinance of the king was necessary in each individual case. Clearly, the law of Napoleon was not *absolute* principle. Napoleon had decreed the subsidy at a time when "religion was just being re-established in France." These conditions no longer existed. Finally, since every cardinal was also an archbishop he was already receiving a handsome salary under this latter title. Their logic did not extend, however, to the admission that since the same law which abolished payments to cardinals also reduced the salary of archbishops by two-fifths no French prelate without a private fortune could afford the purple after 1830. Rome knew it, nevertheless, and refused to name a French cardinal until the payments were restored. It was high time the Deputies faced these facts. The Minister of Religion submitted these observations to the chamber in 1835.[10]

The presentation of the name of Jean Lefebvre de Cheverus to the Chamber of Deputies in June, 1835, had almost immediate effects. If his name was known, it was synonymous with poverty and charity to the poor. No one who wanted him nominated to the cardinalate could deny that he must be subsidized. The finance law of August 17, 1835, was the first step in the direction of achieving his nomination. The budget for the expenses of religion for the coming year added the sum of 20,000 francs to raise the salaries of the Cardinal-Archbishops of Rouen and Auch to 25,000 francs. It was in effect an appropriation for the former subsidy granted under the Empire and the Restoration. True, the amount fell short of the 30,000 francs which they had received independent of any other salary, and merely restored their salaries as archbishops. But the principle was admitted that the first deprivations under the July Monarchy no longer prevailed. The "observations" appended to the budget for religion explained:

> The interests of the Catholic religion as a political factor oppose that France should remain a stranger to the election of popes. However, the Court of Rome is not disposed to confer the dignity of cardinal unless the assurance of a revenue of 25,000 francs is returned to them. This was the salary for archbishops until the Ordinance of 1830. . . . The salary of archbishops having been reduced to 15,000, it became insufficient for those who were at the same time cardinals.[11]

The way was now clear to propose to the Holy See the promotion of Cheverus, and with the naming of Cheverus a cardinal it was easy to overcome the other matter of installation expenses. The Minister of Justice and Religion on March 9, 1836, proposed that a credit of 55,000 francs be opened to raise his salary and pay the costs of installation. The committee which recommended the measure to the Deputies was unanimous on March 23. Deputy Antoine Jay from the Gironde had the pleasure of presenting the report which asserted:

> The dignity of a cardinal is the most eminent of the Church. No

one would want to deprive the French clergy so distinguished by its learning, its piety and enlightment. Honors accessible to the clergy of other nations should equally honor the French. Never since the year of the Napoleonic law was promulgated was the sum of 45,000 francs for installation costs fixed upon as either prodigal or parsimonious.[12]

The measure passed the Deputies on March 29, and the Peers concurred on April 26; the measure received the signature of Louis-Philippe and became law on April 28, 1836.[13]

And so it was that the little former *émigré,* missionary to Maine, and humble Bishop of Boston was instrumental not only in restoring the salary of French cardinal-archbishops but in securing for them as well the appropriations for installation costs. The actions taken by the Orleanist regime in 1835–1836 became precedents cited on later occasions. As a deputy from Haut-Rhin put it in 1840, it was not a matter of executing a decree of Napoleon, but of voting a new, special law. But whether it was a new law or a reversion to an old one, it was the personal character of Cheverus himself that had made the actions possible at the time they were taken. "The unanimity of the vote, without discussion, was a striking homage rendered to the virtues of the saintly prelate. From the moment the nomination of Cheverus was proclaimed, the Chambers hastened to vote his budget of installation and his salary."[14]

The nomination of Cheverus was not only greatly desired by the government and popular with the chambers; it was the earnest wish of the Holy See as well. Although France was one of four powers still retaining in the nineteenth century the right to promote or nominate its cardinals, there were two methods of promotion.[15] These were *de Couronne,* a right the king acquired with his powers, and *de faveur,* those promotions solicited from the good favor of the pope beyond the requests of the king. Of the cardinals created under the Restoration, Talleyrand, Latil, and Rohan were promotions of the Crown; Luzerne, Bausset, Clermont-Tonnerre, la Fare, Croij, and Isoard were promotions of favor. If promotions of the Crown were in a minority under the Bourbons, they were even less likely after 1830. "In fact, several times since that epoch the turn for promotions of the Crown had occurred, and the Holy See had passed them over, encouraged by the lack of accord among the Powers."[16] Since Gregory XVI seemed to enjoy neglecting requests of the Crown, the promotion of Cheverus was sought through favor. This was only good sense on the part of France.[17]

When Louis-Philippe requested Cheverus' promotion, therefore, he said that he was

Relying upon the sentiments of affection which His Holiness wished to demonstrate, on the lively interest which he has always shown for the well-being and dignity of the churches of France . . . on the virtues of Cheverus which for so long entitled him to the veneration of the faithful, on the high qualities which he so strikingly exemplified in the heart of the French Church after having edified a portion of the new world, on the wisdom and talents with which he exercised his holy ministry, on his ardent and enlightened zeal for Religion. . . .[18]

The Holy Father, once satisfied that the French legislature would provide the financial means, was quite prepared to elevate Cheverus. As he privately told one of Cheverus' vicars-general:

If I raise him to that dignity, it is not only because the government has requested it. Independent of that circumstance, I take a special pleasure in making this promotion, because it is due to the merits, the virtues of the archbishop, and to the zeal he exerted in the dioceses of Boston, Montauban and Bordeaux.[19]

When Gregory XVI replied to Louis-Philippe on December 21, 1835, he said:

Being equally persuaded with your Majesty that the promotion of so worthy a subject to the cardinalate will result in ornamenting the sacred college, and increasing the splendor of the clergy of France, we most willingly accede to the request and will propose to give it effect in the next consistory.[20]

As one further proof of the special place Cheverus held in the hearts of his countrymen it should be pointed out here that since he was elevated *de faveur* he was entitled to no money for installation costs at all. Before his elevation only cardinals *de Couronne* received their expenses. The last French cardinal *de faveur,* Isoard, had tried every means direct and indirect to secure them, but his costs were never paid. Even though he was French he was always treated as a foreign cardinal. But Cheverus, "an apostle without patrimony and whose fortune belonged to the poor, could not be abandoned to his own resources. He obtained the 45,000 francs, and besides, when the Chamber of 1836 was called to vote upon the matter, the name of the prelate was received with universal respect, and the allocation passed without any discussion, either in the committee or the public session."[21] As the king said to Cheverus later, "I am happy, Monseigneur, to have the cardinalate re-established in France; and in the actual state of tempers, I could only have done it with you."[22]

What were the feelings of the little man in Bordeaux whose reputation was of such moment to French ecclesiastical prestige in Rome, and to the reconciliation of church and state under the July regime? From the moment he learned of the proposal in 1835 he resisted the promotion with every means he could summon. He pleaded with a member of the government, "You have often protested that you were one of my best friends; prove it now by using all of your influence to prevent the execution of a project that afflicts me. I am already too elevated; let me die as I am." To Latour-Maubourg in Rome he wrote:

After twenty-five years in the episcopacy and forty-five in the priesthood, retreat becomes me better than new dignities. My old shoulders are growing weak and the head on them is growing dull. . . . Try to remove this burden.[23]

His compunctions were increased by the conviction that Hyacinthe de Quelen was the man who ought to have been elevated. The strained relations between the Archbishop of Paris and the July Monarchy carried little weight with Cheverus. He saw human affairs with the eyes of religion and not politics, and Quelen was "an apostle and a martyr," a new St. Vincent de Paul. It was mortifying to receive Quelen's warm congratulations when the news of the promotion began to circulate. The Archbishop of Paris wrote, "The church in Paris unites with that of Montauban and Bordeaux in expressing its joy to you and the share she has in the event which crowns on earth so many virtues. I wish you could read in my heart what interest, devotion, and veneration is enclosed there." Cheverus replied unhappily, "It is you, my mind and heart tell me, who ought to have had this dignity. . . . Imagine, monseigneur, how touched, how honored I am by the interest and friendship of such a prelate." The courage and resignation of Quelen in the midst of so many trials alone deserved the purple; that Bordeaux should take precedence over Paris was mortifying. "It is not to me but to him the honor belongs," Cheverus repeated to those who offered felicitations.[24]

He was alone in his protests. It was the king who spoke for the French people when he told Gregory XVI:

Your Holiness could have done nothing more agreeable to me personally and which at the same time could produce in France more general approbation, a more heartfelt and sincere gratitude shared by all classes of society. . . . The sacred college could not open its doors to a more worthy subject.[25]

The humble protests of the candidate were simply not heard, and Cheverus wrote to Vernou, "They wish absolutely (the Pope as the Government) to make me Cardinal and I am to be proclaimed in a little while." And as always when writing to Guadeloupe, his thoughts turned back to the days when simplicity in service was possible. "I would prefer to be Bishop of Boston and have there as formerly my children with me."[26]

In the Roman consistory of February 1, 1836, two cardinals were proclaimed; one was the nephew of the late Pope Leo XII, Cardinal della Genga, the other was Jean Lefebvre de Cheverus. The Italian cardinal received his red hat in Rome; but Cheverus, according to custom, would go to Paris to receive the symbols of his new dignity. The *Indicateur* of Monday, February 15, informed the citizens of Bordeaux:

A telegraphic despatch dated February 13 announced to M. the Archbishop that the brief of His Holiness which raises him to cardinal has arrived in Paris. He is asked to go as soon as possible to receive the hat which two *auditeurs de Rote* delegated by the Holy Father are charged with giving him.

The first symbol conferred was the small cap or *calotte rouge* which was delivered by a *garde noble*. On February 25 the *Indicateur* described the ceremony on the evidence of their Paris correspondent's report of February 22:

Mgr. the Archbishop of Bordeaux arrived in Paris two days ago and received yesterday the *calotte rouge* at ten o'clock. The chargé d'affaires of His Holiness accompanied by M. le marquis Bourbon del Monte went to M. de Cheverus and gave him the purple with the customary ceremonial. He offered him besides a portrait in miniature of the sovereign pontiff and gave him letters from most of the cardinals of the sacred college. The ceremony took place at the home of Mme de la Vigerie, a relative of the Archbishop of Bordeaux. The new cardinal was attended by his vicar-general and M. l'abbé Grivel, chaplain of the Chamber of Peers and honorary canon of the cathedral.

It was a far cry from the ostentation and luxurious elegance of such ceremonies heretofore. The modest house in Cul de Sac Ferou bore no resemblance to the palatial residences where princes like Croij or Rohan-Chabot had accepted such honors. The men attending Cheverus, too, were symbolic of the new cardinal's simplicity. The vicar-general was, of course, Amadée, who would have been in 1836 the Bishop of Périgueux if his uncle had not resisted this promotion for l'abbé George.[27] Joseph Grivel was just back from bringing the last consolations of religion to Fieschi, whose execution took place that week. Grivel had been made an honorary canon of Saint-André in 1831 and was a favorite Lenten preacher in the churches of Bordeaux. In 1832 Cheverus had asked Marthe-Camille, comte de Montalivet, then in the Ministry of the Interior, to secure a place for this eloquent and exemplary priest in the chapel of Louis-Philippe.[28] Two years later Grivel was made chaplain of the Chamber of Peers. Grivel had been as assiduous in his efforts to help the Fieschi plotters meet death as Christians as Cheverus had been in Northhampton so many years before.[29]

Before wearing the small red cap Cheverus must first demand an audience with the king to secure permission. Strictest usage prescribed that he place it on his head only after leaving the monarch's presence, but he could then wear it while visiting the rest of the royal family.[30] It was understood by everyone that he was only visiting incognito until the actual hat was conferred. It was previously the custom that the *garde noble* who brought the smaller cap should be decorated with the cross of chevalier of the Legion of Honor, but since the guard who brought Cheverus' *calotte rouge* was the Marquis de Bourbon del Monte, Cheverus and Nuncio Garibaldi insisted that he be given a gold cross as only befitting a member of the former ruling family. Louis-Philippe acquiesced but *par exception*, making clear that this was not to set a precedent.[31]

Meanwhile Cheverus had to read the complex instructions sent to him by the secretary of the Sacred Congregation of Rites on the proper procedure of cardinals before kings; and there were letters to be answered. The pope had written:

It is our first care so to form the Sacred College of Cardinals, the venerable Senate of the Universal Church and of the Apostolic See, that it may shine throughout the world, by the eminent merit of its members, as brightly as so elevated a dignity and the decrees of the holy canons require. This consideration had induced us to make you a member of this most august assembly. For your well-known piety, your learning, your prudence, your zeal for the Catholic religion, and your many other virtues, united to an uncommon devotedness to our person and to the Apostolic See, your experience in business, your fidelity and ability, proved in the administration of the diocese of Bordeaux, have placed you so high in our esteem that we cannot doubt your ministry is blessed to the service and honor of the church of God.

In granting Cheverus the special privileges of his new dignity the pope further added:

Looking with paternal regard upon you, who are distinguished by Divine goodness with such eminent gifts of grace, and considering how highly you honor the Roman church of which you are a distinguished member, we deem it not only suitable, but incumbent upon us to grant you [these].[32]

Cheverus answered from the depths of his embarrassment:

We have received Your Holiness' letters with shame and blushes, being conscious of our unworthiness, but at the same time with lively gratitude as a son honored by a beloved father. . . . I experience a feeling of stupor and fear, seeing myself as unworthy as I am, a member of the most eminent college of cardinals of the holy Church. But, placing my confidence in God who is my strength, I pray that He will give me the grace to defend the rights of the Church and of the Holy See and to secure their prosperity.[33]

Then it was March 9, the day of the great formalities. Since it was necessary that a new cardinal enter Paris by one of the ancient gates of the city, Cheverus was staying in Charenton awaiting the arrival of Monseigneur Riario-Sforza, the papal ablegate, who was the bearer of the red hat.[34] In many respects, the personal love of Cheverus for simplicity and the financial situation of an archbishop who gave all his goods to feed the poor changed the details of this particular day of high splendor. Ordinarily Riario-Sforza would have arrived in a carriage furnished by the cardinal; but since Cheverus had never owned his own equipage in his life, the king furnished the carriage which bore his simple monogram and was equipped with grooms in blue. It was flattering not only to Cheverus, but to Rome as well.

The procession from Charenton to the Tuileries, too, would have been more sumptuous. The traditional order of carriages for the entry into Paris called for a carriage of the *introducteur,* another of the queen, the carriage of the king carrying the ablegate and the cardinal, and three other vehicles of the cardinal occupied by his vicars and clergy.

Instead, the king's coach carried the ablegate, the *introducteur,* and Cheverus; three others furnished also by Louis-Philippe carried the rest. This ceremonial was also remarked and recorded by Rome. It was difficult after that to return to the former usage by which cardinals furnished their own conveyances.[35] The arrival of the *introducteur* outside Charenton Gate presented no customary cortège, either. Out of deference to Cheverus he said that the ceremony, where it concerned himself, would also be as simple as possible.

Riario-Sforza received the *introducteur* in the ante-room of Cheverus' hotel and then entered the cardinal's chamber to conduct him to the waiting carriage with its footmen in full red livery. After passing through Charenton Gate the four vehicles drove rapidly into the heart of the city, along the right bank of the Seine, past Pont Neuf with its statue of Henry IV which had been engraved anew with the return of the Bourbons in 1814, past Saint-Germain l'Auxerrois still closed after the sack of both church and presbytery in 1831, the mute monument to the hostility of Archbishop de Quelen toward his king.[36] The little man sitting uneasily in the royal carriage wheeling past these memorials that marked the rise and fall of temporal thrones was himself making history that March morning. The conferring of red hats on French cardinals would never be quite the same again.

The cortège came to a halt before the salon of ambassadors and the ablegate and *introducteur* left Cheverus for their audience with the king. Louis-Philippe, surrounded by the chief ministers of state, stood with head uncovered while Riario-Sforza was conducted by the *introducteur* into the Grand Cabinet. This, too, was new. Formerly the king was covered. The ablegate in Latin presented the brief brought from Rome; the king responded in French. Then the king went to a low Mass in the Tuileries chapel where the red hat reposed on a ruby basin covered with violet silk, on the Epistle side of the altar. Instead of remaining in the sacristy, the ablegate returned to the salon of ambassadors where Cheverus waited. Toward the end of the Mass, Cheverus started toward the sacristy, led by the *introducteur* and an officer of ordinance. Behind them followed Riario-Sforza, Garibaldi, the secretaries of the nunciature, the clergy invited by Cheverus, and finally the laity led by the *garde noble* in full regalia. The procession passed through the sacristy and emerged on the Gospel side of the altar to be on the left of Louis-Philippe. At the door an aide de camp and officer of ordinance went forward to meet the cardinal, and Cheverus was led to the *prie-dieu* of the king just as the *Benedicamus Domino* was being pronounced at the altar. Cheverus saluted the Blessed Sacrament and the monarch, and then knelt to pray on a crimson cushion.

At the close of the last Gospel the ablegate went to the red hat, removed the violet veil, and solemnly carried it to the king where Louis-Philippe sat in an armchair surrounded by the prince royal and his brothers, the chief ministers behind him, the queen and her daughters farther away in the tribune. Then Cheverus went to kneel before the king, and because he was so small a cushion had to be placed on the hassock where he knelt, or his head would not have reached above the top of the royal *prie-dieu*. Louis-Philippe took the hat so long desired for France and placed it on the head of his kneeling subject whose humility had paradoxically occasioned all this ceremony. The harried young priest who had fled to England, the heroic missionary to the Indians of Maine, the beloved first Bishop of Boston, the equally beloved Bishop of Montauban, the tireless and wise administrator of metropolitan Bordeaux, Jean Lefebvre de Cheverus was now a prince of the universal Church under the title of the Trinity of Monte-Pincio.[37] As he rose, removed his cardinal's hat, and saluted the King of the French People, the Church in the persons of the papal dignitaries, the clergy, and the laity rejoiced as did the ministers of the nation. But the tired small man in the brilliant robes and *barette* said heavily to Grivel as they left the chapel, "My dear friend, I fear these robes will consume me."[38]

After the ceremonies in the chapel were over the new cardinal was received by the king in his apartments. With bared head Cheverus made the only kind of speech he had ever known how to make, one from his heart, extemporaneous, simple and sincere:

I beg Your Majesty to add to all his goodness for me that of excusing my difficulty and embarrassment. The eminent dignity for which Your Majesty has deigned to propose me, and to which His Holiness has elevated me, this dignity to which I so little dared to aspire, and which I believe is so little merited, these glorious signs which I have just received from your hand, all this makes me quite confused.

I feel more free and more at ease when I am in the midst of my flock, at Bordeaux. I bless the miraculous Providence which has saved France in preserving the life of Your Majesty and that of your dear sons, when I implore all the blessings of Heaven on Your Majesty and upon your august family.

I restrain myself to assuring Your Majesty, with simplicity but with the sincerity of my heart, of my gratitude and my devotion,

I will manifest these sentiments by doing my best to respond to Your Majesty's intentions. All that our Lord leaves me, of life, of strength, of means in my old age, will be employed with the grace of God to make religion flourish, and to maintain peace and union in my flock, among my fellow citizens. I know that in that way I will conform to the wishes of your royal heart. May the Saviour receive mine and cover with graces and blessings the King and his august family.[39]

Louis-Philippe stood bareheaded as he replied.

Then the cardinal and his party went to present themselves to the queen and the ablegate presented the papal briefs to the queen and to the Duc d'Orleans. In the old days the queen and Dauphin would have been in separate apartments, but the distances were too great, they thought, for the little cardinal and the procedure was happily shortened in 1836. Cheverus felt more at ease in the presence of Her Majesty, knowing what Christian devotion reigned in her heart. He addressed her:

Madame, one approaches the throne with timidity; but when one perceives there piety and goodness even greater than grandeurs one is reassured and approaches with a sweet and respectful confidence, even, to her royal majesty. It is with this sentiment above all that I come to place at the feet of the Queen the homage of my respect. I unite my gratitude to that which inspired the countless benefactions of Your Majesty, and my voice is added to that of all France which praises her and blesses her.[40]

Although Cheverus was now entitled to be called "Cousin" by the king, and to kiss the royal princesses on the cheek, "Cardinal Cheverus did not claim this latter ancient patriarchal privilege." Instead, when he went the following day to take the oath at the hands of the king, he asked a boon of Louis-Philippe. Could His Majesty grant a wish the cardinal so fervently desired, the pardon of Comte de Peyronnet and his companions?

The king was quite unprepared for such a question. Charles-Ignace de Peyronnet was, of course, a diocesan and old friend of Cardinal de Cheverus. But he was also an enemy of the state. After his arrest for high treason against the July monarchy in 1830 he had been sentenced to civic degradation and life imprisonment. In the fortress at Ham he was visited with sciatica, but he bore his painful sentence with noble resignation. "To each his place," he wrote in 1832, "and mine is prison, since God wills it." He spent the long days composing literary articles or even an occasional brochure.[41] Louis-Philippe could not answer a question of such political implications without some thought. He assured Cheverus of his good will and benevolent intentions, but he would not commit himself further at that time. Yet Peyronnet was released that year, and perhaps the request of the cardinal had something to do with it, even though Cheverus was dead when Peyronnet emerged from his "dozen square feet" of solitude on October 17.[42] Peyronnet could at last retire to Montferrand in Guyenne and content himself with his listing in the Academy of Bordeaux as "poet, peer of France and former Minister of Interior."[43]

The first call that Cardinal de Cheverus made after his royal audiences was upon Archbishop de Quelen. Like his request for Peyronnet's release, this act took no cognizance of political sensitivities. Cheverus certainly knew that the brief reconciliation of Quelen with the king after the Fieschi *attentat* was openly repudiated by the Parisian prelate's refusal to call upon the monarch on New Year's Day, 1836. Garibaldi, the papal representative in Paris, had informed Rome on January 11 that this last rebuff placed him in an embarrassing position because of the complaints he had to listen to, not only from the court and the ministry, but from others in religion.[44] On the same day that Cheverus had been proclaimed cardinal, Cardinal Lambruschini who had once served as nuncio in Paris and knew Quelen wrote to the Archbishop of Paris begging him to "destroy the unhappy impression your absence from the court . . . must have produced in the king's spirit." But Quelen had remained adamant on the subject of a regime which he felt was married to irreligion. Let the Archbishop of Bordeaux submit to the Orleanist monarch, if he chose; the Archbishop of Paris could not, even at the price of a cardinal's hat.[45]

None of this mattered to Cheverus. The Archbishop of Paris was the first prelate of the realm, and his friend. Quelen was entitled to the first visit of the new French cardinal; besides, Cheverus wanted to thank him in person for the generosity of Quelen's congratulations. Quelen, on his part, showed nothing but pleasure at Cheverus' elevation. In the days that Cheverus remained in Paris Quelen returned the call and, with an extra courteous gesture, brought the cathedral chapter of Notre Dame to compliment Cheverus in person, in the name of the church of Paris.[46]

Cheverus remained in the capital until the middle of the month and the *Mémorial* announced proudly on March 14, "Yesterday the papal nuncio, the Cardinal-Archbishop of Bordeaux, and several bishops had the honor of being received by the king." He visited the seminaries of the city, Saint-Nicolas and Saint-Sulpice, and the sight of the simple black habit of the young men made him exclaim, "Oh, how I wish I could exchange this red cap for yours!" Was this how Providence fulfilled that Boston dream of spending his last days in the peaceful retirement of a Sulpician house, these heavy robes and heavier responsibilities? He was visited with a profound melancholy.[47]

When all the visits of courtesy and respect were accomplished Cardinal de Cheverus departed for Mayenne.[48] On the left side of the Basilica of Notre Dame de Mayenne a stained glass window later would commemorate the solemn entrance and reception in the square of the Hôtel de Ville.[49] It was the first time Mayenne had received a visit from a cardinal who was a native son, and the reception went beyond description. But when Cheverus mounted the pulpit to speak, he saw only the missing faces. He spoke of death. "It is a lesson for me," he concluded soberly, "that tells me I soon will disappear."

From Mayenne he traveled to Laval to call upon his other relatives and those of Amadée. They stayed from March 23 to 25 with his cousin Julien Lefebvre-Champorin, the son of the man who had helped the young Cheverus escape from Laval forty-four years earlier. Here in Laval the cardinal was saddened, too, by the thought of those no longer living. All those letters he had written from Boston to Mme George, his beloved sister! Now he stood with her son in Laval, his cardinal's array weighing as heavily upon his old shoulders as the thoughts of the past upon his heart. "What does it matter," he reflected, "whether we are buried in red, or violet, or black? How can we attach a price to human things?"[50] But in Bordeaux the papers carried the program for the order of the day of his grand entry. He must push on. All his pleas that he be allowed to return unheralded had been disregarded. The Bordelais would have their day.[51]

On March 29, 1836, Cardinal de Cheverus arrived at the head of the bridge at two o'clock in the afternoon amid the heavy rains of spring. Getting down from his carriage he received the welcomes of all the representatives of the Gironde, the city, and the clergy. In spite of the weather, the whole populace had turned out, and the streets from the bridge to the cathedral were solidly massed behind the National Guard and soldiers of the line who were stationed along the way. The noise of the artillery and the bells was deafening. The procession went, as it had ten years earlier on the occasion of his first arrival, along the *fossés,* up Rue du Hâ, through Place de Rohan, and into Saint-André

Cathedral. Once more the great organ sent its triumphal chords rumbling and rolling among the vaulted arches of that grandest of all naves. Once more the dignitaries took their seats reserved down front. Barrès, who had come to meet him in 1826, had the honor of giving the address inside the church. Once again Cheverus replied. But this time the old prelate could not reach the ears of all that innumerable crowd stretching far beyond and out into the square. The *Mémorial* had to report in deep chagrin the following day, "We were too far away to hear the response that was made and we are unable to give the text to our readers."[52]

But no one really cared. For a decade the deeds of their archbishop had spoken his message of generosity, wisdom, and love. As one Lenten season had followed another, his pastorals had spoken of his deep concern for them all. His most recent one, given just before he had been made a cardinal, reminded them of his perennial admonition:

> Have you ever really meditated on the first and greatest of the commandments of God? Try to really understand what it is to love with all your heart. . . . Remember that without love of God and without fulfilling the duties which He has prescribed, there is no salvation for us. Let us then love this God of goodness who allows us, who ever commands us, to love Him, and prove our love by obeying him with docility.[53]

It was not necessary to hear his words that day. It was not imperative to see the face from which the joy of being home had banished every sign of sorrow and fatigue. The small splash of brilliant color against the gray walls of old Saint-André spoke for itself. It was purest virtue crying in a clear voice: *"Love God with ardor, obey Him with docility, serve Him with zeal; there my dear brethren, is true piety."*[54]

After giving the details of the *entrée* the next day, the *Indicateur* concluded:

> Accustomed to the modest life of M. de Cheverus we would fear wounding his modesty by giving more extended details. It is enough for us to say that that day must have proved to the new cardinal how much we longed for his return among us, and how popular and respected his name is here.[55]

Even if the city could not obey his wishes in permitting him a simple return, Cardinal de Cheverus should know they had acted only out of love. And because Cheverus was never immune to love, momentarily he viewed the red hat with less dissatisfaction.

CHAPTER XXVIII

TO HIS LAST HOME

THE rains which had failed to dampen the enthusiasm of the Bordelais on the day of the cardinal's return were the last remnants of terrible storms that had lashed the seas from March 23 onward. And so it was, that the first news Cheverus heard when the sounds of rejoicing subsided was that of deepest tragedy. On April 1 the *Mémorial* sounded the first notes of lost hope when it announced:

> One is more than ever uneasy about the fate of the fishermen of the Teste. . . . Letters from the various ports of the gulf regard their loss as certain. Several shattered boats have come up on the Arcachon side and corpses have been found on the shores.

Arcachon, across from Cap Ferret, on a sunny summer day was the gayest of seaside resorts southwest of Bordeaux. Merry little craft skimmed the bright blue waters of the gulf while children ran and cried joyously to each other on the white sands which stretched away from the gaudy little town on either side. But the trip from Bordeaux which took fifteen hours in those days, if one stopped at Croix d'Hinx, was taken by others than pleasure seekers. In 1835 Terren de la Roque, a naturalist, had been sent by the prefecture of the Gironde to dislodge a great whale that had come to grief on the beach between the customs houses of the Garonne and Crohot. Others took the trip to visit the castle of Capteaux de Buch and satisfied their interest in medieval architecture. But for most people living in the gulf area life was a serious business of drawing a living from the sea. Croix d'Hinx was a station where fishermen stopped, going and coming, to leave their equipment; the Teste was a village composed entirely of hardy fishermen.[1]

426

On March 23 six fishing boats had left the Teste with seventy-eight men who would never return. After six days of struggling valiantly with the raging waters they had, every one, perished. Twelve had been bachelors, six were married and childless, but the rest were family men and the storm left over 160 children fatherless. The whole village of Teste was plunged into terrible mourning.[2] The city of Bordeaux was roused to a compassion unusual to even that people who had so often witnessed coastal disasters. Every civic device was enlisted to organize means of assistance. Each day the papers published lists of new subscribers to the relief fund. The theater ended its season by a benefit performance for the bereft families; Sunday benefit concerts added to the fund. The city council voted 3,000 francs, and the mayor and prefect worked tirelessly to channel the relief funds. A letter was sent to the Chamber of Deputies bearing the signatures of sixty-five widows, 165 children, and twenty dependents — 250 stricken people begging for help. The *Mémorial,* whose pages during the first two weeks of April were concerned only with the tragedy, announced on April 10, "We learn with pleasure that the Minister of Marine, without waiting for the official report of the events of the Teste, is hastening to send first aid to the families." Louis-Philippe personally gave 1000 francs to the victims. The generous and spontaneous reaction everywhere was heartwarming.[3]

But all of this was aimed at immediate and temporary relief; and Cardinal de Cheverus, who knew human hearts and their lethargy after dramatic and emotional appeals have waned, was more deeply concerned over the ultimate welfare of the destitute families. He had, of course, immediately after the disaster called together in the cathedral a meeting of the faithful to raise money. The Lenten discourses thereafter had been devoted to the Teste victims. To the Teste itself Cheverus immediately sent the Abbé Antoine Dupuch to be the cardinal's "eyes and ears." Dupuch was a man after the cardinal's own heart. He had been ordained the year before Cheverus came to Bordeaux, and since then had served as chaplain to the Petits Savoyards and as spiritual director to the Dames du Sacre Coeur. During the cholera epidemic Dupuch had shown what heroic energies he could summon in human crises.[4]

From Teste Dupuch sent Cheverus a report which the cardinal gave immediately to the Bordeaux papers suggesting a plan of action.[5] It was a public appeal to collaboration with a project Cheverus had already begun to put into action. On the occasion of the solemn service in honor of the lost fishermen, a ceremony calculated to touch the hardest heart, Cheverus explained his plan. An association was to be formed to provide permanent care for the orphans and widows. He hoped to have by the end of May at least 180 associates from the prosperous and kindly families of the archdiocese to act as parents by proxy. Cheverus had shown the way by adopting twenty-five chlidren of his own in the palace whose doors were always open to those in need. "The modesty of the annual contribution, the circumscription of its duration, and the frightful tragedy it would so powerfully help to repair," he urged, ought to make it easy to reach the desired number of associates soon. When the list was complete a ceremony would be held to which all would be invited to witness this wholesale adoption by a generous flock. The funds thus raised would care for the bereft children either in a Bordeaux' children's home or in their mothers' homes if the widows preferred. Even the childless widows and the aged dependents were provided for under this plan of parents-in-love.[6]

It was a beautiful concept and savored of the early Church. Rich orphans of the city, who had suffered the loss of their own families, saw the opportunity as a "sacred right." Even the young students of the Royal College, in addition to collecting 500 francs for the first aid given, adopted an orphan and furnished the expenses of his studies. For his part in conceiving the scheme the Abbé Dupuch was made Chevalier of the Legion of Honor on April 30, 1836.[7] Those who witnessed the success of the plan, however, recorded that it was Cardinal de Cheverus who had "fought for the consolation of all the victims of the disaster."[8]

By the end of the month the Bordelais, like the rest of France, were making preparations to celebrate again the feast day of the king. This time the government's announcement of a new year in the life to which France "owes so many benefits and which Providence has so visibly protected," was received with greater unanimity of good will than ever before. Cheverus heartily told his clergy, "We will celebrate the solemnity of the *fête* of the King of the French, and in imploring for him and all his family the blessings of Heaven, we will ask God to grant the dearest wish of the royal heart — the happiness and prosperity of France." Once again the *Exaudiat,* the *Domine salvum fac Regem,* and the *Quaesumus* for Louis-Philippe would rise from all the churches of the Gironde.[9] Once more the troops would pass in review in the lovely gardens in the spring afternoon, and music would enliven the evening air. The heart of the new cardinal was at rest. Always so susceptible to generosity on the part of others, there was nothing but affection now for his king. Quite apart from all the benevolence of Louis-Philippe in Paris in March, the royal charity toward the victims of the Teste would always stand together with the earlier action of a Bourbon monarch on the occasion of the flood at Montauban. The last *fête* Cheverus celebrated was nearly as happy as those he had so dearly loved when the *Salvum fac Regem* had been sung for a Louis or a Charles. France was truly blessed in her rulers; May 1, 1836, ought to be a day of rejoicing.

In spite of all the confusion attending his new dignity and the vigorous attempts to relieve the misery of Teste villagers, the past crowded in upon the cardinal's thought in a dozen ways. He had found time on April 20 to send word to Vernou.

I have told you of the high dignity with which I have been clothed. I do not need to tell my beloved son that I was far from seeking it or desiring it. They tried to persuade me that it would contribute to the good of Religion & the peace of France. I had to submit, but it is contrary to my nature & exposes me to more display and expenses & only increases my income by 10,000 a year — that is to say, I will receive what I received before 1830, 25,000 francs a year. The costs of the installation, etc. were enormous, and they paid for them. I am therefore no richer, but I am as rich as before, for I owe nothing.

For more than two months I have been agitated, inundated with affairs, visits, letters —. My poor head is not up to it, but my health holds up.

My heart, in spite of all these agitations, is always the same & the old Cardinal loves his children as warmly as the Bishop or rather the Papa of Boston.[10]

Boston was never far from the old man's thoughts; nor was he forgotten there. The Boston gazettes had followed the events in Paris in February and March as faithfully as the *Mémorial* or *Indicateur* in Bordeaux, and when the *Evening Transcript* carried the *Moniteur's* report of February 23 describing the conferring of the *calotte rouge,* the Boston editor added, "Our advices say that expectations are formed that, on the demise of the present Pope — now stricken in years — our enlightened and venerated friend will be elected to fill the pontifical throne."[11] No honor was too high for their former "dear little bishop!" Governor Edward Everett could not deny himself the satisfaction of felicitations and wrote happily, "That you may long live to enjoy in health and happiness the honors of your exalted station and your enviable reputation as a man, a Christian, and a dignitary of the Church is my cordial wish. Your departure from Boston is never spoken of but as a public loss and that of a very serious character." The governor went on to speak of the burning of the Charlestown convent which had recently occurred in Boston and commented sadly, "These things could not have happened in Bishop Cheverus' day."[12]

Cheverus was immeasurably saddened by the news of the anti-Catholic attack on the good nuns he had so happily installed in Boston. Cheverus had learned of the incredible events involving the Ursuline convent from many Bostonians and he wrote to Bryant P. Tilden on February 19, 1835:

> Since the horrid transaction in Charleston I could not feel the courage to write & the result of the trial of the ruffians has heaped sorrow upon sorrow, horror upon horror. Yet I must not neglect my friends. They abhor the savage deed; they, I am sure, blush that an American jury should not do justice. . . . It is sure comfort that a general cry of indignation has re-echoed throughout the United States & has resounded in Europe, but mingled with bitter & unjust invectives against the United States & their government.[13]

When he wrote to the Reverend Thaddeus M. Harris on June 3 he commented, "The shameful and cruel doings at the Ursuline Convent, and the issue of the subsequent trial, have afflicted and astounded me. To this day I can hardly believe it." What had happened to the brotherly tolerance which Catholics and Protestants, led by honorable men like Harris, Quincy, Everett, and the rest, had enjoyed in the old days? He had been rather touched by Harris' request some months earlier that the Archbishop of Bordeaux secure some books for the Protestant minister.

> I wanted to get the two books you desired and I could not procure them before my journey to Paris two months ago. The Rev. J. J. Robertson, of New York, will take charge of them, and I hope you will receive them. I am happy to think that they will be in your hands a memorial of our former relations, and of our continued and mutual friendship and esteem. I thank you for having given me this opportunity of doing something for you.[14]

Young Robertson, who was carrying the books from Bordeaux, was another reminder of happier days. He had been one of Bishop Griswold's seminarians in Bristol when an Episcopalian had courteously offered a Catholic prelate the use of the former's pulpit. The winters of New England had been harsh, but hearts had been very warm then. The cardinal wished with all his heart that times need never have changed. He continued his letter to Harris:

> A dignity which I neither sought nor wished . . . is far from suiting my humble habits and opinions. But considerations of a very high order have obliged me to submit to the appointment. I am confident, however, that you would still find me the plain and humble *little Bishop* of Boston. . . . Remember me kindly and affectionately to your family; to the Rev. Doctors Pierce and Grey. . . . I have not forgotten any of my American friends. . . . It is a treat to me to see an American and above all a Bostonian. He is a fellow citizen and a friend.

This world, in Bordeaux as well as Boston, had enough woe to keep a man humble, certainly. Cheverus had, at long last, been persuaded that May to consider the purchase of his own conveyance. People insisted that his dignity required that he possess an appropriate equipage. But just as he was about to accede a crowd of poor people had assembled in his courtyard, and the money that might have gone for horses and carriage went to the poor. When his relatives wrote in distress after hearing the news, Cheverus denied any hardship. To Sougette he said firmly, "I don't know what the gazettes have told you. . . . My funds are not exhausted. I need nothing; I am rich."[15] As he told Harris, "If religion did not, experience and common sense would convince us of the vanity and emptiness of all grandeur and dignity. They have nothing real, but their cares and anxieties." A cardinal could go without a horse; Cheverus was still the father of the poor.

He was still an assiduous administrator, as well. On Pentecost he had the supreme satisfaction of promulgating new statutes for the Archdiocese of Bordeaux. At last his old yearning to see uniformity achieved throughout his jurisdiction seemed possible of attainment. Like the new catechism and the new ritual, the statutes seemed to emanate from the annual meetings of the clergy, but everyone knew the statutes were "the work of his wisdom and his ardent desire to form a clergy holy and above reproach."[16] For the cardinal, the statutes were the ramparts which were to defend the city of religion.

Unity of conduct will reign in the clergy of this fine Diocese — that unity which honors the priesthood in preserving to earth and to Heaven a single body moved by a single spirit. . . . Everywhere we will see the most perfect harmony, uniformity of principle, and unanimity of conduct. How beautiful the Church of Bordeaux will be, united in discipline as she is in faith and charity, marching along together in serried ranks. How beautiful the clergy of this Diocese, beautiful when seen separately in each of its members, beautiful when viewed as a whole![17]

The statutes were printed by Henry Faye, and the finished work remains even to this day a testimony of the incomparable skill of Cheverus as an administrator. The laws were organized under three headings: divine service, zeal for the salvation of souls, and the ecclesiastical life. These were followed by instructions for the administration of parishes also presented under three categories: the temporal rights of the Church, the temporal rights of the clergy, and the exterior care of religion. The last part of the volume, called "Diverse Matters," furnished a valuable appendix of tables of reserved cases and censures, forms for parish reports, schedules and rules regulating offerings, a model budget, and a model account rendered. In the eyes of the cathedral chapter it was the crowning work of all "the numerous and inestimable monuments of his episcopal administration."[18]

Toward the end of June another attempt was made on the life of Louis-Philippe. This time when the king asked for the prayers of his people Cheverus hurriedly decreed, "The preservation of the precious life of the king is a benefit to all Frenchmen. Let us thank the divine Providence which watches over his days. Sing the *Te Deum* on Sunday, July 10, either after Mass or Vespers."[19] The brevity was due to sheer exhaustion. It was the last decree the cardinal ever issued; when the hymns of thanksgiving rose in the churches of the Gironde on July 10, Jean Lefebvre de Cheverus could scarcely participate for three days before he had been mortally struck down by his old foe, apoplexy.

Cheverus was sixty-eight when Gregory XVI made him a cardinal, and in the ordinary course of events both the Church and the French nation could have anticipated several years of service devoted to the interests of each. A fatal stroke in the summer of 1836 seemed like a premature removal, and the cardinal's contemporaries were tempted to attribute causes pleasing to their own interpretations of human events. Archbishop de Quelen, conditioned by his own sentiments, suspected that Cheverus was unable to bear the burden imposed by Orleanist favor and the consequent divisions that favor must bring to Bordeaux, where "hearts already cooled by some of his words" must inevitably feel Cheverus had succumbed to the flattering recognition of Louis-Philippe. Quelen had seen the cardinal's discomfiture in Paris in March as a sign that Cheverus feared "a new cause for division against him in his diocese."[20] The Abbé Barbier suspected sacerdotal hatreds had hastened the cardinal's death. "The hatreds of priests are terrible," he asserted. "Cheverus died a victim of the hatred of some unhappy men unworthy of belonging to the priesthood."[21] Such judgments might seem reasonable to men who knew the gentle prelate's sensibilities and his pain at being unloved by any one of God's creatures. Over and over again, by his own words, Cheverus was "broken-hearted" during his lifetime. But he did not die of a broken heart; he died of an excess of zeal. The valiant little shepherd whose will had triumphed over emotion for nearly seven decades was laid low in July, 1836, by the heat of his own exertions and the sultry weather, not by any climate of public or private opinion.

June had been a month of terrible heat, but Cheverus had gone about his pastoral visits without any regard for his age or his damaged heart. He had even made a visit to Montauban to please old Trélissac and his flock, who demanded a view of their former bishop in his new regalia.

> There he showed himself more humble, more devoted than ever, preached wherever they wished him to, visited the communities and recommended himself to the prayers of the holy daughters who inhabited them. 'I need more than ever,' he told them, 'the help of your prayers; when one is high on the ladder one risks a greater fall.' But he stayed only a few days among his dear Montalbanais; his zeal recalled him to his diocese.[22]

One of his last visitations in the Gironde had taken him across to Sainte-Foy on the westernmost limit, the same Protestant stronghold which had made the Boston papers back in 1829 when a French item had been copied to describe Cheverus' visit. The report had commented:

> This good prelate addresses us only in the language of peace, union, concord, and toleration. "Do you love one another," said he, "whatever may be your dogmas or opinions? Would that the whole universe was a band of brothers! Such are the precepts of your divine Master! Such are my most ardent wishes." M. de Cheverus in leaving us, carries with him the unanimous regrets of the inhabitants, whether Protestants or Catholic! [23]

Now in 1836 the number of confirmations was larger than ever, and all the people wanted to see him in his new splendor. Day after day, in each of the churches of the various cantons, he had gone through exhausting ceremonies that lasted four and five hours without interruption. At times he had scarcely been able to breathe, yet the old will to sacrifice self for his flock drove him on. When he returned to Bordeaux on the first Saturday in July the old prelate's forces were spent.

Nevertheless, Sunday's schedule called for confirmation ceremonies at Saint-Pierre at one end of the city, and a patronal feast at Saint-Martial at the other. In spite of the protests of his household Cheverus refused to disappoint the Bordelais. As he offered Mass that morning, however, his tongue clove to his palate and for a moment it seemed that death meant to come to the very altar. He muttered in the sacristy, "What did not come will happen soon." The sight of the innocent faces of childhood crowding around him a few minutes later restored him, and the momentary dread that had filled the clergy around him passed.[24] That was Sunday, July 3.

Monday morning the cardinal sent a hasty note to the Hôtel de Richelieu reading:

My dear Félicie,

I need news of you. Give them by voice to the bearer. Shall I have the pleasure of seeing you tomorrow noon with your dear children? Tell good Captain Benquey that I expect him also.

Naturally I expect Henry.[25]

It was signed simply, "Jean." Fatigue or no fatigue, if Félicie de Bonneuil were in Bordeaux with her children and brother-in-law, the cardinal's table would be full on Tuesday. It would never have occurred to Cheverus not to include the captain of her ship, the simple man who had carried so many letters to Guadeloupe for the past ten years.

Two days later Cheverus had the first of the two attacks which were to be his last. This time the mute figure in the pitifully simple bed in Rue Judaïque had nothing to say about the summoning of doctors, who prescribed remedies which they warned the household would not prove permanently effective. Exactly one week later he had a stroke which paralyzed his whole right side and deprived him of his speech. When the *Indicateur* reported the second attack it added:

It seems that the excessive fatigues of his last pastoral visit determined the malady. Last Sunday he was very indisposed but supported by his indefatigable zeal, he kept his suffering quiet in order to assist at the *Te Deum* sung in salute to the King. This unhappy but praiseworthy imprudence will perhaps cost him his life.[26]

Cheverus had known since July 7 that his days were numbered. The *Te Deum* on July 10 was sung not just for the King of the French people; while he still had breath Jean Lefebvre de Cheverus would praise his heavenly King. On July 13 he made one last addition to his will, made his confession to Father Samuel Cooper who spoke the language he had loved so long in Boston, and took a walk in the small, formal garden behind the palace. He had long ago learned to refuse all invitations to stroll for recreation in the charming gardens of the religious houses of Bordeaux. "Since I have been a priest," he was accustomed to say in gentle humor, "I have never walked a quarter of an hour for pleasure; I shall not begin at my age!"[27] But now his days of service were over and he could slowly circle the little paths that had waited outside the tall windows of the palace these ten years. The air was hot and still, but it was good French air with something of the river and the vines of the Gironde rising above the dust and stench of the city.

The next morning at five o'clock the second stroke occurred and he knew nothing of the events which passed around him from that moment until the very end. By July 15 the whole archdiocese understood that "the unanimous prayers of the clergy and faithful are the only hope left." Up in Paris the papers informed the capital:

> Since the beginning of the illness of M. de Cheverus the telegraph daily has brought news of him to the Chateau de Neuilly. It was the first question of the Queen on rising, "What is the news of our worthy archbishop?" We ought to say, to be just, that the Archbishop of Paris often sent to Neuilly to ask for the bulletin of the health of M. de Cheverus. M. l'abbé Guillon, chaplain of the Queen, received a command to have Masses to implore Providence in favor of the august archbishop of Bordeaux.[28]

Inside the hushed rooms of the archbishop's palace Amadée went about his uncle's business with Barrès and Gignoux who had already seen another archbishop die. Antoine Dupuch and Samuel Cooper stood vigil by the bed of the motionless man whose life had been such an inspiration on two continents. Outside, in Rue Judaïque, the crowds milled in dread anticipation, and Lieutenant-General Baron Janin kept soldiers on guard to prevent the people from injuring each other in the frenzy of their grief.

The daily papers gave bulletins on the cardinal's health and on July 16 hope rose briefly. But on July 17 the *Mémorial* reported "Toward six o'clock a feebleness returned, and all hope has vanished." The next day was a sad repetition. During the day Cheverus seemed to rally but toward sunset he plunged into the "despairing state that caused so much anxiety" the night before. In some parts of the city the people were already circulating rumors of his death.[29]

On the morning of July 19 the rumors ceased. When the Mass was being celebrated in his room, as it had been every morning since the cardinal was stricken, at the moment of the elevation just after the words *Quam oblationem tu, Deus, quaesumus . . . fac digneris*, Jean Lefebvre de Cheverus made his last oblation to his God. It was six o'clock in the morning of the feast of Saint Vincent de Paul. The little man of enormous charity had gone to his last home on the feast of his heavenly rival.

The *Mémorial* circulated the sorrowful news with the words:

> Thus passed that beautiful and radiant life so filled with benefactions, love, and mercy; thus escaped from our midst, for a better world, that soul so pure and chaste which has left France and the whole Christian world an imperishable reminder of tolerance and virtue.[30]

The *Mémorial* praised his wisdom and learning, his facility in the classics, in French and English literature, his active intellect. "Monseigneur was one of the most remarkable intelligences of the French clergy," it asserted proudly. The *Indicateur* remarked upon the fine preaching of the departed prelate and listed his good works.

> No man merited more than M. de Cheverus the esteem and affection of men; for, to him, life was all love; he always had ready excuses for the mistakes and weaknesses of human beings; he was always ready to extend his hand in blessing and pardon. In his heart he encompassed all sects, all opinions, all parties; it never occurred to him that love could be measured by degree depending upon character, rank and opinion. Men, as they were, never ceased to be his brothers in Christ. . . .
>
> In an epoch of egotism and intolerance such as ours, the absence

of M. de Cheverus will be particularly noticed. Today, heroism of all kinds is rare. Must we not regret deeply the hero of religion, who, in every hour of his life, in spite of obstacles, fatigues of body and spirit, had only one aim, the happiness of his fellow men?

M. de Cheverus, in the midst of honors, the pomps of this world, loaded with dignities and favors, occupying one of the first places in the hierarchy of the Church, died poor of the riches of earth, but rich in the treasures of friendship which was accorded him by all who had the privilege of knowing him and being with him.[31]

The words of the *Indicateur* remain to this day a remarkable obituary; seldom has a man been so well understood by his own people. Perhaps it was the candor and simplicity of Cheverus in his life that made it possible for a journalist writing in the first press of tragic events to summarize it so exactly. As the bells began to toll the news through the city which had heard such triumphal pealing only four months before, the Bordelais knew what they had lost.

In the days that immediately followed, it seemed that the city could only vent its grief in feverish preparations for a funeral which should be the most impressive ceremony Bordeaux had ever witnessed. The prefect telegraphed immediately to Paris for permission to bury Cheverus in Saint-André, and the ministry telegraphed back a prompt permission. Comte de Preissac who was back in office at the prefecture sent the news over to the vicars-general on July 22 and received their grateful response, "Since it was your immediate intervention which secured this favor for us, please accept our gratitude. All the clergy share it."[32]

Over at the National Guard quarters every man was getting ready. The officers said, "The profound veneration our people have always manifested . . . dispenses the commanding officer from appealing to the zeal of his comrades. All will be proud to accompany to his last home the man who did everything for his brothers and nothing for himself."[33] The cavalry squadron would be mounted; the entire corps, its officers wearing crepe on their arms, would meet at seven sharp in the morning at Cours de Tourney. A battalion would stand guard at the cathedral door.

The 11th Military District was indignant at the suggestion from the vicars-general that a mere fifty men be furnished. Not only would half of Battalion 58 be at Saint-André at seven to keep solemn guard until the ceremonies were over; the cavalry, artillery, sappers, troopers, marines, and grenadiers with regimental band would stand in battle formation at Place Dauphine and at the right and head of Rue de L'Intendance. Cannon would be fired twelve rounds at eight in the morning, and again when the catafalque arrived at Place de Bourgogne, and at the moment of inhumation. In addition the artillery would fire three salvoes, twelve each time. Baron Janin knew how to honor an old friend.[34]

The clergy had been officially notified of the date of the funeral with the words, "The first need of our hearts is to insure for the remains of him we mourn all the honor that piety . . . can procure."[35] The same invitation was sent to the suffragan bishops and to Cardinal Isoard of Auch. To Trélissac in Montauban his old colleagues wrote a more personal message. "You above all, Monseigneur, we think of in our grief. Please come. It would be a consolation to us and all the clergy would be grateful."[36] Of the prelates invited only the Bishops of Rochelle and Périgueux were well enough or free to leave their duties. Old Bishop Trélissac was in the midst of the ecclesiastical retreat at Montauban and he knew the heart of Cheverus in these matters. With the closing of the retreat the Cathedral of the Assumption would give Cheverus its own testimonial on July 27. The eulogy of the Bishop of Montauban left no doubt of the place the Archbishop of Bordeaux had held in his heart.[37]

Bishop Gousset of Périgueux in accepting his invitation added, "What ought to console you, Messieurs, is the confidence we have, confidence so well-founded, that this holy Cardinal . . . will obtain from our Lord for bishops everywhere that apostolic spirit, that spirit of gentleness and charity which was a model to his flock and the most beautiful ornament of the Church."[38] Thomas-Marie-Joseph Gousset, the celebrated propagator of the doctrines of St. Alphonse de Liguori, would himself be a cardinal one day. Cheverus had honored him with his "light and experience," and Gousset felt that not only Bordeaux, the Gironde, and France had suffered an irreparable loss, the whole Roman Church should mourn him as well. He felt privileged indeed, he said gratefully, to walk in that cortège of July 26, 1836.

On Saturday Saint-André was prepared for the last rites. Sunday's office was sung in the Chapel of the Sacred Heart where Cheverus was to rest. That night his remains were moved to the cathedral. On Monday morning Masses rose from the four lateral altars; at three the chapter chanted Vespers; at four they were joined in Matins by the clergy of the parishes; at nine the chapter sang Lauds alone. Throughout the six districts of Bordeaux that Monday night the

Sisters of Charity were distributing bread among the poor at the instructions of the cardinal's relatives. The next morning at eight o'clock the body of the cardinal began its last tour of the city where he was so beloved. Bishop Clement Villecourt of Rochelle missed the first part of the procession because his carriage had broken down *en route* but he would atone by the brilliant eulogy he was to deliver a month later.[39] Through Rue Rohan, Allées d'Albert, Place Dauphine, and the route usually followed by Corpus Christi processions, they moved; then back to Saint-André by Rue Ségur and des Minimes. Because everyone knew whom Monseigneur de Cheverus had always honored most, at the head of the procession, just behind the military, marched the poor of thirteen parishes, fifty-two clothed in white tunics and bearing torches to light their friend's way home.[40] The legitimists, their pique of earlier months forgotten, marched with the rest. Although feeble and trembling with ague, Auguste-Simon Ravez was there. A deputy from the Gironde almost from the start of the Restoration era, Ravez had presided over the Chamber of Deputies until made a peer by Charles X in 1828. Like Cheverus, he had been deprived of his peerage in 1830 but not of his sentiments toward the Bourbons. Now in 1836 veneration and love for Cheverus gave Ravez energy enough to surmount his illness and pay last homage to the prelate whose soul had known no lasting politics. The *Indicateur* of July 27 gave a full description of the procession and when the item was copied in the Boston *Evening Transcript* even the American friends of Boston's first bishop could follow the events of that day almost step by step.

Never before have we beheld a funeral more grand, more solemn, more effective; never has any public occurrence gathered together, in our city, a concourse so immense. The most moderate computation gives 24,000 persons, of both sexes, as the number who thronged the streets through which the procession passed.

From 6 o'clock in the morning these streets were crowded; the windows, balconies, and roofs were alive with deeply interested spectators. Calmness and resignation were in every countenance, and the silence of grief pervaded the whole of this vast assemblage.

As the eighth hour pealed from the tower of the cathedral, a detachment of National Guards, on horseback, with the Lieutenant General of the eleventh division and his staff at their head, began their solemn march. They were followed by muffled drums, and the bands of the civic militia.

The description continued with a complete list of all the groups who made up the gigantic procession, then concluded:

> The procession return to the cathedral at 10 o'clock. The body was deposited upon a platform covered with black and white draperies, and surrounded by a thousand lighted tapers. For ages the ancient cathedral has not beheld a ceremonial of such mournful and solemn grandeur.
>
> Now the tapers are extinguished; the chant has ceased; the remains of the Cardinal Archbishop de Cheverus repose in the chapel of the Sacred Heart. Disturb not the ashes of him who would have desired to sleep by the side of the poor in some humble country burial place.[41]

The ashes were disturbed, of course, by a grateful and loving city which built their cardinal a magnificent tomb in the nave of Saint-André. And the eulogy pronounced on that occasion was only one of countless praises given by men who had known and revered the name of Cheverus.[42] It would be easy to cull from all these judgments the traditional last chapter of the biography of a great man. But with Jean Lefebvre de Cheverus the summary in retrospect is quite unnecessary. His own acts explain his life more precisely than any secondary comment ever could. His was a life of rare consistency; the last events of those months after he was elevated to the College of Cardinals are eulogy enough. His was the thoughtfulness of a man who in the midst of splendid ceremonies in Paris would take time to search out two books for a Protestant minister in Boston. His was the unstinting sacrifice of waning energies that carried him quite unprotesting through the summer heat to Sainte-Foy. His was the spontaneous charity which adopted orphans of the Teste and gave his last francs to the poor who beseiged his door. His was the understanding heart which, perceiving the human desire for reflected glory, led him to Montauban to share his new-found splendor with old friends. "I am not tempted to go there," he had told Vernou in 1827. "They love me too much and would receive me too well." But in 1836 he could stifle his preference to give a moment of pleasure to simple people who yearned to talk of having known a cardinal as a common friend. His was the brilliant administrative capacity which gave to his clergy as a last will and testament the admirable statutes for the Archdiocese of Bordeaux. His was the warmly loving nature which cherished a "daughter" like Félicie de Bonneuil down to his very last gesture of paternal hospitality. His was the humility which made its last confessor a broken old man like Cooper. For a man like Jean Lefebvre de Cheverus memorials in words, in bronze, stained glass or stone must fall far short. The life he lived towers above such earthly tribute. In the end, we need only give him the one thing he demanded of men — completely compassionate and brotherly love for our fellow men of every persuasion.

NOTES

Chapter I — A Youthful Prior

1. A brother, Julien, was only four feet and ten inches tall at the age of twenty-five. The term *Monsieur* is French usage for the ruling king's brother next in succession to the throne.
2. Bertrand de Broussillon, *Une lettre écrite en 1802 par le futur Cardinal de Cheverus* (Le Mans, 1893), p. 6. Cheverus was the first on a list of forty-four tonsured that day. His first biographer, André Hamon, seems to be in error when he states that Bishop Hercé of Dol conferred the tonsure at the Church of the Calvary at Mayenne.
3. Vincent-Gilbert de Cheverus took possession of Torbéchet on March 13, 1725, and held the benefice until his death in 1755. Jean de Cheverus was nominated to the benefice on September 17, 1779. The details of the connection of the Cheverus family with Torbéchet may be found in the Archvies of the Archdiocese of Boston in a folder entitled, "Notes on Cheverus as Chaplain of Torbéchet by M. E. Laurain, Archivist of Dept. of Mayenne."
4. The tithe varied in France from as little as one-fiftieth in Dauphine to as much as one-fourth in Bretagne. On the average, it more often was one-eighteenth rather than the theoretical one-tenth.
5. Adrien Dansette, *Histoire religieuse de la France contemporaine de la Révolution à la troisième République* (Paris, 1948), pp. 8–11.
6. Today the eighteenth-century episcopal palace at Montauban houses the Ingrès Museum; in Bordeaux the palace is now the city hall or Hôtel de Ville.
7. Dansette, *op. cit.*, suggests that there was a much greater intellectual difference between a parish priest and his flock in the eighteenth century than there is today between a much better educated clergy and their present flocks.
8. The duchess was Charlotte-Suzanne des Nos. Clinchamps was prior of Saint-André de Clisson at the time.
9. There are some discrepancies in the account of the benefice given by Hamon in his *Vie du Cardinal de Cheverus*, pp. 5–7. He states that a lawsuit involving the benefice resulted in Cheverus' voluntarily surrendering his rights just prior to the suit's decision in his favor and gives as the required duty a daily recitation of the Little Office of the Virgin Mary. The documents in the Archives de la Mayenne include a declaration of revenues by Cheverus dated December 12, 1790, showing that he had been enjoying the revenues for ten years in return for the required two Masses. In April, 1792, he received his last revenues from Torbéchet. Antoine de Clinchamps well may have thought of disputing the Cheverus claim, since the king did name Clinchamps on April 16, 1780. But Cheverus took possession on April 29 in the presence of lawyers representing both Louis XVI and his brother, suggesting that the defect in the first nomination had been brought to light that month.
10. A. Grosse-Duperon, *Le Manoir de Torbéchet* (Mayenne, 1905), pp. 29–32.
11. Archives de la Mayenne, E, Fonds Bouiller de Branche, no. 40, certificate of the Treasurer of the District of Laval, July 13, 1792. These archives will hereafter be cited as Arch. Mayenne.

12. Arch. Mayenne, no. 44, certificate of baptism recorded February 13, 1773. His mother's name is spelled "Le Marchant de Noyers" in the register. Cheverus was baptized by René Euzanne and his sponsors were his paternal uncle Louis-René and his maternal grandmother, Madeleine Le Marchant.

13. Abbé A. Angot, *Dictionnaire historique, topographique, et biographique de la Mayenne* (Laval, 1903), I, 654; II, 653.

14. Arch. Mayenne, no. 39. According to this certificate of residence dated February 1, 1794, these were the surviving children. If there were others, they did not live to maturity.

15. André Hamon, *Vie du Cardinal de Cheverus* (6th ed., Paris, 1883), pp. 2–3. The first edition of this biography was published in Paris in 1837, the year following the death of Cheverus. In 1839 this first edition was translated into English in Boston by E. Stewart, and in Philadelphia by Robert M. Walsh. After reading some of the additions and corrections made by Stewart in his translation Hamon revised his work and it went through four more editions in 1841, 1842, 1850, and 1858. For the sixth edition the author again "retouched and augmented" his work. For this reason, the author's belief that he had achieved the ultimate truth, the sixth edition is cited whenever it is a matter of the French phases of Cheverus' life.

　　The many editions of Hamon's work gave rise to some confusion. Originally he published the work under the name of an uncle, J. Huen-Dubourg. When the Académie Française honored the book with a prize Hamon had to go through legal forms to obtain the money. This accounts for the fact that the fourth edition of 1850 was published as an anonymous work and that present-day French scholars who happen to use that edition still cite it as an anonymous work. The sixth edition, however, frankly attributes the biography to "M. Hamon, curé de Saint-Sulpice."

　　The will of Anne Lefebvre de Cheverus was drawn up on October 17, 1776, and executed on March 8, 1784. This suggests that she died about the latter date.

16. Archives Nationales, M.M. 325, fo. 49[10], *Boursiers*, 1778–1789, Collège Louis-le-Grand. These archives will hereafter be cited as Arch. Nat.

17. Hamon, *op. cit.*, p. 7.

18. *Almanach Royal* (1781), pp. 476–477. This system was decreed by the king on August 20, 1767.

19. Gustave Dupont-Ferrier, *Du Collège de Clermont au Lycée Louis-le-Grand, 1563–1920: la vie quotidienne d'un collège Parisien pendant plus de trois cents cinquante ans* (Paris, 1921), I, 472–473. Like Cheverus, Dubois went from Louis-le-Grand to Saint-Magloire. Since Dubois was four years older than Cheverus and was ordained in 1786 it is rather unlikely that the two men destined to become American bishops were ever actually classmates.

20. For a brief account of the suppression of the Jesuits in France cf. Annabelle M. Melville, *John Carroll of Baltimore* (New York, 1955), pp. 17–20.

21. Unless otherwise noted, all of the material on Louis-le-Grand is based upon Dupont-Ferrier, *op. cit.*

22. Hamon, *op. cit.*, p. 10.

23. Dupont-Ferrier comments that even though the Jesuits had admitted some Protestants it was "probably only to convert them!" Cf. *op. cit.*, I, 481.

24. *Mémoire pour M. Gerbier, ancien avocat au Parlement* (Paris, 1775); Bécot, *Gerbier et Linguet* (Amiens, 1863), pp. 3–21; Michaud, *Biographie Universelle* (1st ed., Paris, 1816), XVII, 183–185.

25. Hamon, *op. cit.*, p. 7.

26. *Ibid.*, pp. 11–12.

27. Cardinal Louis-François Bausset, "Notice historique sur M. l'Abbé Legris-Duval," in *Sermons de M. l'Abbé Legris-Duval, prédicateur ordinaire du Roi*

(Paris, 1820), I, 1–219. The friends who came to his aid were Jean-Baptiste Matthiew, and Pierre Mignan.
28. Hamon, *op. cit.*, p. 10.
29. *Ibid.*, pp. 9, 12–13. In the Stewart translation the date is given as July 21, 1786, and Augé is identified as the Principal of the College of Stanislas in Paris.
30. R. Limouzin-Lamothe, *Monseigneur de Quelen, Archevêque de Paris* (Paris, 1955–1957), I, 233; II, 279, 282, 318.
31. Joseph Burnichon, S.J., *La Compagnie de Jésus en France* (Paris, 1914), I, 214–216; André Dumege, *Biographie Toulousaine, ou dictionnaire historique des personnages . . . rendus célèbres dans la ville de Toulouse* (Paris, 1823), II, 1–3. Mac-Carthy was forty-nine when he entered the Jesuit novitiate on February 7, 1818. For fifteen years he occupied the greatest pulpits of France. His sermons were published in four volumes in 1834–1836.
32. Hamon, *op. cit.*, pp. 17–18; Abbé Barbier, *Biographie du clergé contemporain par un solitaire* (Paris, 1841), III, 153; Arch. Mayenne, Livre 237, declaration of revenues of Torbéchet, 1789.
33. Bibliothèque de Nantes, Ms. 673, no. 154. The letter is simply addressed to "Madame" and cannot be identified further.
34. Hamon, *op. cit.*, p. 17.

Chapter II — Non-Juring Pastor

1. Angot, *op. cit.*, I, 43.
2. Dom Paul Piolin, O.S.B., *L'Église du Mans durant la Revolution* (Le Mans, 1868), I, 11; Angot, *op. cit.*, I, 43–44.
3. Jean Leflon, *Histoire de l'Église depuis les origines jusqu'à nos jours; La crise révolutionnaire, 1789–1846* (Paris, 1949), pp. 46–47.
4. *Ibid.*, p. 50.
5. Arch. Mayenne, E, fds., Boullier de Branche, doss. 40. An entry dated May 17, 1791, reads: "The said Lefebvre received in 1790 from the treasurer of the district of Mayenne . . . the sum of 909 livres." An entry dated July 13, 1792, reads: "He received all the quarterly payments missing up to last April but no further."
6. Dansette, *op. cit.*, p. 23.
7. Piolin, *op. cit.*, I, 5–6.
8. The distribution of conventual priories was as follows: six Benedictines, four Augustinians, one Chartreux, two each of Dominicans, Cordeliers and Récollets, three each of Capucines and Minims.
9. Piolin, *op. cit.*, I, 2–3.
10. Leflon, *op. cit.*, p. 56.
11. Ernest Lavisse, *Histoire de France contemporaine depuis la Révolution jusqu'à la Paix de 1919* (Paris, 19—), I, 193.
12. These were Paris, Reims, Besançon, Lyon, Aix, Toulouse, Bordeaux, Bourges, Rennes, and Rouen.
13. The three bishops who continued in their jurisdictions were Brienne of Sens, Jarente of Orleans, and Savine of Viviers. Leflon, *op. cit.*, p. 74, corrects the double error of Mgr. Pisani in his work, *l'Épiscopat constitutionnel*, pp. 22–23, when he gave the number to be elected as 83, and the number elected as 82.

14. André Latreille, *L'Église Catholique et la Révolution Française* (Paris, 1946), I, 102.
15. Angot, *op. cit.*, II, 653.
16. The other two candidates were Jean-Baptiste Basile, a canon-regular and pastor of Livré, and René Rondelon de la Touche, a pastor of Genest.
17. The action of Hercé may seem a trifle odd. His own diocese was suppressed in June, 1790, and on December 3 he had adhered to the declaration of the bishops denouncing the Civil Constitution. He himself proved a most loyal son of the Church. Leflon suggests that Hercé may have been anxious to eliminate undesirable men and thus secure to the Diocese of Laval a good bishop. In the interim before Rome condemned the Civil Constitution Hercé may have felt the interests of the faithful demanded some accommodation.
18. There is some disagreement over the age of Louis-René de Cheverus. Piolin refers to him as a septuagenarian in 1791. Broussillon gives his age as fifty-three and a half at the time of his death on January 24, 1792. Since the marriage of his mother and father took place in 1737 it seems that Broussillon is nearer the truth. Both his brothers were in their fifties, in 1792.
19. Piolin, *op. cit.*, I, 168.
20. Arch. Nat., F-7, 3682[10], Report of Michel Puissard on the disorders in Mayenne, June 10, 1791.
21. *Ibid.*
22. Piolin, *op. cit.*, I, 235, 274. Cheverus' brother Louis married a member of the Sougé-Lussault family and another distant relative of his, Jean-Ambroise Sougé, was also related to the unfortunate dead woman.
23. This *mandement* was dated June 18, 1791.
24. Arch. Mayenne, Livre 10, fol. 27, report of procureur-syndic, July 25, 1791. A document in the National Archives in Paris lists the non-juring clergy of Notre Dame as the two Cheverus relatives, Esnault, Jean-Charles Gahier, and Pierre-Joseph Vengeons. The latter may have been the volunteers mentioned in the report of July 25, 1791. Gahier's name was also spelled "Gehier."
25. *Ibid.*
26. Arch. Mayenne, Livre 10, fol. 100, procès-verbal of the meeting of the electors, August 16, 1791.
27. Piolin, *op. cit.*, I, 146.
28. Leflon, *op. cit.*, p. 83.
29. Abbé Barruel, *Histoire du clergé pendant la Révolution française* (London, 1794), p. 149.
30. Piolin, *op. cit.*, I, 273.
31. *Mémorial Bordelais,* July 21, 1836, "Notice necrologique sur Mgr. de Cheverus par Émile Saladin," p. 1.
32. Barbier, *op. cit.*, III, 156. There is no way of determining the exact date of Cheverus' flight from Mayenne. Barbier says he was in Laval two and a half months. Since it is certain that Cheverus was in prison in Laval on June 20, and went to Paris on June 25, he may have arrived in Laval some time early in April, 1792. Hamon, however, says Cheverus left Mayenne three days after he received notice that he had been made pastor of Notre Dame. If Hamon is correct Cheverus would have left nearly two months before the decree compelling the registration at Laval, which seems less likely.
33. Samuel Knapp, "Memoir of Bishop Cheverus," *Boston Monthly Magazine,* I (June, 1825), 19.
34. Barruel, *op. cit.*, pp. 149–155; Piolin, *op. cit.*, II, 35. The Jacobin request was dated May 8, 1792.
35. Hamon, *op. cit.*, p. 21; Piolin, *op. cit.*, II, 56.

36. Alexandre Sorel, *Le Couvent des Carmes et le Séminaire de Saint-Sulpice pendant la Terreur* (Paris, 1863), pp. 138–145.
37. Theodore G. Lenôtre, *Mémoires et souvenirs sur la Révolution et l'Empire* (Paris, 1907), I, 254–283; Sorel, *op. cit.,* pp. 125–137. Sorel gives the number massacred at the Carmes as 115 and the number who escaped as forty-four, among whom was the Abbé Jerome Noël Vialar who escaped over the wall. Both Lenôtre and Sorel reproduce plans of the chapel, courtyard, and corridor where the events at the Carmes took place.
38. Hamon, *op. cit.,* p. 22.
39. Latreille, *op. cit.,* p. 120.
40. Séance of September 7, 1792, of the directory of Département de Mayenne, cited in Piolin, *op. cit.,* II, 55–56.
41. Hamon, *op. cit.,* p. 23.
42. Piolin, *op. cit.,* II, 588–590.
43. Julien Lefebvre de Champorin was arrested as a suspect during the first year of the Terror, but was subsequently released. He was eventually made a judge of the tribunal of Mayenne.

CHAPTER III — ÉMIGRÉ IN ENGLAND

1. Melville, *op. cit.,* p. 114. It has been said that the Lulworth chapel was built to resemble a mausoleum on the recommendation of George III. The foundation stone was laid on Candlemas Day, 1786. In 1953 Lulworth chapel was restored and the late Monsignor Ronald Knox preached the sermon at the consecration of the high altar on July 11, 1953.
2. A good monograph on the subject is Paul de Castro, *The Gordon Riots* (London, 1926).
3. An account of English Catholic life in penal times is found in Dom Basil Hemphill, *The Early Vicars Apostolic of England, 1685–1750* (London, 1954), pp. 78–105.
4. For a detailed account of the progress of the Catholic Relief legislation from 1788–1791 cf. Philip Hughes, *The Catholic Question* (London, 1929), pp. 152–172.
5. Piolin, *op. cit.,* II, 41–42. After October the deportations of the clergy from Laval took place from St. Malo.
6. Cecil Kerr, "What England Owed to France," *Catholic Emancipation* (London, 1928), Series 2, p. 1.
7. Archives of the Archdiocese of Baltimore, 8-G-3, Talbot to Carroll, June 6, 1791. These archives will hereafter be cited as AAB.
8. Augustin Sicard, *Le clergé de France pendant la Révolution: de l'exile au Concordat* (Paris, 1912), III, 15.
9. Kerr, *op. cit.,* p. 6.
10. Sicard, *op. cit.,* III, 45.
11. Knapp, *op. cit.,* p. 4.
12. AAB, 8-B-5, Strickland to Carroll, November 15, 1792.
13. Barruel, *op. cit.,* pp. 349–350.
14. *Ibid.*
15. Sicard, *op. cit.,* III, 23.

16. Kerr, *op. cit.*, p. 16.
17. *Ibid.*, p. 11.
18. Hughes, *op. cit.*, p. 171.
19. *The Gentleman's Magazine*, May, 1796, p. 849.
20. Archives of the Archdiocese of Westminster, Vol. 47, New Series, p. 221, Cheverus to Douglass, August 31, 1798.
21. Barruel, *op. cit.*, p. 358.
22. Kerr, *op. cit.*, pp. 19–20.
23. Hamon, *op. cit.*, pp. 27–28.
24. Cf. note 1, *supra*. The Weld family had been important in the history of the Church in England for centuries. Humphrey Weld acquired Lulworth Castle in Dorset in 1641, and Thomas Weld was the sixth possessor of the property. Cf. C. M. Antony, "Lulworth Castle; Its History and Memories," *Catholic Historical Review*, I (October, 1915), 250–251.
25. Kerr, *op. cit.*, p. 13. Two of Weld's letters to Bishop Walmesley dated in 1794 are printed in Kerr. The Trappists left Lulworth in 1817 for Melleray in Brittany from which place they later founded Mount Melleray in Ireland, Mount St. Bernard in England, and Gethsemani in the United States.
26. Hughes, *op. cit.*, pp. 167–169.
27. F. C. Husenbeth, *Life of Bishop Milner* (Dublin, 1862), pp. 48–56.
28. Kerr, *op. cit.*, p. 7.
29. Melville, *op. cit.*, p. 36.
30. Kerr, *op. cit.*, pp. 9, 11, 21; Charles-François de Lubersac de Livron, *Journal historique et religieux de l'émigration et déportation du clergé de France en Angleterre* (London, 1802), pp. xiii, 16. Buckingham was viceroy of Ireland from 1782–1783 and 1787–1789. *The Gentleman's Magazine*, LXXI (1801), Part II, 592, reproduced the title page of the Bible printed in 1796 for the French clergy.
31. Husenbeth, *op. cit.*, pp. 48–49.
32. *Diary and Letters of Madame d'Arblay* (London, 1842), VI, 11, Burney to d'Arblay, October 4, 1793.
33. Sicard, *op. cit.*, p. 21; Barruel, *op. cit.*, p. 351; Kerr, *op. cit.*, pp. 6, 26. Oddly enough, the French prelate died in England while Mrs. Silburn spent her last days at Roscoff in Brittany. Eventually de la Marche's body was removed to France where he lies buried in his own cathedral at St. Pol de Léon.
34. AAB, 11-A-D-5, Cheverus to Matignon, June 22, 1798.
35. Kerr, *op. cit.*, pp. 9–10.
36. *Ibid.*, p. 9; Lubersac, *op. cit.*, p. 16; *Dictionary of National Biography* (London, 1890), XXI, 540. Wilmot sat for Coventry, 1784–1796.
37. Sicard, *op. cit.*, III, 31, comments that after the return of the exiles to France their only payment to England for 47,000,000 francs spent on them during the years 1792–1806 was words of gratitude.
38. Hamon, *op. cit.*, pp. 24–25.
39. Sicard, *op. cit.*, III, 19.
40. Piolin, *op. cit.*, II, 3; Hamon, *op. cit.*, p. 25. Neither of these writers identifies the school, and Hamon does not even locate it at Wallingford. Knapp, *op. cit.*, p. 5, says that Cheverus lived with a Protestant clergyman who "had five or six young men with him, preparing for the university." Piolin fixes the number of pupils at thirty.
41. Hamon, *op. cit.*, pp. 25–26.
42. Mrs. Bryan Stapleton, *A History of the Post-Reformation Catholic Missions in Oxfordshire* (London, 1906), pp. 245–247. For the origins of Dorchester and Overy cf. Robert Stonor, O.S.B., *Stonor* (Newport, 1952), pp. 31–32. A Father Bruning was the priest who retired in 1788. Whether Cheverus

ever knew him or not is uncertain, but he did send his regards to a Mr. Bruning by Bishop Douglass in his letter from Boston of August 31, 1798. Piolin spells Davey's name "Davay."

43. Piolin, *op. cit.*, II, 3.

44. Hamon, *op. cit.*, p. 26.

45. Piolin, *op. cit.*, II, 6, 47. Vauxponts in turn persuaded Pierre-Louis Dubourg de la Ferrière to come to the Dorchester-Overy area. If Sougé left Jersey with Vauxponts he came to London on March 13, 1793.

46. Stapleton, *op. cit.*, p. 247. The name is spelled "Valpons" and "Desvalpon" in the English accounts. A misprint in Stapleton gives the date of his death as 1793.

47. The records indicate only that Cheverus came to Tottenham "some time in 1793." The first entry of a baptism performed by him is dated March 17, 1794. Since Cheverus himself spoke of having served under Douglass for two and a half years, and it is known that he arrived in Boston in October, 1796, it seems probable that he arrived in Tottenham near the end of the year 1793.

48. Husenbeth, *op. cit.*, pp. 95–96.

49. Although Tottenham appears in the accounts of permanent chapels, the name of Cheverus does not. The humble priest from Mayenne who later became so well known in the history of the Church in both France and the United States seems to have passed unnoticed during his English sojourn.

50. Kerr, *op. cit.*, p. 22; Lubersac, *op. cit.*, pp. 34–49. The eight chapels included, besides the one in Portman Square, Holy Cross in Dudley Street, Soho; Holy Angels in Conway Street, Fitzroy Square; the chapel of the Invocation at Somerstown; St. Louis in St. George's Field; and others at Tottenham Place, Paddington Green, and the Middlesex hospital.

51. This is a translation of the original Latin of the inscription.

52. The first census was not taken until 1801. At that time Tottenham had about 3000 inhabitants. Baptismal and burial figures suggest there were about 2500 when Cheverus arrived.

53. William James Roe, *Ancient Tottenham* (Tottenham, 1949), pp. 15–24. A facsimile of the Domesday Book entry appears on p. 56.

54. This information was furnished by the curator of the Bruce Grove Museum of Tottenham in 1956.

55. Fred Fisk, *History of Tottenham* (Tottenham, 1913), p. 79; *Old and New London* (London, 1897), p. 554.

56. Francis Bayley, "Chronicles of the Tottenham Mission," a manuscript preserved at St. Francis de Sales Parish, Tottenham. Fisk states that Cheverus hired a little upper room, over a beer shop, where he conducted services and founded a mission. Father Bayley's account alleges that Cheverus received a small allotment from the British government, but his chronicles were compiled between 1882–1899 while he was pastor of Tottenham, and were based on secondhand, word-of-mouth sources. Hamon, who knew Cheverus personally, states that Cheverus refused government assistance and asked that the allotment be given to others in greater need. Knapp, who also knew Cheverus and wrote while the latter was still alive to correct him, states, "His father succeeded in making a remittance for his immediate support, which he repeated for some time, so that M. Cheverus was never under the necessity of receiving any portion of that bounty. . . ." From Charles Burney's letter to Fanny d'Arblay in 1793 it appears that the allotment for French priests was eight shillings a week.

There is no clue to the English family who employed Cheverus as tutor in Tottenham.

57. Chanoine F. Plasse, *Le clergé Français refugié en Angleterre* (Paris, 1886),

II, 304. Cheverus entered four baptismal records, the other three being dated June 22, 1794; June 21, 1795; March 18, 1796. These are still preserved in the Tottenham register.

58. Father Fillatrais served from 1796–1801; Father Salmon from 1801–1803; and Father le Tellier from 1803–1823. In the English records the first name is spelled "Filliatrais" but since the French records omit the second "i" the latter form has been used in the present text. Contemporaries of Cheverus from Mayenne of that name were: Jean-Marie-Simeon Laigre de la Fillatrais, tonsured September 20, 1783; Marin-Simeon-René de la Fillatrais, tonsured March 18, 1790; and the Joseph Laigre de la Fillatrais who succeeded him.

59. This will was reprinted in the *Tablet* of May 4, 1878, and in Plasse, *op. cit.,* II, 305. The original is in the Tottenham register.

60. Sicard, *op. cit.,* III, 213–214. The text of the pastoral letter appears in Lubersac, *op. cit.,* pp. 174–177.

61. Hamon, *op. cit.,* pp. 30–31.

62. Arch. Mayenne, E. fds. Bouiller de Branche, doss. 39. The elder Cheverus was given a certificate of citizenship in Saint-Denis on February 23, 1794. He went to Saint-Denis on September 19, 1793.

63. *Ibid.,* Julien de Cheverus enlisted on February 25, 1794, at the age of twenty-five from Saint-Denis. Louis de Cheverus enlisted October 26, 1793, at the age of nineteen; his certificate of enlistment was registered in Mayenne on October 31, 1793.

64. When a group of monarchists marched against the Convention on October 5, 1795, Napoleon who was charged with defending the legislature fired a volley of grapeshot, killing many of the insurgents. On October 26 the Directory and the Constitution of the Year III went into operation.

65. Charles Robert, *Expédition des émigrés à Quiberon* (Paris, 1899), pp. 91–95. Robert published a biography of Bishop Hercé in 1900.

66. Piolin, *op. cit.,* II, 47. Samuel Gauntlett, D.D., was Warden of New College from February 10, 1794, until his death on September 12, 1822.

67. Hamon, *op. cit.,* p. 29.

68. During his stay in England Cheverus is said to have been invited to Cayenne in French Guiana. The first mention of this invitation appears in Knapp's "Memoir," p. 5, where his earliest biographer states that Cheverus "was strongly solicited to take charge of a college at Cayenne." Hamon reiterates this theory and in *Echo de la Mayenne,* XVII (December 18, 1907), fixed the time of the invitation as the later months of 1794 or the early months of 1795. The *History of the Archdiocese of Boston,* I, 524, offers the hypothesis that the invitation may have been related to an American school rather than a college in Cayenne. The Memoirs of Rev. John Pierce of Brookline, entry of September 19, 1818, state, "Dr. Matignon on his arrival in this country, wrote to Mr. Cheverus, to induce him to come over, and take charge of an Academy for the Catholics. On his refusing this, he pressed him to come as an assistant in the ministry, to which he consented."

There is some difficulty in imagining that the design for a college in Guiana was more than a dream in those years. Guiana was a most unhealthful place, was the locale of earlier French failures to colonize successfully, and was from 1792 onward considered by the Paris government as a penal colony. A decree in the spring of 1793 ordered deported to Guiana all non-juring clergy who were *non fonctionnaire.* Deportation to Guiana was called the "bloodless Guillotine" because it brought a slow and terrible death without bloodshed. After the Fructidorian revolt in 1797 the deportations to Guiana were greatly increased. Two thirds of the royalists who reached the South American coast perished there; at least 118 priests died in the French colony.

As a matter of fact, priests who could escape from Cayenne did so. Jean Moranvillé, the first pastor of St. Patrick's Church in Fells Point, Maryland, fled Cayenne several years before the alleged invitation was proffered Cheverus.

In his biography of Cheverus, Hamon cites as Cheverus' reasons for refusing the invitation: his zeal for working in a larger field than the confines of a school, and his conviction that literary pursuits were secondary to the principal occupation of his vocation. Whatever the truth of either the facts of the invitation or its refusal by Cheverus, it can be stated with certainty that Cheverus was fortunate not to have gone to Cayenne at that time.

69. Peter Guilday, *The Life and Times of John Carroll* (New York, 1922), p. 753.
70. AAB, 2-T-6, Carroll to de la Marche, February 19, 1793.
71. Melville, *op. cit.,* p. 203.
72. AAB, 2-M-9, Cheverus to Carroll, January 26, 1797. Douglass' letter to Carroll was lost en route from Boston to Baltimore but something of its nature may be deduced from Cheverus' words to Carroll, "Should his letter come to hand, I must beg you to abate a great deal of what he says. He is in the number of those partial friends who have very much over-rated my feeble abilities."
73. Hamon, *op. cit.,* p. 35. The original was in Latin.
74. Cf. note 50, *supra.* Hamon, *op. cit.,* p. 33, states that Cheverus, fearing the French government might deprive his family of property on the pretext that some might fall to the deported priest, made an irrevocable renunciation of any part of the properties in favor of his brothers and sisters and sent it to his family. The Stewart translation of the first edition says the paper of renunciation was forwarded by the French ambassador to England. Such an act was in keeping with the character of Cheverus, certainly. Some question remains, however, since France and England had severed diplomatic relations three years earlier and it was more likely to be Mrs. Silburn's agency that Cheverus would have used. A second factor involved is the fact that Cheverus continued to receive income from his family until his return to France in 1823. In the absence of any primary documentation the present writer has chosen to relegate the subject to a note.
75. Cf. note 20, *supra.* The exact date of departure from England is not known. If the voyage was uneventful it probably began toward the end of August since the *Galen* arrived in Boston on October 3, 1796.

CHAPTER IV — MISSIONARY TO MAINE

1. Marquise de la Tour du Pin, *Journal d'une femme de 50 ans* (Paris, 1954), p. 172.
2. Jean Pierre Brissot de Warville, *Nouveau voyage dans les États-Unis de l'Amérique septentrionale* (Paris, 1791). This particular portion of Brissot's work relating to Boston is translated in Oscar Handlin, *This Was America* (Cambridge, 1949), pp. 68–76.
3. John Drayton, *Letters Written during a Tour through the Northern and Eastern States of America.* The description of Boston from this work is found in Warren S. Tryon, *Mirror for Americans* (Chicago, 1952), I, 12–14.

4. Hancock Tavern was the former Brasier Inn which took the name of the first Governor of Massachusetts in 1780. The Boston *Traveler* of March 29, 1957, carried a feature story on Corn Court and the tavern.

5. Massachusetts Historical Society, Memoirs of Rev. John Pierce of Brookline, September 19, 1818.

6. Arch. Nat., 0-280, fol. 73, August 5, 1787.

7. AAB, 8-G-3, Talbot to Carroll, June 6, 1791; 8-G-4, Talbot to Carroll, October 20, 1791; 8-B-4, Strickland to Carroll, November 11, 1791.

8. Talbot's letter of October 20, 1791, informed Carroll that Matignon had just gone to Paris to settle his affairs.

9. Talbot wrote to Carroll on January 5, 1792, that Matignon had missed one boat from France and might return to London to sail; but on May 5 he wrote again that Matignon had sailed from France after all. AAB, 8-G-5, 8-G-6.

10. AAB, 2-M-9, Cheverus to Carroll, January 26, 1797. Cheverus said in this second letter to Carroll, "As soon as I landed in this country I made it my first business to write to my new Pastor."

11. George Paré, *The Catholic Church in Detroit, 1701–1888* (Detroit, 1951), pp. 273–277.

12. Department of Archives and Manuscripts of the Catholic University of America, the Carroll Papers, Carroll to the inhabitants of Rivière au Raisin, October 19, 1796. This collection of papers will hereafter be referred to as "Carroll Papers."

13. Carroll wrote to Cheverus on January 10, 1797, but the contents of the letter which is no longer extant can only be surmised from the precise replies which Cheverus made to Carroll's remarks.

14. Melville, *op. cit.,* pp. 234–235.

15. AAB, 2-M-9, Cheverus to Carroll, January 26, 1797.

16. AAB, 5-G-8, Matignon to Carroll, February 24, 1797.

17. Carroll Papers, Carroll to Levadoux, June 26, 1797. A detailed account of the difficulties preceding Matignon's arrival in Boston is given in Robert H. Lord, John E. Sexton, and Edward T. Harrington, *History of the Archdiocese of Boston in the Various Stages of its Development, 1604–1943* (New York, 1944), I, 374–478. This work will hereafter be cited as *Hist. Arch. Bost.*

18. Archives of the Diocese of Portland, Matignon to Indians of Maine, July 22, 1797. The Archives of the Archdiocese of Boston, hereafter cited as AABost., preserve a copy of this letter.

19. AABost., John Welch Foster, "Cardinal Cheverus," a lecture delivered before the Portsmouth Lyceum on February 8, 1842. This lecture was edited and printed in *Memorial of J. W. Foster* (Portsmouth, 1852), pp. 207–238.

20. Hamon, *op. cit.,* p. 56.

21. Archives of the Archdiocese of Quebec, N.B. IV, 1. These archives will hereafter be cited as AAQ.

22. *Hist. Arch. Bost.,* I, 448–453, 483. The text of the letter of the Indians to Carroll is printed in Guilday, *op. cit.,* pp. 608–609; the text of Carroll's reply, pp. 610–611.

23. Melville, *op. cit.,* pp. 166–167.

24. Carroll Papers, Washington to Carroll, April 10, 1792. The text of the complete letter is in Guilday, *op. cit.,* p. 607.

25. Carroll Papers, Carroll to the Select Body of Roman Catholic Clergy, January 28, 1793. Gabriel Richard, who went to Illinois, and Ciquart, who went to Maine, were both Sulpicians.

26. *Hist. Arch. Bost.,* I, 518–519. Ciquart, who received very meager financial support, may have been influenced by Carleton's offer of an annual salary of

fifty pounds sterling. Carroll granted him an *exeat* for the Diocese of Quebec on May 30, 1798.

27. *Ibid.,* pp. 528–529.
28. AAB, 2-N-1[1], Cheverus to Matignon, July 31, 1797.
29. AAB, 2-N-1[2], Cheverus to Matignon, August 10, 1797.
30. AAB, 11-A-D3, Cheverus to Matignon, May 29, 1798.
31. AAB, 2-N-1[3], Cheverus to Matignon, June 7, 1798.
32. *Ibid.*
33. *Hist. Arch. Bost.,* I, 527.
34. AAB, 11-A-D4, Cheverus to Matignon, June 21, 1798.
35. AAB, 11-A-D5, Cheverus to Matignon, June 22, 1798.
36. AAB, 2-N-1[4], Cheverus to Matignon, June 30, 1798.
37. *Ibid.*
38. *Hist. Arch. Bost.,* I, 533–534.
39. Archives of the Archdiocese of Westminster, Vol. 47, New Series, p. 221, Cheverus to Douglass, August 31, 1798.
40. AAB, 2-N-1, Cheverus to Carroll.
41. AAB, 7-E-6, Romagné to Carroll, January 25, 1800.
42. AAB, 5-A-3, Allen to Carroll, May 23, 1791. The text of this letter is found in Guilday, *op. cit.,* pp. 605–606.

CHAPTER V — A LITTLE MATTER OF LAW

1. Louis Philippe, who ascended the throne in the July Revolution of 1830, is said to have been the "M. d'Orlean" who stayed at the Hancock House the year after Cheverus arrived in Boston.
2. Henry Adams, *The United States in 1800* (Ithaca, 1957), pp. 14–16. This work is a reprint by the Cornell University Press of the first six chapters of Adams' *History of the United States of America during the First Administration of Thomas Jefferson* (New York, 1889).
3. *Hist. Arch. Bost.,* I, 545.
4. AAB, 5-H-11, Matignon to Carroll, June 18, 1804.
5. This thesis is documented in great detail in Arthur J. Riley, *Catholicism in New England to 1788* (Washington, 1936).
6. The text of Washington's order is found in Riley, *op. cit.,* pp. 151–152. For a history of "Pope's Day" in the colonies cf. *Researches of the American Catholic Historical Society,* XXIV (1907), 132–136.
7. *Hist. Arch. Bost.,* I, 327.
8. "Hector" St. John de Crèvecoeur was French consul to New York City from 1783. He and a New York merchant, William Seton, tried to establish a packet service between l'Orient and New York. The venture did not succeed and Crèvecoeur was better remembered in the United States for his *Letters of an American Farmer* which in the French edition of 1784 was dedicated to Seton. Crèvecoeur's *Sketches of Eighteenh Century America,* edited by Henri L. Bourdin, Ralph Gabriel, and Stanley Williams, were published by the Yale University Press in 1925.
9. *Hist. Arch. Bost.,* I, pp. 379 ff.
10. *Ibid.,* 478.

11. *Ibid.,* 354.
12. In 1797 thirteen of sixty-nine were French; in 1798 only eleven of 114 were French.
13. Archives of the Archdiocese of Westminster, Vol. 47, New Series, p. 221, Cheverus to Douglass, August 31, 1798.
14. Knapp, *op. cit.,* p. 6.
15. AAB, 5-V-9, Matthew O'Brien to Carroll, September 16, 1812.
16. AAB, Carroll Letterbook I, Carroll to Propaganda Fide, June 17, 1807.
17. AAB, 5-H-9, Matignon to Carroll, April 1, 1803.
18. AABost., Cheverus to Matignon, May 29, 1798.
19. AAB, 3-1-7, Matignon to Carroll, April 6, 1807.
20. These characteristics were attributed to Matignon and Cheverus by Bishop Carroll in a letter to Rome. Cf. note 16, *supra.*
21. Note 19, *supra.*
22. *Hist. Arch. Bost.,* I, 536–537.
23. AAB, 2-N-1², Cheverus to Matignon, August 10, 1797.
24. AAB, 5-G-9, Matignon to Carroll, May 1, 1798. The Communions were: 210 at Boston, fifteen at Plymouth, twenty-one at Newburyport, three at Salem; the baptisms were: fifty-seven at Boston, thirteen among the Indians, thirty-one elsewhere.
25. Thayer remained in Boston from June, 1797, to June, 1798.
26. Tisserant made frequent visits to Boston between 1798 and 1805.
27. AAB, 11-AD-3, Cheverus to Matignon, May 29, 1789. Burke remained in Boston from May, 1798, to January, 1799.
28. *Hist. Arch. Bost.,* I, 547. This letter is printed in *Researches,* VII (1890), 159.
29. AAB, 5-G-9, Matignon to Carroll, May 1, 1798.
30. According to the *Hist. Arch. Bost.,* I, 548, Sougé was at Newtown at least from March 5, 1801, to March 29, 1803. Angot, *op. cit.,* III, 722, errs twice in claiming that Sougé remained in England "to close the eyes" of his relative Vauxponts on March 2, 1798, and that Sougé returned to Laval in 1800.
31. New York Historical Society, Jay Papers, II, 9, Bayley to Jay, November 28, 1796.
32. Carroll Papers, Carroll to Plowden, April 15, 1795.
33. *Columbian Centinel,* August 4, 1798.
34. Hamon, *op. cit.,* p. 59.
35. Note 13, *supra.*
36. Broussillon, *op. cit.,* p. 347, Cheverus to Esnault, January 18, 1802. The story of the first Catholic congregations in Maine is told in William L. Lucey, S.J., *The Catholic Church in Maine* (Francestown, New Hampshire, 1957), pp. 25–49.
37. *Hist. Arch. Bost.,* I, 539. For further details of Kavanagh and Cottrill, cf. William L. Lucey, S.J., "Two Irish Merchants of New England," *New England Quarterly Review,* XIV (December, 1941), 481–490.
38. *Ibid.,* I, 560–561. The Protestant minister was the Reverend Mr. Kiah Bayley.
39. AAB, 2-N-3, Cheverus to Carroll, March 10, 1801.
40. AAB, 5-H-4, Matignon to Carroll, March 16, 1801.
41. AAB, 5-H-3, Matignon to Carroll, October 14, 1800.
42. AAB, 2-N-3, Cheverus to Carroll, March 10, 1801.
43. Note 41, *supra.*
44. Note 42, *supra.*
45. AAB, 5-H-5, Matignon to Carroll, March 19, 1801. The text of the letter Cheverus desired is printed in Guilday, *op. cit.,* p. 442.
46. AAB, 2-N-3, Cheverus to Carroll, March 10, 1801.
47. AAB, 5-H-t, Matignon to Carroll, March 19, 1801.

48. AAB, 5-H-6, Matignon to Carroll, July 3, 1801.
49. AAB, 5-H-8, Matignon to Carroll, January 23, 1802. The register of the Church of the Holy Cross, p. 103, indicates that from August 30, 1801, to January 31, 1802, there were thirty-two baptisms in Maine apportioned as follows: twenty-three in Lincoln County, of which eight were adults; nine in Portland, of which one was adult. The church at Newcastle did not keep separate records until 1808.

Chapter VI — To Go or Stay?

1. AAB, 2-N-3, Cheverus to Carroll, March 10, 1801. Cheverus wrote that Esnault was "The only one out of 4 who survived." The French records show only three active *vicaires* at the time of Cheverus' precarious pastorate. He may have made the simple mistake of giving the number of assistants at Notre Dame de Mayenne while he himself was one and his uncle was pastor. Jean-Charles Gahier and Pierre-Joseph Vengeons seem to have died in England.
2. Leflon, *op. cit.*, p. 168.
3. *Ibid.*, p. 170. The texts of Napoleon's address to the clergy of Milan on June 5, 1800, published in France and in Italy do not agree in every instance.
4. Piolin, *op. cit.*, III, 35–39. Jouffroy de Gonssans died on January 23, 1799, and was buried on February 23 in the cathedral "under the tower commonly called Hossenkamp before the altar of Saint-Liboire."
5. AAB, 2-N-3, Cheverus to Carroll, March 10, 1801.
6. *Ibid.*
7. AAB, 5-H-4, Matignon to Carroll, March 16, 1801; 5-H-5, Matignon to Carroll, March 19, 1801.
8. AAQ, Matignon to Plessis, January 31, 1799.
9. AAB, 5-H-6, Matignon to Carroll, July 3, 1801.
10. AAB, 5-1-12, Matignon to Carroll, September 10, 1801.
11. There is no way of ascertaining the time of Dumourier's letter or Cheverus' reply except by inference. Cheverus said on January 18, 1802, that he had written to Dumourier about three months ago. If he replied immediately he may have received Dumourier's letter in the fall of 1801. The contents of Cheverus' reply may be inferred from this same letter to Esnault of January 18, 1802, in which he stated, "I told him almost the same thing I am sending you." Since his letters on the same subject to several different people usually were duplicates it is a reasonably safe inference.
12. Archives du chateau de Courtilloles, Cheverus to Abbé Bignon, January 18, 1802. This letter was in reality written to Esnault. Esnault, who was the same age as Cheverus, had gone into exile on the continent and returned to France after the Concordat of 1801 where he lived in retirement with his family. Bertrand de Broussillon originally published this letter in the *Union historique et litteraire du Maine*, I (1893), 346–348. A separate reprint in brochure form was published in Le Mans that same year, under the title *Une Lettre écrite en 1802 par le futur Cardinal de Cheverus.*
13. André Latreille, *L'Église catholique et la Révolution Française* (Paris, 1950), II, 32–44; Leflon, *op. cit.*, pp. 191–195.

14. Latreille, *op. cit.*, II, 37.
15. The vote of the cardinals showed: fourteen favored ratification, twelve offered reservations, and two opposed the most ambiguous articles.
16. Latreille, *op. cit.*, II, 44.
17. AAB, 8-D-3, Strickland to Carroll, September 29, 1801.
18. Latreille, *op. cit.*, II, 56–57; Leflon, *op. cit.*, pp. 217–222. In England the adherents of the Petite Église were commonly called "Clementins" or "Blanchardists" after the priests who defended the cause.
19. Toulouse and Besançon went to former constitutional bishops. The See of Lyon went to Napoleon's uncle, Joseph Fesch; Bordeaux got the saintly d'Aviau whom Cheverus was destined to succeed.
20. Cited in a letter of Cheverus to Carroll, March 31, 1803. Cf. AAB, 2-N-4. Duperrier-Dumourier became Bishop of Bayeux in 1823, the year Cheverus returned to France. In 1855 Laval was once more created a separate diocese containing Cheverus' first parish at Mayenne.
21. *Épiscopat français depuis le Concordat jusqu'à la Séparation, 1802–1905* (Paris, 1907), pp. 326–327. The constitutional bishop, Prudhomme de la Bouissinière, handed over the keys of the cathedral to Pidoll.
22. Note 20, *supra*.
23. Latreille, *op. cit.*, II, 53.
24. AAB, 5-H-8, Matignon to Carroll, January 23, 1802.
25. Broussillon, *op. cit.*, p. 347.
26. AAB, 5-H-9, Matignon to Carroll, April 1, 1803.
27. Broussillon, *op. cit.*, p. 347.
28. AAB, 5-H-8, Matignon to Carroll, January 23, 1802.
29. Leflon, *op. cit.*, p. 371; Guilday, *op. cit.*, pp. 542–544.
30. Melville, *op. cit.*, pp. 188–189; J. Herman Schauinger, *Stephen T. Badin, Priest in the Wilderness* (Milwaukee, 1956), pp. 64–65. Father Thayer eventually went to London in November, 1804, and thence to Ireland where he died in 1815.
31. Melville, *op. cit.*, pp. 190–193.
32. AAB, 2-N-4, Cheverus to Carroll, March 31, 1803. This letter quotes verbatim the letters of both Dumourier and the elder Cheverus; it is printed in Guilday, *op. cit.*, pp. 618–619, but is incorrectly dated May 3, 1803.
33. *Ibid.*
34. AAB, 5-H-9, Matignon to Carroll, April 1, 1803.
35. *Boston Monthly Magazine*, I (May, 1825), 20–21, Carroll to Cheverus, April 9, 1803. This letter is incorrectly dated April 20 in the *Hist. Arch. Bost.*, I, 579. Cheverus received the letter on that latter date.
36. AAB, 2-N-5, Cheverus to Carroll, April 29, 1803.
37. AABost., Cheverus to Mme de Cheverus, November 28, 1807. This is a copy of a letter in the Archives privées de Plinval. "Sougette" was a diminutive of the maiden name of the wife of Louis de Cheverus. She had been a Soulge (Sougé) de Lussault.
38. Angot, *op. cit.*, II, 823. Between Paule Gournay and Sougé, for the years 1804–1807, Antoine Motreul was pastor of Notre Dame de Mayenne.
39. AAQ, Carroll to Plessis, July 28, 1806.
40. The complex details of the relations between Napoleon and Pius VII after 1804 are described in Leflon, *op. cit.*, pp. 226–235; 241–273.

CHAPTER VII — A NEW CHURCH OF THE HOLY CROSS

1. AAB, 2-N-5, Cheverus to Carroll, April 29, 1803.
2. Carroll Papers, Carroll to Plowden, February 12, 1803.
3. *Hist. Arch. Bost.*, I, 513.
4. AAB, 5-G-8, Matignon to Carroll, February 24, 1797.
5. *Hist. Arch. Bost.*, I, 544–545. Robert Barry of Baltimore was the nephew of James Barry of Georgetown. The family business activities took the uncle to New York, Boston, and Canada and led the nephew to being named Portuguese consul in Baltimore.
6. The wardens were John Magner, Patrick Campbell, and Michael Burns; the other members of the committee were Edmund O'Connor, John Duggan, and Owen Callahan. This first meeting was held on March 31, 1799.
7. *Hist. Arch. Bost.*, I, 554.
8. AAB, 5-G-11, Matignon to Carroll, May 2, 1799.
9. Joseph W. Ruane, *The Beginnings of the Society of St. Sulpice in the United States, 1791–1829* (Washington, 1935), pp. 97–102.
10. The price expected for a sale to a public house was $4,000. The church committee was later offered $3,000 for the lot.
11. AAB, 5-H-2, Matignon to Carroll, March 18, 1800.
12. AAB, Letterbook I, letters to Fathers Griffin, Lonergan, Doyle, and Tarleton, March 3, 1800, to January 29, 1801; Carroll to Carr, April 22, 1800.
13. AAB, 5-H-3, Matignon to Carroll, October 14, 1800. A faulty translation of the French in the *Hist. Arch. Bost.*, I, 558, reads "the walls had been raised three feet above the ground." From the same letter it is clear that the walls were not begun until the following summer at best.
14. *Ibid.* Adams' gift was not without precedent. President George Washington had contributed to the building of St. Augustine's Church in Philadelphia.
15. AAB, 5-H-3¹,Matignon to Carroll, December 8, 1800.
16. AAB, 2-N-3, Cheverus to Carroll, March 10, 1801.
17. AAB, 5-H-8, Matignon to Carroll, January 23, 1802.
18. *Hist. Arch. Bost.*, I, 580–581, gives the list of these contributions.
19. Jack Frost, *Channels of Grace* (Boston, 1954), not paginated, "Bulfinch in the old North End." Bulfinch was later appointed to succeed Benjamin Henry Latrobe in completing the national Capitol, 1818–1830. For a life of Bulfinch cf. Ellen Susan Bulfinch, *The Life and Letters of Charles Bulfinch Architect* (Boston, 1896). The Cheverus-Matignon letter to Carroll is printed in *Records*, XV (1904), 43.
20. *Columbian Centinel*, October 5, 1803.
21. *Hist. Arch. Bost.*, I, 586.
22. Carroll Papers, Carroll to Mrs. Barry, June 15, 1803; Carroll to Barry, August 25, 1803.
24. *Herald of Freedom*, June 24, 1791.
25. AABost., copy from the Bibliothèque Nationale, *Annales critiques de litterature et de morale* (9ᵉ cahier, 1806), p. 396 ff.
26. *The Laity's Directory* (London, 1806), "America," extract of a letter from Boston, May 16, 1805. It is not possible to identify the one to whom the letter was addressed, but internal evidence identifies Matignon as the author.
27. Archives of Saint Joseph Central House, Emmitsburg, Maryland, Antonio Filicchi to Elizabeth Seton, October 8, 1804. These archives will hereafter be cited ASJCH.

28. *Hist. Arch. Bost.,* I, 611–612, citing Stephen Blyth, *An Apology for the Conversion of Stephen Cleveland Blyth* (New York: 1815).
29. John Quincy Adams, *Memoirs* (Philadelphia, 1876), IX, 35, November 17, 1833.
30. Josiah Quincy, *Figures of the Past from the Leaves of Old Journals* (Boston, 1883), pp. 312–313.
31. Knapp, *op. cit.,* p. 9.
32. *Indicateur Bordelais,* July 20, 1836, "Mort de M. de Cheverus."
33. AAB, 2-N-2, Cheverus to Carroll, April 21, 1800.
34. AAB, 2-N-4, Cheverus to Carroll, March 31, 1803.
35. *Hist. Arch. Bost.,* I, 605, citing Bentley's *Diary,* III, 55.
36. Carroll Papers, Carroll to Barry, December 26, 1803.
37. AAB, 2-N-6, Cheverus to Carroll, March 26, 1804.
38. AAB, 2-O-7, Cheverus to Carroll, June 2, 1812.

Chapter VIII — A Convert by Correspondence

1. The *Manual,* which was a collection of songs and prayers, was printed in December, 1803. Cheverus told Carroll that he had 1500 copies printed, half of which he meant to give away, the others to be sold for 62½ cents. He hoped to get back the $270 printing costs over a ten-year period. AAB, 2-N-6, Cheverus to Carroll, March 26, 1804. For a description of the *Manual* cf. *Hist. Arch. Bost.,* I, 594.
2. AAB, 5-H-12, Matignon to Carroll, July 30, 1804. Matignon contracted with an organ builder named Goodrich to build "a good, well-tuned and sounding organ, composed of fifteen stops . . . and equal to the best in town."
3. *Annales,* cited in *Hist. Arch. Bost.,* I, 613.
4. AAB, 2-N-1⁴, Cheverus to Matignon, June 30, 1798.
5. Carroll Papers, Letterbook I, Carroll to Propaganda Fide, June 17, 1807.
6. AAB, 5-H-9, Matignon to Carroll, April 1, 1803. In this letter Matignon spoke of Cheverus as a missionary who was "adored."
7. AAB, 8-H-2, Tisserant to Carroll, September 26, 1804: *Annales,* p. 396.
8. Filicchi was in the United States at least between 1785 and 1788 the first time, and again in 1789, when he appears to have married Miss Cowper. She went to Italy to join her husband in 1790.
9. Filippo Filicchi was appointed United States Consul in Leghorn by George Washington on December 10, 1794. He had used his influence in Italy to promote the establishment of a Catholic hierarchy in the United States in 1789 and Carroll received news of his appointment via the Filicchi firm and its American connections.
10. Annabelle M. Melville, *Elizabeth Bayley Seton, 1774–1821* (New York, 1951), p. 65 ff. This work will hereafter be cited *Seton.*
11. ASJCH, X, 11, Filicchi to Seton, October 8, 1804.
12. AAB, 5-I-1, Matignon to Carroll, January 29, 1805.
13. AAB, 5-V-4, O'Brien to Carroll, February 19, 1805.
14. ASJCH, Seton-Filicchi Copies, Filicchi to Cheverus, February 19, 1805.
15. With few exceptions the letters of Mother Seton to Cheverus are not extant.

If Cheverus carried them with him on his return to France they may have been lost in the shipwreck he survived in 1823.

16. Archives of the Sisters of Charity of Mount Saint Vincent, Cheverus to Seton, March 4, 1804. The text of this letter appears in *The Life of Mother Elizabeth Boyle* (New York, 1893), p. 25. These archives are hereafter cited AMSV.
17. *Ibid.*
18. ASJCH, Seton-Filicchi Copies, Filicchi to Cheverus, March 16, 1805. This letter is printed in *The Life of Mother Elizabeth Boyle*, p. 25, and in *Hist. Arch. Bost.*, I, 610.
19. ASJCH, I, 1, Seton to Cheverus, no date. Both Code, *op. cit.*, p. 143, and the *Hist. Arch. Bost.*, I, 610, assign the date April 2, 1805, to this letter.
20. Note 18, *supra.*
21. ASJCH, Seton-Filicchi Copies, 10, Seton to Filicchi, April 6, 1805.
22. ASJCH, I, 2, Cheverus to Seton, June 1, 1805. The prayer book is preserved at the Archives of the University of Notre Dame. If Cheverus wrote any inscription it has disappeared with the title page which is now missing. One of the last jottings Mother Seton wrote in the prayer book was, "The virtues of the infirm are *meekness, patience, resignation,* and *gratitude* for help received."
23. Melville, *Seton,* pp. 113–116.
24. ASJCH, I, 25, Tisserant to Seton, April 22, 1806.
25. ASJCH, I, 3, Cheverus to Seton, November 30, 1805.
26. ASJCH, I, 4, Cheverus to Seton, January 28, 1806.
27. ASJCH, I, 22, Tisserant to Seton, March 9, 1806, directly quoting from Cheverus.
28. ASJCH, I, 5, Cheverus to Seton, April 3, 1806.
29. ASJCH, I, 4, Cheverus to Seton, January 28, 1806.
30. ASJCH, I, 121, Matignon to Seton, September 22, 1806.
31. ASJCH, I, 35, Matignon to Seton.
32. ASJCH, X, 26, Filicchi to Seton, no date; X, 33, Filicchi to Seton, November 3, 1806.
33. *Laity's Directory* (London, 1806), letter from Boston, May 16, 1805.
34. ASJCH, I, 3, Cheverus to Seton, November 30, 1805.
35. ASJCH, I, 7, Cheverus to Seton, January 21, 1807.
36. In September, 1796, Carroll appointed Dubourg president of the college at Georgetown where for two years Dubourg gave some éclat to the school. For an account of Dubourg's connection with Georgetown cf. John M. Daley, S.J., *Georgetown University: Origin and Early Years* (Washington, D. C., 1957), pp. 86–101.
37. Ruane, *op. cit.,* pp. 98–100, 104, 133–134.
38. ASJCH, I, 37, Matignon to Seton, November 29, 1806.
39. ASJCH, I, 39, Carroll to Seton, May 23, 1807.
40. AUND, Dubourg to Seton, May 2, 1808.
41. ASJCH, I, 9, Cheverus to Seton, May 12, 1808.
42. ASJCH, Seton-Filicchi Copies, 29, Seton to Filicchi, August 10, 1807.
43. *Ibid.,* 27, Seton to Filicchi, March 30, 1807.
44. *Ibid.,* X, 36, Seton to Filippo Filicchi, November 2, 1807.
45. *Ibid.,* I, 7, Cheverus to Seton, January 21, 1807.

Chapter IX — Reluctant Bishop

1. AAB, 2-O-1, Cheverus to Carroll, July 30, 1808; Lucey, *The Catholic Church in Maine,* pp. 28–34. The land for the church and three acres surrounding it had been deeded to Bishop Carroll two years before on July 28, 1806.
2. *Ibid.* The six priests ordained on June 11, 1808, were: William F. X. O'Bryan, Francis Rolof, James Spink, Leonard Edelen, Enoch Fenwick, and Benedict Joseph Fenwick. The last named did come to Boston, but as the successor to Cheverus in 1825.
3. Ruane, *op. cit.,* pp. 55–57. Carroll's disposition of the new priests may be found in his letter to Robert Molyneux, the head of Georgetown College, dated September 19, 1808, and preserved in the Carroll Papers.
4. Melville, *Carroll,* pp. 214–216; Guilday, *op. cit.,* pp. 568–579. The summer following his consecration in 1790 Carroll mentioned the idea of an auxiliary bishop to John Thorpe in Rome; in November, 1791, he suggested a coadjutor before the Synod of Baltimore; in his report to Propaganda of April, 1792, he recommended either a new diocesan or a coadjutor bishop.
5. AAB, 12-AJ-3, Maréchal to Neale, December 11, 1816, citing Cheverus.
6. AAB, 5-H-13, Matignon to Carroll, November 12, 1804.
7. Carroll Papers, Carroll to Plowden, December 7, 1804.
8. *Laity's Directory,* "Extract of a letter from Boston," May 16, 1805.
9. The other three dioceses recommended were: New York: embracing that state and East Jersey; Philadelphia, comprising Pennsylvania, West Jersey, and Delaware; and some city in Kentucky not yet fixed upon. Bardstown was the final choice. Carroll also anticipated for the future a fifth embracing the Northwest Territory.
10. *Hist. Arch. Bost.,* I, 633.
11. Note 6, *supra.*
12. AAB, 3-I-7, Matignon to Carroll, April 6, 1807. This letter is published in full in *Hist. Arch. Bost.,* I, 635–637, and Guilday, *op. cit.,* pp. 581–583.
13. Carroll Papers, Carroll to Propaganda Fide, June 17, 1807.
14. The briefs were *Ex debito pastoralis officii* and *Pontificii muneris.*
15. Concanen's letter from Rome dated March 25, 1808, reached Archbishop Troy of Dublin on July 4, 1808.
16. ASJCH, X, 38, 39, Filicchi to Seton, November 30, 1808.
17. Carroll Papers, Carroll to Plowden, December 3–5, 1808.
18. ASJCH, I, 10, Cheverus to Seton, April 13, 1809. This letter is printed in facsimile in Madame de Barbery and Joseph B. Code, *Elizabeth Seton* (New York, 1927), pp. 249–251. A reprint of this work was published in 1957 by the Seton Guild of Emmitsburg, Maryland.
19. In a letter to Filippo Filicchi dated February 28, 1809, Mrs. Seton said that Matignon had suggested "this plan for me" before it was thought of in Baltimore. She added, "I have invariably kept it in the background . . . knowing that Almighty God alone could effect it, if indeed it will be realized."
20. ASJCH, Seton-Filicchi Copies, 33, Seton to Filicchi, January 21, 1809.
21. Note 18, *supra.*
22. ASJCH, Seton-Filicchi Copies, 33, 34, 35, Seton to Filicchi, January 21, February 8, November 8, 1809.
23. Note 18, *supra.*
24. ASJCH, X, 39, Filicchi to Seton, November 30, 1808.

25. Carroll Papers, Carroll to Plowden, June 2, 1809.
26. Carroll Papers, Carroll to Plowden, September 19, 1809.
27. AAB, 2-T-1, Concanen to Carroll, August 9, 1809.
28. J. Herman Schauinger, *Cathedrals in the Wilderness* (Milwaukee, 1952), p. 48, suggests without citing a source that Flaget went to enlist Superior-General Emery's support for Flaget's refusal of the Diocese of Bardstown. Carroll told Plowden, however, that Flaget had gone "in order to obtain some of his Brethren [Sulpicians] to go with him into his Diocese." Flaget certainly was trying while in France to recruit assistants, for he wrote, Cheverus from Paris, "Will I have travelling companions or not . . . ? Several are attracted to the thing and seem to desire it ardently, but there are many obstacles to remove. Unless God performs a sort of miracle I won't be able to draw them from their country."
29. AAQ, Cheverus to Plessis, June 26, 1810, quoting directly from Flaget's letter.
30. AAQ, Carroll to Plessis, October 15, 1810. This letter is printed in Guilday, *op. cit.*, p. 588.
31. *Ibid.* Carroll wrote that the copies were sent to "a confidential friend in France." This friend appears to have been Emery, since on March 26, 1810, Concanen wrote from Rome to Ambrose Maréchal that he intended sending the copies to Paris. It is difficult to understand why Guilday, after printing Carroll's statement to Plessis in regard to receiving the French copies, subsequently (*op. cit.*, p. 693) raises the question of Carroll's receiving them, unless he was chiefly influenced by his own error in the date of Flaget's departure from France.
32. Sister Mary Salesia Godecker, O.S.B., *Simon Bruté de Rémur* (St. Meinrad, 1931), pp. 49–50. Bruté, who sailed with Flaget, wrote to Jean and Félicité Lamennais from Bordeaux on June 9, 1810, "on the eve of my departure." Flaget himself in a report to Rome on April 10, 1815, stated that the bulls and briefs (which he brought) arrived in America on August 10, 1810. The *Hist. Arch. Bost.*, Guilday, and Schauinger all appear to err when they state respectively that Flaget arrived August 7, left France on April 10, and was at sea more than three months. Tessier stated that Flaget arrived on August 9. Cf. Archives of St. Mary's Seminary, Baltimore, "Époques," p. 167. These archives are hereafter cited as ASMS.
33. AAQ, Carroll to Plessis, October 15, 1810.
34. *Hist. Arch. Bost.*, I, 642.
35. *Ibid.*, 650.
36. AAQ, Cheverus to Plessis, June 26, 1810.
37. ASMS, Cheverus to Dubourg, October 2, 1810.
38. Joseph M. Finott, *Bibliographia Catholica Americana* (New York, 1872), p. 136. Bernard Dornin of Baltimore published the sermon in a pamphlet, *Instructions on the erection of the four new Catholic Episcopal Sees in the United States and the Consecration of their first Bishops.* A copy is preserved in the library of St. John's Seminary in Brighton, Massachusetts.
    That Cheverus and Carroll reminisced over their Maine experience is evident from a letter, AAB, 7-E-7, Romagné to Carroll, October 8, 1811.
39. Code, *op. cit.*, p. 310; Schauinger, *op. cit.*, p. 52; ASMS, Tessier's Journal, November 11, 1810.
40. Ruane, *op. cit.*, p. 93.
41. The complete texts of these documents are found in Guilday, *op. cit.*, pp. 589–598.
42. Carroll Papers, Carroll to Plowden, January 17, 1812.

43. AAB, 2-J-1, Regulations for the clergy, November 19, 1810.
44. AAB, 2-O-2, Cheverus to Carroll, November 26, 1810.
45. Code, *op. cit.*, p. 312. The niece was Mary Egan; the sisters were Cecilia O'Conway, Mary Ann Butler, and Maria Murphy.
46. ASJCH, Seton-Filicchi Copies, 32, Seton to Filicchi, January 16, 1809.
47. *Ibid.*, 35, Seton to Filicchi, May 20, 1810.
48. ASJCH, VII, Seton to Sadler, November 21, 1810.
49. AAB, 7-N-9, Seton to Carroll, November 29, 1810.
50. ASJCH, Seton-Filicchi Copies, 37, Seton to Filicchi, July 1, 1814.
51. Code, *op. cit.*, pp. 317–318.
52. ASJCH, V, 17, Dubois to Seton, November 23, 1810.
53. AAB, 2-O-2, Cheverus to Carroll, November 26, 1810.
54. ASJCH, I, 10, Cheverus to Seton, April 13, 1809.
55. AMSV, I, 2, Cheverus to Seton, January 4, 1811.
56. ASJCH, XI, 12, Sadler to Seton, December 28, 1810.
57. AMSV, I, 11, Dubourg to Seton, December 30, 1809.
58. Hyde de Neuville, *Mémoires et Souvenirs* (Paris, 1888), I, 451–480.
59. AAB, 2-O-3, Cheverus to Carroll, January 28, 1811; *Hist. Arch. Bost.*, I, 608.
60. *Hist. Arch. Bost.*, I, 650. It is asserted here that "Bishop Cheverus was certainly an active member" of Neuville's association, and that "there is some reason to believe" that Matignon and Cheverus had a part in preparing a catechism for use in New York.
61. ASJCH, XI, B-40, Mary Bayley Bunch to Seton, October 25, 1819. Mrs. Bunch wrote, "Sad is leaving for France this day. . . . At the last moment the French Ambassador received dispatches from Washington City. He and Mme de Neuville are old and intimate friends of Mrs. Sadler." Hyde de Neuville left New York the first time on July 8, 1814. He returned to the United States as minister plenipotentiary in 1816. His third return to France occurred in July, 1822. His influence on Cheverus' return the next year will be discussed subsequently.
62. *Hist. Arch. Bost.*, I, 645. The Literary Institute was closed in 1813 owing to a lack of enough Jesuits to staff the school. At that time it had about seventy-five boarding pupils. When Father Kohlmann described the school on July 26, 1809, he said "It now consists of about 35 of the most respectable children of the city both Catholics and other persuasions." By the time Cheverus saw it in 1810 it had moved from Broadway farther out in the country.
63. Bishop Plessis, *Journal des visites pastorales de 1815–1816,* edited by Henri Têtu (Quebec, 1903), pp. 149 ff.
64. AAB, 2-O-4, Cheverus to Carroll, October 3, 1811; 7-E-7, Romagné to Carroll, October 8, 1811.

Chapter X — The Alien Corn

1. Archbishop Richard J. Cushing.
2. AABost., copy from Arch. Prop. Fide, Cheverus to Litta, February 7, 1817.
3. *Ibid.*, Maréchal to Litta, June 25, 1817.
4. *St. Louis Historical Review,* III (1921), 192, Dubourg to Somaglia, October 6, 1825.

5. AABost., copy from Arch. Prop. Fide, Cheverus to Litta, February 7, 1817.
6. Van Wyck Brooks, *The World of Washington Irving* (New York, 1944), p. 45.
7. Robert H. Lord in *Hist. Arch. Bost.*, II, 30.
8. *Boston Daily Courier*, October 4, 1825.
9. Melville, *Carroll*, pp. 146–147.
10. Archives of the Archdiocese of Westminster, Vol. 47, New Series, p. 221, Cheverus to Douglass, August 31, 1798.
11. AAQ, Matignon to Jones, January 31, 1799.
12. Lengthy quotations from these two articles appear in the *Hist. Arch. Bost.*, I, 569–570.
13. *Ibid.*, I, 571–572.
14. For Carroll's journalistic protests cf. Melville, *Carroll*, pp. 84–99, 134–135.
15. *The Jesuit*, I (February 20, 1830).
16. The London edition was published in 1794 while Cheverus was in Tottenham, England.
17. AAB, 5-H-3, Matignon to Carroll, October 14, 1800.
18. For a discussion of Anglo-Irish relations at this time cf. Philip Hughes, *The Catholic Question*, pp. 223–237.
19. The Democratic-Republican spoke frequently from the pages of the *Independent Chronicle* while the Federalists used the *Columbian Centinel.*
20. *Monthly Anthology and Boston Review*, IV (February, 1807), 71–77.
21. *Ibid.*, pp. 187–190.
22. "Memoir of the Hon. John Lowell," *Proceedings of the Massachusetts Historical Society*, II, 160–169.
23. *Monthly Anthology*, IV (April, 1807), 223–224.
24. Anthology Society, *Journal of Proceedings* (Boston, 1910), pp. 111–112. One of the books he sent was Bossuet's *Exposition of the Catholic Faith;* the other is not identified.
25. Between 1810 and 1823 Cheverus gave the Athenaeum Library some seventy titles and more than 120 volumes. The Athenaeum Library was separate from the Private Library of J. Q. Adams, which was located in a third room of the society's building. The rooms were first located in Congress Street, but in 1810 were in Tremont Street. A description of the Athenaeum in 1817 estimated the library at 10,000 volumes; the reading room received regularly about twenty-one foreign periodicals and twelve American. Cf. Charles Shaw, *A Topographical and Historical Description of Boston* (Boston, 1817), pp. 274–276. For a complete list of the books given by Cheverus cf. Walter Muir Whitehill, *A Memorial to Bishop Cheverus with a Catalogue of the Books Given by Him to the Boston Athenaeum* (Boston, 1951).
26. Samuel Knapp, "Memoir of Bishop Cheverus," *Boston Monthly Magazine*, I (1825), 11. Knapp's opinion was his own, of course. After the death of Cheverus, his first French biographer substantially made the same claim only to be attacked in an American paper for exaggeration. *The Daily Advertiser and Patriot* of January 30, 1839, in reviewing "Huen-Dubourg's Life of Cardinal Cheverus," asserted:

    Now that there were Protestant ladies in Boston who entertained a respect for Bishop Cheverus, and would have deemed his friendship an honor, we have no doubt. That one of a communicative turn might have sought his counsel upon some personal or domestic trial may be true. But that confidence of that kind was common, or that he was resorted to by Protestant ladies, or Protestants of any class as their counsellor, much less as their spiritual advisor, we have no belief.

27. Rev. L. S. Walsh, *Origins of the Catholic Church in Salem*, p. 19.

28. *Diary of William Bentley,* D.D., IV, 20, May 1, 1811.
29. Josiah Quincy, *Figures of the Past* (Boston, 1883), pp. 311–312.
30. Edmund Quincy, *Life of Josiah Quincy* (Boston, 1867), pp. 419–421. The phrases are found in letters exchanged in 1826 while Cheverus was in Montauban.
31. AABost., copy from Bishop Tyler's Diary, entry for September 11, 1836. This story also appears in the appendix of Stewart's translation of the Hamon biography, pp. 379–380.
32. Charles B. Fairbanks, *Aguecheek* (Boston, 1859), p. 242.
33. Boston Public Library, Cheverus to Green, April 8, 1826.
34. Robert H. Lord, "Jean Lefebvre de Cheverus," *Proceedings of the Massachusetts Historical Society,* LXV (1933), 67.
35. A well-documented account of this affair is given in the *Hist. Arch. Bost.,* I, 622–625.
36. Hamon, *op. cit.,* pp. 74 f.
37. *Ibid.,* pp. 74–75. Although Cheverus was not involved in the trial of the men, it is interesting that his exposition of the nature of confession and its relation to public law antedated by seven years the famous case in New York in which Jesuit Anthony Kohlmann defended the inviolability of the confessional.
38. *An Apology for the conversion of Stephen Cleveland Blyth* was first printed in New York in 1815. Blyth later went to Canada where he published another edition in Montreal, 1822, which bears this dedication.
39. Walley's account of his conversion appears in *Records,* XVIII (1907), 46, in a letter written to his daughter Mary, October 13, 1846.
40. AAB, 2-P-2, Cheverus to Carroll, July 13, 1814.
41. AABost., copy from the Archives of the Protestant Episcopal Diocese of Connecticut, Croswell to Hobart, February 8, 1819.
42. Virgil Barber became a Catholic in 1816; Daniel Barber made his decision in 1818; Calvin White announced his in 1819. The story of the Barbers, which is lengthy and complex, is summarized in the *Hist. Arch. Bost.,* I, 740–752.
43. The adult baptisms recorded from 1810–1814, for example, ran 9, 12, 15, 10, and 6.
44. AAQ, Denaut to Plessis, June 18, 1803.
45. Henri Têtu, ed., *Journal des visites pastorales de 1815 et 1816* (Quebec, 1903), pp. 149–151.
46. AAQ, Matignon to Plessis, July 23, 1817.
47. William Tudor, *Letters on the Eastern States* (New York, 1820), p. 71.
48. Bostonian Society Archives, Cheverus to Parkman, June 27, 1816.
49. *Records,* XIV (1903), 359, 469, Cheverus to Bonneuil, July 18, 1815; September 10, 1817.
50. Andrew P. Peabody, *A Memorial of John W. Foster* (Portsmouth, 1852), pp. 220–223.
51. Archives of the Mass. Hist. Soc., Lowell to the *Christian Register,* November 17, no year.
52. *United States Catholic Miscellany, VIII* (April 25, 1829), 331.
53. *New York American,* May 15, 1832. The Reverend William Ware was for several years the sole editor of the *Christian Examiner,* and was the author of *Zenobia* and *Probus.* Cf. Justin Winsor, ed., *The Memorial History of Boston* (Boston, 1881), III, 479.
54. Archives of the Mass. Hist. Soc. Memoirs of Rev. John Pierce of Brookline, entry for September 19, 1818.
55. *Records,* XVIII (1907), 65, Cheverus to Harris, June 3, 1836.

56. *Truth Teller,* November 15, 1828. The writer is not identified.
57. AUND, Cheverus to Bruté, March 23, 1816.
58. AABost., copy from Arch. Prop. Fide, Cheverus to Litta, February 7, 1817.
59. AUND, Cheverus to Bruté, December 17, 1816.
60. Ray A. Billington, *The Protestant Crusade* (New York, 1938), p. 44; *Gazette,* April 22, 1819. The article in the *Gazette* was signed "C. D. E., Cambridge," but Cheverus told Maréchal on May 6, 1819, that Knapp had written it.
61. Whitehill, *op. cit.,* pp. xx–xxi.

Chapter XI — The War Years

1. Arch. Prop. Fide, U.N.S., 61–870, Maréchal to Gradwell, September 10, 1823.
2. AAB, 2-O-8, Cheverus to Carroll, August 31, 1812.
3. AAB, 5-V-9, O'Brien to Carroll, September 16, 1812.
4. AAB, 5-V-10, O'Brien to Carroll, January 5, 1813; *Hist. Arch. Bost.,* I, 645–647.
5. AAB, 2-P-1, Cheverus to Carroll, March 18, 1814.
6. ASJCH, I, 13, Cheverus to Seton, April 12, 1814.
7. Arch. Plinval, Cheverus to Cheverus, January 22, 1815. Although the peace negotiations at Ghent were concluded by December 24, 1814, the news of peace did not reach Boston until February, 1815; Cheverus thus believed the war was still in progress when he wrote this letter to his brother.
8. Bibliothèque St. Sulpice, Montreal, Cheverus to Le Saulnier, April 18, 1815. These archives will be hereafter cited Bibl. St. Sulpice. Copies of the letters of Cheverus and Matignon from this source are located in the Archives of the Archdiocese of Boston.
9. AUND, Cheverus to Bruté, February 14, 1812.
10. AAB, 2-P-2, Cheverus to Carroll, July 13, 1814; ASJCH, I, 14, Cheverus to Seton, January 20, 1815.
11. The Swiss Guard was disarmed on April 7, 1808, and the briefs and bulls for the American dioceses and bishops were issued April 8. It has been suggested that one reason for the appointment of Concanen to the See of New York was the pope's fear that dioceses left vacant might go unfilled indefinitely. Cf. Victor F. O'Daniel, O.P., "Concanen's Election to the See of New York," *Catholic Historical Review,* II (April, 1916), 23.
12. ASJCH, I, 11, Dubourg to Seton, December 30, 1809.
13. AAB, 8-E-6, Strickland to Carroll, April 17, 1810.
14. AAB, 8-E-7, Strickland to Carroll, no date.
15. Carroll Papers, Carroll to Plessis, March 12, 1811.
16. AMSV, I, 3, Cheverus to Seton, January 20, 1812; AUND, Cheverus to Bruté, February 14, 1812.
17. AAB, 2-O-4, Cheverus to Carroll, October 3, 1811.
18. Carroll Papers, Carroll to Plessis, March 2, 1814.
19. ASJCH, I, 45, Carroll to Seton, March 29, 1814.
20. AAB, 2-P-2, Cheverus to Carroll, July 13, 1814.
21. Knapp, *op. cit.,* p. 9.

22. Carroll Papers, Carroll to Enoch Fenwick, June 11, 1814. The pastoral was completed by July 3.
23. AAB, 2-P-2, Cheverus to Carroll, July 13, 1814.
24. Carroll Papers, Pastoral of July 3, 1814. This pastoral is printed in part in Guilday, *op. cit.,* pp. 812–814, and in its entirety in *American Catholic Historical Researches,* VIII (1892), 146 ff.
25. Carroll Papers, Carroll to Grassi, October 14, 1814. Cheverus seems to have received the same report from Bruté by way of Mother Seton. Prince Rohan de Chabot after the death of his wife became a priest, was ordained in 1822, consecrated Archbishop of Bensançon in 1829, and created cardinal on July 5, 1830. He was succeeded at Bensançon in 1833 by William Dubourg, Cheverus' friend.
26. The Baltimore *Federal Republican's* editorial denouncing the war led to a riot which drove the publishers from the city. When they tried to re-establish themselves an actual massacre resulted, lasting during July 27–28, 1812. Baltimore was for a while thereafter notorious throughout the nation for its violence and disorders. Cf. Thomas Scharf, *History of Maryland* (Baltimore, 1879), III, 1–5. Carroll's letter is printed in *Researches,* IX (January, 1892), 2.
27. AAB, 2-O-8, Cheverus to Carroll, August 31, 1812.
28. AAB, 2-O-9, Cheverus to Carroll, December 30, 1812.
29. AAB, 2-O-10, Cheverus to Carroll, January 5, 1813. The veto question dividing the English and Irish prelates involved governmental interference in the nomination of Catholic bishops in Great Britain. This complex subject is discussed in Philip Hughes, *The Catholic Question, 1688–1829* (London, 1929), pp. 261–275. The subject of the Flaget-Badin dissensions is treated by Schauinger in his biographies of these two men, particularly in *Stephen T. Badin* (Milwaukee, 1956), pp. 169–184.
30. Carroll Papers, Carroll to Plowden, November 11, 1813. Carroll did not hesitate to give his own private views to Plowden in later letters dated March 20, 1815, and June 25, 1815.
31. Flaget stayed in Baltimore until April 22, 1813.
32. Carroll Papers, Carroll to Plowden, January 27, 1812.
33. *Ibid.,* March 20, 1815.
34. *Records,* XX (1909), 66–67, Carroll to Cheverus, August 23, 1814. This letter is found also in Guilday, *op. cit.,* pp. 674–675. The account of these conditions is given in Guilday, *op. cit.,* pp. 660–685.
35. This letter in the Carroll Papers is unaddressed and undated, but internal evidence indicates that it was written to Dubourg between Maréchal's arrival in Baltimore in March, 1812, and Dubourg's departure for Louisiana in October, 1812.
36. Carroll Papers, Carroll to Plessis, March 2, 1814. Dubourg intended to leave on October 15, according to a letter to Bruté dated October 13, 1812; Guilday, *op. cit.,* p. 710, states that Dubourg left on October 18.
37. Carroll Papers, Carroll to Plowden, June 25, 1815. There is even a possibility that Carroll forwarded the names of Dubourg and Maréchal to the pope in 1812. The letter cited in note 35, *supra,* reads, "Mr. Maréchal heard from our friend Mr. Garnier that means had been found to place my letter containing your nomination in the pope's hand . . . that a person of great prudence and confidence was employed in making out the necessary writings for filling the Sees of N.O. and N. York."
38. AAB, 2-P-3, Cheverus to Carroll, September 2, 1814.
39. Carroll Papers, Carroll to Plowden, January 5, 1815.

40. Esther Forbes, *Paul Revere and the World He Lived In* (Boston, 1942), p. 423.
41. AAB, 2-P-4, Cheverus to Carroll, October 24, 1814.
42. *Records,* XIV (1903), 322, Cheverus to Bonneuil, September 12, 1814.
43. Forbes, *op. cit.,* p. 423.
44. Isaiah Thomas' *Diary,* cited in *Hist. Arch. Bost.,* I, 660. John Lothrop was a Princeton graduate who was ordained to the second Congregational Church of Boston where he labored until his death in 1816. His name is also spelled "Lathrop."
45. *Columbian Centinel,* October 15, 1814.
46. Forbes, *op. cit.,* p. 424.
47. Guilday, *op. cit.,* pp. 675–676, Neale to Carroll, September 1, 1814.
48. Carroll Papers, Carroll to the Bishops, September 27, 1814; Guilday, *op. cit.,* pp. 677–678.
49. AAB, 2-P-4, Cheverus to Carroll, October 24, 1814.
50. Schauinger, *Cathedrals in the Wilderness,* p. 111.
51. Carroll Papers, Carroll to Flaget, August 12, 1815.
52. *Ibid.*
53. Forbes, *op. cit.,* pp. 424–425, citing a contemporary diary.
54. *Records,* XIV (1903), 340, Cheverus to Bonneuil, February 15, 1815.

Chapter XII — Losses and Gains

1. AAB, 2-O-4, Cheverus to Carroll, October 3, 1811.
2. AAB, 2-O-7, Cheverus to Carroll, June 2, 1812.
3. *Ibid.,* O'Brien to Carroll, attached to Cheverus' letter.
4. AAB, 5-V-10, O'Brien to Carroll, January 5, 1813.
5. Bentley, Diary, IV, 20, 81, 552.
6. AAB, 2-P-1, Cheverus to Carroll, March 18, 1814; *Hist. Arch. Bost.,* I, 666.
7. AAB, 5-V-11, O'Brien to Carroll, May 15, 1814.
8. ASJCH, I, 13, Cheverus to Seton, April 12, 1814.
9. *Ibid.,* 14, Cheverus to Seton, January 20, 1815.
10. *Hist. Arch. Bost.,* I, 667; *Laity's Directory* (New York, 1822), p. 135.
11. *Ibid.,* I, 647–649.
12. AAB, 2-O-9, Cheverus to Carroll, December 30, 1812.
13. AAB, 2-P-1, Cheverus to Carroll, March 18, 1814. The President and Fellows of Harvard voted to hire Brosius on February 21, 1814. Cf. College Records, V, 144; I, 5, 30.
14. *Hist. Arch. Bost.,* I, 772, Dudleian Lecture, May 12, 1813.
15. Archives of Harvard University, College Records, V, 170; I, 5, 30. October 27, 1814.
16. Archives of the Massachusetts Historical Society, Everett Papers, Cheverus to Everett, April 14, 1815. At that time Cheverus had cousins in Paris, sisters in Laval and Ernée, and a brother in Mayenne.
17. AAB, 2-P-7, Cheverus to Carroll, May 22, 1815.
18. *Hist. Arch. Bost.,* I, 645–647.
19. AAB, 2-P-1, Cheverus to Carroll, March 18, 1814.
20. AAB, 2-O-3, Cheverus to Carroll, January 28, 1811.

21. Louisa Stoughton was the half-sister of Anne de Neuville Linzee. There are frequent references in the Cheverus-Carroll correspondence to the fact that John Carroll was Louisa's godfather.
22. AAB, 2-O-4, Cheverus to Carroll, October 3, 1811.
23. *Records*, XIV (1903), 329, Cheverus to Bonneuil, January 26, 1815.
24. *Ibid.*, p. 316, Cheverus to Bonneuil, August 1, 1814.
25. *Ibid.*, p. 322, Cheverus to Bonneuil, September 12, 1814.
26. *Ibid.*, p. 324, Cheverus to Mme de Bonneuil, December 3, 1814.
27. *Ibid.*, p. 326, Cheverus to Mme de Bonneuil, December 21, 1814.
28. Arch. Plinval, Cheverus to Cheverus, January 22, 1815.
29. *Records*, XIV (1903), 328–354, Cheverus to Bonneuil, January 26, 30, February 3, 7, July 4, 1815.
30. ASJCH, I, 11, Cheverus to Seton, January 24, 1810.
31. AMSV, I, 2, Cheverus to Seton, January 4, 1811.
32. *Ibid.*, 3, Cheverus to Seton, January 20, 1812.
33. *Ibid.*, AUND, Cheverus to Bruté, February 14, 1812.
34. ASJCH, I, 12, Cheverus to Seton, February 26, 1812.
35. *Ibid.*, 13, Cheverus to Seton, April 12, 1814.
36. *Ibid.*, 14, Cheverus to Seton, January 20, 1815.
37. Arch. Plinval, Cheverus to Cheverus, January 22, 1815.
38. Carroll Papers, Carroll to Plowden, January 5, 1815.
39. AUND, Cheverus to Bruté, March 17, 1815.
40. The *Tontine* sailed on April 6, 1815.
41. John Talbot Smith, *The Catholic Church in New York* (New York, 1905), I. 56, implies that Cheverus dedicated the church without permission. Since Bishop Connolly's nomination and consecration as Bishop of New York was not known until after the ceremonies his permission could scarcely have been sought. Archbishop Carroll had every right to delegate Cheverus as his substitute during the vacancy of the see. Cheverus clearly states in his report to Carroll of May 9, 1815, "By your direction & on your declining to come . . . I have dedicated the church." Official notification from Rome of Connolly's consecration reached Baltimore the last week in June, 1815.
42. *Independent Journal; New York Gazette and General Advertiser*, May 11, 1815.
43. *Ibid.; Laity's Directory* (New York, 1822), p. 104.
44. AAB, 14-K-37, Cheverus to Maréchal, September 1, 1820.
45. Abbé Lionel Lindsay, "Extracts from the Journal of Bishop Plessis," *Records*, XV (1904), 396. For a more detailed account of St. Patrick's Cathedral cf. Mother Mary Peter Carthy, O.S.U., *Old St. Patrick's, New York's First Cathedral* (New York, 1947), pp. 23–25.
46. AAB, 2-P-5, Cheverus to Carroll, May 9, 1815. This suggests the private ceremonies took place on May 10. Cheverus in 1820 recalled them as having taken place on the day after Ascension Day, or May 8, 1815.
47. *Ibid.*
48. AABost., Cheverus to Grassi, May 9, 1815, copy of a letter in the Fordham Archives, 2-4-14-18. Father Malevé believed the mission in Frederick, Maryland, was too strenuous. According to Grassi, the Frederick mission included Carroll Manor, Maryland Creek, Hagerstown, Martinsburg, Winchester, and Cumberland. Cf. *Notizie Varie* cited in *Researches*, VIII (July, 1891), 102.
49. AAB, 2-P-6, Cheverus to Carroll, May 11, 1815.
50. AAB, 2-P-7, Cheverus to Carroll, May 22, 1815.
51. AAQ, Cheverus to Plessis, May 22, 1815.
52. Bibl. St. Sulpice, Matignon to Saulnier, August 27, 1815.

53. Carroll Papers, Carroll to Plowden, June 25, 1815. Carroll had received the news from Rome a few days earlier. Litta's letter was dated March 15, 1815. Guilday, *op. cit.*, pp. 814–815, is not reliable on the subject of the resumption of Roman-American relations by mail.

54. Dubourg was consecrated by Giuseppe Cardinal Doria Pamphili on September 24, 1815.

Chapter XIII — Troubled Waters

1. AUND, Cheverus to Bruté, December 1, 1815.
2. AAB, 2-P-8, Cheverus to Carroll, August 16, 1815.
3. Bishop Plessis confirmed the Passamaquoddy Indians on August 31, 1815. Father Romagné preached the sermon on that occasion. On August 29, the clergy had been guests at an Indian banquet connected with an Indian tribal celebration at Pleasant Point.
4. Henri Têtu, *Journal des visites pastorales de 1815 et 1816* (Quebec, 1903), pp. 149–151. This portion of the Plessis diaries is also printed in *Records,* XV (1904), 183–187. Some confusion arises from the errors in dates given in the *Hist. Arch. Bost.,* I, 685, and Carthy, *Old St. Patrick's,* p. 25. Plessis arrived in Boston on September 4, 1815, and left on September 7 in the early afternoon for New York. He arrived in New York on September 9 and left for Albany on September 11.
5. AAQ, Cheverus to Plessis, October 30, 1815.
6. Cheverus learned of Connolly's arrival on November 20 by a letter from Benedict Fenwick, S.J.
7. John Carroll was consecrated on the feast of the Assumption, 1790, and the following year placed his diocese under the patronage of the Blessed Virgin. The Sunday within the Octave of the Assumption was thereafter the principal feast of the Diocese of Baltimore. For details of Carroll's death cf. Melville, *Carroll,* pp. 282–284.
8. *Columbian Centinel,* December 9, 1815.
9. AAB, 12-H-3, Cheverus to Neale, December 11, 1815.
10. AAQ, Cheverus to Plessis, March 28, 1816.
11. AUND, Cheverus to Bruté, March 23, 1816.
12. *Records,* XIV (1903), 370, Cheverus to Bonneuil, December 19, 1815.
13. AAB, 12-P-12, Neale to Litta, February 4, 1816; Arch. Prop. Fide, Am. Cent., III, ff. 360–364.
14. AAB, 12-Q-2, Litta to Neale, July 20, 1816.
15. AUND, Cheverus to Brent, February 22, 1816. The will was drawn on November 22, 1815.
16. AUND, Cheverus to Bruté, June 25, 1816.
17. *Records,* XIV (1903), 374–381, Cheverus to Bonneuil, June 28, July 1, 4, 28, August 3, 30, 1816.
18. *Ibid.,* August 30, 1816; Massachusetts Historical Society, Memoirs of Rev. John Pierce, September 12, 1816. The feminine visitors may have been Alice Cogswell, the first deaf-mute to interest Gallaudet, and Sophie Fowler, a deaf pupil who later became Mrs. Gallaudet. Clerc was also entertained by

Lieutenant-Governor William Phillips during this stay in Boston. Pierce commented of Clerc, "He is a good looking man, 28 years old, of elegant manners, and a cheerful countenance. . . . I have seen Abbé Sicard's letter of introduction in favour of M. Clerc to Bp. Cheverus. He mentions him as *plus instruits* of his *élèves*."

19. AAB, 12-H-4, Cheverus to Neale, October 3, 1816.
20. AAB, 12-H-5, Cheverus to Neale, November 5, 1816; 12-A-8, Burke to Neale, November 9, 1816.
21. Arch. Prop. Fide, Am. Cent., III, ff. 512–513, Cheverus to Litta, November 24, 1816.
22. AAQ, Cheverus to Plessis, April 2, 1817.
23. ASJCH, I, 16, Cheverus to Seton, November 28, 1816.
24. ASMS, Tessier's "Époques," November 13–December 11, 1816; ASJCH, II, 37, Moranvillé to Seton, December 4, 1816.
25. ASJCH, XIII, 17B, Bruté to Seton, December 3, 1816.
26. AABost., copy from Fordham Archives, 2-5-W-19, Cheverus to Neale, December 3, 1816.
27. ASJCH, XIII, 18B, Bruté to Seton and Dubois, December 3, 1816; Moranvillé to Seton, December 4, 1816.
28. AMSV, I, 5, Cheverus to Seton, December 30, 1816.
29. AAB, 12-AJ-3, Maréchal to Neale, December 11, 1816; ASMS, Maréchal to Cortal, December 8, 1816.
30. AMSV, I, 5, Cheverus to Seton, December 30, 1816.
31. Arch. Prop. Fide, Lettere, Vol. 297, fol. 200, Litta to Neale, August 17, 1816. This letter did not arrive in Baltimore until after Cheverus had left on December 11. Maréchal notified Neale on January 11, 1817, that he had news from Paris. Cf. AAB, 12-A-J4.
32. AAB, 14-H-3, Cheverus to Maréchal, February 3, 1817.
33. AAB, 12-L-3, Cheverus to Neale, February 3, 1817.
34. Arch. Prop. Fide, Am. Cent. III, ff. 416–417, Cheverus to Litta, February 7, 1817.
35. AUND, Cheverus to Bruté, March 24, 1817.
36. AAQ, Cheverus to Plessis, April 2, 1817.
37. *Records*, XIV (1903), 469, Cheverus to Bonneuil, September 10, 1817.
38. *Ibid.*, pp. 457–460, Cheverus to Bonneuil, May 3, 1817.
39. AAB, 14-H-7, Cheverus to Maréchal, May 1, 1817.
40. *Records*, p. 458, Cheverus to Bonneuil, May 3, 1817.
41. *Ibid.*, pp. 463–465, Cheverus to Bonneuil, May 24, 30, 1817.
42. *Ibid.*, p. 472, Cheverus to Bonneuil, October 4, 1817.
43. AUND, Cheverus to Bruté, June 24, 1817.
44. AAB, 14-H-8, Cheverus to Maréchal, June 25, 1817; 19-A-2, Matignon to Maréchal, September 15, 1817.
45. Arch. Prop. Fide, Am. Cent. III, fol. 600, Maréchal to Litta, June 25, 1817.
46. *Records*, XIV (1903), 475, Cheverus to Bonneuil, November 11, quoting directly from Maréchal's letter of November 6, 1817.
47. *Ibid.*
48. AAB, 14-I-16, Cheverus to Maréchal, November 13, 1817.
49. AAB, 14-I-13, Cheverus to Maréchal, October 9, 1817.
50. AAB, 14-I-14, Cheverus to Maréchal, November 3, 1817.
51. AAB, 14-I-16, Cheverus to Maréchal, November 13, 1817.
52. AAB, 14-I-17, Cheverus to Maréchal, November 18, 1817; AUND, Cheverus to Keating, November 18, 1817.
53. *Records*, XIV (1903), 477, Cheverus to Bonneuil, December 4, 1817.

54. The Sisters of Charity went to Philadelphia in September, 1814, and took formal charge of the orphanage on October 6, 1814. Sister Rose White, whom Cheverus had met in Emmitsburg in 1810, was the first head of the institution in Philadelphia; in December, 1817, Sister Rose was in New York, heading a similar institution.
55. AAB, 14-I-18, Cheverus to Maréchal, December 3, 1817.
56. ASMS, Tessier's "Époques," December 14, 1817.
57. AAB, 14-I-19, Cheverus to Maréchal, January 10, 1818.

CHAPTER XIV — THE OLD ORDER CHANGES

1. Carroll Papers, Carroll to Enoch Fenwick, June 21, 1815.
2. AUND, Cheverus to Bruté, October 9, 1816; AAB, 12-H-4, Cheverus to Neale, October 3, 1816.
3. AAB, 14-H-7, Cheverus to Maréchal, May 1, 1817; *Records,* XIV (1903), 458, Cheverus to Bonneuil, May 3, 1817.
4. *Records,* XIV (1903), 463, Cheverus to Bonneuil, May 24, 1817.
5. Romagné was at Sacé from January, 1819, until November 19, 1836. He and Cheverus died the same year.
6. According to Matignon, Tisserant was in Paris in 1816 but intended to go to Vienna to live with relatives. Records in the Archives Nationales, however, show that he received a salary from the French government after that.
7. Bibl. St. Sulpice, Matignon to Le Saulnier, April 15, August 27, 1815.
8. *Records,* XIV (1903), 449–450, Cheverus to Bonneuil, August 3, 1816, quoting directly from his brother's letter.
9. *Ibid.*
10. AUND, Cheverus to Bruté, October 9, 1816. For the missions of the Restoration era cf. Bertier, *La Restauration,* pp. 435–437 and Dansette, *Histoire Religieuse de la France,* pp. 269–273.
11. AAB, 2-L-2, Carron to Carroll, June 4, 1806. Carron was invited to enter the Diocese of Baltimore and was urged by the Bishop of St. Pol de Léon to go to Louisiana, but he rejected both suggestions.
12. *Records,* XIV (1903), 450, Cheverus to Bonneuil, August 3, 1816.
13. *Ibid.,* August 6, 1816.
14. Bibl. St. Sulpice, Matignon to Le Saulnier, May 11, 1817.
15. *Records,* XIV (1903), 443, Cheverus to Bonneuil, July 28, 1816.
16. AAB, 14-H-11, Cheverus to Maréchal, August 12, 1817.
17. Schauinger, *Cathedrals in the Wilderness,* pp. 154–155.
18. AAB, 14-H-11, Cheverus to Maréchal, August 12, 1817. Eight of the men who accompanied Nerinckx from Europe stayed in Georgetown with the Jesuits; one, James O. Vande Velde, eventually became Bishop of Chicago.
19. ASJCH, XII, 55, Seton to Bruté, September 2, 1816; AUND, Cheverus to Bruté, October 9, 1816.
20. Frederick John Easterly, C.M., *The Life of Rt. Rev. Joseph Rosati, C.M.* (Washington, 1942), pp. 11–26. Rosati was made administrator of the Diocese of New Orleans and St. Louis in 1826; the next year he became bishop of the newly erected See of St. Louis.

21. *Ibid.,* pp. 47–48. The future bishops were Antoine Blanc, Leo De Neckere, Michel Portier. A fourth, Auguste Jeanjean, was offered a diocese but refused.
22. AUND, Cheverus to Bruté, August 21, 1817; AAB, 14-I-13, Cheverus to Maréchal, October 9, 1817.
23. AUND, Cheverus to Bruté, March 24, 1817.
24. Cheverus' letters to Bonneuil in May give the date May 30 as the date of the ordination. Ryan offered his first Mass on Trinity Sunday, June 1, 1817.
25. AUND, Cheverus to Bruté, August 21, 1817.
26. AAB, Cheverus to Maréchal, June 25, 1818.
27. AAB, 14-J-27, Cheverus to Maréchal, January 7, 1819.
28. AUND, Cheverus to Bruté, October 9, 1816.
29. Arch. Prop. Fide, Am. Cent., III, 416–417, copy in the AABost.
30. ASJCH, I, 36, Matignon to Seton, November 10, 1816.
31. *Ibid.,* 16, Cheverus to Seton, November 28, 1816.
32. AMSV, I, 5, Cheverus to Seton, December 30, 1816.
33. Ryan conferred Baptism for the first time on July 20, 1817.
34. AAB, 14-H-12, Cheverus to Maréchal, September 29, 1817.
35. *Records,* XIV (1903), 471, Cheverus to Bonneuil, October 4, 1817.
36. AAB, 14-I-19, Cheverus to Maréchal, January 10, 1818; *Records,* XIV (1903), 487, Cheverus to Bonneuil, May 2, 1818.
37. AAB, 14-I-13, Cheverus to Maréchal, October 9, 1817. The dispensing powers related to *2e Gradu consanguinitatis* and *super disparitate cultus.*
38. AABost., Prefect of Propaganda to Cheverus, December 6, 1817.
39. ASJCH, XII, 56, 79, Seton to Bruté, no dates.
40. AUND, Cheverus to Bruté, April 9, 1818.
41. ASMS, Tessier's "Époques," June 3, 1818.
42. Archives of the Mother Seton Guild at Emmitsburg, Seton to Seton, February 27, 1818.
43. ASJCH, Souvay-Seton Copies, 39, Seton to Seton, March 24, 1818.
44. Archives of the Mother Seton Guild, Seton to Seton, April 1, 1818.
45. AUND, Cheverus to Bruté, April 9, 1818.
46. ASJCH, Seton-Jevons Collection, Seton to Seton, July 21, 1818.
47. AMSV, Letters, August 11, 1818.
48. Seton Guild, Seton to Seton, September 17, 1818.
49. AAB, 14-I-24, Cheverus to Maréchal, July 15, 1818.
50. Bibl. St. Sulpice, Cheverus to Le Saulnier, July 28, 1818; AMSV, Cheverus to Seton, August 11, 1818.
51. Boston Public Library, Cheverus to William Williamson, August 20, 1818.
52. Seton Guild, Seton to Seton, August 29, 1818.
53. AAQ, Cheverus to Plessis, August 26, 1818.
54. *Records,* XIV (1903), 394, Cheverus to Mme Bonneuil, November 19, 1818.
55. Cheverus' account of Matignon's death was given to Le Saulnier in Montreal who gave it to the papers, who printed it under the title, "Bishop Cheverus' Diary." The *Columbian Centinel* on April 21, 1819, reprinted the account from the Montreal papers. The same account appears also in Arthur T. Connolly, *An Appreciation of the Life and Labors of Rev. Francis Matignon, D.D.* (Boston, 1908), Publications of the New England Catholic History Society, no. 7, p. 24. The printed accounts are substantially the same as the one given to Maréchal on October 7, 1818.
56. AAB, 14-J-25, Cheverus to Maréchal, October 7, 1818.
57. Arch. Plinval, Cheverus to Mme de Cheverus, November 14, 1818.

CHAPTER XV — SUNSHINE AND SHADOW

1. American Antiquarian Society, Bentley Papers, Correspondence II, 14, Cheverus to Bentley, October 20, 1818.
2. Boston Athenaeum, fragment of Bentley's letter attached to the Psalter, Bentley to Cheverus, October 21, 1818. For a complete list of books given by Cheverus to the Boston Athenaeum cf. Walter Muir Whitehill, *A Memorial to Bishop Cheverus with a Catalogue of the Books Given by Him to the Boston Athenaeum* (Boston, 1951).
3. *Records,* XIV (1903), 494, Cheverus to Bonneuil, November 19, 1818.
4. ASJCH, Souvay-Filicchi Copies, 51, Seton to Filicchi, November 11, 1818.
5. Arch. Plinval, Cheverus to Mme de Cheverus, November 14, 1818.
6. Arch. Plinval, Cheverus to Louis de Cheverus, March 3, 1821.
7. *Ibid.,* January 22, 1815.
8. ASJCH, Seton-Jevons Collection, Seton to Seton, November 7, 1819.
9. Raymond Walters, Jr., *Albert Gallatin* (New York, 1957), p. 304.
10. *Records,* XIV (1903), 504–507, Cheverus to Bonneuil, October 28, 1820, March 30, 1821.
11. AAQ, Maréchal to Plessis, November 6, 1823; *Records, XVIII* (1907), 451.
12. AAB, 14-J-29, Cheverus to Maréchal, May 6, 1819.
13. Bibl. St. Sulpice, Cheverus to Le Saulnier, May 13, 1819.
14. AAB, 14-J-30, Cheverus to Maréchal, July 16, 1819; *Columbian Centinel,* July 3, 1819.
15. AAB, 14-J-29, Cheverus to Maréchal, May 6, 1819.
16. AUND, Cheverus to Bruté, January 5, 1820. The new organ was installed three years later.
17. *Records,* XIV (1903), 501, Cheverus to Bonneuil, December 27, 1819; *Columbian Centinel,* January 29, 1820; Charles B. Fairbanks, *Aguecheek* (Boston, 1859), 242.
18. AUND, Cheverus to Bruté, January 5, 1820, April 14, 1820.
19. *Records,* XV (1904), 92, Cheverus to Bonneuil, October 23, 1822.
20. AUND, Cheverus to Bruté, March 23, 1816. The valuation of Thayer's property was placed at $10,764. This was later slightly augmented by the sale of his effects in Ireland.
21. *Hist. Arch. Bost.,* I, 708–709. This amount was $2,500. The other two-thirds were left to relatives in France and to Cheverus.
22. AAB, 14-J-30, Cheverus to Maréchal, July 16, 1819.
23. AUND, Cheverus to Bruté, January 5, 1820.
24. *Ibid.,* April 14, 1820.
25. *Ibid.,* June 24, 1817.
26. AAB, 14-J-36, Cheverus to Maréchal, July 18, 1820.
27. AAB, 14-K-37, Cheverus to Maréchal, September 1, 1820.
28. *Ibid.*
29. AAB, 14-J-29, Cheverus to Maréchal, May 6, 1819.
30. ASMS, Tessier's "Époques," August 27, 1820. For Babade's direction of Mother Seton cf. Melville, *Seton,* pp. 166–172.
31. AUND, Cheverus to Bruté, December 19, 1820.
32. *Ibid.*
33. ASJCH, I, 18, Cheverus to Seton, December 17, 1820.
34. John Tracy Ellis, *Documents of American Catholic History* (Milwaukee, 1956),

pp. 209–210, "Maréchal's Report to Propaganda, October 16, 1818." For a description of the designing and building of the cathedral cf. Talbot Hamlin, *Benjamin Henry Latrobe* (New York, 1955), pp. 233–252, 244–245, 251–252.

35. *Maryland Historical Magazine,* XXXIV (December, 1939), 344–345, Maréchal to Hyde de Neuville, October 4, 5, 1819. The paintings were: Karl von Guerin's "St. Louis Burying his Plague-Stricken Troops," and Pierre Guerin's "Descent From the Cross."

36. Latrobe died on September 3, 1820; Carroll had been dead since 1815.

37. *Records,* XIV (1903), 509–510, Cheverus to Bonneuil, May 23, 1821. Cheverus was concerned enough to make out his will on May 21, 1821, before setting out for Baltimore.

38. AAB, 14-K-45, Cheverus to Maréchal, May 3, 1821.

39. AAB, 20-H-12, Roux to Maréchal, May 25, 1821.

40. AAB, 14-K-46, Cheverus to Maréchal, June 15, 1821.

41. AAQ, Maréchal to Plessis, June 25, 1821.

42. AAB, 14-K-47, Cheverus to Maréchal, July 9, 1821; AAQ, Cheverus to Plessis, September 6, 1821.

43. AAB, 14-J-27, 29, Cheverus to Maréchal, January 7, 1819, May 6, 1819.

44. Arch. Plinval, Cheverus to Cheverus, March 13, 1819.

45. AUND, Cheverus to Bruté, April 14, 1820.

46. AAB, 14-J-20, Cheverus to Maréchal, May 6, 1819. The comments of the Sulpician theologians are filed under 20-T-31, "Notes sur le livre de M. Taylor."

47. AAB, 20-F-12, Taylor to Maréchal, February 15, 1821.

48. Father Charles Ffrench, for example, who was troublesome in both the Dioceses of Quebec and New York, eventually proved very satisfactory in the Diocese of Boston under Bishop Benedict Fenwick.

49. AAB, 14-K-45, Cheverus to Maréchal, May 3, 1821.

50. AAB, 14-L-50, Cheverus to Maréchal, November 26, 1822.

51. AAB, 14-K-48, Cheverus to Maréchal, August 17, 1821.

52. AAQ, Cheverus to Plessis, September 6, 1821.

53. AAB, 14-L-49, Cheverus to Maréchal, September 26, 1821.

54. *Records,* XIV (1903), 513, Cheverus to Bonneuil, December 19, 1821.

55. AABost., copy from the Archives of Georgetown University, Cheverus to Fenwick, February 1, 1822.

56. *Records,* III (1887), 18.

57. For Cooper cf. John E. McGarity, "Samuel Sutherland Cooper, 1769–1843," *Records,* XXXVIII (1926), 305–340; for Barber cf. *Hist. Arch. Bost.,* I, 743–746; II, 59–67.

58. Bibl. St. Sulpice, Kohlmann to Cheverus, June 18, 1822.

59. AAB, 14-L-52, Cheverus to Maréchal, January 27, 1823.

60. AAQ, Cheverus to Plessis, September 19, 1822.

61. Baptisms rose from 149 in 1819 to 282 in 1822.

62. Bibl. St. Sulpice, Cheverus to Le Saulnier, September 2, 1822. The churches in 1823 at the close of Cheverus' episcopate were located in: Franklin Street, South Boston, Salem, Claremont, Newcastle, Whitefield, New Bedford, Old Town, and Pleasant Point.

63. This matter of Cheverus' preaching in the Episcopal church in Bristol appears to have been elaborated upon as time passed. The *Historical Magazine* of October, 1873, upon the authority of Dr. Robertson of Saugerties, New York, asserted that "after a brief devotion" Cheverus preached. Robertson had been a seminarian in Bristol at the time. Cf. *Researches* VIII (October, 1891), 187. By 1889 this account was repeated in these words, "The saintly Bishop of Boston . . . read the whole Episcopalian service of 'Morning Prayer' to one

of their congregations and preached to them, all to their great satisfaction and edification." Cf. *Catholic World*, L (December, 1889), 361.
64. *Hist. Arch. Bost.*, I, 756, Cheverus to the Catholics of Hartford, February 7, 1823.
65. AUND, Cheverus to Bruté, December 17, 1820.
66. *United States Catholic Magazine*, III (1890), 216 ff. William L. Lucey, S.J., in *The Catholic Church in Maine*, p. 20, suggests that the Catholic petition concentrated on removing the oath of abjuration since the Baptists and other dissenters were influential enough in securing the removal of the other religious discriminatory clause, the ministerial tax. Lucey further states "it is not easy to determine the exact influence" of the Catholic petition.
67. *The Palladium*, February 18, 22, 1820.
68. The article was signed only "B. G."
69. Library of the American Unitarian Association, Cheverus to un-named person, December 1, 1820.
70. John Pierce, *The Right of Private Judgment* (Cambridge, 1821), p. 23.

CHAPTER XVI — MORE DISTANT HORIZONS

1. AABost., copy from Fordham Archives, 206-S-2a, Benedict Fenwick to George Fenwick, January 14, 1823.
2. Bibl. St. Sulpice, Cheverus to Le Saulnier, February 20, 1821.
3. AAB, 14-K-48, Cheverus to Maréchal, August 17, 1821.
4. AAB, 14-H-6, Cheverus to Maréchal, April 15, 1817.
5. AAB, 14-I-23, 24, Cheverus to Maréchal, June 25, July 15, 1818.
6. AAB, 14-K-40, Cheverus to Maréchal, December 6, 1820.
7. AAB, 12-R-7, rough draft of Neale to Cheverus; 14-H-5, Cheverus to Maréchal, April 16, 1817; 14-I-13, Cheverus to Maréchal, October 9, 1817.
8. AAB, 14-J-28, Cheverus to Maréchal, January 25, 1819.
9. AAB, 14-L-49, Cheverus to Maréchal, September 26, 1821.
10. AAB, 14-J-33, Cheverus to Maréchal, December 20, 1819.
11. Archives of Georgetown University, Transcripts, 316, Taylor to Maréchal, July 8, 1820.
12. AAB, 14-K-39, Cheverus to Maréchal, November 29, 1820.
13. AAB, 14-K-40, Cheverus to Maréchal, December 6, 1820.
14. AAB, 17-F-8, Gradwell to Maréchal, June 23, 1821.
15. AABost., copy from Charleston archives, Fenwick to Wallace, April 10, 1822.
16. AAB, 14-J-33, Cheverus to Maréchal, December 20, 1819.
17. AAB, 14-J-28, Cheverus to Maréchal, January 25, 1819.
18. AAQ, Cheverus to Plessis, January 2, 1821.
19. AAB, 14-K-40, Cheverus to Maréchal, December 6, 1820.
20. AAB, 14-K-38, Cheverus to Maréchal, September 26, 1820.
21. AAB, 2-J-1, Regulations of the First Council, Article 4, November 19, 1810.
22. Melville, *Carroll*, p. 280.
23. Carroll Papers, Carroll to Grassi, November 22, 1813.
24. AAB, 2-Q-4, Clorivière to Carroll, November 16, 1812.
25. AAB, 14-H-7, Cheverus to Maréchal, May 1, 1817, enclosing Cheverus to Litta, April 25, 1817.
26. *Ibid.*

27. AAB, 14-I-13, Cheverus to Maréchal, October 9, 1817.
28. AAB, 14-H-1, Cheverus to Maréchal, December 31, 1817.
29. AAB, 14-I-23, Cheverus to Maréchal, June 25, 1818.
30. AAB, 14-I-24, Cheverus to Maréchal, July 15, 1818.
31. The complete English text of Maréchal's report is found in John Tracy Ellis, *Documents of American Catholic History* (Milwaukee, 1956), pp. 208–225; the Latin text appears in the *Catholic Historical Review*, I (January, 1916), 439–453.
32. AAB, 14-J-26, Cheverus to Maréchal, October 28, 1818.
33. Ellis, *Documents*, pp. 226–228, Trustees to Maréchal, June 14, 1819.
34. AAB, 14-J-30, Cheverus to Maréchal, July 16, 1819.
35. AAB, 14-J-28, Cheverus to Maréchal, January 25, 1819.
36. The bulls making Plessis Archbishop of Quebec arrived five hours after the Canadian's departure for Europe, on July 3, 1819.
37. *Pastoral Letter of the Archbishop of Baltimore to the Roman Catholicks of Norfolk, Virginia* (Baltimore, 1819). Maréchal sent Cheverus a dozen copies.
38. AAB, 14-J-32, Cheverus to Maréchal, December 10, 1819.
39. *Ibid.*
40. AAB, 14-I-23, Cheverus to Maréchal, June 25, 1818.
41. Bishop David was consecrated on August 15, 1819.
42. Schauinger, *Cathedrals in the Wilderness,* pp. 190–191.
43. *Records,* XVIII (1907), 41, Flaget to Plessis, November 3, 1820.
44. Arch. Prop. Fide, Am. Cent. IV, Dubourg to Propaganda, May 12, June 25, 1819; AAQ, Dubourg to Plessis, March 19, 1822.
45. AAB, 14-K-37, Cheverus to Maréchal, September 1, 1820.
46. Sister M. Columba Fox, *The Life of the Rt. Rev. John Baptist Mary David, 1764–1841* (New York, 1925), pp. 115–116, David to Maréchal, July 25, 1820.
47. AAB, 14-I-13, Cheverus to Maréchal, October 9, 1817. Maréchal apparently did not discuss Moranvillé's name with the western bishops, for Flaget in 1820 criticized him for not considering the priest "who has always shown such zeal and aptitude in governing his parish." Cf. Schauinger, *Cathedrals,* p. 192.
48. AAB, 14-H-1, Cheverus to Maréchal, December 31, 1817.
49. AAB, 14-I-20, Cheverus to Maréchal, January 28, 1818. For a biographical sketch of DeBarth cf. Jules C. Foin, "Rev. Louis Barth," *Records,* II (December, 1888), 29–37. His name was really Louis Barth de Walbach.
50. AAB, 14-I-23, Cheverus to Maréchal, June 28, 1818.
51. AAB, 14-J-28, Cheverus to Maréchal, January 25, 1819.
52. AAB, 14-J-33, Cheverus to Maréchal, December 20, 1819.
53. Schauinger, *Cathedrals,* pp. 191–192.
54. *Hist. Arch. Bost.,* I, 786.
55. Ffrench arrived in New York in January, 1818. For an account of his career there cf. Mother Mary Peter Carthy, O.S.U., *Old St. Patrick's* (New York, 1947), pp. 39–44.
56. AAB, 14-J-32, Cheverus to Maréchal, December 10, 1819.
57. AAB, 14-K-38, Cheverus to Maréchal, September 26, 1820.
58. AABost., copy from Arch. Prop. Fide, Plessis to Fontana, September 6, 1820.
59. AABost., copy from Archives of Georgetown University, Taylor to Cheverus, March 21, 1820; Taylor to Maréchal, July 8, 1820.
60. Arch. Prop. Fide, Atti, 1821, Sommario, p. 29.
61. AAB, 14-K-38, Cheverus to Maréchal, September 26, 1820.
62. Arch. Prop. Fide, Atti, 1821, Sommario, pp. 7–8.
63. AAB, 14-K-39, Cheverus to Maréchal, November 29, 1820.

64. AAB, 14-K-40, Cheverus to Maréchal, December 6, 1820.
65. AAB, 14-K-39, Cheverus to Maréchal, November 29, 1820.
66. AAQ, Cheverus to Plessis, January 2, 1821.
67. AAB, 14-K-41, Cheverus to Maréchal, January 30, 1821.
68. Bibl. St. Sulpice, Cheverus to Le Saulnier, February 20, 1821.
69. AAB, 14-K-44, Cheverus to Maréchal enclosing Cheverus to Conwell, April 6, 1821; Francis E. Tourscher, O.S.A., *The Hogan Schism and Trustee Troubles* (Philadelphia, 1930), pp. 40–63; Peter Guilday, *The Life and Times of John England, 1786–1842* (New York, 1927), I, 384–387.
70. Bishop Conwell's sentence of excommunication appears in *Records,* XXIII (1912), 137. The excommunication was upheld by Pius VII on August 24, 1822.
71. *Records,* XVIII (1907), 441, Plessis to Maréchal, April 13, 1821.
72. AAB, 14-K-48, Cheverus to Maréchal, August 17, 1821.
73. AAB, 14-K-46, Cheverus to Maréchal, June 15, 1821; Bibl. St. Sulpice, Cheverus to Le Saulnier, March 9, 1821.
74. AAB, 14-K-47, Cheverus to Maréchal, July 9, 1821.
75. ASJCH, Souvay-Filicchi Copies, no number, Filicchi to Cheverus, November 5, 1821, citing Cheverus to Filicchi, July 31, 1821.
76. AAB, 14-K-48, Cheverus to Maréchal, August 17, 1821.
77. AAB, 14-K-49, Cheverus to Maréchal, September 25, 1821.
78. *Maryland Historical Magazine,* XXXIV (December, 1939), 346–347, Maréchal to Hyde de Neuville, October 5, 1821.
79. *Records,* XVIII (1907), 445, Maréchal to Plessis, October 9, 1821.
80. AAQ, Cheverus to Plessis, October 17, 1821.
81. AABost., copy, Plessis to Connolly, February 23, 1822.
82. AAQ, Cheverus to Plessis, March 8, 1822. After Connolly's death in 1825 Malou's faculties were restored and he served St. Peter's until his own death in 1827. For a brief biographical sketch cf. Patrick J. Dignan, "Peter Anthony Malou, Patriot and Priest," *Records,* XLIII (March, 1932).
83. AAB, 14-K-48, Cheverus to Maréchal, August 17, 1821.
84. AAQ, Cheverus to Plessis, September 6, 1821; AAB, 14-L-49, Cheverus to Maréchal, September 26, 1821. Until Hogan betrayed England's trust in October, 1821, the Bishop of Charleston had been willing to mediate between Hogan and Conwell.
85. ASJCH, Souvay-Filicchi Copies, no number, Filicchi to Cheverus, November 5, 1821.
86. *Records,* XV (1904), 84, Cheverus to Bonneuil, January 17, 1822.
87. AAQ, Cheverus to Plessis, March 8, 1822.
88. Bibl. St. Sulpice, Cheverus to Blyth, June 11, 1822, Cheverus to Le Saulnier, June 11, 1822.
89. Wiliam Leo Lucey, *The Catholic Church in Maine* (Francestown, New Hampshire, 1957), pp. 46–49.
90. *Records,* XV (1904), 86, 88–89, Cheverus to Bonneuil, June 30, July 13, 1822.
91. *Ibid.,* 92, Cheverus to Bonneuil, October 23, 1822.
92. *Columbian Centinel,* July 31, 1822.
93. Bibl. St. Sulpice, Cheverus to Roux, September 23, 1822.
94. AAQ, Cheverus to Plessis, September 19, 1822.
95. Bibl. St. Sulpice, Cheverus to Le Saulnier, September 2, 1822.
96. AABost., copy from the Archives of the Diocese of Portland, Taylor to Kavanagh, September 21, 1822.
97. *Maryland Historical Magazine,* XXXIV (December, 1939), 347–348, Maréchal to Hyde de Neuville, February 16, 1823. Maréchal returned on the ship *Six Frères,* Captain Williams. The voyage was very stormy and they had to put in

to Kinsale, Ireland. He told Neuville, "Thank God, we landed happily at New York on November 21, all in good health though tired."

98. AAQ, Maréchal to Plessis, November 22, 1822, March 11, 1823.
99. James Henry Bailey, II, *A History of the Diocese of Richmond* (Richmond, 1956), pp. 54–55.

CHAPTER XVII — A ROYAL SUMMONS

1. AAB, 14-L-51, Cheverus to Maréchal, January 14, 1823.
2. AAQ, Cheverus to Plessis, March 19, 1823.
3. AAB, 14-L-54, Cheverus to Maréchal, April 8, 1823.
4. *Researches,* VIII (October, 1891), 175. Cheverus probably initiated the collection for the poor on St. Patrick's Day for the records of the society show that he took one up after his own speech in 1817.
5. Boston *Daily Advertiser,* March 26, 1823.
6. *Columbian Centinel,* March 26, 1823.
7. AAB, 14-L-53, Cheverus to Maréchal, March 26, 1823. A priest of Havre also wrote at the same time as Moreau de la Vigerie. *The Hist. Arch. Bost.,* I, 797, suggests that Cheverus gave the news to the papers himself but this is scarcely compatible with the repeated expressions of distress Cheverus felt at all the publicity.
8. Arch. Nat., F19-2538, Prince de Croij to Cheverus, January 18, 1823. The royal ordinance naming Cheverus to Montauban was given at the Tuileries on January 13 and registered on January 17, 1823. Cf. Arch. Nat., F19-699, fol. 18.
9. AAB, 14-L-54, Cheverus to Maréchal, April 8, 1823, enclosing a copy of Neuville's letter.
10. For a brief sketch of Hyde de Neuville cf. A. Boullée, "Hyde de Neuville," *Biographie Universelle,* XX (1858), 239–245; for his own account of his American years cf. *Mémoires* (Paris, 1888). Chapter XII of Volume I covers the first years, 1807–1814.
11. Arch. Plinal, Cheverus to Cheverus, March 3, 1821.
12. *Records,* XV (1904), 90, Cheverus to Bonneuil, July 13, 1822. Cheverus wrote only, "M. de Neuville is returning to France. I hope that he will obtain the retirement of M. de Valnais." Maréchal learned by February, 16, 1823, that Hyde de Neuville was Minister of Interior instead; but as late as May 7 Cheverus still believed Neuville to be in Constantinople.
13. *Maryland Historical Magazine,* XXXIV (December, 1939), 348, Maréchal to Neuville, February 16, 1823.
14. AAB, 14-L-54, Cheverus to Maréchal, April 8, 1823.
15. Bibl. St. Sulpice, Cheverus to Le Saulnier, April 10, 1823.
16. AAB, 32-C-A-9, Gradwell to Maréchal, April 13, 1823.
17. AAB, 17-D-20, Garnier to Maréchal, May 24, 1823.
18. *Records,* XV (1904), 99, Cheverus to Mme de Bonneuil, April 21, 1823.
19. The Gilbert Stuart portrait is in the possession of the Boston Museum of Fine Arts. Steel engravings of this portrait were widely circulated and one was treasured for years by a Bristol boy who in later life was the Protestant

Episcopal Bishop Mark Antony DeWolfe Howe. Cf. Walter Muir Whitehill, *A Memorial to Bishop Cheverus* (Boston, 1951), p. xix.

20. Arch. Nat., F19-2358, Protest of the Boston Protestants to Prince de Croij, April 22, 1823. The protest was sent in both English and French.
21. AAB, 20-I-16, Roux to Maréchal, June 11, 1823.
22. Arch. Nat., F19-2538, Maréchal to Cheverus, April 24, 1823. This more formal copy of Maréchal's first letter was also forwarded to Rome on January 13, 1824.
23. AAB, 14-L-56, Cheverus to Maréchal, April 21, 1823.
24. *Records*, XV (1904), 98–99, Cheverus to Bonneuil, April 21, 1823.
25. Hamon, *Vie du Cardinal de Cheverus*, p. 127.
26. Copies of this letter of Cheverus to Prince de Croij, April 30, 1823, exist in AAB, 14-L-55, Bibl. St. Sulpice copy dated May 7, 1823, and Arch. Nat., F19-2538.
27. Bibl. St. Sulpice, Cheverus to Le Saulnier, May 7, 1823; AAB, 21-A-21, Poynter to Maréchal, September 17, 1823.
28. AAB, 14-L-55, Cheverus to Maréchal, May 9, 1823.
29. Archives de Notre Dame de Mayenne, Cheverus to Cheverus, July 29, 1823.
30. Bibl. St. Sulpice, Cheverus to Le Saulnier, May 7, 1823.
31. AAB, 20-I-16, Roux to Maréchal, June 11, 1823.
32. Arch. Nat., F19-268, Report of August 1, 1823, on the state of bishops and archbishops of France, pp. 72, 86–87.
33. The cardinal's hat was conferred on February 3, 1823.
34. G. de Bertier de Sauvigny, *La Restauration* (Paris, 1955), pp. 416–417.
35. R. Limouzin-Lamothe, *Monseigneur de Quelen, Archevêque de Paris* (Paris, 1955), I, 84, suggests that although the new constitution authorized the king to make treaties "perhaps because the Concordat contained new financial burdens resulting from the creation of some forty new dioceses, perhaps for fear of troubles fomented by the enemies of the Church, the ministry dared not act without parliamentary sanction."
36. Bertier, *op. cit.*, pp. 409–414.
37. Arch. Nat., F19-1929, Address of the French Hierarchy, May 30, 1819. Three cardinals, eight archbishops, and twenty-nine bishops or bishops-elect adhered.
38. *Ibid.*, Pius VII to the French hierarchy, August 19, 1819.
39. Arch. Nat., F19-2538, Corbière to Prince de Croij, July 26, 1823.
40. The *Almanach Royal* of 1823 gave the population of Montauban as 25,232. Cheverus in a letter dated January 24, 1825, said, "There are in this city about 5,000 Protestants."
41. For an account of Napoleon's visit cf. *Journal de Lot,* August 7, 1808. The bull re-erecting the Diocese of Montauban was issued by Pius VII on February 17, 1808.
42. Camille Daux, *Histoire de l'église de Montauban* (Paris, 1886), II, Part VII, 9–24. MacCarthy who was then in his late forties was on the verge of entering the Society of Jesus.
43. Arch. Nat., F19-669, fol. 18, Ordinance 317.
44. Arch. Nat., F19-2538, note attached to Cheverus packet, June 18, 1823.
45. *Ibid.*, Moreau de la Vigerie to Besson, June 18, 1823. Later that year Besson was made Bishop of Metz.
46. *Ibid.*, Corbière to Prince de Croij, July 26, 1823.
47. *Ibid.*, Vigerie to Cheverus, no date. Cheverus replied to this on August 30, 1823. Cf. Vigerie to Besson, October 5, 1823.
48. AAB, 14-J-25, Cheverus to Maréchal, October 7, 1818; Bibl. St. Sulpice, October 9, 1818.
49. Arch. Nat., F19-2538, Prince de Croij to Cheverus, July 12, 1823.

50. *Ibid.,* Cheverus to Prince de Croij, August 30, 1823.
51. AAB, 14-L-57, Cheverus to Maréchal, September 3, 1823.
52. AABost., copy from Arch. Prop. Fide, U.N.S., 61-870, Maréchal to Gradwell, September 10, 1823.
53. *Ibid.*
54. AABost., copy from the Archives of the Diocese of Portland, Taylor to Kavanagh, September 4, 1823.
55. AUND, Cheverus to Bruté, September 24, 1823.
56. Boston Athenaeum, Records, Theodore Lyman, Jr., to Cheverus, September 15, 1823. Complete lists of the Cheverus gifts are preserved both at the Athenaeum and in the Archives of the Archdiocese of Boston.
57. Boston Athenaeum, Cheverus to Lyman, September 25, 1823. This letter was printed in the *Republic,* October 3, 1903, p. 8.
58. *Boston Monthly Magazine,* I (1825), 14–15.
59. *Ibid.,* pp. 15–16.
60. *Ibid.,* p. 16.
61. *Commercial Gazette,* September 22, 1823.

CHAPTER XVIII — PRELATE IN WAITING

1. *United States Catholic Miscellany,* II (1824), 41, Cheverus to Robinson, October 29, 1823.
2. Arch. Nat., F19-2538, Croij to Cheverus, January 18, 1823.
3. AAB, 14-L-50, Cheverus to Maréchal, November 26, 1822.
4. AAB, 14-L-53, Cheverus to Maréchal, March 26, 1823.
5. AABost., copy from Arch. Prop. Fide, Cheverus to Somaglia, January 13, 1824, quoting Maréchal.
6. AABost., Cheverus to McNamara, July 26, 1824.
7. *United States Catholic Miscellany,* II (1824), 41–43, Report of Captain Robinson of the wreck of the *Paris,* November 3, 1823.
8. *Records,* XII (1901), 361, Cheverus to Bonneuil, October 30, 1823.
9. Report of Captain Robinson.
10. AAB, 22-BJ-7, Moranvillé to B. U. Campbell, November 5, 1823. Cheverus offered Moranvillé $100 but Moranvillé declined.
11. *Records,* XV (1904), 198, Cheverus to Mme de Bonneuil, November 4, 1823.
12. Report of Captain Robinson.
13. *Moniteur,* November 17, 1823; *Drapeau Blanc,* same date; *Journal de Tarn-et-Garonne,* November 22, 1823. The *Miscellany,* II (1824), 123, reported the same news copied from *L'Ami de la Religion et du Roi.*
14. *Records,* XV (1904), 198, Cheverus to Mme de Bonneuil, November 4, 1823.
15. Roger G. de la Massonnais, *Deux Frères, Louis-Anne-Abel George de la Massonnais et Jean-Baptiste-Amadée George de la Massonnais* (Paris, 1944), p. 13. Hamon, *op. cit.,* p. 141, states that Cheverus saw his sister before she died.
16. Abbé Barbier, *Biographie du clergé contemporaine par un solitaire* (Paris, 1842), IV, 402–404. Barbier states that Cheverus adopted his nephew but if he meant in a legal sense there is no documentation of his statement. Massonnais, *op. cit.,* p. 13, states that the nephew "passed about two years with his

uncle" at Montauban; this is rather inaccurate since Cheverus did not arrive there until July, 1824, and young George de la Massonnais entered the seminary in Paris the next summer. Actually all the children of his late sister spent their vacations with Cheverus whether at Montauban or Bordeaux.

17. If the Paris newspapers were correct in giving his arrival as Wednesday, Cheverus arrived there on November 12. The *Miscellany* reported the event as taking place November 13. Cheverus in a letter dated November 24 said, "I arrived ten days ago."

18. AABost., copy from Arch. Prop. Fide, Cheverus to Somaglia, November 22, 1823.

19. AABost., copy from Arch. Segret. Vat., Macchi to Somaglia, November 23, 1823.

20. Cheverus to Taylor cited in Taylor to Maréchal, January 20, 1824.

21. AUND, Badin to Edward Fenwick, December 9, 1823.

22. Hamon, *op. cit.,* p. 140.

23. *United States Catholic Miscellany,* II (1824), 123. The sermon was delivered on November 23, 1823.

24. *Le Cardinal de Cheverus* (Laval, 1844), p. 6. This anonymous life of Cheverus was prepared at the time the Cheverus statue was dedicated in Mayenne and seems to have been written by André Hamon.

25. Hamon, *op. cit.,* p. 142, states that Cheverus gave a funeral oration for Sougé while he was in Mayenne.

26. *United States Catholic Miscellany,* II (1824), 173. Cheverus to Taylor, December 26, 1823.

27. *Ibid.*

28. AABost., copy from Vat. Seg. di Stato, Cheverus to Macchi, December 29, 1823.

29. Arch. Nat., F19-2538, Croij to Cheverus, December 29, 1823.

30. *Ibid.,* Cheverus to Croij, January 2, 1823.

31. AABost., copy from Arch. Prop. Fide, Somaglia to Cheverus, December 20, 1823.

32. Arch. Plinval, Cheverus to Cheverus, January 5, 1824.

33. Arch. Nat., F19-2538, Cheverus to Croij, January 7, 1824.

34. AAB, 20-T-26, Taylor to Maréchal, March 23, 1824, citing Cheverus.

35. AABost., copies from Arch. Prop. Fide, Somaglia to Cheverus, February 21, 1824; notes on letters sent February 21, 1824.

36. AABost., copy from Arch. Segret. Vat., Macchi to Somaglia, March 4, 1824.

37. AAQ, Maréchal to Plessis, January 8, 1823. This should read 1824; Maréchal made the common mistake of failing to note the new year.

38. AAB, 17-D-20², Garnier to Maréchal, April 28, 1824.

39. AAB, 19-K-7, Moranvillé to Maréchal, February 19, 1824.

40. AUND, Cheverus to Bruté, April 21, 1824.

41. AAQ, Taylor to Plessis, June 19, 1824, citing Cheverus to Taylor, April 26, 1824.

42. AAB, 19-K-12, Moranvillé to Maréchal, April 26, 1824.

43. Arch. Nat., F19-674, fol. 473, Ordinance of June 23, 1824. Hamon, *op. cit.,* p. 147, telescopes the chronology of these events when, after stating that Cheverus was offended, wrote to the ministry that if after having been called back to France as a French citizen they now refused him as such, threatened to leave Paris the next day and renounce Montauban forever, "this resolution at once cut the difficulties; the bulls were registered immediately and sent that very evening to M. de Cheverus." Taylor wrote to Maréchal after receiving a letter from Cheverus dated June 29 at Paris, "The civil impediment which he so little anticipated and which retarded his departure, had been removed by the

King." Cf. AAB, 21-K-3, Taylor to Maréchal, August 27, 1824. Although Hamon argues that the debate was over Cheverus' naturalization in the United States there is no record that Cheverus ever was a naturalized citizen. The records show, however, that Francis Matignon did apply for naturalization in 1795, and that he was referred to subsequently as a naturalized citizen.

44. Arch. Nat., F19-674, fol. 488, Corbière to Louis XVIII, June 23, 1824.
45. Hamon, *op. cit.*, p. 146.
46. *United States Catholic Miscellany*, III (1824), 43.
47. Hamon, *op. cit.*, p. 146.
48. AAB, 21-Ak-3, Taylor to Maréchal, August 27, 1824, citing Cheverus to Taylor, June 29, 1824.
49. AABost., copy from Arch. Segret. Vat., Macchi to Somaglia, July 13, 1824.
50. Arch. Plinval, Cheverus to Cheverus, July 10, 1824.
51. *Ibid.*
52. The two priests were M. M. Guilleux and Vannier. Vannier went at once but Guilleux did not arrive until later.
53. AABost., Cheverus to McNamara, July 26, 1824.
54. Hamon, *op. cit.*, 147.

CHAPTER XIX — CITIZEN OF TWO WORLDS

1. *Le Tarn-et-Garonne* (Montauban: Association Française pour l'Avancement des Sciences, 1902), p. 175. The chapel was demolished in 1828 to widen the bridge; the arch of triumph was demolished in 1871.
2. Although the cathedral was begun in 1692 it was not consecrated until November 1, 1739. Until 1831 it had two campaniles surmounted by gilded domes. For a description of the cathedral as it appeared in the time of Cheverus cf. Camille Daux, *Histoire de l'église de Montauban* (Paris, 1882), II, Part V, 47–49.
3. Z. Le Bret, Gabriel Ruck and Marcellin Ruck, *Histoire de Montauban* (Montauban, 1841), pp. ii, 6, 330.
4. Burdette C. Poland, *French Protestantism and the French Revolution* (Princeton, 1957), pp. 112–114. Poland refers to the Protestant church of Montauban as "one of the largest and most vigorous in France" at that time.
5. Daux, *op. cit.*, II, Part VII, 19–22; Poland, *op. cit.*, pp. 116–118.
6. Daux, *op. cit.*, II, Part VII; Poland, *op. cit.*, pp. 135, 205–209, 265–270.
7. Daux, *op. cit.*, II, Part VIII, 49–50.
8. *Journal de Tarn-et-Garonne*, July 31, 1824.
9. Vicomte Robert de Mentque, *Le vieux Montauban: six promenades à travers ses rues* (Montauban, 1944), pp. 163–164. The Duc de la Force who was the same age as Cheverus, became an *émigré* in 1791, but returned to Montauban in 1802. Under the Restoration government he was made Maréchal de Camp, Pair de France, member of the Order of St. Louis, and Commandant of Tarn-et-Garonne, 1815–1832.
10. Daux, *op. cit.*, II, Part VIII, 51.
11. *United States Catholic Miscellany*, III (1824), 30, citing *L'Ami de la Religion et du Roi;* Daux, *op. cit.*, II, Part VIII, 52–53.

12. Pierre Genevray, "La 'paix Chrétienne,' l'harmonie des Cultes et les Protestants du Sud-Ouest sous la Monarchie Constitutionelle, 1814–1848," *Bulletin de l'histoire du Protestantisme Français,* XXVI (January–March, 1950), 26.

13. For other accounts of Cheverus' reception cf. E. Forestié, neveu, *Notes historiques ou éphémerides Montalbanaises et du Tarn-et-Garonne* (Montauban, 1882), pp. 110–112; Hamon, *op. cit.,* pp. 148–150.

14. The royal approbation was given on September 18, 1824.

15. Daux, *op. cit.,* II, Part VIII, 55–56.

16. Daux is in error when he states that Cheverus was a former student of Saint-Sulpice. The Congregation of the Mission is commonly called the Lazarists in France.

17. The purchase price was 55,000 francs. The building was used as a woolen spinning factory prior to its acquisition by the Bishop of Montauban.

18. AABost., Cheverus to Eliza Davis, January 24, 1825. There was a Lutheran seminary at Strasbourg, however.

19. *Le Tarn-et-Garonne,* p. 71; *Records,* XV (1904), 224, Cheverus to Bonneuil, June 27, 1826.

20. Édouard Forestié, *Les Anciennes Faïenceries de Montauban* (Montauban, 1876), pp. 106–108.

21. AABost., Cheverus to Eliza Davis, January 24, 1825.

22. Blavian, "Le cardinal de Cheverus, 1768–1836," *Les Contemporains,* no. 252, p. 10.

23. *Ibid.*

24. AUND, Cheverus to Bruté, September 23, 1824. For an account of Bruté's visit to France in 1824 cf. Sister Mary Salesia Godecker, *Simon Bruté de Rémur* (St. Meinrad, Indiana, 1931), pp. 116–123. Bruté's sailing for the United States was delayed by unfavorable winds until October 4.

25. AAB, 20-S-19, Taylor to Maréchal, September 12, 1825.

26. Arch. Plinval, Cheverus to Mme de Cheverus, November 22, 1825.

27. AABost., copy from Fordham Archives, 207-N-12, Fenwick to Dzierozynski, December 24, 1825.

28. Cheverus wrote to Taylor from Montauban, August 25, 1824. Part of this letter was quoted by Taylor in subsequent letters to Maréchal and Plessis on October 20, and November 19, 1824.

29. AAB, 20-S-17, Taylor to Maréchal, May 20, 1825, citing Cheverus to Taylor, March 17, 1825. Benedict Fenwick was named on April 30, 1825. For a detailed account of the Roman considerations in filling the vacancy at Boston cf. *Ristretto con Sommario su la elezione del Vescovo de Boston,* no. 3035, copy in the AABost. To Cheverus himself Propaganda wrote on July 31, 1824, that opinions on Taylor were too diverse to warrant his appointment.

30. Arch. Plinval, Cheverus to Mme de Cheverus, December 27, 1824.

31. Father Romagné died in Sacé on November 19, 1836, four months to the day after Cheverus died in Bordeaux.

32. *Records,* XV (1904), 203–206, Cheverus to Bonneuil, August 26, September 20, 1825; Cheverus to Mme de Bonneuil, September 19, 1825.

33. *Ibid.,* 207, Cheverus to Bonneuil, September 27, 1825. Bonneuil's ship was driven back to Bordeaux by a storm on November 14 and he did not actually depart until November 29.

34. AABost., Cheverus to Eliza Davis, January 24, 1825.

35. Archives Départementales Tarn-et-Garonne, 2-V-1, Cheverus to Capelle, September 23, 1824. These archives are cited hereafter ADTG.

36. ADTG, 2-V-1, Capelle to Cheverus, October 13, 1824.

37. ADTG, 2-V-1, Capelle to Limairac, September 30, 1824. The completed list of nominations included: Vicars-general de Trélissac and Turcq, Canons

Fondomié, Beaufort, Balsac, Carle, Arnac, Durand, Cavalié, Chateau, and Boutang.

38. Arch. Nat., F19-1758, Corbière to Villèle, September 8, 1824; Villèle to Corbière, September 21, 1824.
39. ADTG, 2-V-1, Budget for 1825, item I. The prefect proposed the first 5,000 francs because it was usual in the departements; the council voted 10,000 instead.
40. ADTG, 2-V-1, Limairac to Corbière, October 28, 1824.
41. ADTG, 2-V-1, Budget for 1825, item IV.
42. Arch. Plinval, Cheverus to Mme de Cheverus, November 22, 1825. Daux, II, Part VIII, 49, says Cheverus first occupied the palace on September 20 but Cheverus wrote to Bonneuil on that day, "I have been living in the éveché since Saturday the 17th." Cf. *Records,* XV (1904), 206. Today this house is the Hôtel de Ville de Montauban.
43. *Records,* XV (1904), 214, Cheverus to Mme de Bonneuil, December 5, 1825.
44. Edmund Quincy, *Life of Josiah Quincy* (Boston, 1867), pp. 420–421, Cheverus to Quincy, April 8, 1826.

CHAPTER XX — JEAN VI OF MONTAUBAN

1. Bertier, *La Restauration,* p. 265.
2. Daux, *Église de Montauban,* II, Section VIII, 54; Hamon, *op. cit.,* pp. 155–156.
3. Daux, *op. cit.,* II, Section VIII, 58.
4. *Ibid.*
5. *Journal de Tarn-et-Garonne,* September 25, 1824.
6. Mandement pour le Carême, February 3, 1825, Nègrepelisse collection.
7. Bertier, *La Restauration,* pp. 497–499.
8. Daux, *op. cit.,* II, Section VIII, 66–67.
9. Bertier, *La Restauration,* pp. 420–421.
10. Adrien Dansette, *Histoire Religieuse de la France contemporaine de la Révolution à la troisiéme République* (Paris, 1948), p. 280.
11. *Biographie des cardinaux, archevêques et évêques français vivans, par un Gallican* (Paris, 1826), pp. xxi–xxviii.
12. Daux, *op. cit.,* II, Section VIII, 70.
13. The mission was conducted by P. Passenaud.
14. Daux, *op. cit.,* II, Section VIII, 61–63.
15. Forestié, *Notes historiques . . . montalbanaises,* p. 259; *Journal de Tarn-et-Garonne,* December 24, 1824. The engineer-in-chief was M. Bertheau-Duchesne and the engineer in charge of the work was M. Pellegrini. The medal bore the portrait of Charles X on one side, and on the reverse the facts of the ceremony of December 19, 1824. Under the Second Empire the name of the bridge was changed to Napoleon.
16. The vacancy thus caused in the chapter was filled by Ferdinand Gasc. Cf. Arch. Tarn-et-Garonne, 2-V-1, La Chapelle to Limairac, March 9, 1825. The death of Canon Balsac earlier led to the appointment of Canon Delmar on December 23, 1824.
17. The details are to be found in Daux, *op. cit.,* II, Section VIII, 64–68.

18. Blavian, "Le Cardinal de Cheverus," *Les Contemporaines* (Paris, n.d.), p. 10; Hamon, *op. cit.*, p. 302.
19. Daux, *op. cit.*, II, Section VIII, 67.
20. *Journal de Tarn-et-Garonne,* January 14, 1826.
21. Arch. Nat., F19-682, Frayssinous to Charles X, February 2, 1826.
22. *Records,* XV (1904), 219, Cheverus to Bonneuil, March 9, 1826.
23. Daux, *op. cit.*, II, Section VIII, 68.
24. Leflon, *La crise révolutionnaire,* pp. 389–390; Daux, *op. cit.*, II, Section VIII, 68–69.
25. Arch. Plinval, Guilleux to Mme de Cheverus, March 21, 1826.
26. *Ibid.*
27. *Records,* XV (1904), 220, Cheverus to Bonneuil, April 2, 1826.
28. Hamon, *op. cit.*, pp. 169–170.
29. AAB, 20-T-29, Taylor to Maréchal, January 21, 1826.
30. Arch. Nat., F19-682, ordinance of March 12, 1826; Daux, *op. cit.*, II, Section VIII, 70.
31. Edmund Quincy, *Life of Josiah Quincy* (Boston, 1867), p. 421, Cheverus to Quincy, April 8, 1826.
32. Arch. Nat., F19-683, ordinance of April 19, 1826. The succursales were Saint-Martin de Belcasse, Saint-Grégoire, Caniac, and Saint-Jean du Bouzet.
33. Arch. Nat., F19-683, ff. 3014, report of May 9, 1826.
34. *Records,* XV (1904), 224–226, Cheverus, to Bonneuil, June 27, July 13, 1826.
35. *Le Moniteur Universel,* July 16, 1826.
36. Arch. Nat., F19-683, ff. 3530, 3586. The vicars-general were Pierre Barrès, Philippe-Louis Marginier, and Barthelmy Maurel (sometimes spelled "Morel").
37. Daux, *op. cit.*, II, Section VIII, 71.
38. *Journal de Tarn-et-Garonne,* August 9, 19, 23, 1826.
39. Arch. Nat., F19-2538, Cheverus to Frayssinous, August 4, 1826.
40. *Records,* XV (1904), 234, Cheverus to Bonneuil, September 7, 1826.
41. Archives of the Archdiocese of Bordeaux, Billaud to Gignoux, July 27, September 7, 1826. These archives will hereafter be cited as Arch. Arch. Bord.
42. *Ibid.*, Billaud to Gignoux, October 3, 1826; Arch. Nat., F19-683, ff. 3617, ordinance of August 13, 1826.
43. Daux, *op. cit.*, II, Section IX, 2.
44. *Journal de Tarn-et-Garonne,* August 26, 1826.
45. Dubourg to Mialaret Becknell, September 15, 1826, cited in the *Journal de Tarn-et-Garonne,* September 20, 1826.
46. AAB, 17-D-26, Garnier to Maréchal, December 19, 1826.
47. Archives Départmentales de Bordeaux, II, v 9, 222, Cheverus to vicars-general, August 29, 1826. These archives will hereafter be cited as Arch. Dept. Bord.
48. *Records,* XV (1904), 235, Cheverus to Mme de Bonneuil, October 12, 1826.
49. *Ibid.*
50. Arch. Arch. Bord., Artaud to vicars-general, October 5, 1826.
51. *Records,* XV (1904), 235, Cheverus to Bonneuil, October 12, 1826.
52. Arch. Dept. Bord., II, v 9, 222, Soulan to Barrès, October 26, 1826.
53. *Le Moniteur Universel,* October 25, 1826. Daux gives the date of the confirmation ceremonies as October 13, 1826.
54. *Records,* XV (1904), 235, Cheverus to Bonneuil, October 12, 1826.

CHAPTER XXI — ARCHBISHOP OF BORDEAUX

1. *Moniteur Universel,* November 6, 1826, p. 1511.
2. *Records,* XV (1904), 350, Cheverus to Bonneuil, March 10, 1827.
3. Arch. Nat., F19-282, fo. 1236, F190685, fo. 4040. The ordinance was registered on November 13. The bull itself is preserved in the Archives Departementals de Bordeaux.
4. Arch. Nat., F19-685, fo. 4082, ordinance of November 15, 1826. The indemnity for a bishop was 10,000 francs and for an archbishop 15,000. Since Cheverus already received 10,000 for the cost of establishing at Montauban he received only 5,000 additional for Bordeaux. These sums were determined by customs and a royal ordinance of September 4, 1820.
5. Chateaubriand, *Mémoires d'Outre-Tombe,* edition Levaillant (Paris, 1948), III, 297–298.
6. Arch. Nat., F19*-685, fo. 4087, ordinance of November 15, 1826. Sibourd was referred to as "Pretre du diocese d'Embrun et ancien grand vicaire de la Nouvelle Orleans."
7. Hamon, *op. cit.,* p. 12.
8. *Ibid.,* p. 176.
9. *Records,* XV (1904), 237, 350, Cheverus to Bonneuil, December 19, 1826. March 10, 1827. Morel's name was as often spelled "Maurel."
10. Arch. Nat., F19-1758, Minister of Ecclesiastical Affairs to Minister of Finance, February 10, 1827; Arch. Dept. Bord., II, v9-222, Acte de prise de possession, November 22, 1826.
11. *Receuil des Ordonnances, Mandements et lettres pastorales des archevêques de Bordeaux* (Bordeaux, 1848), II, 498. This work is hereafter cited *Ord. et Mand.*
12. Arch. Dept. Bord., II, v 9, 222, d'Haussez to Barrès, November 24, 1826.
13. *Ibid.,* Acting president of the court to Barrès, December 13, 1826.
14. *Moniteur Universel,* December 18, 1826, p. 1680.
15. This description of the entrance is based upon "Avis officiel de l'arrivée," in *Ord. et Mand.,* pp. 507–508, a printed broadside of the order of the day dated December 14, 1826, in Arch. Dept. Bord., and *Moniteur Universel,* December 20, 1826, p. 1688.
16. For a beautifully illustrated history of the cathedral cf. Pierre Brun, *La Cathédrale Saint-André de Bordeaux* (Bordeaux, 1952). The Porte Royale which was formerly opened for royalty or the *entrée* of an archbishop in 1826 was hidden by a small sacristy which was only demolished in 1888. Cheverus entered by the great door at the rear of the nave. The figure, "old vessel eternally at anchor," is that of François Mauriac, another noted Bordelais.
17. *Moniteur Universel,* December 20, 1826, p. 1688; Hamon, *op. cit.,* pp. 176–177.
18. The Doyenné which served as Cheverus' first episcopal palace was demolished in 1864. The square on which it was located is today named Place Pey-Berland.
19. Hamon, *op. cit.,* p. 177.
20. Arch. Dioc. Port., Kavanagh Papers, Byrne to Kavanagh, March 15, 1827, quoting Taylor, January 10, 1827.
21. *Almanach Royal* for 1827 gave the population of Bordeaux as 93,549 and of the Gironde as 538,151.
22. Bertier, *La Restauration,* pp. 357–358.
23. Jules De Gères, *Table historique et méthodique des travaux et publications de l'Académie de Bordeaux* (Bordeaux, 1877), pp. 10–12.

24. M. Lynch, *Correspondance relative aux évènements qui ont lieu à Bordeaux en 1814* (Bordeaux, 1814).

25. *Moniteur Universel,* December 9, 1823, p. 1433. Vicomte du Hamel was Maréchal-des-logis of the company of royal volunteers commanded by the Marquis de Larochejaquelein. He became mayor of Bordeaux in November, 1823, the same month that Cheverus returned to France.

26. Jacques Moulard, *Le Comte Camille de Tournon* (Paris, 1927), III, 488, 497–502. Tournon was made Peer of France on December 23, 1823.

27. It is rather appropriate that the statue of Comte de Tournon stands at the juncture of important streets of Bordeaux, one of which leads to the present episcopal residence on Rue Croix-Seguey, while the monument to Cheverus is inside Saint-André Cathedral.

28. *Nouvelle Biographie Générale* (Ed. M. de Hoefer, Paris, 1862), XXXIX, 782–783; Hamon, *op. cit.,* p. 216.

29. In 1829 Vicomte de Curzay became Prefect of Bordeaux. For Baron d'Haussez's role in Polignac's ministry cf. Bertier, *La Restauration,* pp. 579–599.

30. These bishops were Jean Jacoupy, Jean-Joseph-Pierre Guigon, Jean-Baptiste de Pouille, Alexandre Rose de Lostanges, Joseph Bernet, and René-François Soyer.

31. The arms of the Chapter of Saint-André show a flesh-colored Saint-André on a golden cross against an oval sprinkled with golden fleurs de lys. Cheverus' arms bore a simple black cross on a white shield. For a history of the chapter cf. Brun, *op. cit.,* pp. 34–38.

32. Arch. Dioc. Port., Kavanagh Papers, Byrne to Kavanagh, March 15, 1827.

33. Hamon, *op. cit.,* pp. 174–175. Le Palais Rohan serves today as the Hôtel de Ville of Bordeaux. For a description of the palace in the time of Cheverus cf. Jacques d'Welles, *Le Palais Rohan, Hôtel de Ville de Bordeaux* (Bordeaux, 1954), pp. 113–140.

34. Arch. Nat., F19*-688, fo. 18, ordinance of July 21, 1827.

35. *Records,* XV (1904), 353, Cheverus to Bonneuil, April 14, 1827.

36. *Ibid.,* p. 350, Cheverus to Bonneuil, March 10, 1827.

37. *Ibid.,* pp. 486, 489, Cheverus to Bonneuil, September 27, November 20, 1828.

38. Hamon, *op. cit.,* pp. 300–302.

39. Arch. Dioc. Port., Kavanagh Papers, Byrne to Kavanagh, March 15, 1827.

40. *Records,* XV (1904), 350, 354, 356, Cheverus to Bonneuil, March 10, July 12, September 6, 1827.

41. *Ibid.,* XVI (1905), 72, Cheverus to Mme de Bonneuil, October 6, 1829.

42. Hamon, *op. cit.,* p. 262. By a decree of April 13, 1809, Napoleon had established a consistory for the Jews of Bordeaux and Andrade was chief rabbi from that time on. Cf. Ad. Detcheverry, *Histoire des Israëlites de Bordeaux* (Bordeaux, 1850), p. 113. This work is of little value for the period after the eighteenth century.

43. Antoine-Louis Bertrand, *Histoire des séminaires de Bordeaux et de Bazas* (Bordeaux, 1894), II, 320–321.

44. *Ord. et Mand.,* II, 509–513, Mandement pour le Careme de 1827, February 8, 1827.

45. Hamon, *op. cit.,* p. 181.

46. Arch. Dept. Bord., II, v10, Cheverus to pastors, October 30, 1827.

47. Arch. Nat., F19*-686, fo. 11, ordinance of January 10, 1827.

48. Arch. Nat., F19*-690, reports like that of March 9, 1828 (fo. 2332) show that applications for scholarships, etc., coming from Bordeaux were received earlier than from most dioceses.

49. Arch. Arch. Bord., Chansarel to Cheverus, January 16, 1827; Cheverus to

Chansarel, January 22, 1827. In this particular exchange a pharmacist complained that the mother of a priest at St. Eloi owed a small debt. Cheverus replied briefly that it did not belong to his province to intervene in affairs of this nature and pointed out that Abbe Leveque personally was foreign to the question.

50. Arch. Dept. Bord., II, v10, Cheverus to pastors, November 30, 1826. The papal bull of December 25, 1825, gave six months for the faithful to share in the benefits of the jubilee. The illness and death of d'Aviau had left Bordeaux unaccounted for.

51. Bertrand, *op. cit.*, III, 183. Four seminarians gave speeches of welcome praising the virtues of Cheverus and comparing him to Bossuet, Saint Francis de Sales, and Fenelon.

52. Arch. Arch. Bord., Cheverus to Peyronnet, February 27, 1827.

53. *Records,* XV (1904), 353, Cheverus to Bonneuil, April 14, 1827.

54. Arch. Arch. Bord., Faye to Cheverus, March 19, 1827; Cheverus to Faye, May 9, 1828.

55. Arch. Arch. Bord., Mandement, April 1, 1827.

56. *Ord. et Mand.*, II, 514–515. Donnet was called to Tours in 1821 to head the Missionaries of Saint-Martin and was a notable preacher of missions and retreats. He was coadjutor Bishop of Nancy from 1835 to 1837 and in that latter year succeeded Cheverus as Archbishop of Bordeaux.

57. Arch. Dept. Bord., II, v9, 222, du Hamel to Cheverus, August 29, 1827; d'Haussez to Cheverus, August 31, 1827; Cheverus to du Hamel and d'Haussez, September 13, 1827.

58. Arch. Dept. Bord., II, v9, 222, Cheverus to du Hamel and d'Haussez, March 10, 1827.

59. Arch. Dept. Bord., II, v9, 222, du Hamel to Cheverus, September 25, 1827; Cheverus to the clergy, September 27, 1827.

60. Arch. Dept. Bord., II, v9, 222, Cheverus to pastors, October 22, 1827.

61. Arch. Dept. Bord., II, v9, 222, Cheverus to du Hamel, November 7, 1827.

62. Hamon, *op. cit.*, p. 178.

63. *Ibid.*, p. 180.

64. *Records,* XV (1904), 360, Cheverus to Mme de Bonneuil, December 29, 1827.

65. *Ibid.*, p. 359, Cheverus to Bonneuil, December 29, 1827.

66. *Ibid.*, p. 361, Cheverus to Bonneuil, January 16, 1828.

Chapter XXII — Peer of France

1. Creagh Library, Brighton, Massachusetts, Cheverus to John McNamara, October 7, 1826.

2. Jacques Moulard, *Le Comte Camille de Tournon, auditeur au conseil d'état, intendant de Bayreuth, préfet de Rome, de Bordeaux, de Lyon, Pair de France* (Paris, 1932), III, 613.

3. On September 5, 1816, sixty-nine new peers were created to strengthen both the ministry and the monarchy. When Comte de Tournon took his oath in 1823 he was one of twenty-four new peers. In 1827 the Villèle ministry produced seventy-six at one stroke.

4. Alexandre Lardier, *Histoire biographique de la Chambre des Pairs depuis la Restauration jusqu'à l'époque actuelle* (Paris, 1829), pp. xliii–liii. The page references are to an essay or preface by C. O. Barbaroux on the institution and influence of the chamber.

5. Bertier, *La Restauration*, p. 392. There were 384 peers in 1830, as contrasted with 210 in 1815, but forty-six were nonparticipating owing either to being under twenty-five years of age or to having failed to be officially admitted at the time the July Revolution broke out. Pensions varied from 12,000 to 30,000 francs; Cheverus fell in the first pension bracket.

6. *Records,* XV (1904), 353, Cheverus to Bonneuil, April 14, 1827.

7. Moulard, *op. cit.,* p. 613. These divisions were extreme conservative, moderate conservative, and radical.

8. *Ibid.,* p. 614. The sessions took place in the building constructed in 1797 for the Assembly of the Five Hundred until it was demolished in August, 1829. After that the deputies met in a temporary wooden building of the Palais-Bourbon grounds and the peers sat in the Palais du Luxembourg. The new parliament building was not ready until 1832, but by that time Cheverus was no longer a peer.

9. *Archives Parlementaires de 1789 a 1860,* Deuxieme Serie, LII, May 15, 1827–March 7, 1828 (Paris, 1883), p. 1. Since Cheverus had already taken an oath at the hands of the king when he became Archbishop of Bordeaux this simpler ceremony was quite normal.

10. Arch. Plinval, Cheverus to Cheverus, May 16, 1827.

11. *Records, XV* (1904), 354, Cheverus to Bonneuil, July 12, 1827. Cheverus merely commented, "I had to go to Paris for the session of peers. I have been back a month."

12. *Ibid.,* p. 358, Cheverus to Bonneuil, November 23, 1827.

13. *Ibid.,* p. 362, Cheverus to Mme de Bonneuil, January 16, 1828.

14. Lardier, *op. cit.,* p. 66.

15. *Records,* XV (1904), p. 479, Cheverus to Bonneuil, May 22, 1828.

16. *Ibid.,* pp. 483–484, Cheverus to Bonneuil, August 1, 1828.

17. Arch. Dept. Bord., II, v 10, Cheverus to pastors, January 12, 1828.

18. Arch. Dept. Bord., II–v–9, 222, Feutrier to Cheverus, May 27, 1828. The other members of the committees were appointed by the prefects of the departments and the rectors of the academies. The composition of the first committees in the Gironde are found in the correspondence of Archbishop Cheverus, Prefect d'Haussez, and Rector Dauzet of August 5–August 26, 1828.

19. Arch. Dept. Bord., II, v 9, 222, Vatimesnil to Cheverus, May 12, 1828.

20. The royal ordinance convoking the special election was given on April 6, 1828.

21. The three electoral districts of Mayenne were Chateau-gontier, Laval, and Mayenne. The third district, Mayenne, was the most populous and had 342 electors as compared with 265 and 326 for the others.

22. Arch. Nat., F_{1e}–III, Mayenne 4, Prefect to Minister of Interior, April 9, 1828. Mayenne had only one brigade of gendarmerie at the time. Reinforcements were furnished from Caen and Beauvais.

23. Archives Municipales de Bordeaux, 135–14 mss, Cheverus to Minister of Interior, April 8, 1828. These archives are cited hereafter Arch. Mun. Bord.

24. Hamon, *op. cit.,* p. 201.

25. Arch. Nat., F^{1e}–III, Mayenne 4, report of Prefect of Mayenne. The other nominees included several former deputies or men of previous experience in other office. Delaunay was a simple *négociant* and his election was a defeat for the king. Delaunay received 168 votes. Mayor Hercé, a former deputy, was second with 90 votes.

26. Arch. Plinval, Cheverus to Mme de Cheverus, May 17, 1828, Cheverus to Cheverus, same date.
27. *Records,* XV (1904), 479, Cheverus to Bonneuil, May 22, 1828.
28. Joseph Burnichon, S.J., *La Compagnie de Jésus en France, histoire, d'un siècle, 1814–1914* (Paris, 1914), I, 289–314; Leflon *op. cit.,* pp. 400–401; Bertier, *op. cit.,* pp. 535–536.
29. Georges Goyau, *Histoire de la France: histoire religieuse* (Paris, 1922), p. 562.
30. R. Limouzin-Lamothe, *Monseigneur de Quelen, archevêque de Paris. Son role dans l'Église de France de 1815 à 1839, d'après ses archives privées* (Paris, 1955), I, 267–269.
31. *Ibid.,* p. 273.
32. Hamon, *op. cit.,* p. 202.
33. AAB, 2-P-5, Cheverus to Carroll, May 9, 1815.
34. AABost., copy from Fordham Archives, 204–H–8, Cheverus to Grassi, May 9, 1815.
35. Adrien Dansette, *Histoire Religieuse de la France Contemporaine* (Paris, 1948), I, 278–279.
36. Limouzin-Lamothe, *op. cit.,* p. 273. The commission met at the home of Archbishop Quelen on June 6, 1828. A fourth article of their report stated that the bishops had violated no law in confiding seminaries to Jesuits.
37. *Ibid.,* p. 274.
38. Hamon, *op cit.,* p. 204.
39. Leflon, *op. cit.,* p. 401; Bertier, *op. cit.,* pp. 564–565; Dansette, *op. cit.,* p. 281.
40. Hamon, *op. cit.,* p. 206.
41. Leflon, *op. cit.,* p. 401.
42. Bertier, *op. cit.,* p. 566; Dansette, *op. cit.,* p. 282; Leflon, *op. cit.,* p. 393. These writers suggest the pope not only had consistently maintained a policy of supporting Charles X in internal affairs but in the present case enjoyed asserting papal authority over the French bishops.
43. *L'Ami de la Religion et du Roi,* LVI (July 12, 1828), 287–288.
44. Burnichon, *op. cit.,* I, 442.
45. Hamon, *op. cit.,* p. 208; Bertrand, *op. cit.,* II, 290. Most of the Jesuits of Bordeaux went to Passage near Saint-Sebastien, where they formed a new college under the auspices of the King of Spain. One or two stayed on in Bordeaux and established a sort of residence, but its existence was brief.
46. *Records,* XV (1904), 489, Cheverus to Bonneuil, November 20, 1828.
47. *Ibid.,* 492, Cheverus to Mme de Bonneuil, December 12, 1828.
48. Léon Aucoc, *Le Conseil d'État avant et depuis 1789: ses transformations, ses travaux et son personnel* (Paris, 1876), pp. 5, 102–105, 399. Cheverus was named to the council on November 5, 1828.
49. Arch. Dept. Bord., II, v 9, 222, Broglie to Cheverus, August 20, 1830.
50. *Archives Parlementaires,* Volumes 58–61, March 31, 1829–July 1, 1829.
51. *Records,* XV (1904), 496, Cheverus to Bonneuil, May 15, 1829.
52. *Ibid.,* XVI (1905), 75, Cheverus to Bonneuil, January 20, 1830.
53. *Mémorial Bordelais,* August 9, 1830, p. 1.
54. *Ibid.,* August 10, 1830, p. 2.
55. *Ibid.,* August 12, 1830, p. 2. The others were Vicomte de Gorgue, Comte de Peyronnet, and Comte de Ravez. Comte de Tournon who did not owe his peerage to Charles X continued to sit after 1830.
56. Barbier, *Clergé contemporain,* III, 203.
57. *Records,* XVI (1905), 82, Cheverus to Bonneuil, September 18, 1830.
58. Hamon, *op. cit.,* p. 216.

59. *Almanach Royal* (1830), p. 276; Comte de Marsy, "La Collection de décorations militaires françaises," no. XII, "Ordre du Saint-Esprit," *Revue Historique Nobiliare et Biographique,* 3ᵉ Série, (1878), III, pp. 32–39. Only nine prelates were granted membership, including the French cardinals and Grand Aumonier. In the Cheverus portraits he was shown wearing a larger cross of the order pinned on his breast and a smaller one on the blue ribbon collar.
60. Hamon, *op. cit.,* pp. 216–217.

CHAPTER XXIII — PASTOR BONUS

1. *Ord. et Mand.,* II, 516–521. The whole *mandement* was quite royalist in flavor and contained the sentence, "Lent always brings back to Bordelais the glorious solemnity of the anniversary of March 14, 1814, when the faithful city proclaimed its love and devotion to the legitimate sovereign."
2. Arch. Dept. Bord., II, v 9, 222, Duhamel to Cheverus, February 2, 1828.
3. Édouard Feret, *Statistique Générale de la Gironde* (Bordeaux, 1878), I, 898.
4. *Biographie Universelle,* VIII, 118.
5. Hamon, *op. cit.,* p. 197.
6. Arch. Plinval, Cheverus to Cheverus, May 17, May 27, 1828.
7. Hamon, *op. cit.,* p. 199.
8. *Ibid.,* pp. 198–199.
9. *Ibid.,* pp. 196–197.
10. Ethel Stanwood Bolten (ed.), *Topliffe's Travels* (Boston, 1916), p. 204.
11. Boston Athenaeum, Cheverus to Topliffe, April 10, 1829.
12. *United States Catholic Miscellany,* VIII (1829), 379
13. Andrew P. Peabody (ed.), *A Memorial of John W. Foster* (Portsmouth, 1852), pp. 230–231. The story was told in a lecture, "Cardinal Cheverus," delivered by John Welch Foster before the Portsmouth Lyceum on February 8, 1842.
14. Hamon, *op. cit.,* p. 302.
15. Arch. Plinval, Cheverus to Cheverus, May 17, 1828.
16. *Mém. Bord.,* July 15–July 18, 1828.
17. *Ibid.,* July 20, 1828.
18. Arch. Dioc. Port., Byrne to Kavanagh, March 15, 1827, citing Taylor to Byrne, January 10, 1827.
19. After Bishop Benedict Fenwick arrived in Boston Father Taylor went to New York with the avowed purpose of joining Cheverus in Montauban. After his arrival in New York, however, he showed no immediate eagerness to sail for France. In February, 1826, he wrote to Archbishop Maréchal of his intentions of translating Fénelon into English and it was not until Cheverus wrote of his transfer to Bordeaux that Taylor talked more specifically of sailing. On October 1, 1826, he informed Maréchal that since he had been assured of "something to do and something to live by" in Bordeaux he expected to depart on November 15. He asked that St. Mary's College grant him an LL.D.since he hoped to educate youth in Bordeaux and the degree might prove helpful.

Meanwhile, Taylor became involved in the unhappy quarrels within the church in New York and a strong suspicion remains that, having been disappointed in episcopal ambitions in Boston, he stayed in New York with hopes of succeeding to the see left vacant by Bishop Connolly's death. Whether it was anger over St. Mary's refusal to grant the degree he requested or frustrated ambition which provoked it, his sermon on the consecration of John Dubois was insulting to the American hierarchy in general and to Conwell of Philadelphia and Dubois of New York in particular. Clerical correspondence on the eve of Taylor's departure from New York was full of the subject, and the news traveled to France. It is inconceivable that Cheverus would not have heard of the affair, from the Sulpicians in Paris, from Maréchal in Baltimore, or from Byrne in Boston, or all three sources.

In any case, Father Taylor who had in 1825 vowed that he meant to live out his days in France, on March 6, 1827 (only a few months after arriving in Bordeaux), began negotiating for bishop of the Diocese of Halifax, Nova Scotia. It seems clear that whatever position he had anticipated under Cheverus did not materialize. Cf. Public Record Office, London: C.O. 217, Vol. 147, pp. 689–696, Taylor to Earl Bathurst, March 6, 1827.

20. *Records,* XV (1904), 486, Cheverus to Bonneuil, September 27, 1828. Other friends of his American years who died in 1828 included Matthew Cottrill, James Kavanagh, and Archbishop Ambrose Maréchal.

21. *Ibid.,* p. 489, Cheverus to Bonneuil, November 20, 1828.

22. Arch. Dept. Bord., II, v 9, 222, Cheverus to Dauzet, August 5, 1828.

23. The six districts of Bordeaux, Libourne, La Réole, Lesparre, Blaye, and Bazas each had its respective committee. The civil authorities tended to name men who were lawyers, doctors, or members of the Council of the Gironde. Cheverus named men like honorary canon Jean-George Roux for the Bordeaux committee, or local pastors as in the cases of Libourne (Saint-Denis) and Lesparre (Saint-Vivien.) Cf. Arch. Dept. Bord., II, v-9, 222, correspondence of August 18–26, 1828, October 8–10, 1829.

24. *Ibid.,* Dauzet to Cheverus, October 9, 1828.

25. The secondary school of Bordeaux was created by an ordinance of October 5, 1814.

26. The school at Bazas was created by an ordinance of June 30, 1819.

27. Antoine-Louis Bertrand, *Histoire des séminaires de Bordeaux et de Bazas* (Bordeaux, 1894), III, 185.

28. Arch. Nat., F19*-693, fo. 90, Report of Minister of Ecclesiastical Affairs, October 1, 1828. According to this report the ordinance approving the transfer of the Bazas Seminary was given on September 29, 1828.

29. Bertrand, *op. cit.,* III, 191. Garnier, like Cheverus, had once labored in the United States. He taught in both the college and seminary of the Sulpicians in Baltimore at one time or another during his stay, 1791–1803. Other Sulpicians consulted by Lacombe were: Augé, Poiloup, Trébuquet, Cartal, Carbon, and Hamon.

30. *Ibid.,* III, 191–192.

31. Hamon, *op. cit.,* pp. 221–223.

32. *Records,* XV (1904), 489, Cheverus to Bonneuil, November 20, 1828.

33. Archbishop d'Aviau's pastorals on the subject were dated June 1, 1804; June 28, 1808; June 23, 1813.

34. It would be incorrect to overemphasize this trend in France generally. As G. de Bertier has pointed out in his essay, "Population Movements and Political Changes in Nineteenth Century France," *Review of Politics,* XIX (January, 1957), 42, urbanization was very slow during the first half of the century. In 1846 the rural population still represented 75 per cent of the whole French

population. Bordeaux, however, was noticeably affected by the increase in foreign commerce which doubled in tonnage in the decade 1820–1830, and by the rise of the thread and textile industries. When the Duchess of Berry visited the Gironde in 1828 she made a point of visiting these industries and the exposition of products of the Gironde held in Bordeaux.

35. *Ord. et Mand.*, II, 522–523, Cheverus to his pastors, December 14, 1828.
36. *Ibid.*, pp. 527–528, Cheverus to his pastors, May 12, 1829.
37. Arch. Dept. Bord., II, v 9, 222, Duhamel to Cheverus, April 11, 1829.
38. The phrase is Chateaubriand's.
39. Arch. Arch. Bord., Billaud to Cheverus, March 31, 1829.
40. *Ord. et Mand.*, II, 524–526, Cheverus to the clergy, February 27, 1829.
41. Arch. Dept. Bord., II, v 10, 221, Pius VIII to Cheverus, June 18, 1829.
42. Hamon, *op. cit.*, p. 229.
43. The association was headed by the Abbé Perreau, vicar-general of the Grand Aumonier. Copies of membership certificates are preserved in the Arch. Arch. Bord.
44. Arch. Dept. Bord., II, v 10, 221 ordinance of September 13, 1829.
45. *Records,* XVI (1905), 75, Cheverus to Bonneuil, January 20, 1830. Abbé George replaced Abbé de Guyannet, who was made pastor of Saint-Croix de Bordeaux. Cheverus did not make his nephew an honorary canon, as former custom would have permitted. Cf. "Mémorial des Curés de la Paroisse Saint André," a manuscript record preserved in the cathedral.
46. Arch. Dept. Bord., II, v 9, 222, Cheverus to Curé Ferrand of Saint-Eloi, October 3, 1828.
47. *Ibid.*, Cheverus to his pastors, May 2, 1829.
48. *Ord. et Mand.*, II, 529, 533, ordinance of October 20, 1829.
49. *Ibid.*, pp. 534–536, ordinance of January 7, 1830.
50. Arch. Dept. Bord., II, v 10, 221, Cheverus to the clergy, September 1, 1831.
51. Hamon, *op. cit.*, p. 186.
52. *Ibid.*, p. 191.
53. Paul Droulers, S.J., *Action Pastorale et problèmes sociaux sous la monarchie de juillet chez Mgr. d'Astros, archévêque de Toulouse, censeur de la Mennais* (Paris, 1954), pp. 3–6, 395–396.
54. First Epistle of Saint Peter, V, 3.
55. Hamon, *op. cit.*, p. 189.
56. *Ibid.*, pp. 192–193.
57. *Ibid.*, p. 211.
58. *Ibid.*, p. 194. Thérèse de Lamoureux, of excellent family, was the head of the house which would correspond to a House of the Good Shepherd in the United States today. She was a close friend of Père Guillaume-Joseph Chaminade, the founder of the *Societé de Marie,* or Marianists, and her spiritual director since 1795. Cf. Michel Darbon, *Guillaume-Joseph Chaminade, 1761–1850* (Paris, 1946), pp. 115–122. Cheverus believed her to be the rival of saints of the early Church.
59. Hamon, *op. cit.*, p. 190.

CHAPTER XXIV — REVOLUTION IN JULY

1. *Mém. Bord.,* December 31, 1829.
2. *Records,* XVI (1905), 75, Cheverus to Bonneuil, January 20, 1830.
3. *Mém. Bord.,* January 1, 1830; Abbe E. Bellemer, *Histoire de la ville de Blaye* (Bordeaux, 1886), pp. 374, 573.
4. *Mém. Bord.,* January 1, 1830.
5. Arch. Dept. Bord., II, v 9, 222, Duhamel to Cheverus, February 1, 1830.
6. Hamon, *op. cit.,* p. 210.
7. *Mém. Bord.,* January 3, 1830.
8. Arch. Dept. Bord., II, v 9, 222, Cheverus to Duhamel, January 16, 1830.
9. *Ibid.,* February 13, 1830.
10. *Ibid.,* II, v 10, 221, Mandement pour Careme, February 5, 1830.
11. *Ord. et Mand.,* II, 537–543.
12. Arch. Arch. Bord., Quelen to Cheverus, March 15, 1830. The relics of St. Vincent de Paul were kept, after the dispersal of the Lazarists, or Vincentians, by the Daughters of Charity. The Lazarists had a new chapel in 1830 (which Quelen had blessed on November 1, 1827) to which the relics were to be taken. The ceremonies began on April 24 with the translation of the relics to Rue de Sèvres and concluded on Sunday, April 25, with a pontifical Mass celebrated by the nuncio, Luigi Lambruschini. A description of the event is given in R. Limouzin-Lamothe, *Monsieur de Quelen* (Paris, 1955), I, 304–309.
13. Arch. Dept. Bord., II, v 9, 222, Guernon-Ranville to Cheverus, Feb. 1, 1830.
14. *Ibid.,* Cheverus to Guernon-Ranville, February 20, 1830.
15. *Ibid.,* Ordinance of February 14, 1830.
16. *Ibid.,* Guernon-Ranville to Cheverus, March 6, 1830.
17. *Ibid.,* Cheverus to Guernon-Ranville, March 22, 1830.
18. *Mém. Bord.,* March 10, 1830.
19. Edmund Quincy, *Life of Josiah Quincy* (Boston, 1867), pp. 436–437, Cheverus to Quincy, April 25, 1830.
20. *Mém. Bord.,* May 12, 1830.
21. *Ibid.,* April 24, 1830.
22. Bertier, *La Restauration,* pp. 595–599.
23. Arch. Dept. Bord., II, v 10, 221, Mandement, May 24, 1830.
24. *Ibid.*
25. *Ord. et Mand.,* II, 547.
26. Leflon, *La crise révolutionnaire,* p. 419.
27. Bertier, *La Restauration,* pp. 586–588.
28. Arch. Dept. Bord., II, v 10, 221, Guernon-Ranville to Cheverus, June 15, 1830.
29. *Ibid.,* Cheverus to pastors, June 18, 1830.
30. *Ibid.,* Cheverus to Guernon-Ranville, June 19, 1830.
31. M. Bernadau, *Histoire de Bordeaux depuis l'année 1675 jusqu'à 1836* (Bordeaux, 1837), pp. 300–302.
32. Hamon, *op. cit.,* p. 217.
33. *Ord. et Mand.,* II, 544–545, Cheverus to pastors, July 1, 1830.
34. Arch. Dept. Bord., II, v 10, 221, Cheverus to pastors, July 5, 1830.
35. Arch. Arch. Bord., Dubourg to Cheverus, July 10, 1830.
36. *Ibid.,* Jacoupy to Cheverus, July 1, 1830.
37. *Mém. Bord.,* July 26, 1830.
38. Bertier, *La Restauration,* pp. 607–611. The events in Paris after July 26 as reported in the *Moniteur* are cited in this work, pp. 611–623.

39. *Mém. Bord.*, July 25, 1830.

40. *Ibid.*, July 27, 1830.

41. *Ibid.*, August 2, 1830.

42. Bernadau, *op. cit.*, pp. 255–256.

43. The *Mémorial* issue of August 2 gives a good summary of the events from July 30 to August 2.

44. Curzay's rescuers were men named Galos, Guillory, Debans, and Holdecocq. The father of Galos was a deputy and gave Curzay sanctuary.

45. The chief sources for this account of the July Revolution in Bordeaux are, in addition to the *Mémorial,* the first and the revised edition of Bernadau's *Historie de Bordeaux,* and Georges Rocal's *La Révolution de 1830 en Dordogne* (Paris, 1936). In addition to the 10th cavalry squadron from Libourne, the 55th Infantry of the Line of Bordeaux became exceedingly unpopular and the officers of the latter had to leave the city disguised in civilian clothes. The common soldiers of the 55th Infantry were imprisoned in Périgueux prisons until August 7, 1830. General quarters at Bordeaux had military divisions 4, 10, 11, 12, and 20 under the command of Lieutenant-General Lemarque during the days of the disorder. The new mayor was Charles de Bryas.

46. Bernadau, *Nouvelle édition* (1839), p. 258.

47. Leflon, *op. cit.*, pp. 418–419; Dansette, *Historie religieuse de la France contemporaine,* pp. 285 f. The best account of the anticlericalism in Paris in 1830 is found in Limouzin-Lamothe, *op. cit.*, II, 11–22.

48. Georges Goyau, *Histoire de la France: histoire religieuse* (Paris, 1922), pp. 565–566.

49. *Records,* XVI (1905), 77, Cheverus to Bonneuil, August 8, 1830.

50. *Ibid.*, pp. 82–83, Cheverus to Bonneuil, September 18, 1830.

51. Arch. Nat., F19-2506, Preissac to Broglie, September 25, 1830.

52. *Records,* XVI (1905), 82, Cheverus to Bonneuil, September 18, 1830.

53. Hamon, *op. cit.*, p. 234.

54. *Ibid.*, p. 222.

55. *Mém. Bord.*, August 10, 1830. Peyronnet was particularly hated for having prepared the text of the July Ordinances. He was arrested in company with Chantelauze, who had prepared the report defending the obnoxious measures. Charles X stayed at Lulworth Castle from August 23 to October 15, 1830.

56. For the arrest, trial and imprisonment of Peyronnet cf. Émile de Perceval, *Un condamné de haute cour, 1830: le comte de Peyronnet, 1776–1854* (Paris, 1830), pp. 228–322.

57. *Records,* XVI (1905), 85, Cheverus to Bonneuil, December 24, 1830.

58. Hamon, *op. cit.*, p. 224.

59. Barbier, *Clergé contemporain,* III, 201.

60. *Records,* XVI (1905), 98, Cheverus to Bonneuil, May 28, 1831.

61. Archives Départementales de Mayenne, Secretary of the Prefecture to Minister of Interior, May 11, 1832. The pastoral referred to was probably the one of May 1, 1832. It is printed in *Ord. et Mand.,* II, 565–567. This particular pastoral seems to have made quite an impression beyond Bordeaux for the Diocese of Orleans requested that Cheverus send a collection of his pastorals. Cheverus replied, "I do not save them, they are not worth the trouble. Nevertheless you encourage me to pay you the courtesy of sending the decree I recently published. . . ." Cf. Arch. Mun. Bord., 135–16 Mss. Cheverus to Mirault, May 12, 1832. Part of the pastoral is quoted in the following chapter, in connection with the cholera-morbus epidemic.

62. Arch. Nat., F19-2506, Preissac to Persil, June 29, 1834.

CHAPTER XXV — THE PRISONER OF BLAYE

1. Lavisse, *Histoire de France contemporaine,* V, 6. Perier replaced banker Jacques Lafitte on March 11, 1831, and remained head of the ministry until his death from cholera-morbus in 1832.
2. Dansette, *op. cit.,* pp. 288–289. The Capucines, Chartreuse, and monks of La Trappe were among those expelled.
3. The Archbishop of Tours and Bishop of Saint-Claude raised these questions respectively on August 15 and August 18, 1830.
4. The Bishop of Agen wrote on August 19, 1830.
5. Jacques Paul Martin, *La Nonciature de Paris, et les affaires écclesiastiques de France sous la règne de Louis Philippe, 1830–1848* (Paris, 1945), p. 50; Leflon, *op. cit.,* p. 420; Limouzin-Lamothe, *op. cit.,* II, 25.
6. Martin, *op. cit.,* pp. 19–20.
7. Leflon, *op. cit.,* p. 421.
8. Martin, *op. cit.,* pp. 39–48. A copy of this brief is preserved in the Arch. Arch. Bord.
9. Arch. Arch. Bord., Quelen to Cheverus, November 16, 1830. This letter is printed in Martin, pp. 48 f, and in Limouzin-Lamothe, II, 28–29.
10. Leflon, *op. cit.,* pp. 420–421; Martin, *op. cit.,* pp. 48–49.
11. Limouzin-Lamothe, *op. cit.,* II, 37–41.
12. *Mém. Bord.,* September 3, 1830.
13. Hamon, *op. cit.,* p. 220. Hamon states that the letter was written to "an influential person" in the government. A "Notice Necrologique" in the *Mémorial Bordelais* of July 21, 1836, states that it was written to Decazes.
14. *Records,* XVI (1905), 85–85, Cheverus to Bonneuil, December 24, 1830, January 16, 1831. Cheverus gave the date in the first letter as December 11, but on later occasions he states that his sister died on December 12.
15. Arch. Dept. Bord., II, v 9, 222, Fougault to Cheverus, December 1, 1830. Fougault was writing for Agent Billaud.
16. Arch. Arch. Bord., Isoard to Cheverus, December 17, 1830. Cardinal Clermont-Tonnerre of Toulouse had died earlier in 1830. Cardinal Rohan-Chabot was created shortly before the July Revolution, having been named on July 5, 1830.
17. Martin, *op. cit.,* p. 57.
18. *Ord. et Mand.,* II, 548–549, December 20, 1830.
19. *Mém. Bord.,* December 30, 1830.
20. Leflon, *op. cit.,* p. 428.
21. Arch. Arch. Bord., Charrier to Gignoux, February 5, 1831.
22. *Ord. et Mand.,* II, 550–551.
23. *Ibid.,* II, 552–553, Cheverus to pastors, February 25, 1831.
24. Brun, *La Cathédral Saint-André de Bordeaux,* pp. 55–56, 104. The cross was erected outside the north transept in 1816. In 1830 it was brought inside and now stands inside the north door of the cathedral.
25. Arch. Dept. Bord., II, v 9, 222, Preissac to Cheverus, February 28, 1831.
26. *Mém. Bord.,* May 4, 1831.
27. *Records,* XVI (1905), 98, Cheverus to Bonneuil, May 28, 1831.
28. *Ibid.,* p. 100, Cheverus to Bonneuil, June 14, 1831.
29. "Mémorial de Curés de la Paroisse Saint-André," a hand-written manuscript preserved in the cathedral. The items are arranged by year. The suppression of the Feu de Saint-Jean appears in 1830.

30. *Ord. et Mand.*, II, 554–555, Cheverus to pastors, August 3, 1831.
31. Arch. Dept. Bord., II, v 10, 221, ordinance of August 26, 1831.
32. *Ibid.*, II, v-9, 222, Brun to Cheverus, December 23, 1835; Cheverus to Brun, December 24, 1835.
33. For an account of the events in Paris in February, 1831, cf. Limouzin-Lamothe, *op. cit.*, II, 45–50.
34. *Ord. et Mand.*, II, 556–557, Cheverus to pastors, November 19, 1831; p. 590, Cheverus to pastors, September 16, 1834.
35. *Records*, XVI (1905), 102, Cheverus to Bonneuil, September 24, 1831.
36. *Ibid.*, p. 100, Cheverus to Bonneuil, June 14, 1831.
37. AABost., Cheverus to Tilden, February 19, 1835.
38. Arch. Dept. Bord., II, v 9, 222, Cheverus to Brun, February 15, 1832.
39. *Ibid.*, Brun to Cheverus (June, 1833), Cheverus to Brun, June 22, 1833.
40. Hamon, *op. cit.*, p. 208. The rejoinder was made in 1828 at the time Cheverus was being bitterly criticized for his theological opinion on the anti-Jesuit ordinances.
41. For an account of the plot cf. G. de Bertier de Sauvigny, *Documents inédits sur la conspiration légitimiste de 1830–1832* (Paris, 1951).
42. Abbé Sabatier, *Premiers mélanges, nouveaux, derniers* (Bordeaux, 1863), p. 370.
43. There are many accounts of the Duchesse de Berry's exploits of which some of the more interesting ones are E. Menière, *La Captivité de Madame la Duchesse de Berry à Blaye, 1833* (Paris, 1882). Dr. Menière attended the duchess from February to June, 1833. Ferdinand Petitpierre, *Journal de la captivité de la Duchesse de Berry à Blaye, 1832–1833* (Paris, 1904), Petitpierre was an officer stationed at Blaye during the duchess' stay. Marc-André Fabre, *La Duchesse de Berry, La Marie Stuart Vendéenne, 1798–1870* (Paris, 1938), a modern biography. Baronne Pigeard, *La Duchesse de Berry à la citadelle de Blaye* (Paris, 1906), an extract from la *Nouvelle Revue* of July 15–August 1, 1906.

   The betrayal of the duchess was effected by a converted Jew named Deutz, who accompanied special police commissioner Louis Joly to Nantes in October. The duchess and her companions tried to hide by a chimney on the roof of the house in Rue Haute-du-Chateau where she was staying, but they were forced out when a fire was lighted below. The Prefect of Loire-Inférieure was Maurice Duval.
44. *Mém. Bord.*, November 21, 1832.
45. Pigeard, *op. cit.*, pp. 8–9.
46. Abbé E. Bellemer, *Histoire de la ville de Blaye depuis sa fondation par les Romains jusqu'à la captivité de la Duchesse de Berry* (Blaye, 1886), p. 589.
47. *Mém. Bord.*, November 17, 1832.
48. Fabre, *op. cit.*, p. 172.
49. *Records*, XVI (1905), 465, Cheverus to Bonneuil, February 3, 1833.
50. Petitpierre, *op. cit.*, pp. 40, 86; Sabatier, *Nouveaux Mélanges*, p. 390. These altar furnishings consisted of some amices and purificators, two corporals, six ordinary candlesticks, a cross, a missal, and a chalice of minimal value. Sabatier estimated their worth at 600 francs; Petitpierre said 770 francs.
51. Bellemer, *op. cit.*, p. 591.
52. Sabatier, *Premiers Mélanges*, pp. 34–342. Sabatier arrived in Bordeaux on December 7, 1832.
53. Bellemer, *op. cit.*, pp. 593–594. Bugeaud also kept a *Journal de la citadelle de Blaye* which was published by comte d'Ideville in *Le Maréchal Bugeaud d'après sa correspondance intime et des documents inédits* (Paris, 1881–1882).

54. Note 49, *supra*. A. de la Coste succeeded Preissac.
55. Bellemer, *op. cit.*, p. 595.
56. *Mém. Bord.*, March 7, 1833, reported Marcellus' remark. In addition to Menière who arrived at Blaye in February, other doctors included the regular doctor of the citadel, Dr. Louis-Charles Deneux, Dr. Gintrac of Bordeaux. In April four others arrived.
57. *Ibid.*, March 4, May 11, May 22, May 27, 1833.
58. Sabatier, *Premiers Mélanges*, pp. 375–376.
59. Bellemer, *op. cit.*, p. 620.
60. Sabatier, *Premiers Mélanges*, p. 393, Cheverus to Sabatier, June 6, 1833.
61. Sabatier, *Nouveaux Mélanges*, pp. 394–395, Cheverus to Sabatier, November 27, 1833.
62. Arch. Dept. Bord., II, v 10, 221, Quelen to pastors, April 11, 1832.
63. *Ord. et Mand.*, II, 562–564, Cheverus to pastors, April 15, 1832.
64. Bernadau, *op. cit.*, pp. 270–272.
65. Hamon, *op. cit.*, p. 237.
66. *Ord. et Mand.*, II, 566–567, Cheverus to pastors, May 1, 1832.
67. *Records*, XVI (1905), 111, Cheverus to Bonneuil, May 7, 1832.
68. *Ord. et Mand.*, II, 568, Cheverus to pastors, November 20, 1832.

CHAPTER XXVI — LONG LIVE THE KING

1. *Records*, XVI (1905), 348, Cheverus to Bonneuil, January 18, 1833.
2. *Ibid.*, p. 468, Cheverus to Bonneuil, June 8, 1833.
3. *Ibid.*, XVII (1906), 98, 104, Cheverus to Bonneuil, July 8, September 26, 1833.
4. *Ibid.*, XVI (1905), 230, Cheverus to Bonneuil, October 15, 1832.
5. *Ibid.*, p. 350, Cheverus to Mme de Bonneuil, January 25, 1833.
6. *Ibid.*, XVII (1906), 355, Cheverus to Bonneuil, July 17, 1834.
7. *Ibid.*, XVI (1905), 228, Cheverus to Mme de Bonneuil, October 15, 1832.
8. *Ibid.*, XVII (1906), 102, Cheverus to Bonneuil, September 4, 1833.
9. *Ibid.*, pp. 216, 218, 358, Cheverus to Bonneuil, January 28, March 26, December 6, 1834.
10. Sabatier, *Nouveaux Mélanges*, p. 352.
11. Sabatier, *Derniers Mélanges*, p. 276.
12. *Records*, XVII (1906), 109, Cheverus to Bonneuil, November 9, 1833.
13. *Ibid.*, p. 100, Cheverus to Bonneuil, July 26, 1833.
14. Hamon, *op. cit.*, pp. 234–235.
15. A good essay on Veuillot is Waldemar Gurian, "Louis Veuillot," *Catholic Historical Review*, XXXVI (January, 1951), 384–414.
16. Alexis de Tocqueville, *Correspondance* inédite, II, 48.
17. *Ord. et Mand.*, II, 579–582, Cheverus to pastors, December 2, 1833. This letter includes the complete letter of the Bishop of Versailles. An explanation of the laws of 1832–1833 is contained in a letter of Guizot to the rectors of academies, reported in the *Mémorial Bordelais* on November 26, 1835.
18. Arch. Dept. Bord., II, v 10, 221, *Rapport sur l'instruction secondaire* presented to the session of the Chamber of Deputies, June 14, 1836.
19. Bertrand, *op. cit.*, III, 197.

20. *Records*, XVII (1906), 356–357, Cheverus to Bonneuil, September 15, October 13, 1834.

21. Bertrand, *op. cit.*, III, 198–200.

22. *Records*, XVII (1906), 361, 364, Cheverus to Bonneuil, February 6, May 26, 1835. Vernou de Bonneuil expected his son to enter business and seems to have felt that a polytechnic institute was preferable.

23. *Ibid.*, p. 487, Cheverus to Bonneuil, July 8, 1835.

24. The *Rapport* of 1836 argued that ecclesiastical schools ought to pay the *impôt* and that "these schools should not be responsible only to bishops."

25. Jacques Paul Martin, *La Nonciature de Paris et les affaires ecclésiastiques de France sous le règne de Louis Philippe, 1830–1848* (Paris, 1949), p. 152. A letter of Antonio Garibaldi to Rome on April 5, 1833, reported Dubourg's insistence that he could not in conscience leave a flock so dear to him in unworthy hands. The see of Besançon was vacant because of the death of Cardinal Rohan-Chabot on February 8, 1833.

26. Daux, *Histoire de l'église de Montauban*, II, Section IX, 36–37.

27. *Records*, XVI (1905), 471, Cheverus to Bonneuil, June 21, 1833.

28. *Ibid.*, XVII (1906), 103, Cheverus to Bonneuil, September 4, 1833.

29. *Ibid.*, p. 98, Cheverus to Bonneuil, July 8, 1833.

30. *Ibid.*, p. 102, Cheverus to Bonneuil, September 4, 1833.

31. The only biographical study of Cooper of any length is that of John E. McGarity, "Reverend Samuel Sutherland Cooper, 1769–1843," *Records*, XXXVII (1926), 305–340. This study gives no clue to the arrival of Cooper other than the assertion that he accepted an invitation of Cheverus in February, 1831. Cheverus himself makes no reference to Cooper by name in the correspondence now extant. It may be that Cooper, after an attack of brain fever, made another European journey and while in Bordeaux was given hospitality which led him to stay on. Hamon, *op. cit.*, pp. 316–317, says of Cheverus:

> Not only all the priests of his diocese, but all strange priests . . . from whatever country, were from their first visit invited to his table, not only once but for the time they stayed in Bordeaux. . . . Often they even stayed in his palace and one could not say how many were offered his hospitality, how many even abused it without his complaining. He excused the strangest indiscretions. . . .

After Cheverus died Cooper went to live at No. 37 Rue Notre Dame where he died in the parish of Saint-Louis on December 18, 1843. He was not buried in Saint-André cathedral, as McGarity stated, but in the cemetery of the Chartreuse across from Saint-Bruno in Bordeaux. While he was in Bordeaux Cooper interested the American consul, George Strobel, in the Catholic Church; when Strobel returned to the United States in 1842 he was received into the Church by Felix J. Barbelin, S.J., and later became a priest himself. Cf. *Researches*, IX (July, 1892), 119.

Cooper was the only one with dry eyes at the deathbed of Cheverus. He is reported to have said, "I would like to cry as you do, but I cannot; because, if I have lost a friend, heaven has gained a saint." Cf. Hamon, *op. cit.*, p. 341.

32. *Ibid.*, p. 109, Cheverus to Bonneuil, November 9, 1833.

33. Double was named to Tarbes on May 26, 1833; Cadalen to Saint-Flour on June 24, 1833.

34. Hamon, *op. cit.*, p. 240.

35. *Ibid.*, p. 241.

36. *Ibid.*, pp. 242–243.

37. *Ibid.*

38. *Records*, XVII (1906), 214, Cheverus to Bonneuil, December 24, 1833.

39. Daux, *op. cit.*, p. 26.
40. *Records*, XVII (1906), 218, Cheverus to Bonneuil, March 25, 1834.
41. *Ibid.*, p. 216, Cheverus to Bonneuil, January 28, 1834.
42. *Ibid.*, p. 215, Cheverus to Bonneuil, January 19, 1834.
43. Arch. Mun. Bord., 135–17, MSS, Cheverus to Decazes, February 6, 1834.
44. *Records*, XVII (1906), 351, Cheverus to Adelaide de Bonneuil, April 12, 1834.
45. *Ibid.*, p. 352, Cheverus to Bonneuil, April 24, 1834.
46. Hamon, *op. cit.*, p. 246.
47. *Records*, XVII (1906), 359, Cheverus to Bonneuil, December 25, 1835. Hamon states that six weeks after the first attack Cheverus suffered a second fall and loss of consciousness, but "happily it had no aftermath, and the next day he could resume his duties." Cheverus himself told Bonneuil, "Since Easter I have not experienced anything serious and now I am really well, much better, I believe, than if I had put myself in the hands of the doctors."
48. For an account of Bruté's nomination to Vincennes cf. Godecker, *Simon Bruté de Rémur*, pp. 198–214.
49. Arch. Arch. Bord., Montalembert to Cheverus, January 1, 1831. The members of the council at the institution of the agency were Bailly de Surcy, Coux, Gerbet, Montalembert, Lacordaire, and Salinis.
50. Leflon, *op. cit.*, p. 445. The so-called "Act of Union" was published on November 15, 1831.
51. Dansette, *Histoire religieuse de la France*, I, 297–303. For a discussion of the nominations of Louis-Philippe cf. Martin, *op. cit.*, pp. 119–135.
52. A printed copy of the petition in both Latin and French is preserved in the Arch. Arch. Bord.
53. Arch. Arch. Bord., D'Astros to Cheverus, July 17, 1832.
54. Arch. Arch. Bord., Faculty of Theology to Cheverus, d'Astros to Cheverus, August 15, 1832. The Archbishop of Toulouse had consulted Sulpicians Carrière, Vieusse, and Boyer in preparing the censure. The full report of the Sulpicians at Bordeaux would prove interesting to a specialist in the controversy.
55. The doctrines particularly condemned were those relating to freedom of conscience, thought, and press, civil and political liberty, the right of insurrection, and separation of church and state. Lamennais received the encyclical accompanied by a letter from Cardinal Pacca in Munich, where Lamennais had gone after his trip to Rome.
56. This conclusion is based upon the scanty evidence remaining today. It is unfortunate that no Bruté-Cheverus correspondence of that period is extant. Bruté certainly continued to take an interest in Lamennais, and when he visited France in 1835 tried to reconcile Lamennais to the Church. Cf. Godecker, *op. cit.*, pp. 263–265.
57. Martin, *op. cit.*, p. 348. Reports were sent on May 5, 7, and 9, 1834. Martin has an excellent summary of the Lamennais affair in the appendix of his book, pp. 340–348.
58. Arch. Nat., F19-1930, printed circular, July 25, 1832.
59. Limouzin-Lamothe, *Monseigneur de Quelen*, II, 151.
60. Arch. Arch. Bord., Cheverus to the Bishops of Agen, Rochelle, Lucon, Poitiers, Périgueux, and Angoulême; Cheverus to Garibaldi, July 26, 1834.
61. *Ord. et Mand.*, II, 586, Cheverus to pastors, September 15, 1834.
62. Although Bishop Bruté was in Mayenne in 1835, and it is reasonable to suspect he had some contact with the Cheverus family at that time, there is no documentary evidence to shed further light on the matter.
63. Martin, *op. cit.*, pp. 147–149. The complete text of the circular is cited here.

64. Limouzin-Lamothe, *op. cit.*, II, 167–168.
65. Hamon, *op. cit.*, pp. 248–250.
66. *Records*, XVII (1906), 363–364, 488, Cheverus to Bonneuil, April 11, May 26, July 8, 1835.
67. Arch. Dept. Bord., II, v 9, 222, Brun to Cheverus, July 23, 1834.
68. *Mém. Bord.*, July 29, 1835.
69. *Ibid.*, July 31, August 5, August 7, 1835.
70. J. Lucos-Dubreton, *Louis-Philippe et la machine infernale*, 1830–1835 (Paris, 1951), pp. 240–246; *Mém. Bord.*, December 6–18.
71. *Ord. et Mand.*, II, 612–613, Cheverus to Pastors, August 4, 1835. This letter repeats the full text of the letter of the king. The original is preserved at Arch. Dept. Bord.
72. Martin, *op. cit.*, p. 95, *Rapport* of August 3, 1835.
73. *Mém. Bord.*, August 7, 1835.
74. Arch. Dept. Bord., II, v 9, 222, Brun to Cheverus, August 7, 1835.
75. *Mém. Bord.*, August 1, 4, 1835. The deputies were Ducos, Hervé, Roul, Wustemberg, Bouthier, Jay, and Guestier. The texts of these addresses were printed in full.
76. *Ibid.*, August 9, 1835.
77. *Mémorial de Curés de Saint-André*, in 1835.
78. *Records*, XVII (1906), 491, Cheverus to Bonneuil, September 3, 1835.

CHAPTER XXVII — JEAN CARDINAL DE CHEVERUS

1. Hamon, *op. cit.*, p. 263. Dupin made his motion on June 8, 1835.
2. *Records*, XVII (1906), 488, Cheverus to Bonneuil, July 8, 1835.
3. Hamon, *op. cit.*, p. 200. Hamon does not identify the minister.
4. Arch. Nat., F19-2446, "Côte sur le Cardinalat," cited hereafter as "Côte," July 21, 1834. Deputy Dessauret from Cantal in his report of April 7, 1841, after referring to the conclave of 1831 continued "et tout aussitôt il forma le projet d'introduire dans le collège des cardinaux un saint prélat dont les vertus si veritablement évangeliques étaient hautement reconnues et honorées par toutes les opinions: l'illustre M. de Cheverus."
5. Leflon, *op. cit.*, pp. 432–435. French troops remained in Ancona until 1838.
6. Arch. Nat., F19-2448, Latour-Maubourg to Sebastiani, March 30, 1832. In 1830 Rohan had fled first to Fribourg, and then — in spite of papal protests — went to Rome where he remained until 1832. For a life of Rohan cf. Charles Baille, *Un Prélat d'ancien regime au XIXe siècle: le cardinal de Rohan-Chabot* (Paris, 1904).
7. Martin, *op. cit.*, p. 83, gives the date of his death as February 13, but the report of the prefect is dated February 8, 1833.
8. Arch. Nat., F19-2446, printed report of the Chamber of Deputies, April 7, 1841.
9. "Côte."
10. Arch. Nat., F19-2446, "Note sur le traitement des Cardinaux," cited hereafter as "Note." The reasons given here are those of the Duc de Broglie.
11. Arch. Nat., F19-2446, Printed Budget for 1836.

12. Arch. Nat., F19–2446, Report of Deputy Golbery of Haut-Rhin, February 1, 1840.
13. Arch. Nat., F19–2446, "Notes sur les lois concernant MM. les cardinaux de Cheverus et de Latour d'Auvergne." These actions were also reported in *Moniteur* of March 10, 24, 30, April 16, 22, 26, 1836.
14. Arch. Nat., F19–2446, "De la promotion des Cardinaux," October, 1839.
15. France, Spain, Austria, and Portugal exercised this right; Sardinia had the right to recommend.
16. *Supra*, note 14.
17. The Minister of Foreign Affairs recommended *de faveur* promotions as a means of saving time.
18. Hamon, *op. cit.*, p. 264.
19. *Ibid.* Hamon does not identify the vicar-general.
20. *Ibid.*, p. 265, note 1.
21. Arch. Nat., F19–2447, Report on the formalities of installation of French cardinals, January 7, 1840. There are many copies of this report in the Arch. Nat., but the original is in the Bibliothèque Nationale.
22. *Mém. Bord.*, July 21, 1836.
23. Hamon, *op. cit.*, pp. 263–264.
24. *Ibid.*, pp. 266–267. Martin, *op. cit.*, pp. 95 f, 102, suggests that the elevation of Cheverus while Quelen was ignored reopened the breach between the Archbishop of Paris and the king. On January 1, 1836, Quelen again refused to present himself at court and when the second attempt on the king's life was made in June, 1836, Quelen's circular announcing the *Te Deum* insolently omitted the title of the king in its references to Louis-Philippe. Quelen's most recent biographer, however, quotes a letter of Quelen to Rome in which the Archbishop of Paris indicated that the government had on several occasions tried to enlist his support through the appeal of the cardinalate but that Quelen preferred no favors. He gave as his reasons for staying away from court: the failure to restore Saint Germain l'Auxerrois, making a public promenade of the grounds of the episcopal palace, turning Saint-Genevieve into a pagan building, the fact that the seminary at Gonflans was still in ruins. "And they would want me to appear to sanction all that by bows and congratulations which would scandalize those who remain pious and fervent Christians?" Limouzin-Lamothe, *op. cit.*, II, 201.
25. Hamon, *op. cit.*, p. 265.
26. *Records*, XVII (1906), 360, Cheverus to Bonneuil, January 9 (1836).
27. When Bishop de Lostanges died on August 12, 1835, the government suggested Father George for the vacant see, but Cheverus opposed the promotion and Thomas-Marie Gousset went to Périgueux. However, when Gousset went to Reims in 1840 George became Bishop of Périgueux.
28. Arch. Mun. Bord., 135–15 Mss, Cheverus to Montalivet, May 1, 1832.
29. Barbier, *Clergé Contemporain*, III, 57–70.
30. Several times in the reign of Louis XIV exception was made because the king himself placed the berettino on the head of the prelate.
31. Arch. Nat., F19–2447, Formalities of installation.
32. Hamon, *op. cit.*, p. 268. The letters are given in both French and Latin.
33. *Ibid.*, p. 269.
34. The ablegate was a papal chamberlain who possessed the rank of envoy extraordinary during his mission. In addition to the hat he brought four briefs: for the king, queen, prince royal, and the Minister of Foreign Affairs.
35. The details of these ceremonies are based upon "Formalities of the installation of French Cardinals" cited above.

36. The statue of Henry IV was replaced on Pont Neuf in May, 1814, with the inscription *Ludovico reduce, Henricus redivivus,* on the occasion of the return of Louis XVIII to Paris. Saint-Germain l'Auxerrois was reopened after a royal ordinance of May 12, 1837.

37. Angot, *op. cit.,* I, 656.

38. Barbier, *op. cit.,* III, 211.

39. *Indicateur,* March 15, 1836.

40. *Ibid.*

41. *Mém. Bord.,* February 23, 1832.

42. Émile de Perceval, *Un condamné de haute cour 1830: le comte de Peyronnet,* 1776–1854 (Paris, 1930), pp. 319–320.

43. Jules De Gères, *Table historique et méthodique des travaux et publications de l'Académie de Bordeaux* (Bordeaux, 1877), pp. 42–43, 201. The Academy which heard a eulogy of Cheverus delivered in 1852 heard one of Peyronnet delivered three years later.

44. Martin, *op. cit.,* pp. 96–97.

45. Limouzin-Lamothe, *op. cit.,* II, 201.

46. Hamon, *op. cit.,* pp. 270–271.

47. *Ibid.,* p. 271.

48. *Indicateur,* March 19, 1836.

49. The window was destroyed in the war of 1939–1945.

50. Hamon, *op. cit.,* p. 271, does not locate these particular remarks as to time or place except to say that "in the middle of so many honors the cardinal was always sad."

51. *Mém. Bord.,* March 24, 1836.

52. *Ibid.,* March 30, 1836.

53. *Ord. et Mand.,* II, 614–617.

54. *Ibid.* The italics were Cheverus' own.

55. *Indicateur,* March 30, 1836.

CHAPTER XXVIII — TO HIS LAST HOME

1. Gustave Labat, *Le Vieux La Teste et le Chateau des Captaux de Buch* (Bordeaux, 1900), pp. 3–4.

2. *Mém. Bord.,* April 3, 1836.

3. *Ibid.,* April 8, 9, 10, 15, 1836.

4. *L'Épiscopat français depuis le Concordat jusqu'à la Séparation, 1802–1905* (Paris, 1907), pp. 31–32. Dupuch was named Bishop of Algier in 1838. For a biography of Dupuch cf. Abbé Pionneau, *Vie de Mgr. Dupuch, premier évêque d'Alger* (Bordeaux, 1860).

5. *Mém. Bord.,* April 13, 1836.

6. *Ibid.;* Hamon, *op. cit.,* pp. 273–274. The *Mémorial* printed the appeal of Cheverus on April 9, 1836.

7. Arch. Nat., F19*-722, fol. 67.

8. J. L. Chabaud, *Éloge de Mgr. de Cheverus Archevêque de Bordeaux* (Bordeaux, 1836), pp. 25–26; Hamon, *op. cit.,* p. 273.

9. *Ord. et Mand.,* II, 623–624, April 19, 1836.

10. *Records,* XVIII (1907), 57, Cheverus to Bonneuil, April 20, 1836.

11. *Boston Evening Transcript,* April 27, 1836.

12. Archives of the Mass. Hist. Soc., Everett Papers, Everett to Cheverus, April 28, 1836.

13. AABost., Cheverus to Tilden, February 19, 1835. For accounts of this tragic affair cf. Robert H. Lord, "Religious Liberty in New England: The Burning of the Charlestown Convent," *Records and Studies,* XXII (1932), 7–31; *Hist. Arch. Bost.,* II, 205–240.

14. *Records,* XVIII (1907), 64–65, Cheverus to Harris, June 3, 1836.

15. Arch. Plinval, Cheverus to Mme de Cheverus, May 20, 1836; Hamon, *op. cit.,* p. 301.

16. Arch. Dept. Bord., II, v 9, 222, Canons to vicars-general, August 8, 1836.

17. Jean Lefebvre de Cheverus, *Statuts du diocèse de Bordeaux suivis d'une instruction sur l'administration temporelle des paroisses* (Bordeaux, 1836), pp. xxvi–xxviii. The statutes were republished with minor modifications by Ferdinand Cardinal Donnet in 1861.

18. *Supra,* note 16.

19. *Ord. et Mand.,* II, 626, decree of July 1, 1836.

20. Limouzin-Lamothe, *op. cit.,* II, 200.

21. Barbier, *Clergé Contemporain,* III, 213.

22. Hamon, *op. cit.,* p. 277.

23. *Truth Teller,* October 3, 1829.

24. Hamon, *op. cit.,* pp. 277–279.

25. *Records,* XVIII (1907), 59, Cheverus to Mme de Bonneuil, July 4, 1836.

26. *Indicateur,* July 15, 1836.

27. *Mém. Bord.,* July 20, 1836; Hamon, *op. cit.,* p. 286.

28. *Indicateur,* July 22, 1836, citing their Paris correspondent of July 19, 1836.

29. *Mém. Bord.,* July 17, 18, 1836.

30. *Ibid.,* July 21, 1836.

31. *Indicateur,* July 20, 1836.

32. Arch. Dept. Bord., II, v 9, 222, Preissac to vicars-general, July 22; vicars-general to Preissac, July 28, 1836. The time involved was only half as long as that required to get permission for D'Aviau's interment in the cathedral.

33. *Mém. Bord.,* July 24, 1836.

34. Arch. Dept. Bord., II, v 9, 222, Janin to vicars-general. The vicars-general had asked Janin for fifty men as a "last sign of respect to the prelate who was happy to count you among his friends."

35. *Ibid.,* Barrès, Gignoux, George to pastors, July 20, 1836.

36. *Ibid.,* to Trélissac, July 20, 1836.

37. *Ibid.,* Trélissac to vicars-general, July 22, 1836. The eulogy is printed in Hamon, *op. cit.,* pp. 345–348.

38. *Ibid.,* Gousset to vicars-general, July 21, 1836.

39. *Indicateur,* July 24, 27, 1836.

40. *Mém. Bord.,* July 24, 1836.

41. *Indicateur,* July 27, 1836; New York *Commercial Advertiser,* September 8, 1836; Boston *Evening Transcript,* September 9, 1836. A copy of the description from the *Indicateur* is preserved in the papers of Dr. John Warren in the Mass. Hist. Soc.

42. André Hamon gave the eulogy on July 30, 1849. Other eulogies, in addition to those of Hamon and Trélissac, include: Clement Villecourt's eulogy of August 30, 1836, which was later read at a public meeting of the Society of Christian Morality on April 17, 1837; J. L. Chabaud, *Éloge de Mgr. de Cheverus, Archevêque de Bordeaux* (Bordeaux, 1836); E. Gaussens, *Éloges*

(Bordeaux, 1854), includes one given August 27, 1844, at the minor seminary of Bordeaux and one written for March 19, 1852, which was crowned by the Academy of Sciences and Belles-Lettres of Bordeaux in a public meeting on January 20, 1853; eulogy in the *Journal de Debats* reprinted in the Boston *Daily Advertiser*, September 9, 1836; John Welch Foster, "Cardinal Cheverus," delivered before the Portsmouth Lyceum on February 8, 1842; J. B. Espic, *Le Cardinal de Cheverus Archevêque de Bordeaux: Poème historique* (Bordeaux, 1841).

BIBLIOGRAPHY

I. Archival Sources

A. American Archives

Archives of the Archdiocese of Baltimore, Maryland
Archives of the Archdiocese of Boston, Massachusetts

These archives preserve authentic copies of documents collected from:
American Antiquarian Society of Worcester
Archives de l'évêché de Quebec
Archives of the Unitarian Historical Society
Archives of the Congregation of Propaganda Fide
Archives privées de M. de Plinval
Athenaeum of Boston
Bibliothèque d'Angers
Bibliothèque de Nantes
Bibliothèque de Saint-Sulpice, Montreal
Diocese of Hartford, Connecticut
Diocese of Portland, Maine
Fordham University, New York
Georgetown University, Washington, D. C.
Massachusetts Historical Society

Archives of the Mother Seton Guild, Emmitsburg, Maryland
Archives of Saint Joseph Central House, Emmitsburg, Maryland
Archives of Saint Mary's Seminary, Roland Park, Maryland
Archives of the Sisters of Charity, Mount Saint Vincent, New York
Archives of the University of Notre Dame, Indiana
Creagh Research Library, Brighton, Massachusetts
Department of Archives and Manuscripts, Catholic University of America, Washington, D. C.

B. English Archives

Archives of the Archdiocese of Westminster
Saint Francis de Sales Church, Tottenham

C. French Archives

Archives of the Archdiocese of Bordeaux
Archives Départmentales, Bordeaux
Archives de la Mayenne, Laval
Archives Municipales de Bordeaux
Archives Municipales de Montauban
Archives Nationales, Paris
Archives de Notre Dame de Mayenne
Archives de Tarn-et-Garonne, Montauban
Bibliothèque Nationale, Paris
La Cathédrale Saint-André de Bordeaux

507

II. Printed Sources

Adams, John Quincy, *Memoirs*, Volume IX (Philadelphia, 1876).

Almanach Royal (Paris, 1780-1789, 1823-1830).

Annales critiques de litterature et de morale, 9e Cahier (Paris, 1806).

Arblay, Madame d', *Diary and Letters of Madame d'Arblay* (London, 1842).

Archives Parlementaires de 1787-1860. Recueil complet des débats legislatifs & politiques, Deuxième Serie, Tomes 52-59 (Paris, 1883-1885).

Barber, Daniel, *Catholic Worship and Piety Explained and Recommended in Sundry Letters to a very near Friend and Others* (Washington City, 1821).

Bertier de Sauvigny, G. de, *Documents inédits sur la conspiration légitimiste de 1830-1832* (Paris, 1951).

Blyth, Stephen C., *An Apology for the Conversion of Stephen Cleveland Blyth to the . . . Catholic . . . Church* (New York, 1815).

Broussillon, Bertrand de, *Une lettre écrite en 1802 par le futur Cardinal de Cheverus* (Le Mans, 1893). (Extrait de l'*Union historique et litteraire du Maine*, I [1893], 346-348.)

Calendrier Écclesiastique (Bordeaux, 1827).

Chateaubriand, Francois-René de, *Mémoires d'Outre-Tombe*, Édition du centenaire . . . établie par Maurice Levaillant, Tome II (Paris, 1949).

Cheverus, Jean Lefebvre de, *Statuts du Diocèse de Bordeaux suivis d'une instruction sur l'administration temporelle des paroisses* (Bordeaux, 1836).

Ellis, John Tracy, ed., *Documents of American Catholic History* (Milwaukee, 1956).

Harold, Reverend William V., *Sermon Preached in the Catholic Church of St. Peter, Baltimore, November 1, 1810, on the occasion of the Consecration of the Rt. Rev. Dr. John Cheverus, Bishop of Boston* (Baltimore, 1810).

Hyde de Neuville, Baron, *Mémoires et souvenirs*, Tome I (Paris, 1888).

Laity's Directory (London, 1806).

Laity's Directory (New York, 1822).

La Tour du Pin, Marquise de, *Journal d'une femme de 50 ans* (Paris, 1954).

Le Coq, F., *Documents authentiques pour servir à l'histoire* (Laval, n.d.).

Lubersac de Livron, Abbé Charles-François de, *Journal historique et religieux de l'émigration et déportation du clergé de France en Angleterre* (London, 1802).

Menière, le docteur E., *La captivité de Madame la Duchesse de Berry à Blaye, 1833. Journal du docteur P. Menière* (Paris, 1882).

Milbert, M., *Itineraire pittoresque du fleuve Hudson* (Paris, 1828).

Mother Seton, Notes by Rev. Simon Gabriel Bruté (Emmitsburg, 1884).

Petitpierre, Lt. Ferdinand, *Journal de la captivité de la Duchesse de Berry à Blaye, 1832-1833* (Paris, 1904).

Plessis, Joseph-Octave, *Journal des visites pastorales de 1815 et 1816*, ed. by Henri Tetu (Quebec, 1903).

Recueil des ordonnances, mandements et lettres pastorales des archevêques de Bordeaux, Tome II (Bordeaux, 1848).

Sabatier, l'abbé Germain, *Premiers Mélanges, Nouveaux, Derniers* (Bordeaux, 1863).

Tudor, William, *Letters on the Eastern States* (Boston, 1819).

III. Biographical Works and Eulogies

Angot, l'abbé A., *Dictionnaire historique, topographique, et biographique de la Mayenne* (Laval, 1903), I, 654-657.

Barbier, l'abbé, *Biographie du clergé contemporain par un solitaire* (Paris, 1841), III, 145–215.

Biographie des cardinaux, archevêques et évêques français vivans par un Gallican (Paris, 1826), pp. 47–50.

Blavian, "Le cardinal de Cheverus, 1768–1836," *Les Contemporains* (Paris, n.d.),

Cauwenbergh, E. van, "Jean-Louis Lefebvre de Cheverus," *Dictionnaire d'histoire et de géographie écclesiastique* (Paris, 1953), XII, 650.

Chabaud, J. L., *Éloge de Mgr. de Cheverus Archevêque de Bordeaux* (Bordeaux, 1836).

Clarke, R. H., *Lives of the Deceased Bishops of the Catholic Church in the United States* (New York, 1888).

Code, Joseph B., *Dictionary of the American Hierarchy* (New York, 1940).

Crawford, Mary Caroline, "When a French Exile Was Boston's Bishop," *The Romance of Old New England Churches* (Boston, 1903), pp. 260–283.

Dassance, l'abbé, *Notice historique sur le cardinal Lefebvre de Cheverus* (Extrait de *Biographie Universelle* de Michaud, premier edition, VIII, 144–120) (Paris, 1842).

Égron, Adrien-Cesar, *Vie abregée du Cardinal de Cheverus* (Lille, 1846).

Espic, J. B., *Le Cardinal de Cheverus Archevêque de Bordeaux. Poème historique* (Bordeaux, 1841).

Finn, Brendan A., "John Cardinal Cheverus: First Bishop of Boston," *Twenty-Four American Cardinals* (New York, 1947), pp. 193–221.

Forbes, Allen, and Cadman, Paul F., *Boston & Some Noted Émigrés* (Boston, 1938).

Foster, John Welch, "Cardinal Cheverus," *A Memorial of John W. Foster* (Portsmouth, 1852), pp. 207–238.

Gaussens, l'abbé E., "Éloge de Mgr. de Cheverus," *Éloges* (Bordeaux, 1854), pp. 248–285.

—— *Éloge du Cardinal de Cheverus archevêque de Bordeaux prononcé à la distribution des prix du petit-séminaire de Bordeaux le 27 aout 1844* (Bordeaux, 1844).

Guilhe, M. H. C., *Éloge de Mgr. de Cheverus* (Bordeaux, 1837).

Hamon, André J. M., *Le Cardinal de Cheverus* (Laval, 1844).

—— "Discours pour l'inauguration du monument de S. E. le Cardinal de Cheverus prononcé par M. Hamon," *Vie du Cardinal de Cheverus* (Paris, 1883), pp. 350–366.

—— *Life of Cardinal Cheverus*, translated by E. Stewart (Boston, 1839).

—— *Life of Cardinal Cheverus*, translated by Robert M. Walsh (Philadelphia, 1839).

—— *Vie du Cardinal de Cheverus archevêque de Bordeaux* (Paris, 1837, 1841, 1842, 1850, 1858, 1867, 1883).

Herpin, Albert, *Sermon . . . pour le centenaire du Cardinal de Cheverus* (Paris, 1936).

Karker, F. X., *Der Cardinal de Cheverus* (Freiburg, 1876).

Knapp, Samuel L., "Memoir of Bishop Cheverus," *Boston Monthly Magazine*, I (June, 1825), 2–22.

Lord, Robert H., "Jean Lefebvre de Cheverus, First Catholic Bishop of Boston," *Proceedings of the Massachusetts Historical Society*, LXV (1933), 64–78.

Loring, J. S., *The Hundred Boston Orators* (Boston, 1852).

"Notice biographique," *Recueil des ordonnances, mandements et lettres pastorales des archevêques de Bordeaux* (Bordeaux, 1848), II, 501–506.

Nouvelle biographie générale, X (1863), 270–271.

O'Donnell, J. H., *The Catholic Hierarchy of the United States, 1790–1922* (Washington, 1922).

Pisani, Paul, *L'Épiscopat français depuis le Concordat jusqu'à la Séparation, 1802–1905* (Paris, 1907), pp. 143–144, 363–364.

Purcell, Richard J., "Jean Lefebvre de Cheverus," *Dictionary of American Biography*, IV (1930), 61–62.

Reuss, F. X., *Biographical Encyclopedia of the Catholic Hierarchy of the United States from 1789 to 1898* (Milwaukee, 1898).

Reville, John C., S.J., "Our Representatives in the Sacred College," *Catholic Builders of the Nation* (Boston, 1923), pp. 1–5.

Saladin, Émile, "Notice nécrologique sur Mgr. de Cheverus," *Mémorial Bordelais*, July 21, 1836.

Shea, John Gilmary, *The Hierarchy of the Catholic Church in the United States* (New York, 1886).

Trélissac, Jean Chaudru de, *Lettre pastorale sur la mort de Mgr. de Cheverus* (Montauban, 1836). The seventh edition of the *Vie* by Hamon carries this letter on pp. 345–348.

Villenave, père, *Éloge de Mgr. le Cardinal de Cheverus lu a la séance publique de la Société de la Morale Chrétienne le 17 avril 1854* (Paris, 1854).

Whitehill, Walter Muir, *A Memorial to Bishop Cheverus* (Boston, 1951).

IV. *Newspapers*

Boston *Daily Advertiser*
Boston *Evening Transcript*
Boston *Gazette*
Columbian Centinel
Indicateur Bordelais
Journal de la Guinne
Journal de Tarn-et-Garonne
Mémorial Bordelais
Moniteur Universel
New England Palladium

V. *General Secondary Works*

Allison, John M. S., *Church and State Under Louis Philippe, 1830–1848* (Princeton, 1916).

Aucoc, Léon, *Le Conseil d'État avant et depuis 1789: ses transformations, ses travaux et son personnel* (Paris, 1876).

Barruel, l'abbé, *Histoire du clergé pendant la Revolution française* (London, 1794).

Bausset, Louis-François, Cardinal de, *Notice historique sur M. l'abbé Legris-Duval*, Preface to the first volume of *Sermons de M. l'abbé Legris-Duval* (Paris, 1820).

Bellemer, l'abbé E., *Histoire de la ville de Blaye depuis sa fondation par les Romains jusqu'à la captivité de la Duchesse de Berry* (Bordeaux et Blaye, 1886).

Bernadau, M., *Histoire de Bordeaux, nouvelle édition revue, corrigée avec vues, portraits, et cartes* (Bordeaux, 1839).

Bertier de Sauvigny, G. de, *Le comte Ferdinand de Bertier (1782–1864) et l'enigme de la congrégation* (Paris, 1948).

——— *La Restauration* (Paris, 1955).

Bertrand, Antoine-Louis, *Histoire des séminaires de Bordeaux et de Bazas*, 3 vols. (Bordeaux, 1894).

Biré, Edmond, *Le clergé de France pendant la Revolution, 1789–1799* (Lyons, 1901).

Bolton, Ethel Stanwood, *Topliffe's Travels* (Boston, 1916).

Bradford, Alden, *Biographical Notices of Distinguished Men in New England* (Boston, 1842).

Brun, l'abbé Pierre, *La Cathédrale Saint-André de Bordeaux* (Bordeaux, 1952).

Bulfinch, Ellen Susan, *The Life and Letters of Charles Bulfinch* (Boston, 1896).

Burnichon, Joseph, S.J., *La Compagnie de Jésus en France. Histoire d'un siècle, 1814–1914,* Volume I (Paris, 1914).

Carré, Henri, *Les émigrés français en Amérique, 1789–1793* (Extrait de la *Revue de Paris,* May 15, 1898) (Paris, 1898).

Carthy, Mother Mary Peter, O.S.U., *Old St. Patrick's, New York's First Cathedral* (New York, 1947).

Code, Joseph B., *Elizabeth Seton* (translation and adaptation of the sixth French edition of Madame de Barberey's biography) (Emmitsburg, 1957).

Connolly, Arthur T., *An Appreciation of the Life and Labors of Rev. Francis Matignon, D.D.* (Boston, 1908).

Cullen, James Bernard, *The Story of the Irish in Boston* (Boston, 1890).

Daly, John M., S.J., *Georgetown University: Origin and Early Years* (Washington, D. C., 1957).

Dansette, Adrien, *Histoire religieuse de la France contemporaine de la Révolution a la Troisième République* (Paris, 1948).

Daux, l'abbé Camille, *Histoire de l'église de Montauban,* Volume II (Paris, 1882).

De Geres, Jules, *Table historique et méthodique des travaux et publications de l'Académie de Bordeaux* (Bordeaux, 1877).

Deney, l'abbé J. M., *Le Petit Séminaire de Bordeaux, 1815–1906* (Bordeaux, 1907).

Detcheverry, Ad., *Histoire des Israélites de Bordeaux* (Bordeaux, 1850).

Droulers, Paul, S.J., *Action pastorale et problèmes sociaux sous la monarchie de juillet, chez Mgr. d'Astros* (Paris, 1954).

Dudon, Paul, *Lamennais et le Saint-Siège (1820–1834) d'après des documents inédits et les Archives du Vatican* (Paris, 1911).

Dumège, André, *et al., Biographie Toulousaine, ou dictionnaire historique des personnages . . . rendus célèbres dans la ville de Toulouse,* Volume II (Paris, 1823).

Dupont-Ferrier, Gustave, *Du Collège de Clermont au Lycée Louis-le-Grand, 1563–1920: la vie quotidienne d'un collège Parisien pendant plus de trois cent cinquante ans,* Volume I (Paris, 1921).

Fabre, Marc-André, *La Duchesse de Berry, la Marie Stuart Vendéenne* (Paris 1938).

Fairbanks, Charles B., *Aguecheek* (Boston, 1859).

Féret, Édouard, *Statistique générale du Département de la Gironde,* Volume III (Bordeaux, 1889).

Forbes, Esther, *Paul Revere & the World He Lived In* (Boston, 1942).

Forestié, Em., neveu, *Notes historiques ou éphémerides montalbanaises et du Tarn-et-Garonne* (Montauban, 1882).

Fourneron, Henri, *Histoire générale des émigrés pendant la Revolution française,* Volume I (Paris, 1884).

Genevray, Pierre, *L'Administration et la vie écclesiastique dans la grand diocèse de Toulouse pendant les dernieres années de l'Empire et sous la Restauration* (Paris, 1941).

Godecker, Sister Salesia, O.S.B., *Simon Bruté de Rémur, First Bishop of Vincennes* (St. Meinrad, 1931).

Goyau, Georges, *Histoire de la France: histoire religieuse,* Tome VI de la série par Gabriel Hanotaux (Paris, 1922).

Greenleaf, J., *Ecclesiastical History of Maine* (Portsmouth, 1821).

Guilday, Peter, *The Catholic Church in Virginia (1815–1822)* (New York, 1924).

—— The Life and Times of John Carroll, Archbishop of Baltimore (1735-1815), 2 vols. (New York, 1922).

—— The Life and Times of John England, 1786-1824, 2 vols. (New York, 1927).

Hamlin, Talbot, *Benjamin Henry Latrobe* (New York, 1955).

Handlin, Oscar, *Boston's Immigrants, 1790-1865* (Cambridge, Mass., 1941).

Hemphill, Dom Basil, O.S.B., *The Early Vicars Apostolic of England, 1685-1750.*

[Hilaire, Émil], *Biographie des archevêques de France par un ancien donneur d'eau bénite* (Paris, 1826).

Hughes, Philip, *The Catholic Question, 1688-1829* (London, 1929).

Husenbeth, F. C., *The Life of the Right Rev. John Milner, D.D.* (Dublin, 1862).

Labat, Gustave, *Le Vieux la Teste et le chateau des Captaux de Buch* (Bordeaux, 1900).

Lardier, Alexandre, *Histoire biographique de la Chambre des Pairs depuis la Restauration jusqu'à l'époque actuelle* (Paris, 1829).

Latreille, André, *L'Église catholique et la Révolution française*, 2 vols. (Paris, 1946-1950).

Lavisse, Ernest, *Histoire de France contemporaine depuis la Revolution jusqu'à la Paix de 1919*: Tome I, *La Revolution, 1789-1792*; Tome V, *La Monarchie de Juillet, 1830-1848* (Paris, 1920-1921).

Leflon, Jean, *La Crise révolutionnaire, 1789-1846*, Tome XX de *L'Histoire de l'église depuis les origines jusqu'à nos jours* de Fliche et Martin (Paris, 1949).

Lenôtre, Théodore G., *Mémoires et souvenirs sur la Révolution et l'Empire*, Tome I, *Les Massacres de Septembre* (Paris, 1907).

Limouzin-Lamothe, R., *Monseigneur de Quelen, archevêque de Paris, son rôle dans l'église de France de 1815-1819, d'après ses archives privées*, 2 vols. (Paris, 1955, 1957).

Lord, Robert H., Sexton, John E., and Harrington, Edward T., *A History of the Archdiocese of Boston, 1604-1943*, 3 vols. (New York, 1944).

Lucey, William Leo, S.J., *The Catholic Church in Maine* (Francestown, New Hampshire, 1957).

—— Edward Kavanagh, Catholic Statesman and Diplomat from Maine, 1795-1844 (Francestown, New Hampshire, 1946).

Lucos-Dubreton, J., *Louis-Philippe et la machine infernale (1830-1835)* (Paris, 1951).

McColgan, Daniel T., *Joseph Tuckerman, Pioneer in American Social Work* (Washington, D. C., 1940).

Martin, Mgr. Jacques-Paul, *La Nonciature de Paris et les affaires écclesiastiques sous le règne de Louis-Philippe, 1830-1848* (Paris, 1949).

Mathew, Archbishop David, *Catholicism in England* (London, 1936).

Melville, Annabelle M., *Elizabeth Bayley Seton, 1774-1821* (New York, 1951).

—— John Carroll of Baltimore, the Founder of the American Catholic Hierarchy (New York, 1955).

Mentque, Vicomte Robert de, *Le Vieux Montauban: six promenades à travers ses rues* (Montauban, 1944).

Moreau, Celestin, *Les prêtres français émigrés aux États-Unis* (Paris, 1856).

Moulard, l'abbé Jacques, *Le comte Camille de Tournon* . . . *(1778-1833)*, 3 vols. (Paris, 1927).

Perceval, Émile de, *Un Condamné de Haute Cour 1830: le comte de Peyronnet (1776-1854)* (Paris, 1930).

Pigeard, Baronne, *La Duchesse de Berry à la citadelle de Blaye (Extrait de la Nouvelle Revue, July 15-August 1, 1906)* (Paris, 1906).

Piolin, Dom Paul, O.S.B., *Histoire de l'église du Mans*, 10 vols. (Paris et Le Mans, 1851-1868).

Plasse, le chanoine F., *Le clergé français refugié en Angleterre,* Tome II (Paris, 1886).

Poland, Burdette C., *French Protestantism and the French Revolution . . . 1685–1815* (Princeton, 1957).

Pondaven, l'abbé Gabriel, *Abbé Legris-Duval, Prédicateur du Roi* (Quimper, 1920).

Quincy, Edmund, *The Life of Josiah Quincy* (Boston, 1867).

Quincy, Josiah, *Figures of the Past from the Leaves of Old Journals* (Boston, 1883).

Riley, Arthur J., *Catholicism in New England to 1788* (Washington, D. C., 1936).

Robert, Charles, *Expédition des émigrés a Quiberon* (Paris, 1899).

———— *Urbain de Hercé dernier évêque de Dol* (Paris, 1900).

Rocal, Georges, *La Révolution de 1830 en Dordogne* (Paris, 1936).

Ruane, Joseph William, *The Beginnings of the Society of St. Sulpice in the United States, 1791–1829* (Washington, D. C., 1935).

Ruskowski, Leo F., *French Émigré Priests in the United States, 1791–1815* (Washington, D. C., 1940).

Schauinger, J. Herman, *Cathedrals in the Wilderness* (Milwaukee, 1952).

———— *Stephen T. Badin, Priest in the Wilderness* (Milwaukee, 1956).

Shaw, Charles, *A Topographical and Historical Description of Boston* (Boston, 1817).

Sicard, l'abbé Augustin, *Le clergé de France pendant la Revolution,* Tome III, *De l'exil au Concordat* (Paris, 1903).

Sorel, Alexandre, *Le couvent des Carmes et le Séminaire de Saint-Sulpice pendant la Terreur* (Paris, 1863).

Stapleton, Mrs. Brian, *A History of the Post-Reformation Catholic Missions in Oxfordshire* (London, 1906).

Tarn-et-Garonne, le, published by the Association Française pour l'Avancement des Sciences (Montauban, 1902).

Thurston, Herbert, S.J., *Catholic Emancipation* (London, 1928).

Tourscher, Francis E., O.S.A., *The Hogan Schism and Trustee Troubles in St. Mary's Church, 1820–1829* (Philadelphia, 1930).

Vidler, Alec R., *Prophecy and Papacy. A Study of Lamennais, the Church and the Revolution* (New York, 1954).

Ward, Mgr. Bernard, *The Dawn of the Catholic Revival in England, 1781–1803,* 2 vols. (London, 1909).

Welles, Jacques d', *Le Palais Rohan, Hôtel de Ville de Bordeaux* (Bordeaux, 1954).

Winsor, Justin, ed., *The Memorial History of Boston, including Suffolk County, Massachusetts, 1630–1880,* 4 vols. (Boston, 1881).

VI. *Periodicals*

Alauzier, comte de, "Les noms des rues de Montauban," *Bulletin Archéologique, historique et artistique de la société archéologique de Tarn-et-Garonne,* LXXIX (1952) (Montauban, 1953).

Bertier de Sauvigny, G. de, "Mgr. de Quelen et les incidents de Saint-Germain-l'Auxerrois en février 1831," *Revue d'Histoire de L'Église de France,* January–June, 1946, pp. 110–120.

———— "Population Movements and Political Changes in Nineteenth Century France," *Review of Politics,* XIX (January, 1957), 37–47.

Brislen, Sister Bernetta, O.S.F., "The Episcopacy of Leonard Neale," *Historical Records and Studies,* XXXIV (1945), 20–112.

Dignan, Patrick J., "Peter Anthony Malou, Patriot and Priest," *Records* of the American Catholic Historical Society, XLIII (March, 1932), 62–95.

Foin, Jules C., "Rev. Louis Barth," *Records* of the American Catholic Historical Society, II (December, 1888), 29–37.

Genevray, Pierre, "La 'Paix Chrétienne' l'harmonie des cultes et les Protestants du Sud-Ouest sous la Monarchie Constitutionnelle, 1814–1848," *Bulletin* de la Société de l'histoire du Protestantisme français, Serie 6e, XXVI (January–March, 1950), 1–59.

Lucey, William Leo, S.J., "Two Irish Merchants of New England," *New England Quarterly Review*, XIV (December, 1941), 481–490.

McAvoy, Thomas T., C.S.C., "The Formation of the Catholic Minority in the United States," *Review of Politics*, X (January, 1948), 13–34.

Marsy, comte de, "La collection de décorations militaires françaises, Ordre du Saint-Esprit," *Revue Historique Nobiliaire et Biographique*, 3e Série, III (1878), 32–39.

Melville, Annabelle M., "Some Aspects of Bishop Cheverus' Return to France in 1823," *Records and Studies* of the United States Catholic Historical Society, XLV (1957), 2–31.

O'Daniel, Victor F., O.P., "Concanen's Election to the See of New York," *Catholic Historical Review*, I (January, 1916), 400–421; II (April, 1916), 19–46.

O'Reilly, Isabel M., "An Interesting Correspondence," *Records* of the American Catholic Historical Society of Philadelphia, XIV (1903), 299–382, 439–514; XV (1904), 191–240, 348–366, 476–496; XVI (1905), 69–111, 225–232, 345–350, 464–472; XVII (1906), 97–110, 213–219, 350–365, 486–492; XVIII (1907), 56–59.

Perkins, Frances, "Cavanagh and Cottrill: Two Historic Houses," *House Beautiful*, XXXII (October, 1912), 148–150.

"Trial of Father Cheverus," *Maine Catholic Historical Magazine*, III (November, 1915), 38–40.

Young, Alfred, "A Plea for Erring Brethren," *Catholic World*, L (December, 1889), 360–361.

INDEX

Adams, John, election, 128; and Holy Cross fund, 91; proclaims fast day, 55

Adams, John Quincy, and Berlin-Milan decrees, 147

Algiers, French expedition, 359–361

Allan, John, and Cheverus, 52; estimate of Indians, 57–58; and General Court, 50; Indian agent, 49

Andrade, Rabbi Abraham, friendship with Cheverus, 320

Anthology Club, Cheverus' letter to, 133–134; founds Athenaeum Library, 134

Arundell, Baron Henry, 32

Astros, Paul-Thérèse-David de, and Lamennais censure, 401–402

Athenaeum Library, 145, Cheverus' gifts to, 134, 207, 266–267; founded, 134

Augé, Antoine-Jean, and Cheverus, 9; vicar-general, 10

Aviau, du Bois de Sanzay de, and American bishops, 174; Cheverus eulogy, 323; Cheverus imitates, 320; death, 306

Babade, Pierre, S.S., 238

Badin, Stephen Theodore, 83; and Flaget, 153–155; in Paris, 276; proposed as bishop, 245

Baltimore, Archdiocese of: Carroll, death of, 178; cathedral completed, 214–216; Cheverus sermon on Carroll, 184; coadjutor question, 179–180, 182–189; creation of, 112–114; Neale, death of, 189; Neale, installation of, 182; Neale, succeeds Carroll, 178–179; provincial council of 1810, 120–121; second council postponed, 152–155; suffragans consecrated, 118–119

Baltimore, city of, British attack, 156–157; first provincial council, 120–121; riots in 1812, 153; St. Peter's Church, 119

Barber, Daniel, and Cheverus, 139

Barber, Virgil, begins ministry, 251;

and New York Jesuits, 139; ordination, 220, 250; pastor of Claremont, 221

Barrès, Pierre, and Cheverus' entry to Bordeaux, 313–314; takes possession of See for Cheverus, 312–313

Barry, James, and Holy Cross, 93, 94

Bausset, Louis-François de, 260

Bazas, College of, La Croix heads, 345

Bazas, Seminary of, moved to Bordeaux, 344–346

Bentley, William, 92; and Carroll, 98; and Cheverus, 135

Berry, Caroline, Duchesse de, conspiracy of, 382; prisoner at Blaye, 383–386, sails for Italy, 387; visit to Bordeaux, 342–343

Blyth, Stephen Cleveland, conversion, 138

Bonaparte, Napoleon, Emperor, 87; Berlin-Milan decrees, 146; and concordat, 74, 78; episcopal nominations, 79; escape from Elba, 173; oath of clergy, 76; Roman negotiations, 77

Bonneuil, Adèle (Adé) de, 166; arrives in Montauban, 292; attends school in Bordeaux, 318, 354; Cheverus' concern for, 308; leaves Bordeaux, 392; visits Cheverus, 294, 305

Bonneuil, Fèlicie de, and Cheverus, 167, 434, 440–441; Cheverus' letters to, 249, 256, 308, 319, 324, 328, 335, 392, 434

Bonneuil, Jean-Vernou, Marquis de, and Cheverus, 166; Cheverus' letters from America, 179, 181–182, 188, 190, 209, 211, 220, 249, 256, 273; Cheverus' letters from Bordeaux, 318, 324; 326, 328, 331, 335, 343, 346, 349, 355, 368, 371, 377, 380, 383, 384–385, 390, 391, 393, 394, 395, 396, 397, 399, 400, 409, 410, 417, 429; Cheverus' letters from Cherbourg, 274; return from Guadeloupe, 180–181; sails for Guadeloupe, 167

Bonneuil, Maxime de, remains at Bazas, 394

515

verus, 342; visit to Cheverus, 340–341

Torbéchet, granted Cheverus, 1

Tottenham, and Cheverus, 35; described, 36–37

Tottenham Chapel, 37; in Cheverus' will, 42

Tournon, Camille comte de, as prefect of Gironde, 316–317

Trappists, at Lulworth, 31

Treaty of Ghent, and Boston, 148, 160

Trélissac, Jean-Armand Chaudru de, in Bordeaux, 319, 396; and Cheverus' entry to Bordeaux, 313; Cheverus, eulogy, 438; consecrated, 397–398; installed in Montauban, 398–399; made vicar-general of Bordeaux, 310, 312; named Bishop of Montauban, 395–396; vicar-general of Montauban, 262–286

Troy, John Thomas, O.P., and American episcopal appointments, 174

Tuckerman, Joseph, founds Seamen's Aid Society, 141; Minister-at-large, 142

Unitarian Controversy, 143

Ursuline Convent, Boston, burning of, 430

Valnais, Joseph de, attached to Cheverus, 264; on Cheverus' return, 263; consul in Boston, 254–255; leaves Boston, 258

Vauxponts, Michel Thoumin des, 16; at Overy, 35; prisoner, 21

Vergennes, Vermont chapel planned, 249–250

Vigerie, Clotilde de la, visits Bordeaux, 319; visits Montauban, 305

Villars, Gabriel-Noël, Bishop, 17; and Cheverus, 18

Villèle, Joseph, ministry, 328

Visitation Convent, Georgetown, Cheverus at, 216; dire straits, 209; founded, 126; Neale's death, 189

Walley, Thomas, Jr., and Bonneuils, 167; conversion of, 138–139, 142, 170; Plessis visits, 177

Wallingford, Cheverus at, 34, 35

Wardour Castle, 27

Ware, William, and Cheverus, 142

Washington, George, and Indian missions, 49–50

White, Calvin, convert, 139

Yellow fever, epidemics, 66; New York quarantine, 94

The Library of Congress has cataloged this publication as follows:

Melville, Annabelle (McConnell) 1910–
    Jean Lefebvre de Cheverus, 1768–1836. Milwaukee, Bruce
Pub. Co. ₁1958₎
    527 p. illus. 23 cm.
    Includes bibliography.

    ———————

    1. Cheverus, Jean Louis Aimé Madeleine Lefebvre de,
Abp., 1768–1836.
BX4705.C465M4   922.273   58–13623 ‡
Library of Congress